MW00811962

THE OXFORD HANDBOOK OF

PUBLIC HERITAGE THEORY AND PRACTICE

THE OXFORD HANDBOOK OF

PUBLIC

HERITAGE

THEORY AND

PRACTICE

Edited by

ANGELA M. LABRADOR

and

NEIL ASHER SILBERMAN

OXFORD

UNIVERSITY PRESS

OXFORD
UNIVERSITY PRESS

Oxford University Press is a department of the University of Oxford. It furthers
the University's objective of excellence in research, scholarship, and education
by publishing worldwide. Oxford is a registered trade mark of Oxford University
Press in the UK and certain other countries.

Published in the United States of America by Oxford University Press
198 Madison Avenue, New York, NY 10016, United States of America.

CIP data is on file at the Library of Congress
ISBN 978–0–19–067631–5

1 3 5 7 9 8 6 4 2

Printed by Sheridan Books, Inc., United States of America

Contents

PART III HERITAGE AND THE USE
OF POWER

PART IV LIVING WITH CHANGE

PART V HERITAGE, MEMORY, AND WELL-BEING

About the Editors

Angela M. Labrador is a cultural anthropologist who has combined her scholarly and professional interest in cultural property issues with the development of participatory action research methods for community-based heritage initiatives. Her dissertation, *Shared Heritage: An Anthropological Theory and Methodology for Assessing, Enhancing, and Communicating a Future-Oriented Social Ethic of Heritage Protection*, drew on real-world heritage practices in New England and the Caribbean to offer a visionary overview of the potential of an inclusive, ethical public heritage.

Neil Asher Silberman is a widely published author, historian, and heritage professional, and the editor-in-chief of the three-volume *Oxford Companion to Archaeology* (2012). He is the author of books on the social and political impact of the past on the present spanning from *Digging for God & Country* (Knopf, 1982) to *The Bible Unearthed* (Free Press, 2001). For the last fifteen years, he has served in various academic and professional capacities to help develop and promote the emerging field of Public Heritage. He served for a decade (2005–15) as president of the ICOMOS International Scientific Committee on Interpretation and Presentation and as a member of the ICOMOS International Advisory Committee.

Silberman and Labrador are colleagues at Coherit Associates, an international heritage consultancy currently coordinating a fourteen-nation heritage capacity-building project in the Caribbean on behalf of the Organization of American States. They are the co-authors of the forthcoming *Oxford Guide to Public Heritage: Managing, Promoting, and Protecting Shared Cultural Assets*.

LIST OF CONTRIBUTORS

Glenn A. Albrecht, The University of Sydney

Christian Barrère, University of Reims

Michael L. Boucher, Jr., Texas State University

Christoph Brumann, Max Planck Institute for Social Anthropology

James Michael Buckley, University of Oregon

Karen L. B. Burgard, Texas A&M University—San Antonio

Terry Nichols Clark, University of Chicago

Giulia Cortellesi, International Child Development Initiatives—ICDI

Marina Dantas de Figueiredo, University of Fortaleza

Sheila Ellwood, University of Bristol

Martin M. Fagin, The New School for Social Research

Martha Frish Okabe, The School of the Art Institute of Chicago

Jessica Harpley, Leiden University

Richard M. Hutchings, Institute for Critical Heritage and Tourism

Ned Kaufman, Pratt Institute

Susan O. Keitumetse, University of Botswana, Okavango Research Institute

Margaret Kernan, International Child Development Initiatives—ICDI

Jenny Kidd, Cardiff University

Marina La Salle, Vancouver Island University

Angela M. Labrador, University of Massachusetts Amherst and Coherit Associates

Denise Lawrence-Zúñiga, California State Polytechnic University, Pomona

Scott A. Lukas, Lake Tahoe Community College

Jim McGuigan, Loughborough University

Steven J. Mock, Balsillie School of International Affairs

Martin Mulligan, RMIT University

Daniel Niles, Research Institute for Humanity and Nature

Eduardo Rojas, University of Pennsylvania

Faye Sayer, Manchester Metropolitan University

David M. Schaepe, Stó:lō Research & Resource Management Centre, Stó:lō Nation, Simon Fraser University, and University of the Fraser Valley

Daniel Shoup, Archaeological/Historical Consultants

Arpakwa O. Sikorei, Ngorongoro Crater, Tanzania

Neil Asher Silberman, University of Massachusetts Amherst and Coherit Associates

Daniel Silver, University of Toronto

Joanie Willett, University of Exeter

Tim Winter, Deakin University

Robert H. Winthrop, University of Maryland, College Park

Luca Zan, University of Bologna

INTRODUCTION

Public Heritage as Social Practice

ANGELA M. LABRADOR AND
NEIL ASHER SILBERMAN

THE field of cultural heritage is no longer simply a past-oriented discipline, dependent on the expertise of art and architectural historians, archaeologists, conservators, curators, and site and museum administrators. It has dramatically expanded across discipli- nary boundaries and social contexts, with even the basic definition of what constitutes cultural heritage being widened far beyond the traditional categories of architecture, artifacts, archives, and art. Heritage now includes vernacular architecture, intangible cultural practices, knowledge and language, performances, and rituals, as well as envi- ronmental landscapes that are inscribed with cultural meanings (Jokilehto 2008, Logan, Nic Craith, and Kockel 2015, Poulios 2014, Waterton and Watson 2015). Cultural her- itage has also become increasingly entangled with the broader social, political, and ec- onomic contexts in which heritage is created, managed, transmitted, protected, or even destroyed (Graham and Howard 2008). Finally, in terms of methodology, heritage pro- tection now encompasses a growing set of methodological approaches whose objectives are not necessarily focused upon the maintenance of material fabric, which has tradi- tionally been cultural heritage's primary concern (Deacon et al. 2004).

Working amidst these expanding dimensions can be both exciting and frustrating. On one hand, cultural heritage professionals are increasingly engaging with projects that have broader social and economic objectives. For instance, museums are no longer seen as stuffy storerooms for dusty relics but as active foci for communities to engage with important contemporary social issues through a historical lens. Heritage site managers are serving growing numbers of cultural tourists who seek enriching per- sonal experiences that go far beyond the facts, dates, and figures presented on inter- pretive panels. Neighborhoods are being planned and reconceived as cultural districts, drawing upon heritage to both create a sense of place and grow local economies. On the other hand, the slipperiness of core concepts such as authenticity, collective memory, landscape, and even heritage itself has contributed to a growing dissatisfaction with universal or standard definitions, typologies, rules, and policies—even as an orientation toward universal human rights has undergirded the contemporary cultural heritage protection discourse (Langfield, Logan, and Craith 2009, Silverman and Ruggles 2007). Thus, heritage scholars have been looking beyond their traditional fields of archaeology, art history, museology, architecture, and history to find potential answers and best practices from other disciplines including political science, economics, urban planning, cultural anthropology, sociology, ecology, geography, psychology, and education. In turn, scholars in these other fields are engaging with cultural heritage as a subject of study, resulting in a body of literature that is increasingly multidisciplinary, interdisciplinary, and in some cases even transdisciplinary.

This handbook charts some of the major sites of convergence between the humanities and the social sciences—where new disciplinary perspectives are being brought to bear on heritage. These convergences have the potential to provide the inter-disciplinary expertise needed not only to critique but also to achieve the intertwined intellectual, political, and socioeconomic goals of cultural heritage in the twenty-first century. Additionally, these convergences more often than not represent some of the crosscutting skills necessary for professional and academic advancement in the contemporary cultural heritage scene.

Why "Public" Heritage?

The decision to preserve something and hand it down to future generations is, at its heart, an ethical one. And like any ethical decision, it is entangled within political, social, cultural, historical, logistical, economic, environmental, and even psychological concerns. However, such decisions about which places or things should be preserved for the future have typically been relegated to small circles of experts, technocrats, and esoteric advocates whose work is often underfunded, underestimated, and misunderstood—or whose values have been critiqued as part of a hegemony that restricts the diversity of values and meanings attributed to cultural heritage (L. Smith 2006). Our usage of the term "public heritage" is a strategic reframing to emphasize that heritage is a matter of wide public concern, in which ethical decisions and management practices must engage with the public directly in the identification, planning, and management of cultural heritage.

This handbook's emphasis upon public engagement tracks with the overall turn toward community participation in the field—a turn that has been paralleled in related fields such as natural resource conservation (Brown, Mitchell, and Beresford 2005), tourism (Richards and Hall 2000, M. Smith and Robinson 2006), international development (Brett 2009, Otsuki 2014), and public policy (Evans and Campos 2013). The contemporary turn toward community in heritage conservation differs markedly from its nineteenth-century and early twentieth-century frameworks, which presumed that heritage was in danger due to the vast changes being experienced under industrialism and modernization, the same forces that projected the romantic ideal of community back in time and focused instead upon the assertion of modern, national, "imagined" communities (Agrawal and Gibson 1999, Adell et al. 2015, Anderson 2006, Macdonald 2013). The romantic ideal of community was associated with heritage in terms of being part of a vanishing rural, pre-modern past. Thus, seeing a constructive role for community in heritage conservation seemed unthinkable.

The tides changed following World War II. In the United States, the sociologist Floyd Hunter penned a study of power structures within urban Atlanta (1953), ushering in new scholarship that framed communities as contemporary, complex, overlapping, and diverse social units with differing relations and access to power. While scholarship in political science, sociology, history, and other fields further developed these ideas, outside the academy the backlash to urban renewal policies, the rising environmentalist movement, and concern over destruction of rural heritage under Eisenhower's highway infrastructure projects shifted public policy toward recognizing the need for increased consultation with local communities in planning projects. Furthermore, the Civil Rights Movement and the American Indian Movement brought attention to how certain communities had been consistently and systemically marginalized throughout the country's history. The ethical imperative to tell multiple and diverse narratives began to emerge. While different ethnic groups and property relationships distinguished the European turn toward community from the post-colonial English contexts (e.g. America, Australia, Canada), a similar trajectory was followed with a clear parallel to be seen between, for instance, the rise of a European discourse around social inclusion to the American discourse around civic engagement (Waterton and Smith 2010: 6).

As the community concept grew in predominance, it rose to a mythic, almost panacea-like status for not only correcting the methodologies of many fields, cultural heritage included, but also in solving any number of social problems (Agrawal and Gibson 1999, Waterton and Smith 2010, Joseph 2002). Waterton and Smith note the "'feel good' factor" of community was infectious—not just in academic circles but in popular press and discourse as well (2010: 6–7). Scholars, especially those coming from a critical theory perspective, contributed helpful reviews of the "community" concept (Agrawal and Gibson 1999, Creed 2006, Crooke 2010, Gibson-Graham 2006a, Hart 2011, Joseph 2002, Waterton and Smith 2010), tracing its genealogy through several turns in Western epistemology, peeling back the "'feel good' factor" to reveal the many layers of meaning hidden underneath—and the discursive work that those hidden meanings were capable of. Such contributions, including Mulligan's in this volume, help to nuance the application of the community concept, and when heeded return us to a more value-neutral usage, which acknowledges the capacity for communities to both work for *and* against specific objectives (Agrawal and Gibson 1999).

This understanding has perhaps brought us back closer to Hunter's original framing of community as a social unit with an evolving internal power structure and differing relations to external power—all of which coexist and overlap in the jumble of lived experience. Postmodern and poststructuralist thought has brought further focus to power, and the ways in which it is exercised, accessed, and experienced by communities and individuals through the social practices that comprise their daily lives and internalized identities. Such work has contributed to the most recent paradigm shift now being experienced, especially influenced by science and technology studies and anthropology: the ontological turn (Pickering 2017). This turn attempts to move beyond the social-constructivist theory that implicitly undergirds most of the "community turn" scholarship. Rather than explaining difference through a culturally relativist lens, difference instead is to be found at an ontological, and thus, material level. The implications for cultural heritage theorists and training of professionals is great: the turn toward community corresponded with a turn away from the material—whether in terms of authenticity in the Nara Document (Larsen 1995) or in definitions of cultural heritage as in the Intangible Cultural Heritage Convention (UNESCO 2003). The ontological turn heralds a return to the material while keeping the knowledge gained from the community turn: that is, the recognition in Pickering's (2017) and Gibson-Graham's (2008) terms of truly "different worlds"—of diversity that runs so deep it reaches the material levels.

Today, the turn toward community in heritage studies is maturing. More and more, the field is placing its focus on the social dynamics and the many values that communities ascribe to cultural heritage while withstanding a wave of self-reflexive critique, especially from the growing critical heritage studies movement. At the same time, the ontological turn is still just beginning as scholars are pushing back against the static foundational definitions and irresolvable contradictions that have comprised cultural heritage epistemology for the last 150 years—especially regarding the binaries of authentic/inauthentic, tangible/intangible, and culture/nature. This handbook's usage of "public heritage" is a way to acknowledge that these binaries are actually just the extreme ends of a spectrum of values ascribed by a multitude of social actors. And the resulting actions taken to preserve, restore, reconstruct, transmit, commemorate, ignore, protect, or even destroy are ethical decisions that depend upon judgments taken along those spectra by every member of society, thereby both being affected by—and affecting—the material world.

The Contribution of the Social Sciences to Public Heritage

The growing interest in the social practices that comprise cultural heritage and its transmission to future generations as well as the recognition of the broader social impacts of and on cultural heritage makes the social sciences a promising realm for several reasons. First and foremost, social science places the social body at the heart of its research questions, enabling us to ask questions about how heritage is understood, valued, and communicated by individuals and collectives within their daily lives. Under the social scientific lens, the focus shifts from whether an expression of cultural heritage is authentic or whether its historical interpretation is accurate to how authenticity is perceived and what impacts various historical narratives have had on differing social groups. As a consequence of this understanding, public heritage may be able to offer a more inclusive foundation for multiple, coexisting identities, rather than its more traditional role in differentiating "us" vs. "them."

As cultural heritage institutions and organizations struggle for financial sustainability and political support, the need to document and communicate the economic and social benefits of cultural heritage has increased—for better or worse. Many scholars have critiqued the impact that neoliberalism has had on traditionally public institutions such as those concerning culture, history, and the arts (e.g. Benhamou 2014, Coombe 2013, Scher 2011, Wilson 2004), but such critiques, although helpful to understand current political forces at work, don't necessarily help those civil servants, executive directors, and advocates who must rally their supporters now. The social sciences' methodological orientation toward data can help in this regard: the disciplines' analytic approaches may translate more effectively to public policy and philanthropic contexts where stakeholders, share-holders, and donors want to know what their return on investment is.

The social sciences can also provide a bridge between the humanities and the natural sciences—bringing environmental sciences, neuroscience, maybe even quantum physics in to the cultural heritage dialogue. Such conversations are even more critical at the present juncture of the Anthropocene, an epoch marked by humanity's global impact upon earth systems at a geologic scale—both the result of and added complication to the intensifying pace of social change. Thus, the exercise of applying social science approaches to cultural heritage should not be seen merely as an idle experiment in interdisciplinarity, but as a theoretical and methodological necessity. In the no-analogue future of our present era, cultural heritage—or as we prefer to call it, public heritage—must be seen as a social process and attendant social ethic that is deeply embedded in the unpredictability of the coming decades, rather than a clearly defined body of knowledge and collection of material objects and sites.

New Ways of Seeing Heritage in Contemporary Society

While the chapters in this volume present the potential contribution of theoretical and methodological approaches from a wide variety of social sciences, many of them share overarching theoretical and methodological shifts in the academy that we find especially relevant to the reconceptualization of public heritage.

We have already mentioned the common use of the concept of "community" in heritage studies, seeing community as the predominant extra-governmental social entity with which to engage in practical heritage work. Yet as we have also seen, the very notion of community has become an analytical concept now ripe for critique.

For cultural heritage, the importance of the emphasis on community—rather than the earlier emphases on the nation-state or universalized World Heritage—is its implicit acknowledgment that heritage values are not intrinsic, but are ascribed to sites, objects, and traditions by multiple communities simultaneously. Thus, a multiplicity—or diversity—of values may coexist in relation to a specific cultural heritage element, and the coexistence of these differing perspectives may not always be peaceful. The increasing incidence of direct conflict over the interpretation or even possession of cultural heritage resources (in issues such as repatriation, conflicting claims to control, and, in the most violent cases, outright destruction) obviously requires serious reflection that moves beyond problems of physical preservation to questions concerning methodologies of dealing with the heritage conflict and dissonance that often ensues. In this respect, the generic use of the term "community" tends to create artificial equivalences between many different social groups as alternative and equally valid perspectives, without examining more deeply how many different kinds of groups are often lumped together under the catch-all term "community."

This tendency naturally leads to the next continuing theme in this volume: a consideration of the role of power—in particular, the relative social, economic, and political power of various groups to control or exclude other groups from the management and interpretation of heritage resources. Although the subject of power has been extensively discussed with regard to the concept of the Authorized Heritage Discourse (AHD) (L. Smith 2006), it has been carried out as an exercise in deconstruction, which, for the most part, is a critique of hegemonic ideologies and state power in their instrumental use of heritage for cultural homogenization and/or marginalization of minority populations and subaltern groups. In recognizing that public heritage is a dynamic social process rather than a single approved canon of heritage resources, it is essential to question the role of power in determining the elements of commemorated collective memory, even *within* subaltern groups. Such an understanding of the workings of heritage power has the potential to transcend postmodern deconstruction of governmentality writ large (primarily in nationalism and capitalism) and the often-times reductive binary between rulers and oppressed. Social scientific research that analyzes the micro-politics of bureaucracies such as Zan and Shoup's chapter reveal how decision-makers don't have it all figured out— especially when trying to work with the idealism of heritage professionals outside the bureaucracy. And frank assessments of such idealism, such as that offered by La Salle and Hutchings in their chapter on collaboration, reveal the ways in which even well-intentioned heritage professionals continue to perpetuate the alienation of subaltern groups. Although a bitter pill to swallow, such contributions can ultimately inform our praxis and ethics when considering how to work in an era of accelerating privatization and social conflict.

Further nuancing our understandings of the social world of public heritage are those theorists engaging with the "ontological turn" (González 2013, Howitt and

Suchet-Pearson 2006, Pickering 2017), who desire to move beyond modernist dualisms (such as nature/culture, public/private, authentic/inauthentic), universalizing "strong theory" (Gibson-Graham 2006b, Walther 2004), and the sometimes self-defeating relativism that results from social constructivist thinking. It has become evident that differing ontologies about the relationship between the past and present can coexist, without privileging any of them as the definitive and exclusive means of valuing heritage, as universal criteria such as Outstanding Universal Value in the UNESCO World Heritage process has done (Jokilehto et al. 2008). Furthermore, recent scholarship has suggested that the impulse to preserve may not be the only management strategy for the significance of heritage, and that "curated decay" may be a valid alternative (DeSilvey 2017). Such recognitions require a transformation in our ways of seeing, and thus in our ways of "doing," as related in Schaepe's auto-ethnographic chapter and in Keitumetse and Sikorei's detailed case study of protected area management. Once again, this volume is meant to present approaches that reject sharp binaries and recognize the social complexities of public heritage as an entangled process of meaning-making that impacts the future (as Willett's chapter proposes) rather than a self-evident and timeless reflection of the past.

A deeper reflection on the dynamics of community and of ontological diversity has not only expanded the cultural heritage field to include non-Eurocentric scholars and political actors but has also resulted in important attempts to reframe authenticity from a discrete and intrinsic quality to an ever-evolving perception of "pastness" that exists in a wide range of simultaneous forms (Holtorf 2013). Continuing scholarly efforts to precisely define the necessary components of authenticity have resulted in ever-wider and, consequently, ever-vaguer definitions to the point where this quality—still so central to existing heritage conservation strategies—has dubious value and is badly in need of thorough reconsideration. Social scientific scholarship around the perceptions of authenticity, such as those contributed by Mock's methodology for "mapping authenticity" and Lukas's reframing of heritage as "remaking" constructively move us toward such a reconsideration for public heritage.

The acknowledgment of the arrival of the proposed Anthropocene epoch and the desire to move beyond postmodernism to a post-post-modernism (Nealon 2012) or some other -ism that enables a more constructive stance has inspired a resurgence of interest in Deleuzean theory and its relevance to emerging approaches to heritage. The idea of heritage as a complexly interconnected assemblage of people, ideas, feelings, and things has opened up new conceptual understandings of the rhizomic extension of heritage values and objects (see Lukas's chapter), the function of heritage in the process of social "becoming" (see Willett's chapter), the deterritorialization of formerly coherent assemblages (see McGuigan's chapter), and "nomadic ethics" (Braidotti 2013). Perhaps the most promising aspect of a Deleuzean speculative realism or new materialism is its philosophical orientation toward pragmatism: on creating and actively testing methods that accept their transformative nature while acknowledging the fluidity and contingency of heritage politics, identity, and authenticity.

MAJOR THEMES IN PUBLIC HERITAGE

Although many of the issues raised in this introduction are thoroughly interconnected, this handbook has been divided into sections that address certain aspects of the impact of contemporary heritage practices and goals.

Heritage, Development, and Global Relations

When Jon Hawkes declared culture the "fourth pillar of sustainability" (2001), the cultural sector within the international development community jumped at the opportunity to finally join the "adults' table" and to be taken seriously as something more than a luxury or optional amenity. At a time of global climate change, worldwide financial volatility, and massive demographic movements, the goal of sustainability has been primary since the United Nations sponsored Brundtland Report was published (United Nations World Commission on Environment and Development 1987). For at least two decades, sustainability had been focused upon three pillars: economic growth, social welfare, and environmental health. Although heritage has been increasingly seen as a field that contributes to social welfare (Jones 2016), its main function in development theory has been economic—with newly established or refurbished heritage sites seen as a platform for increased employment and investment in regions seeking to increase their share in the worldwide traffic in cultural tourism. Although the 1972 World Heritage Convention was not originally intended to be an economic development program, its appeal to states parties has increasingly turned to revenue generation. In his chapter in this section, Brumann traces its historic trajectory, from an exclusive concern with conservation and preservation to a wider range of heritage discourses and lived experiences that sometimes advance, sometimes obstruct.

Yet today, with culture now being recognized as a fourth pillar of sustainability, the cultural sector in general and cultural heritage in particular finds itself moving away from the periphery of the broader development agenda to take its place within the indicators, activities, and even the objectives of development projects. This new status requires heritage and development scholars and professionals to engage with each other's theories and methods and reconcile the sometimes contradictory approaches to measuring success—let alone sustainability itself. Keitumetse and Sikorei's chapter uses two World Heritage sites to demonstrate how such contradictions are embedded in international development policy frameworks, especially with regard to approaches to Indigenous peoples and the triadic relationship between cultural heritage, natural resources, and local people. Rojas and Winter both urge us to shift focus in order to realize the full potential of international heritage initiatives. For Rojas, the field of urban politics can offer heritage studies a critical lens for understanding the decisions made (and their context) regarding heritage conservation in urban contexts. Perhaps most helpful is urban politics' ability to illuminate the diversity of social actors and their roles vis-à-vis urban heritage—moving the field beyond an overly simplistic stakeholder management framework to acknowledge the many different "-holders" that emerge when urban conservation issues arise. Such work can further nuance the conceptualization of "community" for any public heritage project. Winter acknowledges the important work that has been done on conflict within critical heritage studies, but asks us to turn our gaze toward instances in which cultural heritage is part of international diplomatic efforts.

Indeed, better understanding the politics of cooperation as it applies to heritage may lead to a more sophisticated understanding of its use in the international development context. The judicious use of cultural heritage projects as an aspect of diplomatic or "soft" power relations—though far more subtle than military interventions or threats of force—may, in the long run, have a significant social effect among the populations in conflict zones. The utter failure of military force and pressure in such international fora as UNESCO to prevent the destruction of ancient monuments by terrorist groups demonstrates that in many cases the focus on mobilizing international support for the physical preservation of heritage resources may in fact make the monuments more attractive targets for anti-Western fundamentalist groups. A broader vision of development has increasingly come to view heritage as a social resource in the construction of new futures—and Willett's important contribution asks cultural heritage scholars to turn their attention as much to the future as to the past and to begin reflecting upon what future worlds cultural heritage narratives make possible in development contexts at any scale.

Heritage, Markets, and Management

Since the 1980s, with the growing influence of neoliberalism and the enforcement of economic austerity strategies on deeply indebted governments, most countries have seen a steady divestment in public expenditures for social services and non-revenue producing amenities such as cultural heritage protection. Indeed, the era of big government has been steadily replaced by a neoliberal approach to public services once deemed to be the essential responsibilities of the public sector. Market logic and associated audit-based performance management models now permeate the civil service and the growing cadre of non-governmental organizations and public–private partnerships that are stepping in to fill the administrative gaps. Outsourcing and privatization of heritage resources have thus become highly contentious subjects among the professional community (Palumbo 2006), since its results have sometimes not lived up to its projected economic goals (Silberman 2013).

In this section of the volume, the contributors deal with some of the pitfalls and cautionary tales of a Taylorist approach to heritage management—believing that the increased efficiency and productivity of private sector perspectives can indeed achieve the goals of heritage protection and promotion. Dantas de Figueiredo's chapter, for example, unpacks the compound "heritage management" concept, tracing its development and its inherent contradiction to values that cannot be calculated by return on investment metrics. For as we have stated above, the very idea of a "public heritage" must be seen as a dynamic social process in which there are no permanent standards of success that encompass all of its social and economic effects. To concentrate on the performance of heritage within a market economy is to focus on a kind of top-down governance that prioritizes "the trains running on time" to the exclusion of other social effects. And indeed the very management structures, divided among government agencies, cultural institutions, and private interests create internal conflicts and contradictions that create obstacles to the efficiency and productivity that is now sought. The public engagement in cultural heritage sites and practices are ever-evolving, and as Zan and Shoup demonstrate so clearly, neither heritage professionals nor professional management experts have so far succeeded in reconciling their differing approaches or synchronizing their goals. While the path toward effective heritage management may be paved with good intentions, it is costly, conflict-ridden, and chronically unable to achieve either prompt or sustainable results.

One of the most serious uncertainties in a management approach to the protection and promotion of cultural heritage is the question of valuation. Over the years, especially as the economic dimension of cultural heritage has come to the fore, many methods have been proposed, ranging from public surveys of "willingness to pay" to more quantitative appraisal of the value of heritage as real property (Mason 2008). In this section of the volume, Ellwood provides a welcome explanation, from the perspective of accounting, of the various tools available for use, highlighting their pitfalls and their advantages for the valuation of cultural heritage. Indeed, as Barrère points out in his chapter, the very concept of heritage as "cultural capital" is one that must be completely rethought. He suggests that its application may actually create difficulties in evaluating the full range of benefits that society may accrue from an approach to heritage management that is multidimensional.

Another prime challenge in the management of cultural heritage is recognizing its changing role in the twenty-first-century world. In his thought-provoking contribution, Lukas reframes heritage management as a process of remaking rather than carefully managed preservation. He suggests that the establishment, design, and promotion of heritage sites (and the often considerable investment involved in those actions) should be viewed as collective attempts to reinterpret contemporary realities through selective interpretations of the past; that is, heritage management doesn't preserve the past but transforms the present. Concluding this section is Winthrop's thoughtful examination of the social justification for heritage management itself. His description of "culturally reflexive stewardship" moves the discussion from the traditional concerns of *what* should be managed and *how* it should be managed to the more basic, yet harder, questions of *why* and to what ends.

Heritage and the Use of Power

Moving beyond old nationalist frameworks to looking at how power operates in a neo-liberal, global community, this section examines how the deconstruction of traditional sources of power and the long-unquestioned identification of cultural heritage as a public good (rather than the instrumentalization of the remains of the past to serve contemporary interests) requires a reconsideration of the character of heritage landscapes—in terms of both inherited physical monuments and the visibility of cultural heritage in cyberspace. As seen in the ongoing critique of imperial monuments and heritage places that celebrate the heroes and institutions of imperial governance—and in the United States the controversies over heritage sites that celebrate the Confederate defense of slavery and the genocidal successes of Manifest Destiny—intellectual deconstruction is simply not enough. In fact, as McGuigan forcefully argues, the physical retention of monuments of imperial power, especially when accompanied by public debate and re-interpretation of their historical significance, tends to naturalize the monuments in question as inarguably significant, thus allowing their social power to remain uncontested—and failing to displace the very concept of imperial power from a commemorative context.

In sharp opposition to the imperial perspective is the view that the processes of globalization and instantaneous digital communication can become the basis for a new world order, whose physical center is nowhere and whose power can be felt everywhere. The sheer scale of social media—surely just the first, halting steps of evolving technologies of intercultural digital communications—has already begun to serve as a global platform for the dissemination of news and information about cultural heritage (Giaccardi 2012). In this section, Kidd provides an enlightening preview of the promise and perils of social media, suggesting that while its wide reach can offer unprecedented access, it also poses the ethical dangers of trivialization, further downsizing of cultural institutions, and reducing heritage to an entertainment medium.

We have already spoken of the fraught issue of "community," yet while many have regarded this vaguely defined social grouping as a liberatory target, only a few have spoken of the power conflicts and vested interests that every community creates. Mulligan's review of the literature on the relationship of community and heritage reveals some of the unspoken assumptions and misconceptions that a romantic concept of community often overlooks. Furthermore, the practice of community engagement in the existing discipline of archaeology has the unintended consequence of often naturalizing unequal power relations, as La Salle and Hutchings point out. In the case of public commemoration and public history, Burgard and Boucher forcefully call for counteracting the messages of white supremacy that are so deeply embedded in the mainstream narratives of American history—and how education scholars can assist heritage professionals with the challenge. Indeed, if public heritage management could be seen as a collaborative act of ontological reframing, as Schaepe explains in his contribution to this section, it may become possible to conceive of the transformation of power relations between and within communities.

Living with Change

Change has always been central to cultural heritage studies. Yet historically, change has always been seen as the enemy. Indeed, just the term "historic preservation" gives this away. However, the field's relationship to change has been shifting over the past few decades, especially as the inevitability of change grew more apparent and the taxidermic approach to heritage has fallen out of favor. A shift to "managing change" rather than overcoming it has been the subject of considerable controversy in recent years within the international heritage community (cf. Araoz 2011, Petzet 2010). Yet the intensifying environmental, political, and economic transformations that we are now experiencing makes the old approach an entirely nostalgic, even quixotic one. As Kaufman notes in his wide-ranging contribution, heritage must incorporate emerging insights from social science and environmental science to make heritage a more effective instrument of collective adaptation and social equality.

The unprecedented scale of demographic movement has, as mentioned above, created its own constellation of socioeconomic changes, not the least of which is the fragmentation of formerly distinct national heritage traditions and the detachment of tradition from place. The homogenized cultural assimilation of the "melting pot" is no longer the primary means of social cohesion, yet the challenge of truly multicultural heritage has remained elusive. As Buckley demonstrates, a turn toward the shared celebration of cultural expressions and an occasional shift in viewpoint from that of long-settled residents to those of the newcomers may offer avenues to accommodate change through the creation of a more dynamic and flexible cultural environment. The boundaries between public heritage, public art, public amenities, and placemaking are extremely difficult to determine, but Okabe, Silver, and Clark offer a variation of their "scenescapes" approach that can combine the strengths of all of them. In their analysis of urban environments, and the factors that can make them more livable, they show how intentional change and reshaping of the urban landscape need not come in the form of hostility-creating gentrification, but in a shared aesthetic that can offer a distinctive and evolving sense of place.

This section of the volume also addresses the enormous changes that have swept over two other geographic zones, suburbs and rural districts, symptomatic of the transformations brought about by modernity. Lawrence-Zúñiga illustrates how post-1945 suburbs—those planned bedroom communities where modern nuclear families sought to "keep up with the Joneses"—have now become something of a heritage (or more precisely, historic preservation) battlefield. Through case studies of two suburban communities in southern California, she shows how the differing attitudes of residents to the establishment of historic districts are reflective of unresolved and largely misunderstood differences in domestic sensibilities that contribute to a sometimes incoherent heritage landscape. Likewise, the dramatic transformation of rural economies from subsistence agriculture to industrial farming has given birth to a few nostalgic islands of agricultural heritage. As Niles persuasively argues, traditional agricultural methods should be seen as something more than tourist attractions and romantic oddities; their potential value in demonstrating alternative attitudes toward subsistence and their merging of "culture" and "nature" may offer new models for public heritage and strategies for coping with—or countering—the Anthropocene.

Global climate change and the arrival of the unpredictable Anthropocene epoch is perhaps the greatest existential challenge of current generations. Yet in this section's concluding and provocative essay, Albrecht looks beyond the present degradation of our planetary existence to a time when the lessons have all been learned. He imagines that time, far in the future, which he terms the Symbiocene, as an era in which heritage is no longer seen as a nostalgic pearl in the irritated oyster of modernity, but as an invisible and intangible presence deeply embedded in the course of people's reframed symbiotic relationship with the world.

Heritage, Memory, and Well-Being

The last section of this volume seeks to undergird the familiar slogans and often empty clichés about the value of cultural heritage to the individual and to society at large. Advances in behavioral psychology, cognition, collective memory, and intergenerational learning have provided new insights into the influence of cultural heritage on society. Mock's contribution describes how heritage professionals can better understand and analyze perceptions of authenticity and its associated emotions—both positive and negative. In a similar methodological vein, Sayer presents the findings of her ethnographic research of public heritage engagement and suggests an evaluation strategy to more effectively document the social impacts of such projects, especially in terms of public health.

The study of collective memory has been closely connected to heritage sites and monuments since the pioneering work of Halbwachs (1992 [1952]), Nora (1989), Anderson (2006), and Connerton (1989)—and the many other scholars who have dealt with this subject (cf. Olick, Vinitzky-Seroussi, Levy 2011). In this section, Fagin examines the mechanics and function of collective memory through the psycho-social factors that determine its usefulness for identity making—without regard to whether the shared memories are historically factual. This insight may provide a useful understanding of the character of public heritage as something more than the communication of historical or archaeological facts. This section concludes with an analysis by Cortellesi, Harpley, and Kernan of the benefits of intergenerational learning about heritage for both the elderly and the young. As a tool for cultural communication, not only for members of different communities, but also for different generational cohorts, this contribution offers a practical roadmap for productive discussions about the past in the present that bridges some of modern society's most intractable gaps.

CONNECTING WIDER CONVERSATIONS

In addition to the specific foci of this volume's five main parts, several cross-cutting themes are frequently addressed. Global climate change and its devastating physical effects on material culture is an element that goes far beyond preservation techniques and can be seen as both symptom and effect of the dawning Anthropocene epoch. With environmental and social conditions all over the world growing increasingly unpredictable, the basic approach of historic preservation—of overcoming the natural process of decay to enshrine contemporary values in material form and bequeath them to future generations—must take into account the uncertainty of the present governance frameworks of global society and the likely discontinuity of tradition in some places. It is a challenge that public heritage must adapt to, not ignore.

Indeed, in recent decades we have already witnessed the gradual transformation of heritage and visitation to cultural sites from a didactic to a performative activity (Chakrabarty 2002). Certainly part of this change is due to the rise of identity politics, in which heritage is increasingly seen as material legitimization of the rights and history of long-marginalized social groups (Liu and Hilton 2005). Even more significant—at least in sheer numbers and impact on heritage sites and traditions—is the explosive growth of tourism to heritage sites. So much has been written—both positive and negative—about the impact of heritage tourism in our present "Experience Economy" (cf. Pine and Gilmore 2011, and for representative works, see Chhabra 2010, Staiff, Bushell, and Watson 2013, Timothy and Nyaupane 2009) that we chose to concentrate on public heritage as a matter for local governance and participation in heritage activities rather than an as an aspect of the global tourist economy. We trust that this body of literature will continue to grow and encourage scholars to apply the cross-disciplinary perspectives found in this volume to tourism studies.

As disciplinary silos are being breached and bridges built between fields that were once on opposite sides of campuses and libraries in order to address the pressing issues of the twenty-first century, we believe that social science is not only relevant but has a critical part to play. The convergences between the humanities, environmental sciences, and social science as seen in the emerging inter-, multi-, and transdisciplinary literature concerning cultural heritage has been especially fruitful and inspiring. We therefore hope that the essays in this volume will contribute to the redefinition and reshaping of the multi-faceted collective process of public heritage.

REFERENCES

Adell, Nicolas, Regina Bendix, Chiara Bortolotto, and Markus Tauschek, eds. 2015. *Between Imagined Communities and Communities of Practice Participation, Territory and the Making of Heritage.* Vol. 8. Göttingen Studies in Cultural Property. Göttingen: Universitätsverlag Göttingen.

Agrawal, Arun, and Clark C. Gibson. 1999. "Enchantment and Disenchantment: The Role of Community in Natural Resource Conservation." *World Development* 27(4): 629–649.

Anderson, Benedict. 2006. *Imagined Communities: Reflections on the Origin and Spread of Nationalism*. Rev. edn. London: Verso.

Araoz, Gustavo F. 2011. "Preserving Heritage Places under a New Paradigm." *Journal of Cultural Heritage Management and Sustainable Development* 1(1): 55–60.

Benhamou, Françoise. 2014. "Neoliberalism and French Heritage Policy in the Context of Globalization." *Heritage & Society* 7(1): 47–56.

Braidotti, Rosi. 2013. "Nomadic Ethics." *Deleuze Studies* 7(3): 342–359.

Brett, E. A. 2009. *Reconstructing Development Theory: International Inequality, Institutional Reform and Social Emancipation*. New York: Palgrave Macmillan.

Brown, Jessica, Nora Mitchell, and Michael Beresford. 2005. *The Protected Landscape Approach: Linking Nature, Culture and Community*. Gland, Switzerland: IUCN.

Chakrabarty, Dipesh. 2002. "Museums in Late Democracies." *Humanities Research* 9(1): 5–12.

Chhabra, Deepak. 2010. *Sustainable Marketing of Cultural and Heritage Tourism*. Milton Park, Abingdon, Oxon, and New York: Routledge.

Connerton, Paul. 1989. *How Societies Remember*. First Edition edition. Cambridge and New York: Cambridge University Press.

Coombe, Rosemary J. 2013. "Managing Cultural Heritage as Neoliberal Governmentality," in *Heritage Regimes and the State*, ed. Regina F. Bendix, Aditya Eggert, and Arnika Peselmann. 2nd edn. Göttingen Studies in Cultural Property 6. Göttingen: Univ.-Verl. Göttingen, 375–395.

Creed, Gerald W., ed. 2006. *The Seductions of Community: Emancipations, Oppressions, Quandaries*. Santa Fe: School for Advanced Research Press.

Crooke, Elizabeth. 2010. "The Politics of Community Heritage: Motivations, Authority and Control." *International Journal of Heritage Studies* 16(1–2): 16–29.

Deacon, Harriet, Luvuyo Dondolo, Mbulelo Mrubata, and Sandra Prosalendis. 2004. *The Subtle Power of Intangible Heritage*. Cape Town: Human Sciences Research Council.

DeSilvey, Caitlin. 2017. *Curated Decay: Heritage beyond Saving*. Minneapolis: University of Minnesota Press. <http://public.eblib.com/choice/publicfullrecord.aspx?p=4745550>.

Evans, Angela M., and Adriana Campos. 2013. "Open Government Initiatives: Challenges of Citizen Participation." *Journal of Policy Analysis and Management* 32(1) :172–185.

Giaccardi, Elisa. 2012. *Heritage and Social Media: Understanding Heritage in a Participatory Culture*. New York: Routledge.

Gibson-Graham, J. K. 2006a. "Imagining and Enacting a Postcapitalist Feminist Economic Politics." *Women's Studies Quarterly* 34(1–2): 72–78.

Gibson-Graham, J. K. 2006b. *A Postcapitalist Politics*. 1st edn. Minneapolis: Univ Of Minnesota Press.

Gibson-Graham, J. K. 2008. "Diverse Economies: Performative Practices for 'Other Worlds.'" *Progress in Human Geography* 32(5): 613–632.

González, Pablo Alonso. 2013. "The Heritage Machine: A Heritage Ethnography in Maragatería (Spain)." Ph.D. Dissertation, León, Spain: Universidad de León.

Graham, B. J., and Peter Howard. 2008. *The Ashgate Research Companion to Heritage and Identity*. Burlington, VT: Ashgate Pub. Co.

Halbwachs, Maurice. 1992. *On Collective Memory*. Trans. Lewis A. Coser. 1st edn. Chicago: University of Chicago Press.

Hart, Siobhan. 2011. "Heritage, Neighborhoods and Cosmopolitan Sensibilities: Poly-Communal Archaeology in Deerfield, Massachusetts." *Present Pasts* 3(1). <http://presentpasts.info/article/view/33>.

Holtorf, Cornelius. 2013. "On Pastness: A Reconsideration of Materiality in Archaeological Object Authenticity." *Anthropological Quarterly* 86(2): 427–443.

Howitt, Richard, and Sandra Suchet-Pearson. 2006. "Rethinking the Building Blocks: Ontological Pluralism and the Idea of 'Management.'" *Geografiska Annaler: Series B, Human Geography* 88(3): 323–335.

Hunter, Floyd. 1953. *Community Power Structure—A Study of Decision Makers*. Chapel Hill: The University of North Carolina Press.

Jokilehto, Jukka. 2008. "On Definitions of Cultural Heritage." *Heritage Theory* 1(1): 4–26.

Jokilehto, Jukka, Christina Cameron, Michel Parent, and International Council on Monuments and Sites. 2008. *The World Heritage List: What Is OUV? Defining the Outstanding Universal Value of Cultural World Heritage Properties: An ICOMOS Study*. Berlin and Paris: Hendrik Bässler Verlag; ICOMOS, International Council on Monuments and Sites.

Jones, Siân. 2016. "Wrestling with the Social Value of Heritage: Problems, Dilemmas and Opportunities." *Journal of Community Archaeology & Heritage*, July: 1–17.

Joseph, Miranda. 2002. *Against the Romance Of Community*. 1st edn. Minneapolis: Univ Of Minnesota Press.

Langfield, Michele, William Logan, and Mairead Nic Craith, eds. 2009. *Cultural Diversity, Heritage and Human Rights: Intersections in Theory and Practice*. 1st edn. London and New York: Routledge.

Larsen, K., ed. 1995. "The Nara Document on Authenticity," in *Nara Conference on Authenticity in Relation to the World Heritage Convention, Nara, Japan, November 1–6, 1994, Proceedings*. Trondheim: Tapir Publishers.

Liu, James H., and Denis J. Hilton. 2005. "How the Past Weighs on the Present: Social Representations of History and their Role in Identity Politics." *British Journal of Social Psychology* 44(4): 537–556.

Logan, William, Máiréad Nic Craith, and Ullrich Kockel, eds. 2015. *A Companion to Heritage Studies*. Wiley Blackwell Companions to Anthropology. Chichester and Malden, MA: Wiley-Blackwell.

Macdonald, Sharon. 2013. *Memorylands: Heritage and Identity in Europe Today*. London and New York: Routledge.

Mason, Randall. 2008. "Be Interested and Beware: Joining Economic Valuation and Heritage Conservation." *International Journal of Heritage Studies* 14(4): 303–318.

Nealon, Jeffrey T. 2012. *Post-Postmodernism: Or, the Logic of Just-in-Time Capitalism*. Stanford: Stanford University Press.

Nora, Pierre. 1989. "Between Memory and History: Les Lieux de Mémoire." *Representations* 26: 7–24.

Olick, Jeffrey K., Vered Vinitzky-Seroussi, and Daniel Levy, eds. 2011. *The Collective Memory Reader*. 1st edn. New York: Oxford University Press.

Otsuki, Kei. 2014. *Transformative Sustainable Development: Participation, Reflection and Change*. New York: Routledge.

Palumbo, Gaetano. 2006. "Privatization of State-Owned Cultural Heritage," in *Of the Past, for the Future: Integrating Archaeology and Conservation, Proceedings of the Conservation Theme at the 5th World Archaeological Congress, Washington, DC, 22–26 June 2003*. Los Angeles: Getty Conservation Institute, 35.

Petzet, Michael. 2010. *International Principles of Preservation*. Berlin: Bäßler.

Pickering, Andrew. 2017. "The Ontological Turn: Taking Different Worlds Seriously." *Social Analysis* 61(2): 134–150.

Pine, B. Joseph, and James H. Gilmore. 2011. *The Experience Economy*. Cambridge, MA: Harvard Business Review Press.

Poulios, Ioannis. 2014. *The Past in the Present: A Living Heritage Approach—Meteora, Greece*. London: Ubiquity Press.

Richards, Greg, and Derek R. Hall. 2000. *Tourism and Sustainable Community Development*. London and New York: Routledge.

Scher, Philip W. 2011. "Heritage Tourism in the Caribbean: The Politics of Culture after Neoliberalism." *Bulletin of Latin American Research* 30(1): 7–20.

Silberman, Neil A. 2013. "Discourses of Development: Narratives of Cultural Heritage as an Economic Resource," in *Heritage and Tourism: Place, Encounter, Engagement*, ed. Russell Staiff, Robyn Bushell, and Steve Watson. London: Routledge, 213–225.

Silverman, Helaine, and D. Fairchild Ruggles. 2007. *Cultural Heritage and Human Rights*. New York and London: Springer.

Smith, Laurajane. 2006. *Uses of Heritage*. London and New York: Routledge.

Smith, Melanie, and Mike Robinson. 2006. *Cultural Tourism in a Changing World: Politics, Participation and (Re)presentation*. Clevedon, UK: Channel View Publications.

Staiff, Russell, Robyn Bushell, and Steve Watson, eds. 2013. *Heritage and Tourism: Place, Encounter, Engagement*. New York: Routledge.

Timothy, Dallen J., and Gyan P. Nyaupane. 2009. *Cultural Heritage and Tourism in the Developing World: A Regional Perspective*. London and New York: Routledge.

UNESCO. 2003. "Convention for the Safeguarding of the Intangible Cultural Heritage." Paris: UNESCO.

United Nations World Commission on Environment and Development. 1987. "Our Common Future." Oxford: Oxford University Press.

Walther, Bo. 2004. "Big Theory-Strong Theory: The Ontological Ghost of Post-Ontological Epistemology." *Cybernetics & Human Knowing* 11(3): 30–55.

Waterton, Emma, and Laurajane Smith. 2010. "The Recognition and Misrecognition of Community Heritage." *International Journal of Heritage Studies* 16(1–2): 4–15.

Waterton, Emma, and Steve Watson, eds. 2015. *The Palgrave Handbook of Contemporary Heritage Research*. Palgrave Handbooks. Basingstoke and New York: Palgrave Macmillan.

Wilson, David. 2004. "Making Historical Preservation in Chicago: Discourse and Spatiality in Neo-liberal Times." *Space and Polity* 8(1): 43–59.

PART I

HERITAGE, DEVELOPMENT, AND GLOBAL RELATIONS

CHAPTER 1.1

....

CREATING UNIVERSAL VALUE

The UNESCO World Heritage Convention in Its Fifth Decade

....

CHRISTOPH BRUMANN

THE RISE OF WORLD HERITAGE

....

WHILE honoring the relics of the past, the "Convention Concerning the Protection of the World Cultural and Natural Heritage" has itself reached a respectable age: when the General Conference of the United Nations Educational, Scientific, and Cultural Organization (UNESCO) adopted this international treaty in 1972, one of the buildings now on the "World Heritage List"—the Sydney Opera House—was not even completed. One wonders when heritagization will turn on itself here, with the Convention and its organs, discourses, practices, and founder figures becoming the objects rather than the agents of conservation. And indeed, there are indications that the World Heritage Convention will be less of a mobilizing force in the future, both in terms of cultural and natural conservation and for shaping the face of what we see as heritage.[1]

If alone for the active US contribution to its gestation, it is difficult to imagine that this intergovernmental treaty would be adopted today. Yet with the rise of environmental consciousness and modernity's discontents in the late 1960s, it offered itself to combine the efforts of the US National Park Service and the International Union for the Conservation of Nature (IUCN) for a UN-backed register of important nature reserves with UNESCO steps towards a legal tool for cultural conservation. The latter followed up on UNESCO's much-publicized rescue operation for the Nubian monuments of Abu Simbel (Allais 2013, Betts 2015) and other safeguarding campaigns. The drafts of the treaty were finalized in the run-up to the famous 1972 Stockholm UN summit on the human environment and after adoption later that year, ratification had proceeded sufficiently for the Convention to enter into force by 1976 (Batisse and Bolla 2005, Cameron and Rössler 2013, Stott 2011, Titchen 1995). The "World Heritage Committee"—composed of twenty-one (initially fifteen) elected "States Parties" (i.e. treaty states)—assembled for the first of its annual sessions in 1977; in 1978, the Galapagos Islands inaugurated the World Heritage List; and a further year on, the earthquake-stricken "Natural and Culturo-Historical Region of Kotor," Montenegro, was the first entry into the "List of World Heritage in Danger," the sub-list for the most pressing cases.[2]

Yet these were still the days when the Committee sessions attracted only a couple of dozen participants and secretariat duties were fulfilled by no more than two UNESCO employees alongside their regular tasks. The surge into public consciousness was still to come, mostly in the 1990s when Japanese and German TV documentary series celebrating the sites were exported all over the world, converting "World Heritage" into a household name. Participation figures at Committee sessions and the print presence of the phrase in major languages[3] soared in the second half of that decade. A powerful global brand was established, to the surprise of the advertising industry that—as a former World Heritage centre official told me—still marvels at how many waves have been made with so little investment. The potential of World Heritage was also recognized within UNESCO where the secretariat was transformed into an independent unit alongside the conventional visions as the "World Heritage Centre," swelling greatly in staff numbers and attracting considerable "extrabudgetary funding" from the treaty states.

GLOBALIZING THE LIST

World Heritage was already transforming by that time: while there were quite a few inscriptions from the Global South in the first two years, European countries had been quickest in realizing the potential of the World Heritage List and submitting their candidates so that already by the late 1980s, criticism of what appeared to become a Eurocentric affair was rising. While the inclusion of both cultural and natural sites— based on the North American model—had been innovative, the initially intended parity never materialized. Instead, conventional cultural heritage—cathedrals and temples, palaces, and historical town centers—dominated the List.

The World Heritage institutions responded with reform efforts that made the 1990s the "heroic age" of World Heritage. "Cultural landscapes" as a new category, devised for unique kinds of human interaction with the environment rather than pristine wilderness, premiered in 1992; the "Global Strategy for a representative, balanced and credible World Heritage List"[4] promoting a less elite, more vernacular, and broadly anthropological conception of cultural heritage was adopted in 1994; and in the same year, the "Nara Document on Authenticity"[5] widened the potential manifestations of that elusive quality beyond the physical fabric. Listing criteria were reformulated to play down elitist connotations (masterpieces of "human creative genius," rather than of art or architecture; mutual "interchange," not unilateral "influence") and new categories of heritage were introduced (cultural routes, canals, railway lines) or significantly strengthened (vernacular buildings, industrial sites, modern architecture and planning, "sites of conscience" commemorating atrocities and human-rights violations) over the following years (Brumann 2014b: 2180–2183). As Gfeller has outlined (2013b, 2015, 2017), key protagonists of these reforms came from outside Europe or its fringes and from new disciplines, with the earlier hegemony of (Western) European art history and architectural history waning.

In precisely these reform years, however, European countries continued to voraciously push their largely conventional candidates, setting all-time records for single-year World Heritage inscriptions by country (ten Italian properties in 1997) and continent (thirty-four European properties in 2000).[6] The Committee decided to stem the flood in 2000 and imposed a limit of one candidate site per state and year that, however, has been under attack ever since, with the current compromise being two per state and year. Overall European success was hardly affected, given that the well-funded conservation authorities of this continent adapted to the new possibilities smoothly: the most common cultural landscape on the World Heritage List today is the European wine region, not the holy mountains or rice terraces initially evoked,[7] milestones of industrialization and architectural modernism cluster in Europe too, and a maze of national borders together with histories of cooperation ensure that European countries are most likely to profit from the exemption of "transboundary sites" from the national quotas.

Frustration in many other parts of the world was compounded by rising demands: when career diplomats entered the Committee sessions in large numbers around 2000, they found what some perceived as vague decision texts and a lack of transparency, follow-up mechanisms, and accountability. In response, the Bureau—a sub-body of the Committee that heretofore had done much of the work—was stripped of its powers, the Committee sessions were extended, and World Heritage procedures were greatly systematized and elaborated. Yet the Operational Guidelines of the Convention have grown with every update[8] and while nomination documents had a couple of pages in the beginning, some of the voluminous tomes that States Parties submit these days run in the thousands of pages—the nomination manual[9] alone has almost 140. Countries from the Global South are most challenged to play along, and the 2000s saw European nomination machineries in full swing but inscribed sites in the South listed as "in Danger" with disproportional frequency.[10] When first attending a Committee session in 2009, I thus found a clear sentiment among Southern participants that World Heritage was a venture of and for the Northern countries, whatever the world-embracing rhetoric espoused. Fifteen years into the Global Strategy, the European share of the World Heritage List had in fact grown, not shrunk. One may take issue with such counting exercises: is Switzerland with its twelve World Heritage properties better represented than Tanzania when a single one of that country's seven sites—the Selous Game Reserve—is larger than Switzerland? But for many participants in Committee processes, Northern self-serving seemed evident.

"POLITICIZING" THE COMMITTEE

This encouraged a turning of the tables in the memorable 2010 Committee session of Brasilia (Brumann 2014b: 2184–2185). To an unprecedented extent, Committee states supported each other in brushing aside the advice of the International Council on Monuments and Sites (ICOMOS) and IUCN, the Advisory Bodies of the Convention. The Committee relaxed conservation demands for a number of inscribed properties—with the Galapagos Islands again going first—and awarded World Heritage honors liberally. In heated debates resorting to the most far-fetched arguments, three Committee states—Switzerland, Sweden, and Estonia—defended expert advice and proper procedure yet their peers—led by China, Mexico, Egypt, Russia, and the host nation Brazil—overruled them time and again. In a way, the Global South was finally taking its due: all twelve unsupported List inscriptions were from outside Europe and only one of them from a "Northern" country (Australia) whereas the three European resisters embodied past Northern hegemony, leading all their Committee peers in terms of World Heritage properties per population. While the new mode of operation was still controversial in Brasilia, resistance waned over the next years, given that incoming Committee states—North and South—found it agreeable for their interest in maximizing World Heritage titles while minimizing Committee interference. The 2015 session saw peace return to the Committee but also the largest proportion of recommended inscriptions by ICOMOS in a decade.[11] Some amount of lobbying with Committee peers coupled with sheer persistence often suffices to achieve desired outcomes by now, and a decision as in 2009 when anguished Committee delegates voted for ignoring German pleas and deleting the Dresden Elbe Valley from the List has become all but unthinkable. Critics including UNESCO officials have deplored the "politicization" of the Committee, seeing it reduced to intergovernmental horse-trading (Meskell 2015c) and diagnosing "gridlock" (Meskell 2015b) or a "current crisis" (Meskell et al. 2014: 13), but many treaty states have little reason to complain.

They are also less likely to be hindered from appropriating World Heritage for political purposes: China, for example, would instrumentalize the multinational Silk Roads nomination (inscribed in 2014) both for promoting its contemporary "Silk Roads Economic Belt" initiative to its Central Asian neighbors and for disseminating to its own citizens a Sinocentric narrative from which all disturbing elements—such as the Muslim sites—were ultimately cleansed (Cheung 2016), without any questioning by ICOMOS or the Committee. National supremacy extends to challengers such as indigenous peoples who have repeatedly deplored violations of the UN Declaration on the Rights of Indigenous Peoples of 2007 in connection with World Heritage candidacies in recent years. Yet when the respective national delegations claim that all is well, this is to little avail (Brumann 2016a: 306–309), a pattern familiar from the failed attempt to install a World Heritage Indigenous Peoples Council of Experts (WHIPCOE) in the early 2000s (Meskell 2013, Logan 2013).

And neither would most bearers of the World Heritage title complain. It is intriguing how even for the likes of the Great Barrier Reef, news coverage invariably mentions the UNESCO distinction, obviously assuming that this adds significance in the general reader's eyes. The mobilization of people, resources, and enthusiasm around World Heritage candidacies is often impressive, even in the core countries of "old heritage," as just observed for two unsuccessful nominations close to my home (the Francke Foundation in Halle and the cultural landscape around Naumburg Cathedral). The impact of World Heritage on the general heritage boom, the spread of university programs and the rise of the "critical heritage studies" movement (Winter and Waterton 2013) can hardly be overestimated, as is evident from the readiness of States Parties to set up "Category 2 Centres" for World Heritage with UNESCO blessing[12] and the space that World Heritage occupies in heritage handbooks, overviews, and programmatic statements (e.g. Harrison 2012, Logan, Nic Craith, and Kockel 2016, Meskell 2015a, Smith 2006, Tauschek 2013, Waterton and Watson 2015). The Convention has strengthened global "heritage belief" (Brumann 2014a) like little else—which, I hasten to add, is not the same as facilitating conservation or the implementation of other stated goals.

WORLD HERITAGE AND GLOBAL CUSTODIANSHIP

Whether the venture has really managed to transform prime cultural and natural sites into the "common heritage of mankind" is a different question. The extension of this new concept in international law, previously applied to the high seas, outer space, and Antarctica (Höhler 2014), to parts of national territories was an innovative move. By nominating their properties, nation states agree to constrain their own sovereignty, sharing obligations but also rights with all of us, as many as fifty-one times in the case of Italy and for a total of 1052 properties in 165 countries (as of 2016). The components of this quasi-extraterritorial utopia, when taken together, would be the eighth largest country in the world.[13] No state waives its visa requirements for visits to World Heritage sites, however, and neither did the Abu Simbel precedent mobilize huge resources for the World Heritage Fund. Setting up systematic reporting and monitoring procedures took a long time (cf. Cameron and Rössler 2013, 109, 114, 124, 130, 133, 151) and is still largely based on the States Parties' self-reporting. For their personnel and financial capacity alone, the secretariat and the Advisory Bodies can do little in terms of systematic monitoring beyond pursuing the most egregious cases and offering themselves as contact points for whistleblowing. Given that the growth of the World Heritage List outpaces everything around it, this is unlikely to change.

Moral co-ownership on a global scale does not automatically translate into peaceful cooperation either. The ancient Khmer temple of Preah Vihear, listed in 2008, has the dubious distinction of having provoked the first World Heritage war when the troops of Cambodia (nominating the site) and Thailand (claiming it as its own territory) clashed in the aftermath (Hauser-Schäublin 2011a, Silverman 2011, Williams 2011). The "Medieval Monuments in Kosovo" and the Church of the Nativity in Bethlehem and the cultural landscape around Battir, both nominated on an emergency basis by Palestine, are other inscriptions that become the nodes for political conflicts that transcend them, requiring the most delicate closed-door negotiations, and they are all dwarfed by the attention that the Old City of Jerusalem has absorbed over the years (De Cesari 2014, Gfeller 2013a). Tensions also emerge when a hydroelectric dam in Ethiopia has long-distance repercussions for Lake Turkana in Kenya or when a Japanese nomination of early industrial sites fails to mention a history of South (and North) Korean forced labor, bringing the two to loggerheads and having everyone else walk on tiptoes in the 2015 session (Brumann 2016b). Clearly, heritage conservation is often the least of concerns in these conflicts. Yet World Heritage also brings countries together for such multinational sites as the Struve Geodetic Arc (in twelve countries), the architectural work of Le Corbusier (seven countries on three continents), or the Qhapac Ñan, the Andean road network of the Incas (six countries), and participants believably profess that this leads to rewarding international exchanges.

Most of the time, however, the World Heritage title is left to unfold its own, unfunded magic. Once obtained, it can work miracles for investments, development funds by other organizations such as the World Bank, and tourist streams, although there are also cases that disappoint such hopes. For Cologne Cathedral and the historic centers of Vienna, Riga, and Saint Petersburg, the World Heritage title was crucial in suppressing high-rise advances, and the stop of mining in Kakadu National Park, Australia (Logan 2013), or of the highway through the Serengeti was also credited—or conveniently conceded—to the World Heritage Committee. A knowledgeable IUCN official assured me that no other designation of nature reserves is as powerful, and a World Heritage Centre official claimed that without their World Heritage status, the national parks in the Democratic Republic of Congo and their okapis and mountain gorillas would long be gone. Obviously, such claims are difficult to test, and there are scores of cases where Committee reprimands achieve very little against recalcitrant or powerless nation states or against assertive local authorities (as in Dresden or in Liverpool). Sometimes, defeat seems to be almost expected, such as when calling for "visual integrity" and extensive viewing corridors for the Tower or the Westminster sites in the midst of the London skyscraper rush. The construction of the Metro Bridge over the Golden Horn in Istanbul was an instructive case in point: as this affected the famous vistas of the historic peninsula and its mosques, ICOMOS managed to include threats of Danger Listing in the draft decisions, but Turkish lobbying and minor compromises with the size and design of the structure averted this, to the disenchantment of local opponents who had had expected more support from presumably powerful "UNESCO" (Marquart 2015). Whether World Heritage is a boon or a bane here is very much in the eyes of the beholder: it did prevent the worst (from a conservationist perspective) but does it prevent enough? What is safe to say is that the weight it acquires, because of the structural weakness of its core institutions, is precisely the one that national and local actors, in their internal debates, are willing to concede to it—which, depending on the political climate, can still be considerable or even decisive.

WORLD HERITAGE AND HERITAGE CONCEPTIONS

On a conceptual level, World Heritage has contributed to a more democratic and egalitarian notion of cultural heritage, away from the celebration of elite privilege and from ignoring the victims of history. Turning the heritage gaze to the aforementioned new categories either profited from the imprimatur of the World Heritage organizations or, in the case of the cultural landscapes, was largely their brainchild to begin with, and this has left an imprint even in the core countries of "old heritage." World-spanning narratives in the appreciation of cultural heritage have been strengthened alongside, for transboundary properties and for sites of long-distance trade, voluntary and forced migration, cultural routes, pilgrimage, cross-continental communication (such as Varberg Radio Station in Grimeton, Sweden), and cultural fusion (such as the Osun-Osogbo Sacred Grove, Nigeria). Indirectly, World Heritage has also contributed to honoring intangible cultural heritage with its separate UNESCO convention in 2003, both by the discontents it had created in the Global South and by the—sometimes positive, sometimes negative—role model it provided.

World Heritage has done far less in terms of conceptual clarity. Committee debates often feel improvised and there is little consistency and cross-reference over the years in such matters as how to conceptualize and what to include in a cultural route (Brumann 2015), how to treat sites deriving their fame from celebrated individuals (Brumann 2013: 10–12), where to locate the authenticity of a (perennially changing) cultural landscape, or how to operationalize the "in danger" threshold. "Serial" properties combining up to several hundreds of discrete components into a single entry (and narrative) provide challenges of their own, especially when the selection appears arbitrary or when the same site features in two different candidate series (such as San Luis Potosí, Mexico, did in 2010).

Most crucially, the core quality of "outstanding universal value"—"OUV"—demanded for a World Heritage inscription continues to be intuited rather than precisely defined and measured, particularly for the cultural properties; unsurprising for an anthropologist though this is. The required "comparative analyses" in the nominations, too, often content themselves with demonstrating the distinctiveness of a candidate, not its relative rank (Brumann 2017). In the end, the string of expert meetings and "Thematic Studies" by the World Heritage Centre and the Advisory Bodies can only make suggestions, as the right to nominate or not nominate specific sites and categories, of an innovative or entirely conventional character, rests with the States Parties. Future innovation too—battlefields? sports stadiums? subway lines? urban slums?—will depend on the vicissitudes of their uncoordinated initiatives.

It is also not too likely that the residues of Northern hegemony and bias will be removed. Asia competes with Europe now for leading the nomination rush but this largely falls on (the Asian part of) Turkey, Iran, India, China, South Korea, and Japan. These countries team up with the Western European list leaders against anything that might inhibit their submission stream, and the parallels with similar struggles in the World Bank or the International Monetary Fund suggest that the lack of Southern/non-Western solidarity is not germane to heritage (Brumann under review). The World Heritage Unit of IUCN, the World Heritage Advisors of ICOMOS, and the World Heritage Panels of both organizations continue to be dominated by Europeans and North Americans, and the ICOMOS World Heritage Panel is an assembly of practicing conservation architects and elected office-holders, rather than having the scientific credentials that the organization routinely claims and the interdisciplinary composition that the nature of submitted sites might suggest.[14] I see this reflected, for example, in the vastly uneven treatment that cultural landscape nominations from Denmark, Kenya, and Uganda received in the 2015 session cycle (Brumann under review). Yet as long as the larger Southern countries get what they want, the momentum for a more fundamental revision appears unlikely to arise.

WORLD HERITAGE ON THE GROUND

As for what happens with and around World Heritage on the ground, there are as many stories as properties, and the royal road to "benefits beyond borders" (Galla 2012) has not been found yet. Take for example Angkor in Cambodia, a World Heritage site that has seen a quite spectacular international mobilization for conservation activities. Ancient structures have indeed been stabilized and visitor numbers skyrocketed, supporting a struggling national economy, yet the local population sees its old rights and practices—having fish ponds and rice paddies between the ruins, continuing worship in the temples—constrained and is under pressure to resettle, with profits from tourism often bypassing them (Hauser-Schäublin 2011b).

A series of ethnographic site studies co-edited by myself (Brumann and Berliner 2016b) found the loss of local control to be a constant, less to UNESCO bodies than to national authorities that impose their vision of World Heritage glory and propriety (Brumann and Berliner 2016a: 24). The assessment of World Heritage effects is a challenge: for example, in Melaka, Malaysia, the World Heritage listing of the historical center has brought renewed estimation to the city's multiethnic heritage, and the colonial buildings and Sino-Dutch shop houses are, by and large, well-kept and protected from modern incursions. Yet the ring of high-rises just a step outside the buffer zone—often on reclaimed land that removes the famous port ever further from the coastline—is thickening at the same time. Tourism has multiplied, sending an incessant stream of cars, motor rickshaws, and motor boats through the streets and canals, and shop houses re-open as cafés, boutique hotels, or galleries, feeding demand for the high-rise apartments. Most locals approve of the economic boost this brings but old-time shop house residents feel alienated by the loss of local community and the Chetti—descendants of the earliest Indian traders—do not find support in their struggle to protect their neighborhood outside the property, much as it is their downtown temples and sites that are celebrated (De Giosa 2016). Whether World Heritage status has improved things here depends very much on the beneficiaries (or victims?) considered and the standards applied, and the only thing that is certain—as for much other heritage designation—is its contribution to change.

THE FUTURE OF WORLD HERITAGE

That said, I expect World Heritage to play a decreasing role in the future. The growth of the List with an ever larger proportion of sites looking for the title to shine (rather than the other way around) will continue, as so much—happy World Heritage news, the countries' commitment to the venture, UNESCO's and the Advisory Bodies' visibility and perceived importance—depends on it. While almost everyone in the arena is able to name absurd inscriptions, almost everyone points to unlisted sites that deserve the global label. I have yet to meet anyone suggesting immediate closure and Advisory Body personnel confirm that, other things equal, every additional property extends their sphere of legitimate interference. But this directs attention and resources away from other concerns such as the condition of inscribed sites, general questions, and the larger sense of mission. Even the global headlines that the Islamist insurgents then in control of Timbuktu, Mali, had justified their deliberate destructions of the mosques and Sufi tombs with a Committee decision (the Danger Listing of the property a couple of days earlier) did not suffice to give the machinery pause: instead, listing business as usual continued in the 2012 session, delaying an official condemnation of the acts (Brumann 2016a: 309–314).

Yet now when almost all states have joined the treaty and contributions cannot increase any further, added growth strains the resources that have suffered immensely from the financial crisis and the US withdrawal from UNESCO after Palestine's admission in 2011. In the course of subsequent restructuring, the much-reduced personnel of the World Heritage Centre has been reabsorbed into the Culture Sector of the organization. With such a curtailed operational base, conceptual innovation such as in the 1990s or any kind of ambitious change is unlikely to occur. More than ever, the World Heritage institutions' influence on the properties will depend on what the respective country allows, cannot suppress, or even actively seeks, such as when using Committee warnings as a stick against subsidiary government levels. The openness to State Party wishes has reached an all-time high so that the status quo of the World Heritage arena will be, shall we say, conserved.

Yet the World Heritage title will continue to work its magic for the foreseeable future. I do not think that it can be endlessly protected from the reputational damage done by the listing of not-so-impressive sites and by mass media coverage of Committee horse-trading and of (where it applies) the powerlessness of UNESCO site protection. But for the time being, World Heritage still inspires awe and even worries about its unchecked powers (e.g. Meskell 2016: 85–88), and it is a major vehicle for "world-making" (Brumann 2014b), that is for imagining and experiencing the world. This is also confirmed by the frequency with which the "World Heritage" label is (wrongly) applied to the laureates of other UNESCO registers such as those for intangible cultural heritage or the "Memory of the World" archival resources. World Heritage will continue to be harnessed to all kinds of aspirations, uplifting or sinister, conservationist or otherwise. But what is being done in its name will be ever less under the control of the global community and the organizational apparatus set up for this purpose.

NOTES

1. For this chapter, I rely on ethnographic observation of the World Heritage Committee sessions of 2009–12 and 2015, the World Heritage General Assemblies of 2011 and 2013, and other meetings such as the forty-year celebration of the Convention in Kyoto 2012; countless casual conservations with fellow participants; several dozen formal interviews with key individuals from all contributing organizations; and the Committee documents available at <http://whc.unesco.org>. Initial funding was provided by the German Research Association (DFG).
2. Background information, documents, and decisions for all mentioned World Heritage properties can be retrieved from <http://whc.unesco.org/en/list>.
3. Cf. <https://books.google.com/ngrams>.
4. <http://whc.unesco.org/en/globalstrategy>.
5. <https://www.icomos.org/charters/nara-e.pdf>.
6. Cf. <http://whc.unesco.org/en/list/stat>.
7. Cf. <http://whc.unesco.org/en/culturallandscape>.
8. Cf. <http://whc.unesco.org/en/guidelines>.
9. <http://whc.unesco.org/document/116069>.
10. Cf. the figure "Number of World Heritage properties inscribed each year by region" (<http://whc.unesco.org/en/list/stat>) and the list of new "in Danger" entries (<http://whc.unesco.org/en/list/stat#s7>) for that time period.
11. There were only very few natural candidate sites in that session.
12. <http://whc.unesco.org/en/category2centres>.
13. According to the table "Areas of properties inscribed each year" (<whc.unesco.org/en/list/stat>) and assuming that the figures for forests in that table are included in the totals for natural sites, natural and mixed properties have an aggregate surface area of 2,864,697 square kilometers (including some sea) which the usually much smaller cultural properties cannot bring up to the size of country number seven (India).
14. Cf. <https://www.icomos.org/images/DOCUMENTS/World_Heritage/20160613_ICOMOS_2015_Panel.pdf, https://www.iucn.org/theme/world-heritage/our-work/

advisor-world- heritage/iucn-world-heritage-panel> and the information available about the listed individuals on the public internet and the LinkedIn professional network.

REFERENCES

Allais, Lucia. 2013. "Integrities: The Salvage of Abu Simbel." *Grey Room* 50: 6–45.

Batisse, Michel, and Gérard Bolla. 2005. *The Invention of "World Heritage*. Paris: Association of Former UNESCO Staff Members.

Betts, Paul. 2015. "The Warden of World Heritage: UNESCO and the Rescue of the Nubian Monuments." *Past & Present* 226(10): 100–125.

Brumann, Christoph. 2013. "Comment le patrimoine mondial de l'Unesco devient immatériel." *Gradhiva* 18: 5–29.

Brumann, Christoph. 2014a. "Heritage Agnosticism: A Third Path for the Study of Cultural Heritage." *Social Anthropology* 22(2): 73–88.

Brumann, Christoph. 2014b. "Shifting Tides of World-Making in the UNESCO World Heritage Convention: Cosmopolitanisms Colliding." *Ethnic and Racial Studies* 37(12): 2176–2192.

Brumann, Christoph. 2015. "Vom Nutzen der Verbindungen: Die 'Cultural Routes' im UNESCO-Welterbegeschehen," in *Kulturstraßen als Konzept: 20 Jahre Straße der Romanik*, ed. Andreas Ranft and Wolfgang Schenkluhn. Regensburg: Schnell and Steiner, 211–221.

Brumann, Christoph. 2016a. "Conclusion. Imagining the Ground from Afar: Why the Sites Are So Remote in World Heritage Committee Sessions," in *World Heritage on the Ground: Ethnographic Perspectives*, ed. Christoph Brumann and David Berliner. Oxford: Berghahn, 294–317.

Brumann, Christoph. 2016b. "UNESCO-Welterbe, ostasiatische Nachbarn und japanische Altlasten," in *Japan 2016: Politik, Wirtschaft und Gesellschaft*, edited ed. David Chiavacci and Iris Wieczorek. Munich: Iudicium, 93–115.

Brumann, Christoph. 2017. "The Best of the Best: Positing, Measuring and Sensing Value in the UNESCO World Heritage Arena," in *Palaces of Hope: The Anthropology of Global Organizations*, ed. Ron Niezen and Maria Sapignoli. Cambridge: Cambridge University Press, 245–265.

Brumann, Christoph. Under review. "Slag Heaps and Time Lags: Undermining Southern Solidarity in the UNESCO World Heritage Committee."

Brumann, Christoph, and David Berliner. 2016a. "Introduction. UNESCO World Heritage— grounded?," in *World Heritage on the ground: Ethnographic Perspectives*, ed. Christoph Brumann and David Berliner. Oxford: Berghahn, 1–34.

Brumann, Christoph, and David Berliner, eds. 2016b. *World Heritage on the Ground: Ethnographic Perspectives*. Oxford: Berghahn.

Cameron, Christina, and Mechtild Rössler. 2013. *Many Voices, One Vision: The Early Years of the World Heritage Convention*. Farnham: Ashgate.

Cheung, Ah Li. 2016. *De-foreignizing the Past: The Politics of Heritage in Xi'an, Central China*. PhD thesis. Martin Luther University Halle-Wittenberg.

De Cesari, Chiara. 2014. "World Heritage and the Nation-State: A View from Palestine," in *Transnational Memory: Circulation, Articulation, Scales*, ed. Chiara De Cesari and Ann Rignety. Berlin: de Gruyter, 247–270.

De Giosa, Pierpaolo. 2016. *Heritage below the Winds: The Social Life of the Cityscape and UNESCO World Heritage in Melaka*. PhD thesis. Martin Luther University Halle-Wittenberg.

Galla, Amareswar, ed. 2012. *World Heritage: Benefits beyond Borders*. Cambridge: Cambridge University Press.

Gfeller, Aurélie Elisa. 2013a. "Culture at the Crossroad of International Politics: UNESCO, World Heritage and the Holy Land." *Fondation Pierre du Bois Current Affairs in Perspective* 3, <http://www.fondation-pierredubois.ch/Papiers-d-actualite/jerusalem.html>.

Gfeller, Aurélie Elisa. 2013b. "Negotiating the Meaning of Global Heritage: 'Cultural Landscapes' in the UNESCO World Heritage Convention, 1972–1992." *Journal of Global History* 8(3): 483–503.

Gfeller, Aurélie Elisa. 2015. "Anthropologizing and Indigenizing Heritage: The Origins of the UNESCO Global Strategy for a Representative, Balanced and Credible World Heritage List." *Journal of Social Archaeology* 15(3): 366–386.

Gfeller, Aurélie Elisa. 2017. "The Authenticity of Heritage: Global Norm-Making at the Crossroads of Cultures." *American Historical Review* 122(3): 758–791.

Harrison, Rodney. 2012. *Heritage: Critical Approaches*. London: Routledge.

Hauser-Schäublin, Brigitta. 2011a. "Preah Vihear: From Objects of Colonial Desire to a Contested World Heritage Site," in *World Heritage Angkor and Beyond: Circumstances and Implications of UNESCO Listings in Cambodia*, ed. Brigitta Hauser-Schäublin. Göttingen: Göttinger Universitäts-Verlag, 33–56.

Hauser-Schäublin, Brigitta, ed. 2011b. *World Heritage Angkor and Beyond: Circumstances and Implications of UNESCO Listings in Cambodia*. Göttingen: Göttinger Universitäts-Verlag.

Höhler, Sabine. 2014. "Exterritoriale Ressourcen: Die Diskussion um die Tiefsee, die Pole und das Weltall um 1970," in *Global Commons im 20. Jahrhundert: Entwürfe für eine globale Welt*, ed. Isabella Löhr and Andrea Rehling. Berlin: de Gruyter, 53–82.

Logan, William. 2013. "Australia, Indigenous Peoples and World Heritage from Kakadu to Cape York: State Party Behaviour under the World Heritage Convention." *Journal of Social Archaeology* 13(2): 153–176.

Logan, William, Máiréad Nic Craith, and Ullrich Kockel, eds. 2016. *A Companion to Heritage Studies*. Chichester, West Sussex: Wiley-Blackwell.

Marquart, Vivienne. 2015. *Monuments and Malls: Heritage Politics and Urban Struggles in Istanbul*. PhD thesis. Martin Luther University Halle-Wittenberg.

Meskell, Lynn. 2013. "UNESCO and the Fate of the World Heritage Indigenous Peoples Council of Experts (WHIPCOE)." *International Journal of Cultural Property* 20(2): 155–174.

Meskell, Lynn, ed. 2015a. *Global Heritage: A Reader*. Hoboken, NJ: Wiley-Blackwell.

Meskell, Lynn. 2015b. "Gridlock: UNESCO, Global Conflict and Failed Ambitions." *World Archaeology* 47(2): 225–238.

Meskell, Lynn. 2015c. "Transacting UNESCO World Heritage: Gifts and Exchanges on a Global Stage." *Social Anthropology* 23(1): 3–21.

Meskell, Lynn. 2016. "World Heritage and WikiLeaks." *Current Anthropology* 57(1): 72–95.

Meskell, Lynn, C. Liuzza, E. Bertacchini, and D. Saccone. 2014. "Multilateralism and UNESCO World Heritage: Decision-Making, States Parties and Political Processes." *International Journal of Heritage Studies* 21(5): 423–440.

Silverman, Helaine. 2011. "Border Wars: The Ongoing Temple Dispute between Thailand and Cambodia and UNESCO's World Heritage List." *International Journal of Heritage Studies* 17(1): 1–21.

Smith, Laurajane. 2006. *Uses of Heritage*. New York: Routledge.

Stott, Peter H. 2011. "The World Heritage Convention and the National Park Service, 1962–1972." *The George White Forum* 28(3): 279–290.

Tauschek, Markus. 2013. *Kulturerbe: Eine Einführung.* Berlin: Reimer.

Titchen, Sarah M. 1995. *On the Construction of Outstanding Universal Value: UNESCO's World Heritage Convention (Convention Concerning the Protection of the World Cultural and Natural Heritage, 1972) and the Identification and Assessment of Cultural Places for Inclusion in the World Heritage List.* PhD thesis. Australian National University.

Waterton, Emma, and Steve Watson, eds. 2015. *The Palgrave Handbook of Contemporary Heritage Research.* Houndmills: Palgrave Macmillan.

Williams, Tim, 2011. "The Curious Tale of Preah Vihear: The Process and Value of World Heritage Nomination." *Conservation and Management of Archaeological Sites* 13(1): 1–7.

Winter, Tim, and Emma Waterton. 2013. "Special Issue: Critical Heritage Studies." *International Journal of Heritage Studies* 19(6): 529–609.

....

THE SUFFOCATED CULTURAL HERITAGE OF SUB-SAHARAN AFRICA'S PROTECTED AREAS

....

SUSAN O. KEITUMETSE AND ARPAKWA O. SIKOREI

INTRODUCTION AND GENERAL CONTEXT

MANAGEMENT of sub-Saharan Protected areas have been characterized with most countries signing up to a majority of international conventions aimed at protecting not only the natural environment, but also collectively managing political threats that are likely to emanate from other states' interest to harness cross-border environmental resources (Keitumetse 2016b). A typical example in this regard is southern Africa's Okavango River system that extends across three countries and the case of Ngorongoro Crater landscape that extends across two countries. These conservation efforts however are at a broader scale that overlooks geo-place-specific contexts, as well as resources-specific conservation challenges. This chapter looks at the micro scale conservation complexities of African protected landscapes to illustrate some of the gaps that need to be addressed by adopting land management approaches that account for each of the resources found in landscapes that have been dissected from their social and cultural contexts. To achieve this, conservationists should ask questions such as "what diversity of resources do protected landscapes host?"; "how can they all be accounted for?"; "how is each resource of value to the broader conservation of the landscape surrounding it?" This paper focuses on and discusses two World Heritage sites as case studies from sub-Saharan Africa to illuminate on these questions: the Ngorongoro Crater Conservation Area World Heritage site in Tanzania and the Okavango Delta World Heritage site in Botswana.

SUB-SAHARAN AFRICA PROTECTED
LANDSCAPES AND INTERNATIONAL POLICY

At its seventieth session on October 21, 2015, the General Assembly of the United Nations adopted an agenda with a resolution in a document titled "Transforming our World: The 2030 Agenda for Sustainable Development," (United Nations 2017, <http://www.un.org/sustainabledevelopment/development-agenda/>; UNESCO 2017). The preamble section of the document states that seventeen sustainable development goals and sixty-nine targets were outlined ". . . to build on the Millennium Development Goals and complete what they did not achieve . . . . The goals and targets will stimulate action over the next 15 years in areas of critical importance for humanity and the planet." These goals and targets are outlined under declaration number 59 of the same document.

Therefore the Millennium Development Goals have come and gone, and are now followed by the newly adopted 2030 Agenda for Sustainable Development that "call for action by all countries, poor, rich and middle-income to promote prosperity while protecting the planet. They recognize that ending poverty must go hand-in-hand with strategies that build economic growth and addresses a range of social needs including education, health, social protection, and job opportunities, while tackling climate change and environmental protection." Although this declaration is loaded and indeed encompassing in recognizing a way forward for sustainable resources conservation, it does show, in its content, a constant omission by both international and national institutions to recognize beyond vague mention the significance of cultural heritage resources and their specific indicators that should and can inform the process of sustainable development. It is at stages like the formulation of targets where the Millennium Development Goals missed the significant relevance of cultural resources in sustainable development ideals. Once the focus is missed at this stage, member states carry the incomplete baton to the end date, which in this case is the year 2030.

The main question is at what cost? The preceding Millennium Development Goals were also narrow in this regard, focusing almost solely on a mention of indigenous communities as the sole representatives of distinctive community cultural components in protected areas that are perceived as natural resources laden landscapes (Keitumetse 2011). The Botswana's Okavango Delta (Figure 1.2.1) case study's description of "the people" of the area illustrates this well. The focus on "indigenous" people or indigeneity excludes people who can be defined as autochthonous to such landscapes. Autochthony is an affiliation to land and country that is associated with settlement history and land habitation by a community or ethnic community prior to others. Therefore, "autochthony comes with components such as time immemorial; . . . continuous habitation; ethnic pride, sense of land and country; native . . ." (Keitumetse 2016b: 64). Indigenous people are indigenous even across borders, but autochthony denotes people who lay claim to land affiliation and association by virtue of settlement

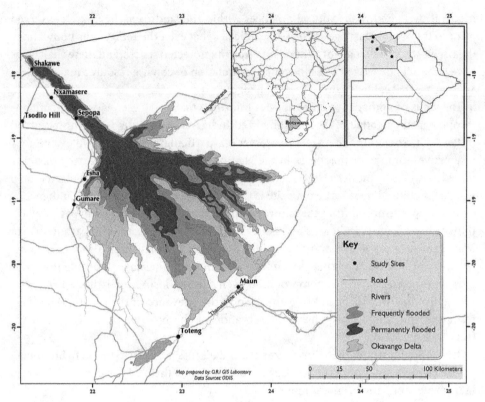

FIGURE 1.2.1 Map showing the location of Okavango Delta in Botswana.

Courtesy of Okavango Research Institute, GIS laboratory.

history enabled by environmental adaptation to land prior to arrival of other communal groups. Over time therefore autochthony can be defined through descriptors such as genealogy (Rosivach 1987), identity (Zenker 2011), and at times as a functional tool (Hilgers 2011).

> *Indigeneity* on the other hand is a term attributed to peoples commonly referred in the literature as "first peoples" who inhabited geographical spaces prior to tribal conquer of landscapes as well as prior to European colonialism of the continent. In particular to southern Africa, examples of these communities are the San/Bushmen/ Basarwa of Botswana and the Khoikhoi and Namaqua in South Africa. In West Africa examples include the Tuareg of the Sahel, the Ogoni people of Nigeria and the Ashanti people of Ghana. In Central Africa examples include the Mbororo and Baka of Cameroon. In North Africa there are the Nubians of Egypt and Sudan and the Berbers of Morocco, Algeria, Libya, Mauritania and Egypt.
>
> (Keitumetse 2016b: 65)

By extension, the Tanzania case study illustrates that though the Maasai communities are recognized within the landscape, they are only useful to the dominant conservation model if they shed their cultural practices within the landscape they have conserved prior to the World Heritage status. This indicates that even the indigenous populations themselves face challenges of cultural retention in protected spaces, and these challenges have to be acknowledged so as to enable formulation of concise resource management approaches that can overcome these challenges.

The focus on indigenous communities informed mainly by the 1960s dominant anthropological narrative of "the marginalized indigene" is proving to be short-sighted in twenty-first-century resources conservation, particularly in a case where the representative "sample" as it appears in the Ngorongoro Crater case is evolving or being forced to evolve by modern times' landscape uses pressured by economic, international and socio-cultural needs. The opposite is the case where the representative indigenous community is removed from the anthropological romanticized context to pave way for protected areas (national parks and game reserves), as is the case of Okavango Delta Management areas of Botswana as well as Serengeti National Park also in Tanzania. Where communities are removed, cultural resources and heritage of people that once lived in protected spaces is compromised even further, losing the latitude to be representative in a way that can bring attention to the relevance of their cultural heritage resources and lead to sustainable conservation of the broader protected landscape (Keitumetse 2016a).

This paper illustrates these predicaments, and discusses the case studies to illuminate neglected challenges of protected area model approach that call for new insights into management of African environments.

Tourism and Economic Dominance of Conservation Indicators

As already indicated, sub-Saharan Africa's protected areas are largely managed with safari tourism in mind (Keitumetse 2016c). Even the new United Nations 2030 Agenda for Sustainable Development has adopted this approach as articulated in its Goal 8; point 8.9 states "By 2030, devise and implement policies to promote sustainable tourism that creates jobs and promotes local culture and products"—however, the policy document fails to recognize that it needs to promote local culture first, and then sieve what is appropriate for economic purposes and what is appropriate for sustaining the cultural integrity of communities. Cultural components of African protected areas exist before and beyond the economic value of tourism. A point of departure such as that suggested within the UN Agenda 2030 sets precedents that compromise cultural and cultural heritage resources value and significance at international level. Suffocation and "breathing" potential of cultural resources are in this chapter illustrated through Okavango and Ngorongoro World Heritage sites case studies. The suffocation factor is the exclusion of people's heritage from protected areas. The people can be either indigenous or autochthonous. The breathing potential is illustrated through the options discussed in the case studies, i.e. finding alternative ways of recognizing and acknowledging cultural heritage resources in protected areas already designated as nature resources hotspots, popularly known as national parks and game reserves (Figure 1.2.2).

Key attributes that the two case studies (Okavango and Ngorongoro) will illuminate are as follows:

- What is missing that could propel inclusion of cultural heritage perspectives?
- What is overstated that overshadows the relevance of the missing cultural resources?
- What could be learnt going forward to inform meaningful inclusion of cultural resources?

The two case studies of Okavango Delta and Ngorongoro Crater World Heritage sites will illustrate that public heritage as social practice in southern Africa's protected areas is very limited even in spaces where communities are allowed to stay in the protected areas such as the Ngorongoro crater. The heritage aspect is largely suffocated by the need to accommodate conservation rules that are not supportive to cultural aspects of landscapes, as observed by Keitumetse (2011) and Sikorei (2015).

FIGURE 1.2.2 Mapping cultural identities in the Okavango, surveying for heritage aspects within a Delta landscape, 2010, with the aid of Botswana Defence Force (BDF) for access.

Case Study 1:   Okavango Delta World Heritage Site and Cultural Heritage Omissions

As already introduced, this case study features a site that has recently been listed, following all the conferences and revisions of most national and international policies, but nonetheless still omits cultural heritage aspects.

The Okavango Delta is an inland delta whose presence is attributed to an extension of the Great Rift Valley system spanning from East Africa downwards (cf. Wolski et al. 2006; McCarthy et al. 1998). The Okavango Delta ecosystem was listed as the 1000th World Heritage site by UNESCO in December 2015 as a natural site, under World Heritage Criterion vii (natural phenomena), Criterion ix (ecological and biological processes), and Criterion x (natural habitats for in situ conservation of biological diversity). These focus solely on nature-related heritage, <http://whc.unesco.org/en/criteria/>. The Okavango Delta system however hosts community cultures from Angola, Namibia, and down to Botswana delta where these cultures are interconnected in a spatio-temporal context. The diverse communities continue to depend on the ecosystem for their livelihood as well as their cultural associations that are outlined in literature such as Tlou (1972), Chirenje (1977), Bock et al. (2004, 2005), Bernard and Moetapele (2005), and Keitumetse and Pampiri (2016). As already observed in earlier works, the site therefore is more suited to category "mixed," rather than "natural" as currently designated (Keitumetse 2016a).

Therefore the UNESCO criteria under which the Okavango Delta site could have been currently listed in addition to the three above are Criterion v (outstanding example of a traditional human settlement . . . representative of a culture . . . or human interaction) and Criterion vi (directly or tangibly associated with events or living traditions).

For Botswana (Figure 1.2.1), during the listing process "Convenience appears to have taken precedence over implications for sustainable conservation (preservation and utilization) going forward" (Keitumetse 2016a: 54). An environment similar to the Okavango Delta, Senegal's Saloum Delta is listed as a cultural landscape, and as a cultural site, and is described in a way that reflects a delta life that could not be easily ignored by human populations surrounding it. The following description from Senegal fits the Okavango Delta life use very well: "Fishing and shellfish gathering have sustained human life in the 5,000 km^2 property, which is formed by the arms of three rivers. The site comprises brackish channels encompassing over 200 islands and islets, mangrove forest, an Atlantic marine environment, and dry forest" (<http://whc.unesco.org/en/list/1359>).

Under protection and management requirements of the World Heritage list accessible in UNESCO's World Heritage website the description focuses exclusively on the indigenous population, and ignores the autochthonous populations as described earlier that have inhabited the Okavango Delta system in Angola, Namibia, and Botswana over a considerable length of time stretching as far back as the eighteenth century and even earlier (Tlou 1972, Chrenje 1977). Therefore the suffocation occurs in that the majority of the people are autochthonous and not indigenous, and their heritage is left out because policy is only looking at indigenous people's heritage. Efforts to map these alternative cultural heritages comprise Keitumetse's work as depicted in Figure 1.2.2 below.

The statement that describes people for Okavango Delta World Heritage site in the UNESCO listing website reads as follows:

> The Delta has been inhabited for centuries by small numbers of indigenous people, living a hunter-gatherer existence with different groups adapting their cultural identity and lifestyle to the exploitation of particular resources (e.g. fishing or hunting). This form of low-level subsistence use has had no significant impact on the ecological integrity of the area, and today mixed settlements of indigenous peoples and later immigrants to the area are located around the fringes of the delta, mostly outside the boundaries of the property. Continued special attention is needed to reinforce the recognition of the cultural heritage of indigenous inhabitants of the Delta region.... Efforts should center on ensuring that indigenous peoples living in the property are included ... [that] their views are respected and integrated into management planning and implementation, and that they have access to benefits stemming from tourism.
>
> (<http://whc.unesco.org/en/list/1432>)

This description does not only minimize the Okavango Delta communities that could be acknowledged as communities associated with such landscapes during the listing process stage, but also creates unnecessary conflicts between communities identifying with the Okavango Delta and similar landscapes. The emphasis of the statement on only "indigenous people ... integrated into management planning ... and ... hav[ing] access to benefits ... from tourism" is one of the issues that are causing conflicts related to economic benefits sharing in most natural-resources rich areas of southern Africa. It is thus pertinent that a World Heritage status recognize the various communities that inhabit and lay claim to the identities within the Okavango Delta. There are two concepts that define the general group of people affiliated and associated with the Okavango Delta World Heritage site as a landscape where their heritage has been deposited through time. These are indigenous and autochthonous groups.

In addition to indigenous communities of Bugakhwe, Dxereku, and Xanekwe there are also communities that are autochthonous (cf. Gausset et al. 2011, Keitumetse 2016b) to the Delta area and landscape: Wayeyi, Hambukushu, and Tawana communities that have been interacting with the landscape and indigenous people for a very long time deserve mention and their cultural identity to the landscape deserve recognition, in a heritage identity listing such as at the World Heritage stage. Wayeyi in particular are well-known water people (Tlou 1972, Chirenje 1977, Nyati-Ramahobo 2002). The indigenous people in accordance with the ILO Convention No. 169 that are associated with the Okavango Delta water systems are the River San (Saugestad, 2001; Bolaane and Sudo 2013) who interacted with the Wayeyi long before the demarcation of borders of the Ramsar site (Ramsar Bureau, 1971 <http://www.ramsar.org/>) as well as the recently listed World Heritage site (cf. Chirenje 1977, Tlou 1972, Nyati-Ramahobo 2002, Bernard and Moetapele 2005, Keitumetse and Pampiri 2016).

The African indigenous is perceived as less high maintenance than the autochthonous partner community (identified as immigrants in the Okavango description above) who interrogate their rights and go to the extent of challenging their own governments in courts, as is the case of Wayeyi of the Okavango region (Nyati-Ramahobo 2002). In this case therefore the indigenous who is already known and described in international fora of UNESCO level, becomes convenient "people" representative of such landscapes, as opposed to being 'inconvenient' (Saugestad 2001) when they have to be relocated from land for development. These approaches ultimately lead to the exclusion of cultural heritage aspects represented by these communities in a landscape such as the Okavango Delta because people's cultures consequently harbor cultural heritage and the subsequent cultural meanings deposited within the environment over a period of time.

Whereas the Okavango case study illustrated how cultural aspects are suffocated at the source of the listing, the case study that follows will extend this understanding by showing how our contemporary conservation approaches still suffocate cultural aspects of protected areas even where they are in abundance, in particular in situations where these aspects are represented by the internationally described indigenous people living in these landscapes.

Case Study 2: Ngorongoro Conservation Area World Heritage Site, Tanzania: Cultural Heritage

This case study will illustrate how a World Heritage site with indigenous communities living inside it still experiences aspects of cultural heritage suffocation/exclusion as a result of approaches that are conventional and convenient for modern day conservation practices that prioritize wilderness and wildlife romanticism at the expense of the social and cultural aspects of protected landscapes of sub-Saharan Africa that have now become or are assuming World Heritage status.

The Ngorongoro Conservation Area (NCA), Northern Tanzania, was established in 1959 under the game ordinance (Cap 413). The indigenous Maasai people were evicted from Serengeti (Siringet) to create the current Serengeti National Park (Shivji and Kapinga 1998; Rogers 2009; Olenasha 2014). The Maasai continued their traditional ways of life subject only to close control of hunting in the NCA.[1] The law of NCA safeguards the triple purpose of conserving its natural resources, safeguarding the interests of indigenous Maasai residents of the area, and promoting tourism. This was made clearer when the British governor of Tanganyika spoke to the Maasai Federal Council in 1959, saying that "I should like to make it clear to you all that it is the intention of the Government to develop the Crater in the interests of the people who use it. At the same time the Government intends to protect the game animals of the area, but should there be any conflict between the interests of the game and the human inhabitants, those of the latter must take precedence" (Homewood and Rogers 1991). In addition, Saibull (1968: 11) states that the conservation agreement of Ngorongoro is that "[a] basic requisite for the area is a stable environment in which its human and animal inhabitants, including livestock can prosper." However, "only if all these resources are in balance, will it be possible to maintain the rights of the existing residents, preserve unscathed the scenic attraction, safeguard the wildlife, perpetuate the value of the area for research, and so ensure that both the national and international obligation are honored." The NCA's management is in the hands of the Ngorongoro Conservation Area Authority (NCAA), a Parastatal under the Ministry of Natural Resources and Tourism (MNRT). Both the Chief Conservator (CN) and the Chairman of the Board of directors are the President's appointees, while the rest of the members are appointed by the Minister responsible to the Ministry.

Ngorongoro Conservation Area (NCA) as a World Heritage Site (WHS)

The site became a World Heritage site (WHS) under natural category in 1979, Criteria vii, ix, and x of the UNESCO World Heritage Convention (http://whc.unesco.org/en/criteria). After several years, the site was re-nominated in June 2010, on cultural category Criteria iv, as recognition of its richness on archaeological and paleontological sites (Oldupai and Laitole); hence it is now referred to as a mixed World Heritage site (UNESCO, ICOMOS and IUCN 2012). In principle and in theory this is befitting the status of people (Maasai) and wilderness in the area. However, it is important to note that the cultural category is associated with the archaeological heritage more than the living people of Maasai origin heritage—espoused in the UNESCO (2003)'s convention on safeguarding intangible cultural heritage—that are depicted in Figure 1.2.3.

The management system is such that within the park, pastoral lands are alienated from wildlife spaces. Beside the NCA is a mixed site where both wild animals and stocks stay and graze together, but there have been continuous alienations of pastoralists with some places in the site (including Ngorongoro crater and highland forests). The gradual elimination of pastoral resources use patterns, and mostly the Maasai community's cultural heritage that ties people's life and their ecosystems within the Ngorongoro landscape illustrates a case for suffocation of cultural practices and cultural heritages in the protected landscape globally designated as a World Heritage site.

With the advent of tourism in the Ngorongoro landscape, lodges and campsites are mushrooming around the World Heritage site of Ngorongoro and areas that were before prime lands of both wildlife and livestock in the NCA are occupied by tourism establishments (Figures 1.2.4 and 1.2.5). The tourism lodges are however tolerated and allowed by both the government and the international conservation institutions that query the growing presence of Maasai domestic animals and livestock. The irony of the situation is that as preservationists complain about the human and livestock population increase, more investors are given bigger plots of land in the prime forests that were for a long time primarily reserved by pastoralists as reservoirs for wildlife and livestock, a practice that helped to safeguard the pristine quality of the natural landscape. An example of such a lodge is provided by Asilia Africa Highland Campsite[2] depicted

FIGURE 1.2.3 Last rite of passage for Ilmirishi age-group in Ngorongoro.

FIGURE 1.2.4 Asilia Campsite built recently in the prime forest of wild animals and livestock in Olchaniomelock village.

in Figure 1.2.4, opened in 2016 in Olchaniomelock Village. The campsite occupies part of the livestock grazing area. In addition, due to its proximity to Maasai *bomas* (homes), in certain cases tourists roam into *bomas*, invading their privacy and not asking their consent prior to taking photos of their homestead, children, and/or surroundings on the entire site.

The economic occupation of the Ngorongoro crater through tourism lodges that prioritize business operations contradicts findings from different scholars who have

FIGURE 1.2.5 Asilia Africa tourist vehicles in the MAASAI Boma in Olchaniomelock Village, NCA (2016).

concluded that sustainable utilization of the landscape occurs when Maasai ecology and right of occupancy in the area are recognized (cf. Olenasha 2014). Homewood and Rogers (1991) and Lissu (2000) stated that NCA is not only important for its beauty, ancient history, and wildlife, but also home to about eighty thousand Maasai and Tatoga pastoralists and numerous Hadzabe hunter-gatherers (Government of Tanzania Prime Minister office 2013; Olenasha 2014). The sustainable use by people of NCA is exhibited by Maasai who continuously move with their herds of cattle, goats, and sheep as a way to optimize the use of dry and wet season pastures offered by the different resource niches in the NCA (Lissu 2000). In so doing, they avoid large herds of wildebeest which carry a viral disease, Malignant Catarrh Fever (MCF), which is fatal to cattle, but they also create existence for both wildlife and livestock. Homewood and Rogers's (1991) research indicated that the Maasai have practiced the rotation without substantial change for over two centuries, while pastoralism has been practiced in the area for at least seven millenia (Lissu 2000). Ngorongoro has, therefore, been an area where people coexisted with wildlife for thousands of years, long before it was classified as a World Heritage site that is now valued predominantly for its wildlife and tourism potential. A recent decision made by the Prime Minister Majaliwa Kassim to stop cattle from entering Ngorongoro crater throughout the year has led to imbalances in the use of the landscape by the Maasai people, exemplifying a worldview that derives from a "pure conservationist" perspective that does not subscribe to the concept of multiple use of the NCA landscape. This fundamental change in the philosophy and approach to use of the landscape by government, extrapolated from an international convention perspective of world heritage as nature, rather than a cultural aspect of being, suffocates the cultural heritage of the NCA that is under the custodianship of people such as the Maasai community. The approach fails to consider that cultural value in nature landscapes is important in that it preserves a practical useful intelligence of people such as art, cultural products, and cultural industries that constitute a balanced system in utilizing the land, derived from the groups' values customs, beliefs, and traditions (Throsby 2015). The Maasai of NCA, Datoga, and Hadzabe have culture heritage values that are strongly connected to the landscape, wildlife, and the conservation of these areas (Sikorei 2015). However, these traditional relationships, values, and practices have not been recognized nor inventoried in the documents that guide management and conservation of NCA for the last General Management Plan (GMP) (2006–16), where the cultural elements were vaguely mentioned but not implemented. Practitioners of cultural heritage in areas like the NCA can be enabled to continue expressing their cultural practices as espoused in some of the UNESCO Conventions such as the one on Safeguarding Intangible Cultural Heritage, which insists that "intangible cultural heritage, transmitted from generation to generation, is constantly recreated by communities and groups in response to their environment" (UNESCO 2003, Art. 2.1). An approach such as this will enable cultural heritage resources to "breathe" in nature-dominant spaces such as the NCA.

Discussion and Analysis

Whereas the Okavango Delta provides an example of world heritage as it was originally intended (without people), it nonetheless exposes the deliberate ignorance of aspects of conservation that are acknowledged and contained only in international policy papers such asthe cultural landscape clause in the World Heritage listing process and Criteria v and vi of the World Heritage Convention listing criteria. The omission is later compounded at the national policy level as espoused and expressed by the Botswana government's exclusion of cultural aspects of the Okavango Delta listing process, as well as the Tanzanian government's NCA–GMP document (2006–16) on the use of the Ngorongoro landscape that is conflated with a unique and rich heritage community of Maasai people.

The case study on Ngorongoro, where the Maasai community resides within a World Heritage site, illustrates that people are representative of culture and cultural heritage. However, for the Okavango Delta, unlike the Ngorongoro, people's cultural identities are excluded in landscape expression, save for a passing mention of indigenous communities in documents. Autochthonous communities are still excluded from document mention as illustrated by the description of what constitutes people in the Okavango Delta World Heritage listing document. For Ngorongoro, while the people are indeed acknowledged and remain in the World Heritage site, this commendable approach and effort is threatened by the narrow focus of conservation for wilderness and wildlife concern expressed by the high priority given to lodges at the expense of Maasai grazing grounds. The wilderness and wildlife fanaticism as representative of the conservation of protected areas of sub-Saharan Africa is also clearly illustrated in the Okavango, where people and/or people's identities within these landscapes are not at all recognized nor acknowledged.

In the Ngorongoro, people are included in the site but the expectation is that they limit cultural practices imbued in their socioeconomic and sociocultural life, thus suffocating their culture. For instance, the current NCA management plan under review has only a small reference to cultural heritage on paleontological cultural evolution, noting that tourists should respect the indigenous culture's norms and customs. Nothing substantive on cultural heritage is mentioned, even in a thick document of NCA–GMP (2006–16), no single part discusses culture or cultural heritage, its values, and its attributes, and nothing indicates the link of cultural heritage with tourism and the conservation of natural heritage in the site. The focus on archaeological resources in NCA is similar to the focus on wilderness and wildlife. They both represent a distant heritage that cannot be claimed by living communities.

Another example is the current status of cultural *bomas* (Maasai community dwellings) operating in the area that might be a significant place to value and recognize cultural heritage. In the NCA, some practices of business actors in the site knowingly or unknowingly suffocate cultural heritage and endanger its sustainability and survival, for example by breaching the myth and allowing tourists to visit each Maasai *boma* in the villages for enjoyment and leisure. This has a significant detrimental effect on the cultural heritage of the society and on children, disturbing social cohesion and bringing conflict by interfering with their normal work activities, especially the rearing of livestock. Sustainable management will demand that Maasai communities in *bomas* become substantive stakeholders rather than passive ones.

All in all culture and hence cultural heritage provide values of aesthetic, spiritual, social, historical, and symbolic authenticity (Throsby 2015), which will make the NCA a most remarkable World Heritage site, if these cultural heritages could be respected and sustainably managed for the future generation and development.

CONCLUSION

The case studies used in this chapter have illustrated that although there are numerous efforts towards sustainable conservation of sub-Saharan protected areas, there is room for improvement particularly where cultural resources are concerned. The focus on wilderness and wildlife provides a single-angle perspective. There is a still a huge opportunity left untapped of incorporating cultural aspects of these landscapes as key drivers towards sustainable conservation. It is apparent from the case studies' narratives that the activities that lead to shortchanging sustainable development initiatives (UNESCO 2017) in sub-Saharan protected landscapes of World Heritage status can be traced in several areas of recently launched international policy frameworks such as UN Millennium Goals and UN Agenda 2030 (United Nations 2017, <http://www.un.org/sustainabledevelopment/development-agenda/>). Nation states such as Botswana and Tanzania follow these leads by default and by so doing suffocate existing cultural and cultural heritage resources found in most of their African protected landscapes. It is important that approaches are redefined by questioning how each resource can be of value to the broader conservation debate, rather than prioritizing one form of resources by virtue of its historical economic value that may not necessarily cater for other components that enable sustainable conservation, use, and management of a particular protected area.

NOTES

1. The government of Tanganyika, 1958.
2. <http://www.ultimateafrica.com/asilias-highlands-camp-at-ngorongoro-to-open/>.

REFERENCES

Bernard, T., and N. Moetapele. 2005. "Desiccation of the Gomoti River: Biophysical Process and Indigenous Resource Management in Northern Botswana." *Journal of Arid Environments* 63(1): 256–283.

Bock, J. 2005. "Farming, Foraging, and Children's Play in the Okavango Delta, Botswana," in *The Nature of Play: Great Apes and Humans*, ed. A. D. Pellegrini and P. K. Smith, 254–281.

Bock, J., and S. E. Johnson. 2004. "Subsistence Ecology and Play among the Okavango Delta Peoples of Botswana." *Human Nature* 15(1): 63–81.

Bolaane, M. M., and K. Sudo. 2013. *Chiefs, Hunters and San in the Creation of the Moremi Game Reserve, Okavango Delta: Multiracial Interactions and Initiatives, 1956–1979*. Osaka: National Museum of Ethnology.

Chirenje, M. J. 1977. *A History of Northern Botswana: 1850–1910*. London: Associated University Presses.

Gausset, Q., J. Kenrick, and R. Gibb. 2011. "Indigeneity and Autochthony: A Couple of False Twins?" *Social Anthropology* 19(2): 135–142.

Government of Tanzania Prime Minister office. 2013. Taarifa ya Tathmini ya Watu na Hali ya Uchumi Tarafa ya Ngorongoro. Dar es Salaam, and Loliondo-Tanzania [An assessment report of the People and Social economic in the Ngorongoro Division, Ngorongoro District, Arush].

Hilgers, M. 2011. "Autochthony as Capital in a Global Age." *Theory, Culture, Society* 28(34): 34–51.

Homewood, K and Rogers W. A. 1991. *Maasai Ecology: Pastoralists Development and Wildlife Conservation in Ngorongoro, Tanzania*. Cambridge: Cambridge University Press.

Keitumetse, S. O. 2011. "Sustainable Development and Cultural Heritage Management in Botswana: Towards Sustainable Communities." *Sustainable Development* 19(1): 49–59.

Keitumetse, S. O. 2016a. "International Conventions as Frameworks of Management and Identity for African Cultural Heritage," in *African Cultural Heritage Conservation and Management*. Basel: Springer International Publishing, 23–61.

Keitumetse, S. O. 2016b. "The Politics of the Past: Evolving Ethnic Cultural Identities in African Traditional Governance Systems," in *African Cultural Heritage Conservation and Management*. Basel: Springer International Publishing, 63–87.

Keitumetse, S. O. 2016c. "Heritage Enterprising: Cultural Heritage and Sustainable Tourism in Southern Africa," in *African Cultural Heritage Conservation and Management*. Basel: Springer International Publishing, 157–179.

Keitumetse, S. O., and M. G. Pampiri. 2016. "Community Cultural Identity in Nature-Tourism Gateway Areas: Maun Village, Okavango Delta World Heritage Site, Botswana." *Journal of Community Archaeology & Heritage* 3(2): 99–117.

Lissu, T. 2000. "Policy and Legal Issues on Wildlife Management in Tanzania's Pastoral Lands: The Case Study of the Ngorongoro Conservation Area." *Law, Social Justice & Global Development Journal (LGD)* 2000 (1). <https://warwick.ac.uk/fac/soc/law/elj/lgd/2000_1/lissu>.

McCarthy, Terence S., A. Bloem, and P. A. Larkin. 1998. "Observations on the Hydrology and Geohydrology of the Okavango Delta." *South African Journal of Geology* 101(2): 101–17.

Ngorongoro Conservation Area Authority (NCAA). 2006–16. *General Management Plan 2006–2016, Ngorongoro*. Arusha-Tanzania: NCAA.

Nyati-Ramahobo, L. 2002. "From a Phone Call to the High Court: Wayeyi Visibility and the Kamanakao Association's Campaign for Linguistic and Cultural Rights in Botswana." *Journal of Southern African Studies* 28(4): 685–709.

Ole Sikorei, Arpakwa M. 2015. *Community Traditional Practices and Cultural Heritage for Tourism Management and Living Sustainability: Case Study of Ngorongoro Conservation Area*. Master thesis. Turin: International Labor Organization Centre and University of Turin.

Olenasha, William. 2014. "A World Heritage Site in the Ngorongoro Conservation Area: Whose World? Whose Heritage?," in *World Heritage Sites and Indigenous Peoples' Rights*, ed. Stefan Disko and Helen Tugendhat. Copenhagen: IWGIA 2014, Forest Peoples Programme and Gundjeihmi Aboriginal Corporation doc. no. 129.

Ramsar Bureau. 1971. *Ramsar Convention on Wetlands*. Switzerland: Ramsar Bureau. <http://www.ramsar.org/> [accessed: April 30, 2017].

Rogers, Peter J. 2009. "International Conservation Governance and the Early History of the Ngorongoro Conservation Area, Tanzania." *Global Environment* 4: 78–117. <http://www.environmentandsociety.org/node/4811>.

Rosivach, V. J. 1987. "Autochthony and the Athenians." *The Classical Quarterly* 37(2): 294–306.

Saibull, S. A. 1968. "Ngorongoro Conservation Area." *East African Agricultural and Forestry Journal* 33(1): Special Issue.

Saugestad, S. 2001. *The Inconvenient Indigenous: Remote Area Development in Botswana, Donor Assistance and the First People of the Kalahari*. Uppsala: Nordic Africa Institute.

Shivji, I., and W. Kapinga. 1998. *Maasai Rights in Ngorongoro, Tanzania*. Dar es Salaam: IIED/HAKIARDHI.

Tanganyika. 1958/9. *Ngorongoro Conservation Area: An Act, 1959 for the Ngorongoro Conservation Area Ordinance, No. 43, September 19, 1963*. Dar es Salaam government Print. FAOLEX No: LEXFAOC017716. 65.

Throsby, David. 2015. *Cultural Capital and the Theory of Development*. Turin: International Training Centre of the ILO, Università di Torino, Politecnico di Torino, UNESCO World Heritage Centre.

Tlou, Thomas. 1972. "A Political History of Northwestern Botswana to 1906." PhD thesis. University of Wisconsin.

United Nations, 2017. The Sustainable Development Agenda—17 Goals to Transform our World. <http://www.un.org/sustainabledevelopment/development-agenda/> [accessed April 27, 2017].

UNESCO. 2003. Convention on Safeguarding Intangible Cultural Heritage—Article 2.1. <http://www.unesco.org/new/en/santiago/culture/intangible-heritage/convention-intan-gible-cultural-heritage/>.

UNESCO. 2017. The Ngorongoro Declaration: African World Heritage and Sustainable Development – Signed Monday, June 6, 2016. <http:// whc.unesco.org/ en/ news/ 1506> [accessed, April 29, 2017].

UNESCO, ICOMOS, and IUCN. 2012. *Report on the Joint WHC/ICOMOS/IUCN Mission to Ngorongoro Conservation Area, Republic of Tanzania, April 10–13, 2012.* Paris: World Heritage Centre.

Wolski, P., and Hubertus Henricus Gerardus Savenije. 2006. "Dynamics of Floodplain-Island Groundwater Flow in the Okavango Delta, Botswana." *Journal of Hydrology* 320(3): 283–301.

Zenker, O. 2011. "Autochthony, Ethnicity, Indigeneity and Nationalism: Time-Honouring and State-Oriented Modes of Rooting Individual–Territory–Group Triads in a Globalizing World." *Critique of Anthropology* 31(1): 63–81.

SUSTAINABLE CONSERVATION OF URBAN HERITAGE

The Contribution of Governance-Focused Studies

EDUARDO ROJAS

As cities grow and develop they confront complex choices including whether to protect their material heritage or let new development take its place. These topics are not well researched and call for a more systematic treatment from studies focused on urban governance.

THE GOVERNANCE OF CITIES

Urban politics—a branch of the social sciences—studies the forces influencing the decisions made by elected officials, city managers, entrepreneurs, communities, and households that affect the development of a city (Stone 2008). In the last two decades urban politics expanded the scope of its concerns into the study of "the governance of cities" (McCann 2016) including "the processes through which public and private resources are coordinated in the pursuit of collective interests" (Pierre 2011: 20). A large body of work in urban governance studies is concerned with the positioning and competitiveness of cities in the globalized economy (Gupta et al. 2015), the challenges posed by neo-liberal approaches to the provision and financing of urban services such as water, sewerage, health, and education (Swyngedouw 2005), the management of urban environmental issues (Biermann et al. 2010), and the integration of different segments of society to the benefits of urban development (Harvey 2003). The urban governance approach also contributed to the study of the institutional and financial issues related to the redevelopment of deteriorated urban areas in Europe (Newman and Thornley

1996, Roberts et al. 2017, Lees 2008), the United States (Tiesdel et al. 2013, Frieden and Sagalyn 1994), and Latin America (Rojas 2004), and to better understanding the factors affecting the sustainability of urban renewal processes (Wei Zhen et al. 2013). There are other urban development issues that are yet to benefit from this approach, including the rapid expansion of the urbanized area in most cities (Angel 2012) and the persistent and often growing inequalities in wealth, access to opportunities, and services in cities of developed (Musterd and Ostendorf 2013) and developing countries (Cornia 2014).

In need of attention from the urban governance perspective are the dilemmas confronted by urban communities when development pressures impact their city's "urban heritage"—the stock of buildings, public spaces, and infrastructures inherited from previous generations. The theory and practice of urban heritage conservation could greatly benefit from more "governance-focused" studies to complement the existing corpus of scientific documents, international agreements, and professional standards that guided the practice in the last fifty years (ICOMOS 2017, UNESCO 2017). This chapter discusses the challenges and potential contributions of this field of studies and makes reference to the findings of governance-focused analyses of the experiences of four Latin American cities that are conserving urban heritage areas included in UNESCO's World Heritage List (Rojas 2014b).

Conservation of Urban Heritage: Emerging Demands

Urban heritage conservation is facing challenges that go beyond those foreseen by the Venice Charter of 1964 and subsequent international agreements and ensuing technical documents (see ICOMOS 2017 for a compendium of these documents). The most critical include:

Mounting development pressures. In most cities there is a growing demand for residential, craft manufacture, and commercial space in central locations that impact the city's historic centers and neighborhoods. These pressures—the result of changing needs and preferences of households, consumers, and entrepreneurs—confront urban communities with complex trade-offs between conserving the material heritage of these areas or allowing its disappearance to make room for new developments.

Wider appreciation of the values of urban heritage. Communities have a broader appreciation of the cultural and economic services provided by the urban heritage. According to Throsby (2012) they value the streams of sociocultural (historic, religious, aesthetic, social) and economic (use for contemporary needs, increased real estate value) benefits that the heritage areas can provide. This interest confronts communities with the need to use public funds to protect the urban heritage and bequest it to future generations or to maintain the option to use it in the future. Balancing the interest in conserving the urban heritage and the limitations of public funds requires broad-based agreements among the different social actors that can only be mediated by the city governance mechanisms.

Expanded significance of urban heritage in development. The role of culture and heritage in socioeconomic development is recognized and considered a significant component of the social and economic development of communities. Its preservation and development play a significant role in the United Nations' Sustainable Development Goals (UN 2015) and in the implementation of the New Urban Agenda (UN HABITAT 2016). The challenge is how to incorporate urban heritage conservation into city development priorities and investment programs.

Increased use of adaptive rehabilitation strategies. Cutting-edge practice puts urban heritage monuments, buildings, and sites to contemporary uses that are compatible with the preservation of their heritage values. The "adaptive rehabilitation" of urban heritage properties, neighborhoods, and central areas is proving effective in promoting the development of depressed historic centers (Rojas 2004) or rebalancing the use of heritage areas in high demand from tourism and recreational activities to their carrying capacity (Zanini 2017). Its implementation, however, challenges many of the tenets of the traditional approaches that advocate the full conservation of the heritage properties and severely limit their adaptation to contemporary uses.

More social actors interested in the conservation of urban heritage. What once was the concern of the cultural elite is today the concern of a much wider set of social actors. In addition to the few scholars and philanthropists concerned with the aesthetic, historic, or religious importance of the urban heritage that were active in the mid-twentieth century, today whole communities are actively protecting the material heritage of their neighborhoods and cities—monuments, significant buildings, and public spaces—that support their social practices and festivities or are symbols of their identity. Also governments (central or local) are demanded by their constituencies to spend funds in the conservation of the urban heritage to ensure its bequest to future generations. Furthermore, property owners, enterprises, and households are increasingly interested in the capacity of heritage properties to accommodate urban uses and generate profits (Rojas 2016).

Growing need for public-private cooperation. There is growing awareness among conservators that setting self-sustainable conservation conditions for the urban heritage requires: a wide variety of users demanding and occupying rehabilitated heritage properties for residential, commercial, service, cultural, and recreational activities; private investors supplying rehabilitated space and maintaining privately owned heritage buildings; and governments guaranteeing the adequate provision of public goods including the conservation of the monuments and heritage public spaces. The free operation of the real estate market does not ensure these outcomes requiring the concerted intervention of public and private sector actors.

To respond to the emerging demands the practice of urban heritage conservation should strengthen the on-going departure from its initial monument-focused concerns towards a more integrated approach that focus on historic urban landscapes (UNESCO 2011) and take full advantage of the adaptive rehabilitation of heritage properties for contemporary uses as a viable conservation strategy. In addition to finding consensual answers to the key questions of why to conserve and what to conserve, communities must also decide how to conserve, including setting priorities to allocate to this end the always scarce public resources available. Confronted with these complex trade-offs urban heritage conservation practitioners and the interested social actors need to agree on principles of urban heritage governance that complement the preservation principles advocated by the international charters and agreements (Rojas 2014a).

GOVERNANCE-FOCUSED ANALYSES OF THE CONSERVATION OF THE URBAN HERITAGE

Governance studies are concerned with the ways communities agree on rules and practices that would produce acceptable outcomes for the majority of their members. In its broadest interpretation, governance studies analyze what Foucault (1984) calls society's "mechanism," that is the links among institutions, rules, and laws, administrative procedures, scientific knowledge, philosophical and moral propositions, even physical infrastructures that govern, guide, or condition human behavior in society. Although urban governance interests are not as wide as Foucault's yet—according to McCann (2016)—the field of enquiry is still ample as its concerns include "not only why cities are the way they are at a particular time, or only how urban built environments, societies and political economies are shaped and reshaped in reference to wider forces and processes, but also how they are made to be the way they are, through the concerted actions of the state, other public and private institutions, social movements, civil society and the practices of everyday life" (2).

Urban governance research in cities of democratic market economies (developed and developing) that adopted a neo-liberal approach to economic development concentrate mostly on the study of "urban managerialism" (MacLeod 2011) or what Swyngedouw (2005) calls "governance-beyond-the-state" the study of the expanded role that private economic actors and parts of civil society play in city policy-making, administration, and provision of urban services. Similar analyses are not available for issues concerning the private public interface that occurs in the conservation of the urban heritage.

Governance studies in urban heritage conservation are few in spite of the growing awareness about their significance (Borch and Kornberger 2015, Pierre 2011, Shipley and Kovacs 2008). Available works focus in two interrelated concerns: the integration of urban heritage conservation into the urban development planning and management processes, and the challenges of involving the community in the heritage conservation decisions that such integration requires. According to Rodwell (2014) governance studies must help urban heritage conservation to become a central activity in urban planning and development and not a specialized and peripheral activity in the cultural realm. The adoption of this approach confronts urban governments with decisions commonly adopted by cultural institutions including determining what to preserve, how to do it, and with which resources (Gupta et al. 2015). Valverde (2011) argues that in facing these challenges urban government institutions get limited help from the traditional land use control tools of the urban planning profession.

Fully incorporating urban heritage conservation into urban planning means assigning more responsibilities to local communities (Ripp and Rowell 2016) in decisions related to the heritage and significantly broadening the diversity of social actors engaged in the process. There is the need to establish local institutions and structures of authority capable of managing their interactions and guide their activities towards the attainment of the common goal of a well and sustainable conserved heritage (Rojas 2016). The absence of a large body of research on these issues indicates that there is still a long way to go before the practice of urban heritage conservation can fruitfully integrate its concepts and methodologies with those of urban development planning and management.

Practical Implications of Governance Studies for the Conservation of the Urban Heritage

Addressing the governance challenges of the urban conservation discipline within the limitations of the present work benefits from a concise definition of governance like that proposed by Bell (2002: 1): "the use of institutions and structures of authority to allocate resources and coordinate or control activities in society or in any other relevant environment." This definition directs the attention to key components of governing urban heritage conservation: the public and private institutions responsible or directly related to conservation, the structures of authority used to control or regulate the activities of the social actors, the social actors involved, and how the interactions among these components affect the allocation of public and private resources. The analysis of these components brings to light issues and opportunities that are not evident in the canonical approach that dominates the practice of urban heritage preservation. In the following sections these components will be discussed starting from the social actors and moving to the structures of authority and institutions. Examples of the contribution of this approach to the sustainable conservation of the urban heritage come from a governance-focused analysis (Rojas 2014b) of 1995–2010 conservation experiences benefiting four Latin American historic centers in the World Heritage List (UNESCO 2017): Oaxaca in Mexico (Quartesan and Romis 2011), Quito in Ecuador (Jaramillo

2011), Salvador de Bahia in Brazil (Mendes Zancheti and Gabriel 2011), and Valparaiso in Chile (Trivelli and Mishimura 2011).

A Diverse Set of Social Actors: The More Inclusive the Better

Governance-focused studies of the social actors holding an interest in the conservation of urban heritage allow a better understanding of their objectives and incentives, reveal the complex network of relations among them, and identify the conflicts that could emerge from their often diverging views and interests.

Individuals and institutions care for what brings them benefits; thus they would assign importance to the urban heritage considering the flow of sociocultural and economic benefits that it may bring. According to Thorsby (2012) these flows of benefits are the main factor in assessing the heritage's values. It follows that the wider the variety of sociocultural and economic benefits generated by the urban heritage the more social actors interested and the greater the probability that the heritage sites receive attention and investments boosting the sustainability of the conservation effort. This is the thesis proposed by Rojas (2012) and supported by the analysis of the cases mentioned herein that provides evidence pointing in this direction (2014b).

In Latin America there is a parallelism in the growing awareness about the diversity of the urban heritage values and the variety of social actors interested in its conservation (Rojas 2016: 239 Table 13.1). Initially urban heritage conservation was a concern of the cultural elites—scholars, intellectuals, and philanthropists—interested in protecting the aesthetic and historic values of monuments and sites. Later the urban heritage came to the attention of governments interested in preserving its bequest value. Laterly the values of the urban heritage called the attention of residents and neighborhood associations interested in its symbolic or social values, and of entrepreneurs engaged in creative industries or tourism that would benefit from the economic use value of the heritage area. In the cases discussed here the range of values at play and interested social actors involved is much wider in Oaxaca than in Salvador with Quito and Valparaiso lying in between (Rojas 2014b Table 4.1 and Figure 1.2.1).

The social actors that have an interest in conservation are a varied lot. Applying to urban heritage conservation the concepts of Schmitter (2000) that focus on the interests "held" by social actors in a given social process, it is convenient to characterize the following types of actors. Social actors owning property in a heritage area would be "share-holders" and those that know about the issues "knowledge holders." The electors of the local officials with jurisdiction on the heritage area would be "right holders" while those whose properties are directly affected by conservation programs are "stake holders." Additionally it is convenient to differentiate, among social actors that hold a permanent interest in the urban heritage, the "committed" holders from those with only a temporary or passing interest, who can be called "marginal" holders (Rojas

2016). Comparing the World Heritage cases hereto mentioned Rojas (2014b) found that there is a positive relationship between the presence of a diversified base of committed holders and the sustainability of the conservation process. Oaxaca and Quito had a wide set of committed holders from the public and private sectors investing and using the rehabilitated properties while the investments in Salvador and Valparaiso depended mostly on a small number of public actors with a marginal commitment to the heritage sites (Rojas 2014b: Figure 4.1). Not surprisingly, Oaxaca and Quito showed signs of a more sustainable conservation processes than Valparaiso and Salvador by having a higher proportion of well-maintained properties and more diversified uses of their historic centers (Rojas 2014: Table 4.3 and Figure 4.3).

The more diverse the set of social actors interested in conservation the more complex their relations. Some actors would favor the full conservation of the urban heritage while others would advocate for its redevelopment. Landowners would resent the restrictions imposed by the conservation regulations while proponents of conservation often find them insufficient. It is not uncommon that residents of heritage areas do not see advantages in the listing and do not fully support the conservation regulations, as is the case with Valparaiso's inclusion into the World Heritage List (Trivelli and Nihsimura 2011). Addressing these conflicts early in the conservation effort and taking advantage of the synergies that may exist among social actors can go a long way in ensuring a more stable and sustainable conservation process. This is the case of Oaxaca that for over twenty years has sustained conservation activities promoted by a variety of social actors: private non-profit and for-profit and public local, regional, and national (Quartesan and Romis 2011).

Structures of Authority, Rules, Regulations, and Instruments: Rigid or Flexible?

The legal and institutional traditions of a country determine the structures of authority, the institutions to govern, and the instruments used in the conservation of the urban heritage. In countries following the British legal tradition laws and rules originate in customs and precedents and in abstract legal norms in countries adhering to the Napoleonic tradition (Newman and Thornley 1996). These differences lead to historic preservation laws and regulations that allow interpretation in the British tradition and are prescriptive and rigid in the Napoleonic. Each tradition confronts conservationists with different challenges. In the British social actors face regulatory uncertainty as heritage intervention proposals are decided on their merits and precedent, but also enjoy the greater flexibility allowed to decision-makers to consider adaptive rehabilitation proposals of urban heritage properties to better match contemporary needs. Regulations based on the Napoleonic tradition define the level of conservation desired by the regulators for each heritage property or public space providing more certainty to the social actors involved at the cost of losing flexibility to adapt to changing circumstances.

Latin American countries inherited the Napoleonic legal tradition that originated in France and disseminated via Spain and Portugal to their former colonies. In Quito the Municipality adopted a Conservation Plan that defined the level of conservation for each building within the area included in the World Heritage List (Jaramillo 2011) so landowners, prospective investors, and public entities knew in advance what they could do in the properties. However, these regulations focused mostly on what "not to do" with the heritage buildings and required a separate program from the Municipality to induce private actors to do what was convenient for the sustainable conservation of the historic center (see next section). Valparaiso had only general land use and building regulations for its heritage area causing uncertainty among investors on what they would be allowed to do in the protected properties and lacked an institutional framework to induce private actors to contribute to the attainment of public objectives (Rojas 2014b).

Legal and administrative traditions also determine the local governments' capacity to use the most common instruments in urban heritage conservation. Of the five tools for urban heritage preservation discussed by Schuster et al. (1997)—ownership and operation of heritage properties, land use and building regulations, economic incentives, restrictions to property rights, and information—only a few are available to most Latin American countries. Concerning economic incentives through taxes, low rates and poor compliance with land and income taxes restrict the use of tax exemptions and credits as incentives and drive most countries to use direct public investment as a stimulus to private investors. Most countries face difficulties in enforcing property rights over the urban heritage and reach local social actors with information about their value and the importance of its conservation. This difficulty originates in the fact that the institutions concerned with the urban heritage are part of ministries of the Central Government concerned with culture and have difficulties reaching local communities. Governments end up having to use the onerous instrument of direct ownership and operation of heritage properties where the public cultural institutions bear all the expenses of restoring and maintaining them.

Lacking sufficient resources to own, restore, and operate heritage properties, government's tool of choice is the enactment of conservation regulations that define a technically optimal level of conservation for urban heritage properties and make owners responsible for fulfilling the regulations. When used as the only tool for conservation this instrument does not lead to the desired results. Constrained in their options to develop the properties and lacking incentives to conserve them it is not uncommon that owners abandon the heritage properties in the hope that physical decay forces the authorities to allow their demolition.

The analysis of the structures of authority in the cases studied call for more flexibility to adapt the heritage assets to current needs focusing on conserving the characteristics that give them their heritage value: their typological features defined by their function, materiality, and aesthetics (Caniggia and Maffei 2001). This approach has succeeded in the historic center of Cartagena in Colombia (Rojas 2014b) but is very demanding in institutional capacity to manage the flexible norms and regulations.

Heritage Conservation Institutions: Sector-Based or Territorial?

Institutions and processes matter as they have significant impacts on the quality and sustainability of the urban heritage conservation effort. History and tradition determine the institutional structure of nations and in particular the balance between central and local government as the locus of decision-making capacity to allocate resources and regulate the activities of society. There is ample variation between unitary and federal countries: the former being more centralized than the latter, but in most countries the listing of urban heritage areas and monuments falls under the purview of the national cultural institutions (although there are countries that have sub-national listing procedures managed by the states and municipalities) (UNESCO 2016: Part One). Heritage conservation commissions are the most common decision-making bodies in listing and regulating urban heritage and they usually have strong representation of the cultural elites and central government bureaucracies, place much emphasis on cultural issues in the rules and regulations they enforce, and use top-down modes of decision-making. Central government commissions are prevalent in most developing countries and represent a barrier to fully integrate urban heritage conservation with urban development planning—a condition to turn conservation into a local priority fully supported by the communities and attracting the resources of a wider variety of social actors.

The impact of the institutional arrangements in the sustainability of the conservation effort is evident in the cases referred to in this chapter. In Salvador the Cultural Institute of the State of Bahia undertook most of the conservation activities. Specialists from the Institute using funds provided by the Government of the State of Bahia evaluated the conditions of the buildings and monuments, designed and executed the conservation works, and implemented cultural and entertainment programs to attract visitors and users to the rehabilitated historic center (Mendes Sancheti and Gabriel 2011). As a result, the conservation process was based on a sector-biased view of the values of this heritage (that of the cultural elite and conservators in the Institute), promoted few new uses in the center beyond public culture and entertainment, and did not mobilize the resources of property owners and potential investors or residents (Rojas 2014b). At the other end of the spectrum of the cases discussed here lies the Municipality of Quito that established a mixed-capital corporation for the historic center to enter in partnerships with property owners and investors to conserve and rehabilitate the heritage area. Adopting a territorial approach to the problem and attracting a variety of holders to cooperate in the effort, the Corporation managed in a decade to conserve more than half of the area included in the World Heritage List, retaining users, attracting new economic activities, and engaging the resources of a variety of holders to match the resources allocated by the Municipality (Jaramillo 2011). The case of Quito achieved many of the conditions of sustainable conservation while that of Salvador had all the marks of an unsustainable conservation processes (Rojas 2014b).

Financing Urban Heritage Conservation: Public or Private?

Advances in academic studies and the practice of public finance provide guidance for the efficient allocation of public resources in the conservation of the urban heritage. The advice for decision makers is to use public resources to achieve public objectives and to encourage private actors to finance investments that in addition to generating private benefits contribute to attaining socially desirable objectives. Urban heritage conservation would benefit from following these orientations but unfortunately this is rarely the case. In most developing countries the listing of monuments and heritage areas invariably comes with a call for public resources to finance its preservation. In the cases of Salvador and Valparaiso the government (State and Central respectively) financed most of the urban heritage conservation activities. In Salvador the government fully financed even the rehabilitation of private properties to prevent their collapse due to deterioration. Two results were observable: the public resources were insufficient to benefit the whole area included in the World Heritage List, and the conservation effort lacked continuity due to resource shortages or changes in government priorities (Rojas 2014b). In addition to subsidizing property owners that may have been able to contribute, government spending crowded out private investment that may have come to the conservation areas.

The conservation of the urban heritage would benefit from a careful analysis of the most efficient and equitable ways of financing these activities. Such analysis will provide evidence of the suitability of devoting public resources to finance conservation activities that generate public benefits and to incite the private sector to do the rest within the framework of flexible and well-enforced conservation regulations. The right approach also includes incentives and transfers to private investors and property owners to induce them to contribute to the public good that represents the sustainable conservation of the urban heritage valued by the communities and that the majority of its members agree to protect. The good use of public funds includes the conservation and adaptive reuse of significant public buildings for public purposes (educational, social, or cultural) as it is done when turning monuments into public museums or cultural institutions (provided that careful attention is paid to their proper operation and maintenance). Another adequate use of public resources is the conservation and adaptive rehabilitation of public spaces. Also there are solid reasons to use public funds to assist property owners to conserve the features of their properties that contribute to the heritage character of public spaces that is a public good. Examples are investments to conserve the façades of private buildings including the conservation of the structure and roofs and fire prevention measures to ensure that they stay in place. In cases where the heritage areas are in need of revitalization or re-equilibrium to their carrying capacity it is also reasonable to spend public funds to induce users to expand (or reduce) their usage of the heritage sites.

Attaining the right balance for the contributions of public and private financial resources is an area of urban governance studies in need of more development. The results of further research on these topics will provide evidence-based recommendations for the most efficient and equitable allocation of the public resources devoted by communities to the conservation of their heritage without crowding out the private resources that could flow to the areas.

CONCLUSION

The study of the governance of urban heritage conservation is one of the less developed branches of this field of the social sciences notwithstanding the evidence that governance matters for the sustainability of the conservation process and that its study can make significant contributions to enhance its effectiveness. Governance-focused studies bring to the attention of conservators and city managers the institutional, regulatory, and financial underpinnings of the conservation process that are not commonly discussed when listing monuments or when establishing rules and regulations for their conservation. Among many other contributions, governance studies help to identify the variety of social actors holding an interest in the urban heritage, better understand their interactions and conflicts, implement more effective institutional arrangements, and better allocate the available resources. A more systematic research of these topics will make a significant contribution to the sustainable conservation of urban heritage and enhance its contribution to the social and economic development of urban communities in all regions of the world.

REFERENCES

Angel, S. 2012. *Planet of Cities*. Cambridge, MA: Lincoln Institute of Land Policy.

Bell, S. 2002. *Economic Governance and Institutional Dynamics: The Market, the State, and Networks*. Melbourne: Oxford University Press.

Biermann, F., M. Betsill, J. Gupta, N. Kanie, L. Lebel, D. Liverman, H. Schroeder, B. Siebenhuner, and R. Zondervan. 2010. "Earth System Governance: A Research Framework." *INEA* 10(4): 277–298.

Borch, C. and M. Kornberger, eds. 2015. *Urban Commons: Rethinking the City*. Milton Park Abingdon: Routledge.

Caniggia, J. F., and G. L. Maffei. 2001. *Architectural Composition and Building Typology: Interpreting Basic Buildings*. Florence: Alinea.

Cornia, G., ed. 2014. *Falling Inequality in Latin America: Policy Changes and Lessons*. Oxford: Oxford University Press.

Foucault, M. 1984. "El juego de Michel Foucault (Saber y Verdad)." Madrid: Ediciones de la Piqueta, 127–62; quoted by S. Dallorso, "Notas sobre el uso del concepto de dispositivo para el análisis de programas sociales" (2010), *Espiral: Estudios sobre Estado y Sociedad* 19(54): 43–74.

Frieden, B., and L. Sagalyn. 1994. *Downtown, Inc.: How America Rebuilds Cities*. Cambridge, MA: MIT.

Gupta, J., K. Pfeffer, H. Verrest, and M. Ros-Tonen, eds. 2015. *Geographies of Urban Governance: Advanced Theories, Methods and Practices*. London: Springer.

Harvey, D. 2003. "The right to the City." *International Journal of Regional Research* 27(4): 939–941.

International Council on Monuments and Sites (ICOMOS). 2017. *Charters and Other Doctrinal Texts*. Paris: ICOMOS. <http://www.icomos.org/en/charters-and-texts> [last accessed April 23, 2017].

Jaramillo, P. 2011. "Quito," in *City Development: Experiences in the Preservation of Ten World Heritage Sites*, ed. E. Rojas and F. Lanzafame. Washington, DC: Inter American Development Bank, 59–86.

Lees, L. 2008. "Gentrification and Social Mixing: Towards an Inclusive Urban Renaissance?" *Urban Studies* 45(12): 2449–2470.

MacLeod, G. 2011. "Urban Politics Reconsidered: Growth Machine to Post-Democratic City?" *Urban Studies* 48(12): 2629–2660.

McCann, E. 2016. "Governing Urbanism: Urban Governance Studies 1.0, 2.0 and Beyond." *Urban Studies: virtual special issue editorial essay*, <http://journals.sagepub.com/doi/abs/10.1177/0042098016670046>.

Mendes Sancheti, S., and J. Gabriel. 2011. "Salvador de Bahia," in *City Development: Experiences in the Preservation of Ten World Heritage Sites*, ed. E. Rojas and F. Lanzafame. Washington, DC: Inter American Development Bank, 87–131.

Musterd, S., and W. Ostendorf, eds. 2013. *Urban Segregation and the Welfare State: Inequality and Exclusion in Western Cities*. Abingdon: Routledge.

Newman, P., and A. Thornley. 1996. *Urban Planning in Europe: International Competition, National Systems and Planning Projects*. London: Routledge.

Pierre, J. 2011. *The Politics of Urban Governance*. London: Palgrave Macmillan.

Quartesan, A., and M. Romis. 2011. "Oaxaca," in *City Development: Experiences in the Preservation of Ten World Heritage Sites*, ed. E. Rojas and F. Lanzafame. Washington, DC: Inter American Development Bank, 13–58.

Ripp, M., and D. Rodwell. 2016. "The Governance of Urban Heritage." *The Historic Environment: Policy and Practice* 7(1): 81–108.

Roberts, P., H. Sykes, and R. Granger, eds. 2017. *Urban Regeneration*. 2nd edn. New York: Sage.

Rodwell, D. 2014. "Celebrating Continuity." *Context* 136: 54.

Rojas, E. 2004. *Volver al centro: La recuperación de áreas urbanas centrales*. Washington, DC: Banco Interamericano de Desarrollo.

Rojas, E. 2012. "Governance in Historic City Core Regeneration Projects," in *The Economics of Uniqueness: Investing in Historic Cores and Cultural Heritage Assets for Sustainable Development*, ed. G. Licciardi and R. Amirtahmasebi. Washington, DC: The World Bank, 143–181.

Rojas, E. 2014a. "Historic Cities and the Venice Charter." *Change Over Time* 4(2): 196–203.

Rojas, E. 2014b. "Governance Matters for the Conservation of the Urban Heritage: The Case of Four World Heritage Sites in Latin America." PhD thesis. Lisbon: Universidade Lusófona de Humanidades e Tecnologías, <http://recil.grupolusofona.pt/handle/10437/6112?show=full>.

Rojas, E. 2016. "The Sustainable Conservation of Urban Heritage: A Concern of All Social Actors," in *Urban Heritage Development and Sustainability: International Framework, National and Local Governance*, ed. S. Labadi and W. Logan. Abingdon: Routledge, 235–255.

Schmitter, P. 2000. "Governance." Paper presented at the Conference "Democratic and Participatory Governance: From Citizens to 'Holders,'" European University Institute, Florence (quoted by Swyngedouw 2005; Page 1995).

Schuster, M., J. de Mocheaux, and C. Riley II, eds. 1997. *Preserving the Built Heritage: Tools for Implementation*. London: University Press of New England.

Shipley, R., and J. Kovacs. 2008. "Good Governance Principles for the Cultural Heritage Sector: Lessons from International Experience." *Corporate Governance: The International Journal of Business in Society* 8(2): 214–28.

Stone, C. 2008. "Urban Politics Then and Now," in *Power in the City: Clarence Stone and the Politics of Inequality*, ed. M. Orr and V. Johnson. Lawrence, KS: University Press of Kansas, 267–316.

Swyngedouw, E. 2005. "Governance Innovation and the Citizen: The Janus Face of Governance beyond the State." *Urban Studies* 42(11): 1991–2006.

Throsby, D. 2012. "Heritage Economics: A Conceptual Approach," in *The Economics of Uniqueness: Investing in Historic Cores and Cultural Heritage Assets for Sustainable Development*, ed. G. Licciardi and R. Amirtahmasebi. Washington, DC: The World Bank, 45–73.

Tiesdell, S., T. Heath, and T. Oc. 1996. *Revitalizing Historic Urban Quarters*. 2nd edn 2013. London: Routledge.

Trivelli, P., and Y. Nishimura. 2011. "Valparaiso," in *City Development: Experiences in the Preservation of Ten World Heritage Sites*, ed. E. Rojas and F. Lanzafame. Washington, DC: Inter American Development Bank, 133–180.

United Nations. 2015. *Sustainable Development Goals*. New York: United Nations, <https://sustainabledevelopment.un.org/sdg11>.

United Nations Education, Science and Culture Organisation (UNESCO). 2011. *Recommendation on the Historic Urban Landscape*. Paris: UNESCO, <http://whc.unesco.org/en/activities/638>.

United Nations Education, Science and Culture Organisation (UNESCO). 2016. *Culture Urban Future: The Global Report on Culture for Sustainable Urban Development*. Paris: UNESCO.

United Nations Education, Science and Culture Organisation (UNESCO). 2017. *World Heritage Convention, Publications*. <http://whc.unesco.org/en/publications/> [last accessed April 24, 2017].

United Nations (UN HABITAT). 2016. *New Urban Agenda*. New York: UN HABITAT, <https://habitat3.org/the-new-urban-agenda>.

Valverde, M. 2011. "Seeing Like a City: The Dialectic of Modern and Premodern Ways of Seeing in Urban Governance." *Law and Society* 45(2): 277–312.

Wei Zheng, H., G. Qiping Shen, and H. Wang. 2013. "A Review of Recent Studies on Sustainable Urban Renewal." *Habitat International* 41: 272–279.

Zanini, S. 2017. "Tourism Pressures and Depopulation in Cannaregio: Effects of Mass Tourism on Venetian Cultural Heritage." *Journal of Cultural Heritage Management and Sustainable Development* 7: 2.

CHAPTER 1.4

....

HERITAGE AND THE
POLITICS OF COOPERATION

....

TIM WINTER

HERITAGE studies has seen a lively debate emerge in recent years concerning its place in the academy. As a field that crosses conventional disciplinary boundaries, important questions have been raised as to whether critical analyses of heritage are best constituted through inter- or multi-disciplinary modes of enquiry. Those working outside Europe and North America have also highlighted the shortcomings of a field that has long been rooted in the experiences of Europe, such that heritage is often read as a product of modernity and associated with shifts towards deindustrialization. The closely related field of conservation has also been firmly anchored by those theorists and institutions that emerged in Europe from the nineteenth century onwards.

The need to question, and perhaps even transcend, such "Eurocentric" paradigms, together with the various ways in which they have come to be embedded within international heritage policy, has formed part of a critical heritage studies movement that has called for alternative epistemologies and methodologies for understanding cultural heritage. Implicit to these arguments has been an awareness of the politics of scholarship and knowledge production, which has its roots in domains like post-processual archaeology, critical regionalism in architecture, and the postcolonial turns of anthropology, history, and museum studies. The field of archaeology provides ample evidence of how the epistemologies scholars use and the arguments that arise from these can both reflect and contribute to state-based politics and ethnocultural hostilities. Indeed, archaeological researchers whose work has directly or indirectly advanced claims of territory, sovereignty, and identity have defined the contours of religion and heritage in places like India, Israel, and Palestine (Kohl et al. 2007).

One area where the links between academic scholarship and wider political forces have become particularly pronounced in recent years has been maritime archaeology in the South China Sea. Looking beyond the media coverage of man-made islands, researchers in think tanks and university-based institutes within the disciplines of law, international relations, and defence studies have formed the backbone of an expertise that has often been located close to national centers of power across the Asia Pacific.[1] But in the effort to establish knowledge certainties around territories and jurisdictions, political science has converged with military studies, and marine scientists have collaborated with underwater archaeologists (Adams 2013).

China's first forays into state-funded maritime archaeology began back in November 1987 with the establishment of the Underwater Archaeological Research Center (UWARC). In 1989 new legislation was passed regulating underwater archaeology in territorial waters, with a specific prohibition on any unlicensed commercial salvage operations. Jeff Adams has argued the operations of UWARC have been closely tied to China's territorial interests in the South China Sea and beyond. Accordingly, he cites UWARC's first open water project in the mid-1990s, which took place in the Paracel Islands, a location that has been the focal point of contested ownership claims between China and Vietnam since 1974 (Adams 2013: 274). Investments made into maritime museums and the salvaging of wrecks from waters around China's coast form part of a state-funded program for maritime archaeology which has gathered momentum over the past twenty years or so. In 2010 China joined a select group of countries with manned submersibles capable of operating below depths of 1000 m. These have been used to conduct surveys of the seabed in deeper waters beyond the continental shelf. The Philippines, Taiwan, South Korea, and Vietnam have all pursued similar strategies, with each establishing national maritime archaeology centers and conducting underwater surveys in recent years. In this regard, maritime archaeology scholarship and research has become deeply entangled in government foreign policies across East Asia and the politics of hotly contested waters.

Toward the Diplomacy of Heritage

Stepping back from such examples, it is clear that over the years the sub-field of heritage politics has endeavoured to reveal the ways in which the material culture of the past comes to be politicized, as well as how researchers themselves might be entangled therein. With the nation-state often providing a key anchoring point for analysis and debate, the focus has overwhelmingly been on contestation and excavating the roots of ownership, sovereignty, or even enmity. Heritage has, after all, been a key vector of identity politics in modern times, a language through which ideas about lands, borders, and cultural pasts are carved out in exclusionary ways. It is a domain of scholarly research that has, however, paid much less attention to the political dynamics at play when institutions and social groups pursue heritage as a space for cooperation. More recently, studies into preservation and heritage diplomacy have begun to address this issue, opening up new and, I believe, important questions concerning the international politics of heritage (Akagawa 2014, Luke and Kersel 2013, Winter 2016).

The concept of heritage diplomacy considers how the cultural past—and the discourses and practices that have come to surround it in the modern era—intersects with international relations, diplomacy, geopolitics, and wider structures of global emergence (see Winter 2015). It is a set of relations that raises important questions about methodology, epistemology, and the ways in which wider political forces shape how knowledge about the past is produced. Understanding the drivers of international preservation and heritage today means asking fresh questions about the boundaries of heritage diplomacy and its proponents. It demands researchers to rethink who they might talk to as their informants. It broadens the scope of organizations that might be engaged with in order to understand the political and economic drivers of heritage and conservation. To historicize heritage and conservation through a lens of international relations and diplomacy also means exploring archives and libraries that have traditionally sat outside the scope of heritage studies. It also means reading the connections between archives, both within and across national boundaries. As critical theorists in heritage and archaeology seek to interpret the political forces that enmesh the past and its material culture, there is real benefit in considering such questions in greater detail.

I wish to consider one issue in particular: how knowledge about the cultural past can be shaped and crafted in particular ways by diplomatic relations, international trade, and geopolitics. To do this I return, in part, to the seas of Southeast and East Asia, but expand outwards to highlight how the cultural past of these regions has come to be enmeshed in one of the most ambitious trade and foreign relations initiatives ever conceived, "One Belt One Road." My principal concern here are the ways in which Belt and Road creates new assemblages of knowledge production, whereby history and cultural heritage are reframed and realigned in ways that serve the ambitions of states to cooperate and build multilateral and bilateral relations in a fast-changing global economy.

The Silk Roads

Launched by Chinese President Xi Jinping in September 2013, One Belt One Road has been described as "the most significant and far-reaching initiative that China has ever put forward" (Jianmin 2015). The Belt and Road Initiative (BRI), as it has since come to be known in English, is framed around a narrative of re-establishing the two Silk Roads, overland and maritime, for the twenty-first century. BRI is ostensibly a strategic initiative to foster economic and political integration across the Asia region in order to maintain growth in the Chinese economy, and accelerate the development of the country's northwest provinces, home to large numbers of minorities, including the primarily Muslim population of Uyghers. In an attempt to re-center global trade towards Asia, five components of connectivity and cooperation—policy, facilities, trade, finance, people-to-people ties—underpinned the "Visions and Actions on Jointly Building Silk Road Economic Belt and 21st-Century Maritime Silk Road" program announced by the Ministry of Foreign Affairs and Ministry of Commerce in March 2015.[2] The project reflects China's strategic interests in expanding its influence westwards, including towards the Persian Gulf.

In addition to securing and exploiting Middle Eastern energy supplies, Belt and Road seeks to build corridors of development stretching across national boundaries and create a platform of finance for constructing the physical infrastructure—special economic zones, rail, road, and air and sea ports—required for cross regional trade. As Figure 1.4.1 illustrates, BRI involves the development of several economic corridors, which together straddle both the overland and maritime silk roads. Three years after launch it was clear major developments were being made along each of these corridors. To advance the China–Indochina Economic Corridor, in 2015 The Malacca Gateway Project featured a 10 billion USD investment loan from Beijing to develop the largest deep water port in Southeast Asia over the coming decade (Chew 2016, Bromby 2013). In 2016 China continued its developmental aid to Cambodia, with Xi Jinping visiting Phnom Penh to sign BRI agreements regarding the construction of road and energy infrastructures and special economic zones worth hundreds of millions of dollars.[3] As part of the Bangladesh–China–India–Myanmar Corridor, agreements were signed for multi-billion dollar Chinese investments in the development of deep-water ports in Chittagong, Bangladesh, and Kyaukphyu, Myanmar.[4] For the China–Central Asia– West Asia Economic Corridor, Iran rapidly emerged as a major partner of the scheme. Bilateral trade with China increased from 4 to 13 billion USD between 2003 and 2013, a

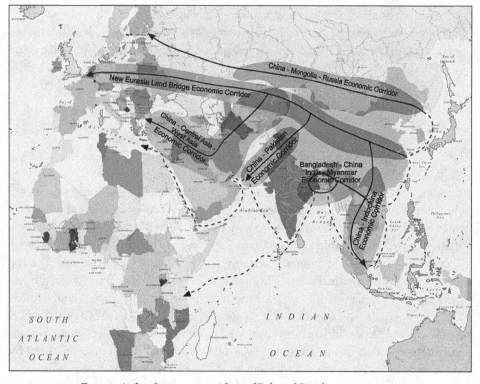

FIGURE 1.4.1 Economic development corridors of Belt and Road.

© Toyah Horman and Tim Winter.

trend that is expected to increase significantly as BRI projects and agreements come into operation (Ramachandran 2016). Once again, massive urban development, energy, and transport infrastructure projects form the basis of agreements tying Iran's economy into Chinese companies and investors.[5] With international sanctions on Iran being lifted, in early 2016 the two governments agreed to increase bilateral trade to 600 billion USD in the following ten years (DAWN 2016). In Pakistan, China has provided a loan of over 1.5 billion USD to cover 85 percent of the cost of an oil pipeline linking to the Iranian border (Saeed 2015). In May 2017, a major Belt and Road summit was held in Beijing. Twenty-eight heads of state were among those in the audience applauding Xi Jinping's declaration that his government would increase its BRI funding by a further 124 billion USD (FORTUNE—International 2017). This would build on the various bilateral trade and infrastructure agreements already signed, such as those above, and a 40 billion USD Silk Road Fund earmarked as part of the 100 billion USD establishment fund of the newly operational Asian Investment Infrastructure Bank.

Central to the discourse of "reviving" the Silk Roads of previous centuries has been an emphasis on the development of people-to-people connections, one of BRI's five pillars. Here the language of cultural heritage has taken on particular importance, with connectivity, routes, hubs, and corridors underpinning the ambitions of Belt and Road, countries are using the Silk Road as a concept of shared heritage to find cultural connections and use these as leverage across Belt and Road's other sectors of cooperation. Cities and countries across Asia, East Africa, and Southern Europe are now showcasing their place on the historic Silk Roads to help legitimize their participation in twenty-first-century trade and commerce. World Heritage nominations for Silk Road properties are among the mechanisms through which countries across the region are collaborating to build historic and cultural ties. Maritime archaeology across the region has also emerged as a key space for collaboration, with China funding salvage operations across the Indian Ocean in an effort to find evidence of former historic connections between China and other countries.

As we can see then Belt and Road has significantly increased interest in the historic Silk Roads and their material culture across a number of countries. More complex though is understanding how this is happening precisely, and how the "celebration" and "revival" of this trans-boundary heritage is being shaped and driven institutionally and politically.

PRODUCING HERITAGE FOR COOPERATION

Interesting questions are now arising concerning how Belt and Road is transforming and assembling scholarly knowledge pertaining to Silk Road material culture and cultural heritage. In the wake of the 2013 Belt and Road launch an extraordinary array of One Belt One Road–themed conferences took place across the world. In this regard, it rapidly became a container for re-branding existing areas of enquiry. But in a significant

number of instances, the geographic and economic possibilities Belt and Road promised afforded new configurations of knowledge production. Political scientists have
been brought into dialogue with anthropologists and archaeologists. Indeed for those
working across the humanities and social sciences, Belt and Road has further increased
the gravitational pull China exerts upon debates about development and globalization, neoliberalism and neo-colonialism. It has also created new dynamics between
nationalism and internationalism, with maritime archaeology serving as an interesting example in this regard. As noted above, a number of maritime archaeology research centers have been established across Asia in the last two decades. State funding
has meant national and territorial interests have quietly underpinned the parameters
of maritime exploration and the salvaging of artifacts. This has been strongly reflected
in the delivery and production of academic papers for the field.[6] Given the intense
sensitivities concerning archaeological discoveries in the South China Sea, shifting to
a language of win-win cooperation is far more complex than collaborations over serial
World Heritage nominations for overland Silk Road properties.

Interestingly, the "Maritime Silk Road of the Twenty-First Century" brings Hong
Kong and Singapore into this picture, with both having a much greater investment in
the development of maritime heritage sectors than before. Indeed, both cities reveal the
confluence between scholarly research on Silk Road histories, Belt and Road futures,
and governmental interests. As part of a wider public diplomacy program on Belt and
Road, the Hong Kong Government instructed its public sector institutions to develop
initiatives addressing the city's future in the Maritime Silk Road. In response, the city's
art and history museums ran events exploring the cultural and historic roots of Silk Road
cooperation.[7] During the 2016 conference "The Belt and Road Initiative—Combining
Hard with Soft Power," maritime archaeology was among the topics debated as an asset
for trade and diplomacy.[8] And in late 2017, the city's maritime museum contributed to
the hosting of the tri-annual Asia-Pacific Regional Conference on Underwater Cultural
Heritage. In Singapore, academic activity around maritime histories has also acceler-
ated in recent years. Topics for university based conferences have included mercantile
connections established during the Śrīvijaya kingdom of Southeast Asia and between
China and the Persian Gulf.[9] Both cities have hosted a number of maritime heritage
exhibitions in recent years, and in each case it is common for experts in academia
and the public museum and heritage sectors to be familiar with each other. Scholars
in history, archaeology, and anthropology are regularly called upon to offer guidance
on exhibition planning. Equally, academics frequently look to cultural sector public
institutions for event hosting and collaborative funding. Singapore and Hong Kong are
also among a select few cities in Asia whose universities have the funding and international connections required for hosting large scale scholarly events and conducting
high-impact research projects.

The idea of reviving a Maritime Silk Road gives a new inflection to the politics of
underwater archaeological material in the East and South China Seas. The recovery
of shipwrecks from the seabed shifts from claims of historical presence and territorial ownership towards a much larger and more diplomatically expedient language of

region-wide trade, encounter, and exchange. Conducting underwater archaeology surveys is an expensive affair, and only the wealthier governments in the region are able to commit the funds required to run such programs. Belt and Road's emphasis on maritime connections helps China bolster its claim that it ranks alongside its European counterparts as one of the great naval powers in world history. One figure in particular, Admiral Zheng He, embodies this grand narrative. A Muslim eunuch who led seven fleets across to South Asia, the Arabian Peninsula, and West Africa between 1405 and 1433 during the Ming dynasty, Zheng He is widely celebrated as a peaceful envoy in both China and by the overseas Chinese living in Malaysia, Indonesia, and elsewhere. In addition to the museums, mosques, and artifacts now appearing around the region celebrating his voyages, China has given millions of dollars and technical assistance to Sri Lanka and Kenya in the search for Zheng He's treasure ships. As part of this cultural aid, funds have also been committed in Kenya to a new maritime heritage museum and the training of maritime archaeology researchers. Both countries are key nodes in the Belt and Road infrastructure network, with Beijing financing the construction of major infrastructure projects such as deep-water ports and road, rail, and airport developments.

The examples of Sri Lanka and Kenya help illustrate how Beijing's desire to build diplomatic and trade relations with key strategic partners, as exemplified by Belt and Road, strongly influences where, when, and in what form scholarly knowledge about the maritime histories of the region emerges. In all these cases, it is important to remember that where archaeology starts, heritage invariably follows. To return to the point made earlier, in Sri Lanka, Singapore, and Hong Kong the links between university-based scholarship and public heritage discourses are often readily discernible. And as cities across the region look to host exhibitions, develop archaeological sites, and build heritage tourism attractions such connections between scholarly expertise on Silk Road histories and government heritage policies are likely to strengthen further.

HERITAGE DIPLOMACY
AND ACADEMIC ENTREPRENEURSHIP

This interface between academia and wider discourses of heritage means influences flow in both directions, such that we have also seen extant discourses of heritage inform academic knowledge production. A collaboration between Nanyang Technological University and the International Zheng He Society in 2015 is illustrative of this point. A conference held in Singapore led to a book, titled "China's One Belt One Road Initiative," published in London a year later (Lim 2016a). The premise of the project was to understand the "central OBOR concept of connectivity" (Lim 2016b), and with a particular focus on Southeast Asia the book's arguments are buttressed by lengthy accounts of trade and vassal kingdoms of the tenth to fourteenth centuries. To this end, Tseng (2016: 141) states: "The entire world system functioned smoothly when the connection through China operated well. Actually, this was the original apparatus upon which the 21st century OBOR initiative was sketched out." The volume further cements these temporal and spatial connections through assertions that the twenty-first-century "maritime route is almost identical with Zheng He's seven maritime voyages" (Lim 2016b: 5). Indeed, Tan Ta Sen, the President of the International Zheng He Society and owner of the museum in Melaka argues Zheng He's "Art of Collaboration" holds important insights for building cordial relations today:

> Cheng Ho's voyages to the Western Ocean showed such features of Confucian ethics as humanism, benevolence, righteousness, forgiveness, morality, harmonious inter-personal relationships, as well as a stable social order. He incorporated Confucian ethics into his foreign policy as a form of the "Art of Collaboration". . . . The Cheng Ho spirit could be a model for contemporary international relations and foreign relations. Reliving Cheng Ho's spirit in international relations based on mutual respect, non-invasion, non-intervention and fostering good relationships with foreign states will result in the creation of a world order where multipolar powers are in a partnership to achieve world peace, universal harmony and equality. (2016: 57–59)

Belt and Road has also blurred the boundaries between academic research, policy think tanks, and commercial enterprise. This has meant scholarship in the humanities and social sciences is now being drawn into entirely new political relations. Belt and Road impacts the energy, construction, security, and foreign policy portfolios of dozens of governments around the world, and given the think tank template is a now well established medium for building expert advisory capacities and the international partnerships required for diplomacy and commercial ventures, a number of new BRI-related think tanks and university based research institutes were established in the three year period of 2014–16. Many of these are multi-disciplinary, with the majority orienting their intelligence building capacities towards the cooperation pillars of the 2015 Belt and Road "Visions and Action Plan." It is an area many universities have been eager to play in, often by pooling existing expertise across faculties in an effort to secure funding, government or otherwise, or establish networks for international student recruitment.

The approach institutions have taken has, in part, been shaped by their location. In the case of the Collaborative Innovation Center of Silk Road Economic Belt Research, at Xi'an Jiaotong University, Xi'an, for example, the priority has been to build ties with a number of Central Asian countries, as well as with Russia and India. In proposing collaborations across multiple fields—law, economics, engineering, trade—the Center has aimed to contribute to the diplomatic dimensions of BRI by building an "academic belt of the Silk Road," in order to improve "exchanges between experts from different countries and their ability of knowledge production, tackling key problems by a collaborative innovation which was transnational, transregional and transboundary" (Xi'an Jiaotong University 2015). The mantra of "win-win cooperation" has also included nurturing a "dialogue among civilizations" as a priority area. For those universities nearer the coast, the assemblages look a little different. In Xiamen,

Huaqiao University's Institute of Maritime Silk Road is using its location on the Taiwan Strait and the university's historical connections with overseas Chinese to build a series of partnerships, including ones focused on "cultural exchanges" with countries across Southeast Asia.[10] Further south, City University of Macau has established the "Macau One Belt One Road Research Center," with a particular focus on strengthening connections between China and Portuguese-speaking Belt and Road countries. Maritime histories linking Portugal, Timor Leste, Mozambique, and Macau underpin a networking strategy revolving around the twenty-first-century Maritime Silk Road. With Belt and Road holding profound consequences for Hong Kong, the city has witnessed a flurry of related academic production, including institutes created across a number of universities. Within portfolios of expertise built around trade, banking, and the shipping and air transport sectors, an interest in understanding Hong Kong's place in the historic Maritime Silk Road has been typically couched within the discourses of public diplomacy and international cooperation.[11]

Belt and Road has also become a vehicle for Chinese-funded research centers in other countries in the region. In 2016, the Royal University of Phnom Penh created such an initiative, the Maritime Silk Road Research Center. For the Cambodian government, a long-term recipient of Chinese aid and investment, the center would provide a gateway for sourcing further funds from the Asian Investment Infrastructure Bank and its Silk Road Fund.[12] In June 2015, the Confucius Institute of Maritime Silk Road was inaugurated as a collaboration between twenty-seven educational institutions across Thailand. Designed to be a model for similarly named entities in other BRI countries, the institute's key remit would be to build educational and cultural exchanges between Thailand and China. Such educational bilateralism has also extended into various multilateral configurations. These include the "The Silk Road Think Tank Network," "The New Silk Road Law Schools Alliance," "Maritime Continental Silk Road Cities Alliance," "Belt and Road Think Tank Association," "University Alliance of the New Silk Road," and the "International Silk Road Think Tank Association." In November 2014, the Silk Road Universities Network was also established with the premise of fostering academic connections that revive the "Silkroadia" spirit of the ancient Silk Roads, a commitment laid out in the organization's constitution and mission statement:

> We aim to realize our vision of "serving the world" by undertaking diverse projects that restore the historical value of the ancient Silk Road which, as the birthplace of four major civilizations, has been a source of immense pride for centuries. The most valuable lesson from the history of the Silk Road is that the key to peaceful coexistence and collective prosperity is to treat individual differences as a cause for celebration rather than segregation, best captured in Silkroadia—the spirit of ancient Silk Road. In line with this thinking, we believe that the coming together of universities can help realize this vision through fostering an exchange of ideas culminating into decisive action between intellectuals transcending national, religious and cultural boundaries.
>
> Mission Statement, Silk Road Universities Network (2016)

To this end, annual conferences have provided the focal point for the development of the associated International Association for Silk Road Studies, involving scholars from universities in more than twenty countries, including Iran, Malaysia, Pakistan, Sri Lanka, Portugal, and Greece. Not surprisingly, the number of academic and policy conferences dedicated to Belt and Road also expanded rapidly in the aftermath of its launch.

In these examples the academic entrepreneurialism which has formed around Belt and Road is clearly evident. Some institutes and networks will undoubtedly be more successful than others over the longer term. What we also see in the examples of Hong Kong, Singapore, Xiamen, and Xi'an is the incorporation of universities into government strategies for making cities economically competitive. In this regard Belt and Road significantly advances a neoliberal model of higher education funding, one that is oriented by national priorities and rearranges scholarship into new configurations, both intellectually and institutionally. It is an arena that involves Silk Road histories and cultural pasts being invoked in multiple ways.

In certain contexts, this idea of building contemporary trade and business relations on the foundations of links established more than half a millennia ago is being critically interrogated. But as we have seen here, the notion of "ancient" overland and sea-based connections is also being deployed as a vehicle for universities to conduct public diplomacy, recruit students, undertake cultural exchanges, and build networks of high-value commercial and scientific research. Once again then we see a political economy at play shaping how the past is conceived, moulding which histories are brought into focus and how they come to be funnelled through a language of exchanges and partnerships. In the developments cited from Singapore we also see how certain interpretations of Southeast Asia's maritime history give intellectual weight to analyses that advance the government's ambitions of ensuring the country remains tightly integrated in Asia's networked economy.

Since its 2013 launch, Belt and Road has proved to be an extraordinary catalyst of knowledge production. From a starting point of twenty-two in 2014, a Google Scholar search returns over a thousand "One Belt One Road" articles published in English two years later.[13] The majority of these fell within the domain of political geography, foreign affairs, and business. Belt and Road research themes and topics will continue to diversify and proliferate.

CONCLUSION

The aim of this chapter has been to point to the ways in which cultural heritage knowledge can be shaped and rearranged within particular political conditions. By addressing such themes at the international level and within the fast changing political economy of twenty-first-century Asia, the themes highlighted here link heritage discourses to geopolitics, international relations, and different modes of diplomacy. The idea of "reviving" the Silk Roads through the Belt and Road Initiative is creating new institutional and political relationships around cultural heritage, processes that will significantly contribute to remapping the narratives of Eurasia and Indian Ocean history. It is a situation that is likely to open up important spaces for understanding previously neglected historical events and under-researched locations. But as we have seen, the forms of re-territorialization that Belt and Road delivers steers these histories along certain intellectual and geographic corridors and across institutional networks and hubs. Belt and Road also offers a vivid example of how discourses of heritage come to be reimagined and reconfigured as countries seek to use their past to facilitate forms of trade and physical connectivity. In effect then, we see a distinct politics of heritage in play within a complex landscape of cooperation, one that warrants our critical attention.

ACKNOWLEDGMENTS

This work was supported by the Australia Research Council Discovery Scheme under Grant DP140102991—The Crisis in International Heritage Conservation in an Age of Shifting Global Power. The author would also like to acknowledge the support of Toyah Horman.

NOTES

1. Shannon Tiezzi provides a nice overview of this issue in the article, "China's Academic Battle for the South China Sea." See: Tiezzi, Shannon. "China's Academic Battle for the South China Sea." <http://thediplomat.com/2014/02/chinas-academic-battle-for-the-south-china-sea/>.
2. National Development and Reform Commission, Ministry of Foreign Affairs and Ministry of Commerce of the People's Republic of China. "Vision and Actions on Jointly Building Silk Road Economic Belt and 21st-Century Maritime Silk Road." <http://en.ndrc.gov.cn/newsrelease/201503/t20150330_669367.html>.
3. In late 2016, the development aid tracking project AidData reported over two hundred active Chinese assistance projects in Cambodia. See: China Aid Data. "Geospatial Dashboard." <http://china.aiddata.org/geospatial_dashboard?q=Cambodia&l=12.70604 2123782732,104.23112999999998,9>. See also: Janelle Retka. "Cambodia Positions Itself along New Silk Road." <https://www.cambodiadaily.com/news/cambodia-positions-itself-along-new-silk-road-114629/>; and Ben Paviour. "For China, Cambodia Is a Sideshow, But It's a Loyal One." <https://www.cambodiadaily.com/news/china-cambodia-sideshow-loyal-one-119475/>.
4. See for example Ananth Krishnan. "China Offers to Develop Chittagong Port." <http://www.thehindu.com/news/international/china-offers-to-develop-chittagong-port/article245961.ece>; and Shannon Tiezzi. "Chinese Company Wins Contract for Deep Sea Port in Myanmar." <http://thediplomat.com/2016/01/chinese-company-wins-contract-for-deep-sea-port-in-myanmar/>.
5. See PressTV. "Chabahar Port to Harbor Chinese Industrial Town." <http://www.presstv.com/Detail/2016/04/27/462797/China-CMI-Iran-mega-port>.
6. The role the nation, past and present, plays in orienting research undertaken by scholars employed in institutions across the region is reflected in the published literature and was

evident in the 2014 Asia-Pacific Regional Conference on Underwater Cultural Heritage held in Hawaii. For program details see National Marine Sanctuary Foundation and Marine Option Program University of Hawaii. "Final APCONF 2014 Program." <http://www.apconf.org/wp-content/uploads/Final-APCONF-2014-program.pdf>.

7. In October 2016 Hong Kong Museum of History ran the exhibition "Across the Oceans: The Local Connections and Global Dimensions of China's Maritime Silk Road."

8. See Maritime Silk Road Society. "Leaders from Top-Notch Enterprises Speak at 'The Belt and Road Initiative—Combining Hard Power with Soft Power' Conference." <http://maritimesilkroad.org.hk/en/news/newsReleasesDetail/102>.

9. Since 2014 the National University of Singapore has run Muhammad Alagil Arabia Asia Conference series. These have been titled: "Arabia-Asia Relations, Then and Now" (2014), "Silk Roads, Muslim Passages: The Islam Question" (2015), and "China-Arabia Encounters and Engagements" (2016).

10. See Ding Yi. "Huaqiao Univeristy—A Think Tank for 'One Belt, One Road' Strategy." <http://www.sino-us.com/433/15021790078.html>.

11. Within the City University of Hong Kong Research Center on One Belt One Road for example, a program of building "cultural intelligence" has been established to effectively deal with cross-cultural settings. See City University of Hong Kong Research Centre on One-Belt-One-Road. "Introduction." <http://www.cb.cityu.edu.hk/obor/>.

12. See Xinhua. "Cambodia Launches China-Backed Maritime Silk Road Research Center." <http://news.xinhuanet.com/english/2016-06/13/c_135432581.htm>.

13. A Google Scholar search conducted in February 2017 for articles titled "One Belt One Road" identified the following totals: 22: 2014, 547: 2015, 1030: 2016. Articles with titles including "The Silk Road Economic Belt" totalled: 620: 2014, 1520: 2015, 1550: 2016.

REFERENCES

Adams, Jeff. 2013. "The Role of Underwater Archaeology in Framing and Facilitating the Chinese National Strategic Agenda," in *Cultural Heritage Politics in China*, ed. T. Blumenfield and H. Silverman. New York: Springer, 261–282.

Akagawa, Natsuko. 2014. *Heritage Conservation and Japan's Cultural Diplomacy: Heritage, National Identity and National Interest*. London: Routledge.

Bromby, Robin. "Down the Maritime Silk Road." *The Australian*, <http://www.theaustralian.com.au/business/in-depth/down-the-maritime-silk-road/story-fnjy4qn5-1226776242929> [last modified December 6, 2013].

Chew, Amy. "China, Malaysia Tour New 'Port Alliance' to Reduce Customs Bottlenecks and Boost Trade." *South China Morning Post*, <http://www.scmp.com/news/asia/southeast-asia/article/1934839/china-malaysia-tout-new-port-alliance-reduce-customs> [last modified April 9, 2016].

DAWN. "Iran, China Agree $600-Billion Trade Deal after Sanctions." *DAWN*, <http://www.dawn.com/news/1234923> [last modified January 23, 2016].

Erickson, A., and K. Bond. 2015. "Archaeology and the South China Sea." <http://thediplomat.com/2015/07/archaeology-and-the-south-china-sea/>.

FORTUNE—International. "Xi Jinping Says the Rejection of Protectionism Is Part of What 'One Belt, One Road' Is About." FORTUNE—International, <http://fortune.com/2017/05/15/china-xi-jinping-belt-road-summit-protectionism/> [last modified May 15, 2017].

Jianmin, Wu. "'One Belt and One Road', Far-Reaching Inititaive." *China–US Focus*, <http://www. chinausfocus.com/finance-economy/one-belt-and-one-road-far-reaching-initiative/> [last modified March 26, 2015].

Kohl, P. L., et al. 2007. *Selective Remembrances: Archaeology in the Construction, Commemoration, and Consecration of National Pasts*. Chicago: University of Chicago Press.

Lim, T. W., et al., eds. 2016a. *China's One Belt One Road Initiative*. London: Imperial College Press.

Lim, T. W. 2016b. "Introduction," in *China's One Belt One Road Initiative*, ed. T. W. Lim et al. London: Imperial College Press, 3–18.

Luke, C., and M. Kersel. 2013. *U.S. Cultural Diplomacy and Archaeology: Soft Power, Hard Heritage*. New York: Routledge.

Paviour, Ben. 2016. "For China, 'Cambodia Is a Sideshow, But It's a Loyal One." <https://www. cambodiadaily.com/news/china-cambodia-sideshow-loyal-one-119475/>.

Ramachandran, Sudha. "Iran, China and the Silk Road Train." *The Diplomat*, <http:// thediplomat.com/2016/03/iran-china-and-the-silk-road-train/> [last modified March 30, 2016].

Retka, Janelle. 2016. "Cambodia Positions Itself along New Silk Road." <https://www. cambodiadaily.com/news/cambodia-positions-itself-along-new-silk-road-114629/>.

Saeed, Shah. "China to Build Pipeline from Iran to Pakistan." *The Wall Street Journal*, <http:// www.wsj.com/articles/china-to-build-pipeline-from-iran-to-pakistan-1428515277> [last modified April 9, 2015].

The Silk Road Universities Network. "Purpose and Background of SUN." *The Silk Road Universities Network*, <http://www.sun-silkroadia.org/eng/view/sun.php?pid=2> [last modified 2016].

Tan, T. S. 2016. "Cheng Ho Spirit and World Dream," in *China's One Belt One Road Initiative*, ed. T. W. Lim et al. London: Imperial College Press, 57–59.

Tseng, K.H-Y. 2016. "The South China Sea and the Maritime Silk Road Proposal: Conflicts Can Be Transformed," in *China's One Belt One Road Initiative*, ed. T. W. Lim et al. London: Imperial College Press, 133–147.

Winter, T. 2015. "Heritage Diplomacy." *International Journal of Heritage Studies* 21(10): 997–1015.

Winter, T. 2016. "Heritage Diplomacy: Entangled Materialities of International Relations." *Future Anterior* 21(1): 16–34.

Xi'An Jiaotong University. "Collaborative Innovation Center of Silk Road Economic Belt Research Started by XJTU." Xi'An Jiaotong University, <http://en.xjtu.edu.cn/info/1044/ 1572.htm> [last modified January 23, 2015].

....

CULTURE, HERITAGE, AND THE POLITICS OF BECOMING

....

JOANIE WILLETT

INTRODUCTION

....

SPATIAL cultures and the tangible and intangible heritage that supports them are made up of both objective truths (such as objects, historical sites, dates and key moments, and practices), and deeply subjective ideas, meanings, and interpretations. As peoples and cultures mediate the spaces within which they live, work, and pass leisure time (see Lefebvre 1974 [1991], Cosgrove 1998), they discursively produce and construct the imaginary localities within which they are situated (Soja 1996, Massey 2005, Thrift 2008, Cresswell 1996, Hetherington 2008, Sibley 1995).

However, whilst we understand *how* people create the cultures and spaces of which they are a part—and the relationship between the past and the present—the literature about the production of place overlooks future temporalities. Spatial narratives have three key elements. (1) The past, from which heritage is drawn. (2) The present, where things that used to happen in the past are interpreted by the people that produce a place in the present. Stories about previous times are used to give meaning or explain things that happen in the here and now. (3) The future: the story of "who we are" also contains the seed or kernel of "what we might become" (or "what we are becoming") as we move forward into the future (Willett 2016). This future needs to be consistent and congruent with the stories that are told about the past and present. To illustrate, it would be incongruent or unrealistic for a region that drew its primary narrative of itself from an agricultural, rural past to decide that its future economy is going to be based around rocket science. Further creative and conceptual narrative development would be required to make such a claim carry weight.

Moreover, the narratives that we weave around a culture and heritage have important implications for the ways that peoples are perceived by both persons within a culture and by others; Eriksson (2008) demonstrates this. Drawing on Hechter's (1975) model of internal colonialism, Eriksson claims that urban parts of Sweden construct the rural North of the country in ways that emphasize economic stagnation, social backwardness, and dependency on the urban "core." Here, the ways that a space is discursively (re)produced can significantly impact the kinds of economic activity that are able to be supported and practiced in an area (Galani-Moutafi 2013). Bürk et al. (2012) call this "stigmatization" whereby a set of negative characteristics attach themselves to a place, affecting the capacity of regional individuals and industries to do business with the outside world. These studies appear to claim that powerful (often urban) economically core regions have the ability to disproportionately affect how a region and its culture is perceived and imagined by the outside world. Part of the mechanism is through knowledges generated through rural tourism activities, but also from arts, cultural, heritage, and economic institutions which operate at a national level. Deacon (2004) claims that because such bodies have an incomplete understanding about the cultures and practices of peripheries, they can tend to draw on regional stereotypes (which may be inaccurate, outdated, or otherwise value-laden because of complex historic relationships between core and peripheral spaces). However Willett and Lang (forthcoming) challenge the notion that power flows in such a linear format, arguing that peripheral regions contain the agency and capacity to resist "peripheralizing" narratives of place which further marginalize such localities.

It is clear that as places produce their cultures and heritage they are creating stories or narratives that feed back into not only how local people imagine themselves, but also how others perceive local people. This has important implications for future activity. In the remainder of this chapter, I am going to argue that as heritage theorists and professionals we need to pay close attention not only to what the narratives that we produce are saying about the present and the past, but also about the kinds of futures that are made possible through them. Nor should we be shy of recognizing the economic implications of heritage. Indeed, if culture is about how people behave whilst they are producing means of survival, cultural heritage is infused with economic activity. Consequently, we should not be surprised that the futures imagined within cultural narratives *also* have a close link with economic fortunes or otherwise. Acknowledging this can better enable researchers to contribute to the ongoing social, cultural, and economic development of the spaces that we work with.

To explore this further, I will analyze a case study of Cornwall in the far South-West of the United Kingdom through the phenomenologies of Merleau-Ponty, the temporality of Bergson, and the assemblages of Delueze and Guattari. I will explore two differing narratives of culture and heritage in Cornwall, and the implications that these have for the future development of the region.

Cornwall

Cornwall is a peninsula with over 549,400 inhabitants (Nomis 2017), characterized by economic uncertainty and what Cloke and Edwards (1986) describe as "peripheral rurality." Over recent decades the region has been on a downward economic spiral and is now positioned at the bottom of the UK and EU economic league tables, meaning that over a period of five decades Cornwall had gone from being poor, but better off than the poorest parts of Britain, to being the poorest itself (Willett 2010). From 1999 the region has received European Union structural funds on the basis that its Gross Domestic Product (GDP) was below 75 percent of the European average (Willett 2013). Cornwall is still in receipt of structural funds until the United Kingdom exits the European Union.

Although there are no longer the high levels of unemployment that were seen up until the end of the 1990s (Perry 1993, Payne et al. 1996), the economy is still weak. Average earned incomes are 13 percent lower than UK averages (Nomis 2017) (down from 18 percent lower in 2013, Willett 2016), and the economy has been characterized by low skills, high outward migration, and a dispersed population (Williams 2003, Cornwall Council 2016, Cornwall Council 2017, Nomis 2017). This is often attributed to the decline of traditional industries such as mining, farming, and fishing, and over the later twentieth century, the economy had come to be dominated by tourism (Cornwall and Isles of Scilly Economic Forum 2007, Nomis 2017).

As an industry, tourism has influenced how the region is perceived by others and, over the course of time, the image of a region where residents can experience a good lifestyle has come to dominate despite the challenging local socioeconomic conditions (Willett 2016). It is this opposition between regional poverty and perceived high quality of life that makes Cornwall an interesting case study with regards to narrative and the production of place. Indeed, there are two competing narratives of place in Cornwall. In one, it is a desperately economically poor region with a proud cultural heritage and traditions. In the other, derived from the use of counter-urbanization and tourism heritage as a means of combating rural decline, it is a great place to experience a high quality of life.

The latter has been a central theme of Cornish economic development strategies since at least the late 1960s (Willett 2010). As in other rural regions, it is predicated on the idea that in-migrants to rural spaces gain a higher quality of life based around a rural idyll, and in return the enterprises that they bring with them provide a much needed boost to the rural knowledge economy (Halfacree 2012). Latterly, this has drawn heavily on the discourse of "Creative Regions," (Miller 2009) whereby, following Florida (2002), educated, dynamic, geographically mobile entrepreneurs are motivated to relocate their knowledge economy enterprises on the basis of the strength of cultural industries.

However, there is still a need to stem the ongoing problem of economic and population decline. The paradox of the narrative that seeks to attract people to the region on the basis of the lifestyle that can be lived there is that it has not managed to stop existing residents from moving away. Although the population of Cornwall continues to rise, and gained around 100,000 people between the 2001 and 2011 censuses (Nomis 2017), there is also a form of "population exchange" where young people in particular feel that "to get on, you have to get out" (Williams 2003). This indicates that there may be a sharply contrasting difference of experience between newer residents and those who have had a more long-term stake in the region. To an extent, this is not necessarily surprising given the continued reluctance of the Cornish economy to recover on a par with the rest of the United Kingdom.

Both narratives provide an interpretation of cultural heritage for the present, but largely draw on *different* heritages. One sees time as part of a trajectory that stretches to the deep past, and the other borrows from a more recent past. What we don't know yet but will explore below is the kinds of futures imagined by these histories.

The primary data is taken from a series of semi-structured interviews with senior regional development personnel and political actors, followed by interviews with members of the public. In total thirty-two interviews were conducted using a grounded theory methodology (Charmaz 2006; Strauss and Corbin 2008), and participants were selected on the basis of the insights that they offered to emerging theories. Interview transcripts were textually analyzed with Foucauldian discourse analysis grounded in the intricate relationship between power, discourse, knowledge, and truth. This looked at how Cornwall as the "discursive object" was constructed by different actors, in differing historical moments, and the sites of power that this exposed (Foucault [1969] 2002).

BECOMING AND THE NARRATIVES OF CORNWALL

"Narrative" implies a particular, single, agreed-upon story which encapsulates an experience for a people, an individual, an isolated event, or a series of events. But narratives are always inherently political and to imagine the story of place as made up of only one story is to deny the multiplicity of competing, contrasting, or complementary stories which are also told in any given context. A singular narrative is merely a story which has gained dominance, closing off differing versions, but always containing possible slippages into alternative stories.

Because of their multiplicity, narratives can be imagined as assemblages, collections of networked signs, symbols, practices, and institutions which coalesce around a given point (see Deleuze and Guattari 2004). Although they might give the appearance of being a unity, the relationship between the assembled parts is always unstable, capable of readily absorbing the new, but also creating fractures between apparently fixed elements, and slippages between one group of signs and another entirely different assemblage. The relationship between assembled elements is not arbitrary, but built on what Connolly (2008) calls "resonance," or a recollection of similarity which has left an affective impact or mark on the memory. Elements are absorbed on the basis of resonance with some physical or emotional prior meaning amongst and between the assembled actors, which leaves a complex and layered affective impact on an individual or group (Ahmed 2004). The thoughts and feelings that become attached to certain memories, material objects, institutions, or things affects how we relate to those same objects, drawing matter and ideas into an assemblage, and expelling other things. Over the course of the following argument, we will see how these symbolic and emotive affects impact how narratives slip, slide, develop, and grow.

The dimension of time is critical for understanding narratives beyond just what they are, but also what they will become. Human narratives do not follow a predictable path towards the future but instead have multiple possibilities for becoming (Bergson [1907] 1944, Connolly 2011, Delanda 2011, Merleau-Ponty [1945] 2002). The past actively shapes how events, ideas, and objects within the assemblage are understood, which in turn affects how the future is built. Becoming is a complex process involving a multiplicity of elements, and so is inherently unpredictable, which means that although becoming can indicate a trajectory, it cannot predict the future. However, what becoming does is to open up spaces of possibility from which possible futures can emerge.

The interview data is divided into two distinct categories that emerged from the analysis. "Insider types" tended to have grown up in Cornwall, and "outsider types" tended to have relocated on the basis of lifestyle. Both groups used different perceptions of Cornwall's culture and heritage to generate different kinds of narrative futures, or becoming. These should be imagined as Weberian "ideal types," representing the polar ends of a spectrum rather than being representative of the broader population in Cornwall. I start the analysis with an examination of the outsider-type narrative, before moving to the response of the insider type. Later, I consider how these differing groups construct each other, what this tells us about the discursive construction of Cornwall, and the implications that these different versions of culture and heritage have for Cornwall's strategic becoming.

Outsider Types

The Outsider-type narrative assemblage coalesced around quality-of-life type discourses. This provided a way for disparate in-migrants from diverse backgrounds to derive a sense of shared experience. In common with a more general perception of the rural, (Murdoch and Lowe 2003), this assemblage presented Cornwall as a place to consume, resonating with the hopes and desires of in-migrants, and frequently incorporating the language and ideas underpinning creative industries discourse. For example, when asked to describe the region, one senior manager of a publicly funded county-wide development body moved swiftly into a discussion of a wide range of cultural activities, naming high profile restaurants and elite destinations, that made it great for "young rich trendies" (R19). Other persons expressed the work/life balance that they felt could be achieved in the region. The owner of a relocated business describes her experience in this way:

> We literally did work around the children, I mean we finish work at 3, and then we are
> a family until around 7, and the children go off to bed and then we work again, and

> that time we're out walking, and it sounds so idyllic but its true, we're making jam and surfing and all of that sort of jazz, . . . I think that there's a true understanding between businesses within Cornwall. It's work life balance. (R14)

Within this lifestyle assemblage, running a business in Cornwall means that individuals do not need to make compromises about the balance between work and play because the imagined reality of life in Cornwall is a nicer environment to work, with more opportunities for relaxation and spending time with the family. We also see an intersection with visitor/tourism assemblages. The activities engaged in borrow from symbolisms and cultural resonances such as beach-going and other outdoors style pursuits that are shared with the visitor experience. These conjure up and incorporate pleasurable emotional affects, full of the rosy glow of memories of carefree happy holidays. Within this version Cornwall is not enjoyed for its business opportunities for dynamic entrepreneurs, but for its leisure pursuits and hedonistic affective register. Borrowing from visitor assemblages in this way suggests that for these in-migrants, running a business from Cornwall is a bit like an extension of a holiday. Economic development is a matter of enhancing and facilitating the consumption of place which the visitor demands, and extending the visitor experience to those desiring a permanent holiday in the region.

Moreover, these respondents are focused on the present with little sense of where the story of Cornwall that they construct is moving toward. Progress and their sense of becoming is a negotiated relationship between their pasts and the present, emphasizing their personal enjoyment whilst still addressing the necessity to earn money. Far from appearing like dynamic entrepreneurs, these individuals seem to be "downshifting," making the conscious decision to trade economic or career ambition for quality of life. The line of time is actually turning backwards on itself, rather than moving forward with a sense of becoming. This may indicate that regional development borrowing of the symbols and affective register of visitor assemblages might not attract the most dynamic group of people.

The concept of becoming implies that the present is filtered through memory and the past to create something new (see Bergson [1907] 1944, Connolly 2002, 2011). But the question here relates to whether the "new" in this instance represents social and economic progress or not. Economic development decision-makers clearly recognize the need to reinvigorate the economy, and in an attempt to do this they are drawing on a set of tourism-related symbolisms and meanings which are deeply embedded in cultural memory. Coincidentally this coheres with development orthodoxy which claims that dynamic entrepreneurs will relocate to somewhere where they can enjoy a great lifestyle. However in another sense little really new is actually emerging from what might be considered as the absorption of the creative industries assemblage by the visitor assemblage, replacing Florida's "dynamism" with visitor "consumption." In other words, whilst purporting to look to the future, this narrative actually represents "more of the same," and so consequently has little real becoming.

The Insider-type Response

The insider-type group often explicitly attempted to distance itself from the alternative narrative, rejecting outsider-type consumption of place as something "other" people do. Sometimes this group drew on a sense of nationhood and shared origin as a people which has underpinned the recent grant of "national minority" status to the region (BBC 2014). Some respondents referred to the "kings and rulers" that had governed the territory up until the time of eleventh century Athelstan, the uniqueness afforded by the Cornish language, or to a pride in the industrial heritage which had once made Cornwall a wealthy centre of the industrial revolution. This group saw themselves as situated not just in terms of a shared discourse or common enjoyment of place, but as embedded in the fabric of Cornish history.

Insider types understood the intricate link between the tourist affective assemblage and the relocation choices of outsider types, believing that the moves that this precipitated were not about the career development of migrants, but their desire to "escape," and "get away from it all." This is combined with an acute awareness of how "lifestyle" type symbolisms and emotive affects overlaid others' perceptions of Cornwall and the activities that occur within the space. To illustrate, a cultural sector manager told an amusing story of how the makers of a popular TV drama set in Cornwall had expected that they would be able to find "vintage" type medical equipment in the region's main hospital.

In the minds of the insider-type group, quality of life narratives contain a baggage of slippages that resonate with a perspective that imagines Cornwall, and therefore its inhabitants, to be at best "behind the times," and at worst to be completely backward. This carries important repercussions for local businesses trying to expand their markets as discussed by a young local businessman, trying to forge networks further afield. He stated that:

> The original impression when we started the meeting or this networking, was that we closed shop at one o clock, that we don't really do "proper" business, we just muck around a bit. They thought that we worked very hard but then would go surfing for the rest of the day, that was the general feeling. Afterwards it became clear to them that we were working possibly harder than some of them up there. (R4)

The issue in this example is that the slippage of signs and symbols between economic development promotion and tourist imaginings and experiences has become central to how Cornwall is perceived by external businesses and actors. In the above quote, the dominance of lifestyle type representations of Cornwall, both related to holiday experiences or later acquaintance with creative industries branding, cloaks how Cornish businesses are perceived (Bergson [1907] 1944), and the quality of their imagined offer. The strength of outsider-type symbols has meant that people outside of the region can struggle to take Cornish enterprises seriously.

A prominent politician stated that:

> Mostly because Cornwall's seen as a holiday destination, people, their first reaction is "oh what a lovely place to live, you're really lucky, and so on," and being in the kind of trade that I'm in, which is a fairly middle class trade, the assumption is "when did I first move here," that it wouldn't be possible for someone who was born up here to have succeeded to represent their own area. Someone would clearly have to come down to do the job. (R13)

This is not a story which says "in-migrants take our jobs," but one that borrows from, and echoes with Fanon's ([1952] 2008) exposé of colonial myths, stating that in-migrants are naturally more skilled and capable than local insider types. To borrow from Bürk et al.'s (2012) work on peripheral cities, not only the territory, but also the people become stigmatized by a narrative which asserts that the inhabitants of a peripheral region are backward.

The Made in Cornwall logo (Figure 1.5.1) exemplifies these contestations. Developed in the early 2000s, it depicts a roofless, decayed, long abandoned engine house—a romanticized relic of the region's impressive mining heritage, and a ubiquitous visual in many parts of the contemporary landscape. The image was deeply contentious because it made the statement to an international audience that the Cornwall of the twenty-first century is defined by a long-since lost economic activity. It might well reflect the impact of the past on the landscape of the present, but it has no sense of what people in Cornwall actively *do* in the present, or might be able to do in the future. Indeed, it can even be interpreted as stating that Cornwall is nothing more than its long lost mining heritage. This might not trouble the outsider-type position, whose experience of the present is rooted in a romanticized consumption of place which is not affected—indeed might be enhanced— by these kinds of visual narratives. However for insider-types concerned about using heritage as a spur to action in the present and future, it was much more problematic.

The narrative of economic development within the insider-type position not only rejects fragments, meanings, and resonances associated with the quality-of-life type discourse, but actively holds it responsible for the entrenchment of the economic difficulties which Cornwall has faced for generations. It claims that reliance on physical

FIGURE 1.5.1. "Made in Cornwall" logo.

and emotive symbolisms which recall visitor experiences closes off progressive development. Instead, it's line of time and becoming which opens possibilities for the future looks to a reassertion of Cornwall's cultural identity as a hope for the future—i.e. through Cornish devolution, strengthening Cornish governance institutions and looking to the symbolisms from Cornwall's industrial past.

These two narrative positions exist at opposite ends of the spectrum with very few points of intersection. They proclaim different points of origin; one based on territory and continuity, the other on consumption and enjoyment. One group embraces migration and is suspicious of those with a more temporal attachment to place, the other has a temporal attachment to place and is suspicious of the motivations and actions of newer residents, constructing instead a story of colonization. One group sees progress and economic development as bound up by the consumption of place, and the other imagines it as a reassertion of place, territory, and identity. Each ideal type is deeply aware of its other, often consciously positioning itself in terms of difference, which in true Nietzschean fashion can be constructed as the scapegoat and cause for regional problems. However, despite the recent success of the campaign for national minority status, and the importance of insider-type narratives in obtaining EU structural funding (Willett 2013), it is the lifestyle of the outsider-type response which has been dominant in policy-making.

This is a problem in terms of development narratives because this cultural story is reliant on pleasure and consumption in the here and now. Its "lifestyle" has neither future nor past, only middle and present. If becoming is the emergent production of the new (see Connolly 2002), the only "new" that can happen here has little help from its past beyond the promise of a great quality of life. The role of culture and heritage is limited to providing an interesting diversion for the visitor experience, or a tourist and economic development marketing line about a romanticized rurality. This makes it difficult to move beyond the conceptual return of tourism discourses that are always looking backwards to an imagined more gentle period. In turn, this becomes a structural trap that the narrative finds itself in, where it is forever returning to an imagined past.

Conclusion

The problem with regards to Cornwall and development has been that policy discourse has imagined culture and heritage as part of a narrative which has little or no sense of becoming. This means that people both inside and outside of the space become locked in a series of (mis)perceptions which constructs the region in ways that do not help its capacity to redevelop its struggling economy. The region has gone on to be discursively (re)produced in harmful ways which can only repeat the failed policies of recent decades, whilst having little real sense of new possibilities for the future. Moreover, in othering the narratives at the other end of the spectrum, it closes off the opportunity for growing the narrative, and finding alternative, progressive forms of becoming beyond its perpetual backwards churn.

Whilst this chapter has focused on a single case study, the narrative movements and contentions are familiar in other peripheral regions with contested discursive constructions of place (see Eriksson 2008, Bürk et al. 2012). For Critical Heritage Studies, this means that we need to pay close attention to the kinds of things that we are saying about the spaces that we analyze, including the trajectories, lines of time, and narrative becoming which lies in interpretations about culture and heritage. Telling a story about a place is not only a story about the past and the present. It is also a story about the future, and we need to be mindful about what kinds of future possibilities we are creating with our analyses and interpretations.

REFERENCES

Ahmed, Sara. 2004. *The Cultural Politics of Emotion*. Edinburgh: Edinburgh University Press.

BBC. 2014. 'Cornish People Granted Minority Status Within UK' http://www.bbc.co.uk/news/uk-england-cornwall-27132035 [accessed February 7, 2018].

Bergson, Henri. [1907] 1944. *Creative Evolution*. New York: Random House.

Bürk, Thomas, Manfred Kühn, and Hanna Sommer. 2012. "Stigmatisation of Cities: The Vulnerability of Local Identities." *Raumforschung und Raumordnung* 70(4): 337–347.

Charmaz, Kathy. 2006. *Constructing Grounded Theory: A Practical Guide through Qualitative Analysis*. Delhi: Sage Publications.

Cloke, Paul, and Gareth Edwards. 1986. "Rurality in England and Wales 1981: A Replication of the 1971 Index." *Regional Studies* 20(4): 289–306.

Connolly, William. 2002. *Neuropolitics: Thinking, Culture, Speed (Theory out of Bounds)*. Minneapolis: University of Minnesota Press.

Connolly, William. 2008. *Capitalism and Christianity, American Style*. Durham: Duke University Press.

Connolly, William. 2011. *A World of Becoming*. Durham: Duke University Press.

Cornwall and Isles of Scilly Economic Forum. 2007. *Strategy and Action, the Economic Development Strategy for Cornwall and the Isles of Scilly 2007–2021*. Truro: Cornwall and Isles of Scilly Economic Forum.

Cornwall Council. 2016. *Understanding Cornwall: Equality Data for Cornwall*. Truro: Cornwall Council.

Cornwall Council. 2017. *State of the Economy March 2017*. Truro: Cornwall Council.

Cosgrove, Denis. 1998. *Social Formation and Symbolic Landscape*. Wisconsin: University of Wisconsin Press.

Cresswell, Tim. 1996. *In Place, out of Place: Geography, Ideology and Transgression*. Minneapolis: University of Minnesota Press.

Deacon, Bernard. 2004. "Under Construction: Culture and Regional Formation in South-West England." *European Urban and Regional Studies* 11(3): 213–225.

Delanda, Manuel. 2011. *A New Philosophy of Society: Assemblage Theory and Social Complexity*. London: Continuum.

Deleuze, Giles, and Felix Guattari. 2004. *A Thousand Plateaus*. Continuum: London.

Eriksson, Madeleine. 2008. "(Re)Producing A 'Peripheral' Region—Northern Sweden in the News." *Geografiska Annaler Series B* 90(4): 369–388.

Fanon, Frantz. [1952] 2008. *Black Skin, White Masks*. London: Pluto Press.

Florida, Richard. 2002. *The Rise of The Creative Class*. New York: Basic Books.

Foucault, Michel. [1969] 2002. *The Archeology of Knowledge*. London: Routledge.

Galani-Moutafi, Vasiliki. 2013 "Rural Space (Re)Produced—Practices, Performances and Visions: A Case Study from an Aegean Island." *Journal of Rural Studies* 32, October: 103–113.

Halfacree, Keith. 2012. "Heterolocal Identities? Counter-Urbanisation, Second Homes, and Rural Consumption in the Era of Mobilities." *Population, Space and Place* 18(2): 209–224.

Hechter, Michael. 1975. *Internal Colonialism: The Celtic Fringe in British National Development, 1536–1966*. London: Routledge and Kegan Paul.

Hetherington, K. 2008. *In Capitalism's Eye: Cultural Spaces of the Commodity*. London: Routledge.

Lefebvre, Henri. 1974. *The Production of Space*. Trans. D. Nicholdson Smith. 1991. Oxford: Blackwell.

Massey, Doreen. 2005. *For Space*. Sage: London.

Merleau-Ponty, Maurice. [1945] 2002. *A Phenomenology of Perception*. London: Routledge Classics.

Miller, Toby. 2009. "From Creative to Cultural Industries." *Cultural Studies* 23(1): 88–99.

Murdoch, Jonathan, and Philip Lowe. 2003. "The Preservationist Paradox: Modernism, Environmentalism, and the Politics of Spatial Division." *Transactions of the Institute of British Geographers* 28(3): 318–332.

Nomis. 2017. "Labour Market Profile Cornwall." <https://www.nomisweb.co.uk/reports/lmp/la/1946157349/report.aspx?town=Cornwall> [accessed April 24, 2017].

Payne, Sarah, Brenda Henson, David Gordon, and Ray Forrest. 1996. *Poverty and Deprivation in West Cornwall in the 1990s*. Bristol: Statistical Monitoring Unit, School for Policy Studies, University of Bristol.

Perry, Ronald. 1993. "Economic Change and Opposition Economics," in *The Making of Modern Cornwall: Cornwall Since the War*, ed. Philip Payton. Redruth: Institute of Cornish Studies, 48–83.

Sibley, David. 1995. *Geographies of Exclusion*. London: Routledge.

Soja, Edward. 1996. *Thirdspace: Journeys to Los Angeles and Other Real-and-Imagined Places*. Oxford: Blackwell.

Strauss, Anselm, and Juliet Corbin. 2008. *Basics of Qualitative Research: Grounded Theory Procedures and Techniques*. London: Sage.

Thrift, N. 2008. *Non-Representational Theory: Space/Politics/Affect*. London: Routledge.

Willett, Joanie. 2010. "Why Is Cornwall So Poor? Narrative, Perception and Identity." PhD diss., University of Exeter.

Willett, Joanie. 2013. "National Identity and Regional Development: Cornwall and the Campaign for Objective 1 Funding." *National Identities* 15(3): 297–311.

Willett, Joanie. 2016. "The Production of Place: Perception, Reality, and the Politics of Becoming." *Political Studies* 64(2): 436–451.

Willett, Joanie, and Thilo Lang. Forthcoming. "Peripheralisation: A Politics of Place, Perception, and Representation." *Sociologia Ruralis*. <http://onlinelibrary.wiley.com/doi/10.1111/soru.12161/abstract>

Williams, Malcom. 2003. "Why Is Cornwall Poor? Poverty and In-Migration since the 1960s." *Contemporary British History* 17(3): 55–70.

PART II

HERITAGE, MARKETS, AND MANAGEMENT

CHAPTER 2.1

....

PROBLEMATIZING THE IDEA OF HERITAGE MANAGEMENT

....

MARINA DANTAS DE FIGUEIREDO

INTRODUCTION: VALUING WHAT IS VALUABLE

....

HERITAGE management (HM) is a nebulous concept, composed of two contemporary buzzwords, which each carry the traditions and contradictions of their meanings from differing academic and practical domains. Both heritage and management have to do with value, but in distinct yet complimentary ways. The first term—heritage—is associated with something that is distinguished by the value of rarity, antiquity, and scarceness. In the academic field of Heritage Studies, it is commonsense that value relates to the authenticity of an object, a place, or a practice in the realm of a situated past or within a tradition (Holtorf 2010). The second term—management—relates to the act of preserving value, or caring for goods in order to keep their content, importance, or meaning. In the domain of management studies, value is something that ultimately has an economic worth that can be enhanced (Jensen 2001), added (Goold and Luchs 2006), and created (Ravald and Grönroos 1996). The juxtaposition of both terms forms a thought-provoking tautology: HM might be an issue of "valuing what is valuable."

The authorized heritage discourse (Smith 2006, Smith and Waterton 2012) stresses that objects, places, and practices that come to be formally recognized as heritage have to be actively protected, according to assumptions of inherent value. That is, the value of an item of heritage is somehow perceived to be intrinsic to the object itself, as the "authentic" and the "old" are defined as innately valuable and meaningful. Perhaps because the inherent value of heritage reflects assumed losses of individual and group identity, a great deal of attention has been given to define heritage from a materialistic standpoint. The idea that "the materiality of monuments and ancient places embodies elements from which knowledge, values, and meaning are derived" (Pace 2012: 4) precipitates the conclusion that heritage value relies on things. Likewise, "concerns about cultural, natural, tangible, and intangible heritage have caused governments to enact protective legislation, courts to impose penalties, and organizations to conduct awareness campaigns" (Edson 2004: 334). As such instruments and actions enclose heritage within concrete bounds, the existence of a material substratum for heritage becomes true even for the so-called immaterial assets. The emphasis within the authorized heritage discourse therefore is on the preservation of things to ensure that heritage be kept safe by delimiting their meanings and isolating them from mischaracterization no less than physical deterioration.

In instrumental business discourse (Grant, Idema, and Oswick 2011) the *métier* of managers is to maintain and increase value. For management, "the public" are all of the stakeholders who have some vested interest in a business. Indeed, the stakeholder concept is deceptively simple (Freeman and Reed 1983); that is, there are other groups to whom the corporation is responsible in addition to shareholders: those who have a stake in the actions of a corporation. This includes anyone that can be affected—benefited or harmed—by the corporation's activity (Freeman 1984, Savage et al. 1991). But this concept becomes more complex when it is recognized that stakeholders are not passive; they also affect the corporation's activities while pursuing some particular interest in their relationship with it. It follows that stakeholders and the corporation try to influence each other's actions toward the fulfillment of their own expected rational benefits.

In the terms of stakeholder theory analysis, "stakeholders are identified by their interest in the affairs of the corporation and . . . the interests of all stakeholders have intrinsic value" (Donaldson and Preston 1995: 81). The idea of intrinsic value means that each group of stakeholders merits consideration for its own sake and not merely because of its ability to further the interests of some other group, or their common interests. That is, each group of stakeholders possesses a self-interested attitude toward the corporation and the other stakeholders. This assumption is consistent with the rational choice perspective, which asserts that interest-based action is driven by the expected values and payoffs associated with the consequences of that action. From this perspective, stakeholders are rational actors driven by the utility of their actions, in terms of achieving their own interest (Savage et al. 1991).

Since the value of heritage depends on the evolving assessments of experts and the general publics, its value is not stable nor absolute; it may range according to the interests of multiple groups that are involved in the issue of heritage while they are enjoying rights and benefits or fulfilling obligations that come from it. As the number of stakeholders might be infinite—because the category of people called "the general public" will always persist, even in exhaustive definition attempts—the different claims are in many cases irreconcilable. If there is no absolute value for heritage under the epitome of stakeholders, the emphasis thus turns toward the preservation of interests, or at least in the preservation of the interest of some groups.

On the one hand HM can be defined as the process of caring for and maintaining the material and immaterial assets from the past in order to make their value endure for the sake of future generations (Carman 2012). On the other hand it is about the decision-making regarding the use of such assets by contemporary people, according to circumstantial interests on heritage value and revenues (Millar 2006). These two perspectives are not oppositional, but are counterparts that entwine around a fundamental issue: the complex of social and moral transformations that have equated "management" with "business" (Anteby 2017) in the present day. These transformations can be summed up in the development of a managerial logic (Chandler 1977, Dalton 1959, Mintzberg 1973) that orients social life and has become more prevalent as corporations have risen in prominence as a social form. As this logic has pervaded the heritage field, HM's reasoning came to be constrained by a capitalistic-business ethic of performance optimization (Nielsen 2005). Therefore, the emphasis on preserving value typifies a conservative ethic toward heritage. Yet, such a standpoint is in conflict with the aforementioned emphasis of preserving the interest of all present and future stakeholders.

Along these lines the aim of this chapter is to "problematize" HM, focusing on the way the concept has come to be framed and how it has turned into a practice. "Problematizing" calls for "assembling and aligning actors and arguments such that a measure of agreement is achieved" (Mennicken and Miller 2014: 4). It does not imply the search for a consensus that could elaborate a conceptual schema for HM, but in the quest for a line of reasoning through which HM can be understood as an inherently contradictory idea and thus undertaken as a complex practice. A useful starting point is to elaborate the ways through which the issue of value can be addressed in the HM practices of the fields of public archaeology and the branches of heritage studies particularly infused with a managerial logic, such as tourism and leisure studies. The chapter then reviews the differences between the concepts of "the public" and "the stakeholders" and how the relationships between heritage and community have been re-elaborated in the practice of HM. While acknowledging the importance of care and maintenance of heritage assets in the dynamics of contemporary societies, this chapter closes by recognizing that HM in its most basic sense is a complex concept that needs further theorizing.

CAN HERITAGE VALUE BE CREATED? CAN ITS VALUE BE MAINTAINED?

Either because heritage is something rare, valuable, and treasured, or because it is ubiquitous to post-industrial, developing, and industrialized societies (Harrison 2013, Lowenthal 1996), HM is a concern for many academic fields. The past decades have been marked by substantial contributions to the topic of HM coming from public archaeology (Carman 2012), museology (Graham, Gregory, Ashworth, and Tunbridge 2005), tourism and leisure studies (Millar 1989, Moscardo 1996) and other social sciences such as geography and economics (Graham, Ashworth, and Tunbridge 2000, Ready and Navrud 2002). Even though such contributions might be grouped under the umbrella of heritage studies, there are sensible differences in the ways through which the concept of HM is elaborated and the HM practices are carried out in each. Some of these differences shall now be analyzed with an emphasis on the issue of value maintenance and creation and how it poses dialectic challenges to HM.

Although the academic field of management studies does not engage explicitly in the research and practice of HM, the relationship between management and value maintenance, creation, and exploitation of heritage seems to echo the managerial perspective in some other academic fields. This is particularly the case in tourism and leisure studies, where there is frank debate over the economic value of heritage (Chhabra 2009, Kim, Wong, and Cho 2007, Salazar and Marques 2005), the uses of heritage for generating revenues (Fyall and Garrod 1998, Ho and McKercher 2004, Hughes and Carlsen 2010) and marketing issues related to the increase of the flow of visitors and capital in heritage sites (Boyd and Timothy 2006, Fyall and Rakic 2006).

In others fields, particularly in public archaeology, the relation of HM with the broader idea of management in the business discourse (Grant, Iedema, and Oswick 2011) seems to be kept in the shadows. For example, Carman (2000) once said that even though archaeologists do engage with the major concerns of heritage studies, they prefer to name what they do as public archaeology. Heritage studies would be more closely connected to museology, tourism, and leisure studies, while public archaeology would designate "all those areas where archaeologists have to deal with the lay population and the wider world" (Carman 2000: 303). Public archaeology is primarily concerned with archaeological outreach—that is how archaeologists access the past and present representations of that past to inexpert audiences—but also with rendering services to the public, as part of environmental conservation, the preservation of ancient remains, their care and maintenance (Carman 2000).

However, public archaeologists have to be concerned with HM, as they play a very important role in choosing what material and cultural evidence of the past shall be retained, and what research frameworks shall be possible for future archaeologists. Archaeological heritage management (AHM) is the specific branch of that field where "the concerns are with material remains as expression of *culture* in the anthropological sense; with their contemporary use, often as some kind of *resource*; and with the management of that *resource*" (Carman 2000: 304). Although seemingly focused exclusively on archaeology, AHM is more adequately described as a multi-disciplinary and multi-practical domain. As stated in the Charter for the Protection and Management of Archaeological Heritage (ICOMOS 1990: 1), "the protection of heritage cannot be based upon the application of archaeological techniques alone." This opens up the possibility for effective collaboration between professionals from many disciplines. Besides, as AHM also requires the active involvement of policymakers, it necessarily integrates the interests of several groups: government authorities, academic researchers, private or public enterprise, and the general public.

Just like any manager, the task of archaeological heritage managers—a category that includes public archaeologists along with site managers, interpreters, technocrats, and others—is to make decisions about the use of resources; however, they undertake this in a context where resources are not necessarily limited, but presumably fast fading. It might be paradoxical, but as much as the remains of the past are disappearing, the "past" is not an exhaustible resource. This raises the questions "as to whether archaeological resources are finite and non-renewable, or whether they are in fact renewable" (Pace 2012: 3).

As counterintuitive as it sounds to suggest that heritage is a distinctively modern notion, the concern with the production of heritage is part of a modern conception of time, in which the past is made to appear distant and the present appears as a "contemporary past" (Harrison 2013: 1). The dichotomies that are typical of modern thought conceptualize the [present] time of modernity as contemporary and new, and oppositional to the past. Inside a modern present, there is always a latent past that is about to become whilst it anticipates the future. In other words, modernity creates for itself a past which is perceived to be both immanent (contained within) and imminent (impending) in the present (Harrison 2011, 2013). The rapid changes in late modern societies summarized by Harrison (2013: 4) created the urgency of preserving "the past," or at least the objects, structures, and ways of living that come to us from that past and that are vulnerable, as framed in a context of risk (Beck 1992). As Harvey (2008: 32) stated, "the recognition of heritage as malleable present-centred and future oriented appears to bring us full circle," as people from the present elaborate heritage in a way that enable them to reveal the past inside the present, and to use it according to meta-narratives of heritage purposes.

Indeed, there are almost infinite remains of the past to be listed and cataloged as heritage when "one generation after another creates and discards structures and manufactured objects" (Pace 2012: 3). Protecting old things is part of the modern obsession with the past that eventually can lead to "bequeathed by has-beens" (Lowenthal 1996). This means there might be a penchant for safeguarding almost everything—for example objects, places, and buildings that are old enough to be considered valuable, but also the cultural practices and embodied knowledge that fit the list of immaterial heritage—just because heritage seems to be important in itself. "The cult of heritage" (Lowenthal 1996, Carman 2012) eventually could turn any remain of the past into a manifestation of anthropological/archaeological resource, but there are reasons why this does not happen. Partially this has to do with the philosophical and ethical roots of AHM (Lowenthal 1998, Pace 2012), but also simply because caring for everything that could fit the label of heritage demands massive-scale safeguarding mechanisms that are too onerous to maintain.

AHM is management after all. And managing requires appraising assets in terms of their actual value, the cost to keep it, and their value in the future, according to certain profit expectations. Notwithstanding humankind's propensity to create material culture (Pace 2012) maintaining its value is a difficult endeavor: it demands efforts and spending: obvious reasons why modern people cannot preserve every single element of the past. The administration of cultural heritage might be thought of as an international practice that acknowledges, if not mandates, the existence of HM systems in every nation, regardless of wealth (Long 2000). Once heritage became an element of sovereignty, owned or regulated by government bureaucracies, heritage care depended on the government's budget. But today's neoliberal regimes of heritage "increasingly make simple state–society dichotomies difficult to maintain when heritage governance is constituted synergistically through international policy, national legislation, local rules, and market demands" (Coombe and Weiss 2015: 45).

Managing heritage therefore involves making specific decisions on the why's and how's something—place, building, ruin, object, cultural practice, and even embodied know-how—shall be preserved. Even in the post-processual perspective in archae-ology, it is hard to escape from criteria for heritage valuing, whether such criteria are official or not. AHM professionals do not like to think about their working practice as "management" according to a managerial logic that seems to encompass the neoliberal governmentalities of HM (Coombe 2012). According to Carman (2000: 305) the task of AHM is "too important to be left to those who wish to limit heritage studies to an agenda concerned only with presentation or tourism or development, and should be one that attracts a wider interest." Notwithstanding public archaeology's commitment to the interests of "the public," there are interests that come to be considered more im-portant than others, as HM is part of the struggle to control the use of heritage within society (Harvey 2008).

STAKEHOLDERS, MANAGEMENT LOGIC, AND THE PUBLIC VALUE OF HERITAGE

Much as public archaeology is concerned with "the public," the issue of interests cannot be thought of as an externality. Merriman (2004: 1) helpfully defines what is meant by "public" in recognizing two definitions for the word. The first is the association of "the public" with the state and its institutions (public bodies, public buildings, public office, the public interest). The second is the concept of "the public" as a group of individuals who debate issues and consume cultural products, and whose reactions inform public opinion. According to Merriman (2004: 2), "these two notions of 'the public'—the state and the people—have always been potentially in tension" and such tensions have imposed themselves to the work of archaeology. On one hand, there is the state appa-ratus for archaeology that does not reflect the diversity of interests embodied by the public. On the other hand, there is a public which is disenchanted with the archaeology provided by the state and that may prefer other ways of relating with the past that better suit their interests.

When the term public archaeology entered widespread archaeological use (McGimsey 1972), the idea of the public participating in archaeology relied on the support that was necessary to convince legislators and government agents that archae-ological sites needed protection. From that moment on, heritage could be considered a public endeavor that depended on the continuous struggles of institutions, policies, professionals, and communities on defining what may or may not be considered heritage as well as on performing specific practices of heritage protection. But in a time when heritage appears to be "both universal and ever-present" (Harrison 2013: 1), public engagement may happen alongside the work of public archaeology. Public archaeology nowadays includes archaeologists, and other professionals, collaborating with and within communities, supporting civic engagement, and embracing the struggles of groups for social justice (Little 2011, Little and Shackel 2014). Heritage can now be used as an instrument in collective policies of social representation and political cohesion. However, as the acknowledgement of the value of heritage brings visibility to sites and cultural practice, there is a risk of heritage being "directly used as a resource in many commercial heritage industries, in which aspects of a commodified past are selected and packaged into heritage products for sale on various contemporary markets" (Ashworth 2014: 3).

Under the neoliberal regimes of heritage (Coombe and Weiss 2015: 43), the idea of "the public" has also enlarged, relying increasingly upon "the self-empowerment of capacitated citizens and self-organized communities in marketized relationships which position cultural heritage as a resource." This includes opinion leaders, taxpayers, indigenous people, museum directors, collectors, heritage officials, teachers, students, law enforcement officials, archaeologists and other specialists, government managers, private owners of heritage places and items, and a number of others. Such a complex assemblage of actors are today more properly identified as "stakeholders."

The term stakeholder has a long tradition in economic and business thought where it is associated with an interest-based view for explaining the actions of individuals in relationship with a corporation (Donaldson and Preston 1995). Yet, the definition of stakeholders becomes more intricate when it takes into account that such individuals or groups also may hold interests in past, present, and future property or rights related to a corporation's activity (Clarkson 1995). Such rights or interests may be legal or moral, individual or collective. This results in a complex set of relationships between and among interest groups with different rights, objectives, expectations, and responsibilities.

The fact that the stakeholder concept has become taken-for-granted within HM means that the conceptualization of stakeholders within its originating context of management theory deserves attention. Stakeholder theory is managerial in the broadest sense of that term, "it does not simply describe existing situations or predict cause-effect relationships; it also recommends attitudes, structures, and practices that, taken together, constitute the idea of stakeholder management" (Donaldson and Preston 1995: 67). Fundamental to the concept is the fact that stakeholders' interests have to be managed in order to reach the consensus that best fits the business strategy (Savage et al. 1991). It does not imply that all stakeholders should be equally involved in all processes and decisions, but that some claims shall be dealt with under general policies and that certain anomalous situations may require case-by-case decision making (Donaldson and Preston 1995). From the managerial perspective, the corporation has to show responsiveness in the management of social issues (Clarkson 1995); however, in the normal course of conducting their business, managers will not focus on attending to stakeholders' interests, but reconcile them with the strategic ones.

The concept of stakeholders within HM has developed alongside the growth of the so-called "heritage industry" (Millar 1989), especially as tourism has become an area of development for many countries (AlSayyad 2001, Mowforth and Munt 1998). From a managerial standpoint, as the concept of stakeholders is applied to other academic and practical domains, such as HM, ways of thinking formerly constrained to business interests can be extended to the management of other social issues. It means that the narrow boundaries of rational interest may be taken as the motives of stakeholders' behavior, even when the affairs under focus might not exactly be defined as a business. Such is the case with heritage. HM has taken on the logic of contemporary economics and business management in adopting the underlying assumption that heritage value can be (re)produced to serve the interests of stakeholders, treating heritage as a commodity within a market for heritage experiences (Ashworth 2014). At the same time there is a vast global increase in the number of places which are classified and managed as heritage sites, (Harrison 2013) Pace (2012: 6) asserts that, "heritage consumption thrives on itself and on market forces, placing antiquities at risk of exhaustion, depletion, or damage."

The issues to be addressed, though, are: what are the strategic interests in HM and who are the relevant stakeholders. Heritage is created to serve many contemporary uses, both individual and collective, and there are many interests around it in both the private and public realms (Ashworth 2014). But as dominant ways of thinking, writing, and talking about HM frames, constrains, or (de)legitimizes debates about the meaning, nature, and value of "heritage" (Smith and Waterton 2012), the interests of some stakeholders prevail over others. Ashworth (2014) argues that the heritage process, for whatever reason it is pursued, has a fundamental economic dimension: namely that all heritage has economic costs, but equally all heritage has at least the potential to reap economic benefits.

The managerial logic of HM—according to which heritage value can be (re)produced—implies that the exploitation of heritage resources in economic activities is possible and feasible. The problem, however, is that the hegemonic authorized heritage discourse (Smith 2006) perpetuated the assumption that heritage is intrinsically unique, irreplaceable, and non-renewable. The resulting conservation philosophy, which focuses on physical preservation, imposes implicit limits on the economic exploitation of heritage resources. As Ashworth (2014: 7) asserts, "preservation and development are by definition contradictory ideas," while, as he explains, a broader view of "heritage and development are not" (Ashworth 2014: 7).

The ideal of the harmonious symbiosis of heritage and development (Ashworth 2014), as well as the application of the managerial logic for valuing heritage assets (Hooper, Krenis, and Green 2005) has not gone unchallenged. Perhaps this is because heritage theorists and professionals recognize that economic rationality is a dangerously reductive way of dealing with such a complex issue. The current practices of HM, in which stakeholder management plays a major role, implies that certain values can become naturalized while others can become marginalized (Smith 2006). Likewise, the stakeholders that are now frequently mentioned in the heritage studies literature do not always act according to the assumption of rationality that underlies traditional economic models of managerial and corporate behavior. For example, under certain circumstances managers may find that a cost-benefit calculation is not an effective method for predicting stakeholder action.

Rather, stakeholders' interests could be more coherently framed within an identity-based model of stakeholder group mobilization (Rowley and Moldoveanu 2003), in which group action can be motivated by a desire to express identity as well as to protect interests. Stakeholder group action, according to this view, is not instrumental but expressive; it emphasizes that identity is a value that can create social change and influence institutions such as corporations and the state. In such situations, individuals may still mobilize even though the chances of economic gain are very small or nonexistent, because participation in the group has a symbolic utility that surpasses any instrumental utility (Rowley and Moldoveanu 2003).

This identity-based model of stakeholder behavior is more consistent with approaches to heritage value elaborated by theorists or proponents who conceive of heritage as a sociocultural process (Smith 2006). From this perspective, the value of heritage lies ultimately in the meanings that people construct or ascribe in their daily lives. That is, heritage is not inherently valuable; its value derives from the identity, memory, and associated social behaviors of contemporary social groups. This perspective challenges the emphasis placed on material authenticity and historical veracity. Thus, it also offers the opportunity to redefine the idea of heritage through the consequences of HM concepts and practices in people's lives (Smith 2006).

If some stakeholders act according to the assumptions of identity-based group action, then the principles of HM can be elaborated as a negotiation of new ways of being and the active expression of identity through the use of the past and its collective remembering. Recent HM policies, for example the ICOMOS Ename Charter on the Interpretation and Presentation of Cultural Heritage Sites (ICOMOS 2008, Silberman 2009), give support to the inclusion of multiple stakeholders' interests and conceiving heritage as an ongoing, contemporary social process. Interpretation is "both a personal and collective activity that could and should be carried out by everyone, layperson and expert, child or adult, local resident and outside tourist alike" (ICOMOS 2008: Definitions). Heritage is not so much of a "thing" but the result of "cultural and social processes, which engages with acts of remembering that work to create ways to understand and engage with the present" (Smith 2006: 2).

Thus the positive impacts of HM may be widened if we take into account the dynamics of the practices of appropriation and re-appropriations of heritage items by stakeholders—along with the focus on issues of physical conservation. The relationship of stakeholders with cultural goods can lead to creative elaboration of the relationship between culture, heritage, and daily practices. Thus HM can be reframed within a post-heritage perspective that favors the ideal of stewardship. According to Pace (2012: 18), "the term stewardship generally means the care and prudent use of something or resources entrusted to one's care." The ideal of stewardship applied by HM should reinforce an ethical commitment to the long term, sustainable care of heritage and, no less important, to the social processes that generate its perceived value. HM should be approached as a complex public exercise that requires the involvement of many stakeholders, with an emphasis on ensuring participation for all. This requires new ways of assessing the value of heritage that goes beyond a two-dimensional classification of economic and non-economic values. Studies based in such post-heritage approaches suggest that the integration of tourism with other value chains enables the construction of different (or new) cultural dynamics, which can incorporate a wide range of contemporary interests into public heritage activities (Pace 2012, Taylor 2004).

References

AlSayyad, Nezar. 2001. "Prologue," in *Consuming Tradition, Manufacturing Heritage: Global Norms and Urban Forms in the Age of the Tourism*, ed. Nezar AlSayyad. New York: Routledge, 1–33.

Anteby, Michel. 2017. "Management and Morality/Ethics—The Elusive Corporate Morals," in *The Oxford Handbook of Management*, ed. Adrian Wilkinson, Steven J. Armstrong, and Michael Lounsbury. Oxford: Oxford University Press, 1–17. DOI: 10.1093/oxfordhb/9780198708612.013.22.

Ashworth, Gregory J. 2014. "Heritage and Economic Development: Selling the Unsellable." *Heritage and Society* 7(1): 3–17.

Beck, Ulrich. 1992. *Risk Society: Towards a New Modernity*. London: Sage Publications.

Boyd, Stephen W., and Dallen J. Timothy. 2006. "Marketing Issues and World Heritage Sites," in *Managing World Heritage Sites*, ed. Anna Leask and Alan Fyall. Oxford: Elsevier, 55–68.

Carman, John. 2000. "Theorising a Realm of Practice?: Introducing Archaeological Heritage Management as a Research Field." *International Journal of Heritage Studies* 6(4): 303–308.

Carman, John. 2012. "Towards an International Comparative History of Archaeological Heritage Management," in *The Oxford Handbook of Public Archaeology*, ed. Robin Skeates, Carol McDavid, and John Carman. Oxford: Oxford University Press, 1–23. DOI: 10.1093/oxfordhb/9780199237821.013.0002.

Chandler, A. D. 1977. *The Visible Hand: The Managerial Revolution in American Business*. Cambridge, MA: Belknap Press.

Chhabra, Deepak. 2009. "Proposing a Sustainable Marketing Framework for Heritage Tourism." *Journal of Sustainable Tourism* 17(3): 303–320.

Clarkson, M. E. 1995. "A Stakeholder Framework for Analyzing and Evaluating Corporate Social Performance." *Academy of Management Review* 20(1): 92–117. DOI: 10.5465/AMR.1995.9503271994.

Coombe, Rosemary. 2012. "Managing Cultural Heritage as Neoliberal Governmentality," in *Heritage Regimes and the State*, ed. Regina Bendix, Additia Eggert, and Arnika Peselman. Gottingen: Universitatsverlag Gottingen, 375–387.

Coombe, Rosemary, and Linda Weiss. 2015. "Neoliberalism, Heritage Regimes, and Cultural Rights," in *Global Heritage: A Reader*, ed. Lynn Meskell. Hoboken: Wiley-Blackwell, 43–69.

Dalton, M. 1959. *Men Who Manage: Fusions of Feeling and Theory in Administration*. New York: Wiley.

Donaldson, Thomas, and Lee E. Preston. 1995. "The Stakeholder Theory of the Corporation: Concepts, Evidence, and Implications." *The Academy of Management Review* 20(1): 65–91.

Edson, Gary. 2004. "Heritage: Pride or Passion, Product or Service?" *International Journal of Heritage Studies* 10(4): 333–348.

Freeman, R. Edward. 1984. *Strategic Management: A Stakeholder Approach*. Boston: Pitman.

Freeman, R. Edward, and David. L. Reed. 1983. "Stockholders and Stakeholders: A New Perspective on Corporate Governance." *California Management Review* 25(3): 88–106. DOI: 10.2307/41165018.

Fyall, Alan, and Brian Garrod. 1998. "Heritage Tourism: At What Price?" *Managing Leisure* 3(4): 213–228.

Fyall, Alan, and Tijana Rakic. 2006. "The Future Market for World Heritage Sites," in *Managing World Heritage Sites*, ed. Anna Liesk and Allan Fyall. Amsterdam: Butterwhorf Hinemann, 159–175.

Goold, Michael, and Kathleene Luchs. 2006. "Why Diversify? Four Decades of Management Thinking," in *The Oxford Handbook of Strategy: A Strategy Overview and Competitive Strategy*, ed. David O. Faulkner and Andrew Campbell. Oxford: Oxford University Press, 1–36. DOI: 10.1093/oxfordhb/9780199275212.003.0017.

Graham, Brian, Gregory J. Ashworth, and John E. Tunbridge. 2000. *A Geography of Heritage: Power, Culture and Economy*. London: Arnold.

Graham, Brian, Gregory J. Ashworth, and John E. Tunbridge. 2005. "The Uses and Abuses of Heritage," in *Heritage, Museums and Galleries: An Introductory Reader*, ed. Gerald Corsane. New York: Routledge, 26–36.

Grant, David, Rick Idema, and Cliff Oswick. 2011. "Discourse and Critical Management Studies," in *The Oxford Handbook of Critical Management Studies*, ed. Mats Alvesson, Todd Bridgman, and Hugh Willmott. Oxford: Oxford University Press, 1–25. DOI: 10.1093/oxfordhb/9780199595686.013.0010.

Harrison, Rodney. 2011. "Surface Assemblages: Towards an Archaeology *in* and *of* the Present." *Archaeological Dialogues* 18(2): 141–196.

Harrison, Rodney. 2013. "Heritage," in *The Oxford Handbook of the Archaeology of the Contemporary World*, ed. Paul Graves-Brown and Rodney Harrison. Oxford: Oxford University Press, 1–21. DOI: 10.1093/oxfordhb/9780199602001.013.021.

Harvey, David. 2008. "The History of Heritage," in *The Ashgate Research Companion to Heritage and Identity*, ed. Brian Graham and Peter Howard. Hampshire: Ashgate Publishing Company, 19–36.

Ho, Pamela S., and Bob McKercher. 2004. "Managing Heritage Resources as Tourism Products." *Asia Pacific Journal of Tourism Research* 9(3) 255–266.

Holtorf, Cornelius. 2010. "Heritage Values in Contemporary Popular Culture," in *Heritage Values in Contemporary Society*, ed. George Smith, Phillis Messenger, and Hilary Soderland. Walnut Creek: Left Coast Press, 43–54.

Hooper, Keith, Kate Krenis, and Ruth Green. 2005. "Knowing 'the Price of Everything and the Value of Nothing': Accounting for Heritage Assets." *Accounting, Auditing and Accountability Journal* 18(3): 410–433.

Hughes, Michael, and Jack Carlsen. 2010. "The Business of Cultural Heritage Tourism: Critical Success Factors." *Journal of Heritage Tourism* 5(1): 17–32.

ICOMOS. 1990. "Charter for the Protection and Management of Archaeological Heritage, 9th General Assembly of the International Council for Monuments and Sites, Lausanne." <http://www.icomos.org/images/DOCUMENTS/Charters/arch_e.pdf> [accessed July 7, 2017].

ICOMOS. 2008. "Charter for the Interpretation and Presentation of Cultural Heritage Sites, 16th General Assembly of the International Council for Monuments and Sites, Québec.

<http://www.icomos.org/images/DOCUMENTS/Charters/interpretation_e.pdf> [accessed July 6, 2017].

Jensen, M. C. 2001. "Value Maximization, Stakeholder Theory, and the Corporate Objective Function." *Journal of Applied Corporate Finance* 14(3): 8–21.

Kim, Samuel, Kevin Wong, and Cho Min. 2007. "Assessing the Economic Value of a World Heritage Site and Willingness-to-Pay Determinants: A Case of Changdeok Palace." *Tourism Management* 28(1): 317–322.

Little, Barbara J. 2011. "Envisioning Engaged and Useful Archaeologies," in *Archaeology in Society*, ed. Marcy Rockman and Joe Flatman. New York: Springer, 277–289.

Little, Barbara J., and Paul A. Shackel. 2014. *Archaeology, Heritage, and Civic Engagement: Working toward the Public Good.* Walnut Creek, CA: Left Coast Press.

Long, Darrin Lee. 2000. "Cultural Heritage Management in Post-Colonial Polities: Not the Heritage of the Other." *International Journal of Heritage Studies* 6(4): 317–322.

Lowenthal, David. 1996. *Possessed by the Past: The Heritage Crusade and the Spoils of History.* New York: Free Press.

Lowenthal, David. 1998. "Fabricating Heritage." *History and Memory* 10(1): 5–24.

McGimsey, Charles Robert. 1972. *Public Archaeology.* New York: Seminar Press.

Mennicken, Andrea, and Peter Miller. 2014. "Michel Foucault and the Administering of Lives," in *The Oxford Handbook of Sociology, Social Theory, and Organization Studies: Contemporary Currents*, ed. Paul Adler, Paul du Gay, Glenn Morgan, and Mike Reed. Oxford: Oxford University Press, 1–36. DOI: 10.1093/oxfordhb/9780199671083.013.0002.

Merriman, Nick. 2004. "Introduction: Diversity and Dissonance in Public Archaeology," in *Public Archaeology*, ed. Nick Merriman. New York: Routledge, 1–17.

Millar, Sue. 1989. "Heritage Management for Heritage Tourism." *Tourism Management* 10(1): 9–14.

Millar, Sue. 2006. "Stakeholders and Community Participation," in *Managing World Heritage Sites*, ed. Anna Liesk and Allan Fyall. Amsterdam: Butterwhorf Hinemann, 37–54.

Mintzberg, Henry. 1973. *The Nature of Managerial Work.* New York: Harper and Row.

Moscardo, Gianna. 1996. "Mindful Visitors: Heritage and Tourism." *Annals of Tourism Research* 23(2): 376–397.

Mowforth, Martin, and Ian Munt. 1998. *Tourism and Sustainability: New Tourism in the Third World.* New York: Routledge.

Nielsen, Richard. 2005. "Organization Theory and Ethics: Varieties and Dynamics of Constrained Optimization," in *The Oxford Handbook of Organization Theory*, ed. Christian Knudsen and Haridimos Tsoukas. Oxford: Oxford University Press, 1–28. DOI:10.1093/oxfordhb/9780199275250.003.0018.

Pace, Anthony. 2012. "From Heritage to Stewardship: defining the sustainable care of archaeological places," in *The Oxford Handbook of Public Archaeology*, ed. Robin Skeates, Carol McDavid, and John Carman. Oxford: Oxford University Press, 1–25. DOI: 10.1093/oxfordhb/9780199237821.013.0015.

Ravald, Annika, and Christian Grönroos. 1996. "The Value Concept and Relationship Marketing." *European Journal of Marketing* 30(2): 19–30.

Ready, Richard, and Ståle Navrud. 2002. "Why Value Cultural Heritage?" in *Valuing Cultural Heritage: Applying Environmental Valuation Techniques to Historic Buildings, Monuments and Artifacts*, ed. Ståle Navrud and Richard Ready. Cheltenham and Northampton: Edward Elgar, 3–9.

Rowley, Timothy I., and Mihnea Moldoveanu. 2003. "When Will Stakeholder Groups Act? An Interest- and Identity-Based Model of Stakeholder Group Mobilization." *Academy of Management Review* 28(2): 204–219.

Salazar, S., and J. Marques. 2005. "Valuing Cultural Heritage: The Social Benefits of Restoring an Old Arab Tower." *Journal of Cultural Heritage* 6(1): 69–77.

Savage, Grant T., Timothy W. Nix, Carlton J. Whitehead, and John D. Blair. 1991. "Strategies for Assessing and Managing Organizational Stakeholders." *Academy of Management Executive* 5(2): 61–75. DOI: 10.5465/AME.1991.4274682.

Silberman, Neil A. 2009. "Process Not Product: The ICOMOS Ename Charter (2008) and the Practice of Heritage Stewardship." *CRM: The Journal of Heritage Stewardship* 6: 7.

Smith, Laurajane. 2006. *The Uses of Heritage*. London: Routledge.

Smith, Laurajane, and Emma Waterton. 2012. "Constrained by Commonsense: The Authorized Heritage Discourse in Contemporary Debates," in *The Oxford Handbook of Public Archaeology*, ed. Robin Skeates, Carol McDavid, and John Carman. Oxford: Oxford University Press, 1–23. DOI: 10.1093/oxfordhb/9780199237821.013.0009.

Taylor, Ken. 2004. "Cultural Heritage Management: A Possible Role for Charters and Principles in Asia." *International Journal of Heritage Studies* 10(5): 417–433.

CHAPTER 2.2

··

HERITAGE AND MANAGEMENT, PROFESSIONAL UTOPIANISM, ADMINISTRATIVE NAIVETÉ, AND ORGANIZATIONAL UNCERTAINTY AT THE SHIPWRECKS OF PISA

··

LUCA ZAN AND DANIEL SHOUP

INTRODUCTION

··

THIS chapter examines the organizational dynamics that emerged from the 1998 discovery of seventeen well-preserved Roman shipwrecks in Pisa, Italy (the *Navi di Pisa*). The excavation, conservation, and museification of the finds have now stretched over nineteen years, and present interesting elements for analyzing heritage from a management studies perspective. We are particularly interested in how heritage professionals manage uncertainty, allowing us to explore the interaction of professional utopianism, bureaucratic myopia, and administrative naiveté in project outcomes.

As management scholars, we are close to the literature on "strategy as process" (from Normann 1977, onward), strategic change (Mintzberg 1978, 1994, Quinn 1980, Pettigrew 1987), and processes of organizational becoming (with attention to the notion of "fit": Venkatraman and Camillus 1984, Garlichs 2011). More generally, our perspective is non-positivist, open to interactions among subjects where sense-making processes are crucial (Weick 1977). We are sympathetic to a contextualist approach (March 1978), and consider the literature on decision-making processes a crucial element for understanding organizational dynamics. Since we focus on arts, culture, and heritage, we also draw on New Public Management literature (NPM), because public administration plays a central role in the heritage sector (Gruening 2001). This might sound strange for North American readers who assume a minimal role for the State, but is essential for understanding heritage in most countries, where the public sector strongly shapes cultural activities.

Over the years, we have developed an approach to cultural organizations that could be defined as the "ethnography of administrations." We use interview research and primary and secondary documents to reconstruct the tension between professional discourse (archaeology, history, curatorship, museology, etc.) and the attention to client orientation and resources that has emerged internationally in the last thirty years as fundamental aspects of NPM (Wirick, 2009; OECD, 2010; Hood and Dixon 2015). In our research, the trade-off among these three partially conflicting dimensions typically appears as a dialogue between the dimensions of effectiveness (professional and consumer-oriented) and efficiency (financial and human resources).

In our study of the *Navi di Pisa*, we investigate professional values, public administration, and their interaction—understood as discrete but interconnected management phenomena—through archival and field research, based on a systematic reading of the historical archives of the Archaeological Superintendency of Tuscany (*Soprintendenza per i Beni Archeologici della Toscana* or SBAT), plus a series of interviews with SBAT staff during 2012–14.[1] Since no report providing a synoptic view of the project existed, the authors had to use primary and secondary sources to reconstruct the project's chronology, budget, policy decisions, and organizational structures. An interesting observation in itself: why was it outside researchers, and not the protagonists, who had to create a holistic view of the project?

⁘ Management Research and Heritage: Some Preliminary Notes

Heritage is a multidisciplinary field, involving a variety of professions, bodies of knowledge, and research traditions. To create a trans-disciplinary perspective, we use the notion of Heritage Chain (Zan, 2013; Zan et al. 2015), to reconstruct all aspects of the story, including excavation, preservation, conservation, academic research, and public access through museum development. However, disciplines tend to resist an interdisciplinary approach, and archaeology played a particularly crucial role in this story, having "imprinted" the project from the earliest stages of discovery.

Archaeology is often thought of as an academic pursuit, where a specific organization develops an excavation or survey program in which the nature of the finds can confirm or disprove preselected hypotheses. Such "on-purpose" research projects are typically conducted by universities, foundations, or research institutes, who create a research design, pursue funding, and hope to find specific types of archaeological information. However, most global archaeology is now "salvage archaeology," where excavation is incidental to development of housing, bridges, subways, or dams, in compliance with laws on cultural heritage.

Here, archaeological surveys or excavations are either conducted in advance—to verify that the proposed activity will not destroy important archaeological materials ("preventive archaeology": Demoule 2012, Bradley et al. 2010, Bozóki-Ernyey 2007)— or are initiated on an emergency basis when archaeological deposits are found *during* construction and must be recovered before their destruction ("rescue" archaeology). Salvage archaeology is interesting for its huge and growing quantitative significance (perhaps 90 percent of all archaeological discoveries worldwide; a multibillion-dollar industry), but also in a qualitative sense: salvage projects witness direct conflicts between time, resources, the logic of site protection, and the construction of infrastructure related to economic development. It is unsurprising, therefore, that it is a highly regulated activity, and that regulation varies strongly across countries.

Above all, it is the degree of uncertainty that distinguishes salvage from research excavation. In an "on-purpose" excavation there is high uncertainty (it is unknown whether you will find what you are looking for), but at least you are looking for something specific on the base of previous studies and hypotheses. In preventive or rescue archaeology, there is no hypothesis to prove, nor do you know what you are looking for: excavation attempts to understand "if" an archaeological deposit exists, and whether it deserves protection or recovery. In such cases uncertainty is an absolute, constitutive condition.

The nature of preventive and rescue archaeology, then, introduces ontological uncertainty to the story of the *Navi di Pisa*, which had to be "managed," one way or another. Yet the conditions for managing are set within the Italian public sector, whose behavior presents a set of distinct elements worthy of investigation. In Italy, the State plays a determinative role in the heritage sector, in both positive and negative ways. The conceptualization of cultural heritage in Italian law is among the most rigorous and generous in the world, with a centuries-old tradition of protection embedded within the current, highly centralized system. Even where the "cultural good"—the cultural resource as defined by the law—is privately owned, some of its values (e.g. the view, the historical meanings) belong to the community and nation. While in other countries this collective ownership is an exception (think of the list of protected buildings in the UK, or the largely voluntary listing system in the USA), in Italy it is embedded in centuries of professional tradition and administrative law (Settis 2002): this explains why Italy has so many historical centers, wherein overall protection is better than many (or any) other countries.

However, this is only a partial picture. On the "negative" side, Heritage is just one of many public services that the State provides, and the heritage sector is structured by the same general administrative rules applied to the rest of the public sector, where the lack of differentiation (Lawrence and Lorsch 1967) is one of the most common problems. It is a law-driven system (Panozzo 2000), based on the Roman code tradition, where administrative lawyers play a hegemonic role ("Administrative Directors" of public sector entities are usually lawyers rather than accountants). The whole public sector is ruled by "one size fits all" regulations, particularly in terms of *human resource* management, which makes hiring, firing, or changing the composition of the labor force in individual offices extremely complicated. The whole public sector uses a cash accounting system, which imposes obstacles to multi-year financing and creates serious problems in planning *financial resources*; even creating a new spending category within ministerial ordinary funds can take over a decade. The amount of red tape is simply astonishing, making *administrative procedures* incredibly complex and difficult to manage (even when human and financial resources are available): a situation sometimes referred to as "over-bureaucratization" (Robinson 2004) or "bureau-crazy" (Ferri and Zan 2014). When such inflexible administrative traditions interact with the inherent uncertainty of rescue archaeology, serious contradictions can arise.

The *Navi di Pisa*: An Extraordinary Preventive Archaeology Discovery

The discovery of the first shipwreck on December 7, 1998, resulted in an extremely complex project lasting almost twenty years and involving many distinct organizational activities including excavation, conservation, and development of a museum that is still incomplete as of 2017. The finds are of a unique value: the *Navi di Pisa* were sunk by periodic tsunami-like flooding events on the river Serchio between the fifth century BC and seventh century AD. The ships sunk into oxygen-free mud that beautifully preserved ship timbers and other organic materials such as rope, cloth, and baskets. Their exquisite preservation and complex cargoes allow the reconstruction of coastal trade routes and give insight into ancient maritime technology (Camilli and Setari 2005).

Our reconstruction of the organizational story is based on primary source material from the archives of the SBAT in Florence, including four interviews and 288 documents totaling over 1900 pages from the period 1997–2014. Space limitations allow us to tell the story only briefly, structured in four main phases. A more detailed narrative with references (though many source documents are not publicly available) is provided inside a virtual appendix to this chapter that the reader can find at SSRN <https://papers.ssrn.com/sol3/papers.cfm?abstract_id=3061161#>.

Phase 1: Preventive Prelude and Discovery of the Ships (1997–2000)

In October 1997, Italian State Railways (hereafter FS, *Ferrovie dello Stato*) hired a private archaeological cooperative to carry out preventive excavations for a new directional center at San Rossore, 1 km northwest of Pisa's city center. A Roman-era archaeological deposit was soon found, 2 m below ground surface. The first of the *Navi di Pisa* was discovered a year later, 3 m below ground surface. Between December 1998 and August 1999, nine well-preserved ships (Ships A–I) and fragments of eight more were found

(Table 2.2.1). Suddenly, San Rossore was a globally important maritime archaeology site. During 1999 FS covered most of the excavation costs, and local company Teseco donated a warehouse in a nearby village for a temporary conservation laboratory. SBAT's funding requests from the Ministry of Cultural Goods & Environment (hereafter "the Ministry"), however, were only partially fulfilled.

A grand institutional vision for the ships was articulated even before the scale of the finds was fully understood. In January 1999—just weeks after the first ship was found—SBAT Superintendent Bottini presented the concept of a "museum with three vertices" to the Ministry in Rome. The excavation site, conservation laboratory, and a museum "dedicated to the history of Pisa on the sea," would be developed as interconnected institutions open to the public. Bottini also suggested a location for the laboratory and museum: the Medici Arsenal (*Arsenali Medicei*, hereafter "the Arsenali"), a dilapidated seventeenth-century cavalry stables on the north side of the Arno, 500 m from the famous leaning tower and 800 m from the excavation site. The archaeological finds at San Rossore could thereby be leveraged to redevelop another neglected cultural heritage site.

As the Ministry discussed Bottini's proposal, the FS began to withdraw. Realizing that the "archaeological problems" would not be resolved on a "less than geological time scale," FS cancelled the directional center in August 1999, withdrew funding, and ceded the site to SBAT. Here the preventive archaeological investigation suddenly became a rescue excavation, even though (paradoxically) the construction project no longer threatened the site. The change in management required emergency measures during 2000: huge amounts of ancient wood were left exposed, requiring constant irrigation to prevent shrinkage. The temporary conservation warehouse was prepared, along with plans to encase the ships in water-filled fiberglass caskets before lifting them from the site; in the laboratory they were later to be impregnated with a formaldehyde-melamine resin to replace the natural cellulose that degrades in waterlogged wood. The worksite was over 6 m deep and crisscrossed by a series of groundwater faults, requiring retaining

Table 2.2.1. Excavating the ships.

Date	Activity
1999–2001	Ships C and F excavated
2001	Ship F lifted, placed in tanks, taken to TESECO
2002	Ship C lifted, placed in tanks, taken to TESECO
2002–4	Most of Ships A and H plus prows of Ships P and G excavated and lifted, taken to TESECO
December 2005	CRLB opened, Ships C and F moved there in early 2006
2005–6	Excavation and lifting of Ship D, identification of ship I
2009	Ship I had not yet been lifted; part 2 of Ship A and Ship B awaited lifting
2011	Public bids issued for lifting Ship B and second part of Ship A

walls and an elaborate pumping system to protect against collapse: the Public Works Agency of Tuscany agreed in mid-2000 to manage these major engineering issues, which were beyond the SBAT's expertise. The costs for the *Cantiere delle navi* ("worksite of the ships") grew faster than available funding: in 2000, the Ministry provided only €1 million of Bottini's €1.8 million budget request.[2]

Despite the ongoing emergency in Pisa, a special Ministry committee in Rome endorsed Bottini's "museum with three vertices." The excavation site would be a working museum, the laboratory would be a national training center for wet archaeological materials, while the museum would focus not only on the *Navi di Pisa*, but the history of Mediterranean navigation. The whole Arsenali (6000 m^2) was to be used, even though the University of Pisa had just leased part of the complex and the rest was partially in ruins. An ad hoc administrative structure was to manage the threefold entity.

The plan, however, featured no numbers, financial or otherwise. Bottini, though enthusiastic for the vision, stressed the crucial importance of funding and presented the Ministry with a €6.3 million budget for 2001–3—exclusive of the Arsenali restoration. But even as the grand vision took shape, SBAT had trouble covering mundane costs: in November 2000 Bottini had to beg the Ministry for €25,000 to cope with site flooding after a rainstorm.

Phase 2: The "Dirty Job," Professional Challenges and Solutions (2001–3)

The next three years saw professional progress tempered by financial and institutional uncertainty. The sole source of funding for 2001–3 was the Italian State Lottery (hereafter "Lotto"), which provided an average of €2.2 million per year. This allowed two ships (F and C) to be moved to the conservation laboratory, but a shortage of funds in late 2001 stopped work for months.

Andrea Camilli, a SBAT staff archaeologist, was appointed director of the excavation site and the proposed conservation center in early 2002.[3] In response to funding shortage, Camilli produced an alternatives assessment for the *Cantiere* that presented three options: closing it to the public, stopping the excavations for two or three years, or filling in and closing the site forever. These "alternatives" seem *pro forma*, however: after opaque calculations (including very optimistic cost estimates), the report concludes by affirming that with only "€1,000,000 in the first three years and a minimal amount thereafter, it will be possible to recover all of the ships already found, [and] conduct additional excavations." The "best" choice, unsurprisingly, was the one that reinforced the preferences of professionals—to proceed with excavations.

In Rome, a Ministry working group discussed the organizational statute and communication strategy for the new museum, but avoided discussing budgets and resources. A separate commission to plan the conservation laboratory was established only in September 2003—four years after the discovery.

Phase 3: Instability and Improvisation: Digesting the Discovery (2004–8)

In this period, the project's funding stream—still dependent on Lotto—fluctuated wildly, threatening degradation of the half-excavated ships (Table 2.2.2). In 2004 Lotto declined to fund the *Navi di Pisa*, and only a last-minute allocation from leftover Lotto 2003 funds avoided major disruption. Lotto funding in 2006 and 2007 averaged €1.2 million, falling to just €370,000 in 2008. The Ministry provided funds only in 2006. Unpredictable funding threatened to close the excavation and laboratory except for basic maintenance, and to cancel the international partnerships and conservation projects already underway.

Archaeological progress, however, continued. At the excavation site, now 3500 m^2 and 5.5–9.5 m deep, ships A and H and the prows of P and G were removed to the Teseco warehouse laboratory by late 2004. However, high rents, the increasing number of finds, and the imminent arrival of equipment donated by the Ministry's Central Conservation Institute (*Istituto Centrale di Restauro*, hereafter "ICR") made a permanent conservation lab essential. Since the Arsenali were still half-ruined, SBAT decided in January 2004 to construct the Wet Wood Conservation Center (*Centro di Restauro del Legno*

Table 2.2.2. Funding the *Navi di Pisa*, 2001–11 (€).

	Funding Source						
Year	Lotto	CIPE 17/2003	FO cap 1321	FO Cap 7723	FO cap 7723 spec.	ARCUS	Total
2001	2,169,119						2,169,119
2002	1,807,599						1,807,599
2003	2,582,285						2,582,285
2004	1,925,509						1,925,509
2005	1,143,101						1,143,101
2006	1,379,788	1,200,000	600,000				3,179,788
2007	368,640						368,640
2008	290,395						290,395
2009	129,766					964,000	1,093,766
2010	290,000						290,000
2011			210,000	200,000	2,000,000		2,410,000
Total	12,086,202	1,200,000	810,000	200,000	2,000,000	964,000	17,260,202

* Original Lotto allocation for 2004 was €224,829; after an emergency appeal an additional €1,700,680 was allocated from Lotto funds remaining from FY 2003.

Bagnato, hereafter "CRLB") next to the excavation site. Construction moved rapidly: the 1700 m² facility was functional and open to visitors by late 2005, and ships C and F were moved to the new facility in early 2006 (Camilli 2007). Between December 2005 and April 2009, the CRLB conserved over eight thousand artifacts and began to fulfill its role as "national reference point" for wet archaeological materials by providing consulting services to other Superintendencies in Italy and internationally. A torrent of academic publications also emerged during this period, including a book-length academic guide, numerous papers, several major conferences, a traveling museum exhibit, and theatrical performances at the site.

These professional accomplishments depended on extensive management improvisation by SBAT, with much informal outsourcing to "get things done" despite funding constraints. In 2004 SBAT renewed the agreement with the Public Works Agency to manage guards, cleaning staff, pumps, and shoring. As part of his strategy to reduce the excavation to "zero budget," Camilli invited universities to take over excavation and conservation work, and built a guest house to house visiting scholars. By 2007, twenty-two universities had worked at San Rossore, enabling work to continue despite funding averaging only €335,000 in 2007–8. There is an impressive contrast between unstable funding and the importance of academic results in this period.

Though plans for the Arsenali were on hold, the City of Pisa supported their renovation as a museum, and commissioned cultural management experts from Bocconi University in 2004 to create a museum feasibility study. The report estimated €20 million to restore the Arsenali and develop the museum, to open in 2015. The report estimated annual costs of €2.6 million and revenues of €500,000—an indefinite annual loss of €2.1 million. This is the first estimate of running costs in any of the project documents. In February 2007 SBAT and the City of Pisa signed an agreement: SBAT staff would design and install the museum and manage construction; by 2008, Camilli and SBAT had prepared a project design for the museum.

Phase 4: Jan 2009–20(?), Managerialization and Urban Politics

By 2009, excavation was largely finished, though it took until 2011 to lift the final three ships. Meanwhile, managerial and financial unpredictability continued. The Public Works Agency withdrew at the end of 2009, leaving SBAT to manage engineering tasks and costs. In 2010, the excavation and laboratory complex experienced another budget crisis, when only €290,000 was allocated from Lotto funds. Work was put on hold until 2011, when the Ministry allocated €2.4 million to the project from Ordinary Funds (that is, its normal annual budget)—only the third time in thirteen years that the Ministry gave money to the project and the first time that it assumed primary financial responsibility.

The Arsenali renovation and museum project gained momentum in 2009, when a coordination agreement was concluded under the rubric of PIUSS (*Piani Integrati di Sviluppo Urbano*), an urban sustainability initiative for Tuscany funded by European Regional Development Funds. Signatories included not only SBAT and Pisa, but forty-five other government bodies and foundations who were to work together under four different coordination plans. The PIUSS agreement inserted the project into the urban politics of Pisa, adding a politicized approach to budgeting and increased use of strategic management jargon.

The 2009 PIUSS Executive Management Plan proposed a dual management structure for the project area, which expanded from the *Arsenali* to include three other buildings within the historic Citadel of Pisa. The complex would have a managing director, a technical-scientific director, ten permanent staff, and outsourced services. The budget proposal included the *Museo delle Navi* and surrounding buildings, but no funding for archaeology or conservation. Projected completion was in 2014, with annual operating costs of €1.5 million. The plan forecasted €1.3 million in annual income from tickets, gift shops, and restaurants, for a small operating loss. Four years after the ASK study, this report presents only the second mention of running costs in any project document.

This new managerial approach was taken up by the SBAT in its "Strategic Analysis and Business Plan" (2010) for the excavation site, conservation laboratory, and museum. The document leans heavily on generic strategic management tools, including a mission statement, SWOT, and analysis of resources, demand, and competitors. The plan estimated €3.4 million in investment for the three institutions, with an annual operating cost of €1.61 million, of which only 35 percent would be self-funded by conservation consulting for other entities. The business plan makes for peculiar reading, given that the archaeologists had never used such managerial language in the previous twelve years of project documents. It also shows a fundamentally different logic than previous SBAT budgets, attempting to distinguish between operating costs and investment costs over time while estimating the long-term running costs of permanent institutions.

The PIUSS and SBAT plans both provide cost estimates for the *Museo delle Navi*, but are organized in fundamentally different ways, with different categories, numbers, and organizational logics. Moreover, both conflict with the 2004 Bocconi report, as well as with the SBAT's own budgets (Table 2.2.3). The Ministry's Scientific Commission for the *Navi di Pisa* convened a meeting in March 2010 to compare estimates, and noted that the Bocconi estimates were much less optimistic, showing an operating deficit of €2 million per year for the "museum with three vertices."[4] The report's appendices outline the cost estimates for the PIUSS project for 2010–15, which are €5.9–9.1 million per year in 2010–14 with a running cost of €4.8 million in the regime phase. By contrast, the scientific project received a mere €290,000 in 2010! Strangely, the political will to spend money on excavation and conservation emerged only after both were mostly complete.

Despite these contradictions, sufficient Ministry ordinary funds were allocated to allow museum construction to begin. By January 2011 over €1 million of restoration work had been completed at the museum, including light and heating systems, the courtyard, entrance hall, bathrooms, and ticket area. In 2011, a €2 million tender was prepared to

Table 2.2.3. Comparative estimates of operating costs (€).

	2004 Bocconi Study		2010 City of Pisa	
	2010	2015	Start Up	Regime
Other operating cost	277,300	508,700	314,060	402,220
Personnel	969,199	1,281,558	668,000	1,132,000
Exhibit maintenance	10,000	150,000	0	60,000
Ordinary and extraordinary maintenance, Citadel Area			0	80,000
Ordinary and extraordinary maintenance, Arsenali Medicei			0	80,000
Promotion and Marketing	200,000	100,000	120,000	80,000
General Costs	50,000	75,000	25,000	30,000
Contingencies	500,000	500,000	50,000	105,000
Total Annual Cost	2,006,499	2,615,258	1,177,060	1,969,220

cover removal of the final ships from the excavation site (A and B) and restoration of the removed ships and their installation in the museum (C, D, F, H). It was not until the end of 2016, however, that the first two halls of the museum were completed. The Ministry's total investment in the project was then reported to be €14 million (Fabiani 2016)—almost all of which appears to have been spent on the museum. In mid-2017 the museum was still under construction, and open only to limited groups of visitors by reservation.

DISCUSSION

The *Navi di Pisa*'s complex history, full of uncertainty and unstable solutions, is fascinating from a management point of view. In the end, its achievements are significant. Far from the worst examples of salvage excavation, the project recovered and conserved nine mostly complete Roman shipwrecks and thousands of stunning small finds, conserved them with innovative and successful techniques, and designed a museum to display them, which will (perhaps) open in 2017. All this was accomplished in the midst of constant organizational conflicts and lack of systematic planning. Throughout the whole narrative, there is a striking contradiction between the grand vision of the "museum with three vertices," and the (in)ability of professionals to implement it within the context of the Italian public sector. Funding for even basic operations remained problematic and irregular for more than a decade, delaying the realization of the vision, and creating fundamental uncertainty about project outcomes.

Substantive and professional effectiveness was achieved, despite a general lack of efficiency. How was this possible? What are the conditions under which even inefficient approaches can end up being effective? What seems to matter is the relationship between actors' behavior and the specific context of their action: similar behavior in a different context (say, archaeological survey in the United States) would have probably resulted in a less unusual situation, where lack of efficiency would have probably led to lack of effectiveness. More specifically, if management is an issue of addressing attention (March 1978), in what ways is the Pisa situation likely to address attention (or mis-address it)? To understand the issue, it may be useful to recall the basic uncertainty characterizing salvage excavation, before discussing the specific dynamics between professionals and the state at Pisa (Figure 2.2.1).

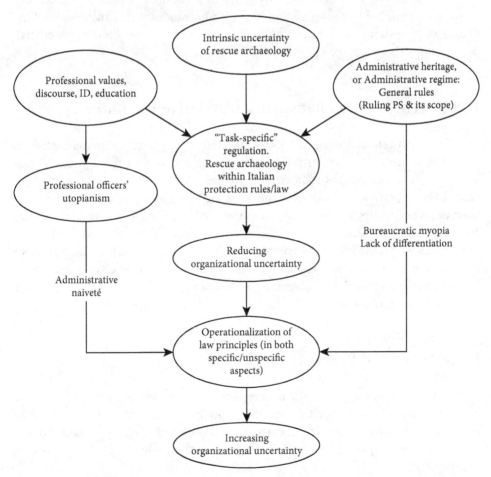

FIGURE 2.2.1. Managing uncertainty, professional utopianism, and bureaucratic myopia.

Archaeological Excavation, Intrinsic Uncertainty, and Organizational Uncertainty

Uncertainty is unavoidable in archaeology: by definition, preventive (and rescue) archaeology is characterized by an inability to know what will be found. Excavations are carried out to determine if something that deserves protection is buried in the ground; yet even if something is found, its significance is not always apparent until after substantial work has been done.

Though uncertainty is unavoidable in these situations, its impacts can be better or worse depending on the administrative and professional traditions used to approach it—which differ greatly among countries. In other words, there is an intrinsic component of uncertainty, which cannot be eliminated; but there is an additional component related to the organizational context and dynamics. We refer to this as "organizational uncertainty." In our view, the enormous organizational uncertainty surrounding the *Navi di Pisa* affected the project negatively, due to a less-than-positive interaction between archaeological professionals and their own bureaucracy: still, the long-term influence of professionalism on the state bureaucracy plays a more hidden, yet crucial, positive role in heritage protection.

Long-Term Professionalism in a Law-Driven Country

The heritage system as a whole is highly protected in Italy, and rescue archaeology is part of this heavy administrative apparatus. Italian archaeologists are proud of the Italian protection law (Settis 2002): they share the values behind "task-specific" regulation of heritage. Indeed, historically speaking, professionals have been able to impose their views and values in lawmaking, an indispensable influence in such a law-driven country. This long-lasting tradition has created professional-friendly legal structures that provide ways of reducing uncertainty in archaeology, define ad hoc administrative routines, and provide a suite of solutions that are usually quite effective in protecting heritage resources over the long-term, regardless of mistakes and misbehaviors which might occur on a "short-term" basis.

Uncertainty and Bureaucratic Myopia

However, this is only a part of the picture. Because when you are part of the public sector, it is not only "task-specific" rules that apply, but the general rules for any public entity: here some of the major "cons" emerge, notably the lack of differentiation and inability of the law to cope with intrinsic elements of heritage projects—particularly rescue archaeology.

This combination of inflexibility and structural limitations gives the centralized administrative system an inability to "see" and cope with individual, non-generalizable problems, which we call "bureaucratic myopia." Any individual problem that might emerge—say, the discovery of a shipwreck, or emergency repairs at Pompeii—must navigate the same generic administrative regulations as *every other public sector project*, before the intrinsic, substantive and specific needs and values of an individual discovery can be addressed.

In the operationalization of general law principles, administrative action in the heritage field is the sum of task-specific rules and regulations, deeply embedded in the value of heritage professionals, *and* the day-to-day general procedures affecting the Italian public sector as such.

Professional Utopianism

In this context of bureaucratic myopia, the professional optimism of archaeologists can create problems, despite its positive role in long-term regulation of task-specific elements. At San Rossore, archaeologists pursued their own professional values but did not foresee the likely reactions and behavior of their own bureaucratic institutions, showing a lack of "strategic" attitude.

Professional optimism, manifested through the visionary idea of three open, interconnected institutions, created an initial condition of extreme complexity that became a barrier to action for a long period. Reading the project correspondence and meeting memos, it seems as if the more complicated solution was always chosen: a museum not only for the ships of San Rossore but one focusing on four thousand years of Mediterranean navigation; not a temporary conservation lab to process the ships and associated finds, but a permanent international center of reference for the study of wet archaeological materials; and a museum plan that did not just focus on an appropriate space for the ships, but included the redevelopment of a whole district of Pisa in partnership with forty-seven(!) different entities.

Three elements in professional decision-making can be highlighted here, each with huge consequences.

- *The lack of attention to alternatives*. Excavations started over a large area, and even when the first ships were discovered, other possible ways of running archaeological excavations were not seriously debated: for instance slowing the process, focusing on only one ship at a time, moving the first ship *before* expanding excavations. Despite words from Cordaro of ICR—"it seems useful to suggest the creation of multiple proposals for recovery and restoration in this preliminary phase, so as to take overall effectiveness into consideration"—alternatives to fast, large-scale excavation were never seriously considered. Reburial was suggested rhetorically in a couple of situations, but only as a threat to get more money from the Ministry.

Rapid work during the emergency phase created a structure for future costs and decision-making: having exposed the ships, it became impossible to stop working.

- *The lack of attention to internal consistency.* It took many years before the visionary dream of the threefold museum was thought of in terms of feasibility. But early operations (and decisions about the laboratory) focused on "investments" (capital expenditure, e.g. instruments and tools that will be used for years or decades), without addressing the issue of the resources needed for running operations on a day-to-day basis. Indeed the concept of current costs first appears in 2004 for the museum (the Bocconi study) and 2010 for the excavation and conservation lab (in Camilli's 2010 project budget). Estimates of the operating deficit of the museum ranged from €1.9 to 2.6 million—nearly as much as was spent each year on the excavation in its highest-funded years—a cost which in theory, would be permanent.

- *The lack of a notion of a flow of resources.* That two of the components of the threefold museum (the excavation site and conservation laboratory) had different organizational natures compared to the core function of a museum never appears in the discussion. The "open excavation," for instance, could never have been a permanent institution, since excavations were never planned to last forever. The conservation laboratory was also needed for only a finite period, with nothing in the long run for the visitor to see after primary conservation of the finds from San Rossore was finished. Yet from the beginning, the plan was for three permanent institutions open to the public. This is the opposite of the stereotype of the "ivory tower" archaeologist, disconnected from the public: but at the same time, heritage professionals' naïve obsession with the project as public spectacle seems to have corrupted it.

Administrative Naiveté: Increasing Organizational Uncertainty

Professional utopianism combined with bureaucratic myopia produce "administrative naiveté," that is an inability to forecast problems, costs, and obstacles associated with the project. The grandiose initial vision of the "museum with three vertices" created a situation of extreme path-dependency that was exacerbated by the inability of the State bureaucracies to bring the project "down to earth."

Funding patterns for the project clearly demonstrate the lack of managerial logic, which is consonant with the overall practice of the Italian heritage bureaucracy. For the decade 2001–10, the whole project was funded almost exclusively with extraordinary funds from Lotto. Operating costs—mostly for the excavation and conservation lab—were relatively small compared to the cost of the visionary museum that the Ministry also wanted to develop. But the problems of the Italian public sector are knowable (and in fact known) to archaeologists, who are mostly public employees; and if you know of a problem, you can avoid it, or at least try to minimize its perverse effects.

This is exactly what the archaeologists were unable to do: their own value-driven professional utopianism ended up increasing confusion, rather than helping to find an effective solution that could support their day-to-day operating needs. This applies to the three-fold museum, but also to the initial professional choices (the decision to excavate over a large area and uncover numerous ships in the early period substantially predetermined the structure of costs for the following decade). Professional optimism, linked with an inability to understand their own institutional and bureaucratic context, caused trouble, costs, and risks—and added huge doses of organizational uncertainty to the unavoidable uncertainties of rescue excavation.

Learning to Keep It Simple

The incompatibility between vision and reality created consequences that made professionals' lives harder and riskier than necessary. It took four years to understand that the time, costs, and logistics to restore the Arsenali as a laboratory were incompatible with the timeline for restoring the ships, and to adjust the assumptions for the laboratory project. Ironically, when the excavation area was finally opened to the public in 2005, most of the excavation activities were finished or on hold.

It does seem that professionals learned their lessons. As soon as institutional and organizational confusion declined, things began to "get done." The "optimistic" and beautiful plan for a hybrid, public laboratory-museum in the Arsenali placed the conservation facilities in a four-year limbo—but once the initial plan was abandoned it took just eighteen months to build the new structure and get to work. Conservation, moreover, seems to have been efficient and effective. In museum construction, progress was swift once structural decisions were made: the PIUSS agreement was signed in March 2009, major work was underway in 2010, and the museum is mostly complete today. Moreover, the managerial approach of PIUSS and the City of Pisa began to include realistic estimates of investments and running costs, allowing projection of future costs—generating much-delayed political controversy over the operating subsidies required.

When complexity was reduced, professional optimism could play a more positive role: archaeological managers could pursue clever survival practices vis-à-vis the unresponsive bureaucracy to achieve their professional goals, such as informally outsourcing maintenance of the site to another government agency and research to a consortium of universities, "at zero cost."

Though the turn toward "modern" managerial rhetoric approach in project documents after 2010 is reassuring in some ways, some doubts remain about its efficacy: for instance when the SBAT's 2010 business plan undertakes a "competitor analysis" for archaeological wet wood restoration services; or the manipulation of cost and revenue estimates within the PIUSS project to make the museum project more politically appealing. Furthermore, the actual meanings associated with the museum constantly changed over time, without making the underlying assumptions explicit (for instance, to what extent the exhibitions within the Arsenali Medicei will coincide with the initial idea of a general museum of Mediterranean navigation, rather than just of the San Rossore ships, is still unclear to us). The Ministerial commission that affirmed and developed Bottini's 1999 proposal for three interconnected museums created a situation of "professional optimism" against which the archaeologists of the SBAT constantly had to struggle. The City of Pisa also attempted to change the agenda of the project by subsuming it into overall urban planning projects; however the City's insistence that the State fund the museum project seems to have allowed professionals within the SBAT to substantially control the process of museum development.

CONCLUSIONS

All in all, the Pisa discovery could be defined as a story with a happy ending: a success, despite the mess; professional effectiveness despite an overall lack of efficiency. Our analysis however underlines the risk of failure not only in general administration, but also of professional values (the potential loss of the ships themselves). Despite being effective, they could have been even more effective under a professional lens. Finally, the delicate and contradictory role played by professional values in dealing with uncertainty is the hidden part of the story, with long-term professional values creating a positive way of reducing uncertainty, while professional utopianism in the short term, with its associated administrative naiveté, tended to dangerously increase complexity.

A couple of comments are possible here. Italian heritage professionals as a whole seem to have "resisted" what is normally perceived as a kind of hostile attack on their professional jurisdiction by "non-experts," i.e. the bearers of general management knowledge (Settis 2002). So far at least, they have been able to keep control of the overall process, with their persistent love for complexity and radical resistance to any need for systematic reporting. Interestingly enough, however, they indeed appear very open to the "new" notion of client orientation which is normally perceived as positive in NPM literature, and whose lack characterized the old-fashioned approach of heritage professionals, according to NPM rhetoric. But this enthusiastic adoption of a client-oriented approach appears to have been too much, and too early in Pisa: less obsession with public access (to the excavation area, the conservation center, and the universalist museum) would have reduced risks and simplified the achievement of professional results.

In addition, it is interesting to notice how, paradoxically, the end of the emergency situation made things harder: emergencies seem to allow organizational behaviors and decisions that are difficult to implement in day-to-day routines. This may also explain why excavation and protection (urgent, emergency activities) achieved better performance than the museum (a more routine development project).

At a more general level, the *Navi di Pisa* outline an important research agenda for management scholars. Heritage entities, like most arts and cultural entities, are professional organizations, where professional values play a crucial (sometimes counterproductive) role. Understanding this role would help to better understand hidden processes in sense-making and the reproduction of meanings within the thousands of organizations that could be labeled as "professional." This might help overcome the recent seduction of management by a small part of the arts sector, the so called "creative" industries, which are looked at instrumentally, as ways to understand how creativity works for better (general) management uses (Bilton 2006). In addition to understanding value-driven aspects of creativity, highlighting how professional values engage with uncertainty is likely to open up interesting venues for general reflection.

NOTES

1. We would like to thank the Superintendency for generous access to the data archive, and Dr. Andrea Camilli for several in-depth interviews.
2. We express all monetary values in Euro, though the currency was Italian Lira until 2001.
3. He remains director today, and is the key figure in the management of the project.
4. Note how budget estimates politically justify the project *post facto*: Pisa wants to build it, so finds "cheaper" numbers.

REFERENCES

Bilton, C. 2006. *Management and Creativity: From Creative Industries to Creative Management*. Oxford: Blackwell.

Bozóki-Ernyey, K. 2007. *European preventive archaeology. Papers of the EPAC Meeting, Vilnius 2004*. Budapest: Hungarian National Office of Cultural Heritage.

Bradley, R., C. Haselgrove, M. Van der Linden, and L. Webley, eds. 2010. *Developer-Led Archaeology in North-Western Europe*. Oxford: Oxbow Books.

Camilli, A. 2007. L'esperienza delle navi antiche di Pisa: attività e programmi futuri. In F. Gravina, ed., *Comunicare la memoria del Mediterraneo. Strumenti, esperienze e progetti di valorizzazione del patrimonio culturale maritimo*. Naples: Centre Jean Bérard/Centre Camille Jullian, 217–224.

Camilli, A., and E. Setari, eds. 2005. *Le navi antiche di Pisa. Guida archaeologica*. Milano: Electa.

Demoule, J-P. 2012. "Rescue archaeology: A European view." *Annual Review of Anthropology* 41: 611–626.

Fabiani, T. 2016. "Navi antiche di Pisa: tutto pronto per l'apertura dei primi due padiglioni," <http://www.pisatoday.it/cronaca/apertura-museo-navi-antiche-pisa.html>.

Ferri, P., and L. Zan. 2014. "Ten years after. The rise and fall of managerial autonomy in Pompei." *Critical Perspectives on Accounting* 25: 368–387.

Garlichs, M. 2011. *The concept of strategic fit*. Hamburg: Diplomica Verlag.

Gruening, G. 2001. "Origin and theoretical basis of NPM." *International Public Management Journal* 4, no. 1: 1–25.

Hood, C., and R. Dixon. 2015. "What we have to show for 30 years of New Public Management: higher costs, more complaints." *Governance* 28(3): 265–7. DOI: 10.1111/gove.12150.

Lawrence, P., and J. Lorsch. 1967. "Differentiation and Integration in Complex Organizations." *Administrative Science Quarterly* 12: 1–30.

March, J. G. 1978. "Bounded rationality, ambiguity, and the engineering of choice." *The Bell Journal of Economics* 9: 587–608.

Mintzberg, H. 1978. "Patterns in strategy formation." *Management Science* 24, no. 9: 934–48.

Mintzberg, H. 1994. *The Rise and Fall of Strategic Planning.* New York: The Free Press.

Normann, R. 1977. *Management for growth.* Chichester: John Wiley and Sons.

OECD. 2010. Value for Money in Government. Public Administration after "New Public Management." <http://www.oecd-ilibrary.org/docserver/download/4210191e.pdf?expires=1453113101&id=id&accname=ocid195206&checksum=5A500F3766F43CAA35A0F39A7265C1F3> [last accessed January 2016, 2018].

Panozzo, F. 2000. "Management by decree. Paradoxes in the reform of the Italian public sector." *Scandinavian Journal of Management* 16, no. 4: 357–373.

Pettigrew, A., ed. 1987. *The management of strategic change.* Oxford: Basil Blackwell.

Quinn, J. B. 1980. *Strategy for change: Logical instrumentalism.* Homewood IL: Irwin.

Robinson, S. E. 2004. "Punctuated Equilibrium, Bureaucratization, and Budgetary Changes in Schools." *The Policy Studies Journal* 32, no. 1: 25–39.

Settis, S. 2002. *Italia S.P.A. L'assalto al patrimonio culturale.* Turin: Einaudi.

Venkatraman, N., and J. C. Camillus. 1984. "Exploring the Concept of Fit in Strategic Management." *Academy of Management Review* 3: 513–525.

Weick, K. E. 1977. "Enactment process in organizations," in *New directions in organizational behavior,* ed. B. M. Staw and G. B. Salancik. Chicago: St. Clair Press, 211–244.

Wirick, D. 2009. *Public-Sector Project Management: Meeting the Challenges and Achieving Results.* Hoboken, NJ: John Wiley & Sons.

Zan, L. 2013. "Economic discourse and heritage conservation. Towards an ethnography of administrations." *Heritage & Society* 6, no. 2: 167–184.

Zan, L., S. Bonini Baraldi, M. Lusiani, D. Shoup, P. Ferri, and F. Onofri. 2015. *Managing Cultural Heritage. An International research Perspective.* London: Routledge.

....

ACCOUNTING FOR WHAT WE TREASURE

Economic Valuation of Public Heritage

....

SHEILA ELLWOOD

INTRODUCTION

....

PUBLIC heritage embraces World Heritage sites, palaces, castles, parks, museums and art collections. As such it represents huge wealth, but this wealth is often invisible in the financial statements of government bodies and charities. In recent decades, however, several countries took steps to include public heritage in the annual financial statements and reports. When attempting to account for what we treasure recognition and measurement of heritage assets is conceptually and practically difficult. Items recognized on balance sheets should conform to economic definitions and be capable of reliable measurement. But methodological assessment of the value of heritage assets is fraught with difficulties. There are many kinds of value (economic, cultural, social, political, etc.) and different measurement tools none of which seem wholly appropriate. Moreover, values change over time and are strongly shaped by contextual factors such as economic opportunities and cultural trends. After reviewing the accounting problems of recognition and measurement a wide view of economic valuation is considered covering several methodologies. Accounting is used for accountability and decision-making. While there is generally agreement on providing information on public heritage for stewardship and accountability, it is argued that partial information on economic values may distort decision-making and including only economic information may affect perceptions of cultural value (Ellwood and Greenwood 2016). It is therefore important to also consider the purpose of accounting for what we treasure. The valuation of public heritage serves many purposes: an understanding of tools and aims (targets) bridging accounting, economics, and other social cultural disciplines can be helpful in ensuring appropriate reporting and decision-making for public heritage.

Accounting for Heritage Assets

Recognition and Measurement

In common parlance, public heritage is implicitly taken to be an asset. Mautz (1988) questioned—how can a Treasure not be an asset? But in accounting, items should conform to recognition and measurement criteria before they can be included in financial statements such as the balance sheet. To be recognized an item must meet the accounting definition of an element of the financial statements (e.g. asset, liability, expense) and be able to be measured reliably.

In 2009, the UK Accounting Standards Board (ASB) provided the following definition of a heritage asset in Financial Reporting Standard (FRS) 30:

> A tangible asset with historical, artistic, scientific, technological, geophysical or environmental qualities that is held and maintained principally for its contribution to knowledge and culture.
> (FRS 30 Heritage assets)

The accounting standard setter considered cultural or heritage items as assets. But this required a different definition from the conventional one used in accounting conceptual frameworks that is based on an economic (cash) flow—"a resource controlled by an entity as a result of past events and from which future economic benefits are expected to flow to the entity." Paragraph 4.4, IFRS (2010).

In the definition of a heritage asset provided by the ASB, the *intent* of the holder is to contribute to culture. These *benefits* in contribution to knowledge and culture rather than *cash flows* are considered by the standard setter to be sufficient to meet the accounting asset definition. Therefore, heritage assets are not conventional assets in accounting terms and the accounting asset definition requires some reworking before heritage assets can be recognized. The attributes of heritage assets are different from business assets. Heritage assets tend to have long lives (which can span over a thousand years, e.g. Stonehenge in Wiltshire, England). It may be difficult to estimate their useful lives (depreciation may be irrelevant) and they may incur high maintenance costs. They are often unique or irreplaceable and their value may increase over time even if their physical condition deteriorates. They are rarely held for their ability to generate cash inflows or sale proceeds; they are often donated and are sometimes inalienable (cannot be sold without external consent). Their value in cultural, environmental, educational, and historic terms is unlikely to be fully reflected as a financial value. These characteristics give rise to fundamental problems in relation to asset definition and measurement.

Developments in Accounting for Heritage Assets

Despite difficulties in definition and accounting valuation, accounting standard setters and governments have increasingly required the inclusion of heritage assets in financial statements.

The United Kingdom has addressed accounting for heritage assets in recent years. In 1999 the UK ASB required that heritage assets should be capitalized at historic cost with a revaluation option (FRS 15 Tangible Fixed Assets). Operational heritage assets, for example, a listed building used for office accommodation, would be valued on the same basis as other operational assets. For non-operational assets, most entities only valued purchases after 2001. The Financial Reporting Advisory Board (FRAB) on government accounting expressed concern regarding this partial coverage of heritage assets in accounting statements.

In 2006 the ASB issued a *Discussion Paper: Heritage Assets—Can Accounting Do Better?* The paper proposed the adoption of current value and the capitalization of all heritage assets where practicable. This was embodied in the ensuing exposure draft which received an unprecedented level of response that showed furious rejection. There was a clear preference for non-capitalization (i.e. not including a value for heritage assets on the balance sheet), but support for disclosures. The ASB back-tracked: a later exposure draft followed by FRS 30 in 2009 largely reverted to the previous position but kept the disclosure requirements. Thus FRS 30 required, as a minimum historic cost, capitalization for acquisitions on or after 2001, but with a current value option, and additional disclosures on how heritage assets are managed. The financial statements should contain an indication of the nature and scale of heritage assets held by the entity and disclose—

> the policy for the acquisition, preservation, management and disposal of heritage assets. This should include the description of the records maintained . . . of its collection of heritage assets and information on the extent to which access to the assets is permitted. (Paragraph 7, FRS 30)

Central and local government bodies in the UK follow accounting manuals and codes that require inclusion of heritage assets at valuation wherever information is available and further descriptive information must be disclosed. Despite FRAB's concerns, information on heritage assets in financial statements is not identified separately in the UK's Whole of Government Accounts and remains partial in the reports of individual entities. For example, the National Portrait Gallery (included as part of the Department for Culture Media and Sport) values only those heritage assets acquired from 2001 onwards; it is estimated that about 4 percent of the primary collection of approximately twelve thousand portraits is capitalized and only about 0.1 percent of the reference collection of a further eighty-five thousand portraits (Ellwood and Greenwood 2016). The National Trust has over five hundred historic houses, castles, and monuments, 280,000 hectares of land, and 775 miles of coastline but places no value on them in its financial statements. It does, however, provide disclosure of the nature, scale, and significance of heritage asset holdings and policies for acquisition, management, and care of the property (National Trust 2016).

In a wider international context, there is little uniformity of accounting treatment; for example, expenditure on heritage assets is expensed on acquisition in US financial statements (no inclusion on the balance sheet) whereas in New Zealand and Australia capitalization on the balance sheet is required. The inclusion of heritage assets could make a vast difference to the net assets of a nation shown on government financial statements. Ouda (2014) claims Luxor in Egypt hosts one-third of the Pharaonic monuments and antiquities of the whole world; and with other Pharaonic assets in other cities and Greco-Roman antiquities, Islamic-Coptic antiquities, and "recent" antiquities "we will find that Egypt possesses around two-thirds of heritage assets of the whole world . . . if these heritage assets will be capitalized in the balance sheet of the Egyptian government, nobody can imagine the volume of positive net worth" (2014: 27).

The Debate on Accounting Recognition

In one of the earliest contributions to the literature on heritage assets Mautz (1988) used the example of the Washington Monument to argue whether what we treasure should be considered to be an asset.

> The Washington Monument . . . is a national treasure, an historical structure of great significance exemplifying the spirit and sustaining the morale of our country. We would all be the losers without it. Of course, it is an asset. How could anyone think otherwise? And as an asset, it should appear in our national balance sheet. (1988: 123)

Mautz contended that the Monument represented an obligation for future cash outflows rather than inflows and therefore was more characteristic of a liability than an asset. He argued for a new categorization of "facilities" which transfer benefit to others. In subsequent years, several authors added to the debate (Table 2.3.1).

Pallot (1990) considered heritage assets as akin to community assets and similarly argued for their separate treatment. However, Rowles (1992) considered that many arguments deployed against the inclusion of heritage assets in the financial statements could equally apply to some non-heritage assets. Factory manufacturing plant, for example, may have no market value but is included in the financial statements. Similarly, land has an indefinite life and the value of other assets such as schools can be recovered through social benefits and so on. However, Carnegie and Wolnizer (1995, 1996) argue that as heritage assets often cannot be sold they should not be matched against liabilities and they cannot be valued in monetary terms. It is misleading to show net liabilities (net debt) after reducing liabilities for items such as heritage assets that cannot be sold. This point is developed further by Barton (2000) who argues that the government is often only the custodian of heritage assets:

Table 2.3.1. Arguments surrounding accounting recognition of public heritage.

View on accounting recognition	Authors
Heritage assets are not conventional assets and if included on balance sheets should be categorized as "facilities."	Mautz (1988)
Heritage assets are community assets.	Pallot (1990)
Heritage assets frequently cannot be sold (are inalienable). They should not be valued and matched against liabilities in the balance sheet.	Carnegie and Wolnizer (1995, 1996)
Heritage assets can be treated as conventional assets and representational faithfulness requires their inclusion.	Rowles et al. (1992), Micallef and Peirson (1997)
As trust assets for which the government is custodian, heritage assets should not be included in the balance sheet.	Barton (2000), Nasi et al. (2001),
Recognition is less important than disclosure of other financial issues: maintenance efforts, preservation.	Hooper et al. (2005), Aversano and Christiaens (2014)
Classify heritage assets as restricted (saleable) or not. Unrestricted are capitalized on the balance sheet; related revenue and expenses in the operating statement. Restricted included in a separate Trust Statement (unvalued); revenues and expenses shown against a Trust Fund balance.	Ouda (2014)
Accounting recognition of financial value can distort perceived cultural value.	Ellwood and Greenwood (2016)

The government holds the heritage assets in trust for present and future generations and has a responsibility to protect and preserve them. The costs of protecting and maintaining them should be borne by each generation as they enjoy the benefits from them. As trust assets, public heritage assets should not be included in the government's own statement of assets and liabilities. (2000: 231)

He goes on to regard them as public goods: they are often non-excludable and non-rival, all can enjoy them and one person enjoying them does not prevent others (Barton 2000, 2005). However, other writers such as Micallef and Peirson (1997) argue that representational faithfulness requires that heritage assets, as assets, should be included in financial statements: following Rowles' argument above, there are assets with the same characteristics as heritage assets that are included.

More recent studies look at the user needs of accounting information and question the value of including heritage assets on the balance sheet. Hooper et al. (2005) in a study of New Zealand independent museums found that museum managers sought to reflect curatorship values in their annual reports and rejected the application of accounting standards requiring the inclusion of heritage assets. Aversano and Christiaens (2014) find that Italian local government politicians regard information on heritage assets in government financial reports as important for financial and public accountability reasons.

> The politicians are mainly interested in accounting information such as financial value, cost of the preservation, sources used for the acquisition of heritage assets, the cost of custody, performance indicators and descriptive information such as the conservation policies, the physical condition and the description of the assets. (2014: 170)

Ouda (2014) extends Barton's argument that the government (or charity) is only a custodian for many heritage assets. As such he recommends the government adopt a practical approach, it should account for heritage according to whether its use is restricted. If it has unrestricted use of the heritage assets they should be capitalized on the balance sheet and revenue and expense recorded in the operating (performance) statement. For restricted heritage assets, the government is merely acting as custodian and should use a separate Trust Statement with revenues and expenses shown against a Trust Fund balance.

Although accounting has in recent decades sought to include public heritage on balance sheets, there has been concern about how such inclusion could be misleading or that financial value could diminish their cultural value (Ellwood and Greenwood, 2016). On the other hand, additional disclosures to accompany financial statements (on the nature, conservation, and access to public heritage) are largely welcomed. Intertwined with whether public heritage should be recognized is the difficulty of determining a financial value.

Problems of Accounting Measurement

Items included in financial statements must be capable of reliable measurement (IFRS 2010) and are subject to audit verification. Reliable measurement of heritage assets can occasionally be unproblematic (for example experts may be able to provide immediate valuations on some works of art), sometimes difficult (the Washington Memorial), sometimes impossible (the Rosetta Stone). Accounting approaches commonly adopted in the valuation of assets are historical cost, replacement cost, fair value, and value in use, but all have problems in relation to heritage assets.

Historic cost is adopted on acquisition of assets, but often heritage assets have not been purchased in recent years (if ever); they are frequently bequeathed or donated. Historic cost, the traditional accounting approach, is often unavailable or irrelevant. Smith (2007) notes that Stonehenge was sold in 1915 for £6000 only to be bequeathed to the nation a few years later. The historic cost of £6000 holds little meaning.

In accounting, replacement cost is often adopted for specialist assets, particularly public-sector assets, but heritage assets are largely irreplaceable. The cost of reconstructing Stonehenge by hewing stone from the Welsh mountains, transporting them to Wiltshire, and constructing a stone circle would again be considered to be a figure with very little meaning by most people.

Fair value or market value assumes there is a market for the same or similar assets. This valuation approach is increasingly put forward as the most appropriate accounting measurement approach in business accounting. Even where this is an active market for the heritage asset (e.g. there may have been recent sales of a painting by the same artist), the prices are often volatile and each asset would have differing subjective value. Market valuations are also argued to be futile as frequently the organization holding the heritage asset is not permitted to sell the item (Barton 2000, Ellwood and Greenwood 2016).

"Value in use" is an income approach commonly used in accounting. "Value in use" is the discounted future cash flows generated by the asset. Although fees that would maximize revenue without jeopardizing targets for visitors are frequently applied (Steiner 1997) many heritage assets are freely available or subsidized because of their cultural, social, or educational benefits. Furthermore, there are often externalities such as tourist income generated by those visiting the locality to view the asset which would not be assessed in accounting "value in use," which is entity-specific. Zan et al. (2000: 336) claim that "to visit the Pompei site with a 6 Euro ticket, a visitor normally spends as much as twenty or thirty times this amount in the regional economy (transport, accommodation, food, etc.)."

All the commonly used methods of accounting measurement have deficiencies when applied to heritage assets and an organization is unlikely to be able to employ consistent, reliable policies.

ECONOMIC VALUATION METHODOLOGIES

Dimensions of Value

There are various dimensions of the value of public heritage: economic, cultural, social, and so on. Public value or human well-being regards any benefit as important, not merely cash; a benefit is anything that increases human well-being and a cost decreases human well-being. The view can be individual or collective value (Hutter and Rizzo 1997, Peacock 1998), private or public value. Accounting usually takes an individual, private view of an entity's worth, but there are wider approaches that could be used to place a non-market value on public heritage.

There is an extensive literature on methodologies that can be used when accounting or market values are absent or inadequate. The methods available to a public heritage context use preferences—revealed or stated.

Revealed Preferences

Revealed preference methods estimate preferences for non-market goods by "willingness to pay" (WTP) behavior. The methods include hedonic price, travel cost, and maintenance cost.

The hedonic price method is based on the extra price paid to enjoy the public heritage; the idea is that property is affected by its characteristics which may include non-market cultural factors. Price differentials can therefore reflect the "willingness to pay" for public heritage, but the approach is inevitably limited to property and an efficient functioning property market. Furthermore, non-use and alternative options are not measured.

The travel cost method uses differences in travel costs of visitors to a public heritage site to infer the value of the site. The travel costs act as a surrogate for the price paid to acquire available benefits. Under this approach, the cost of visiting a public heritage site is not only the entrance fee, but includes the cost associated with travel and an estimated cost of traveling time (based on the travel time of participants multiplied by a specified wage rate). The approach is only useful for sites entailing significant travel and only measures active or passive use benefits and cannot incorporate non-use benefits such as preservation or option values. Nevertheless, the travel cost information can enable a demand curve to be drawn to estimate an entrance fee for different zones of travel and the fee can be incorporated into a net present value model to estimate the value of the public heritage site.

The avoided maintenance approach would take the costs of cleaning, repairing, and restoring the fabric of a public heritage structure as a proxy for value. This approach does not consider the benefits derived from public heritage and is therefore very deficient as an estimate of economic value.

Stated Preferences

Stated Preferences methods use hypothetical markets. Usually a survey elicits preferences where there is no market for the public heritage good or service. Contingent valuation is the most popular stated preference method (Mourato and Mazzanti 2002) used in developing and developed countries. Hanemann (1994) argues that when public valuation is the object of measurement, a well-designed contingent valuation survey is one way of consulting the relevant experts—the public itself. The approach is similar to market research undertaken for a new or modified product: a random sample of people are directly asked to express their willingness to pay (or willingness to accept) for a hypothetical change in the level of provision of a good. Theoretically, contingent valuation is based on welfare economics and assumes that stated "willingness to pay" (WTP) amounts are related to respondents' underlying preferences. Unlike revealed preference techniques, contingent valuation is able to capture all types of benefits including non-use values. The US National Oceanic and Atmospheric Administration (NOAA) was able to assess contingent valuation studies as reliable to be used in judicial process natural resource damage assessment including non-use values (Arrow et al. 1993).

The contingent value questionnaire has three stages: first, identifying the good (public heritage), the valuation scenario, and eliciting monetary values; second, questions on attitudes and knowledge together with demographic and debriefing questions; and third, the piloting stage. Mitchell and Carson (1989: 120) point out the importance of making "the scenario sufficiently understandable, plausible, and meaningful to respondents so that they can and will give valid and reliable values despite their lack of experience with one or more of the scenario dimensions." Bateman et al. (2002) provide guidelines for using contingent valuation in UK studies. However, Hausman (2012) argues that contingent valuation is laden with so many problems as to be "hopeless." He contends that three long-standing problems continue to exist: hypothetical response bias that overstates value; large differences between willingness to pay and willingness to accept; and the embedding (including scope) problem—"respondents to contingent valuation surveys are often not responding out of stable or well-defined preferences, but are essentially inventing their answers on the fly" (43).

Choice modeling is increasingly used by valuation practitioners partly to overcome problems incurred in contingent valuation studies (Mourato and Mazzanti 2002). The choice modeling technique is based on "the characteristics theory of value" (Lancaster 1966) in which a good is taken as consisting of a bundle of component attributes and their levels. For example, a museum can be described by information on conservation level/activity, access policy (visit hours), additional services, and entry fee (Mazzanti 2003). Choice modeling is survey-based, respondents are given various alternative descriptions of the good, differentiated by their attributes and levels. They are asked to:

- rank the various alternatives in order of preference; or
- rate each alternative according to a preference scale; or
- choose the most preferred alternative out of the set.

One of the choice options is usually given as the status quo. One attribute typically represents a monetary variable (known as the 'payment vehicle') which facilitates implicit prices. Variants of choice modeling were widely used in market research and transport literatures before application to public heritage. Choice modeling, unlike contingent valuation, is capable of dealing with multidimensional changes. Mourato and Mazzanti (2002: 65) summarize:

> CM has explicit advantages over the CV method in the analysis of goods of a multidimensional nature. As far as cultural heritage is concerned, CM brings together a structured economic theoretical framework, a powerful and detailed capacity of evaluation, and a great variety of application possibilities.

However, Kaminski et al. (2007) observed that of seventeen non-market economic valuations of cultural sites in Europe fifteen solely used contingent value while only two used choice modeling.

WHY ACCOUNT FOR WHAT WE TREASURE?

Information Needs

Public heritage is an important resource: governments are held accountable for the use of resources (stewardship) and require information to ensure the efficient use of those resources when making decisions.

Governmental accountability is based on the belief that the citizenry has a "right to know" (GASB 2013), this principle going back to ancient times has recently applied to heritage assets. However, there is confusion over appropriate information for accountability purposes. There are three main (but entangled) types of decision-making surrounding public heritage: management, financing, and resource allocation. Table 2.3.2 provides examples under each category drawing on schedules in Mourato and Mazzanti (2002). It is particularly the problems of resource allocation that prompts accounting standard setters to require the inclusion of heritage assets, but relevant information is required for a whole range of decisions.

Mourato and Mazzanti (2002: 52) claimed "apart from what can be inferred from data on visitors and from maintenance and restoration expenditure, little is known about the actual magnitude of the economic value of non-market cultural resources." As we have seen, the conventional accounting approaches to the valuation of assets present difficulties in the context of public heritage. In recent years, however, there has been increasing recognition and measurement of public heritage on the financial statements of governments and charities internationally. There has also been development of more comprehensive empirical studies using wider economic evaluation. But there is also dissension to translating all values to monetary terms, some argue for enhancing or supplanting the accounting valuation of heritage with more cultural and social appreciation of heritage (Biondi and Lapsley 2014).

Accounting value and cultural value may not correspond. For example, in the UK National Portrait Gallery—"not all of the gallery's portraits are works of art. In many cases the subject is of more significance than the artist" (*The Times*, June 16, 2017: 21). Ellwood and Greenwood (2016) use the analogy of a thought experiment from quantum physics to argue that measurement can affect the phenomenon perceived; the act of measuring a treasure may affect how it is viewed. Treasures have economic, cultural, and social values however, decisions may be made on largely financial grounds, the recent enthusiasm for disposing of heritage assets when public organizations are suffering "austerity" provides a compelling case for taking a wider view of value. In a large survey of local authority asset managers in the United Kingdom, just over half indicated they had sold or leased heritage buildings in the last five years (Green Balance Report 2012).

There are also huge practical problems to generating economic information for accountability and decision-making. For example, it is estimated that it would take twenty-seven

Table 2.3.2. Decisions on public heritage.

Management of public heritage	Assessing changes (exhibitions; improvements) in cultural locations
	Evaluating tourism, development damage, pollution
	Assessing conservation work (restoration, replacement, cleaning)
	Estimating current and future demand
Financing public heritage	Assessing willingness to pay
	Analysing pricing policies
	Determining policy effects on different socioeconomic groups
	Quantifying net benefits (costs) of public heritage
	Informing different funding policies/levels of subsidies
Resource Allocation	Strategic policy: public heritage and other areas of public spending
	Allocating within competing public heritage institutions/locations
	Measuring public satisfaction and ranking institutions
	Appraising and ranking interventions (grant allocation)
	Allocating a specific budget among competing projects/locations
	Whether a specific cultural asset is to be conserved and at what level

person years and cost £1.3 million to place a value on all items held by the National Portrait Gallery (Ellwood and Greenwood 2016). Furthermore, information should be tailored for specific decisions, for example there may be legal impediments to the sale of heritage assets. There is a shortage of expertise to enable many empirical economic valuations (Bateman et al. 2002) and their interpretation. More innovative ways of achieving information needs could be considered. For example, Barker (2006) suggests a virtual tour of the heritage assets would be a better mechanism for accountability with the possibility of interrogation of the guardians on-line rather than trying to force a number value on them.

Conclusions

Accountability and decision-making for public heritage is inhibited by conceptual concerns surrounding accounting recognition and measurement, the difficulties of wider economic valuation tools such as contingent valuation and choice modeling, and unease about the dominance of economic calculative practices.

In addition to conceptual problems, there are a raft of contextual and practical problems associated with the valuation and reporting of public heritage. Public policy is made in the context of budgets and levels of public net debt. The absence of a budget consideration in contingent valuation studies can have a distorting effect (Hausman 2012); the partial inclusion of public heritage on government financial statement may distort accountability and decision-making; but the economic valuation of public heritage can also have an immense (distorting) effect on the wealth of the nation and the level of net debt (Ouda 2014).

However, public heritage is a vast and important resource that has implications for public well-being of current and future generations. Pragmatic solutions which provide a range of information (economic valuation together with cultural and social disclosures) must be sought. Information is needed for accountability purposes and public policy. Government agencies and Parliament/Congress should make informed decisions. Despite difficulties in recognizing and measuring value, decision-making on public heritage will do better if it is informed by expert opinion across accounting, economics, and cultural and social disciplines.

REFERENCES

Accounting Standards Board. 2006. *Heritage Assets: Can Accounting Do Better?* FRC Publications.

Accounting Standards Board. 2009. "FRS 30 *Heritage Assets.*"

Arrow, K., R. Solow, P. R. Portney, E. E. Leamer, R. Radnor, and H. Schuman. 1993. "Report of the NOAA Panel on contingent valuation." *Federal Register* 58(10): 4601–4614.

Aversano, N., and J. Christiaens. 2014. "Governmental Financial Reporting of Heritage Assets from a User Needs Perspective." *Financial Accountability & Management* 30(2): 150–174.

Barker, P. 2006. "Heritage Assets: Can Accounting Do Better?" *Accounting Ireland* 38(4): 48–50.

Barton, A. D. 2000. "Accounting for Public Heritage Facilities—Assets or Liabilities of the Government?" *Accounting, Auditing & Accountability Journal* 13(2): 219–235.

Barton, A. D. 2005. "The Conceptual Arguments Concerning Accounting for Public Heritage Assets: A Note." *Accounting, Auditing & Accountability Journal* 18(3): 434–440.

Bateman, I., R. T. Carson, B. Day, M. Hanneman, N. Hanley, and T. Hett. 2002. *Economic Valuation and Stated Preference Techniques: A Manual.* Cheltenham, UK: Edward Elgar.

Biondi, L., and I. Lapsley. 2014. "Accounting, Transparency and Governance: The Heritage Asset Problem," *Qualitative Research in Accounting & Management* 11(20): 146–161.

Carnegie, G. D., P. W. and Wolnizer. 1995. "The Financial Value of Cultural, Heritage and Scientific Collections: An Accounting Fiction," *Australian Accounting Review* 5(1): 31–47.

Carnegie G. D., and P. W. Wolnizer. 1996. "Enabling Accountability in Museums." *Accounting, Auditing & Accountability Journal* 9(5): 84–99.

Ellwood, S., and M. Greenwood. 2016. "Accounting for Heritage Assets: Does Measuring Economic Value 'Kill the Cat'?" *Critical Perspectives on Accounting* 38: 1–13.

Governmental Accounting Standards Board. 2013. *Why Governmental Accounting and Financial reporting Is—and Should Be—Different.* GASB.

Green Balance. 2012. *Local Authority Heritage Assets: Current Issues and Opportunities.* Report to English Heritage and the Heritage Lottery Fund, Grover Lewis Associates Ltd.

Hanemann, W. M. 1994. "Valuing the Environment through Contingent Valuation." *Journal of Economic Perspectives* 8(4): 19–43.

Hausman, J. 2012. "Contingent Valuation: From Dubious to Hopeless." *Journal of Economic Perspectives* 26(4): 43–56.

Hooper, K. C., K. N. Kearins, and R. Green. 2005. "Knowing the Price of Everything and the Value of Nothing: Accounting for Heritage Assets." *Accounting, Auditing and Accountability Journal* 62(4): 181–184.

Hutter, M., and I. Rizzo. 1997. *Economic Perspectives of Cultural Heritage*. London: Macmillan.

IFRS. 2010. *The Conceptual Framework for Financial Reporting*. International Accounting Standards Board, The IFRS Foundation.

Kaminski, J., J. McLoughlin, and B. Sodagar. 2007. "Economic Methods for Valuing European Cultural Heritage Sites (1994–2006)," in *Perspectives on Impact, Technology and Strategic Management, vol. 1*, ed. J. McLoughlin, J. Kaminski, and B. Sodagar. Budapest: EPOCH, 98–121.

Lancaster, K. J. 1966. "A New Approach to Consumer Theory," *Journal of Political Economy* 74: 132–157.

Mautz, R. K. 1988. "Monuments, Mistakes and Opportunities." *Accounting Horizons* 2(2): 123–128.

Mazzanti, M. 2003. "Valuing Cultural Heritage in a Multi-Attribute Framework: Microeconomic Perspectives and Policy Implications." *Journal of Socio-Economics* 32: 549–569.

Micallef, F., and G. Peirson. 1997. "Financial Reporting of Cultural, Heritage and Scientific Collections." *Australian Accounting Review* 7: 31–37.

Mitchell, R., and R. Carson. 1989. *Using Surveys to Value Public Goods: The Contingent Valuation Method*. Washington, DC: Resources for the Future.

Mourato, S., and M. Mazzanti. 2002. "Economic Valuation of Cultural Heritage: Evidence and Prospects," in *Assessing the Values of Cultural Heritage*, ed. Marta de la Torre. Los Angeles: Getty Conservation Institute, 51–76.

National Trust. 2016. "National Trust Annual Report 2015/16."

Nasi, S., K. Hansen, and H. Hefzi. 2001. "Off Balance Sheet Assets in Central Governments: Are They Unique or Are They Really Assets?" *Journal of Interdisciplinary Studies* 14(2): 137–54.

Ouda, H. A. G. 2014. "Towards a Practical Accounting Approach for Heritage Assets: An Alternative Reporting Model for the NPM Practices." *Journal of Finance and Accounting* 2(2): 19–33.

Pallot, J. 1990. "The Nature of Public Sector Assets: A Reply to Mautz." *Accounting Horizons* 42: 79–85.

Peacock, A. 1998. *Does the Past Have a Future? The Political Economy of Heritage*. London: Institute of Economic Affairs.

Rowles, T. 1992. "*Financial Reporting on Infrastructure and Heritage Assets by Public Sector Entities.*" *Discussion Paper no. 17*. Melbourne: Australian Accounting Research Foundation.

Smith, P. 2007. "Money and Monuments." *Accountancy* UK February 23–25.

Steiner, F. 1997. "Optimal pricing of museum admission." *Journal of Cultural Economics*, 21: 307–333.

Zan, L., A. Blackstock, G. Cerutti, M. C. Mayer. 2000. "Accounting for Art." *Scandinavian Journal of Management* 16: 335–347.

....

CULTURAL HERITAGE
Capital, Commons, and Heritages

....

CHRISTIAN BARRÈRE

CULTURAL HERITAGES AND ECONOMIC ANALYSIS

....

CULTURAL economics attempts to accord culture its rightful place, that implies considering cultural heritages (CH), i.e. culture that has stood the test of time, making the transition to heritage status. It is difficult because CH have very diverse and complex economic and social consequences (Rizzo and Mignosa 2013). Both Westminster Abbey and San Marco of Venice are famous churches providing utilities to Christians (for worship) and tourists (for visits). Beyond these two groups, they also provide utility to English and Italian inhabitants proud of their civilization, who use their images as symbols of national identity, and so on. A lot of connected activities (mainly touristic) allow professionals to earn money by selling touristic services. Today many CH have an increasing economic value, leading to the development of competition about heritages. Firms compete for the use of traditional heritages not yet governed by private property rights; pharmaceutical firms seek access to traditional indigenous medicines and transform them in new, private, patents; French clothing firms and luxury groups compete to internalize the collective heritage of French Haute Couture and the French luxury image. An institutional competition emerges to organize new global institutions by specific heritages: is the new regulation of international exchanges recognizing the European institution of geographic labels of origin—or just the trademarks?

At the same time, some CH disappear. Interest in indigenous medicines does not prevent the disappearance of indigenous languages: this shows private (market) value and public (social) value do not coincide, thus leading to favor the preservation of the heritages with a high private value and to abandon those with a low private value, even if their social value is very high. Interest in reputation capital by the founders of luxury companies does not prevent the loss of highly specialized know-how among dressmakers, feather workers, embroiderers, etc., when production units are closed: this shows some holders, at a given moment of the time, award to a part of their CH a strong value and to another a nil or very small, even if in the future this part would be productive and increase its value. So market evaluation cannot be capable of measuring the long term and social value of these heritages.

Any attempt to use economic analysis to manage CH is confronted with their complexity:

- They have different components: private and public, individual and collective.
- They have different dimensions: economic, cultural, social—and sometimes aesthetic.

Nevertheless, economic theory not only provides tools for their management but also suggest different ways of conceiving them: CH are variously conceived of as cultural capital, cultural commons (Bertacchini and et al. 2012), or community heritages. Far from being the natural results of the past, heritages result from social and cultural constructions (Tunbridge and Ashworth 1996) and far from being the application of indisputable economic tools, the economic management of heritages results from economic constructions.

So, the main thrust of this chapter is that how CH are conceived of carries implications as to how they should be managed. Defining CH (mainly as capital or not capital) depends on author preferences as to the best ways to manage them; in other words it depends on their preferences as to the various goals and results of the different management logics. To put it crudely, touristic firms prefer to define famous heritages as capital, with a logic of earning money, whereas archeologists and communities probably prefer to define them as common heritages, with a logic of preservation— witness the problem of protecting local traditions and ways of life as tourism expands in a globalized world!

We try to show that, rather than falling back CH on traditional economic analysis categories (capital and commons), another approach is to elaborate an economic conception of CH that respects their diversity and complexity. Construction of such a category could allow their management to be governed by the substantive properties of their components, according to their various stakeholders. Instead of dodging the question of their multi-dimensionality, we use it as a starting point in explaining the debates about how they should best be defined and managed, and the necessity of considering the differing points of view and interests (material and symbolic) of the various stakeholders. And this often leads to their being managed through both market and non-market relations, procedures, and institutions.

Cultural Heritage:
An Economic Resource

Cities and States have long sought to protect their CH and capture the CH of their competitors. Think of the Republic of Venice. The city organized the protection of its production know-how via secrecy (the Arsenal for shipbuilding, and Murano for the glass industry were protected: no foreigners were allowed anywhere near them) and craft workers attempting to sell these secrets or leave Venice for foreign countries were stabbed to death with glass daggers, adding a signature to the Republic's retaliation (Huyghe 2000, Laroque 1997). At the same time, the Republic tried to convince talented foreign craft workers to join it, and financed espionage aimed at pirating the know-how of foreign competitors (Marchis 1999).

Cultural Heritages as Economic Resources

Consideration of the costs of preservation and the benefits of CH led to the definition of public policies for their management, mainly for those official, formal heritages combining material and immaterial dimensions—such as museums and monuments (Greffe 2003, Hutter and Rizzo 1997, Rizzo and Towse 2002). Yet CH includes a whole range of elements, many of which remain informal (Barrère 2016): from know-how heritage found in *Maisons de couture* to recipes that are typical of a culinary culture or a common language used within a territory. Individuals, families, companies, industries, territories, societies, and humanity inherit cultural resources from the past.

In some cases, CH appears strongly on markets and capital exchanges. By producing over time, companies build heritages—specific resources that pass through time and can be used for new production. The case of the luxury industry is spectacular: luxury companies create and produce on the basis of both craftsmanship heritages (handed down through generations of workers) and creative knowledge. When Lagerfeld became head designer of Chanel, his first decision was to spend a great deal of time visiting every Chanel *Maison* department, to immerse himself in its heritage. He sought to be inspired by (rather than to copy) the Chanel style in order to create a new Chanel in the style of Coco Chanel (Lipovetsky and Roux 2003: ch. 4). This also allows customers to identify a style, and companies to accumulate reputation or good will. Bernard Arnault, the owner of LVMH, used to say that the source of the incredible success of Louis Vuitton is its 150-year history (Arnault and Messarovitch 2000).

Insofar as informal heritages acquire a rising value, they must be considered. Think of The Third Italy model (Bagnasco 1977), an important analysis focusing on the role of cultural heritage interpreted as a set of specific, individual, collective, and social assets, allowing the development of economic cooperation and stimulation of innovation. In the

1950s and '60s, falling transport costs and the extension of economies of scale encouraged most economists to envisage a world of very large companies of indifferent location. However, the outstanding success of the "industrial districts"—in these clusters, in spite of the level of the Italian wages compared to the Asian ones, small companies developed production, local income, jobs, and exports in chocolate products, eyewear, footwear, tannery and leather goods, but also in rubber and steel industries (Becattini 1998)—completely contradicted this expectation, and this success is now clearly related to cultural and social proximity, mainly relating to strong local heritages. If the production of standard pieces of basic goods can be relocated abroad, it is different for sophisticated pieces, high-quality goods, or for design of goods and processes. Districts and clusters develop an internal productive atmosphere, similar to the industrial atmosphere defined by Alfred Marshall (1890, 1919), but clearly related to these heritages—which constitute specific assets. Firstly, these districts set a common culture capable of lowering coordination costs: mutual trust, sharing of tacit knowledge, easy circulation of information, forms of cooperation in spite of competition, and so on. Secondly, they developed idiosyncratic effects, causing producers to benefit from the local specificities of resources, cultivated throughout history, from the Middle Ages, and the source of decisive comparative advantages.

Today, CH play an increasing role in the growth of a creative economy (Florida 2002, Zukin and Braslow 2011). Just as a modern economy develops semiotic values and cultural goods based on creativity, CH are used to increase supplier reputations and nourish creativity.

The Economic Value of Cultural Heritages: Cultural Capital

The first author to explicitly define and analyze heritages as economic resources was Austrian art historian Aloïs Riegl ([1903] 1982). He defined a social value of (mainly cultural) heritages as well as an economic value, and suggested that historical monuments be managed according to these, rather than out of political duty (for instance, preserving them for future generations).

In order to manage the politics of public preservation of selected monuments, the value to be considered must include their various utilities as:

- contemporary values (practical use value and artistic value);
- commemorative values (values of old artifacts, produced in the past and, then, unique), generally including:
  - historical value, depending on the role played by the artifact in the historical development of art;
  - age value, based on the emotion created by the passage of time;
  - deliberate commemorative value, connected to the original meaning of the artifact, which people want to keep.

Even if Riegl's analysis mainly considers monuments (and in so doing, material capital) it can apply to CH insofar as monuments are connected to culture and meaning.

Today, economists seek to define the value of CH to help define their efficient management: since money for their preservation and development is scarce, every expenditure has a direct cost and an opportunity cost, so that choices have to be made—is it better to allocate money to restoring this monument, or to contribute to the elimination of illiteracy?

Throsby (2001), whose concern is the specific cultural dimension of cultural assets, suggested distinguishing between cultural value and economic value as distinct entities. The latter includes individual and collective value (which can be estimated via techniques mimicking exchange and market as contingent valuation methods), while the former refers to many components (aesthetic, spiritual, historical, etc.) affecting economic value but cannot only come down to individuals' willingness to pay (Throsby 2001: 32–33). We cannot suppose that individuals, at a given moment, are interested in a lot of effects which do not directly and totally modify their utilities, surpassing them by acting on other people (in space) and other generations (in time); moreover they cannot give a rational or only reasonable evaluation of these positive and possibly negative effects. Unhappily, many economists now lose sight of this cultural specificity, using a formalist approach according to which it is possible to abstract the substantive specificities of goods to consider only their formal economic characteristics (scarcity, utility in consumption or production area, etc.). Tangible CH, such as monuments and museums—and, even intangible CH, such as described in Becker's analysis of human and social capital (Becker 1996)—are directly defined as economic capital and, thus, heritages are reduced to capital. CH becomes a stock of components producing flows of utilities through time.

Cultural Heritages as Economic Constraints

Though the CH considered by economic theory can gather economic resources, they can also represent economic constraints—and even economic obstacles. North (1991) has been one of the most important authors to focus on the legacy of the past and analyze its effects on path developments. North et al. (2000) applied the framework to the history of economic development. They started out with a simple empirical observation: prior to colonization, South America and North America had eminently comparable levels of development, whereas, today, global and average wealth between both areas strongly differ and there is a widening gap in living standards between Latin America and North America. Initial endowments in factors of production are unable to explain this, since both have significant and comparable resources. The difference could arise out of the incentive institutions provide to development. They showed how to distinguish between what we might call two heritages—one transmitted by England, the market organization, and the other by Spain and Portugal, the imperial-bureaucratic model. English colonization imposed a horizontal and decentralized model—the market model—which multiplied incentives to seek profit through innovation and productivity. The Iberian colonization developed a second model—vertical and centralized—based on rent seeking and withdrawal from productive activities, which discouraged productive effort, increased transaction costs and weakened development. Both colonizations created an institutional arrangement, including an incentive system, selecting defined types of normal behaviors. These rules, behaviors, incentives, and institutions passed through time, constituting an institutional heritage, and thus self-reinforced. Heritages do not disappear with the end of the colonial system. Moreover, heritages prevent efficient adaptation via a lock-in effect. These CH cannot obviously be identified to capital!

The development of the economic consideration of CH shows that the consequences of formal and informal heritages are both very wide and potentially very complex; in some cases, as just seen, CH do not produce utilities but inefficiency and lock-in situations. Is it then possible to capture all the economic consequences of CH through the category of capital?

The Limits of the Reduction of Cultural Heritages to Cultural Capital

Adam Smith and David Ricardo, the founders of the Classical economic analysis, used the notion of capital to distinguish consumption good and production good (or factor of production). Capital is an economic resource, used to produce consumption goods, so its value is gradually transmitted to them. Later, economists developed a more formal definition of capital in order to apply economic calculus to it and to efficiently manage resources producing flows of utilities through time. In the first point we question the identification between CH and capital. In the second one, we wonder whether using the framework of Cultural Commons allows surpassing the limits of the Cultural Capital framework.

Heritage versus Capital: Limitations of the Formalist Approach

The formalist approach reduces Cultural Heritages to Cultural Capital. With the case of the Iberian colonization we just saw that, sometimes, CH do not produce utilities but inefficiency and lock-in situations. Moreover the reduction of CH to a variety of capital misses several main characteristics of CH, related to the temporal dimension of cultural resources. We now study the four specificities of the temporal dimension of cultural resources which avoid identifying CH and Cultural Capital:

The Uses of the Resource are Frequently Non-Rival

Defining an economic resource as capital generally allows an efficient management. When its uses are rival (using it for a specific task prevents from using it for an another one) market Property Rights leads to allocate the resource to its most efficient use. In the case of CH, it is not always true. Sometimes there is rivalry. Congestion effects (think of the frequentation of famous beaches) and conflicts between different uses of CH (think of the problems of mass tourism in star destinations as Venice) may occur. Nevertheless—that shows the complexity of heritage compared to capital—using cultural resources does not generally create rivalry *through space* because their use does not destroy them (even if it can damage them, cf. the next point, it does not consume them) and does not prevent others simultaneously using them. On the contrary, network effects sometimes increase the utility of individual consumption when other people use them too. Moreover, cultural resource uses are often non-rival *through time*. Reading Hamlet today is unaffected by generations and generations having read it before us.

The Specific Profile of User Cost of Cultural Capital

The value of standard capital is supposed to decrease with previous use. Some uses of CH obey this principle: mass tourism damages sites and monuments (which implies monetary costs) and living conditions of local populations (which implies non-monetary costs). But the user cost of CH has some specificities. Earlier readings of Hamlet provide contemporary readers with comments and explanations that allow a more interesting reading. Previous use of cultural capital thus reinforces its present productivity. It follows that the conditions of the obsolescence of capital are different, mainly for the intangible dimension of CH. In the case of cumulative knowledge old resources are replaced by new ones, and become obsolete—but it is different in the case of non-cumulative knowledge. The works of Donatello and Shakespeare are very old, yet continue to fascinate audiences and teach new artists. On the contrary the value of some CH can disappear, even if they physically survive (think of the Soviet statues of Stalin and Lenin), because heritages are social and cultural constructions and are, also, destructions.

The Creative Working of Cultural Capital

The creativity framework undermines cultural capital reasoning since it does not work according to the traditional scheme of the production function, i.e. according to a regular and reproducible relation between a clearly identified input and a production of value. If production uses heritages, how can their contribution be measured? How can we measure the contribution through time (in terms of consumption and production) of the cultural capital incorporated in Chambord and Borobudur, or in the works of Keynes and Ricardo? Picasso used to say he would never have painted as he did without Cézanne, Puvis de Chavanne, Poussin and Ingres, or Vélasquez; but how can we identify and separate these different "inputs" (mainly those related to heritage and those related to the creative use of heritage)?

A Non-Generic Capital—But a Localized and Idiosyncratic Capital

The notion of capital is useful in comparing the outcome of each feasible combination of inputs to choose the most efficient. This presupposes the possibility of investing to reproduce the most efficient combination. Yet cultural resources are not generic. They are generally included in larger sets resulting, through time, from given historical and spatial conditions; it is therefore impossible to reproduce and adopt them anywhere else with the same result. It is sometimes possible to borrow from a cultural production (adapting Toyotism to the Western world, for instance) but it is often impossible to do it due to the idiosyncratic character of cultural resources.

These four specificities are not marginal, allowing identification of cultural resources and capital using the notion of cultural capital. The aim of the economic concept of capital is to connect outlay in capital (a consumption of value) and output (an increase in value), to efficiently manage this relation through economic calculus. As long as the expenditure dimension is not the key element and the output is not indicative of the effects of cultural capital, the concept becomes inappropriate. It would be better to say that cultural resources *are not* Cultural Capital (CK), but, in some conditions, they may *work as* capital, even if this does not exhaust all their economic consequences. In some other conditions, cultural resources do not work according to the capital scheme.

Consideration of the different dimensions of CH reinforces this argument. CH, rather than being a collection of things, is a cultural process of meaning-making, a mentality, "a way of knowing and seeing" (Smith 2006: 54), frequently connected to a group or community identity, sustaining their stability and continuity. In post-modern societies two different trends frame the role of CH. The first increases the economic and *capitalistic* dimension of CH. As noted by the Frankfurt School, the development of a mass culture adapted to a mass society (according to an industrialist framework previously only typical of industrial goods) leading to a submission by the field of culture to capital working. Similarly, culture and CH are increasingly used in the production process, as illustrated by the creative framework. Nevertheless, there is a second trend, corresponding to the willingness to preserve CH from pure economic logic and develop their *sacred* character, mainly in terms of their relation to the specificity and identity of a group and its historical roots. This being the case, CH also belongs to the world of ethics and values. Cultural Heritage is precisely what is not mainly (or not only) cultural capital, which means that resources conceived as cultural heritage are those that are not mainly (or not only) economic resources capable of being described and managed as capital!

Using the Framework of Cultural Commons to Surpass the Limits of the Cultural Heritage Framework?

Some economists, using the commons framework recently developed by Oström (1990), consider cultural commons (Hess and Oström 2003). The commons analysis began with the observation of the inefficiency of the free-access to common resources: the absence of property rights is an incentive to waste resources and leads to the famous "tragedy of commons" (Hardin 1968). Then, economists recommend privatization or state control to manage the common-pools of natural resources rather than maintaining their open access. Nevertheless, the development of practices and analyses has revealed the limitations of quota politics (for instance, through the Maine's Lobster Fishery case, Wilson 1997) and the market's failures giving the possibility of anti-commons tragedy caused by the multiplication and partitioning of property rights (Heller 1998, 2008). Ostrom (1990) clarified these matters by distinguishing between CPR (Common-Pool Resources) and open access. Common-Pool resources can be managed according to specific rules excluding free access. She analyzed the different forms of common property as specific institutions that gave rise to complex ownership organization. Her study mainly concerned natural resource commons—but this framework was also used for cultural commons (CC). CH then appears as cultural commons, that is, cultural resources that have to be managed through common institutions in view of the market's failure to minimize transaction costs.

The literature on CC is interesting by surpassing the formalist approach which proposes management of all economic resources either through markets, or by mimicking them. Nevertheless its resource management approach remains embedded in the mainstream approach to efficiency, limits the diversity of economic resources to their transactional properties, and does not set the institutions in their *time* and *space* context. This is obvious in the naturalist—perhaps technical—presentation of commons as a fourth type of economic goods (or resources): private goods (strong subtractability and easy exclusion), club goods (low subtractability and easy exclusion), public goods (low subtractability and costly exclusion), and commons (strong subtractability and costly exclusion). Commons, then, are resources held in common according to technical characteristics—whereas other resources are held by clubs, by the state, and by private ownership. The relation between type of property and technical characteristics (exclusivity and subtractability) derives from the constraint of minimizing transaction costs.

In the case of CC, as the use of cultural resources is generally non-rival, the efficiency question is not about exploiting natural resources avoiding waste and overuse, but about producing and developing cultural resources (Madison, Frischmann, and Strandburg 2010). Moreover, CH are not reducible to CC (even though they can, in some cases, be managed as CC), since their connection to both time and place is fundamental. CH thus have a structure, a logic, a coherence, resulting from a selection and a specific building, and are more than mere unstructured collections of resources, of *things*. Being connected to *meanings*, they include a subjective dimension and represent a relation between objects and subjects. As elements of a global project and of meaning, they are not an aggregate but are structured to define the sense of the construction. Let us consider the enlightening case of gastronomy.

The recipes of gastronomy are shared resources and collective creations, which have been passed on through time. Nevertheless a gastronomic heritage is a specific kind of commons for four main reasons:

- A gastronomic commons is related to the identity of one group, in relation to other groups, and expresses its specificity through a collective idiosyncrasy. Fischler (1993) mentions that in popular language people are often designated by the special food they are supposed to like: in France, the Italians are called "macaroni" and the British "rosbif," while in England the French are "frogs" or "frog eaters."
- Generally, a gastronomic commons is not a collection of resources but is structured by norms: for instance, these norms define what must be eaten at feasts and ceremonies in relation to the ordinary consumption of food; they define luxury goods in relation to standard ones.
- Gastronomic heritages result from a social and cultural building of local communities and societies. English cuisine is different from French and Italian cuisines; local and regional cuisines are also different. Their development paths are not the same.
- They pass through time, by a process of cultural transmission, for instance through the conservation of the guild traditions and the mother–daughter transmission within families. The concept of heritage underlines the historical dimension of culinary and gastronomic commons that determines their main characteristics.

Cultural Heritages as Social Resources

Many CH play a strong role in both economic and social life, without public protection and without explicit management—these are the main institutions connecting history, territory, and society, and defining the cultural context of social life. T. H. Marshall (1950) has taken a particular interest in the relation between social heritage and social life. He analyzed the socialization process by focusing on citizenship. For him, citizenship includes a social component in addition to its civil (rights necessary to individual freedom) and political (right to participate in the exercise of political power) components. This social component covers "the whole range from the rights to a modicum of economic welfare and security to the right to share to the full in the social heritage and to live the life of a civilized being according to the standards prevailing in the society" (Marshall 1950: 149). The formal and informal components of the social heritage thus form the basis of the individual's social life as well as providing social cohesion.

French *Solidarisme* suggested a close, and more systematic, analysis. The *Solidarist* approach (Bourgeois 1902) used the idea of social interdependence between individuals to surpass the dichotomy between individualism and holism by considering socialized individuals, and defining society as a society of individuals. The *Solidarists* argue that every individual is born into a society that allows them to benefit from a social and cultural heritage: language, education, institutions, and many other aspects that allow each personality to develop. Without their relation to society, no one would survive. Social time is, then, longer than individual time. People benefit from this social and cultural heritage and, in return, they participate in its preservation, evolution, and enlargement.

This framework can be read in economic terms. Heritage is simultaneously both cultural and economic resource. A society produces goods and institutions; yet most of the goods disappear in consumption (both unproductive and productive). Some—both material and immaterial—remain, and, together with institutions, these constitute a social and cultural heritage. Obviously, the stock of material capital (equipment, machines, buildings, etc.) is an important part of this social heritage. Yet rules, institutions, mentalities, and creative goods (artistic products, knowledge, and so on) are another important part of the heritage. Thus, CH refers to sets of elements, coming from the past, handed down from generation to generation, either on the basis of explicit and voluntary procedures or by tradition, and connected to a place, a territory. Even when informal, CH result from such a selection that only some elements of the past pass through time. Those that do achieve this have a particular value, generally connected to the specificity and identity of its holder, individual, group, or community. Within heritages, cultural assets may be tangible (buildings, structures, cultural artefacts such as paintings, sculptures, etc.) or intangible (ideas, practices, beliefs, values, traditions, and goods in the public domain, such as literature and music).

Since individuals and groups (as well as institutions and common resources) use present inputs to produce their output, perhaps social wealth depends as much on social heritage as it does on present choices and on the individual resources of economic agents. Conversely, society has to manage this heritage (in addition to the natural heritage) for future generations. The development of the creative economy (which uses culture for producing and consuming, for communicating and cooperating, and for enjoyment of life) reinforces the scope of these observations. The right way to capture all these economic and social effects of CH is to reduce it to neither capital nor commons, but rather to use an economic conception of CH—including (as a source of dissonance) the different components and contexts in which heritage is used.

CONCLUSION: THREE PRINCIPLES FOR THE MANAGEMENT OF CULTURAL HERITAGES

In economics, the mainstream erects market management of all goods (regardless of their substantive characteristics) as the key norm—except when the market fails. It matters little whether the goods in question are children (as on the adoption market), personal goods (as on the organ markets), cultural goods, or a standard industrial commodity; any goods (or resources) can be exchanged on either an explicit (standard markets using monetary prices) or implicit market (exchange relations using an exchange rate that can be understood as an implicit price). The previous argument has shown that, contrary to the formalist framework, CH have significant specificities that prevent both identification of management of the economic dimension of CH and that of market management. Management of the economic dimension of CH has to first consider each of their different dimensions, and second, each of the substantive characteristics of their components.

Making Cultural Heritages Management Explicit

No natural principle justifies the identification of CH as CK or CC. The CH category is richer than either, and CH components cannot be reduced to formal economic resources having economic costs and values. They are linked to time and space, to meanings and social values, and their economic management has to be connected to the full range of their dimensions. Since some of these components have an economic value, individuals and groups are interested in managing them in line with their own interests; implicit managements thus often develop without clarification or justification of how the public rates their goals and consequences. The first principle is then to make explicit all CH managements, clarifying their different dimensions, consequences and stakes, including economic aspects as well as social, material, and symbolic dimensions.

Defining Management According to the Social Values Attributed to Cultural Heritages

Management of the economic dimension of CH may be important—but this does not necessarily make their economic dimension the dominant or unique dimension. Thus, given that CH results from a social construction, society has to debate the relative importance of the dimensions and goals of management of the different components of CH and, then, of the various criteria included in a multi-criteria policy. No technical reason can justify whether entrance to the museum should be free, or not.

The public debate must also identify the different demands concerning CH management. As in the case of tourism, demands can be very different—and often, conflicting. Such conflicts are all the more frequent because definition of the holders does not usually derive directly from the natural characteristics of things—who is entitled to decide on the use and management of the Venetian lagoon: the inhabitants of Venice, of the regional area, of Italy, the touristic suppliers, the tourists, humanity . . . Who should be designated as having dominion over the territory, the landscape, the traditions?

Debate is necessary—because different ways of managing CH obey different logics. The logic of the market is the selection of users according to their willingness to pay and the competition to minimize monetary costs; the logic of the commons is different. Should the paintings of the Italian Renaissance be owned by private collectors, or freely accessible in museums, and how can either be justified?

Adapting Management to the Substantive Characteristics of their Components

By considering their transactional characteristics, the transaction cost framework does introduce some (limited) substantive characteristics of economic goods. It is necessary to go further, introducing all the substantive characteristics of the different components of CH, because the option of managing them via economic procedures and institutions differs hugely, depending on these characteristics. Regardless of social choices regarding free access to artistic creativity belonging to CH, it is generally more difficult to protect it using intellectual property rights (IPR) than technological creativity. For instance, even though IPR are generally able to manage industrial patents, they are incapable of protecting creative heritages and avoiding creative piracy, in the field of fashion (Barrère and Delabruyère 2011). Moreover, fashion companies inherit intangible assets (such as name, reputation, and know-how). They attempt to protect their informal heritages by transforming them into more formal heritages, but do not always protect every component of fashion CH. New luxury groups generally succeed in transferring the positive image of the great fashion creators, who founded their own *Maisons*, to the name of the company; they move from the name of the fashion designer, the *griffe* (an association between the creative products and the name of the creator, a personal IPR) towards the trademark (an association between the products and the company name, a market IPR). Such a transfer allows the value of the designer's name to be extended over time and space.

The use of CH cannot generally avoid conflicts between different stakeholders. Thus public administrations, communities, and associations are interested in tools to manage them and they turn to economists for it. This demand encounters the economists' supply. Economists often pretend to hold a scientific framework able to solve public choices when interests and preferences are competing. They found their propositions on their analysis of the market working and transfer the market solutions to public area. Market is really an institution managing the conflicts related to the allocation of economic resources by choosing between competing projects and claims. Different individuals claim for the same economic resources and have different subjective valuations of their use. The working of the market gives a solution: the resource is attributed to the best offer; the different subjective valuations are eclipsed by a unique monetary valuation, the market price. Then there is no more conflict. In the case of resources giving utilities through time, the market price takes the form of the price or value of capital and we have a unique and global criterion to manage the allocation of capital. It would be wonderful if economists could give managers a unique evaluation of all the costs and benefits of CH!

Unhappily, as we saw it, it is impossible to reduce the different valuations of costs and benefits—by different individuals and groups, according to different dimensions, and on a long time surpassing the period of a whole generation—to a unique indicator, a global indicator of the net value of CH. It would imply transforming heterogeneous consequences of preservation and different uses of CH in homogenous ones, summing them in a homogenous unity, and comparing the costs and benefits of each use. How to compare the "value" of the touristic frequentation of Venice and the "cost" of eviction of the local population from their houses to transform them in hotels, restaurants, and souvenir shops?

Moreover the application of the logic of market management to CH is generally refused by a lot of stakeholders. Is the willingness to pay a socially acceptable criterion to decide the allocation of CH, for instance when a very rich person propose to buy a Scottish medieval castle or a Venetian palace, to destroy it and rebuild it in another place, five thousand miles further? The logic of the UNESCO World Heritage list is to define humanity as the holder of these elements in order to put CH out of the market logic.

In response to the demand of evaluation coming from heritage managers, the economic analysis can do less and more. Less because it cannot give a simple criterion to evaluate CH (the "economic value" of CH as capital) and define the best way to manage them (to use market valuations, to mimic the working of market exchanges, to use regulations or commons management, to mix them, and so on). More because it can help stakeholders by analyzing all the economic consequences of CH and of their type of management. Such an analysis is the basis for multicriteria analysis using different measures of heterogeneous effects and costs: costs of preservation and touristic earnings can be measured in monetary terms; effects on employment in number of jobs created or suppressed; social or environmental costs measured by quantitative but non-monetary indicators (changes in the rate of pollution . . .). Nevertheless the economic analysis of cultural heritages is still in its early stages and the road to supply a theory of their management is still a long way off.

References

Arnault, B., and Y. Messarovitch. 2000. *La passion créative*. Paris: Plon.

Bagnasco, A. 1977. *Tre Italie: La problematica territoriale dello sviluppo economico italiano*. Bologna: Il Mulino.

Barrère, C. 2016. "Cultural Heritages: From Official to Informal." *City, Culture and Society* 7: 87–94.

Barrère, C., and S. Delabruyère. 2011. "Intellectual Property Rights on Creativity and Heritage: The Case of Fashion Industry." *European Journal of Law and Economics* 32(3): 305–339.

Becattini, G. 1998. *Distretti industriali e made in Italy: Le basi socioculturali del nostro sviluppo economico*. Turin: Bollati Boringhieri.

Becker, G. 1996. *Accounting for Tastes*. Cambridge: Harvard University Press.

Bertacchini, E. E., G. Bravo, M. Marrelli, and W. Santagata, eds. 2012. *Cultural Commons: A New Perspective on the Production and Evolution of Cultures*. Cheltenham: Edward Elgar.

Bourgeois, L. 1902. *Solidarité*. New edn 1996. Toulouse: Presses du Septentrion.

Fischler, C. 1993. *L'homnivore*. Paris: O. Jacob.

Florida, R. 2002. *The Rise of the Creative Class and How It's Transforming Work, Leisure and Everyday Life*. New York: Basic Books.

Greffe, X. 2003. *La valorisation économique du patrimoine*. Paris: Ministère de la culture; Département des Études de la Prospective et des Statistiques (DEPS).

Hardin, G. 1968. "The Tragedy of the Commons." *Science* 162: 1243–1248.

Heller, M.A. 1998. "The Tragedy of the Anticommons: Property in the Transition from Marx to Markets." *Harvard Law Review* 111: 621–688.

Heller, M.A. 2008. *The Gridlock Economy: How Too Much Ownership Wrecks Markets, Stops innovation, and Costs Lives*. New York: Basic Books.

Hess, C., and E. Ostrom. 2003. "Ideas, Artifacts, and Facilities: Information as a Common-Pool Resource." *Law and Contemporary Problems* 66: 111–145.

Hutter, M., and I. Rizzo. 1997. *Economic Perspectives on Cultural Heritage*. London: Macmillan.

Huyghe, E., and F. B. Huyghe. 2000. *Histoire des secrets: De la guerre du feu à l'Internet*. New York: Hazan. <http://www.huyghe.fr>.

Laroque, F. 1997. *Histoire et secret à la Renaissance*. Paris: Presses de la Sorbonne Nouvelle.

Lipovetsky, G., and E. Roux. 2003. *Le luxe éternel: de l'âge du sacré au temps des marques*. Paris: Gallimard.

Madison, M. J., B. M. Frischmann, and K. J. Strandburg. 2010. "Constructing Cultural Commons in the Cultural Environment." *Cornell Law Review* 95: 657–710.

Marchis, V. 1999. "De la soie et d'autres choses in De la diffusion des sciences à l'espionnage industriel: XV°–XX° siècles," in *Cahiers d'histoire et de philosophie des sciences 47: Actes du colloque de Lyon (30–31 mai 1996) de la SFHST*, ed. A. Guillerme. Paris: ENS Editions.

Marshall, A. 1890. *Principles of Economics*. London: Macmillan.

Marshall, A. 1919. *Industry and Trade*. London: Macmillan.

Marshall, T. H. 1950. *Citizenship and Social Class and Other Essays*. Cambridge: Cambridge University Press.

North, D. C. 1991. *Institutions, Institutional Change and Economic Performance*. Cambridge: Cambridge University Press.

North, D. C., W. Summerhill, and B. R. Weingast. 2000. "Order, Disorder and Economic Change: Latin America vs. North America," in *Governing for Prosperity*, ed. Bueno de Mesquita and H. Root. New Haven: Yale University Press.

Ostrom, E. 1990. *Governing the Commons: The Evolution of Institutions for Collective Action*. Cambridge: Cambridge University Press.

Riegl, A. [1903] 1982. *Moderne denkmalkultus: sein wesen und seine entstehung*. Vienna: Braumûller. English translation: "The Modern Cult of the Monument: Its Character and its Origin," *Oppositions* 25 (fall, 1982): 21–51.

Rizzo, I., and A. Mignosa. 2013. *Handbook on the Economics of Cultural Heritage*. Cheltenham: Edward Elgar.

Rizzo, I., and R. Towse. 2002. *The Economics of Heritage: A Study in the Political Economy of Culture in Sicily*. Cheltenham: Edward Elgar.

Smith, L. 2006. *The Uses of Heritage*. London and New York: Routledge.

Throsby, D. 2001. *Economics and Culture*. Cambridge: Cambridge University Press.

Tunbridge, J. E., and G. J. Ashworth. 1996. *Dissonant Heritage: The Management of the Past as a Resource in Conflict*. New York: Wiley.

Wilson, J.A., 1997. "Maine's Lobster Fishery. Managing a Common Property Resource", in *Increasing Understanding of Public Problems and Policies*, ed. S.A. Halbrook and K.W. Ward., Oak Brook, Illinois, Farm Foundation: 145–160.

Zukin, S., and L. Braslow. 2011. *City, Culture and Society*. Amsterdam and London: Elsevier.

HERITAGE AS REMAKING

Locating Heritage in the Contemporary World

SCOTT A. LUKAS

THE ninth-century Castle of Matrera in Villamartín, Spain, is an unlikely yet apt place at which to begin a discussion of heritage. The castle has been the subject of numerous popular journalistic stories and blog discussions as a result of the curious controversy that has surrounded its recent remaking. The ninth-century castle, like so many other historic sites in Europe, began to show the effects of time. Instead of rebuilding the structure as it might have looked originally, firm Carquero Arquitectura chose to combine remnants of the original structure with a stark, abstract modern structure that essentially highlights the volume and texture of the original (Figure 2.5.1).

Critics spoke of Carquero Arquitectura's restoration as nothing short of a "heritage massacre" (Jones 2016). Presumably, the combination of the old and the new evident in the firm's play with architectural remaking has been deemed as inappropriate, even disrespectful. Castle Matrera is one of many such curiosities that are part of a new genre of heritage that is made famous as a result of its "botched nature." Cecilia Giménez's questionable restoration of a fresco of Christ in Borja and the restoration of the Roman theater in Sagunto, both in Spain, remind us of the vast public interest in issues of heritage, particularly when there is a significant dispute in terms of how that heritage should be staged or re-presented to the public. Lowenthal reminds us that "heritage by its very nature *must* depart from verifiable truth" (Lowenthal 1998: 250), and while most scholars of heritage would recognize this fact of the re-presentation of heritage, many would be unsatisfied to leave heritage study to the realm of pure relativism. As Harrison suggests, "definitions of heritage have expanded to such an extent that almost anything can be perceived to be 'heritage'" (Harrison 2013: 3). So, what exactly can we know of heritage?

The word "heritage" connotes "that which may be inherited" and "transmitted from ancestors" (Online Etymology Dictionary). These meanings of "inheritance"

FIGURE 2.5.1. Castillo de Matrera en Villamartín.

Ignacio Palomo Duarte, Creative Commons Attribution-ShareAlike 4.0 International.

and "transmission" are present in many peoples' minds—whether they are academics who study it or lay individuals who appreciate its many didactic and life-enriching qualities—and it is common to experience heritage through reflections on the didactic, even the sublime. Heritage may include official forms as defined by UNESCO, official versions as defined by another governmental or influential agency (such as The National Register of Historic Places), as well as unofficial or lay forms that are defined as significant by everyday people, their cultures, and communities. Clearly, though all of these forms imply heritage, the legitimacy of any given form is connected to dynamics of power, representation, and politics in society. Heritage is a form of the social imaginary that implies issues of collective meaning, political contestation, and experiential and interpretive depth (Ashley and Frank 2016).

In this writing, I focus on five arenas of heritage—each of which is connected to an overarching question of heritage and an explanatory metaphor, as well as a suggested replacement metaphor appropriate to the worlds and contexts of remaking. I will argue for a new perspective on the topic, one that is influenced by the representational, critical, political, and existential tendencies of the prefix "re-." While I will engage in specific rumination on sites of heritage, this writing is intended to consider it as a way of thinking and orienting ourselves in the world, and less as an analysis of specific sites, people, and contexts of heritage.

REFRAMING HERITAGE

One of the curious ironies that was missed in many of the critical discussions of Castle Matrera is the role that heritage law (Article 39.2 of Spanish Historical Heritage Law) played in the Carquero Arquitectura firm's design decisions at the site. The firm's choices were less a matter of postmodern architectural experimentalism, but ones of necessity mandated by law. Symbolically, we may use Castle Matrera's presumed "heritage massacre" as entry into the curious, complex, and contentious world of heritage. As well, we may allegorize the final design of the castle—in its curious incommensurability of the old and the new—for the purpose of more clearly situating heritage contexts in the world of remaking. As a form of cultural production, we often recognize that heritage practice "depends on display to give . . . dead sites a second life as exhibitions of themselves" (Kirshenblatt-Gimblett 1998: 7).

Smith reminds us that the second life afforded in heritage practice is not, necessarily, based on inherent value of the place, thing, intangible practice, person, or historical event involved in that life; provocatively, she offers that "Stonehenge, for instance, is basically a collection of rocks in a field" (Smith 2006: 3). Historians, archaeologists, and members of the general public would likely not appreciate Smith's rather radical constructivist point; yet, we would be amiss to avoid her greater insights in that heritage is something added to—or upon—something tangible or intangible in the world. We select certain things, contexts, and places as legitimate of a heritage label, and because of heritage's rather monumental nature, we are often inclined to ignore the processes that underpin it. This is the predicament of heritage. In its moments of public display, its remade form—whether showing signs of its Janus nature or not—has an initial appearance of surface and knowability. Yet, beneath its layers of patina, there are other motivations that belie its surfaces. All heritage—whether the complex material layering of Castle Matrera or a historical interpretive plaque attached to a heritage site—illustrates the multiple contexts of remaking that are implied in its realization, whether acknowledged or not.

In 2015, during a discussion at an international conference on heritage, I encountered such an example of the predicament of heritage. Following the presentation of a graduate student who aspired to bring traditional heritage concerns into the worlds of the theme park, a more traditional conference attendee took issue with the first individual's sense of the issue. The student envisioned a retelling of classic Chinese folktales through immersive and multisensory theme park attraction technologies. The attendee, who was quite dismissive, suggested that the student "get his work on track," to paraphrase, particularly as "this was no way to re-present heritage for the public."

What the disagreement emphasizes is the degree to which heritage is a matter of perspective. In the contemporary world, there are no absolutes in terms of what heritage is, how it should be presented to the public (as in this example from the conference), what people should make of it, and how academics and experts should act on it all. Because heritage is always a form of re-presentation, a key to understanding the dynamics of heritage rests on their "virtuality, whether in the presence or the absence of actualities" (Kirshenblatt-Gimblett 1998: 149). While the traditional conference attendee would claim otherwise, both heritage and theme parks (and associated tourist spaces) deal in the "intangible, absent, inaccessible, fragmentary, and dislocated" (Kirshenblatt-Gimblett 1998: 167).

Contemporary theories and practices of heritage remind us of the challenge of answering the question, *what is heritage?* It would be quite easy for the academic or the layperson to define heritage through reference to any number of conceptual terms that include: old, significant, historic, monumental, interesting, didactic, shared, public, valuable, transcendent, and sublime. And while any and all of these notions do likely define many of our understandings of what is heritage, their over-deployment, particularly in public debates like those surrounding Castle Matrera or the heritage conference that I described, may result in damage to the future possibilities of heritage in all of its senses.

UNESCO and numerous other less influential official heritage and history-granting agencies have actually responded quite pragmatically to these postmodern, relativistic, and constructivist tendencies within heritage studies. UNESCO's Nara Document on Authenticity (1994) focused on expanding the scope of heritage established, in part, in the Venice Charter (1964) to include a broader conceptualization of heritage. Realizations including the lack of attention given to marginal or subaltern cultures, people, places, and practices; the fact of heritage's intangibility; the Eurocentric practice of defining "masterpieces" of the world through heritage; and the notion of the threats faced to indigenous cultures and places due to warfare, globalization, and other factors, are all indications of heritage catching up with the times, so to speak. At the same time, such adjustments in the conceptualization and practices of heritage are necessarily incomplete—a reminder of how heritage shares much in common with the impossible and undefined nature of the culture concept in anthropology.

All heritage, at some level, is metaphor and metacultural (Holtorf 2010, Kirshenblatt-Gimblett 2006: 161). Yet, in some cases, only certain metaphors are chosen as bridging devices to "carry meaning" to lay people who visit heritage sites and academics and heritage professionals who study their uses. A common metaphor of heritage is the tree—that which is rooted, grows, and transmits knowledge or cultural meaning. Especially in recent interventionist notions of heritage, such as in UNESCO's idea that "the cultural heritage of each is the cultural heritage of all" (UNESCO 1994), the concept's arborescent tendencies speak to the idea of heritage acting as a tree for all humanity and all cultures. While this is a noble idea that bridges with contemporary human rights and intercultural movements, such as The Universal Declaration of Human Rights (adopted in 1948), it is also one that is at odds, ironically, with the tenets of cultural diversity and cultural relativism (Kirshenblatt-Gimblett 2006: 186).

As an alternative to the tree, we may consider reconstituting and remaking conceptually heritage as a rhizome—that subterranean plant which contrasts with the tree for its sprouting, haphazard, and random growth patterns. The rhizome challenges the arborescent metaphor of heritage and its notion of descent (Russell 2010: 34–35,

Kirshenblatt-Gimblett 2006: 170) by suggesting, in its place, a much more "middle," in-between, and connected framing—a focus on alliance, as opposed to filiation (Deleuze and Guattari 1987: 25). In this sense, heritage becomes a connector of things, people, and places, not a final resting place.

HERITAGE AS RETROSPECTION

In the United States, a curious sort of mock heritage plaque has begun to appear in numerous small-town restaurants, attractions, and storefronts. The seemingly innocuous "On This Site in 1897 Nothing Happened" signs, which have been designed with typefaces, patina, and other stylizations to appear old and historic, remind us of the perplexing heritage implications of the current era. Many viewers of these signs often react with the presumably intended response that is implied with such jokes, but there is a much deeper and more interesting analysis that we may undertake. These signs remind us of the monumental, overbearing, and didactic implications of the constructions of heritage. As we analyze the (existential) weight of heritage, we should ask the framing question, *to what extent is heritage retrospective?* How does it reflect the past and how might its focus be reframed?

Heritage has been said to be a type of "cultural production in the present that has recourse to the past" (Kirshenblatt-Gimblett 1998: 149), and most significant in this definition, surprisingly, is the implication of "recourse." As we ruminate on the retrospective "pastness" (Holtorf 2013) of heritage, we may be inclined to focus on its recourse in terms of the meanings of "return" and "back," yet we may begin to see, particularly in light of remaking, the greater significance of the meanings of "retreat" and "course." Whether the faux-historic patina of an Irish pub, a blue historical plaque proclaiming the significance of a site, or an "On This Site in 1897 Nothing Happened" sign, we are confronted continually with the pressures of the past as a return to something that is familiar, even nostalgic.

The Denver International Airport, like the other spaces in this writing, offers a surprising connection to heritage, as well as to its retrospective tendencies. Denver's airport has had considerable notoriety (Figure 2.5.2). There are nascent conspiracy theories related to the airport's never-realized baggage transport system—and the space that it occupies being part of a big government conspiracy—and related interpretations of the many art pieces in the airport. Apocalyptic murals, gargoyle sculptures, and a mustang horse sculpture dubbed "Blucifer" (which actually fell on and killed the artist who created it) are among the many aesthetic and symbolic trappings that have led some to suggest a peculiar conspiratorial symbolic order at the airport (Wenzel 2016). Theories of the New World Order have also been offered in regards to the place's main "heritage" feature—Michael Singer's unnamed installation that resembles Incan and Mayan ruins, as well as Japanese gardens. Singer's project, which is worthy of its own aesthetic analysis, is one of a small but growing number of heritage experiments being undertaken

FIGURE 2.5.2. Concourse C, Denver International Airport, Michael Singer Studio.

Photo by Scott A. Lukas.

by artists. Such projects have the frame of a "culturematic" or a device that represents a playful remaking of or experimenting with culture (McCracken 2012). Heritage remakes, not unlike filmic versions, imply a duplicitous meeting of past and present, of previous and future versions.

What makes Singer's project remarkable in a pedagogical sense is the fact that one could, on first glance, accept the ruins as being some sort of reconstructed, or even transplanted, project of an archaeological sort. Yet, on closer inspection, one notes surfaces, traces, and patina of the past, not an actual chronology of it. There is retro-spection in terms of looking back on an imagined past, but, more importantly, there is acknowledgment of an ominous future as the ruins lie near the retrofuturism of the airport's airplane exhibits and the terminal monorail. With the ruins we are reminded of Harrison's view that "heritage is primarily *not* about the *past*, but instead about our relationship with the *present* and the *future*" (Harrison 2013: 4). Singer's ruins are retro-spective in the traditional modality of heritage, yet only for the purpose of forcing us to think about the implications of our often obsessive and uncritical reflection on what has come before us.

Another recent experiment with heritage is found at the Staten Island Ferry Disaster Memorial Monument. The project, designed by the visual artist Joe Reginella, imagines the loss of the ferry *Cornelius G. Kolff* as a result of a giant octopus attack. The disaster, which is expressed in a cast-bronze sculpture of an octopus devouring a ferry, never happened—a fact lost on the many visitors who frequent the monument at Battery Park in Manhattan. Accompanying the monument is an extensive fake Web site, mockumentary, and announcements for a non-existent Staten Island Ferry Disaster Memorial Museum. The extensive nature of Reginella's joke is reminiscent of the Museum of Jurassic Technology in Culver City, California (a museum that blurs the line between fact and fiction). Like the museum, the Staten Island Ferry Disaster Memorial Monument asks visitors to consider critically the nature of reality, re-presentation, and memorialization before their eyes.

As we ruminate on both of these projects and their connections to reminiscence, we identify the metaphor that governs this historical side of heritage in the battery—the common device of storage that involves accumulation and then dissemination. Heritage, in returning to its "ancestral" meaning, is something passed down to us—"of timeless values and unbroken lineages" (Smith 2006: 48, quoting Graham et al.)—and, thus, it is worthy of our attention. In its retrospective gaze, heritage is meant to be perceived though not interrogated, appreciated though not considered critically. Ultimately, the presence of the past within heritage often "denies historical process, and radiates only historical surfaces." (Walsh 1992: 182).

As we consider reworking this metaphor, we may imagine, in its place, the Rube Goldberg machine. Not unlike the Staten Island Ferry Disaster Memorial Museum, the Rube Goldberg machine might be appreciated only through a comedic register. Reframing this device, we may interpret a more critical register—one suggesting the realm of the fantastic, improvised, and impractical. In reframing heritage through the Rube Goldberg machine, we jettison not its preoccupation with the past but its tendencies to value an uncritical and unexamined past. The impractical side of the Rube Goldberg machine (its circuitous route to accomplishing a task) may be interpreted as an opportunity for more clear and critical rumination on the past. As such machines, both Michael Singer's ruins and Reginella's monument joke remind us that the retrospective glances of heritage are not so much illegitimate as they are incomplete, unaware of the full potential that "looking back" may have.

THE SERVICE OF HERITAGE

In the small resort town of Incline Village, California, is the curious O. M. Henrikson Poplar Trees Mall (Figure 2.5.3). The mall was built in the 1960s by the eccentric Libertarian figure Oliver Henrikson who, in the 1950s, imagined a resort motel that might accompany the 1960 Winter Olympics that were held in the nearby Squaw Valley, California. Over time, Henrikson modified his plans for a motel and instead began a different project—a multi-tenant shopping mall. As such, his project was nothing remarkable. Yet, as he worked to imagine his vision in a material sense, he eschewed traditional design practices and worked in the style of a *bricoleur*, assembling what he could

FIGURE 2.5.3. O. M. Henrikson Poplar Trees Mall.

Photo by Scott A. Lukas.

with materials available. Henrikson added unapproved and illegal structures to the site, including an indoor swimming pool, much to the chagrin of local commissioners who battled the builder in court and in the realm of public opinion.

The mall is nothing short of a construction palimpsest—mismatched beams, odd juxtapositions of colors, layers of repurposed building materials, blocked passageways, and construction shortcuts (many of which are nothing short of hazardous). The mall relates to other such spaces that have an eccentric approach to design and use and that rely on a handmade, *bricolage* approach to construction—Robber's Roost Ranch in Inyokern, California; Juan Pollo's Route 66 Museum in San Bernardino, California; Tio's Tacos in Riverside, California; Dr. Evermor's Forevertron in Sumpter, Wisconsin; and Haw Par Villa in Singapore. As of 2017, many years since the passing of Henrikson, the mall sits in inheritance limbo. Many locals look at the mall, which has become even more dilapidated over the years, as an eyesore—a place that contrasts greatly with other European-themed properties down the street. There have been only a few members of the local community who have argued for the designation of the mall with a landmark, historic, or exceptional status. In the public debate about the property in the local newspaper, one such person expressed that the mall and its architecture was worthy of official historical designation as a heritage site, to which many others expressed strong negative reaction (Siig 2012).

Presumably, unless more locals express the rather subversive sentiment that the Poplar Trees Mall—due to its relationship to the Olympics, its eccentric local builder, and the uniqueness of the design and construction choices—is worthy of preservation, the mall will be razed to make way for a much cleaner mixed-use site (full of chain and branded stores, that will, no doubt, lack authenticity and heritage). The fate of the mall reminds of another key orienting question for the study: *should heritage save?* And, if so, what should it save and how?

In speaking of the "service" of heritage a typical expression is that a given site in question is to be revered—a monument, in a metaphorical sense. In the case of certain sites that are already been imbued with the status of the monument, such as the Buddhas of Bamiyan, we are told that the damage to or loss of the said "monument" is of detriment to specific cultures, if not humanity as a whole. The monument, especially as it is deployed in political senses, illustrates its etymological meaning of "something that reminds." Thus, preservation or conservation efforts exhibit significance in the material sense of maintaining the site-in-question's essence as well as its "being" or the non-material and ideological traces of it.

The very popular tourist attraction, Bodie, near Bridgeport, California, offers one of the most interesting reflections of heritage, particularly as it suggests an alternative to traditional conservation and preservation efforts reflected in the monument. Since its having been acquired by the California Department of Parks and Recreation, a process of "arrested decay" has been implemented. In short, the process focuses on "[keeping the town] exactly as it was when the final residents moved away . . . the interiors remain just as they were, furniture and other objects left in place . . . no improvements or alterations are made" (Walser 2015). Like other sites that have a heavy focus on interpretation and storytelling, Bodie offers visitors a look at life as it once was, though the experience is told through the buildings and material culture themselves, devoid of technological or other contemporary means of re-telling. As the years pass, Bodie's buildings wear, and with only minor efforts to preserve the structures, the effect of the town's re-presentation of a heritage past is one of freezing time. As well, the unique efforts at Bodie remind of DeSilvey's concept of curated decay, a "mov[ement] away from the rigidity of preservation and conservation to change and transformation" (DeSilvey 2017: 132), to the uncanny and subversive realms of remaking.

Bodie's alternative preservation recalls the point that heritage reflects consensus—the public's interest in a place, a declaration of the things deemed important to keep for future generations (Clark 2001: 7, Houston 2012: 107). The declaration of Bodie's significance as a place to be saved, even in its arrested decay sense, contrasts with the lack of similar sensibility in terms of Henrikson's Poplar Trees Mall. On the surface, it would appear that the "service" of heritage is not universal, and to recall the often forceful metaphor of the monument, we may discover a more curious figure of the souvenir. This form, whose meaning suggests a "coming to mind" and (from *sub*) "up from below" (Online Etymology Dictionary). As a subterranean form, the souvenir recalls traces of previous places, things, and intangible contexts, yet it displaces the urge to attribute absolutism to the entities that it references. As a metaphor, it reminds of the power of remaking to confront our deepest existential desires.

HERITAGE AND HUMAN RIGHTS

In March 2001, the Buddhas of Bamiyan—the giant fifth-century statues located in central Afghanistan—were destroyed by the Taliban. The action, which included no less than dynamite and rocket launchers, was condemned almost universally. At the time, the United States was engaged in a war whose impetus was the September 11 terrorist attacks. For many, the Buddhas and their destruction came to represent the brutality of fundamentalist terrorism *and* the loss of valuable historical and heritage culture. Yet, the curious question in this case of the threat against heritage was whose heritage was being threatened? Afghani locals, Buddhists, or citizens of the world? More globally, we are left asking, *for whom or what does heritage exist?*

The Buddhas, as they are situated within the complex geopolitical contexts of September 11, remind us of the didactic metaphor of heritage as a lecture. While few would debate the destruction of the fifth-century sculptures as anything but a heritage and cultural crime, their use as icons in the larger political debates about the Taliban, terrorism, and the changing order of the post–Cold War world suggest that heritage is never an innocent party to larger political, cultural, and representational issues that are typically attributed to other realms of culture, such as religion and politics. The decision to use the Buddhas in a symbolical manner reflects the use value of heritage in the didactic sense of redeploying historically significant places or objects as new political vessels. The Buddhas remind us that heritage can very easily enter the fray over the geopolitical contexts of the contemporary world.

In contrast with the metaphor of the lecture, which implies a monovocal and hierarchical foundation, we may apply the replacement metaphor of dialogue. The meaning of dialogue implies conversation and, more importantly, the idea of movement "across," such that the conversation at hand involves covering as much space, time, and context as possible. In this sense, we are reminded of the power of the middle voice—that figure which, in contrast with the active and passive voices, suggests that the speaker is a part of, not above or against, the context at hand—as well as Actor Network Theory (ANT), which suggests a similar constitutive approach to the contexts at hand. Applied to the world of heritage, we may begin to imagine new polyvocal ways of engaging with the tangible or intangible worlds around us (Harrison 2013: 216).

HERITAGE IN THE ANTHROPOCENE

In 2006, the Svalbard Global Seed Vault broke ground in a rural part of Norway. Called by some the "doomsday seed vault," the goal of the facility is to preserve the world's biodiversity. It currently holds nearly one million botanical seeds, and has a capacity of five million. The 2016 removal of gene bank seeds in Aleppo, Syria illustrates the core principles of the vault in terms of its preservation efforts. In 2017, near the location of the seed vault, a second space known as the Arctic World Archive was built. The archive has been dubbed the "doomsday library" for its promise to house (and protect forever) any and all data or information that is provided to Piql, the company that has initiated this Library of Alexandria for a new time. The operators of the archive store data on a type of photosensitive film that has been deemed impervious to the elements, essentially an indestructible storage form.

The loss of the world's biodiversity that is imagined in and acted upon at the seed vault reminds of the significant epoch of the Anthropocene. The Anthropocene—or the geologic epoch in which humans have dramatically and negatively impacted the Earth, its environments, and biodiversity—has, more and more, begun to define our understandings of all forms of heritage. The Anthropocene necessitates a final question in terms of heritage: *What will become of heritage and us as a result of it?*

In its many metaphorical formations, whether tree, battery, monument, or lecture, heritage has always implied a certain level of missionary zeal. A final metaphor that continues such tendency is that of the library or archive. Both the Svalbard Global Seed Vault and the World Data Archive suggest a literal figuration of this metaphor. In these two examples, we are presented with projects that aim to deal with the vast uncertainty of the future—what many social scientists have referred to as the perils of "risk society" (Beck 1992). Both the vault and the archive store and preserve forms of heritage— whether natural or intangible—for future generations. Yet, more significantly in the context of the Anthropocene, both imagine the possibility of a post-apocalyptic future in which, presumably, no or very few humans will be around to grow the crops from the seeds in the vault or read the data sources in the archive. While in today's turbulent and uncertain world such archives seem natural and beneficial to humanity, we might re-frame them for one final replacement metaphor of the open source community.

The open source metaphor extends the previous focus on dialogue to the realm of public, civic participation. Unlike a library or archive, which tends to store and protect, the open source movement is characterized by its commitments to democracy, sharing, repurposing, and, to also recall the previous replacement metaphor, dialogue. Open source, as it extends the dialogue beyond non-human actors (as Harrison has called for in his notion of "connectivity ontologies," 2015: 27) and to other species, ecosystems, and contexts beyond the human world will, no doubt, open up possibilities for the fu-ture framing—and remaking—of heritage. While we may never agree on exactly what constitutes heritage, we may begin to see that framing heritage in such a way that it promotes a deeper understanding of its construction may be a necessity.

This chapter has argued for a new perspective on heritage, one that is informed by the contexts of remaking. It began with a rumination on the restoration of Castle of Matrera as a reflection on the challenging politics of the "truth" of heritage. While her-itage often connotes meanings of "inheritance," we learned that the concept has much broader and more political implications than we may have imagined. Heritage may in-clude both official and unofficial demarcations of places, sites, and cultural activities. The first of five considerations of heritage asked the question, what is heritage? In this context, the writing focused on the transformation of heritage from a metaphor of a tree to that of a rhizome. The next focus addressed the question of heritage and retrospection. The metaphor of the battery was contrasted with that of the Rube Goldberg machine. Consideration then shifted to the question of whether heritage should be deployed to save certain places, things, or cultural constructions. The metaphor of the monument was considered as was the replacement metaphor of the souvenir. The next segment on heritage and human rights asked, for whom or what does heritage exist? The lecture, in which heritage is passed down to people, was contrasted with the metaphor of dialogue, in which it was argued that heritage could be remade as a more collaborative entity or process. Finally, the writing concluded on Heritage in the Anthropocene, asking the question, what will become of heritage and us as a result of it? The metaphor of the library or archive, specifically in reference to the Svalbard Global Seed Vault and the World Data Archive, was discussed in relationship to the open source metaphor, which suggested a reframing of heritage as something more accessible to the public.

References

Ashley, Susan L. T., and Sybille Frank. 2016. "Introduction: Heritage-Outside-In." *International Journal of Heritage Studies* 22(7): 501–503.

Beck, Ulrich. 1992. *Risk Society: Towards a New Modernity*. London: Sage.

Clark, Kate. 2001. "Preserving What Matters: Value-Led Planning for Cultural Heritage Sites." Conservation, the CGI Newsletter 16(3): 5–12.

Deleuze, Gilles, and Félix Guattari. 1987. *A Thousand Plateaus: Capitalism and Schizophrenia*. Minneapolis: University of Minnesota Press.

DeSilvey, Caitlin. 2017. *Curated Decay: Heritage Beyond Saving*. Minneapolis: University of Minnesota Press.

Harrison, Rodney. 2013. *Heritage: Critical Approaches*. London: Routledge.

Harrison, Rodney. 2015. "Beyond 'Natural' and 'Cultural' Heritage: Toward an Ontological Politics of Heritage in the Age of Anthropocene." *Heritage and Society* 18(1): 24–42.

Holtorf, Cornelius. 2010. "Heritage Values in Contemporary Popular Culture," in *Heritage Values in Contemporary Society*, ed. George S. Smith, Phyllis Mauch Messenger, and Hilary A. Soderland. Walnut Creek, CA: Left Coast Press, 43–54.

Holtorf, Cornelius. 2013. "On Pastness: A Reconsideration of Materiality in Archaeological Object Authenticity." *Anthropological Quarterly* 86(2): 427–444.

Houston, Donna. 2012. "Junk into Urban Heritage: The Neon Boneyard, Las Vegas." *Cultural Geographies* 20(1): 103–111.

Jones, Sam. 2016. "'What the Hell Have They Done?' Spanish Castle Restoration Mocked." *The Guardian*, March 9.

Kirshenblatt-Gimblett, Barbara. 1998. *Destination Culture: Tourism, Museums, and Heritage*. Berkeley: University of California Press.

Kirshenblatt-Gimblett, Barbara. 2006. "World Heritage and Cultural Economics," in *Museum Frictions: Public Cultures/Global Transformations*, ed. Ivan Karp et al. Durham: Duke University Press, 161–202.

Lowenthal, David. 1998. *The Heritage Crusade and the Spoils of History*. Cambridge: Cambridge University Press.

McCracken, Grant. 2012. *Culturematic*. Boston: Harvard Business Review Press.

Online Etymology Dictionary. <http://www.etymonline.com/index.php?term=heritage>.

Russell, Ian. 2010. "Heritages, Identities, and Roots: A Critique of Arborescent Models of Heritage and Identity," in *Heritage Values in Contemporary Society*, ed. George S. Smith, Phyllis Mauch Messenger, and Hilary A. Soderland. Walnut Creek, CA: Left Coast Press, 29–41.

Siig, Melissa. 2012. "The Key to the City." *Moonshine Ink*, August 10.

Smith, Laurajane. 2006. *Uses of Heritage*. London: Routledge.

UNESCO. 1994. "Information Note: Nara Document on Authenticity." <http://whc.unesco.org/archive/nara94.htm>.

Walser, Lauren. 2015. "Preserving Decay: Exploring the Ghost Town of Bodie, California." National Trust for Historic Preservation. <https://savingplaces.org/stories/preserving-decay-exploring-the-ghost-town-of-bodie-california#.WPrbY1dWKmM>.

Walsh, Kevin. 1992. *The Representation of the Past: Museums and Heritage in the Post-Modern World*. London: Routledge.

Wenzel, John. "The Definitive Guide to Denver International Airport's Biggest Conspiracy Theories." *The Denver Post*, October 31.

......

CULTURALLY REFLEXIVE STEWARDSHIP

Conserving Ways of Life

......

ROBERT H. WINTHROP

INTRODUCTION

......

THIS chapter is concerned with caring for place, the interweaving of community, landscape, and social memory. It is intended as a cross-disciplinary communiqué from a cultural anthropologist to colleagues specializing in heritage conservation and interpretation. From an anthropological perspective the sites and landscapes that are the concern of heritage research and practice are special cases of a far broader human capacity to transform physical *space* into inhabited *place* (Tuan 1977). The emphasis here is on this wider domain of social life, in a sense building on the principles recognized in the ICOMOS Charter for the Interpretation and Presentation of Cultural Heritage Sites (ICOMOS 2008), which acknowledged the role of living communities in interpreting the meaning and considering the authenticity of sites and landscapes.

Two objectives shape the direction of this chapter, the first theoretical, the second practical. First, I emphasize approaches that can clarify the nature of the connections binding community and place, treating these as elements of *coupled human and natural systems*. From this perspective, {humans—communities—social organization} and {nature—landscape—environment} are given equal analytic weight, and through their mutual influence constitute a single system, considered at a variety of spatial and temporal scales (Liu et al. 2007: 639). Second, I examine how the ties of community and place can foster actions intended to conserve a way of life—the shared experience of living in a certain manner, in a certain place—making local agency a matter of practical as well as theoretical concern.

Here is an example. In southeastern Oregon in the mid-1980s the US Department of Energy undertook an environmental cleanup of radioactive mill tailings, a legacy of uranium mining and milling. This required collecting, transporting, and storing over 700,000 tons of radioactive waste.[1] One of the storage sites under final consideration lay at the base of a mountain holding significant associations for a Northern Paiute Indian community. Voicing strong opposition, the tribal government stated in a letter to the Energy Department: "It was at these sites (Drake Peak, Hart Mountain, and Steens Mountain) that members of the aboriginal Northern Paiute Bands sought communion with the Ancient Power. And it is at these same sites, like the Drake Peak area, that now, centuries later, Gidutikad people continue to seek spiritual help" (in Winthrop 1990: 129). As one elder said to me:

> MR. WASHOE: We pray to the mountain. We pray when we drink the water that comes off the mountain. That's our God. Everything on the mountain. [...]
> WINTHROP: You said that Drake Peak was sacred. Is that right ... there's spirits there?
> MR. WASHOE: Yeah, that's the old Indians. They never leave. They're over there now. All the dead Indians. Their spirits are still there.
>
> (Winthrop 1990: 129)

What follows is organized in three parts. First, I consider two resource regimes which reflect fundamentally different ways of understanding the relation between people, place, and meaning. One is based on a logic of tradeoffs and markets, the other on a logic of stewardship. Second, I present the key characteristics of culturally reflexive stewardship (CRS) as a specific expression of stewardship ethics, consider its relationship to social organization, and offer examples of CRS in three modes, which I term "living in place," "conservation and recovery," and "polarization and protest." Third, I consider the implications of these arguments for theory and practice.

THE LOGIC OF STEWARDSHIP

There are multiple ways to organize the control and use of land. In the logic of tradeoffs, the world of environmental goods is vast, but nothing is unique or irreplaceable. Markets for land and resources are based on this principle. In 1953 Disneyland was built on 160 acres of former orange and walnut orchards in Anaheim, California.[2] Disneyland quickly became one of the world's most popular amusement parks—in 2015 the park welcomed over 18 million visitors.[3] These 18 million visitors—or more correctly, the money these 18 million visitors paid annually to be entertained—define the value of Disneyland, vastly exceeding the value of the orchards it replaced.

In contrast, the value of America's Civil War battlefield at Gettysburg has a very different basis: historical events and their shared symbolism in American life. As Mark Sagoff noted of Gettysburg, "to say that the nation has a duty to pay homage to those from whom it received the last full measure of devotion is to state a moral fact," not to report an economic preference (Sagoff 2004: 39). Americans recognize the value of Gettysburg primarily as *citizens*, just as Buddhists recognize Sarnath and Jews recognize

Jerusalem as members of those religious communities. Over a million visitors travel to Gettysburg each year.[4] Yet if the number of visitors were reduced to zero, Gettysburg would retain its value in American life. Here a conventional economic account of value is irrelevant.

Anonymity, alienability, and fungibility are key attributes in the logic of tradeoffs, particularly as elaborated through neoclassical economic analysis (Pritchard, Folke, and Gunderson 2000: 38). In contrast, for the Northern Paiute community contesting the siting of radioactive waste, or for Americans respecting the sacrifice commemorated at Gettysburg, none of these attributes apply. Rather than anonymity, the social identity of those asserting the value of place and heritage is fundamental. Rather than alienability, long-term responsibility for a place or landscape is both a virtue and an obligation. Rather than fungibility, such places and landscapes have unique significance for particular families, communities, or even nations. In the words of an old advertising slogan, they "accept no substitute."

This contrast can be developed further by considering *resource regimes*, the rules and institutional structures that shape the control and management of land and resources, including rights of access, use, and sale (Vatn 2005: 252–257). The problem of identifying which regime best fits a particular set of circumstances can be examined along three dimensions (after Vatn 2005: 419–422). A first dimension concerns the *aims* of managing a resource: whether this involves an individual logic maximizing personal advantage, or a social—cooperative logic seeking a collective benefit. A second dimension involves the form of *interaction and choice*: whether this is technical—instrumental, involving explicit criteria (how to maximize return on investment), or deliberative, weighing matters of symbolic and ethical complexity (applying broad cultural principles to determine action in specific circumstances). A third dimension involves the *nature of the good* being managed: whether private (a single-family home) or some variant of shared or public good (commonly held pasture).

The conditions of individual rationality, instrumental choice, and private goods define the logic of tradeoffs—the world of markets. In contrast, the conditions of social rationality, deliberative choice, and shared, common-pool, or public goods are consistent with the logic of stewardship. Yet while this analysis defines a space for stewardship within a typology of resource regimes, it does not capture the subjective experience of the Paiutes' concern for Drake's Peak, or many Americans' reverence for Gettysburg. Understanding these aspects requires another perspective.

CULTURALLY REFLEXIVE STEWARDSHIP

For Aboriginal communities of Australia, the English word *country* refers to:

> the traditional habitat of a particular group ... but implies not only geographic territory but human interaction with it. *Country* is more than dirt and rock; it is alive, it is part of interaction, it has its myths and songs and traditions that are proper to it and necessary

to its continued health. It is humanized landscape. . . . Ownership of country is complex but strict and elaborately worked out; it entails a firm requirement for the owners to manage the landscape as well as they can to maintain productivity . . . Country is crossed by countless tracks ("songlines") of mythic and historic creators. These tracks were well known, as were the stories associated with them, which often included detailed recommendations about the treatment and management of particular areas.

(Anderson 2014: 99)

If stewardship as commonly understood involves "the careful and responsible management of something entrusted to one's care" (Barrett 1996: 11), the Aboriginal notion of *country* involves a far more specific sense of relationship and care, a more specific linking of human and natural systems. Nor is the Aboriginal example unique. While the specifics of place, belief, and moral obligation vary, the depth and intensity of this relationship are found in societies around the world. As Keith Basso notes in his masterful ethnography of Western Apache cultural landscapes, "Apaches view the landscape as a repository of distilled wisdom, a stern but benevolent keeper of tradition, an ever-vigilant ally in the efforts of individuals and whole communities to maintain a set of standards for social living" (Basso 2007: 62–63).

The type of "caring for place" reflected in these examples I term *culturally reflexive stewardship* (CRS).[5] As a working definition, CRS involves *actions to sustain a way of life, motivated by a shared appreciation of place, landscape, and region, and expressed through practices that transmit cultural knowledge and affirm a social identity.*[6] Place, landscape, and the narratives that describe them are affective and compelling: affective in carrying strong emotional content and compelling in exerting moral obligation. These qualities derive in part from the "forest of symbols" that grows from the linkage of human ideas about the world with their tangible qualities, joining ideological and sensory aspects of environmental experience, and expressed with particular intensity through ritual (Turner 1967: 29–30).

In many societies, water offers such a symbol, linking personal experience to landscape. Among American Indian communities of the arid Columbia Plateau (US Pacific Northwest), water can be a "medicine," possessing healing properties when gathered from streams at particular elevations in a mountain environment. Traditional meals in these communities still begin with a sip of water and an exclamation of thanks: in the Sahaptin language, *čuuš* ("water!"). In the hierarchy of native environmental values on the Columbia Plateau, water is "primordial and ultimate" (Schuster 1975: 436).

WHOSE LAND—WHOSE KNOWLEDGE?

Thus far stewardship has been examined without considering the social systems that shape attachment to places and landscapes. Communities are seldom if ever fully consistent in cultural outlook or unified in solidarity (McCay 2001). Multiple groups may value the same landscape, or at least the same environment. As migration, conflict, conquest, and displacement are recurring themes of history, it follows that there are few tracts of land claimed or revered by only a single group. In the case of the San Pedro River watershed in southeast Arizona, at least four tribes have ties to this landscape: Hopi, Zuni, Tohono O'odham, and Western Apache, each using this "in the construction of contemporary social identity and in the retention and transmission of historical knowledge" (Ferguson and Colwell-Chanthaphonh 2006: 27).

Indigenous and non-indigenous groups may encounter the same landscape in quite different ways. Crater Lake, in the southern Oregon Cascades, is a volcanic caldera important for Klamath and several other American Indian tribes of the region. Primarily it was a place of power and peril, renowned as a spirit quest site, but also feared for the dangerous beings residing in the lake, described in a number of Klamath myths. First encountered by Anglo travelers in the 1850s, Crater Lake admirably met their desire for a sublime and inspiring experience of nature. One visitor wrote, "It is at once weird, fascinating, enchanting, repellent, of exquisite beauty and at times terrifying in its ... oppressing stillness" (Winthrop 1997: 7). Both American Indians and Euro-Americans recognized the alien and numinous in this ancient caldera. Unlike the Indian visitors to Crater Lake, Euro-Americans lacked the cultural models—the cognitive templates encompassing myths, rituals, and knowledge of local spirit beings—which allow such encounters to yield a message, to produce lasting understanding and personal change.

An example from New Zealand illustrates the ways in which expressions of stewardship can be shaped by both political and ethnic differences. In *Calling the Station Home* Michele Dominy provides a vivid account of sheep pastoralism in the High Country of New Zealand's South Island. These sheep farmers are New Zealanders of European descent, leasing Crown lands. As such their identity is framed by a double contrast: as Europeans in contrast to native Maoris who contest their rights to leases in the High Country; and as ranchers in contrast to environmental advocates who wish the High Country to be managed for aesthetic and ecological values, freed from productive human uses. For many contemporary *pakeha* (non-Maori) New Zealanders, social identity is in flux as they, along with indigenous Pacific peoples, "are simultaneously exploring what it means to have a Pacific identity" (Dominy 2001: 27). This is evident in a statement by one of the sheep farmers profiled in *Calling the Station Home*: "After 25 years working in the back country as a shepherd and then after a lucky break, as a lessee, I still look every day with a feeling of awe on the mountains, the rivers and the bush that make up our high country lands. My hope is that this awe, felt no doubt by many men and women, will transcend so called cultural differences and unite us, so we will go into the next decade as one, with the best management of our fragile resources as a collective goal" (Dominy 2001: 221).

STEWARDSHIP OUTCOMES

CRS is manifested in a variety of ways, reflecting the degree of social and political polarization, and the presence or absence of forced environmental change. I consider these under three somewhat arbitrary categories: living in place, conservation and recovery, and polarization and protest.

Living in Place

Writing of Appalachian communities in rural Virginia, Melinda Wagner comments, "Here land is social space. . . . [it] is identified with the people who have lived there; the land is given meaning by the human activities that have happened and are happening on it" (Wagner 2002: 125). Conversations that touch on locations and directions refer to named geological features or local landmarks with cultural resonance, not state or county road numbers. Even in giving directions to strangers, a reference to "John's road" is more likely than "Route 624" (Wagner 2002: 125).

The undramatic, everyday quality of this Appalachian example suggests why stewardship as "living in place" is widespread, important, and yet easily overlooked. As Yi-Fu Tuan observed regarding a sense of *homeland*, "Attachment of a deep though subconscious sort may come simply with familiarity and ease, with the assurance of nurture and security, with the memory of sounds and smells, of communal activities and homely pleasures accumulated over time" (Tuan 1977: 159).

Conservation and Recovery

Stewardship is more obvious in cases of deliberate efforts to conserve local knowledge and practices. Many American Indian tribes sponsor culture camps for young people to provide an organized way to share traditional knowledge, impart skills, and provide language instruction. The Sault Ste. Marie Tribe of Chippewa Indians in northern Michigan offers a range of programs throughout the year at the Mary Murray Cultural Camp, including "camps for winter survival, sugar bush, lodge teachings and smoked fish; workshops to make moccasin, baskets and moose hide mittens; and field trips such as sweetgrass, birch bark, and medicine picking."[7] In Sand Point, Alaska, in the Aleutian Islands, the Qagan Tayagungin Tribe sponsors an annual culture camp for kindergarten through twelfth grades. Classes include basket weaving, net mending, Aleut dance, and preparing tradition foods.[8]

Community-based environmental monitoring can also serve to enhance awareness and appreciation of a local environment. Potential benefits include increased scientific literacy, social capital, and citizen participation in environmental management (Conrad and Hilchey 2011: 279–281), all of which can support stewardship. Keeping Track is an environmental nonprofit operating primarily in Vermont and New Hampshire, which trains citizens to observe and inventory wildlife, particularly wide-ranging mammals such as black bears and bobcats. The aim is to provide data to support local and regional plans to maintain or enhance species habitat (Mitchell and Diamant 2001: 221–223).

Bioregionalism offers a program for cultural/ecological conservation and recovery through a commitment to place, at the scale of biogeographical regions and watersheds. As the poet Gary Snyder wrote, bioregionalism "calls us to see our country in ... its whole natural history before the net of political jurisdictions was cast over it" (in Lockyer and Veteto 2013: 9). Ozark bioregionalism provides an interesting example because of the merging of traditional ecological knowledge and practices with contemporary economic and environmental concerns, the multiplicity of practical activities established, and the explicit contrast between unsustainable urban living and what is perceived to be a more responsible and sustainable rural way of life.

As an intentional movement, Ozark bioregionalism dates to the 1970s, as back-to-the-land ex-urbanites sought a simpler, more ecologically sustainable life. Traditional Ozark communities are characterized by simple living, innovation, and a reliance on local resources and ecological knowledge. Contemporary Ozark homesteaders sought to adopt these traits by choice (Campbell 2013: 59). Here CRS is manifested through a range of practical actions. These include regional organizing (the Ozark Area Community Congress), an entity promoting responsible waste management (the National Water Center), a research station (the New Life Farm), the Ozark Regional Land Trust, the Ozark Organic Growers Association, and a community loan fund (Financing Ozarks Rural Growth & Economy) (Campbell 2013: 67–72).

Polarization and Protest

The ties of CRS can prompt political as well as legal opposition to imposed environmental change. Where more conventional responses prove ineffective, demonstrations and civil disobedience may follow.

Pollution in North America's Great Lakes prompted two Canadian Anishinaabe women elders to lead "Water Walks" to raise awareness. Beginning with a walk around Lake Superior in 2003, the Water Walks had by 2017 included all of the Great Lakes, and several other lakes and rivers, on both Canadian and US territory.[9] The walks involve an Anshinaabe water ceremony and a feast, with participating grandmothers taking turns to carry a water vessel and eagle staff (Whyte 2016: 573–574). "The goal of each walk is to raise awareness about water and to change the perception of water from that of a resource to that of a sacred entity" (McGregor 2012: 13).

Indian fishing rights in America's Pacific Northwest have been a source of legal and political controversy for more than a century. The anadromous salmon that travelled along the Columbia and other rivers of the region, including chinook, coho, sockeye, and steelhead, provided abundant and valued food for Indian communities. Moreover, fishing was a critical cultural practice. Being a skilled fisherman involved detailed knowledge of the various runs of fish, the characteristics of particular fishing sites, their mythical associations, the respect with which the fish must be treated, and the norms and values that governed sharing of the catch. By the late nineteenth century Anglo settlements blocked Indians from many traditional fishing sites. Over the

next century commercial fishing took an ever-larger share of the salmon catch, while
construction of a series of dams on the Columbia River injured or killed a sizeable
proportion of the salmon runs (Hunn and Selam 1990: 148–155). State regulations also
served to restrict Indians' rights to fish, despite the strong protections afforded by
treaties.

From the early 1940s, Indian fishermen undertook acts of civil disobedience, for
example, challenging state regulations that prohibited use of a dip net. Beginning in
the 1960s, tactics shifted from individual acts of defiance to group actions of non-
violent civil disobedience—"fish-ins"—gatherings at customary fishing sites to
fish without state licenses, courting arrest. As the name implied, the "fish-in" was
influenced by the "sit-in" of the Civil Rights movement unfolding in the American
South (Parham 2013: 11–13). Some of the acts of civil disobedience led to landmark
federal rulings in the 1970s that greatly strengthened the fishing rights of Pacific
Northwest tribes (Hunn and Selam 1990: 284–294). The combination of legal and political action across the Pacific Northwest helped affirm social identity as native peoples of the region. As Vera Parham has noted, "each counter move against protesters,
each rebuttal in the court room, embedded the expanding and multiple identities as
fishermen and fisherwomen into Pacific Northwest Native American consciousness"
(Parham 2013: 12).

IMPLICATIONS

What CRS conserves.

The specific situations linking communities and landscapes vary widely: the Northern
Paiutes sought to maintain Drake Peak as a place of spiritual power; Indian tribes of the
Pacific Northwest sought to preserve access to traditional fishing sites and practices. Yet
there is a common intention underlying these disparate actions: preserving the basis for
a way of life. The latter aim could be termed second-order cultural choice. In this sense,
first-order choice involves the ability to undertake particular practices; *second-order
choice* involves the ability to conserve the physical and cultural context within which
these practices remain meaningful. Traditions can be transmitted to the extent that they
can be enacted (Winthrop 2002: 165–173).

Linking communities and landscapes.

For western observers, the notion of landscape carries the pictorial assumptions
of European aesthetics: landscape as an attractive depiction of rural scenery. Yet
as considered here cultural landscapes are far more than vistas: they have intellectual content, reproduced through local practice and beliefs (Ferguson and Colwell-
Chanthaphonh 2006: 27). The former perspective is captured in the Anglo travelers'

reaction to Crater Lake: emotion without the cognitive dimension of cultural knowledge. For most of the communities considered here, in contrast, the affective and compelling qualities of stewardship stem from linking traditional knowledge of place and region with perception of their tangible qualities.

Contrasting logics of place.

CRS was introduced by contrasting the logic of tradeoffs and the logic of stewardship, where assumptions of individual rationality, instrumental choice, and private goods contend with an alternate perspective involving social rationality, discursive choice, and shared goods. The contrast is most apparent where dominant legal principles conflict with those of less powerful, enclaved, often indigenous groups, as with American Indian struggles to secure fishing rights. Many conflicts over claimed cultural rights stem fundamentally from disagreement over which logic should prevail. Yet it is also important to recognize that the logic of tradeoffs and the logic of stewardship may compete within a single social system. Anglo ranchers in the American West offer a notable example, many of whom pursue ranching as a way of life shaped by ties of community and landscape, rather than pursuing the more profitable uses of their land suggested by a logic of tradeoffs and markets (Sheridan 2007: 129–133).

Implications for heritage research and practice.

Place and landscape have been foundational concepts for heritage studies. I argue for considering explicitly the social systems that frame the experience and shape the value of place. I suggest further that the phenomenon of stewardship can contribute to a better understanding of the integration of human and natural systems. Translating this into the context of heritage management, where "significance" (historical, archaeological, or cultural) looms large, we should be as concerned to ask *how* sites and landscapes become significant for communities (a question of social and semiotic process) as to ask *why*. This is a multidisciplinary and transdisciplinary endeavor, to which heritage scholars have much to contribute.

The examples of stewardship considered here involve systems of knowledge about places and landscapes. Such systems are often referred to as "local," "traditional," or "indigenous" knowledge, and as such contrast with (mainstream) scientific knowledge in such fields as geology, botany, or wildlife ecology. Since the 1990s interest has grown in finding ways to integrate these disparate forms of knowledge, though such efforts are challenged by formidable epistemological and organizational barriers (Ross et al. 2011: chs 1–3). There are good reasons to seek this integration, for the two worlds of knowledge have much to offer one another. Nonetheless there is a risk in exploring the compatibility of such systems while failing to acknowledge their fundamental difference. This is the ethical dimension of much local or traditional knowledge, the affective and compelling qualities which provide the motive force for stewardship.

NOTES

1. Department of Energy, Long-term surveillance plan for the Collins Ranch Disposal Site, Lakeview, Oregon, December 1993, page 1-1. <http://www.osti.gov/scitech/servlets/purl/10112124> [accessed May 7, 2017].
2. The Construction of Disneyland. <https://www.designingdisney.com/content/construction-disneyland> [accessed April 22, 2017].
3. Most Popular Theme Parks By Attendance. <http://www.worldatlas.com/articles/most-popular-theme-parks-in-the-world.html> [accessed April 22, 2017].
4. Gettysburg—Adams Chamber of Commerce: Tourism. <http://www.gettysburg-chamber.org/business-resources/tourism> [accessed April 24, 2017].
5. For examples of CRS from American Indian communities of the Pacific Northwest, see Winthrop 2014.
6. Whether a particular form of stewardship actually promotes objectively defined conservation outcomes is a matter for investigation. This point needs emphasis, particularly when citing examples from indigenous communities, given the sometimes romanticized notions of indigenous peoples as inherently "exemplary conservationists" (Ross et al. 2011: 84–92, Smith and Wishnie 2000).
7. Sault Ste. Marie Tribe of Chippewa Indians, Mary Murray Culture Camp. <http://www.saulttribe.com/membership-services/culture/14-membership-services/culture/21-mary-murray-culture-camp> [accessed May 4, 2017].
8. The Qagan Tayagungin Tribe of Sand Point. Culture Camp. <http://www.qttribe.org/index.asp?Type=B_BASIC&SEC={FFA82E17-6631-44E6-BD6D-E9222DF73C12}> [accessed May 4, 2017].
9. A list of Water Walks is available at <http://www.motherearthwaterwalk.com/> [accessed May 5, 2017].

REFERENCES

Anderson, E. N. 2014. *Caring for Place: Ecology, Ideology, and Emotion in Traditional Landscape Management*. Walnut Creek, CA: Left Coast Press.

Barrett, Christopher B. 1996. "Fairness, Stewardship and Sustainable Development." *Ecological Economics* 19(1): 11–17.

Basso, Keith H. 2007. *Wisdom Sits in Places: Landscape and Language among the Western Apache*. Albuquerque: University of New Mexico Press.

Campbell, Brian C. 2013. "Growing an Oak: An Ethnography of Ozark Bioregionalism," in *Environmental Anthropology Engaging Ecotopia: Bioregionalism, Permaculture, and Ecovillages*, ed. Joshua Lockyer and James R. Veteto. New York and Oxford: Berghahn Books, 58–75.

Conrad, Cathy C., and Krista G. Hilchey. 2011. "A Review of Citizen Science and Community-Based Environmental Monitoring: Issues and Opportunities." *Environmental Monitoring and Assessment* 176(1): 273–291.

Dominy, Michèle D. 2001. *Calling the Station Home: Place and Identity in New Zealand's High Country*. Lanham, MD: Rowman and Littlefield.

Ferguson, T. J, and Chip Colwell-Chanthaphonh. 2006. *History Is in the Land: Multivocal Tribal Traditions in Arizona's San Pedro Valley*. Tucson: University of Arizona Press.

Hunn, Eugene S., and James Selam. 1990. *Nch'i-wána, "The Big River": Mid-Columbia Indians and Their Land*. Seattle: University of Washington Press.

International Council on Monuments and Sites. 2008. "ICOMOS Charter on the Interpretation and Presentation of Cultural Heritage Sites." <http://www.international.icomos.org/charters/interpretation_e.pdf> [accessed May 28, 2017].

Liu, Jianguo, Thomas Dietz, Stephen R. Carpenter, Carl Folke, Marina Alberti, Charles L. Redman, Stephen H. Schneider, et al. 2007. "Coupled Human and Natural Systems." *Ambio: A Journal of the Human Environment* 36(8): 639–649.

Lockyer, Joshua, and James R. Veteto. 2013. "Environmental Anthropology Engaging Ecotopia: An Introduction," in *Environmental Anthropology. Engaging Ecotopia: Bioregionalism, Permaculture, and Ecovillages*, ed. Joshua Lockyer and James R. Veteto. New York and Oxford: Berghahn Books, 1–31.

McCay, Bonnie J. 2001. "Community and the Commons: Romantic and Other Views," in *Communities and the Environment: Ethnicity, Gender, and the State in Community-Based Conservation*, ed. Arun Agrawal and Clark C. Gibson. New Brunswick, NJ: Rutgers University Press, 180–191.

McGregor, Deborah. 2012. "Traditional Knowledge: Considerations for Protecting Water in Ontario." *International Indigenous Policy Journal* 3(3).

Mitchell, Nora J., and Rolf Diamant. 2001. "Stewardship and Sustainability: Lessons from the Middle Landscape of Vermont," in *Wilderness Comes Home: Rewilding the Northeast*, ed. Christopher McGrory Klyza. Hanover: University Press of New England, 213–233.

Parham, Vera. 2013. "'It Was a Spearhead of Change'—The Fish-Ins of the Pacific Northwest and the Boldt Decision, Shifting Native American Protest Identities in the 1960s and 1970s." *Native Studies Review* 22: 1–26.

Pritchard, Lowell Jr., Carl Folke, and Lance Gunderson. 2000. "Valuation of Ecosystem Services in Institutional Context." *Ecosystems* 3(1): 36–40. DOI: 10.1007/s100210000008.

Ross, Anne, Kathleen Pickering Sherman, Jeffrey G. Snodgrass, Henry D. Delcore, and Richard Sherman. 2011. *Indigenous Peoples and the Collaborative Stewardship of Nature: Knowledge Binds and Institutional Conflicts*. Walnut Creek, CA: Left Coast Press.

Sagoff, Mark. 2004. *Price, Principle, and the Environment*. Cambridge and New York: Cambridge University Press.

Schuster, Helen H. 1975. "Yakima Indian Traditionalism: A Study in Continuity and Change." PhD thesis. Seattle: University of Washington.

Sheridan, Thomas E. 2007. "Embattled Ranchers, Endangered Species, and Urban Sprawl: The Political Ecology of the New American West." *Annual Review of Anthropology* 36: 121–138.

Smith, Eric Alden, and Mark Wishnie. 2000. "Conservation and Subsistence in Small-Scale Societies." *Annual Review of Anthropology* 29(1): 493–524.

Tuan, Yi-Fu. 1977. *Space and Place: The Perspective of Experience*. Minneapolis: University of Minnesota Press.

Turner, Victor W. 1967. *The Forest of Symbols: Aspects of Ndembu Ritual*. Ithaca, NY: Cornell University Press.

Vatn, Arild. 2005. *Institutions and the Environment*. Cheltenham: Edward Elgar.

Wagner, Melinda Bollar. 2002. "Space, Place, Land and Legacy," in *Culture, Environment, and Conservation in the Appalachian South*, ed. Benita J. Howell. Urbana and Chicago: University of Illinois Press, 121–132.

Whyte, Kyle Powys. 2016. "Indigenous Environmental Movements and the Function of Governance Institutions," in *The Oxford Handbook of Environmental Political Theory*, ed.

Teena Gabrielson, Cheryl Hall, John M. Meyer, and David Schlosberg. Oxford: Oxford University Press.

Winthrop, Robert H. 1990. "Persistent Peoples: Mechanisms of Cultural Survival in Southern Oregon and Northwestern California," in *Living with The Land: The Indians of Southwest Oregon (Symposium Proceedings)*, ed. Nan Hannon and Richard K. Olmo. Medford, OR: Southern Oregon Historical Society.

Winthrop, Robert H. 1997. "Crater Lake in Indian Tradition: Sacred Landscapes and Cultural Survival." *Nature Notes from Crater Lake* 28: 6–12.

Winthrop, Robert H. 2002. "Defining a Right to Culture, and Some Alternatives." *Cultural Dynamics* 14(2): 161–183.

Winthrop, Robert H. 2014. "The Strange Case of Cultural Services: Limits of the Ecosystem Services Paradigm." *Ecological Economics* 108: 208–214.

PART III

HERITAGE AND THE USE OF POWER

....

NEOLIBERALISM AND THE EQUIVOCATIONS OF EMPIRE

....

JIM MCGUIGAN

The [British] Empire brought blood and tears and dispossession to millions of people but it also brought roads and railways and education.

Jeremy Paxman, presenter of the BBC TV Series *Empire*, 2012

INTRODUCTION

....

WHAT has neoliberalism to do with Empire? Neoliberal thought and practice command the world today in a quasi-imperial manner, that's what. The most extensive empire of the past was the British Empire, of which there remains a contested heritage. British "liberal capitalism"—in the older term of political-economy, *laissez-faire*—was at the heart of modern imperialism. Economic exploitation and political domination supported by the Royal Navy "ruled the waves," so to speak. Britain no longer commands anything of the sort. But, "Empire" persists, if only in the mind and sustained by the concrete symbols of "heritage." Moreover, a limited recognition of past evils, which is taken for granted today, effectively inoculates against serious criticism, thereby neutralizing the memory and present-day sense of imperialism in public culture.

Michael Hardt and Antonio Negri have conjured up a postmodern conception of "Empire" to describe the imperial process today. According to them, this latter-day notion of Empire has four outstanding characteristics that differentiate it at least partly from the older sense of empire: (1) it has no boundaries; (2) it is not the result of historical conquest but the freezing of history, "fix[ing] the existing state of affairs for eternity"; (3) "the rule of Empire operates on all registers of the social order, extending down to the depths of the social world . . . the paradigmatic form of biopower"; (4) "although the practice of Empire is bathed in blood, the concept of Empire is always dedicated to peace" (Hardt and Negri 2001 [2000]: xiv–xv). Hardt and Negri's concept of Empire is extremely abstract and diffuse. Moreover, it draws too sharp a demarcation line between the curiously ethereal "Empire" of today—global, yet still dominated by the United States—and the substance of yesterday's European empires. Nevertheless, the persistence of something like imperialism in the form of the world-wide hegemony of neoliberal capitalism is suggestive of the contemporary operations of culture, power, and economy.

On the street, the most visible manifestations of imperial heritage, concrete traces from the past, are statues and monuments. Walk around Central London today, for instance, you will see many statues of Britain's imperial heroes, some of whom would otherwise be forgotten, and also monuments to imperial warfare in general, most notably the Cenotaph in Whitehall.

Yet, as well as enduring memorialization, loss of empire, in contrast, is often marked by the removal of statues and monuments. When the Bolsheviks seized power in Russia in 1917 one of their first acts was to bring down the statue of the Czar in Petrograd long before the man himself was executed. And, when Soviet Communism in turn collapsed, statues of Lenin similarly hit the dust. Perhaps the greatest monument to Eastern Europe's communist past today is the collection of statues that have been parked on the outskirts of Budapest. And, of course, one of the most famous images of recent times, circulating instantly around the world on television, was the pulling down of Saddam Hussein's statue in Baghdad's Firdos Square by the US military in 2003 on the formal conclusion to the second Gulf War.

To mark a post-colonial heritage in the British Isles now, perhaps it is time to blow up Nelson's Column in Trafalgar Square, as the IRA did with his Pillar in Dublin in 1966.

NEOLIBERALISM AND NEOCONSERVATISM

Is there a culture of neoliberalism (McGuigan 2016)? Straight away, in addressing such a question, there is a problem. Neoliberalism is not especially cultural at all. It is, first and foremost, economic, recalling the Romantic opposition between culture and commerce, but in reverse.

Neoliberalism treats the economy as a force of nature, comparable to gravity. In order to appreciate how deeply entrenched is the economic reductionism of neoliberal thought and practice, then, it is essential to compare it to and differentiate it from *neoconservativism*. Although the terms, "neoliberal" and "neoconservative," are sometimes used interchangeably and their referents are often bound up together in reality, they are not the same. Here, these two names of the game are dealt with artificially as contrasting ideal types for analytical purposes.

Neoconservatism is about conserving and defending something, probably defined in national-culture terms: "the British way of life" or "the American way . . . ," say. The late but unlamented Tory politician, Enoch Powell, was a neoconservative. In the 1960s, he famously articulated in an exemplary manner what came to be known as *cultural racism*. He wanted to protect the British way of life from the incursion of post-colonial Otherness, which was represented for him by immigrants from the Indian sub-continent. Unlike his imperial forebears, Powell did not necessarily regard Asians living in his Wolverhampton constituency in the 1960s as inferior beings to the English. Rather, he saw them as irredeemably different in a cultural sense, unwilling or unable to adapt to English customs or even, for house-bound women, to learn the language. Therefore, to use a medical metaphor, perhaps inappropriately, Asians represented contagion to Britishness. That is why Powell wanted to exclude them from Britain. Powell was also an old imperialist who, similar to many self-regarding Britons still, found it impossible to come to terms with the dissolution of the British Empire.

Samuel Huntington's (1996) much praised "clash of civilisations" thesis is similar to Powell's earlier neoconservative position in that it is also *cultural racist*, the leading mode of contemporary racism. None the less, bizarrely, it has been misrecognized in socially liberal circles by insouciant observers as somehow manifesting respect for the Other.

In the post–Second World War period, liberals and social democrats argued that Britain could no longer afford the Empire: that is, they made an economic argument for the dissolution of empire which prefigured neoliberal reasoning. This gave rise to the historical myth that the British relinquished their imperial possessions peaceably. That was not always so—or even usually the case. The collapse of the British Empire was, in fact, often a bloody affair, as epitomized by the peremptory execution of Irish rebels in 1916, the appalling Amritsar massacre of protesters in 1919, and the savage treatment of insurgents in Kenya as late as the 1950s, to mention some of the better-known instances of state-sanctioned violence. The British Empire always put down protest severely and took sadistic vengeance on troublemakers. There was, in truth, considerable military resistance to liberation movements throughout the British Empire.

Unlike neoliberal economism, neoconservatism is much more comfortable with military power and its excesses. Take, for instance, Donald Trump's presidential desire to "make America great again," not just by asserting national superiority, but by backing it up with increased military expenditure, money taken from reductions elsewhere such as in the environment budget, which is a thoroughly neoconservative thing to do, as is his economic nationalism.

Commenting on the inaugural conference for the neoliberal reaction to creeping socialism that was held in Paris in 1938, forty years later, Michel Foucault remarked that it proposed an economic model for life itself. People were to be made up more or less solely as economic actors, calculating entrepreneurs as well as sovereign consumers. Market forces and competition ruled the natural order. Everything else was epiphenomenal and, at best, secondary. As Foucault (2008 [2004]: 239) said, this (re)emerging episteme—to use one of his earlier terms—is *"[t]he application of the economic grid to social phenomena."* He went on to ask (p. 242): "What is the function of this generalization of the 'enterprise' form? . . . [I]t involves extending the economic model of supply and demand and of investment-costs-profit so as to make it a model of social relations and of existence itself, a form of relationship of the individual to himself, time, those around him, the group, and the family." The most straightforward application of neoliberal reasoning in the cultural field would be the cessation of state intervention and withdrawal of public subsidy from arts and heritage, as recommended by the highly respected American economist, Tyler Cowan (1998). The only residual role remaining for government under neoliberal conditions, reasoned Cowan, should be as a customer (perhaps by commissioning statues of neoliberal heroes and for monuments to American victims of terror?).

Although neoliberalism has, indeed, had a negative impact on public expenditure in the cultural field and foisted capitalistic rationality on public sector organizations, it goes yet further than these obvious matters by establishing a largely subterranean structure of feeling that is commensurate with capitalism today. In his original formulation of the concept, Raymond Williams (1961) argued that a structure of feeling in the most profound sense negotiates between and reconciles together more or less successfully rival and contradictory tendencies (or, "social characters," as he put it) within the society. He later refined the concept with the aid of Gramscian hegemony theory by tracing alternative, oppositional and residual processes of emergence and incorporation (Williams 1973).

Since the 1970s there has been an epochal shift away from the hegemony of organized capitalism in the West and proto-socialism in capitalist as well as communist countries across the world in the direction of free-market orthodoxy, the neoliberal order that is currently hegemonic globally.

What, then, distinguishes neoliberalism from the *laissez-faire* liberalism of the nineteenth century? Because it is agnostic or merely neutral towards culture, neoliberal political economy may coexist with social and cultural progressivism, both apparent and real. Witness the "cool" liberalism of Bill Clinton's Democratic presidency during the 1990s and, similarly, Tony Blair's New Labour governments into the 2000s. These examples illustrate a moment of contingent articulation between the political economy of neoliberalism and social and political "liberalism" in the American sense. It was a contradictory amalgam which appeared elitist and provoked, in hostile response, the right-wing populism of Trump and others in recent years. Another example of such a contradictory amalgam, though questionably progressive, was the "cool" phenomenon of Young British Art (McGuigan 2016: 63–83). This combination of extreme capitalism and apparent cultural progress may encompass, furthermore and most notably for the purpose in hand, limited recognition of, say, the past evils of British imperialism.

IMPERIALISM—THE HIGHEST STAGE OF BRITISH CAPITALISM

The British Empire originated with audacious acts of criminality, plundering booty around the Americas, endorsed by the Crown back in England. In the sixteenth and seventeenth centuries, Spain was the most advanced imperial power. Parts of South

America and the Caribbean had already been colonized by the Spanish who were attracted to the gold and silver that could be culled from these territories. "Privateers"— that is, swashbuckling pirates like Francis Drake—attacked Spanish galleons and stole their cargoes. Such activity proved even more lucrative for Drake than his earlier slave-trading. He became one of the heroes of the Elizabethan age, celebrated for circumnavigating the globe in the Golden Hind and admired for his audacity in less auspicious respects too. Drake was knighted by Queen Elizabeth the First for robbing Spanish galleons of *their* ill-gotten gains and, thus, contributing handsomely to the coffers of "perfidious Albion."

There is to this day an imposing statue of Sir Francis Drake with his hand on the globe overlooking the Hoe in Plymouth where, according to legend, he finished his game of bowls before going out to face the Spanish Armada as Vice-Admiral of the fleet in 1588. The nearby base for the Royal Navy is still named after him, "Drake Island." Playing games, especially cricket from the nineteenth century onwards, much later furnished a light-headed metaphor for what young "chaps," just out of public school (that is, expensive private school) and Oxbridge, did on their imperial adventures overseas.

When a royal charter was issued to the East India Company in 1600, the transition from outright criminality to a more or less legitimate form of economic enterprise nurtured the embryonic British Empire, particularly through the ruthless activities of Robert Clive in India during the following century. This was a commercial company dedicated to trade, not political domination in the first instance. Spices from the East and Indian textiles were the main attractions as well as sugar from the Caribbean and elsewhere. Britain, of course, could supply weapons and other manufactured goods to the colonies, increasingly so by the nineteenth century when the Company eventually morphed into the official branch of the British state in the Empire. Other imperial countries had East India companies too, such as the great rival, France, and also the more advanced imperial power, Holland. When he was invited to do so, the Protestant William of Orange seized the throne from the Roman Catholic James II in 1688, the so-called "Glorious Revolution," which was, in effect, a little remembered invasion by the Dutch. It became convenient then to combine British and Dutch commerce in the East. On the other hand, French imperial competition was dealt with militarily and, only to some extent, diplomatically in the Caribbean, Canada, and India.

In one way or another, England/Britain surpassed its rivals and cultivated overseas territories effectively, with a model of occupation pioneered by Scottish Protestant plantations in the North of Ireland. As well as providing land for hard-pressed migrants, administrative loyalty was sought from sections of indigenous populations, including leadership roles for "Nabobs," and rewarded accordingly.

Economic exploitation and commercial activity supported militarily preceded the articulation of an imperial mission to civilize "savages," which supposedly transcended the profit motive and mere domination. At the heart of Britain's do-good imperial propaganda were Christianity and ideas of Britishness, European civility, and knowledge. Colonial peoples were not thought to be necessarily inferior to Europeans but, instead, in need of guidance.

However, inhumane treatment of subjected people, especially Africans forced into slavery and transported perilously across the Atlantic to work on the sugar plantations, was criticized on the grounds of Christian decency. Lobbying by William Wilberforce and the Clapham Sect resulted in the official abolition of slavery throughout the Empire. Slaves became wage laborers and their efforts were supplemented by indentured labor from, for instance, India to the Caribbean and Mauritius.

The British anti-slavery movement was a progressive feature of missionary Christianity which also, during the nineteenth century, sought to save colonial souls from various strains of "superstitious" belief and heathenism. The civilizing process aimed to inculcate European values and modes of conduct, ideally represented by British customs. The issues at stake were often complex and multi-sided, such as over the imperial prohibition of *sati* in Bengal, the practice whereby widows were required to be burnt to death alongside the remains of their dead husbands on funeral pyres. Not all aspects, then, of the civilizing mission represented ethnocentric oppression. Some challenged cruel practices and enabled modernizing "enlightenment" in education and medicine.

Quite apart from the delusions of Britain's self-righteous civilizing project during the nineteenth century, whether good or bad, few Britons were entirely unaware of the atrocities committed in the colonies: to mention just a few, such as the famine in Ireland of the 1840s that could have been easily averted by governmental intervention ("the Irish poor were sacrificed on the altar of free trade and economic liberalism"— Newsinger 2013 [2006]: 43); and bullying China over the opium trade from India ("[t]he British Empire was the largest drug pusher the world has ever seen"—Newsinger 2013 [2006]: 56). Drug-trafficking, in fact, financed the administration of India from the 1830s until late in the century.

There was also the ferocious suppression of rebellion on the sub-continent during the 1850s, involving torture and sadistic execution. Indian nationalist revolt was misnamed "the Indian Mutiny" and exemplified by the horror story of "the black hole of Calcutta" where colonists were incarcerated. British violence was overlooked and the "savagery" of colonial subjects exaggerated in gory detail during outbreaks of conflict. All of which continued into the twentieth century.

The killing of the absurd General Gordon of Khartoum in 1885 by Sudanese warriors, which became a popular tableau at Madame Tussaud's waxworks on Baker Street, was avenged immediately by killing the insurgent leader, the Mahdi himself and, much later, by Kitchener's troops slaughtering Dervishes at Omdurman in 1898, witnessed disapprovingly by the young journalist, Winston Churchill. As Niall Ferguson (2004 [2003]: 272) has remarked, "The lesson of Omdurman seemed to be the old and unambiguous one that no one challenged British power with impunity."

It was only in the second half of the nineteenth century that "scientific racism" was formulated in order to legitimize British supremacy over colonial subjects. Francis Galton's flawed psychology in close association with the bowdlerization of his uncle, Charles Darwin's evolutionary theory—Social Darwinism—seemed to provide a scientific justification for imperialism. In the words of Herbert Spencer, "the survival of the fittest," usually attributed wrongly to Darwin himself, made white Britons feel naturally superior to subordinate peoples. British imperial propaganda reached a high pitch of hysteria towards the end of the century, no doubt due to anxiety over the looming prospect of being matched and eventually surpassed by Germany and the United States. The largest empire, manufacturing, and trading economy in the capitalist world was not secure for long in its global pre-eminence.

Prime Minister Benjamin Disraeli had made Queen Victoria the Empress of India in 1876, which was followed by a series of festivals—including the Golden Jubilee of 1897—that served as ostentatious displays of the British Empire well into the next century. This was a period of immense popular imperialism in Britain, traces of which are still felt in the working and middle classes. Such popularity, no doubt, was due to real material though unequally distributed benefits deriving from the empire for most Britons. Imperialism was stirred up further by adventure stories in magazines and novels as well as by jingoistic song in the music halls and classical music in concert halls. Moreover, the general public were said to be hungry for news about events such as "the relief of Mafeking," especially if relatives were involved, during the war with the Boers of Dutch origin in the Transvaal.

The Boers were eventually defeated and the Union of South African territories was accomplished. The unification had been long sought and maneuvered by the most controversial British imperialist, Cecil Rhodes. Yet, due to insufficient immigration from the United Kingdom, the Boers remained in *de facto* power. Harking back to the heroism of Empire at its height and the manly virtues learned "out there," the Boy Scout movement was founded by the old imperial warrior, Robert Baden Powell, in the early twentieth century.

The greatest propagandist for the British Empire and, indeed, the idea of Empire itself was the writer Rudyard Kipling, born in Bombay in 1865, and brought up on the South coast of England from the age of six, returning to India subsequently in his late teens as a journalist. His literary writing, which included verse and fiction, for children and adults, met with great acclaim not only at home but also abroad. His famous *Jungle Book* set in India was especially popular, not only in Britain. Although he was a dedicated right-winger in politics, Kipling's writing was admired by the German communist, Bertolt Brecht. He became a multimillionaire from his literary earnings, which was unusual for a poet even at the turn of the nineteenth and twentieth century. Kipling was also the first Briton to be awarded the Nobel Prize for Literature.

Kipling's famous poem, "The White Man's Burden" (1899), is normally read as representing British imperialism's sense of responsibility towards subordinate races in the colonies. However, the poem was actually written to encourage the United States to colonize the Philippines. As a recent biographer, David Gilmour (2003 [2002]: 125), has remarked: "The Americans had stopped regarding British imperialists as robbers and hypocrites. They were taking up the same tasks themselves and in consequence some of them received highly patronizing advice from a man who claimed to know all about it."

"The White Man's Burden" of 1899 was originally subtitled "The United States and the Philippine Islands." Here is its first stanza:

> Take up the White Man's burden—
> Send forth the best ye breed—
> Go bind your son's to exile
> To serve your captives' needs;
> To wait in heavy harness
> On fluttered folk and wild—
> Your new-caught, sullen peoples,
> Half devil and half child.
>
> (Kipling 2013: 92)

After reading such words, it is difficult to understand the typical English commentator's enduring ambivalence towards Kipling, the "Yes, but" attitude, acknowledging the arrogant racism but still expressing admiration for him. Curiously, such ambivalence was encouraged by George Orwell, a critic of imperialism and of Kipling's own "jingoism and brutality," which he regarded as "morally insensitive and aesthetically disgusting" (2000: 204). Yet Orwell disagreed with the unqualified hostility towards him of "the middle-class Left" (2000: 206). In his famous essay on the author of "The White Man's Burden," Orwell praised Kipling's English patriotism, sincerity, and popular appeal "as a good bad poet" (2000: 215). Kipling's only son died in the First World War, which may explain why he became heavily involved in the Commonwealth War Graves Commission and the erection of monuments to the war dead.

Probably the most controversial figure in the history of British imperialism was Cecil Rhodes. As a precocious teenager like Kipling, he went not to India to write but to South Africa to make his fortune at the age of seventeen in 1871, at first by cultivating cotton. Very quickly cotton was abandoned and Rhodes switched to diamond mining at Kimberley. Simultaneous to making a fortune, during his early years, Rhodes returned to England periodically to pick up a degree at Oriel College, Oxford. The South African undertaking was financed by the Rothschilds bank. This arrangement resulted in the establishment of the De Beers mining and diamond company in 1888 with Rhodes as chairperson.

When Rhodes first went to South Africa, it was a tapestry of different territories mainly ruled by Africans. He settled in Cape Colony and entered politics, becoming Prime Minister in 1890. Although he may not have gone to Africa with racist opinions, Rhodes became increasingly prejudiced and discriminating with the passage of time. For instance, he was responsible for withdrawing the franchise from black Africans in the Cape, thereby effectively laying the foundations for apartheid in the future Republic of South Africa. He also developed an ambitious plan for the expansion of the British Empire stretching from North to South in Africa, from Cairo to the Cape.

Rhodes's later pronouncements in speeches and writings eventually fired up racism and pride in the expanding Empire among the British population, the great majority of whom had never set foot in the overseas possessions. He was a white supremacist of a distinctly Social-Darwinian persuasion: "Whites have clearly come out top . . . in the struggle for existence and achieved the highest standard of human perfection. Within the white race, English-speaking man, whether British, American, Australian or South African, has proved himself to be the most likely instrument of the Divine Plan to spread Justice, Liberty and Peace . . . over the widest possible area of the planet" (Rhodes, quoted by Thomas, 1996: 114). Although he was himself an Atheist, Rhodes asserted that the white man's colonization of the Earth was to "God's purpose." He tricked and outmaneuvered chiefs throughout southern Africa in order to grab territory and create a huge country named after himself, Rhodesia (now Zaire and Zimbabwe), and South Africa itself. In such expansionist operations he was normally supported by the British government and feted in Britain for his bold imperialism. However, annexing the Boer territory of Transvaal with its valuable deposits of gold proved more difficult for Rhodes to accomplish in the short run.

Rhodes was obliged to resign his premiership in the Cape on the ignominious failure of his associate, Storm Jameson's Raid on Paul Kruger's Transvaal. Kipling's poem *If*, which, according to a recent poll, is the most popular English poem, was written in honour of Jameson—"If you can keep your head when all about you are losing theirs and blaming it on you . . . You'll be a Man, my son!" It was not until the century had turned that the British prevailed over the Boers and eventually united South Africa under the Crown. The effective strategy was to attack and burn down the farmsteads of the Boers. Women and children were corralled into concentration camps, a fact which Hitler was always eager to mention.

Even at the height of his power and influence in Africa there were suspicions over Rhodes's devious methods and general skulduggery. In spite of anti-imperialist criticism, he was determined, however, to leave behind a lasting legacy to himself. His legacy included statues and monuments, the country of Rhodesia, and especially the prestigious Rhodes Scholarships to the University of Oxford, which were supposed to create a freemasonry of Rhodesians.

A statue was also erected at the front of his old college, Oriel, in Oxford. Students have campaigned in recent years to have the statue removed from the college but to no avail. Cecil Rhodes's statue at Oriel College is now protected by a metal wire mesh. There have been similar but more successful campaigns in the South of Africa to remove statues and other monuments to Rhodes.

YES, BUT—(MIS)REMEMBERING EMPIRE

During the post–Second World War period and throughout the decolonization process that accumulated in the 1950s and '60s, but began with India and Pakistan in 1947

FIGURE 3.1.1. Rhodes bestrides Oxford, at Oriel College on the High Street.

Photo by J. McGuigan, March 2017.

and continued up to the 1980s, it became increasingly implausible to project a positive image of Britain's commanding role overseas in the past and to encourage nostalgia for its imperial way of life. In 1972, the BBC television series *The British Empire* interrogated the past record of imposition and atrocity to the chagrin of the corporation's management and political apologists for empire in parliament. There was plenty of scope for criticizing what many in Britain would have preferred to forget. Since then, though, critical denunciation of the British Empire has become comparatively muted in mainstream culture with the possible exception of satire, though not in the academic preserve of Post-Colonial Studies. Preference for public forgetfulness is brought up short, however, by the sometimes thoroughly inappropriate presence of concrete monuments to imperial heritage in our midst, particularly statues to the fallen heroes of Empire like Cecil Rhodes.

However, there is emerging a much less damning indictment for the British Empire of old. This reappraisal bears a corresponding relation to nineteenth-century imperial pride that *neoliberalism* does to *liberalism*. Although neoliberalism signals a return to certain aspects of the nineteenth century's "liberal" political economy—most notably, "free trade" capitalism rather than "fair trade"; selfish individualism instead of generous cooperation; "private affluence and public squalor," as J. K. Galbraith (1970 [1958]) put it; tolerance of astonishingly high levels of inequality throughout the world and within countries—to mention just a few of the acid refluxes. It is now impossible to ignore or tacitly approve of exploitation and oppression in the global Empire by denying the evil record of European imperialism yet, at the same time, it is acceptable to recall its good points. Thus, the neoliberal order is legitimized by *the inoculation effect*, as Roland Barthes put it in his classic essay, "Myth Today": "One immunizes the content of the collective imagination by means of a small inoculation of acknowledged evil; one thus protects it against a generalized subversion. This *liberal* treatment would not have been possible only a hundred years ago" (1972 [1957]: 150). So, in 2015, the Conservative Prime Minister of Britain, David Cameron, witnessed the unveiling of Mahatma Ghandi's statue in Westminster's Parliament Square across from Cameron's great hero and the Mahatma's most implacable enemy, Winston Churchill. Nelson Mandela had also found a place in Parliament Square in 2007 under New Labour.

On a less symbolic but equally argumentative note, consider, for instance, the Scottish economic historian, Niall Ferguson's (2004 [2003]) book and Channel Four television series: *Empire—How Britain Made the Modern World*. Ferguson is a more than competent historian and a very good writer. He is also dedicatedly neoliberal in his economics and political views. With regard to the pros and cons of imperialism, he says, "It is nowadays quite conventional to think that, on balance, it was bad. Probably the main reason for the Empire's fall into disrepute was its involvement in the Atlantic slave trade" (xi–xii). Yet, having said that, Ferguson (2004 [2003]: xxii) goes on blithely to stress the main point of the work in hand: "[N]o organization in history has done more to promote the free movement of goods, capital and labour than the British Empire in the nineteenth and early twentieth centuries. And no organization has done more to impose Western norms of law, order and governance around the world." And, he then says:

> [T]he legacy of Empire is not just "racism, racial discrimination, xenophobia and related intolerance"—which in any case existed long before colonialism—but
>
> – the triumph of capitalism as the optimal system of economic organization;
> – the Anglicization of North America and Australasia;
> – the internationalization of the English language;
> – the enduring influence of the Protestant version of Christianity;
>
> and above all-the survival of parliamentary institutions, which far worse empires were poised to extinguish in the 1940s. (xxvii)

Yes, but by what right does public heritage in Britain, at the same time, continue to celebrate the shameful history of Empire as exemplified by the well-protected statue of Cecil Rhodes at the University of Oxford?

Indian writer, Sashi Tharoor, author of *Inglorious Empire* (2016a), whilst noting the prevalence of a neoliberal discourse on imperialism today, exemplified here by Ferguson's sophisticated reasoning, has objected strenuously to such a "reasonable" whitewashing of history:

> Many modern apologists for British colonial rule in India no longer contest the basic facts of imperial exploitation and plunder, rapacity and loot, which are too deeply documented to be challengeable. Instead they offer a counterargument: granted, the British took what they could for 200 years, but didn't they also leave behind a great deal of lasting benefit? In particular, political unity and democracy, the rule of law, railways, English education, even tea and cricket . . . The process of colonial rule in India meant economic exploitation and ruin to millions, the destruction of thriving industries, the systematic denial of opportunities to compete, the elimination of indigenous institutions of governance, the transformation of lifestyles and patterns of living that had flourished since time immemorial.
>
> (Tharoor 2016b: 7, 9)

The memorialization of Empire raises difficult issues for the management of heritage today. Winston Churchill, for instance, is remembered fondly because he led Britain successfully in the war against Nazi Germany yet earlier in the twentieth century, as Home Secretary, he had called upon troops to be prepared to shoot striking workers at Tonypandy in Wales if necessary and he sent the "Black'n'Tan" mercenaries into Ireland to put down nationalist rebels; and later, as Prime Minister during the Second World War, he denounced Ghandi, his companion statue now in Parliament Square, in racist terms when the Mahatma was leading the Indian campaign for independence. How do you square that circle?

REFERENCES

Barthes, Roland. 1973 [1957]. "Myth Today," in his *Mythologies*. London: Paladin, 109–159.

Ferguson, Niall. 2004 [2003]. *Empire—How Britain Made the Modern World*. London: Penguin.

Foucault, M. 2008 [2004]. *The Birth of Biopolitics—Lectures in the College de France 1978–79*. Trans. G. Burchill. London: Palgrave Macmillan.

Galbraith, John Kenneth. 1970 [1958]. *The Affluent Society*. Harmondsworth: Penguin.

Gilmour, David. 2003 [2002]. *The Long Recessional: The Imperial Life of Rudyard Kipling*. London: Pimlico.

Hardt, Michael, and Antonio Negri. 2001 [2000]. *Empire*. Cambridge, MA: Harvard University Press.

Huntington, Samuel. 1996. *The Clash of Civilizations and the Remaking of World Order*. New York: Simon and Schuster.

Kipling, Rudyard. 2013. *The White Man's Poet*. Ostara Publications.

McGuigan, Jim. 2016. *Neoliberal Culture*. London: Palgrave Macmillan.

Newsinger, J. 2013 [2006]. *The Blood Never Dried: A People's History of the British Empire*. London: Bookmarks.

Orwell, G. 2000. "Rudyard Kipling," in *George Orwell's Essays*. London: Penguin, 203–215.

Tharoor, Shashi. 2016a. *Inglorious Empire: What the British Did to India*. London: Hurst and Company.

Tharoor, Shashi. 2016b. "A Legacy of Ruin and Exploitation." *Guardian* 2, March 9: 7–9.

Thomas, Anthony. 1996. *Rhodes: The Race for Africa*. London: BBC Books.

Williams, Raymond. 1961. *The Long Revolution*. London: Chatto and Windus.

Williams, Raymond. 1973. "Base and Superstructure in Marxist Cultural Theory," in *New Left Review* 82. Reprinted in McGuigan, ed., 2014, *Raymond Williams on Culture and Society*. London: Sage, 119–138.

....

PUBLIC HERITAGE AND THE PROMISE OF THE DIGITAL

....

JENNY KIDD

OUR encounters with cultural heritage have become increasingly multimodal, collaborative, and mediatized. They are also nomadic: shifting online, offline, and collapsing the spaces in between. How digital media are impacting our understandings of heritage, and how those understandings in turn intersect with the public realm, are questions of considerable interest. Margarita Díaz-Andreu asserts that "the digital revolution has . . . affected the way in which the interaction between heritage and the public takes place" (2017: 404–405). It is certainly the case that heritage "making" is a thing made hyper-visible by digital media, open to constant and continuous negotiation, potentially against a backdrop of global scrutiny.

The "promise" of the digital has been a democratization of the very notion of heritage, and a disruption of ideas about ownership, authorship, and authenticity that might have seemed more straightforward in the recent past. This has consequently raised searching questions about cultural value: how it is ascribed, on what basis, and by whom (Adair et al. 2011). These developments have received significant attention and some scrutiny in scholarly debates (in, for example, Giaccardi 2012, Drotner and Schrøder 2013, Kidd 2014, Ridge 2014). Much has been made of the role of the digital in overturning our long-established "authorised heritage discourse" (Smith 2006), in safeguarding intangible heritages including those in minority languages (Antonaci et al. 2013, Hubin et al. 2013), and in curating previously hidden or marginalized histories (Kidd et al. 2014). "Open" versus "closed" heritage practices have also been brought sharply into focus in debates about the affordances of different hardware and software "solutions" (Owens 2016).

Alongside the argument that digital media might democratize cultural heritage is the related assumption that such media might also aid heritage institutions in their ongoing attempts to remain relevant. As Gertraud Koch notes "cultural heritage can only remain a living part of cultural practice as long as it can incorporate social and technological change and thus remain contemporary" (Koch 2013: 169). There is a seductive logic underpinning claims that young people in particular might respond positively to digital manifestations of heritage, or that reaching them might be only a matter of tapping into the latest social media platform, seeking them out and engaging with them *where they already are*.

Joel Taylor and Laura Kate Gibson have however identified a "notable reluctance" to critique digital practices ostensibly designed with democratization in mind (2016: 408). Their own incredibly valuable intervention in the literature explores a disconnect "between increased access and increased democracy" (2016: 409) which although established within communications studies, does seem to have been overlooked in the heritage discourse. They raise valuable questions about the extent to which digital media in and of themselves can be expected to facilitate more and better democratization of heritage.

Following Barbara J. Little (2009: 30) in her taxonomy of approaches to public archaeology, I would like to suggest that digital heritage intersects with notions of "the public" in four distinct ways. Firstly, digital heritage work can be funded by the public, for example through state support, the work of research councils, or directly via crowdfunding initiatives. Secondly, such work often happens as part of outreach and education initiatives bringing heritage into commune with communities variously defined, in digital storytelling workshops and through online games for example. Thirdly, there is digital heritage work designed to "solve societal problems," such as that done under the auspices of European Union–funded schemes. And lastly, there is the not insignificant work carried out by non-professionals through, for example, citizen science and citizen humanities initiatives. This is then a complex picture, with many and much invested at the points where notions of heritage, the public, and the digital intersect.

This contribution appraises and problematizes the logics which often bolster talk about digital media's potential to radically alter the grounds upon which heritage is (co)produced and circulated. It will highlight a range of ethical dimensions to those debates, dimensions which are often sidelined or revealed only through close scrutiny at the interstices of heritage studies with other disciplines, such as media and communications studies or the digital humanities. There has been some attempt to bring this more reflexive agenda to scholarship on heritage and digital media, but it has thus far been somewhat limited (see for example Marstine 2011, Fouseki and Vacharopoulou 2013, Holdgaard and Klastrup 2014, Hartley 2015, Pantalony 2016, Kidd and Cardiff 2017).

In this chapter I will explore the promises and challenges of three practices currently being positioned as game-changers in the pursuit of a more authentically public conceptualization of heritage. These are: the turn toward social media, crowd-based methods more broadly, and immersive mobile encounters. Although the particular projects and platforms referenced here may well prove to be ephemeral, the questions raised will be with us for some time to come, and the critiques themselves will likely become amplified.

Social Media

Social media communications provide much in the way of promise for a more open and dynamic understanding of heritage, offering scope for dialogue, sharing, and play-fulness in our negotiation of the past (Kelly 2013, Giaccardi 2012, Parry 2011). Such networks are seen to represent a shift from a broadcast or "transmission" model of com-munications by heritage institutions, to a networked communication model, one that is purported to be less hierarchical and exclusionary (Drotner and Schrøder 2013). This has led to great claims about the prospects of social media for more and better public heritage: "Social media starts by offering a way to 'widen the audience,' 'reach new constituencies' but it ends by changing heritage and by asking everyone to participate in its construction, encouraging openness not closure of interpretation and valuation, making flux, uncertainty and doubt critical" (Fairclough 2012: xvi–xvii). Social network sites—for example Facebook, Instagram, and Twitter—are no doubt intriguing in light of these claims. Critically, given the interests of this volume, such platforms operate on a basis of openness as a default, privileging the public over the private as core to their business models. They foreground sharing, conversation, and debate, lowering barriers to enter into those debates, and offering the potential for impressive reach and a diver-sity of voices. They also allow users to upload their own content and to respond in real time to real world events and stimuli. All of the time, of course, they are also making "visible the museum's networks of social relations" (Sánchez Laws 2015: 6) in ways that might be institutionally compelling, and which seem to offer a rebalancing of power. At face value, the capacity of such platforms to "change heritage" might seem self-evident.

There are a great number of heritage institutions being recognized for their work within social media spaces,[1] especially noteworthy given the incredible competition for attention that is now a given within such environments, and the sobering assessment of Henry Jenkins et al. that "if it doesn't spread it's dead" (2013). The popularity of projects such as Culture 24's VanGoYourself attest to the spreadability of forms of user-created content and playful remix[2]. The award-winning VanGoYourself platform offers users the opportunity to produce and circulate their own re-creations of paintings, including those of the "masters," with a view to "get[ting] inside them and discover[ing] art in a whole new way" (Culture 24 nd). Sharable content is the holy grail of digital communi-cations and promotions, as evidenced also in the wildly popular #MuseumSelfie initi-ative. It is events like the #AskACurator day held annually in September that we might also look to in order to assess the capacities of social media to open up understandings of and interest in heritage. #AskACurator has become a global event premised on the idea that digital provides a platform for genuine exchanges between those with different kinds and levels of expertise, both amateur and professional museum and heritage "makers."

However research into uses of social media sites within heritage organizations has offered mixed readings of their capacity to enable *more* and/or *better* democratic exchanges around, or in the production of, heritage content. I have found in my own research (Kidd 2011, 2014) that uses of social media by museums (for example) are often shallow and dominated by marketing and brand messaging. Taylor and Gibson have found that where interactions do happen in social media spaces, they tend to be focused on pre-selected subject matters which leave little room for people to "[define] their heritage according to their own values" (2016: 10). Ana Luisa Sánchez Laws too has studied participation, sustainability, trust, diversity, and questions about representation as they map onto museums' social media presence, and cautions that "[s]ome assumptions about the potential of social media to foster broader public engagement and participation (and to therefore be always beneficial to museums, regardless of their type) need to be examined" (Sánchez Laws 2015: 3).

There has been an assumption that "the more people can be actively involved in discussion, debate and consensus-building, the more legitimate the insights" (Albert 2013: 6), yet this idea of legitimacy is a slippery one. Who gets to decide what the measure of legitimacy is? What is the relationship between "more people" and better insight? And is consensus always practicable and desirable? Vincent Miller (2008: 399) has posited that communication within social network sites tends toward "phatic" small talk rather than meaningful conversation or debate, and there have been more troubling assessments of the level and tone of discussions in recent years (deemed especially problematic within the Twittersphere (Kidd 2015)).

There are issues too about the kinds of infrastructures and permissions that have become normative within these environments, and questions about platform politics and uses of data that heritage institutions and researchers may not be attuned to. Social design is at the core of these platforms (White et al. 2013: 390), but it has its limitations. Perennial problems around access mean that reach within such spaces is multiply skewed, and any understanding of community likely flawed (Baym 2010: 74). In addition, the sharing of content turns networking into cultural capital which largely accrues to heritage institutions rather than individuals, or economic capital which accrues to the owners of the platforms which underpin the projects. Savvy users may be unwilling to enter into interactions on those bases.

When evaluating projects that have involved the use of social media, heritage institutions and organizations need to think about the measures for success that have become normative. Reach is only one measure, assessed by quantitative means, and may of course not be the best one in the final analysis. It says nothing about the depth or quality of interactions from either the user perspective, or that of the institution. Sánchez Laws (2015: 6) proposes that we need to do much more in order "to understand when, how and why these activities may have a positive, neutral or negative result," for their impacts might be ambiguous at best. This raises also the specter of intentionality and motivation for the program in the first instance, and how considered and well-articulated that is.

There are then problems with the premise that social media *per se* are a viable route to more public negotiations of heritage. But what might be said about seemingly more involved direct appeals to "the crowd" to problem solve with and alongside heritage institutions? The next section will explore this thematic in more detail.

CROWD-BASED METHODS

Since the mid-2000s we have witnessed an explosion in rhetoric about the capacities of digital media to leverage the "wisdom of crowds" (Surowieki 2004) and to make use of our "cognitive surplus" (Shirky 2010). The discourse speaks of participation, community, and empowerment, and is thus also incredibly seductive for heritage practitioners keen to democratize the stories they work with. Underpinning these developments is an assumption that the involvement of "citizens" in heritage work will render it in some way more genuinely public, and that the kinds of knowledge produced and circulated as a result will be more representative and authentic. Such outcomes are however never inevitable.

"Crowdsourcing" for example has been defined as "inviting members of the public, often referred to as "the crowd," to tag and classify, transcribe, organize, and otherwise add value to digital cultural heritage collection content" (Owens 2013: 121). Such approaches are often used as part of citizen science and citizen humanities initiatives about which there is an emerging literature (see for example Dobreva et al. 2014, Carletti et al. 2013, Ridge 2013, 2014). These are projects that—whether situated within University research programs, or the Education Departments of museums and heritage sites—are touted as opening up knowledge production.

There are many examples of citizen science programs that could be cited here but I shall briefly focus on the offers from two institutions. The Natural History Museum in London has no fewer than five science projects live as of May 2017 which encourage "citizens" to get involved in activities varying from exploring the distribution of seaweed around the United Kingdom as part of the "Big Seaweed Search," to transcribing microscopic slide labels for the "Miniature Lives Magnified" initiative.[3] According to the museum these projects "invite you [the citizen] to actively contribute to our science research" (Natural History Museum nd), making the data richer, and more comprehensive than is practicable otherwise without major project investment. Similarly, the Australian Museum has no fewer than six current projects, including "Australasian Fishes" which sees "citizens" uploading and identifying their own observations of marine life, and "Solar-powered Ibis" which calls upon people to keep their eyes open for birds with wing tags and to email the project if they happen to see any[4]. In terms of citizen humanities projects, there are again many options for people to get involved; on the Smithsonian website people can head to the transcription center to become a "digital volunteer" (Smithsonian nd), "History Unfolded" encourages citizens to work with the United States Holocaust Memorial Museum, searching online local news archives for articles and submitting them to the online database[5], and "annoTATE" asks people to help transcribe documents from the Tate collection of artists' diaries and letters.[6]

But there are challenges associated with these approaches also, and as noted above, ethical dimensions that we are only beginning to consider. One of the major concerns with the crowdsourcing approach has been around assessment of the labor involved;

why "outsource" that work to members of your community rather than pay somebody to do it? Is it exploitative? Does it *under*value and even *de*value the work involved? Why do people participate in the numbers that they do? What in fact is being traded? There are broader debates about digital labor happening across the disciplines (Terranova 2000, van Dijck 2012, Fuchs and Sevignani 2013, Owens 2013, Fuchs 2014), and the case for how and why heritage crowdsourcing might be considered exempt from those criticisms has yet to be adequately argued.

As with the consideration of social media above, there are also questions about access, sustainability, and trust that emerge within this kind of work. Just who is this crowd that heritage organizations are appealing to? And who does it exclude (and it always excludes somebody)? We know that there continue to be inequalities in digital access along the lines of age, geography, ethnicity, disability, and education (for example), so how might these be overcome? How we create interfaces that enable and encourage participation in such initiatives is the subject of ongoing exploration, but perhaps not enough reflection. We might also note potential issues around how to manage peoples' expectations of what being involved in a project means, and their sense of what might happen to the associated outputs, including the extent to which their contribution is likely to influence the way that particular subject matter will be worked with and articulated in the future.

IMMERSIVE MOBILE ENCOUNTERS

Another area of exploration is the increased number of immersive mobile encounters that are available for visitors and users to interact with. As Sánchez Laws notes, there are many heritage organizations "experimenting with hybrid physical–digital combinations enabled by mobile technologies," a fact that demonstrates that the "shape of online narratives continues to evolve" (Sánchez Laws 2015: 2). There are of course a multitude of mobile applications (apps) which serve a wayfinding and interpretive function on-site at museums and heritage sites, and those have been the subject of quite some reflection in the literature (Lagoudi and Sexton 2010, Cromartie 2012, Robson et al. 2016), but here I wish to focus on more intriguing and (perhaps) ambiguous apps that encourage atypical interactions between members of the public and the heritages on offer.

One emergent format for such encounters is the "subtle mob," which has been trialed by both the Museum of London ("A Hollow Body")[7] and Amgueddfa Cymru—National Museum Wales ("Traces"/"Olion") in recent years.[8] Whereas *flash* mobs are noisy, hyper-visible interventions in public spaces, *subtle* mobs are quite the opposite. They are quieter, slower, more considered, and invisible to the onlooker. They are designed to make participants respond to and view their environments, or the "stage," in new ways, and they are expressly performative.

"Traces" for example ("Olion" in the Welsh language version) is an attempt to create a digital heritage encounter via a mobile application that changes peoples' relationship

with the space of the St Fagans National History Museum. Rather than a faithful interpretation of the site which might overlay the existing interpretation, the experience is
conceived instead as an artistic narrative composition *inspired by* the site. "Traces" was
created in partnership with a street gaming company (yello brick), and is designed to
be game-like, story-like, and interpretation-*lite*. But this raises questions also about the
ways in which "truth" and "fact" might be being negotiated, and to what extent their disruption might be consequential. At a time when heritage institutions are trusted by the
general public (in the global North at least) more than media or government sources, is
it the right time to foreground playfulness, or to engender a more questioning and critical approach in citizens toward the truth-claims that such institutions have made and
continue to make?

Other formats raise fewer such questions, and are notable in their attempts to
offer a plurality of perspectives that might otherwise be missing from a heritage encounter. The Holocaust Memorial mobile app for Miami Beach[9], the 9/11 Memorial
Guide app[10], or the Slavery at Monticello app for example all allow access to stories in
different voices. The last of these, Slavery at Monticello, is an app created by the Thomas
Jefferson Foundation for use at the Monticello World Heritage Site, a former plantation
and home to the Jefferson family[11]. The app introduces stories of slavery through multiple perspectives and promises that "Once you hear their stories you will never forget
them . . . this app presents a small piece of their story." The app presents mixed-media
insights into seventeen peoples' stories, including those of James Hubbard "A Runaway"
slave, Sally Hemings "Domestic Servant and Devoted Mother," and Thomas Jefferson
"American President, Slave Owner." The app seeks to present an insight into "The
Messiness of History" via a rich and immersive mediascape that people can navigate on
their own terms.

Such projects produce or curate what might be termed "multimodal" digital heritage
encounters; they utilize multiple modalities including sounds, smells, gestures, but also
spatial resources and other inputs from the environment. Sarah Kenderdine has noted
the multimodal "real" in her analysis of embodiment in digital heritage encounters: "embodiment is multisensory and results from effects of visual, auditory, tactile, olfactory,
and gustatory cues. Embodiment is entanglement through, and with, context and environment" (2016: 29; see also Hanna Schraffenberger and Edwin van der Heide). These
approaches demonstrate institutions starting to think more carefully and creatively
about how they can encourage symbiosis between space and content, interactions which
enable new kinds of experience or knowledge to emerge, and which implicate the user
in the experience. They show an understanding of the environment as a "sense-scape"
(Young 2007 quoted in Kenderdine 2016), an accumulation of unique spatial and historical elements that can themselves be significant resources. They work beyond traditional
conceptions of "visitor" and "visiting" which have been exploded in recent years, and
they seek to embrace increased fluidity between digital and physical, online and offline,
hoping to create frictionless hybrid encounters.

But there are challenges here also, and a re-emergence of questions about accessibility,
usability, and platform politics. Sustainability is also a concern, especially given the not

insignificant amounts of money set aside for such initiatives. The ongoing frustration with mobile applications is of course getting people to download them in the first instance, and they can be fiendishly difficult things to evaluate also (Groppel-Wegener 2011). Indeed, evaluating digital heritage projects generally is often an area of quite considerable unease for those who are involved at the sharp end of project delivery and reporting.

Conclusion

The above attests to the creativity and excitement that is a facet of our current explorations in using digital for the benefit of public heritage variously defined. What it also demonstrates however is the need for reflexivity and care as key components of professional practice in this area. If those fail there is a real risk that the very public[s] heritage institutions actively court within the digital mediascape will be misunderstood and (ultimately) ill-served. There is a tendency to see the digital as a way of opening up access, democratizing heritage and broadening its scope, but these things are never inevitable, and need to be subject to honest and repeated appraisal. Taylor and Gibson diagnose this problem acutely when they note that "[m]obilising people to engage with heritage is valuable and interesting, but the role of digitization and social media in the democratization of heritage needs to be better understood. Understanding the implications, particularly unintended, that come from digitising or digital engagement becomes increasingly important" (Taylor and Gibson 2016: 417). Their reference here to unintended implications is a reminder that heritage organizations need to gain a better grasp of questions around platform politics, privacy, data misuse, and how all of these things intersect with questions about power. As Pickover has said, "digitisation and digital interaction with heritage today cannot be seen as a 'neutral' activity divorced from the entangled power relations of our past" (Pickover 2014 in Taylor and Gibson 2017: 409).

Elsewhere I have argued that recognizing these issues is akin to a new professional literacy for those who work in, through, and with digital heritage (Kidd 2018). This needs to involve scrutiny of practice along a number of evaluative criteria; Why digital public heritage? Which public(s) are represented? Whose measures of success are being privileged and what do they amount to? How have choices about formats, platforms, framing, moderation, and institutional voice impacted the kinds of engagement and/or "democracy" that are possible? Only close and considered reflexivity *with* those publics, and perhaps also with those who are excluded, will offer insight into whether the promises of digital public heritage have been met, or are achievable. We do our communities no service at all if we skate over these issues, and are instead in danger of replicating the problematics of past heritage practices that the very process of becoming digital was supposed to overturn.

NOTES

1. See for example those recognized by the annual Museums and the Web GLAMI awards, <http://mw2016.museumsandtheweb.com/glami-winners/>.
2. <http://vangoyourself.com/>.
3. <http://www.nhm.ac.uk/take-part/citizen-science.html>.
4. <https://australianmuseum.net.au/australian-museum-centre-for-citizen-science>.
5. <https://newspapers.ushmm.org/>.
6. <https://anno.tate.org.uk/#!/>.
7. <http://www.ahollowbody.com/>.
8. <https://museum.wales/stfagans/whatson/traces/>.
9. <http://holocaustmemorialmiamibeach.org/learn/a_brand_new_experience/>.
10. <https://www.911memorial.org/guide>.
11. <https://www.monticello.org/site/visit/download-free-slavery-monticello-app>.

REFERENCES

Adair, Bill, Benjamin Filene, and Laura Koloski. 2011. *Letting Go? Sharing Historical Authority in a User-generated World*. Philadelphia: The Pew Center for Arts and Heritage.

Albert, Marie-Theres. 2013. "Introduction," in *Understanding Heritage*, ed. Marie Theres Albert, Roland Bernecker, and Britta Rudolff. Berlin and Boston: de Gruyter, 169–181.

Antonaci, Alessandra, Paolo Bravi, Lutzu Dagnino, Francesca Maria Marco, Michela Ott, Sebastiano Pilosu, and Francesca Pozzi. 2013. "Digital Technology and Transmission of Intangible Cultural Heritage: The Case of Cantu a Tenore." Digital Heritage International Congress Proceedings, 11.

Baym, Nancy K. 2010. *Personal Connection in the Digital Age*. Cambridge, MA: Polity Press.

Carletti, Laura, Derek McAuley, Dominic Price, Gabriella Giannachi, and Steve Benford. 2013. "Digital Humanities and Crowdsourcing: An Exploration," in *Museums and the Web 2013*, ed. Nancy Proctor and Rich Cherry. Silver Spring, MD: Museums and the Web.

Cromartie, Nicole. 2012. "ArtClix Mobile App at the High Museum of Art." <http://www.museumsandtheweb.com/mw2012/papers/artclix_mobile_app_at_the_high_museum_of_art.html> [accessed May 19, 2017].

Culture24. nd. "About VanGoYourself." <http://vangoyourself.com/about/> [accessed May 18, 2017].

Díaz-Andreu, Margarita. 2017. "Introduction to the Themed Section 'Digital Heritage and the Public.'" in *International Journal of Heritage Studies* 23(5): 404–407.

Dobreva, Milena, and Daniela Azzopardi. 2014. "Citizen Science in the Humanities: A Promise for Creativity," in *Cyprus Library: The 9th International Conference on Knowledge, Information and Creativity Support Systems*, ed. G. A. Papadopoulos, University of Cyprus, Nicosia, Cyprus, available at <https://www.um.edu.mt/library/oar/bitstream/handle/123456789/987/KICSS2014%20dobreva_azzopardi.pdf?sequence=1&isAllowed=y> [accessed April 21, 2017].

Drotner, Kirsten, and Kim Christian Schrøder. 2013. *Museum Communication and Social Media: The Connected Museum*. New York and London: Routledge.

Fairclough, Graham, 2012. "Foreword," in *Heritage and Social Media*, ed. Elisa Giaccardi. London and New York: Routledge, xiv–xvii.

Fouseki, Kalliopi, and Kalliopi Vacharopoulou. 2013. "Digital Museum Collections and Social Media: Ethical Considerations of Ownership and Use." *Journal of Conservation and Museum Studies*, <http://www.jcms-journal.com/collections/special/museum-ethics/> [accessed July 26, 2016].

Fuchs, Christian. 2014. *Social Media: A Critical Introduction*. London: Sage.

Fuchs, Christian, and Sebastian Sevignani. 2013. "What Is Digital Labour? What Is Digital Work? What's their Difference? And Why Do These Questions Matter for Understanding Social Media?" *tripleC* 11(2): 237–293.

Giaccardi, Elisa, ed. 2012. *Heritage and Social Media*. London and New York: Routledge.

Groppel-Wegener, Alke. 2011. "Creating Heritage Experiences through Architecture," in *Performing Heritage*, ed. Anthony Jackson and Jenny Kidd. Manchester: Manchester University Press.

Hartley, Julian A. "Museums and the Digital Public Space: Researching Digital Engagement Practice at the Whitworth Art Gallery." PhD thesis. <https://www.research.manchester. ac.uk/portal/en/theses/museums-and-the-digital-public-space-researching-digital-en-gagement-practiceat-the-whitworth-art-gallery(8eebb8f4-b0b5-4e40-a419-50be3c2e6e9a). html> [accessed May 18, 2017].

Holdgaard, Nanna, and Lisbeth Klastrup. 2014. "Between Control and Creativity: Challenging Co-Creation and Social Media Use in a Museum Context." *Digital Creativity* 25(3): 190–202.

Hubin, Yin, Bamo Qubumo, Guo Cuixiao, and Li Gane. 2013. "Achive/Base/Network: A Threefold Solution for Safeguarding Ethnic Minorities' Oral Heritage in China." Digital Heritage International Congress Proceedings, 177–180.

Jenkins, Henry, Sam Ford, and Joshua Green. 2013. *Spreadable Media: Creating Value and Meaning in a Networked Culture*. New York and London: NYU Press.

Kelly, Lynda, 2013. "The Connected Museum in the World of Social Media," in *Museum Communication and Social Media: The Connected Museum*, ed. Drotner, Kirsten, and Schrøder, Kim Christian. New York and London: Routledge, 54–71.

Kenderdine, Sarah. 2016. "Embodiment, Entanglement, and Immersion in Digital Cultural Heritage," in *A New Companion to Digital Humanities*, ed. Susan Schreibman, Ray Siemens, and John Unsworth. Chichester and Malden: John Wiley and Sons Ltd., 22–41.

Kidd, Jenny. 2011. "Enacting Engagement Online: Framing Social Media Use for the Museum." *Information, Technology and People* 24(1): 64–77.

Kidd, Jenny. 2014. Museums in the New Mediascape: Transmedia, Participation, Ethics. London and New York: Routledge.

Kidd, Jenny. 2015. *Representation: Key Ideas in Media and Culture*. London and New York: Routledge.

Kidd, Jenny. 2018. "Digital Media Ethics and Museum Communication," in *The Routledge Handbook of Museums, Media and Communication*, ed. K. Drotner, V. Dziekan, R. Parry, and K. C. Schrøder. London and New York: Routledge.

Kidd, Jenny, and Rosie Cardiff. 2017. "'A Space of Negotiation': Visitor Generated Content and Ethics at Tate." *Museum and Society* 15(1): 43–55.

Koch, Gertraud. 2013. "Studying Heritage in the Digital Era," in *Understanding Heritage*, ed. Marie Theres Albert, Roland Bernecker, and Britta Rudolff. Berlin and Boston: de Gruyter, 169–181.

Lagoudi, Elena, and Charlotte Sexton. 2010. "Old Masters at Your Fingertips: The Journey of Creating a Museum App for the iPhone & iTouch." <http://www.museumsandtheweb.com/mw2010/papers/lagoudi/lagoudi.html> [accessed May 19, 2017].

Little, Barbara J. 2009. "Public Archaeology in the United States in the Early Twentieth Century," in *Heritage Studies: Methods and Approaches*, ed. Marie Louise Stig Sørensen and John Carman. London and New York: Routledge, 29–51.

Marstine, Janet, ed. 2011. *Routledge Companion to Museum Ethics: Redefining Ethics for the Twenty-First Century Museum*. London and New York: Routledge.

Miller, Vincent. 2008. "New Media, Networking, and Phatic Culture." *Convergence* 14(4): 387–400.

Natural History Museum. nd. "Citizen Science." <http://www.nhm.ac.uk/take-part/citizen-science.html> [accessed May 18, 2017].

Owens, Trevor. 2013. "Digital Cultural Heritage and the Crowd." *Curator: The Museum Journal* 56(1): 121–130.

Owens, Trevor. 2016. "Curating in the Open: A Case for Iteratively and Openly Publishing Curatorial Research on the Web." *Curator: The Museums Journal* 59(4): 427–442.

Parry, Ross. 2011. "Transfer Protocols: Museum Codes and Ethics in the New Digital Environment," in *Routledge Companion to Museum Ethics: Redefining Ethics for the Twenty-First Century Museum*, ed. Janet Marstine. Routledge. 316–331.

Pantalony, R. E. 2016. "Dances with Intellectual Property: Museums, Monetization and Digitization," in *Museums, Ethics and Cultural Heritage*, ed. Bernice L. Murphy. New York and Oxon: Routledge, 71–78.

Ridge, Mia. 2013. "From Tagging to Theorizing: Deepening Engagement with Cultural Heritage through Crowdsourcing." *Curator: The Museum Journal* 56(4): 435–450.

Ridge, Mia, ed. 2014. *Crowdsourcing our Cultural Heritage*. Surrey: Ashgate.

Robson, Tricia, Gary Castro, Mark Paddon, and Alexa Beaman. 2016. "The de Young Museum App by Guidekick as a Model for Collaborative Development, Technological Innovation, and Visitor Behavior Insight." <http://mw2016.museumsandtheweb.com/paper/the-de-young-museum-app-by-guidekick-as-a-model-for-collaborative-development-technological-innovation-and-visitor-behavior-insight/> [accessed May 19, 2017].

Sánchez Laws, Ana Louisa. 2015. *Museum Websites and Social Media: Issues of Participation, Sustainability, Trust and Diversity*. Oxford and New York: Berghahn Books.

Schraffenberger, Hanna, and Edwin van der Heide. 2014. "Everything Augmented: On the Real in Augmented Reality." *CITAR Journal* 6(1): 17–29.

Shirky, Clay. 2010. *Cognitive Surplus: Creativity and Generosity in a Connected Age*. London, New York, and Toronto: Penguin.

Smith, Laurajane. 2006. *The Uses of Heritage*. London: Routledge.

Smithsonian. nd. "Smithsonian Digital Volunteers: Transcription Centre." <https://transcription.si.edu/> [accessed May 18, 2017].

Surowieki, James. 2004. *The Wisdom of Crowds: Why the Many Are Smarter Than the Few*. London: Little and Brown.

Taylor, Joel, and Laura Kate Gibson. 2017. "Digitisation, Digital Interaction and Social Media: Embedded Barriers to Democratic Heritage." *International Journal of Heritage Studies* 23(5): 408–420.

Terranova, Tiziana. 2000. "Free Labor: Producing Culture for the Digital Economy." *Social Text* 18(2): 33–58.

van Dijck, J. 2012. "Facebook as a Tool for Producing Sociality and Connectivity." *Television and New Media* 13(2): 160–176.

White, Martin, Zeeshan Patoli, Tudor Pascu. 2013. "Knowledge Networking through Social Media for a Digital Heritage Resource." Digital Heritage International Congress Proceedings, 389–392.

....

ON THE NEED FOR A NUANCED UNDERSTANDING OF "COMMUNITY" IN HERITAGE POLICY AND PRACTICE

....

MARTIN MULLIGAN

The community and heritage connection is one that is considered so natural an affinity that it hardly needs justification or explanation.

Elizabeth Crooke, 2010

INTRODUCTION

....

ACCORDING to Watson and Waterton (2010: 1) the benefits derived from involving
communities in "cultural resource management" have become such an article of faith
within the "heritage community" that few people have stopped to think critically about
how the word "community" is deployed. However, the feeling that "the very notion of
'community' seemed to have ossified into a set of assumptions and practices that were
now rarely examined" became a subject for discussion at the Sixth World Archaeology
Congress held in Dublin in 2008 (ibid.). Here it was acknowledged that any success in
engaging communities in heritage practice could increase public support for "otherwise
arcane activities" and the growth of the "heritage industry" over the previous twenty
years had "an effect in motivating and energising individuals and communities to engage with the past" (ibid.). The 2008 discussion led to the publication of a special edition
of *International Journal of Heritage Studies* in which Crooke (2010) and Waterton and
Smith (2010)—in particular—argued strongly for working with more open-ended, con-
testable, and dynamic understandings of what community means. Waterton and Smith

argued that the link between community and heritage can be used to feed nostalgia for an "imagined" "golden age" (2010: 7) while Crooke noted that this link can be used to feed divisive representations of national identity in rather fragile political communities such as that found in Northern Ireland. Both these papers stressed the need to distinguish between the "production" and "representation" of community, with contestability being especially important for the latter. Whilst Crooke, in particular, noted that representations of community apply at scales ranging from the local to the national, neither of these papers considered how the concept of "community" has been stretched to refer to processes of identify formation and representation which have little or no link to particular geographies.

Given that the "turn to community" in heritage policy and practice began to gather force in the 1990s—first in the United Kingdom before spreading globally (Waterton and Watson 2015: 7)—critical reflection on how the term has been deployed was rather slow to emerge. The contributions to the debate by Crooke and Waterton and Smith demonstrated the need for heritage scholars to engage more fully with sociological and political studies literature on the topic. Yet these two papers worked with a limited sampling of that literature and there is little evidence to suggest that their efforts have subsequently been extended by others in the field, even though pitfalls associated with uncritical use of the concept have intensified since 2010.

Silberman has noted that "heritage places" have never had an exclusive affinity with particular communities—serving as everything from "objects of state power" (2016: 32–3) to sites of "symbolic resistance" (35). Earlier he had argued (2012: 435) that new global developments—such as mass migration and the rise of "sub-national identity politics"—have posed the need to work with understandings of community that are not only "local and fixed" but also "scattered across the world." However, while the work needed to stretch and deepen the ways in which the concept of community engagement is deployed in international heritage policy and practice is far from finished, Silberman noted that a "rhetorical turn toward the goals of environmental sustainability, regional economic development, poverty alleviation, social cohesion, and urban regeneration" may overwhelm the focus on community engagement (ibid.). This chapter will argue that heritage policy and practice cannot escape its association with representations of community identities at multiple scales so that work needs to continue on better understanding that inevitable affinity even if the rhetorical focus has shifted.

The turn to community in heritage policy and practice occurred at a time when a range of sociologists and historians were suggesting that the very concept had lost its relevance in a world of global mobilities (e.g. Sennett 1986, Bauman 1993, Hobsbawm 1994). Others, however, noted that the appeal of community appears to be strengthening rather than fading (e.g. Williams 1983, Cohen 1985, Nancy 1991, Rose 1996, Delanty 2003) as I have also found in my research on the evolution of community art practices in a wide range of local communities in Australia (see Mulligan et al. 2006). However, as a range of authors have stressed (e.g. Young 1990, Joseph 2002, Creed 2006), the romantic appeal of community can mask efforts to legitimate hierarchies of power and forms of social exclusion so it can be far from being the common good that many imagine. The contributions by Crooke and Waterton and Smith, discussed above, demonstrated the need for heritage scholars and practitioners to be familiar with the way community has been debated in wider fields of social theory and practice and this chapter aims to deepen that engagement.

WHERE, WHEN, AND WHY THE "TURN TO COMMUNITY" EMERGED

In their review of heritage research interests, Waterton and Watson (2015) argue that the role of heritage (primarily in museums) in the promotion of "national development" only came under serious critique in the 1980s. One source of critique emerged in "settler/colonial states"—such as Australia, the United States, New Zealand, and Canada—where Indigenous people attacked the role of museums in the theft of their heritage. Such critiques led to the publication in 2000 of *A Geography of Heritage: Power, Culture and Economy* (Graham et al.) which lifted the lid on previously neglected debates about the exercise of power and control in selection of heritage items and sites. According to Waterton and Watson, Britain led the way in debating the social consequences of heritage policies and practices and they suggest that it was Prime Minister Tony Blair's "fixation" with "communitarianism" (2015: 7) that sparked the turn to community in UK heritage policy and practice which was subsequently globalized. Growing public interest in heritage matters—as reflected in the global popularity of heritage-related films and TV shows—subsequently stimulated interests in things like "national heritage versus local heritage," "the role of memory and oral history," and the "role played by heritage within contemporary public policies, particularly those concerned with multiculturalism and national cohesion" (ibid.). Such developments led Waterton and Watson to conclude that "community" had become "one of the most influential themes to have impacted the field . . . along with its tropes of participation, dissonance and identity" (ibid.).

Reflecting on her experiences working in Northern Ireland, Crooke's aforementioned paper (2010: 21) notes that the concept of "community" has a very different resonance because a "community worker" is commonly seen as one who fiercely defends particular traditions against others. Heritage there has long been a politically charged idea with "loyalists" and "republicans" fighting pitched battles over public celebrations of their separate and competing traditions. "Even with a changing political context, community is still burdened with this past legacy," she notes, and this led her to conclude that "community" and "heritage" are both "malleable concepts" which are "also highly emotive, closely guarded and used to stake control and define authority" (ibid. 27).

Crooke's rather bleak assessment of how "community" is deployed in heritage practice in Northern Ireland may not match practice in less divided social and political contexts. However, in their contribution to the same special edition of the *International*

Journal of Heritage Studies, Chirikure et al. (2010: 30–44) argue that practice has rarely, if ever, lived up to the rhetoric about community engagement in heritage practice in Africa, severely frustrating those who had welcomed it as a departure from old colonial practices. Others (e.g. Perkin 2010: 107–22) have pointed to much more positive experiences with community engagement in heritage practices. Nonetheless, Waterton and Smith (2015: 5) were led to conclude: "A form of rhetoric that is ostensibly about challenging our privileged stewardship and control over the past has thus essentially become quite the opposite: a mechanism that ensures the continued misrecognition of a range of stakeholders within the heritage management process, particularly those that are already at risk."

According to a range of reviews (e.g. Bauman 2001, Joseph 2002, Delanty 2003, Studdert 2005, Walmsley 2006) it is the fact that the word "community" can mean many different things that has frustrated many social science scholars. This ambiguity was noted by the pioneering cultural historian Raymond Williams (1983: 76) when he observed that "community" is a "warmly persuasive word" which "never seems to be used unfavourably" because different people can use it to serve very different purposes. However, Williams included the word in his compilation of "keywords" in the English language precisely because it has strong and enduring evocative appeal. Many such "keywords" accumulate layers of sometimes contradictory meanings but, as Cohen later noted (1985), it is critically important to interrogate the enduring symbolic power of an idea like "community" in order to discuss openly how that power is being mobilized.

COMMUNITY AS ASPIRATIONAL, FRAUGHT, AND CONTESTABLE

In their incisive reviews of social science literature on community, both Gerard Delanty (2003, 2010) and Roberto Esposito (2010) note that the English word "community" has its origins in the language and thinking of the ancient Greeks and Romans, with Esposito exploring the layers of meaning embedded in the ancient Greek word *koinos* and the Latin word *communitas*. Going even further, Delanty (2003: 11) asserts that some notion of community "exerts itself as a powerful idea of belonging in every age." However, he goes on to argue that there has always been an ambivalence embedded within the idea because it has been used to refer to both "locality and particularness" (the "domain of immediate social relations") and a sense of belonging to a "universal community in which all humans participate" (2003: 12). For both Delanty and Esposito the desire to participate in community is part of what Hannah Arendt (1958) called "the human condition" with Esposito (2010: 8) arguing that it represents "the most suitable, indeed the sole dimension" of what it means to be human.

The age-old hope of finding community does not mean, however, that the search will end well. Indeed, Esposito (ibid.) argues that the search for community is a rather dangerous preoccupation because it can also be understood as "the hole into which the common thing continually risks falling." Noting that the Latin word *communitas* includes the word *munus* which refers to the interplay of gift and obligation (p. 4), he suggests that there can be no guarantee of a safety net at the bottom of the hole and that helps to explain why talk of community can evoke emotions of both hope and despair. Similarly, Delanty (2003: 11) argued that "as a discourse of loss and recovery, community can be at the same time utopian and nostalgic." Increasing mobilities—of people, goods, and ideas—means that community formations are less likely to be stable and enduring than in past periods of human history and this undoubtedly makes the search for community even more fraught. Increased mobility not only means that particular representations of a particular community can become dated more easily, it also means that past-oriented representations can seek to exclude newcomers or stand against the ways in which a nation is being constantly transformed.

The word "community" is probably deployed most commonly to refer to local, or place-based, social formations but it applies equally to metropolitan communities, the nation as a community, international networks or communities of practice, and a wide range of "identity communities" that can operate across geographic and sociopolitical scales. In his seminal work on the "symbolic construction of community," Anthony Cohen argued against efforts to understand the social functioning of community in order to concentrate instead on efforts made by members of a community—operating at different scales—to distinguish themselves "in some significant way from the members of other putative groups" (1985: 12). This always involves a process of boundary-setting because physical and conceptual boundaries are used to define a community which includes some and excludes others. However, Cohen pointed out that any boundary will enclose differences as well as sameness and he went on to argue that it is much more important to consider how communities form around symbols of shared identity rather than the delineation of territory, even if geography has played an important role in the evolution of the culture represented by such symbols. Cohen's work on community was influenced by the work of his anthropology mentor Victor Turner who, like Delanty and Esposito later, examined the origins of the word in the Latin *communitas* and concluded that community forms "in resistance to structure, at the edges of structure, and from beneath structure" (Turner 1969: 128).

The suggestion that communities form around symbols of shared identity rather than through a process of territorial boundary-setting has obvious implications for heritage policy and practice. Items, objects, or places which gain a heritage status are local in origin but their role in the formation of communities at scales ranging from the local to transnational means that their symbolic power commonly transcends their origins and they might end up in a national museum or as a site used to celebrate national, sub-national, or even transnational identities. Of course, the same items/objects or sites may be claimed by different identity formations, as seen, for example, in intense contestation between Jews and Muslims over the Temple Mount/Haram esh-Sharif site in Jerusalem or, less problematically, in the way that a temple at Kataragama in southeastern Sri Lanka serves as a pilgrimage site for both Sri Lankan Buddhists and for

Hindus coming from across Sri Lanka and India. Of course, distinct identity formations often have common origins and the long processes of identity formation involve inter-action and forms of hybridity as much as processes of separation. However, Silberman notes (2016: 33) that nation-states commonly seek to claim "heritage places" as sites for "ethno-national commemoration . . . where loyalty to the nation-state was literally or symbolically mobilized." In his view this has often led to "the twin evils" of extending territorial claims to include such places or otherwise neglecting sites which do not fit the "national narrative" (ibid.). As noted earlier, Elizabeth Crooke (2010) referred to po-litically charged and contested representations of heritage sites in Northern Ireland to argue that the assumed "natural affinity" between community and heritage needs to be treated with much more diligence. The danger of using the link between community and heritage to serve divisive political agendas did not lead Crooke to argue that the link should be avoided. Rather she argued that heritage scholars and practitioners need to work with a "multi-layered" understanding of what community means so that divisive representations of the link can be contested.

I came across a good example of how heritage sites can be used to promote divisions at a national scale when I took a group of RMIT University Students on a study tour to Sri Lanka in July 2016. Visiting the "heartland" of Sri Lankan Buddhism in the ancient, yet long abandoned, city of Anuradhapura we were able to secure the services of a very knowledgable and skilled local guide who was able to draw on his deep knowledge of Buddhist philosophy to interpret sites ranging from the central temple, where offshoots of a Bodhi tree brought from the site where the Lord Buddha meditated in India in 288 BC still live, to elaborate monasteries built in surrounding hills. At the central temple our guide noted that it had been attacked by members of the Tamil Tigers separatist army during the recent civil war but throughout the day he had represented the ancient city as a place of peace and tranquillity. However, at the end of the day, he unleashed a surprising rant against Tamils in the country's north and Muslims "taking over" cities such as Kandy in order to suggest that ever since Anuradhapura was abandoned in the thirteenth century, Buddhism in Sri Lanka has always been under siege from "foreign" interests. This reflects a paranoid account of Sri Lanka's history which underpins post-independence efforts to assert Buddhism and the Sinhalese language as primary markers of the nation's identity; a view of history which played a significant role in the long and costly civil war which came to a bloody and inclusive end in 2009.

COMMUNITY AS ALWAYS IMPERMANENT AND INCOMPLETE

The suggestion that community is essentially an ageless human aspiration which can never be actually realized is most commonly associated with an influential essay by French philosopher and art critic Jean-Luc Nancy published in 1983 but only in English in 1991 under the title *The Inoperative Community*. Delanty (2003: 135) has suggested that a similar argument was made in a 1988 book by Maurice Blanchot while Esposito has argued that Georges Bataille discussed similar ideas in an essay published in 1985 (Esposito 2010: 115–16) and there are clear echoes of Nancy's ideas in a book titled *The Coming Community* by Giorgio Agamben in 1993. Perhaps Nancy's rendition of the argument has reverberated most strongly because he outlined similar arguments to those of Cohen about the symbolic importance of community even if it is more likely to be experienced as something lost rather than gained. Nancy (1991: 35) stressed that while "incompletion" is the necessary "principle" of community we should think of "incompletion in an active sense . . . as designating not an insufficiency of lack, but the activity of sharing." In his later book titled *Being Singular Plural* (2000) Nancy developed the argument that the search for community represents the process of constant co-becoming for our individual and collective selves.

As mentioned earlier, Delanty (2003, 2010) was among those who argued that rising insecurities in a world of increased global integration had increased rather than decreased the desire for community. In 2010 (152) he suggested that community "is neither a form of social integration nor a form of meaning, but an open-ended system of communication about belonging." On the one hand, he argued (2003: 193) the growing "fragmentation of society has provoked a worldwide search for community" and, on the other hand, "cultural developments and new global forms of communication of facilitated the construction of community." The rising global influence of "neoliberal" conceptions of relationships between self and society has undoubtedly valorized the individual over the collective and Delanty (2003: 192) noted the irony of this when he suggested that the "finality" of community is impossible because it "ends up [being] destroyed by the individualism which created the desire for it."

Whilst Delanty, Esposito, and others have pointed out that the search for community reflects deep human needs, it still seems reasonable to wonder if the tensions at play within the idea can continue to coexist in the "global age" (see Mulligan 2015). As mentioned earlier, Delanty (2003: 11) has argued that community has always carried undertones of nostalgia even as it sought a path towards utopia and events like the 2016 UK decision to leave the European Union and the election, in the same year, of Donald Trump as US president confirm the fears expressed by Waterton and Smith (2010: 7) that community can be deployed to argue for a return to a supposed "golden age" and heritage can too easily be framed as a past-oriented set of ideas and practices. Nikolas Rose has argued that the "idea of community" is now being seen as an "antidote or even cure to the ills that the social has not been able to address" (1999: 89) and it is this hope that feeds nostalgia for romanticized views of the past. However, Rose went on to argue that "to community as essence, origin, fixity, one can . . . counterpose community as a constructed form for the collective unworking of identities and moralities" (1999: 195). Both Delanty and Rose argue that new communication technologies have made it much easier to contest representations of community identities at all scales and they are convinced that the idea can never be fully captured by anyone. Delanty (2003: 130) argued that globalization has meant that community only exists to the extent that it is "wilfully constructed" and, as mentioned above, he suggests that opportunities for more people to participate in the creation of community have increased.

In his influential essay on the "incompletion" of community, Nancy (1991: 11) anticipated the later argument by Rose by suggesting that "community, far from being what society has crushed or lost, is what happens to us—question, waiting, event, imperative—in the wake of society." While this can be seen as a rather unsettling rendition of a term that is commonly deployed without much thought or care, it presents community making as a process, rather than end result, and this, in turn, points to boundless possibilities for negotiating the terms of our co-existence. The question for heritage workers is how can references to the past inform, rather than narrow, the choices that can be made.

RESISTING SHALLOW OR DIVISIVE
REPRESENTATIONS

As Delanty, in particular, has emphasized, the global revolution in communication technologies that has occurred in recent decades has greatly expanded the range of both "real" and "virtual" communities that people can decide to participate in. Like it or not we co-exist with other people in geographically based communities but some choose to participate actively, perhaps at particular times in their lives (see Mulligan et al. 2006), while others pay little attention to the strengths or weaknesses of the communities in which they reside, unless the weaknesses become a threat to their social needs or aspirations (see below). Most people participate in political communities/nations by dint of citizenship rights and responsibilities but here also levels of participation vary enormously. Some may choose to prioritize workplace communities or spatially extended professional associations. Others join interest groups, communities of practice, or social networks facilitated by various social media platforms which have little or no reference to locations or territories. Increased global mobility has resulted in the rapid growth of extended "diasporas" of people who share common origins and many such migrants feel a need to keep in contact with communities of origin, even if that desire may fade for their children.

Such an expansion in the range of "virtual" communities we can all participate in prompted the influential sociologist Manuel Castells (1996) to argue that geographically based communities have essentially been supplanted by spatially extended communities which grow out of communication networks. However, Delanty (2003: 177) countered this argument by suggesting that many "virtual" communities are "thin" and "ephemeral" and cannot replace the deep and enduring human desire for a more secure sense of belonging. I have argued (Mulligan 2015) that there is no apparent reason to counterpose geographically based and "virtual" communities. In fact, "grounded communities" (of place) are gaining renewed importance in a world of uncertainty, with the onset of global climate change posing the need to rethink our relationships with ecological systems which operate across the scales from the local to the global. A range of scholars (e.g. Jackson 2016) have argued for the need to relocalize our economic and social practices in order to reduce our impacts on global ecological systems. While it seems counterproductive to counterpose "real" and "virtual" communities we have to acknowledge that the explosion of choice makes it even more important to think carefully about when and where we use the term community and to relate the choices we make to our local and global ecological impacts. The relationship between heritage and community clearly applies to local communities, national communities, and subnational religious or "ethnic" communities. However, it also applies to transnational diasporic communities and to other "virtual" communities that use forms of heritage to justify their existence.

While increased global mobility and new communication technologies have brought the transnational dimensions of community formation into view, Burrawoy et al. (2000) have highlighted the fact that people are moving between local communities both within and across national boundaries. This focus on "translocalism" has led to the suggestion that, whereas the arrival of "outsiders" is often seen as a destabilizing influence for a local community, people moving between local communities can carry with them forms of social or cultural capital which can enhance the adaptive capacity of the communities they join (Brickell and Datta 2011: 5). According to this argument, cultural diversity can help a local community function more effectively in a globally connected world. However, this raises some complex questions about the extent to which separate forms of heritage can be shared by "multicultural" communities. Doreen Massey (2005) has argued that such questions need to be addressed in a transparent way by people who find themselves coexisting within the shared spaces. It is highly likely that aspects of heritage will be part of such deliberations and heritage experts need to consider if interpretations of heritage are facilitating or undermining the prospects for peaceful coexistence.

Given the emotive power of community discussed above, it is not surprising that politicians and policy advocates often seek to deploy the rhetoric of community well-being to promote their policies or ideologies. As early as 1981 the Australian sociologists Martin Mowbray and Lois Bryson suggested that talk of community can often be described as a "spray-on solution" for complex social and economic challenges. There is no doubt that rhetorical and shallow use of the word has hollowed it out in some ways (Creed 2006, Walmsley 2006). Yet, as both Rose (1999) and Delanty (2003, 2010) have argued it has become easier for shallow or misleading representations of community to be publicly challenged.

While Waterton and Smith (2010: 9) argued that "community" works best when it creates forums for working on a wide range of tensions—such as difference versus unity and self-interest versus mutuality—a range of authors (e.g. Young 1990, Bauman 2001, Jha 2010) have pointed out that such tensions can easily turn into forms of exclusion or conflict. Building on the work of Young, Miranda Joseph (2002) has demonstrated that the romantic appeal of community is commonly used to entrench hierarchies of power and forms of social exclusion. In reflecting on the way in which references to the past can exacerbate local conflicts Manoj Jha (2010: 318) noted that communities sometimes draw on stories of past humiliations as "chosen traumas" to justify various forms of chauvinism. While Jha's analysis was based on a sudden eruption of violence directed against Muslim communities in the Indian state of Gujarat in 2002, it helps to explain how multi-ethnic communities all over the world can be torn apart by sudden eruptions of communal tension and violence, as was the case across the United Kingdom in August 2011. When past grievances become "chosen traumas," Jha argued, historic truth becomes largely irrelevant and rational analysis becomes very difficult (ibid.). Nevertheless, Waterton and Smith are undoubtedly right in arguing that the tensions which exist within all complex geographically based communities need to be openly debated in order to work out terms of coexistence which maximise tolerance or respect for differences. As Jha's analysis confirms, aspects of heritage can be deployed to either increase or reduce tolerance of difference and in a world of increased mobilities and information exchange this is creating new and complex, yet potentially exciting, challenges for heritage scholars and practitioners.

In my study of post-tsunami recovery in Sri Lanka, I found a local community in which pre-existing respect for cultural diversity became a feature of post-disaster social recovery. When the tsunami struck the town of Hambantota on Sri Lanka's southeast "corner" in December 2004 nearly half the local residents were Tamil-speaking Muslims in a wider district dominated by Sinhalese-speaking Buddhists. Muslim settlers had lived around the harbor town for centuries, with some originating from the Malay peninsula and others from the Indian sub-continent, and a community of Muslims living in close proximity to the fishing harbor were hit hardest by the destructive waves. When local authorities decided that a historic mosque, located where the decimated fishing community had lived, would be relocated further away from the sea, the Sinhalese community strongly supported the Muslim community in rejecting the decision and supported plans to rebuild the damaged mosque. At the same time, a small Muslim community organization had taken the lead in getting international aid for the rebuilding of a badly damaged Buddhist temple, which was not included on a list of temples to be rebuilt by the national Buddhist organizations. Soon after the tsunami hit, community organizations in Hambantota formed an inclusive local committee to monitor the delivery of aid and the development of reconstruction plans in order to ensure that tolerance of religious and cultural diversity was not undermined by any kind of preferential treatment (see Mulligan and

Nadarajah 2012). In this case shared heritage was valued over the pursuit of separate interests.

BRINGING A MORE NUANCED UNDERSTANDING OF COMMUNITY INTO HERITAGE PRACTICE

The paper by Waterton and Smith discussed earlier goes a long way towards disabusing the sector of what they called "reified and unreflexive notions of community" (2010: 5). While noting that heritage can be used to feed a nostalgic longing for a supposed "golden age" (2010: 7) they echoed the work of scholars discussed above in noting that representations of community are often contested and rather fraught because they evoke a wide range of emotions as either "motivating" or "disruptive" energies (2010: 8). They argued that community needs to be seen as a process because it is constantly "(re) constructed through ongoing experiences, engagements and relations, and not all of these need to be consensual." (ibid.). They cited Burkett (2001: 9) in saying that community "is about difference as much as it is about unity, about conflict *and* harmony, selfishness *and* mutuality, separateness *and* wholeness, discomfort *and* comfort." This means, they concluded, that "communities are not always sources of empowerment and positive identity" yet they suggested that thinking about community as a process rather than outcome "can retain the sociality of the process."

The paper by Waterton and Smith refers to the influential work of Anthony Cohen, Jean-Luc Nancy, and Zygmunt Bauman discussed above and it usefully links the need to contest representations of community to Nancy Fraser's work on the "politics of recognition" through often competing "representations" of complex reality (Waterton and Smith 2010: 10–11). However, this is still a rather limited engagement with the extensive social science literature on community and this chapter has emphasized the need to work with a multi-layered understanding of community formation which was flagged, but only briefly discussed, by Elizabeth Crooke (2010).

Since the special edition of the *International Journal of Heritage Studies* was published in 2010, global ideological clashes have intensified, especially between radical Muslims and those who argue that "western" values are superior. World heritage sites—such as those at Palmyra—have become among the targets of warfare. Waterton and Watson note (2015: 13) that the "emblematic and symbolic value of heritage continues to place it at the forefront of conflict of all kinds," so that it can become everything from "a rallying call, a locus of resistance and opposition, a symbol of domination and of subjugation, objects to be venerated or destroyed." In a world of heightened tensions local conflicts can reverberate widely and heritage professionals need to be very mindful that they work in politically charged environments. They cannot avoid the need to think carefully about how heritage values that draw on their work can be used to promote either divisive or tolerant and inclusive community formations.

CONCLUSIONS

The concept of community has frequently polarized scholars and practitioners alike in many fields of scholarship and practice (see Joseph 2002, Studdert 2005, Creed 2006, Mulligan 2015). As I have noted (Mulligan 2015), numerous scholars, over more than a century, have predicted the death of community, trampled underfoot by the relentless march of urbanization and globalization. However, Rose (1999), Bauman (2001), and Delanty (2003) were prominent among those who noted that the desire for community has experienced a renaissance in a world of increasing uncertainties. The fact that the word can be used to mean very different things to different people drives many scholars mad; yet, Day and Murdoch noted in 1993 that it is a concept which "although badly wounded . . . just will not lie down" (as cited by Waterton and Smith 2010: 6).

As mentioned earlier, the international "turn to community" in heritage policy and practice which first emerged in the 1990s has been overshadowed to an extent by a more recent "rhetorical turn toward the goals of environmental sustainability, regional economic development, poverty alleviation, social cohesion, and urban regeneration" (Silberman 2012: 435). However, the enormous symbolic importance of heritage means that heritage professionals are involved in the constant creation and representation of community, whether they like it or not, and this takes place in a world that is more politically charged than ever. By trying to remain "professionally neutral" heritage professionals may inadvertently promote divisive representations of community identities; indeed there is no normatively neutral position to take. Heritage and community are joined at the hip through their interconnected symbolic power, especially when representations of community are more easily disrupted and contested than ever before in a world of global flows and real time connectivity.

As a number of authors have stressed, the idea of community has romantic and rather seductive appeal (see Joseph 2002, Creed 2006) and it is easy for heritage professionals to adopt an uncritical stance towards the idea. However, as Waterton and Smith (2010) argued, heritage values can be mobilized to justify nostalgia for a romanticized "golden age" while Joseph (2002) explained that the romance of community can mask the fact that the idea can be deployed to legitimate hierarchies of power and forms of social exclusion. The 2010 special edition of the *International Journal of Heritage Studies* opened an important dialogue about the need for heritage scholars and practitioners to work with dynamic, open-ended, and multi-layered understandings of the idea of community. However, the possibilities for using representations of community to serve different social, cultural, and political agendas have continued to evolve and it has become even more important for every person who is obliged to work with the idea of community to think critically about how it is deployed in particular settings and contexts ranging from the local to the global. More than ever before, heritage professionals can unwittingly support socially and politically divisive representations of community yet reflexive community engagement also promises to make this work more socially relevant and constructive.

References

Agamben, G. 1993. *The Coming Community*. Minneapolis: University of Minnesota Press.

Arendt, H. 1958. *The Human Condition*. Chicago: University of Chicago Press.

Bauman, Z. 1993. *Postmodern Ethics*. Oxford: Blackwell.

Bauman, Z. 2001. *Community: Seeking Safety in an Insecure World*. Cambridge: Polity Press.

Brickell, K., and A. Datta. 2011. "Introduction: Translocal Geographies," in *Translocal Goegraphies: Spaces, Places, Connections*, ed. K. Brickell and A. Datta. Burlongton: Ashgate, 3–22.

Burkett. L. 2001. "Traversing the swampy terrain of postmodern communities: towards theoretican revisionings of community development" *European Journal of Social Work* 4 (3): 233–246.

Burrawoy, M., J. A. Blum, S. George, Z. Gille, T. Gowan, L. Haney, M. Klawiter, S. H. Lopez, S. Ó. Riain, and M. Thayer 2000. *Global Ethnogrophy: Forces, Connections and Imaginations in a Postmodern World*, Berkeley and Los Angeles: University of California Press.

Castells, M. 1996. *The Rise of the Network State, Vol. 1: The Information Age*. Oxford: Blackwell.

Chirikure, S., M. Manyanga, W. Ndoro, and G. Pwiti. 2010. "Unfulfilled Promises? Heritage Management and Community Participation in Some of Africa's Heritage Sites." *International Journal of Heritage Studies* 16(1–2): 30–44.

Cohen, A. 1985. *The Symbolic Construction of Community*. London: Tavistock.

Creed, G.W. 2006. "Reconsidering Communities," in *The Seductions of Community: Emancipation, Oppression, Quandaries*, ed. G. W. Creed. Santa Fe: School of American Research Press, 3–22.

Crooke, E. 2010. "The Politics of Community Heritage: Motivations, Authority and Control." *International Journal of Heritage Studies* 16(1–2): 16–29.

Delanty, G. 2003. *Community*. London: Routledge.

Delanty, G. 2010. *Community*. 2nd edn. London: Routledge.

Esposito, R. 2010. *Communitas: The Origin and Destiny of Community*. Stanford, CA: Stanford University Press.

Graham, B., G. J. Ashworth, and J. E. Tunbridge. 2000. *A Geography of Heritage: Power, Culture and Economy*. New York: Oxford University Press.

Hobsbawm, E. 1994. *The Age of Extremes: The Short History of the Twentieth Century, 1914–1991*. London: Michael Joseph.

Jackson, T. 2016. *Prosperity without Growth: Foundations for the Economy of Tomorrow*. 2nd edn. London: Routledge.

Jha, M. 2010. "Community Organisation in Split Societies." *Community Development Journal* 44(3): 305–319.

Joseph, M. 2002. *Against the Romamce of Community*. Minneapolis: University of Minnesota Press.

Massey, D. 2005. *For Space*. London: Sage.

Mowbray, M., and L. Bryson. 1981. "'Community': The Spray-On Solution." *Australian Journal of Social Issues* 16(4): 255–62.

Mulligan, M. 2015. "On Ambivalence and Hope in the Restless Search for Community: How to Work with the Idea of Community in the Global Age." *Sociology* 49(2): 340–355.

Mulligan, M., K. Humphery, P. James, C. Scanlon, P. Smith, and N. Welch. 2006. *Creating Community: Celebrations, Arts and Wellbeing within and across Local Communities.* Melbourne: Centre for Global Research, RMIT University.

Mulligan, M., and Y. Nadarajah. 2012. *Rebuilding Communities in the Wake of Disaster: Social Recovery in Sri Lanka and India.* New Delhi: Routledge.

Nancy, J-L. 1991. *The Inoperative Community.* Minneapolis: University of Minnesota Press.

Perkin, C. 2010. "Beyond the Rhetoric: Negotiating the Politics and Realising the Potential of Community-Driven Heritage Engagement." *International Journal of Heritage Studies* 16(1–2): 107–122.

Rose, N. 1996. "The Death of the Social." *Economcy and Society* 25: 327–356.

Rose, N. 1999. *Powers of Freedom: Reframing Political Thought.* Cambridge: Cambridge University Press.

Sennett, R. 1986. *The Fall of Public Man.* London: Faber and Faber.

Silberman, N. A. 2012. "Changing Visions of Heritage Value: What Role Should the Experts Play?" ICOMOS-ICIP: 433–445.

Silberman, N. A. 2016. "Heritage Places: Evolving Conceptions and Changing Forms," in *A Companion to Heritage Studies,* ed. W. Logan and M. N. Craith. Oxford: John Wiley and Sons, 29–40.

Studdert, D. 2005. *Conceptualising Community: Theories of Sociality beyond State and Society.* Basingstoke: Palgrave Macmillan.

Walmsley, J. 2006. "Putting Community in Place." *Dialogue* 25(1): 5–12.

Waterton, E., and L. Smith. 2010. "The Recognition and Misrecognition of Community Heritage." *International Journal of Heritage Studies* 16(1–2): 4–15.

Waterton, E., and S. Watson. 2015. "Heritage as a Focus of Research: Past, Present and New Directions," in *The Palgrave Handbook of Contemporary Heritage Research,* ed. E. Waterton and S. Watson. London: Palgrave Macmillan, 1–17.

Watson, S., and E. Waterton. 2010. "Editorial: Heritage and Community Engagement." *International Journal of Heritage Studies* 16(1–2): 1–3.

Williams, R. 1983. *Keywords: A Vocabulary of Culture and Society.* London: Flamingo.

Young, I. M. 1990. "The Ideal of Community and the Politics of Difference," in *Feminism/Postmodernism,* ed. L. J. Nicholson. New York: Routledge, 300–323.

CHAPTER 3.4

"WHAT COULD BE MORE REASONABLE?" COLLABORATION IN COLONIAL CONTEXTS

MARINA LA SALLE AND RICHARD M. HUTCHINGS

INTRODUCTION

COLLABORATION is often claimed to be North American archaeology's cure-all. It can, if its proponents are to be believed, fix virtually every heritage problem under the sun (Atalay et al. 2014, Martindale and Lyons 2014). Some contend collaboration is ubiquitous in contemporary North American archaeology and point to how "sophisticated and nuanced" today's archaeology is when it comes to engaging "different publics" and "stakeholders," particularly Indigenous descendent communities (Colwell 2016: 115). Interpreting the collaborative turn as the ethical rebirth of a once colonial project, the transformation is used to justify archaeology's authority over all forms of heritage, tangible and intangible (Hogg et al. 2017). Others use it to legitimize cultural resource management (CRM), philosophically and morally (Connaughton et al. 2014). Collaboration, it seems, can do no wrong. Yet very little critical study has been done of collaborative archaeology, meaning much is taken for granted and much remains unquestioned and unchallenged.

In this chapter, we take a critical approach to the collaborative turn, deconstructing claims made about collaboration and how it has affected North American archaeology. Special attention is given to Indigenous archaeology, often used synonymously with collaborative archaeology. Towards this, we ask: What is collaborative archaeology? What is Indigenous archaeology? Who defines it? Who does it? To what end? How is "success" measured? How is "transformation" measured? These questions are relevant not just to North American archaeology but for heritage practice everywhere.

We begin our survey with a brief historical review of the factors that prompted the collaborative turn and the concomitant development of Indigenous archaeology. We then examine how proponents of collaboration envision the practice. Thereafter we provide our critique foregrounding power in colonized contexts and offer a revised vision for what we believe collaboration in archaeology really is.

THE COLLABORATIVE TURN

A full understanding of the collaborative turn in archaeology requires confronting colonialism in all its contexts, past and present. This is the central focus of Ian McNiven and Lynette Russell's (2005) book *Appropriated Pasts: Indigenous Peoples and the Colonial Culture of Archaeology*. Taking a historical approach, they examine Western representations of Indigenous peoples and argue "atrocities against Aboriginal people were aided by prevailing ideologies and mainstream scientific theories that held Aboriginal people to be primitive savages little removed from apes" (2005: 76). Archaeology played a fundamental role in that agenda, providing "scientific support" to legitimize expropriation of Indigenous lands and the enslavement and genocide of Indigenous peoples (2005: 92). An outcome of the "colonial culture of archaeology" was the co-optation of Indigenous heritage by archaeologists on behalf of the colonizing state: "Under the guise of writing a world prehistory for all humanity, Indigenous people's pasts and interests have been subsumed" within a colonial vision of heritage (McNiven and Russell 2005: 216; see also Smith 2004, Smith and Waterton 2012).

In the introduction to their book *Indigenous Archaeologies: Decolonizing Theory and Practice*, Claire Smith and Martin Wobst (2005: 5) demonstrate that colonialism is ongoing, not a thing of the past: "At heart, archaeology is a colonialist endeavor. It is based on, and generally perpetuates, the values of Western cultures. Privileging the material over the spiritual and the scientific over the religious, archaeological practice is solidly grounded in Western ways of knowing the world." Secure in their power and privilege, academic archaeologists have dominated story-telling about Indigenous history and reaped the benefits in socioeconomic capital. This legacy of taking and not giving back is central in Vine Deloria Jr.'s (1969, 1997) critiques of anthropology and archaeology.

Pressure to redress the power imbalance between archaeologists and Indigenous peoples emerged from events of the 1960s and 1970s: (1) the formation of increasingly organized and empowered Indigenous resistance groups such as the American Indian Movement (AIM), who fought for, among other things, the inalienable right of Indigenous people to steward their own land and heritage (Deloria 1969, Watkins 2000); and (2) the establishment of legally defined state heritage regimes governing archaeology (Gnecco and Dias 2015, Hutchings 2017, Hutchings and Dent 2017, King

2009, 2012, Smith 2004). The passage in the early 1990s in the United States of the Native American Graves Protection and Repatriation Act (NAGPRA) further emphasized the need for archaeologists to be responsible to descendant communities, with interest peaking later that decade with the Society for American Archaeology's new "principles of archaeological ethics" (Swidler et al. 1997). Thus, while collaboration may be viewed as a transformation or "turn" in North American archaeology (Colwell 2016: 115–119), archaeologists cannot claim credit for initiating this change, as it was largely a reactive process born of necessity, not a proactive one.

Archaeologists subsequently responded to those pressures by calling for increased community participation in archaeology (McNiven and Russell 2005: 230, Smith and Wobst 2005, Zimmerman 2006). Martin Wobst (2005: 18), for example, suggests that "Indigenous and non-indigenous archaeologists should look for their common ground, learn from an alliance with one another, and support each other's projects as long as they are beneficial to Indigenous and non-Indigenous populations alike." This he sees as part of "decolonization" (2005: 29), which "requires non-Indigenous archaeologists to reinvent themselves so that they are thoroughly grounded in the problems of their Indigenous contemporaries, sensitive to Indigenous needs, and willing to further Indigenous projects and agendas."

Thus, collaboration as power-sharing is the solution presented by archaeologists to the problem of the discipline's colonial legacy, with the intended outcome being decolonization. So what is the nature of this collaboration? Chip Colwell-Chanthaphonh (2012: 271) characterizes it as "a kind of intellectual synergy that provides all participants with equal power and benefits—the construction of even-handed relationships which are ethically driven and committed to a shared purpose of better understanding the past." Thus, equality is a central premise of collaboration. Other elements include "virtues such as civility, benevolence, generosity, loyalty, dependability, thoughtfulness, and friendliness" (Colwell-Chanthaphonh and Ferguson 2008: 13). Colwell (2016) elaborates on this vision of collaborative archaeology, describing it in such terms as rich, positive, active, inclusive, vital, improved, and admirable; as something that helps, redresses, recovers, empowers, fosters, and enriches; leading to advantages, quality, advancement, evolution, benefits, activism, social justice, and stewardship.

Colwell (2016: 119) argues collaboration is "a paradigm shift" and "a fundamental change" that has helped to "transform archaeology into a science that is driven by an ethical engagement" (2016: 113), in the process becoming more "sophisticated and nuanced" in its relations with Indigenous peoples (2016: 115). Indeed, a new practice called Indigenous archaeology developed in parallel to collaborative archaeology (Watkins and Nicholas 2014: 141–142), and was originally defined as "archaeology with, for, and by Indigenous peoples" (Nicholas and Andrews 1997). Because of their overlapping focus on a community-based approach and the shared goal of "decolonization" (Atalay 2006, Bruchac et al. 2010), collaboration and Indigenous archaeology have come to be closely aligned and the terms are at times used synonymously (e.g., Colwell 2016). In this chapter, we argue such conflation is problematic.

RETHINKING COLLABORATION

Faced with its colonial past, collaboration with Indigenous communities has been offered as the way forward by archaeologists, with self-identified goals of equality and decolonization. From this perspective, archaeology is no longer colonial as it has been transformed into something laudable, "radical" and even "revolutionary" (Atalay et al. 2014).

We suggest this characterization of archaeology is biased and does not accurately represent the practice. Below, we address what we see as the three most problematic features of collaboration: how archaeology is defined, how power is conceptualized in collaboration, and the stated goal of decolonization.

Defining Archaeology by Exception

We have been studying the different ways archaeologists define their practice for a number of years now (Hutchings and La Salle 2014, 2015a, 2015b, 2015c, 2017b, La Salle 2010, 2014, La Salle and Hutchings 2012, 2016). Not including such vital psychosocial elements as ego, emotion, and cultural cognition (Hutchings and La Salle 2015c, Kahan et al. 2011), the primary factor determining how archaeologists represent their practice is their worldview or ideology (Bernbeck and McGuire 2000, Custer 2005, Fowler 1987). Minimally, ideology affects how archaeologists see the world—their vantage or standpoint (Hicks and McAtackney 2007).

Advocates of collaboration define archaeology by excluding those aspects of the practice that contradict their view. We suggest that how researchers define archaeology strongly influences how they portray its social impact. Archaeologists whose research focuses on academic and especially collaborative archaeology describe it in positive, progressive, even celebratory terms—for example, as "admirable" and "ethical" (Colwell 2016). Alternatively, researchers who define archaeology to include cultural resource management (CRM) tend to represent the practice in a very different light—for example, as a "technology of government" (Smith 2004) and "a sham" (King 2009).

However, as Figure 3.4.1 illustrates, academic archaeology is, in fact, the exception, not the rule. The rule is cultural resource management, accounting for up to 97 percent of archaeological projects and most of the money involved in the industry (La Salle and Hutchings 2012, Ferris and Welch 2014: 74, Green and Doershuk 1998: 122). Yet, CRM is marginalized in academic archaeology insofar as it is rarely discussed (Hutchings and La Salle 2014), and literature espousing the benefits of collaboration contributes to this situation. Case studies in these publications nearly always refer to collaborative projects between academic archaeologists and Indigenous communities (e.g., Atalay et al. 2014, Martindale and Lyons 2014). The collaborative turn, articulated as representing the

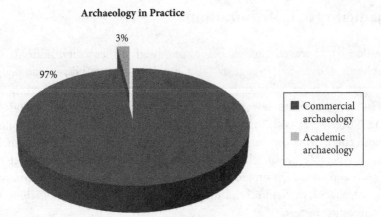

Archaeology in Practice

3%

97%

Commercial archaeology

Academic archaeology

FIGURE 3.4.1. Proportion of academic versus CRM archaeology as measured in British Columbia, Canada in 2011 (La Salle and Hutchings 2012).

"transformation" of archaeology, is thus only really relevant to academic settings—the overwhelming minority of the discipline as it is practiced.

Further, collaboration is marginalized even within academic archaeology. To assess whether collaborative or Indigenous archaeology projects are representative of North American academic archaeology more broadly, we reviewed the three most prestigious academic archaeology journals in North America: *Journal of World Prehistory, Journal of Archaeological Research,* and *American Antiquity* (Scimago Journal and Country Rank 2015; see also Guerrero-Bote and Moya-Anegón 2012). We analyzed the articles and reports in these three journals over the last five years (2012 to 2016) to identify projects that either focused on Indigenous or collaborative archaeology or acknowledged collaboration with local communities. We specifically searched for and manually reviewed the following terms:

- public;
- Native, (First) Nation;
- Indian, Indigenous;
- collaboration, community.

In the three journals analyzed, these topics are addressed in just 4.7 percent (14 of 295) of the publications. As a proxy for North American academic archaeology, these results confirm the limited attention given to Indigenous and collaborative approaches.

Given that most archaeology is CRM and most academic archaeology is not collaborative, it is not just misleading to suggest that archaeology in North America has been radically transformed by collaboration (Atalay et al. 2014, Colwell 2016); it is blatantly wrong. It is also dangerous, for such an assertion enables archaeologists to whitewash the colonial culture of archaeology and the heritage crimes committed against Indigenous peoples through cultural resource management (Hutchings and La Salle 2017a).

The Inequality of Collaboration

Collaboration is characterized as being premised on equality; indeed, Colwell-Chanthaphonh (2012: 271) suggests "the gulf" between Indigenous people and archaeologists has been bridged. How this transformation is measured, however, is unclear. Indeed, there are few publications that directly address methodology for evaluating "success" in collaboration. Recent examples include David Guilfoyle and Erin Hogg (2015), who use self-evaluation by archaeologists to assess collaborative outcomes; predictably, these self-evaluations are largely positive (Kahan et al. 2011). Craig Cipolla and James Quinn (2016) likewise rely on self-evaluation to consider their Indigenous archaeology field school project, but their analysis does include views of both collaborating parties.

There are, however, other ways of evaluating equality; for example, income and education are often used as indicators (e.g., UNECE 2015). In a review of data available for British Columbia, Canada, for example, we found that salaries for academic archaeologists are nearly six times the average annual income for Indigenous people (La Salle 2014). Moreover, most CRM archaeologists have a Bachelors degree, and academic archaeologists have at least a Master's, usually a Doctorate. Conversely, less than 10 percent of Aboriginal people in Canada have a university degree (Statistics Canada 2011). Add to this that most archaeologists in North America are white, and any claims of equality or a bridged "gulf" between archaeologists and Indigenous communities become problematic.

Evaluating power within collaborative archaeology, Colwell (2016: 117, fig. 1) has delineated a spectrum with "colonial control" at one end and "collaboration" towards the other. In his paradigm, Colwell sees collaboration as the end goal. However, if collaboration is about *sharing power equally*, then it should be in the middle of his table, as we illustrate here in Table 3.4.1. We suggest Colwell identifies collaboration as the end goal because archaeologists are not willing or able to move beyond collaboration and surrender control over Indigenous heritage. Collaboration is thus a compromise that ensures archaeologists get to keep their jobs and all the social, political, and economic benefits that result.

As discussed above, collaboration is also largely limited to academic archaeology. In CRM, *consultation* with Indigenous communities is the standard, not collaboration, and requires only minimal contact with the affected community. However, consultation has been critiqued as lip-service, manipulation, and cooptation (Gnecco 2012, La Salle 2013). Even where CRM projects are framed as collaborative (e.g., Connaughton et al. 2014, Connaughton and Herbert 2017), Indigenous participants are paid by the consulting firm or project proponent for their participation, typically as "monitors." This has been described as a form of tokenism (Devries 2014) and corporate heritage discourse that manipulates social responsibility in the name of capitalist development (Baird 2017, Coombe and Baird 2016). Such financial incentive to be involved makes "collaboration" in CRM a form of coercion; it does not afford both parties free, prior,

Table 3.4.1. Spectrum of power and control in archaeology. Adapted from Colwell (2016: 117).

COLONIAL ARCHAEOLOGY/EXTERNAL ◀◀◀ POWER & CONTROL ▶▶▶ *INDIGENOUS ARCHAEOLOGY/INTERNAL*

	Colonial Resistance	Colonial Dominance	Indigenous Participation	Collaboration	Colonial Participation	Indigenous Dominance	Indigenous Resistance
Goals	Goals of colonial states and their archaeologists develop in opposition to sovereign Indigenous peoples	Goals are set by colonial states and their archaeologists	Goals develop independently	Goals develop jointly between colonial states and sovereign Indigenous peoples	Goals develop independently	Goals are set by sovereign Indigenous peoples and their archaeologists	Goals of sovereign Indigenous peoples and their archaeologists develop in opposition to colonial states
Information	Information is controlled and secreted	Information is extracted and removed from Indigenous peoples	Information is disclosed by colonial states and their archaeologists to Indigenous peoples	Information flows freely between colonial states and sovereign Indigenous peoples	Information is disclosed by Indigenous peoples and their archaeologists to colonial states	Information is extracted and removed from colonial states	Information is controlled and secreted
Involvement	Indigenous involvement is resisted	Indigenous peoples are not involved in archaeology except as labor	Limited Indigenous involvement	Equal involvement of colonial states and sovereign Indigenous peoples	Limited state involvement	States are not involved in archaeology except as labor	State involvement is resisted
Voice	Resistant to Indigenous voices	Full state voice	Some Indigenous voice	Voices of colonial states and sovereign Indigenous peoples heard equally	Some state voice	Full Indigenous voice	Resistant to colonial voices
Support	No Indigenous support is given/obtained	Acquiescence is enforced by the state	Indigenous support is solicited	Power shared equitably between colonial states and sovereign Indigenous peoples	State support is solicited	Acquiescence is enforced by Indigenous peoples	No state support is given/obtained
Needs	Indigenous needs resisted	Needs of states privileged	Needs of both parties are somewhat met	Needs of both colonial states and sovereign Indigenous peoples met	Needs of both parties are somewhat met	Needs of Indigenous peoples privileged	State needs resisted

and informed consent. Thus, in CRM—and therefore most archaeology—power remains firmly in the hands of archaeologists and the colonizing states they represent.

The Myth of Decolonization

It is unclear how proponents of collaborative archaeology conclude their practice is decolonizing. Indeed, decolonization was once the goal of Indigenous archaeology, defined as "with, for, and by" Indigenous peoples; however, collaboration, defined as power sharing, is also framed as decolonizing.

The central tenet of decolonization is that the colonized retake control (Adams 1995, Alfred 2009). Frantz Fanon (1963: 37) has described this as "the last shall be first and the first last." Linda Tuhiwai Smith (2006: 98) envisions decolonization as "a long-term process involving the bureaucratic, cultural, linguistic and psychological divesting of colonial power." Aman Sium and colleagues (2012) suggest a vision of decolonization must necessarily be an Indigenous one or risk becoming hegemonic. Eve Tuck and Wayne Yang (2012) insist decolonization is not a metaphor and must involve the repatriation of and control over Indigenous land and life.

By these definitions, archaeology is not decolonized when non-Indigenous scholars are the primary or even co-directors of research. Decolonization in academia would minimally entail Indigenous archaeologists replacing non-Indigenous professors who study Indigenous pasts, yet this is a trend not yet observed. In North America, there are only a few Indigenous archaeologists employed as professors at universities and, in our experience, these positions have not replaced but rather added to those already existing. As described above, most archaeology does not involve collaboration with Indigenous communities, and few authors are Indigenous (see, for example, Hillerdal et al. 2017). Instead, mostly non-Indigenous archaeologists employed at state institutions continue to study Indigenous pasts. Likewise, in CRM, Indigenous archaeology firms are few and far between compared with non-Indigenous consulting companies (La Salle and Hutchings 2012). This is a far cry from decolonization as imagined above.

The assertion of collaborative archaeology as decolonizing is especially problematic when considering how the definition of Indigenous archaeology has changed. Originally defined as "with, for, and by" Indigenous peoples (Nicholas and Andrews 1997), Indigenous archaeology emphasized control over archaeology by Indigenous people (Atalay 2006: 283). Such approaches are represented in the three columns to the right of collaboration in Table 3.4.1.

Since first articulated, the definition of Indigenous archaeology has broadened to include "with, for, *or* by" Indigenous communities (Nicholas 2008: 1665, emphasis added), such that Indigenous people are not necessarily involved. Indeed, Indigenous archaeology is now defined by vague criteria including "a political statement" and "a postcolonial enterprise" (Nicholas 2008: 1660). Most recently, Colwell (2016: 117–119) suggested Indigenous archaeology does not need to either include Indigenous people or be about Indigenous history at all. Rather than decolonization, Colwell (2016: 117, citing Nicholas 2010) suggests the goal of Indigenous archaeology *is to end it* "by fully integrating these scholars and their views into everyday practices." This is hegemony in action.

Something is fundamentally wrong when Indigenous archaeology does not involve Indigenous people, sites, or history, and when sharing power is seen as giving up power. This represents a watering down and whitewashing of the politics of Indigenous archaeology and decolonization, theorizing both until they mean nothing. If decolonization were truly the goal, the far-right column in Table 3.4.1 would be the objective, where Aboriginal groups are in full control of their own heritage (e.g., Nicholas 2006, 2017, Watkins 2000, 2012, Yellowhorn 2002). Instead, collaboration is framed as both the means *and* the end, coopting Indigenous archaeology and ultimately giving *less* power to Indigenous communities (Cipolla and Quinn 2016), not more.

This should come as no surprise. Writing about the "colonized mind," Peter d'Errico (2011: n.p.) notes how easily:

> We might say that collaboration among Indian nations and [the colonizing state] is the best of both worlds. Even here, however, we must be careful. To "collaborate," in its root meaning, is to "work together"; but there is also a different meaning: "traitorous cooperation with the enemy." Which of these we mean—and which we engage in—depends on whether our minds are decolonized. "Working together" requires all participants to work on themselves, their thinking, assumptions, perspectives, beliefs, and habits of mind. Decolonization is personal and political.

The message is clear: until decolonization is a reality, collaboration must be considered co-optation.

CONCLUSION

> What could be more reasonable than a desire to ensure that you are the custodian of your own cultural heritage? And what could be more unreasonable than holding another people's cultural heritage, of ongoing significance to them, in your hands?
>
> Michael Asch (2009: 394)

Collaboration can have positive outcomes for those involved (see Atalay et al. 2014), but there is little evidence that the structure of archaeology has shifted away from its colonial origins. Our review of collaborative archaeology illustrates significant bias in how archaeology is defined (by the exceptions), how power is represented (as equal), and how collaboration is viewed (as decolonizing). When considered as it is practiced, archaeology remains a colonial technology of government designed to control living Indigenous people by controlling their heritage. Not only is the identified goal of decolonization not being met, but it is questionable whether this is truly the goal or just rhetoric.

In our analysis, archaeology has not been reborn, nor has it become "sophisticated and nuanced" in its associations with Indigenous people. As Anne Pyburn (2014: 198) notes, "[o]ne of the primary lessons of colonialism is that interference is damaging to local groups and Indigenous cultures, and that what outsiders think will help is often not at all helpful." We see no evidence to suggest this statement is any less true about collaboration. Instead, we maintain North American archaeologists should continue to be viewed "with wary eyes" (Watkins 2005). Such a gaze lends a very different view of collaboration than the vision provided by its proponents, who prefer to see their practice through rose-colored glasses.

Collaboration as a cure-all is a myth that absolves archaeologists of their colonial past and present. Yet, in our estimation, the only needs that are consistently met are those of the archaeologists and the colonizing states they represent. We thus call upon archaeologists to be honest about what collaboration is, what specific problems they are fixing, and whether archaeologists even have the power to accomplish these goals.

Postscript

We provided in this chapter a counter to the official discourse surrounding collaborative archaeology, which we feel is simplistic, celebratory, and lacking in critical reflection. Here, as with our other work, responses by archaeologists to our "ruthless criticism" (Marx 1978 [1844]: 13; see also Smith 2012: 534–5) have been strong and defensive, condemning our "negative tone" and "stark" outlook (Hutchings and La Salle 2015a, 2015b, 2015c, 2017b). The response by reviewers to this chapter did not deviate significantly from this pattern. For example, one reviewer suggested "It is a poor archaeologist that does not have a positive view of the discipline"; another said, "We want to hear about heritage theory and practice, not the sorry state of the world." Reviewers instead asked us to emphasize "positive" solutions. We offer here our response to these requests.

We have seen no evidence to suggest that focusing on the positive stories will bring about the radical change necessary if equality and decolonization are really the goals; indeed this is the central thesis of our chapter here. Moreover, as d'Errico notes above, "decolonization is personal and political," thus the process should and will be unsettling to the colonizers. Furthermore, most archaeologists today are operating within the powerful structural constraints of corporate and state policies and laws; most archaeologists probably feel they have little or no control in this structure, regardless of what power they may actually have. Thus, our story is not a simple one of "good guys" and "bad guys" and quick fixes; indeed, it is increasingly likely there will be no happy ending (Hutchings 2017, 2018). This is not Disney.

A major gap thus exists between our worldview and those expressed by proponents of collaboration: they believe archaeology can be decolonized, while we believe decolonization means the end of archaeology. Points of departure for our perspective are Laurajane Smith and Emma Waterton's (2009) argument to "take archaeology out of heritage" and Marie Battiste's (2005) recognition that "you can't be the colonial doctor if you're the colonial disease." Decolonization means dismantling not just the state apparatus of archaeology/CRM, but the colonizing state itself. Until archaeologists see themselves as part of colonization and not the solution to it, they will remain entangled in a practice that disempowers Indigenous people and destroys the very heritage it claims to protect.

Acknowledgments

We are grateful to the editors for inviting us to contribute this chapter, and to the reviewers for their comments and suggestions.

References

Adams, Howard. 1995. *A Tortured People: The Politics of Colonization*. Penticton, BC: Theytus Books Ltd.

Alfred, Taiaiake. 2009. *Peace, Power, Righteousness: An Indigenous Manifesto*. 2nd edn. Oxford: Oxford University Press.

Asch, Michael. 2009. "Concluding Thoughts and Fundamental Questions," in *Protection of First Nations Cultural Heritage: Laws, Policy, and Reform*, ed. C. Bell and R. K. Paterson. Vancouver, BC: UBC Press, 394–411.

Atalay, Sonya. 2006. "Indigenous Archaeology as Decolonizing Practice." *The American Indian Quarterly* 30(3–4): 280–310.

Atalay, Sonya, Lee Rains Clauss, Randall H. McGuire, and John R. Welch, eds. 2014. *Transforming Archaeology: Activist Practices and Prospects*. Walnut Creek, CA: Left Coast Press.

Baird, Melissa F. 2017. "Extractive Industries, Corporate Disourse and Indigenous Heritage," in *Archaeologies of "Us" and "Them": Debating History, Heritage and Indigeneity*, ed. Charlotta Hillerdal, Anna Karlström, and Carl-Gösta Ohala. London: Routledge, 53–63.

Battiste, Marie. 2005. "You Can't Be the Global Doctor if You're the Colonial Disease," in *Teaching as Activism: Equity Meets Environmentalism*, ed. P. Tripp and L. Muzzin. Montreal, QC: McGill-Queen's Press, 120–133.

Bernbeck, Reinhard, and Randall H. McGuire. 2000. "A Conceptual History of Ideology and its Place in Archaeology," in *Ideologies in Archaeology*, ed. R. Bernbeck and R. H. McGuire. Tucson, AZ: University of Arizona Press, 15–59.

Bruchac, Margaret, Siobhan Hart, and H. Martin Wobst. 2010. "Preface," in *Indigenous Archaeologies: A Reader on Decolonization*, ed. Margaret Bruchac, Siobhan Hart, and H. Martin Wobst. Walnut Creek, CA: Left Coast Press, 11–14.

Cipolla, Craig N., and James Quinn. 2016. "Field School Archaeology the Mohegan Way: Reflections on Twenty Years of Community-Based Research and Teaching." *Journal of Community Archaeology & Heritage* 3: 118–134.

Colwell, Chip. 2016. "Collaborative Archaeologies and Descendent Communities." *Annual Review of Anthropology* 45: 1–15.

Colwell-Chanthaphonh, Chip. 2012. "Archaeology and Indigenous Collaboration," in *Archaeological Theory Today*, ed. Ian Hodder, 267–291. Cambridge: Polity Press.

Colwell-Chanthaphonh, Chip, and T. J. Ferguson, eds. 2008. *Collaboration in Archaeological Practice: Engaging Descendant Communities*. Lanham, MD: AltaMira Press.

Connaughton, Sean P., and James Herbert. 2017. "Engagement Within: An Anthropological Exploration of First Nations Engagement and Consulting Archaeology within a Transnational Corporation." *Archaeologies*. DOI: 10.1007/s11759-017-9317-7.

Connaughton, Sean P., Mike Leon, and James Herbert. 2014. "Collaboration, Partnerships, and Relationships within a Corporate World." *Canadian Journal of Archaeology* 38: 541–562.

Coombe, Rosemary J., and Melissa F. Baird. 2016. "Heritage: Corporate Interests and Cultural Rights on Resource Frontiers," in *A Companion to Heritage Studies*, ed. W. William Logan, Mairead Nie Craith, and Ullrich Kockel. Hoboken, NJ: John Wiley & Sons, 337–354.

Custer, Jay F. 2005. "Ethics and the Hyperreality of the Archaeological Thought World." *North American Archaeologist* 26: 3–27.

d'Errico, Peter. 2011. "What Is a Colonized Mind?" *Indian Country Today* December 12. <http://indiancountrytodaymedianetwork.com/2011/12/12/what-colonized-mind>.

Deloria, Vine, Jr. 1969. *Custer Died for your Sins*. New York: Macmillan Press.

Deloria, Vine, Jr. 1997. *Red Earth, White Lies: Native Americans and the Myth of Scientific Fact*. New York: Scribner.

Devries, Megan. 2014. "*Cultural Resource Management and Aboriginal Engagement: Policy and Practice in Ontario Archaeology*." Unpublished Master's Thesis, Department of Anthropology, University of Western Ontario.

Fanon, Frantz. 1963. *The Wretched of the Earth: The Handbook for the Black Revolution That Is Changing the Shape of the World*. New York: Grove Press.

Ferris, Neal, and John R. Welch. 2014. "New Worlds: Ethics in Contemporary North American Archaeological Practice," in *Ethics and Archaeological Praxis*, ed. Cristobal Gnecco and Dorothy Lippert. New York: Springer, 69–92.

Fowler, Don D. 1987. "Uses of the Past: Archaeology in the Service of the State." *American Antiquity* 52: 229–248.

Gnecco, Cristobal. 2012. "Europe and the People without Archaeology," in *European Archaeology Abroad: Global Settings, Comparative Perspectives*, ed. Sjoerd J. Van der Linde, Monique H. van de Dries, and Corijanne G. Slappendel. Leiden: Sidestone Press, 387–399.

Gnecco, Cristobal, and Adriana S. Dias, eds. 2015. "Special Issue: On Contract Archaeology." *International Journal of Historical Archaeology* 19(4): 687–842.

Green, William, and John F. Doershuk. 1998. "Cultural Resource Management and American Archaeology." *Journal of Archaeological Research* 6(2): 121–67.

Guerrero-Bote, Vicente P. and Félix Moya-Anegón. 2012. "A Further Step Forward in Measuring Journals' Scientific Prestige: The SJR2 Indicator." *Journal of Informetrics* 6: 647–688.

Guilfoyle, David R., and Erin A. Hogg. 2015. "Towards an Evaluation-Based Framework of Collaborative Archaeology." *Advances in Archaeological Practice* 3(2): 107–123.

Hicks, Dan, and Laura McAtackney. 2007. "Introduction: Landscapes as Standpoints," in *Envisioning Landscape: Situations and Standpoints in Archaeology and Heritage*, ed. Dan Hicks, Laura McAtackney, and Graham Fairclough. Walnut Creek, CA: Left Coast Press, 13–29.

Hillerdal, Charlotta, Anna Karlström, and Carl-Gösta Ohala, eds. 2017. *Archaeologies of "Us" and "Them": Debating History, Heritage and Indigeneity*. London: Routledge.

Hogg, Erin, John R. Welch, and Neal Ferris. 2017. "Full Spectrum Archaeology." *Archaeologies* 13(1): 175–200.

Hutchings, Richard M. 2017. *Maritime Heritage in Crisis: Indigenous Landscapes and Global Ecological Breakdown*. London: Routledge.

Hutchings, Richard M. 2019. "Meeting the Shadow: Cultural Resource Management and the McDonaldization of Heritage Stewardship," in *Human-Centered Built Environment Heritage Conservation: Theory and Evidence-Based Practice*, ed. Jeremy C. Wells and Barry Stiefel. New York: Routledge.

Hutchings, Richard M., and Joshua Dent, eds. 2017. "Archaeology and the Late Modern State." *Archaeologies* 13(1): 1–25.

Hutchings, Richard M., and Marina La Salle. 2014. "Teaching Anti-Colonial Archaeology." *Archaeologies* 10(1): 27–69.

Hutchings, Richard M., and Marina La Salle. 2015a. "Archaeology as Disaster Capitalism." *International Journal of Historical Archaeology* 19: 699–720.

Hutchings, Richard M., and Marina La Salle. 2015b. "Arqueologia como Capitalismo do Desastre." *Revista de Arqueologia da Sociedade de Arqueologia Brasileira* 28(2): 20–44.

Hutchings, Richard M., and Marina La Salle. 2015c. "Why Archaeologists Misrepresent their Practice: A North American Perspective." *Journal of Contemporary Archaeology* 2(2): S11–S17.

Hutchings, Richard M., and Marina La Salle. 2017a. "Archaeology as State Heritage Crime." *Archaeologies* 13(1): 66–87.

Hutchings, Richard M., and Marina La Salle. 2017b. "Arqueología como Capitalismo del Desastre," in *Crítica de la Razón Arqueológica: Arqueología de Contrato y Capitalismo*, ed. Cristóbal Gnecco and Adriana Dias. Bogotá: Instituto Colombiano de Antropología e Historia, 29–57.

Kahan, Dan M., Hank Jenkins-Smith, and Donald Braman. 2011. "Cultural Cognition of Scientific Consensus." *Journal of Risk Research* 14: 147–174.

King, Thomas F. 2009. *Our Unprotected Heritage: Whitewashing the Destruction of our Cultural and Natural Environment*. Walnut Creek, CA: Left Coast Press.

King, Thomas F. 2012. *Cultural Resource Laws and Practice*. 4th edn. Lanham, MD: AltaMira Press.

La Salle, Marina. 2010. "Community Collaboration and Other Good Intentions." *Archaeologies* 6(3): 401–422.

La Salle, Marina. 2013. "'Capital-C' Consultation: Community, Capitalism, and Colonialism." *New Proposals* 6(1–2): 72–88.

La Salle, Marina. 2014. "The Trouble with 'Co-'." *Institute for Critical Heritage and Tourism Bulletin* 2014-2.

La Salle, Marina, and Richard M. Hutchings. 2012. "Commercial Archaeology in British Columbia." *The Midden* 44(2): 8–16.

La Salle, Marina, and Richard M. Hutchings. 2016. "What Makes Us Squirm: A Critical Assessment of Community-Oriented Archaeology." *Canadian Journal of Archaeology* 40(1): 164–180.

Martindale, Andrew, and Natasha Lyons, eds. 2014. "Special Issue: Community-Oriented Archaeology." *Canadian Journal of Archaeology* 38(2): 425–562.

Marx, Karl. 1978 [1844]. "For a Ruthless Criticism of Everything Existing," in *The Marx–Engels Reader*, ed. R. C. Tucker. 2nd edn. New York: W. W. Norton, 12–15.

McNiven, Ian, and Lynette Russell. 2005. *Appropriated Pasts: Indigenous Peoples and the Colonial Culture of Archaeology*. Oxford: Altamira Press.

Nicholas, George P. 2006. "Decolonizing the Archaeological Landscape: The Practice and Politics of Archaeology in British Columbia." *American Indian Quarterly* 30(3–4): 350–380.

Nicholas, George P. 2008. "Native Peoples and Archaeology." *Encyclopedia of Archaeology* 3: 1660–1669.

Nicholas, George P. 2010. "Seeking the End of Indigenous Archaeology," in *Bridging the Divide: Indigenous Communities and Archaeology into the 21st Century*, ed. Caroline Phillips and Harry Allen. Walnut Creek, CA: Left Coast Press, 233–252.

Nicholas, George P. 2017. "Culture, Rights, Indigeneity and Intervention: Addressing Inequality in Indigenous Heritage Protection and Control," in *Archaeologies of "Us" and "Them": Debating History, Heritage and Identity*, ed. Charlotta Hillerdal, Anna Karlström, and Carl-Gösta Ohala. London: Routledge, 199–217.

Nicholas, George P., and Thomas D. Andrews. 1997. "Indigenous Archaeology in the Postmodern World," in *At a Crossroads: Archaeologists and First Peoples in Canada*, ed. George P. Nicholas and Thomas D. Andrews. Burnaby, BC: SFU Archaeology Press, 1–18.

Pyburn, K. Anne. 2014. "Activating Archaeology," in *Transforming Archaeology: Activist Practices and Prospects*, ed. Sonya Atalay, Lee Rains Clauss, Randall H. McGuire, and John R. Welch. Walnut Creek, CA: Left Coast Press, 197–214.

Scimago Journal and Country Rank. 2015. "Journal Rankings." <http://www.scimagojr.com/journalrank.php?category=3302&country=Northern%20America>.

Sium, Aman, Chandni Desai, and Eric Ritskes. 2012. "Towards the 'Tangible Unknown': Decolonization and the Indigenous Future." *Decolonization: Indigeneity, Education & Society* 1(1): I–XIII.

Smith, Laurajane. 2004. *Archaeological Theory and the Politics of Cultural Heritage*. London: Routledge.

Smith, Linda Tuhiwai. 2006. *Decolonizing Methodologies: Research and Indigenous Peoples*. London: Zed Books.

Smith, Laurajane, and Emma Waterton, eds. 2009. *Taking Archaeology Out of Heritage*. Cambridge: Cambridge Scholars Press.

Smith, Laurajane, and Emma Waterton. 2012. "Constrained by Commonsense: The Authorized Heritage Discourse in Contemporary Debates," in *The Oxford Handbook of Public Archaeology*, ed. Robin Skeates, Carole McDavid, and John Carman. Oxford: Oxford University Press. DOI: 10.1093/oxfordhb/9780199237821.013.0009.

Smith, Claire, and H. Martin Wobst. 2005. "Decolonizing Archaeological Theory and Practice," in *Indigenous Archaeologies: Decolonizing Theory and Practice*, ed. Claire Smith and H. Martin Wobst. London: Routledge, 5–16.

Statistics Canada. 2011. "The Educational Attainment of Aboriginal Peoples in Canada." <http://www12.statcan.gc.ca/nhs-enm/2011/as-sa/99-012-x/99-012-x2011003_3-eng.cfm>.

Swidler, Nina, Kurt E. Dongoske, Roger Anyon, and Alan S. Downer, eds. 1997. *Native Americans and Archaeologists: Stepping Stones to Common Ground*. Walnut Creek, CA: AltaMira Press.

Tuck, Eve, and K. Wayne Yang. 2012. "Decolonization Is Not a Metaphor." *Decolonization: Indigeneity, Education and Society* 1(1): 1–40.

United Nations Economic Commission for Europe (UNECE). 2015. "Indicators of Gender Equality." Report prepared for the Task Force on Indicators of Gender Equality. <https://www.unece.org/fileadmin/DAM/stats/publications/2015/ECE_CES_37_WEB.pdf>.

Watkins, Joe. 2000. *Indigenous Archaeology: American Indian Values and Scientific Practice*. Lanham, MD: AltaMira Press.

Watkins, Joe. 2005. "Through Wary Eyes: Indigenous Perspectives on Archaeology." *Annual Review of Anthropology* 34: 429–449.

Watkins, Joe. 2012. "Public Archaeology and Indigenous Archaeology: Intersections and Divergences from a Native American Perspective," in *The Oxford Handbook of Public Archaeology*, ed. Robin Skeates, Carole McDavid, and John Carman. Oxford: Oxford University Press. DOI: 10.1093/oxfordhb/9780199237821.013.0034.

Watkins, Joe, and George P. Nicholas. 2014. "Why Indigenous Archaeology Is Important as a Means of Changing Relationships between Archaeologists and Indigenous Communities," in *Indigenous Heritage and Tourism: Theories and Practices on Utilizing the Ainu Heritage*, ed. Mayumi Okada and Hirofumi Kato. Japan: Hokkaido University Center for Ainu and Indigenous Studies Report, Hokkaido University, 141–151.

Wobst, H. Martin. 2005. "Power to the (Indigenous) Past and Present! Or: The Theory and Method behind Archaeological Theory and Methods," in *Indigenous Archaeologies: Decolonizing Theory and Practice*, ed. Claire Smith and H. Martin Wobst. London: Routledge, 17–32.

Yellowhorn, Eldon C. 2002. "Awakening Internalist Archaeology in the Aboriginal World." Unpublished Ph.D. dissertation, Department of Anthropology, McGill University.

Zimmerman, Larry J. 2006. "Sharing Control of the Past," in *Archaeological Ethics*, ed. Karen D. Vitelli and Chip Colwell-Chanthaphonh. Lanham, MD: Altamira Press, 170–175.

....

THE SPECIAL RESPONSIBILITY OF PUBLIC SPACES TO DISMANTLE WHITE SUPREMACIST HISTORICAL NARRATIVES

....

KAREN L. B. BURGARD AND
MICHAEL L. BOUCHER, JR.

INTRODUCTION: THE ADDITIVE HISTORICAL CURRICULUM OF MUSEUMS

IN September 2016, President Barack Obama spoke to a crowd at the opening of the National Museum of African American History and Culture (NMAAHC). After decades of discussion, debate, and legislation, Washington DC finally had a Smithsonian museum dedicated to the significance of African American contributions to the history of the United States. The Washington Post chronicled the historic day (Contrera 2016): "In a speech filled with reminders of America's dark and not-so-distant past, and hopes for a brighter future, President Obama helped to inaugurate the National Museum of African American History and Culture today in Washington. The country's first black chief executive stood before a crowd of more than 7,000 official guests—and thousands more gathered on the National Mall [stating] 'African American history is not somehow separate than the American story. It is not the underside of the American story. It is central to the American story.'" Despite the President's exhortation that African American history is not "separate," the addition of museums on the National Mall dedicated to the lived experiences of Native Americans (est. 2004) and African Americans (est. 2016) are indicative of the additive model museums take when including the experiences of people of color and under-represented groups to the American story. These museums are, in fact, separate from the National Museum of American History (NMAH) (est. 1964) that primarily focuses on political history, military history, and popular culture. The need for these museums that specialize in other histories arose from the inability of the NMAH to adequately represent the histories of marginalized groups.

While we celebrate the creation of these museums and their missions, the work of dismantling White supremacist narratives in our museums and public spaces still has not been undertaken with enough intentionality (Bonilla-Silva 2001, Inwood and Alderman 2016). To history educators tasked with inspiring the next generation of civically engaged citizens, all museums, signposts, markers, and public monuments compose a tapestry of historical curriculum that tells the official story of the United States. That story, though many are reticent to see or admit, is overwhelmingly a whitewashed and colorblind version of America that centers White[1] supremacy and it is the special responsibility of the curators of these public spaces to recognize, and then decenter, White supremacy in that curriculum (Goodman 2008, Loewen 1999, Painter 2010).

POSITIONALITY AND THEORETICAL FRAMEWORK

As to our positionality, both authors are former secondary social studies teachers with a background in teaching both US and world history. Both of us have decades long experience advocating for social studies and history education at the state, national, and international level and in the study of curriculum and instruction. We have served on the board of the National Council for the Social Studies and have been part of writing teams for history standards in three states. Currently we are educational researchers focusing on curriculum and instruction. In addition, we are teacher educators who train future K–12 educators to use inclusive, culturally relevant pedagogy. Burgard is White, of mostly German and English descent and Boucher is descended from multiple European ancestries and Native American.

When discussing race, it is important that it not be confused with culture, and to understand that it is not a scientific, but a social construction created by, and for the benefit of, people considered White (Frankenberg 1993). It is not static who is considered White, Black, or other races, as the parameters of racial categorization are historically fluid, changing with the political and social needs of the times (Brodkin 1998, Hargrove 2009, Monroe 2017, Painter 2010, Roediger 2005). Yet, whiteness and its hegemonic and normative power is a daily reality. Race and whiteness were created by White people to provide them with structural, material, and personal advantage; thus these concepts are as real as the other foundational ideas in American history. Bestowing upon or withholding whiteness from individuals and groups has been a driving force behind American history, laws, social mores, and historical memory, and continues to be a determining factor in our social, economic, and political life (Lipsitz 2006, Painter 2010).

To examine the implications of whiteness, White supremacy, and erasure at historic sites, we have chosen the framework of Critical White Studies (CWS). CWS is a way for White scholars to engage with the work of Critical Race Theorists (CRT) like Derrick Bell who encouraged White scholars to begin their own examinations of the effects of whiteness in America (Delgado and Stefancic 1997, 2001, 2005). In education, the work of CRT scholar Gloria Ladson-Billings (Ladson-Billings and Tate 1995, Ladson-Billings 1998) set the foundations for scholars who have challenged White supremacy in education (Crowley 2016, Dixson and Rousseau 2005, Ledesma and Calderon 2015, Matias 2016, Taylor, Gillborn, and Ladson-Billings 2016). CRT has guiding propositions that frame the discussion of racism and racial inequities: (1) racism and White supremacy are foundational in US history and current US policy; (2) whiteness is a form of property that ensures White people will have economic and social benefits that are excluded from other people who are not considered White; (3) progress in law and politics for African Americans, e.g. *Brown v. Board of Education* (1954) are the result of interest convergence where White people's goals are met while White supremacy remains un-challenged; and (4) to uncover the experiences of racialized persons, CRT scholars use "counternarratives" to illustrate the nature of the racism, decenter whiteness in narratives, and challenge the normativity of whiteness (Dixson and Rousseau 2005, Ladson-Billings and Tate 1995, Ladson-Billings 1998). Critical White Studies accepts these propositions and uses the tools of CRT to expose White normativity, challenge White supremacy, and give a vehicle for White people to tell their stories about their own whiteness, leading to social action toward a more equitable society (Delgado and Stefancic 1997, Sleeter 2017).

WHITENESS AND THE HISTORICAL NARRATIVE

The theme that flows through all discussions of race in America is the one that is seldom spoken, as it is so normal that to name it has only recently been allowed; the ideology of White supremacy (Bonilla-Silva 2001, Leonardo 2004). White supremacy permeates our nation's museums and historic sites and overwhelms our efforts at inclusion. White supremacy is more than its most extreme version of violence and terrorism and means more than an individual or personal hatred of the Other. It manifests in more subtle ways in our public spaces and is expressed in the narratives of White progress, goodness, and innocence perpetuated in historical landmarks and museums as an exhibition of cultural power and cultural chauvinism (Burgard and Boucher 2016). As Leonardo (2004: 149) explained: "When it comes to official history, there is no paucity of repre-sentation of whites as its creator. . . . However, when it concerns domination, whites suddenly disappear, as if history were purely a positive sense of contribution. Their previous omnipresence becomes a position of nowhere, a certain politics of undetectability. When it comes to culture, our students learn a benign form of multiculturalism, as if culture were a purely constructive notion free of imperialist histories and examples of imposition." Using research on historical understanding, racialized historical understanding, historical understanding in museums and public spaces, and the concept of erasure in history, we contend that public historical spaces hold a powerful role in teaching our American story but the loud narrative of whiteness erases histories that would decenter White people. For those who identify as White, whiteness also blinds them to the intricacies of the American tapestry and drowns out the diverse cultures in the woven fabric of our national story and identity (Bonilla-Silva 2013, Spencer 2006). Consequently, for people of color to see their history, or hear the stories of their heritage above the deafening roar of whiteness, they must often create separate spaces or segregated historical areas within the larger White dominated spaces of museums and historical landmarks. This tendency to create separate spaces or to use an additive model of historical depiction allows whiteness to remain undisturbed and impedes historical understanding for all participants.

Our public sites, museums, and monuments, are used by citizens to conceptualize their past, regardless of what they may have formally learned in school, yet the contributions of populations not considered central to the White historical narrative are excluded or left to the margins, creating a historical understanding that centers only White people in history and leaves others as a sideline curiosity. Even when the narratives of marginalized, oppressed, and underrepresented groups were included, our study referenced in this chapter found that White supremacist and White progressive narratives, where the White majority gradually bestowed rights to people of color, still influenced students' understanding and interpretations, leading to a misunderstanding of the events and a mischaracterization of the historical sites (Burgard and Boucher 2016).

Normative Whiteness and Color-Blindness

Some argue that history is colorblind and factual (see Carr 1962), but our investigation challenges that assumption. According to Frankenberg (1993), whiteness is not seen as a separate racialized category, but is perceived as merely normal. She explained that three dimensions of whiteness allow this normality to occur. First, whiteness has a "structural advantage" of the power structure that fosters privileges that are only bestowed upon White people. Secondly, whiteness is a "standpoint" or positionality where White people see the world through a lens where they are set apart from other people and cultures. "Thirdly, [whiteness] carries with it a set of ways of being in the world, a set of cultural practices, often not named as 'white' by White [people], but looked on instead as 'American' or 'normal'" (p. 54). Being the norm in all parts of the culture including clothing, religion, values, and speech gives a deep misconception to White people as they grow up, and as they navigate the world in adulthood. Thus, when discussing the "American way of life," the narrative seldom includes people who are not White in the imaginations of the speaker. Whiteness is seen as normal, continuous, forthright, and mainstream. Diverse viewpoints of people who are not in this normative narrative include people of color, people who identify as Gay, Lesbian, Bisexual, or Transgendered, immigrants, colonized or conquered peoples, the enslaved, and the victims of mass slaughter.

Bonilla-Silva (2013: 2) explained that there is a pervasive practice in American discourse known as "color blind racism." Hayes and Juarez (2012: 7) stated, "Holding on to a color-blind framework allows people to address only the egregious forms of racism." However, the need to understand, and then extract White supremacist narratives requires more than a color-blind approach to historical memory. The color-blind discourse assumes that the experiences of White people in America are so normal that others who are not White must have their same experiences. Thus, the people who adhere to color-blind racism will say that they "do not see color," thereby erasing the historical and cultural context of the people who are not White and imposing whiteness upon them. Color-blindness, then, is not blind, but the refusal to see people for who they really are (Bonilla-Silva 2015). Color-blindness is also a way to circumvent race as a topic, avoiding discomfort and a possible challenge to White supremacy (Leonardo 2004). As White teachers and history educators, we have learned that colorblindness erases the lived experiences of our students and inhibits their understanding of the past. This race evasion and unconscious, unquestioned acceptance of White normalcy provides the framework from which the stories of history, and by extension the sites that contain those stories, are told. And any attempts to problematize the normalization of whiteness is often met with profound resistance or condemned as practicing presentism or political correctness.

HISTORIC SITES AS CURRICULUM

Public sites, museums, and markers are placed in specific geographical locations to teach people about the past. They are more than just places of remembrance or heritage, they are spaces whose specific purpose is the learning of history. Thus, the presented history in these sites and the places themselves are all *curriculum*. To help non-educators understand the meaning of curriculum, Egan (1978) explained in his foundational work, *What Is Curriculum?*, that it is the set of knowledge and skills desired from a student, or in the case of public histories, from the viewer, or recipient. The curriculum of a specific museum at an historic site will teach the visitors about the events that made that place significant. They may have certain desired outcomes of pride, patriotism, or look to trouble assumed notions about a place. But curriculum also encompasses all the historic sites across the country. A particular site can then be viewed in the same way that a single class will have a curriculum that is nested in the larger curriculum of a four-year degree.

Generally, curriculum is the mechanism to transmit the knowledge, understandings, and ideology of the older generations to the younger, or from the expert to the novice. As Egan (1978: 9) explained, in that way, curriculum is used to transmit culture and traditional frameworks: "In all human societies, children are initiated into particular modes of making sense of their experience and the world about them, and also into a set of norms, knowledge, and skills which the society requires for its continuance. In most societies most of the time, this 'curriculum' of initiation is not questioned; frequently it is enshrined in myths, rituals, and immemorial practices, which have absolute authority." Thus, when educators use the term curriculum, they are discussing the mechanisms to transmit both culture and knowledge.

Scholars have identified that public historical spaces have a curriculum that creates historical understanding (Baron 2012, Dean 2013, Evans 2013, Falk and Dierking 2000, Glassberg 1996, Handler and Gable 1997, Hooper-Greenhill 2007, Lewis 2005, Marcus and Levine 2011, Marcus, Levine, and Grenier 2012, Segall 2014, Wood and Wolf 2008, Woods 1995, Wunder 2002). This understanding can be increased through the questioning of accepted narratives, but instead, many historical sites seek not to trouble White supremacist narratives, and in most cases, choose to reinforce them. Due to its ideological nature, curriculum is then laden with unquestioned suppositions about how the world works.

The Hidden Historical Curriculum

To illustrate, "history books" are often assumed to be the authorities about the past and both students and adults rarely question the veracity of the historical narratives inside (Bain 2006, Loewen 2007, Luke, de Castell, and Luke 1989). The authority of historical sites is even less questioned than in textbooks so that receivers do not even imagine that there may be things deliberately left out of the story they are being told. Beyond the missing history, the "hidden curriculum" of White dominance in history education centers the stories of White people over all others that creates a progressive narrative of White Americans as center to US and world history (Giroux and Penna 1979, Jackson 1990). Thus, the fact that these pieces are missing is a hidden curriculum that histories of people who are not perceived as White are unimportant to the overall narrative. This intentional centering of White Americans and the omission of the stories and identities of marginalized and oppressed groups creates an unequal, ahistorical space allowing for a normative, White supremacist narrative while simultaneously further marginalizing the importance and significance of the historical contributions of other groups.

The Historical Erasure Curriculum

The concept of historical erasure is rooted in the belief that marginalized and oppressed populations have a valuable and important story to tell but societal structures, ideology, political agendas, and power differentials make that nearly impossible. Beyond the *leaving out*, or the *ignoring of* perspectives of people who are not perceived as White, erasure is a project specifically to accomplish at least one of the following: (1) establish ownership by White settlers of a particular piece of land; (2) establish a narrative of progress that reinforces White narratives of goodness, responsibility, hard work, and/ or the preferential treatment by God; (3) provide counterfactual narratives of White innocence or that erase White complicity in historical conflicts; (4) provide a historical narrative that devalues the contributions of aboriginal, enslaved, or marginalized peoples in a geographical area or for a particular event.

This phenomenon of *making blank* or enacting *erasure* has been a focus of education scholarship on historical texts, historic sites and museums, public memory, and public narratives in the United States and around the globe (Anglin 2004, Bigelow 2011, Byrne 2003, Foster 2010, Garcia 1993, Mattingly 2008, Santiago 2017). Historical erasure of marginalized groups presents the mechanism for a monolithic view of the past where those in power, often White wealthy men, are over-represented and centered in our history to the erasure of others. The rightness of their cause is unexamined, their heroism is extolled, their morality is heralded, and their brilliance in business, politics, or invention is raised as a role model for the youth of today. On the other side of that triumphant march is the erasure of the Other.

Scholars have explained that historical erasure is often transmitted through history textbooks (Garcia 1993, Hall 2008, Lee 2017, Loewen 2007). Erasure in history creates an incomplete narrative of who we are as a people and who we are as a nation. Santiago (2017: 47) discussed an example of historical erasure in the context of students' historical understanding of Mexican-American history. "People of color might be included, but under specific parameters. They are often 'injected' into the curriculum as a token example of how people of color were also present at historical events, but without changing the overall story." This tokenism further illustrates the White supremacist narrative. By including people of color in the historical discussion only as an addendum, a footnote, or only as an additive to the accomplishments of Whites further distances non-White populations from full participation in the national heritage, no matter what their historical contributions have been.

The Color-Blind Erasure Curriculum

Color-blindness and the centering of normative whiteness have resulted in a curriculum that has erased the lived experiences of those who are not part of the normative historical narrative. Even when politicians engage in this dialogue, they are often unwilling to extend the lesson to deal with the histories of the public curriculum because it takes more than removal of a statue to decenter whiteness. Inwood and Alderman (2016: 11) addressed the issues of historical erasure in national monuments to the Confederacy: "As state governments throughout the nation acted to remove the vestiges of Confederate symbolism from their public grounds and spaces, we suggest that these politicians, far from addressing the material and social consequences of the histories and geographies of racism, are in fact engaging in a process of historical and geographical erasure. Erasing or simply removing those symbols perpetuates forgetting the past, and presumably moving forward (for some) without engaging in true memory work." It is important not to engage in a different type of presentism and erasure around these statues and assume that they represent *heritage*. The purpose of their installation was to intimidate the African American populations and, if only symbolically, to defy desegregation (Applebaum 2017).

America's history has always had race at the center and so America's artifacts and sacred places all have a racialized element. The question for keepers of our history becomes whether that element is hidden, or displayed. This decision has deep consequences for the receivers of that information. Researchers have found that the racialized and cultural historical understanding of students directly impacts their understandings of events and artifacts (Barton 2001b, Burgard and Boucher 2016, Dimitriadis 2000, Epstein 2009, Howard 2004, Terzian and Yeager 2007, Trainor 2005).

The removal of the Confederate battle flag from the South Carolina Statehouse in 2015, the renaming of Lake Calhoun in Minneapolis, the renaming of Calhoun College at Yale University, and the removal of confederate memorials in New Orleans in 2017 have all caused controversy and a backlash from Confederate enthusiasts who insist that these symbols of White supremacy are not racist, and should remain (Holloway 2017, Inwood and Alderman 2016, McCrummen and Izadi 2015, Namakkal 2015, Rockeymoore 2017, Selk 2017, Yale News 2017). These monuments and names are more than just remembrances, they are tools to teach the history of the area, or building. As these examples show, people inject their own meaning into historical spaces and, by extension, their own historical understanding. However, these controversies also exemplify incomplete understandings and purposeful forgetting of the intent behind the erecting of these curricular monuments.

Complicating Curriculum: Racialized Historical Understanding

Complicating the research on curriculum of historic sites, is the research in racialized historical understanding. Understanding how people interpret history and make meaning and sense of the past is a well-researched field in education (Barton 2001a, 2004, 2005, Barton and Levstik 2004, 2011, Davis, Yeager, and Foster 2001, Doyle 2002, Foster 2010, Graff 1999, Grant 2001, Lee and Ashby 2000, Mandell 2008, Mayer 2006, Schocker 2014, Seixas 1994, 1998, Stearns, Seixas, and Wineburg 2000, Van Sledright and Afflerbach 2000, Van Sledright 2002, 2004, Wineburg 2001). To summarize, historical understanding is a process used by the consumer of the historical site, book, photo, or artifact to make meaning from the historical narrative (Burgard 2009, Burgard and Boucher 2016). While the research focuses primarily on P–12 students or student teachers in their early twenties, we are comfortable applying it to the rest of the public since most people do not continue to study history in a formal way after leaving a school setting. Through our study, we have learned that no matter the intent of the presenter, the curriculum *learned* is a uniquely individual experience and the parts of the curriculum that are accepted or rejected by the learner is complicated by their own biases and lived experiences. This narrative is grounded in individual lived experience and cultural background and heritage (Burgard and Boucher 2016).

Epstein (2009) connected race and historical understanding, showing that there are commonalities based on racialized lived experiences (Epstein and Shiller 2005, 2015, Epstein 1997, 1998, 2000, 2001). In one study, Epstein (2000: 202) found that African American students "constructed a nation in which White racism, rather than individual rights and democratic rule, played a significant role in the nation's formation, development, and contemporary conditions." The receivers of curriculum create a narrative of connections between historical events, places, and ideas and use available knowledge to decide what is historically significant based on their understanding. The shortened story of America, as it is most often told at historic sites, is one of triumph of thrifty, godly, White *settlers* over a hostile and savage continent, and our historical public curriculum is the most prominent purveyor of that facile and simplified narrative (Loewen 2007, Takaki 2008). However, while museums and historic sites truncate history for consumption by the multitudes, the decisions about what tales to tell and what to leave out are intentional and reflect the historical understanding of the creators and funders of the site.

To sum up, the historical narrative in museums and sites is viewed as authoritative, but the understanding that comes from the curriculum depends on the prior experiences of the receiver. This complex relationship between the message sent and the message received is the space the teacher occupies in the curriculum. Teachers guide students through curriculum to make sure they understand what is being read, heard, and seen. They create context for students, give them frameworks to understand new information, and assess students' understanding. The teacher provides opportunities to question and challenge those authoritative narratives. This is not to say that people do not learn from public curricular experiences, but the curriculum does not guarantee that it will be received as intended. Baron (2012: 845) explained, "The historic site ceases to be a historical moment encased in amber, but begins to speak to the ways in which contemporary interactions with the past can affect our ability to get to any particular historical 'truth.'" In public spaces, there is seldom a person there to guide and assess understanding so the curriculum must be created in a way that increases understanding and assumes that receivers will come with a combination of understandings and misunderstandings when they enter the site.

The Centering of Whiteness in Public Historic Curriculum

As Leonardo (2004: 144) explained, "To the extent that racial supremacy is taught to white students, it is pedagogical. Insofar as it is pedagogical, there is the possibility of critically reflecting on its flows in order to disrupt them." To investigate erasure and White supremacist narratives in public historical spaces, we asked high school students who were involved in touring historical spaces in Indiana, *who creates the narrative and whose voices are included in that narrative?* The details of method and sampling are available in a previously published article (Burgard and Boucher 2016). In this chapter, we hope to speak to a new audience using education literature on racialized historical understanding to challenge public history specialists to look at their own sites with the purpose of decentering whiteness and dismantling White supremacist narratives in our public curriculum. It is essential that when we begin to operationalize the dismantling of the White supremacist narratives that form our museums and historic sites that we look critically at how this history is being consumed and (mis)understood.

We have found through this work that it is not an easy task to portray the intricate web of events and the power relationships that move history. Understanding the past is made more difficult by factors like personal heritage, racial, cultural, and ethnic identity, and the racial consciousness of those consuming the history (Burgard and Boucher 2016, Barton 2001b, Dimitriadis 2000, Epstein 2009, Howard 2004, Terzian and Yeager 2007, Trainor 2005). People of color are often erased from historical narratives but even White people who do not meet the criteria of goodness can become excluded from historical narratives. Anglin (2004) found erasure is not limited to people who do not identify as White and social/economic class can also be a point of erasure in the historical narrative; for example, Anglin found that historians have been especially dismissive of Appalachian Whites. However, while class makes a difference in whose stories are told, lower-class Whites are eulogized in public histories all over the country. As an example, a search of "miners" on the Historical Marker Database yielded over three hundred markers documenting mining disasters and the accomplishments of mine workers (<http://www.hmdb.org>). Thus, while class can be an important marker for including the marginalized, the erasure of people of color should be a far more prevalent concern for educators.

Race, class, gender, power, and wealth all come together to create our past, but the challenge to portray the past in all its dirt and glory can, and should, be done for our children and their progeny. Taking these into account, we are calling for a reexamination of the mechanisms for content delivery in historical sites and museums and for how they are used in school curriculums.

WITNESSING THE POWER
OF PUBLIC HISTORY AS A REFLECTION
OF CULTURE AND HERITAGE

When museums and heritage sites work to make the invisible *visible*, our study showed that it is still difficult to create a narrative that does not erase (Burgard and Boucher 2016). However, even imperfect attempts have a deep effect on students from marginalized groups. In our study, we participated in a trip with both Black and White students who were exposed to historical sites and museums around the events of the Underground Railroad and segregation. We found that Black students had more dissatisfaction with their school history curriculum and were, at times, critical of the progressive narratives at the sites. White students approached the experience with a mental framework of American progress. There was a striking difference between the White students' uncomplicated progressive narrative and the Black students' more critical look at the history they were taught inside and outside of their classrooms. One White male stated: "I just thought it was really cool . . . how you know I've grown up that we're all integrated all times. We don't care about color and it's just such a big deal that people back then were so set in their ways. Some people did this and some people did that. Like Blacks weren't allowed to do this and Whites were allowed to do that" (White male). This participant argued that the modern day United States is one of integration and "not caring" about color or being "color blind" whereas people in the past focused on race as part of their daily lives. However, the African American students were more pessimistic in their view of US history taught in schools. One African American female stated: "I mean a lot of people think that segregation, I mean racism and stuff like that's, [all] over with, that slavery's over with. No, it just has a different name. It's just different. Like I guess any oppression kind of gets, like the oppression of people being in captivity . . . but that's not over with. It's still going on" (African American female).

These quotes, pulled from our previous work (Burgard and Boucher 2016), show that there are differences in how the two groups understood American history. The White students incorporated a progressive narrative and accepted historical sites as remnants of an older time when people were not as intelligent, advanced, and informed as we are today. Black students connected their current experiences with enslaved and segregated peoples of the past and had more complex narratives than did the White students. The differences in students' conceptions of the past using the same input from sites shows that these are not static memorials, but curricular artifacts that have meaning beyond the words in the placards. Historical understanding does not happen in a vacuum, nor is it easily controlled by the messenger. It is, therefore the responsibility of the decision makers to intentionally create curriculum to dismantle White centered erasure narratives in our public spaces.

CONCLUSIONS AND DISCUSSION

Public spaces that include historic sites, monuments, and museums have a special responsibility to create learning spaces that center the culture and heritage of underrepresented groups (Connerton 2008, Fischer, Swarpa, and Moore 2017, Forest, Johnson, and Till 2004, Holloway 2017, Inwood 2012, Inwood and Alderman 2016, Mahoney 2015, Rockeymoore 2017, Silverman 2011, Tyner, Inwood, and Alderman 2014). These spaces should strive to rework the average citizen's understanding of the American narrative.

Erasure creates a glaring gap in how Americans construct mental frameworks of the past. Further, to ignore the White supremacy in historical narratives and the racialized difference of understanding of the content is fundamentally ahistorical and amounts to an erasure of minority voices from our history. If we ever hope to begin tackling the White supremacist narrative that permeates through these public spaces, we must start by understanding who creates those narratives and then identify whose voices are left out, or silenced, and why. There must be an intentionality behind the decisions that are made regarding these public spaces. As Fischer, Swarpa, and Moore (2017: 26) explained: "even as antiracism policies and strategies are put into place and more people of color enter the field, political, economic, and intellectual power remains with white professionals. It is incumbent upon those in power to work as allies with those who have dedicated their careers to pushing the boulder of antiracism efforts up the mountain of institutional inertia." The culture and heritage presented in museums demonstrates a public power, a sense of worth, a sense of identity, and all groups should be able to embrace that power. Epstein (2000: 137) agreed: "Teaching history in ways that promote the examination of the failings of the nation's past, as well as its virtues, may better equip young people to acknowledge and understand the roots of contemporary racism and inequality, to learn about the existence and effectiveness of cross-racial alliances, and to imagine themselves and act as citizens capable of change in a contemporary society."

Research has shown that excellent history teaching questions dominant histor- ical narratives and decenters whiteness, however, the use of dominant histories still pervades History classrooms, despite the efforts of teacher educators (Alridge 2006, Foster 2010, Garcia 1993, Santiago 2017). The curators of historical sites can support teachers by teaching the non-school population and deepening their understanding of our history. Historic sites can complicate the pervasive narrative that only pow- erful, White, wealthy men made significant contributions to the American cloth and in doing so, work to create a new, bolder, more colorful tapestry that more accurately describes who we are as a nation. As educators, we are asking the community of curators and preservationists to engage with educators to meet this goal. Specifically, we would like more museums to engage with a combination of curriculum scholars, curriculum specialists, classroom teachers, and students to build curriculums that enlighten, en- gage, and include those that have been historically erased, not as tokens, but as a central part of the American story.

Civil Rights leader and U.S. Representative John Lewis from Georgia, whose ded- ication for over fifteen years led to the completion of the AAMHC, said this, "There were some who said it couldn't happen, who said 'you can't do it,' but we did it . . . This place is more than a building. It is a dream come true." (Contrera 2016). A female stu- dent in our study explained that she was seeing things on a deeper level after a visit to a museum that included history that made her feel included, "It is important to me be- cause it is my ancestors' stories, the things they did and went through. Being bi-racial, I get both stories' sides and I can relate to this." Another student used the Indiana ex- perience to connect to her heritage: "Just my family, they're from Mississippi or my

African-American side of the family is from Mississippi so I was able to talk to my grandfather about how they came up from the South up to the North and the trip just sparked that to just keep talking, keep asking more questions, and just knowing where you came from and how your family history is very important to remember. And all history is important to remember. It just made me want to delve more into preserving what my family had to go through and remembering that."

Minorities, marginalized and underrepresented groups should not have to wait decades to have their stories be told. We should all demand that those stories be told now and told authentically in order to provide a multi-layered, complicated, and intricate portrait of the past. Our museums and public spaces have an ability to do just that.

NOTE

1. Critical race theorists often use the capital "W" when writing about White people to illustrate that it is not a neutral description of skin color, but a social construction and racial designation. Some quoted materials used the lowercase "w" and those have remained intact.

REFERENCES

Alridge, D. 2006. "The Limits of Master Narratives in Textbooks. An Analysis of Representations of Martin Luther King, Jr." *Teachers College Record* 108(4): 662–686. DOI: 10.1111/j.1467-9620.2006.00664.x.

Anglin, M. 2004. "Erasures of the Past: Culture, Power, and Heterogeneity in Appalachia." *Journal of Appalachian Studies* 10(1/2): 73–84.

Bain, R. B. 2006. "Rounding Up Unusual Suspects: Facing the Authority Hidden in the History Classroom." *Teachers College Record* 108(10): 2080–2114.

Baron, C. 2012. "Understanding Historical Thinking at Historic Sites." *Journal of Educational Psychology* 104(3): 833–847.

Barton, K. C. 2001a. "A Picture's Worth: Analyzing Historical Photographs in the Elementary Grades." *Social Education* 65(5): 278–283.

Barton, K. C. 2001b. "A Sociocultural Perspective on Children's Understanding of Historical Change: Comparative Findings from Northern Ireland and the United States." *American Educational Research Journal* 38(4): 881–913.

Barton, K. C. 2004. "Research on Students' Historical Thinking and Learning." *Perspectives* 42(7): 19–27.

Barton, K. C. 2005. "'Best Not to Forget Them': Secondary Students' Judgments of Historical Significance in Northern Ireland." *Theory and Research in Social Education* 33(1): 9–44.

Barton, K. C., and L. S. Levstik. 2004. *Teaching History for the Common Good*. Mahwah, NJ: Lawrence Erlbaum Associates.

Barton, K. C., and L. S. Levstik. 2011. *Doing History: Investigating with Children in Elementary and Middle Schools*. New York: Routledge.

Bigelow, A. 2011. "Memory and Minority: Making Muslim Indians." *Numen* 58(2/3): 375–403.

Bonilla-Silva, E. 2001. *White supremacy and Racism in the Post-Civil Rights Era*. Boulder, CO: Lynne Rienner Publications.

Bonilla-Silva, E. 2013. *Racism without Racists: Color-Blind Racism and the Persistence of Racial Inequality in America*. New York: Rowman and Littlefield Publishers.

Bonilla-Silva, E. 2015. "The Structure of Racism in Color-Blind, 'Post-Racial' America." *American Behavioral Scientist* 59(11): 1358–1376.

Brodkin, K. 1998. *How Jews Became White Folks and What That Says about Race in America*. New Brunswick, NJ: Rutgers University Press.

Burgard, K. 2009. "Hollywood and History: A Qualitative Study of High School Students' Historical Understanding." PhD thesis. Retrieved from Eric ProQuest. (ERIC: ED513804).

Burgard, K., and M. L. Boucher. 2016. "Same Story; Different History: Students' Racialized Understanding of Historic Sites." *The Urban Review* 48(5): 696–717.

Byrne, D. 2003. "The Ethos of Return: Erasure and Reinstatement of Aboriginal Visibility in the Australian Historical Landscape." *Historical Archaeology* 37(1): 73–86.

Carr, E. H. 1962. *What Is History?* New York: Knopf.

Connerton, P. 2008. Seven Types of Forgetting. *Memory Studies* 1(59): 59–71.

Contrera, J. 2016. "African American Museum Opening: 'This Place Is More Than a Building. It Is a Dream Come True." <http://www.washingtonpost.com/news/arts-and-entertainment/wp/2016/09/24/african-american-museum-opening-a-historic-day-on-the-national-mall/?utm_term=.4a5a0d61973e> [accessed April, 2017].

Crowley, R. 2016. "White Teachers, Racial Privilege, and the Sociological Imagination." *Urban Education*. DOI: 10.1177/0042085916656901.

Davis, O. L., E. A. Yeager, and S. J. Foster. 2001. *Historical Empathy and Perspective Taking in the Social Studies*. Lanham, MD: Rowman and Littlefield.

Dean, D. 2013. "Museums as Sites for Historical Understanding, Peace, and Social Justice: Views from Canada." *Peace and Conflict: Journal of Peace Psychology* 19(4): 325–337.

Delgado, R., and J. Stefancic, eds. 1997. *Critical White Studies: Looking Behind the Mirror*. Philadelphia, PA: Temple University Press.

Delgado, R. and J. Stefancic, eds. 2001. *Critical Race Theory: An Introduction*. New York: New York University Press.

Delgado, R. and J. Stefancic, eds. 2005. *The Derrick Bell Reader*. New York: New York University Press.

Dimitriadis, G. 2000. "'Making History Go' at a Local Community Center: Popular Media and the Construction of Historical Knowledge among African American Youth." *Theory and Research in Social Education* 28(1): 40–64.

Dixson, A. D., and C. K. Rousseau. 2005. "And We Are Still Not Saved: Critical Race Theory in Education Ten Years Later." *Race and Ethnicity in Education* 8(1): 7–27.

Doyle, C. L. 2002. "Teach These Boys and Girls Nothing but Facts." *Perspectives* 40(4): 33–36.

Egan, K. 1978. "What Is Curriculum?" *Curriculum Inquiry* 8(1): 66–72.

Epstein, T. 1997. "Sociological Approaches to Young Peoples' Historical Understanding." *Social Education* 61: 28–31.

Epstein, T. 1998. "Deconstructing Differences in African-American and European-American Adolescents' Perspectives on U.S. History." *Curriculum Inquiry* 28(4): 397–423.

Epstein, T. 2000. "Adolescents' Perspectives on Racial Diversity in U.S. History: Case Studies from an Urban Classroom." *American Educational Research Journal* 37(1): 185–214.

Epstein, T. 2001. "Racial Identity and Young People's Perspectives on Social Education." *Theory into Practice* 40(1): 42–47.

Epstein, T. 2009. *Interpreting National History: Race, Identity, and Pedagogy in Classrooms and Communities*. New York: Routledge.

Epstein, T., and J. Shiller. 2005. "Perspective Matters: Social Identity and the Teaching and Learning of National History." *Social Education* 69(4): 201.

Epstein, T., and J. Shiller. 2015. "Race, Gender, and the Teaching and Learning of National History," in *Social Studies Today: Research and Practice*, ed. W. Parker. 2nd edn. New York: Routledge, 113–119.

Evans, S. 2013. "Personal Beliefs and National Stories: Theater in Museums as a Tool for Exploring Historical Memory." *Curator: The Museum Journal Curator* 56(2): 189–197.

Falk, J. H., and L. D. Dierking. 2000. *Learning from Museums: Visitor Experiences and the Making of Meaning*. Walnut Creek, CA: AltaMira Press.

Fischer, D., A. Swarpa, and P. Moore. 2017. "Coming Together to Address Systemic Racism in Museums." *Forum* 60(1): 23–31.

Forest, B., J. E. Johnson, and K. Till. 2004. "Post-Totalitarian National Identity: Public Memory in Germany and Russia." *Social and Cultural Geography* 5(3): 357–380.

Foster, S. J. 2010. "The Struggle for American Identity: Treatment of Ethnic Groups in United States History Textbooks." *History of Education* 28(3): 251–278.

Frankenberg, R. 1993. "Growing Up White: Feminism, Racism and the Social Geography of Childhood." *Feminist Review* 45: 51–84.

Garcia, J. 1993. "The Changing Image of Ethnic Groups in Textbooks." *The Phi Delta Kappan* 75(1): 29–35.

Glassberg, D. 1996. "Public History and the Study of Memory." *The Public Historian* 18(2): 7–23.

Giroux, H. A., and A. N. Penna. 1979. "Social Education in the Classroom: The Dynamics of the Hidden Curriculum." *Theory and Research in Social Education* 7(1): 21–42.

Goodman, A. H. 2008. "Exposing Race as an Obsolete Biological Concept," in *Everyday Antiracism: Getting Real about Race in Schools*, ed. M. Pollock. New York: The New Press, 4–8.

Graff, H. J. 1999. "Teaching [and] Historical Understanding: Disciplining Historical Imagination with Historical Context." *Interchange* 30(2): 143–169.

Grant, S. G. 2001. "It's Just the Facts, or Is It? Teachers' Practices and Students' Understanding of History." *Theory and Research in Social Education* 29(1): 65–108.

Hall, L. 2008. "Strategies of Erasure: U.S. Colonialism and Native Hawaiian Feminism." *American Quarterly* 60(2): 273–280.

Handler, R., and E. Gable. 1997. *The New History in an Old Museum: Creating the Past at Colonial Williamsburg*. Durham, NC: Duke University Press.

Hargrove, M. 2009. "Mapping the 'Social Field of Whiteness': White Racism as Habitus in the City Where History Lives." *Transforming Anthropology* 17(2): 93–104.

Hayes, C., and B. Juarez. 2012. "There Is No Culturally Responsive Teaching Spoken Here: A Critical Race Perspective." *Democracy and Education* 20(1): 1–14.

Holloway, K. 2017. "Georgia Civil War Museum Shuts Down Rather Than Surrender Its Confederate Flags." <http://www.alternet.org/news-amp-politics/georgia-civil-war-museum-shuts-down-rather-surrender-its-confederate-flags>.

Hooper-Greenhill, E. 2007. *Museums and Education: Purpose, Pedagogy, Performance*. London: Routledge.

Howard, T. C. 2004. "'Does Race Really Matter?' Secondary Students' Constructions of Racial Dialogue in the Social Studies." *Theory and Research in Social Education* 32(4): 484–502.

Inwood, J. F. J. 2012. "The Politics of Being Sorry: The Greensboro Truth Process and Efforts at Restorative Justice." *Social and Cultural Geography* 56(1): 9–15.

Inwood, J. F. J., and D. H. Alderman. 2016. "Taking Down the Flag Is Just a Start: Toward the Memory-Work of Racial Reconciliation in White Supremacist America." *Southeastern Geographer* 13(6): 607–624.

Jackson, P. 1990. *Life in Schools*. New York: Teachers College Press.

Ladson-Billings, G. 1998. "Just What Is Critical Race Theory and What's It Doing in a Nice Field like Education?" *Qualitative Studies in Education* 11(1): 7–24.

Ladson-Billings, G. and W. F. Tate. 1995. "Toward a Critical Race Theory of Education." *Teachers College Record* 97(1): 47–68.

Ledesma, M. C. and D. Calderon. 2015. "Critical Race Theory in Education: A Review of Past Literature and a Look to the Future." *Qualitative Review* 21(13): 206–222.

Lee, E. 2017. "Why Are Asian Americans Missing from our Textbooks?" *Pacific Standard*, <https://psmag.com/why-are-asian-americans-missing-from-our-textbooks-6319bd4ed0d6> [accessed April, 2017].

Lee, P., and R. Ashby. 2000. "Progression in Historical Understanding among Students Ages 7–14," in *Knowing, Teaching, and Learning History: National and International Perspectives*, ed. P. N. Stearns, P. C. Seixas, and S. S. Wineburg. New York: New York University Press, 7–14.

Leonardo, Z. 2004. "The Color of Supremacy: Beyond the Discourse of 'White privilege.'" *Educational Philosophy and Theory* 36(2): 137–152.

Lewis, C. M. 2005. *The Changing Face of Public History: The Chicago Historical Society and the Transformation of an American Museum*. DeKalb, IL: Northern Illinois University Press.

Lipsitz, G. 2006. *The Possessive Investment in Whiteness: How White People Profit from Identity Politics*. Philadelphia: Temple University Press.

Loewen, J. 1999. *Lies across America: What our History Sites Get Wrong*. New York: New Press.

Loewen, J. 2007. *Lies my Teacher Told Me: Everything your American History Textbook Got Wrong*. New York: Touchstone.

Luke, C., S. de Castell, and A. Luke. 1989. "Beyond Criticism: The Authority of the School Textbook," in *Language, Authority, and Criticism: Readings on the School Textbook*, ed. C. Luke, S. de Castell, and A. Luke. New York: The Falmer Press, 245–60.

Mahoney, S. 2015. "'Faced with Courage': Interpreting and Presenting Sites of African American Heritage to the Public." *Conservation and Management of Archaeological Sites* 17(1): 56–66.

Mandell, M. 2008. "Thinking like a Historian: A Framework for Teaching and Learning." *OAH Magazine of History* 22(2): 55–62.

Marcus, A. S., and T. H. Levine. 2011. "Knight at the Museum: Learning History with Museums." *The Social Studies* 102(3): 104–109.

Marcus, A. S., T. H. Levine, and R. S. Grenier. 2012. "How Secondary History Teachers Use and Think about Museums: Current Practices and Untapped Promise for Promoting Historical Understanding." *Theory and Research in Social Education* 40(1): 66–97.

Matias, C. 2016. *Feeling White*. New York: Sense Publishers.

Mattingly, C. 2008. "Women's Temple, Women's Fountains: The Erasure of Public Memory." *American Studies* 49(3/4): 133–156.

Mayer, R. H. 2006. "Learning to Teach Young People How to Think Historically: A Case Study of One Student Teacher's Experience." *The Social Studies* 97(2): 69–76.

McCrummen, S. and E. Izadi. 2015. "Confederate Flag Comes Down on South Carolina's Statehouse Grounds." *Washington Post* <www.washingtonpost.com/news/post-nation/wp/2015/07/10/watch-live-as-the-confederate-flag-comes-down-in-south-carolina/?utm_term=.4ca32d3dfe06> [accessed April 2017].

Monroe, C. 2017. *Race and Colorism in Education*. New York: Routledge.

Namakkal, J. 2015. "Re-Naming Colonization." *Counter Punch*, <http://www.counterpunch. org/2015/06/26/re-naming-as-decolonization/> [accessed April 2017].

Painter, N. I. 2010. *The History of White People*. New York: W.W. Norton and Co.

Rockeymoore, M. 2017. "Removing Civil War Statues the First Step in Finally Defeating the Confederacy." *The Hill*, <http://thehill.com/blogs/pundits-blog/civil-rights/336276-removing-civil-war-statues-the-first-step-in-finally>.

Roediger, D. R. 2005. *Working toward Whiteness: How America's Immigrants Became White: The Strange Journey from Ellis Island to the Suburbs*. New York: Basic Books.

Santiago, M. 2017. "Erasing Differences for the Sake of Inclusion: How Mexican/Mexican American Students Construct Historical Narratives." *Theory and Research in Social Education* 45(1): 43–74.

Schocker, J. B. 2014. "A Case for Using Images to Teach Women's History." *The History Teacher* 47(3): 421–450.

Segall, A. 2014. "Making Difficult History Public: The Pedagogy of Remembering and Forgetting in Two Washington DC Museums." *Review of Education, Pedagogy, and Cultural Studies* 36(1): 55–70.

Seixas, P. 1994. "Students' Understanding of Historical Significance." *Theory and Research in Social Education* 22(3): 281–304. DOI: 10.1080/00933104.1994.10505726.

Seixas, P. 1998. "Student Teachers Thinking Historically." *Theory and Research in Social Education* 26(3): 310–341.

Selk, A. 2017. "New Orleans Removes a Tribute to 'The Lost Cause of the Confederacy'—with Snipers Standing By." *Washington Post*, <www.washingtonpost.com/news/post-nation/wp/2017/04/24/new-orleans-removes-a-tribute-to-the-lost-cause-of-the-confederacy-with-snipers-standing-by/?utm_term=.094eddfb85f4> [accessed April 2017].

Silverman, H. 2011. "Contested Cultural Heritage: A Selective Historiography," in *Contested Cultural Heritage: Religion, Nationalism, Erasure, and Exclusion in a Global World*, ed. H. Silverman. New York: Springer, 1–49.

Sleeter, C. E. 2017. "Critical Race Theory and the Whiteness of Teacher Education." *Urban Education* 52(2): 155–169.

Spencer, S. 2006. *Race and Ethnicity: Culture, Identity, Representation*. New York: Routledge.

Stearns, P. N., P. C. Seixas, and S. S. Wineburg. 2000. *Knowing, Teaching, and Learning History: National and International Perspectives*. New York: New York University Press.

Takaki, R. 2008. *A Different Mirror: A History of Multicultural America*. New York: Back Bay Books.

Taylor, E., Gillborn, D., and Ladson-Billings, G., eds. 2016. *Foundations of Critical Race Theory in Education*. New York: Routledge.

Terzian, S. G., and E. A. Yeager. 2007. "'That's When We Became a Nation': Urban Latino Adolescents and the Designation of Historical Significance." *Urban Education* 42(1): 52–81. DOI: 10.1177/0042085906294027.

Trainor, J. S. 2005. "'My Ancestors Didn't Own Slaves': Understanding White Talk about Race." *Research in the Teaching of English* 40(2): 140–167.

Tyner, J., J. F. J. Inwood, and D. H. Alderman. 2014. "Theorizing Violence and the Dialectics of Landscape Memorialization: A Case Study of Greensboro, North Carolina." *Environment and Planning D: Society and Space* 32(5): 902–914.

Van Sledright, B. A. 2004. "What Does It Mean to Think Historically . . . and How Do You Teach It?" *Social Education* 68(3): 230–233.

Van Sledright, B. A. 2002. "Confronting History's Interpretive Paradox While Teaching Fifth Graders to Investigate the Past." *American Educational Research Journal* 39(4): 1089–1115.

Van Sledright, B. A., and P. Afflerbach. 2000. "Reconstructing Andrew Jackson: Prospective Elementary Teachers' Readings of Revisionist History Texts." *Theory and Research in Social Education* 28(3): 411–444.

Wineburg, S. S. 2001. *Historical Thinking and Other Unnatural Acts: Charting the Future of Teaching the Past.* Philadelphia, PA: Temple University Press.

Wood, E., and B. Wolf. 2008. "Between the Lines of Engagement in Museums: Indiana University and The Children's Museum of Indianapolis." *Journal of Museum Education* 33(2): 121–130. DOI: 10.1179/jme.2008.33.2.121.

Woods, T. A. 1995. "Museums and the Public: Doing History Together." *The Journal of American History* 82(3): 1111.

Wunder, S. 2002. "Learning to Teach for Historical Understanding: Preservice Teachers at a Hands On Museum." *The Social Studies* 93(4): 159–163.

Yale News. 2017. "Yale to Change Calhoun College's Name to Honor Grace Murray Hopper." *Yale News*, <http://news.yale.edu/2017/02/11/yale-change-calhoun-college-s-name-honor-grace-murray-hopper-0> [accessed April 2017].

PUBLIC HERITAGE AS TRANSFORMATIVE EXPERIENCE

The Co-occupation of Place and Decision-Making

DAVID M. SCHAEPE

"Colonialism"—A practice of domination, which involves the subjugation of one people to another . . . [that] involves political and economic control over a dependent territory.

Margaret Kohn, *The Stanford Encyclopedia of Philosophy* (Spring 2014 Edition)

When Gregor Samsa woke up one morning from unsettling dreams, he found himself changed in his bed into a monstrous vermin.

Franz Kafka, *Metamorphosis* (1915)

INTRODUCTION: PUBLIC HERITAGE AS A TRANSFORMATIVE EXPERIENCE

I begin by riffing off Franz Kafka's opening line to *Metamorphosis*—I woke up one morning from unsettling dreams to find myself changed in my bed into a social scientist, an archaeologist faced with the prospect of metamorphing into a "monstrous vermin," an agent of public heritage working amongst a colonial society. Throughout this chapter I work these opening lines into the meaning of public heritage provided by the editors of this volume. I also work this into common definitions of "public" as (1a) an adjective describing something of concern to "a people" as a whole; and (1b) the perception of something in open view; and (2) a noun referring to ordinary people in general community. A connective element of public and heritage is one definition of colonialism presented above, as a major theme of this essay and factor of both individual metamorphosis and public transformation. As central themes of this chapter I transpose concepts and processes of metamorphosis against trans- formation. Metamorphosis invokes a subliminal awareness of and action within the monstrous societal dynamics entrenched within bureaucracies of colonial paradigms and agency. Those constraining forces affect the definition and man- agement of public heritage within the agendas of our currently dominant societies. Transformation invokes a mindful awareness and decolonizing processes affecting inclusiveness and the broadening of public heritage across cultural paradigms and institutional controls incorporating Indigenous perspectives. As individuals and members of the public we all are connected to some manifestation of these processes and thus factors in determining and addressing contemporary issues and practices in public heritage.

This chapter is a humanistic, personal, auto-ethnographic, and self-reflexive case study. I aim to assess and address central challenges embedded in and presently affecting the relationship between archaeology and heritage landscape management as aspects of public heritage. The content of this chapter is pieced together from presentations (McHalsie and Schaepe 2010, Nicholas and Schaepe 2008, Schaepe 2003, 2004, 2008, 2011, 2015) and experiences between 1997 to now. It is messy, like public heritage itself (Piccini and Schaepe 2014), and requires some effort on the part of the audience to piece things together. I present current cases and issues arising from the field of cul- tural heritage relations in British Columbia, Canada. This account is based on my per- sonal involvement in these cases as a non-Indigenous archaeologist with, now, thirty years of experience; the last twenty of those years, and counting, spent working within an Indigenous context of and for the Stó:lō [Sta-lo] Nation. As such, I present a view- point from within a community-based archaeological and cultural heritage manage- ment framework and field of relationships, messily linked to government, industry, and the public at large.[1]

OCCUPYING THE FIELD
AND DESCRIBING RELATIONS

For the past twenty years, I have assisted the Stó:lō Nation in occupying the field of cul- tural heritage relationships. The field being occupied is primarily one made of political- economic relations and negotiations (Bourdieu 1977, 1980, Roseberry 1988). The purpose of occupying this field is to xólhmet te mekw' stám ít kwelát [hoth-met ta mek-stam eet kwa-lot] ("we have to care of everything that belongs to us") (Stó:lō Nation 2003, McHalsie 2007). This central principle has guided our occupying process. Our aim has continually been to broaden the scope of recognition, participation, and inclusion of Stó:lō people in areas of research, management, decision-making, and protection of their tangible and intangible heritage, including but not limited to what are commonly understood as "archaeological sites." Many strategies have been employed to create community-based legislation, policy, protocols, and mechanisms including Halq'eméylem heritage definitions, inventories, database structures and classification systems, curation systems, interpretation and educational outcomes, permitting processes, and management plans. The scope of this occupation and related strategies exceeds the scope of this chapter. I thus focus on a few current issues arising from and related to the implementation of this holistic community-based Stó:lō heritage stewardship initiative.

Central to this piece is the concept of placing archaeology within Indigenous heritage landscapes, and within the "monstrous" realm of inter-community public heritage relations—monstrous in its domination by colonial influences. "Monstrous" describes the current scope of division between Indigenous and non-Indigenous worldviews and political economies, and the colonial nature of these public relations affecting public heritage. These relations remain metamorphosed and badly scarred by centuries of severely imbalanced power, occupation of place, and decision-making. These scars remain largely invisible to the vast majority of the general public, a habitus of public heritage (Bourdieu 1977). I present a case study derived from my experiences within S'ólh Téméxw [Solth Tumuk], which is the Halq'eméylem [Halk-a-maylem] word for "Our World" or "Our Land" and which generally refers to the traditional, unceded lands of the Stó:lō (Figure 3.6.1). S'ólh Téméxw is located within the context

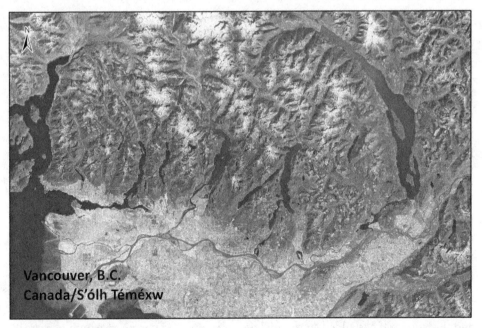

FIGURE 3.6.1. S'ólh Téméxw (Our World; Our Land)—the lower Fraser River Watershed of southwestern, British Columbia, Canada.

(Google Earth 2017).

of southwestern British Columbia, Canada, and extends into northern Washington State in the United States (Carlson et al. 2001). The geographical term S'ólh Téméxw is grounded in an understanding of Stó:lō-Coast Salish worldview and interconnected sets of relationships between people, places, and things; shared as commonly held beliefs and customs—forming a world of relations and obligations connected to land, water, and resources.

Too often, unrecognized Indigenous knowledge underlies and cradles the archaeological sites and features of S'ólh Téméxw, the lower Fraser River Watershed of southwestern British Columbia and ancestral home of the Stó:lō—People of the River (see <http://www.digitalsqewlets.ca>). Coupling Indigenous knowledge with that gained from archaeological research works to establish new relationships of theory and practice. This cross-fertilization communicates between cultural, institutional, and disciplinary paradigms to foster alternative ways of knowing. Halq'eméylem place names are imbued with Indigenous knowledge and perspectives and are fundamental elements of S'ólh Téméxw. Such elements integrate people, geography, and material culture—people, places, and things. Stó:lō sqwelqwel (personal histories) and sxwōxwiyám (narratives of the distant past related to the travels and transformations of Xexá:ls [xha-xhals], the Transformers) ground archaeological explorations of the Fraser Valley within a framework of Indigenous knowledge, cultural landscapes, and relationships of interconnected senses of space and place within the land (McHalsie et al. 2001) (Figures 3.6.2 and 3.6.3).

CRADLING ARCHAEOLOGY IN INDIGENOUS LANDSCAPES: LEARNING TO SEE

Perception is a core element of "public" heritage with regard to a collective view and visibility, by which something exists in a public (adjective) realm. A substantial issue facing public heritage is a division of power within our society(ies) that limits visibility of and understanding of what exists in open view. It is absolutely clear in my experience that we, as a general public, do not share a common view of the cultural landscape. As some Indigenous spokespeople, archaeologists, and heritage resource managers have increasingly come to point out over the past two decades, per Angela Labrador (pers. comm., 2017) "this is not just the isolation of indigenous heritage from the general public, but the isolating of indigenous people from the general public when we theorize or use 'general public' in archaeology and heritage" (e.g. Atalay 2006, Atalay et al. 2014, Deloria, Jr. 1969, Ferris and Welch 2015, Ferguson 2009, Lyons 2013, Nicholas 2006, Sassaman 2014).

Cradling archaeology within relationships of material culture, intangible knowledge, and the land itself has added substantial new meaning and perspective both personally and within the local field of public heritage over the twenty years that I have worked for the Stó:lō as an archaeologist and heritage resource manager (Schaepe 2007, 2009, Stó:lō

Sxwōxwiyám is the time, long ago when the world was 'mixed up'; when there was no veil between people and spirit; when animals and people could talk to and transform from one to the other. It is also the narratives of the actions of X̱exá:ls (the Transformers). Through sxwōxwiyám we are all connected; this is integral to Stó:lō survival as people.

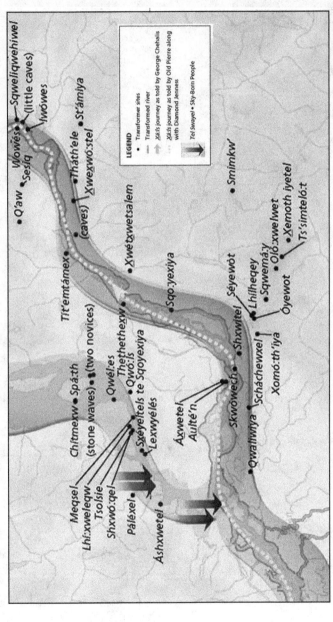

FIGURE 3.6.2. Stó:lō sxwōxwiyám in Sólh Téméxw, generally unseen elements of public heritage.

X̱exá:ls were given the responsibility to walk through our lands and make things right. In walking through our lands they were confronted by people and different situations that were going against the laws of the land and rules given by the Creator. X̱exá:ls were given the task of making those things right, turning those people into stone.

(SRRMC 2016).

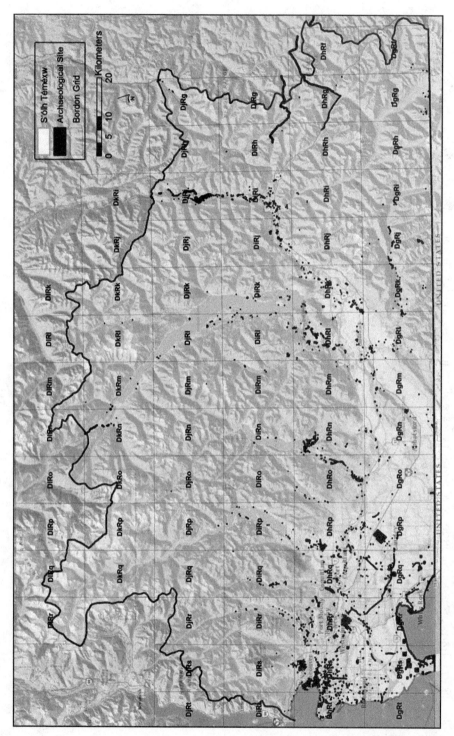

FIGURE 3.6.3. Documented archaeological sites c.2015 within the lower Fraser River Watershed—aspects of sqwélqwel cradled within Stó:lō sxwōx̱wiyám and Canadian federal/provincial legislation.

(SRRMC 2015).

Nation 2003). I gained, sometimes slowly and sometimes in sudden cathartic moments, an ability to see a range of cultural landscapes—Indigenous and colonial—that surround and cradle my archaeological work. This began when I was hired and began working at Stó:lō Nation in the Aboriginal Rights and Title Department in 1997, to carry out an inventory of the Chilliwack River Valley. I soon thereafter moved into the Chilliwack Valley, in 1998. I was surrounded by Stó:lō people, whose political existence was lived within a context of treaty negotiations and nation-building and assertion of aboriginal rights, about which I had no education, training, or real understanding.

I gained what I refer to as my initial training at "Stó:lō University" working with a fieldcrew of three Stó:lō men—Larry Commodore, the late Riley Lewis, and Dean Jones. We had many daily excursions and "boots on the ground" in-field discussions throughout nearly a year of archaeological survey work inventorying the Chilliwack River Valley—following a survey design that focused on Mt. McGuire. "Boots on the ground," I began to gain an awareness and appreciation of the social, political, and cultural context within which I was working.

At that time I had read the core ethnographies and archaeological reports and publications relevant to this part of the world. I had ten years of experience as a working archaeologist. I had a Bachelors of Arts in Anthropology from New York University. I came out of the theoretical and methodological traditions of "New Archaeology" and the developing debates associated with the emergence of post-Processualism. I was, academically and technically, a fully equipped and professionally trained archaeologist. Yet, I knew nothing of the context in which I found myself practicing archaeology as an employee of Stó:lō Nation, one of the largest and most progressive aboriginal organizations in Canada and certainly so in British Columbia.

After living in the Chilliwack Valley for a couple of years and looking at the view of Mt. McGuire (Figure 3.6.4) every day from my home, literally from my bed, I quite suddenly realized one day that this mountain is in fact a transformed persona (i.e. a living entity transformed into that mountain), alive and a result of the superhuman transformative actions of X̱ex̱á:ls as directed by Chíchelh Siyá:m (Cheech-elth See-am)—the Creator. It is sx̱wōx̱wiyám, one of the ancestral transformed mountain-scapes of intrinsic heritage value to the Stó:lō that carries with it teachings, laws of the land, and is understood to be a person that is still alive but transformed into that mountain form. The mountain has a Halq'eméylem name, Támiyehó:y [Tami-hi]. As is common among Stó:lō Coast Salish place names and places, Támiyehó:y has multiple meanings in this case related to both sx̱wōx̱wiyám and sqwelqwel. What suddenly struck me was the form of this mountain as a "hermaphrodite," a person with male and female biological features. This is one of its core meanings. Every time I show and explain this to some unknowing friend or visitor they arrive looking at Mt. McGuire and they leave seeing Támiyehó:y. They leave more consciously aware of multiple worldviews and therefore transformed as a participant in public heritage. They are new members of the broader public community sharing a broadened connection to this mountain persona.

Can you see the Stó:lō heriṭage in this landscape?

FIGURE 3.6.4. A view of Támiyehó:y and/or Mt. McGuire, as a matter of knowledge and (in)visibility of the cultural landscape; and as seen from my bedroom window (inset).

Photos: David Schaepe.

I have since come to understand Támiyehó:y as also referring to "the place of Wren" who provided the Ts'elxwéyeqw Tribe of Stó:lō with the knowledge of fish weirs; as a burial grounds known as "the place of the deformed" where deformed babies were brought and left to die; as a name for the creek that flows into the Chilliwack River; as the name of the pre-contact settlement that was located at the confluence of that creek and river; and as a reference to a place(s) of contemporary spiritual practice associated with the mountain; as a place that is alive and actively holds knowledge and laws that are part of collective Stó:lō identity, socialization, constitution, and system of governance (Schaepe and Ts'elxwéyeqw Tribe 2017). This mountain was one of the influences that changed the way in which I understand and practice archaeology and heritage landscape management. And yet, it is neither recognized nor protected as a heritage feature by Canadian provincial or federal law.

Keith Basso (1996) is another social scientist who similarly brought attention to an indigenous world full of intangible heritage that occupies the landscape (see Zedeno 2000). Such recognition poses three central questions and strategies of heritage policy and protection: (1) what is it? (2) how should it be inventoried?; and (3) how do you treat it? All three of these elements must be situated within appropriate cultural contexts in order to effectively contribute to the transformation of public heritage. These questions and strategies have played out in Stó:lō Nation development of the *Stó:lō Heritage Policy Manual* and an array of other heritage management plans and tools (e.g. the S'ólh Téméxw Use Plan [Schaepe, Brady, et al. 2016]).

GLOBAL PARALLELS ON THE SIGNIFICANCE OF MATERIAL CULTURE AND HERITAGE LANDSCAPES

Integrating archaeology within the broader heritage landscape and peoples' heritage raises a fundamental issue regarding the assignment of significance: How does one assess the significance of the transformation places inscribed in Stó:lō's cultural landscape? The very concept of transformation blurs the lines between the usual static types of heritage sites in official inventories. Primordial actions, like those resulting from the actions of X̱exá:ls in altering the character of the mountain Támiyehó:y are not recognized as historical "facts" in Canadian law. In the face of non-recognition, what difference does it make if a transformation place is disturbed or destroyed?

Támiyehó:y. What if somebody builds a road through the rib-cage of this transformed person; or blows up a breast; or mines her/his forehead? What knowledge is lost? What laws are broken? How is shxwelí [shwa-lee] (life force; collective, interconnected spirit) affected? We have to understand the impact of such actions in terms of significance across cultures on a broad basis; across common human sensibilities; across comparative foundations of meaning. I suggest that there are relevant parallels of significance derived from the global scope of view and experiences.

For example, the Bible tells how Moses went to the top of Mt. Sinai and received the Ten Commandments written by God on a stone table. If instead, Moses was given one commandment and was himself turned into a rock outcrop, or the mountain itself was inscribed with that law (as snowyelth [snow-ay-eth], laws of the land), then this would parallel the actions of X̱exá:ls.

In the modern industrial world, the Twin Towers in New York City were significant landscape features within the deep mythology of New Yorkers, the citizens of the United States and worldwide socio-cultural, socioeconomic relations—creations of superhuman power marking the landscape of lower Manhattan. The sudden and violent loss of the Twin Towers on 9/11 resulted in significant long-lasting suffering, sickness, grief, imbalance, and irreplaceable loss; a "perosis" of our cultural infrastructure. There was huge power in that transformative event taking those material structures and dissolving them into an intangible place, creating sacred ground. Such powerful actions parallel 110-plus transformed places that "constitute" S'ólh Téméxw and provide guidance to Stó:lō (Figures 3.6.5 and 3.6.6).

Global Parallels of Significance:

• **Moses, Mount Sinai and the Ten Commandments**

If as Moses went to the top of Mount Sinai and received the
Ten Commandments written by God on a stone tablet he was
instead given one Commandment and himself turned into
stone or the mountain itself as the inscription of that law on
the land, THEN this would parallel the actions of X̱exá:ls
and transformations of S'ólh Téméxw.

• **Twin Towers / 9-11**

Significant landscape features / significant loss and sickness
/ transformation into sacred ground

FIGURE 3.6.5. Global parallels of significance—transformative actions and public heritage.

Photo of Twin Tower Memorial: David Schaepe.

A Stó:lō Constitution

*The creator in his wisdom decided to take
certain people and make an example of them,
and so throughout the Nation you have these
stone figures which represent rules or values
that we have actually now in stone. And our
constitution has always been here then, our
rules of conduct, our rules of behavior, and
the way that we think, our moral values...*

– Xwelikweltal (Steven Point), in Joe et al (2006).

FIGURE 3.6.6. A Stó:lō Constitution—"Written in Stone."

Such extreme transformative power—fusing or confusing tangible and intangible, animate and inanimate, life and death—is, I suggest, a commonly felt and understood force of interconnecting people with place.

PLACING AND GUIDING ARCHAEOLOGY IN PUBLIC INTERACTION AND RELATIONS

From my home, I see other types of features—conical earthen mounds approximately 10 meters in diameter and 3 meters high. These are currently under investigation as "*site class*: precontact; *type*: human remains; *descriptors*: earthwork features; mounds" per the provincial archaeological site recording typological options. Under British Columbia's *Heritage Conservation Act* (RSBC 1996), these features may be recognized as a "heritage object(s)" meaning "*personal property* that has heritage value to British Columbia, a community or an aboriginal people" (emphasis added); and as a "heritage site" meaning "land, including land covered by water, that has heritage value to British Columbia, a community or an aboriginal people"; where "heritage value" means the "historical, cultural, aesthetic, scientific or educational worth or usefulness of a site or object." From a Stó:lō-Tsʼelxwéyeqw perspective they are remains connected to the ancestors, whose presence remains with them. These landscape features in my neighborhood are currently at the heart of a public heritage issue involving the government, the Tsʼelxwéyeqw Tribe, Stó:lō Nation, private properties/owners, and my neighbors. The bi-cultural recognition (what is coming to be referred to as two-eyed seeing [Bartlett et al. 2012]) by which I saw and understood these features, and the question of what actions to take upon their recognition as a public heritage resource manager, raised both the specter of metamorphosis and prospect of transformation.

This archaeological scenario also raised three core questions and issues: How do I act? Whose laws apply? What is an archaeological site? Addressing these questions initiates a dialogue related to professional ethics, legislation, and archaeological site definition, influencing actions moving toward either metamorphosis or transformation.

CROSS-CULTURAL IMPACTS ON ANTHROPOLOGICAL AND ARCHAEOLOGICAL ETHICS OF ACTION

The first question is one of professional ethics: What am I supposed to do? How do I act? I am an archaeologist, the Senior Archaeologist for the Stó:lō Nation; I am a neighbor and member of the local public community; not Stó:lō but standing in feet set within both Stó:lō and settler communities. With the aid of my staff I compiled statements of ethical practice from nine professional anthropological/archaeological associations worldwide.[2] Of these I found that the Society for American Archaeology (SAA), American Anthropological Association (AAA), and Stó:lō Nation Heritage Policy establish a fulsome set of ethical principles and guidelines needed to address this situation of community-based "public archaeology," placed within the context of indigenous and settler–colonial cultural landscapes and heritage. Five points constitute the ethical framework of action developed for this situation: Do No Harm, Stewardship, Consent, Collaboration, and Respect—set within the context of an indigenous Stó:lō worldview and health model (Schaepe et al. 2017) and are, I suggest, ubiquitously applicable.

Do No Harm

Primary for the AAA is "do no harm." Why isn't there a statement of "do no harm" among the archaeological societies? Social science research with human subjects requires strict ethical practice; medical doctors, MDs, physicians, maintain the Hippocratic Oath to "do no harm" in interacting with human subjects within the practice of medicine. Yet the same framework does not currently apply to our treatment of cultural materials and resources in our archaeological practice. Generally, a Western legal framework of "harm" deals with damage to a person or personal property, physical, tangible. Intangible harms such as pain, emotional trauma, and social impacts are also recognized.

The Western framework underlying the common application of "do no harm" doesn't entirely work for Stó:lō because factors of "harm" go beyond the personal, physical, material world. Stó:lō, within an Indigenous worldview, maintain a model that recognizes at least five elements of health: physical, mental, emotional, spiritual, and shxwelí (Schaepe et al. 2017). The concept and understanding of "harm" conventionally understood within the Westerly ethic of "do no harm" does not adequately address the full set of relationships associated with ancestral Stó:lō heritage features. Stó:lō heritage is alive; ancestral connections are maintained through extant spiritual relationships. Landscape features and objects are understood to exist as entities to be considered within the collection of relations fundamental to the well-being of Stó:lō society and therefore public heritage.

Stewardship

For the SAA, another central ethical point is "stewardship"—taking care of archaeological resources and educating the public about their significance. Archaeologists are thus "caretakers" of the archaeological record, but apparently not of human welfare. Recognizing Stó:lō principles extends stewardship more explicitly to caring for both things and people, in light of their deep interconnections—not just teaching people to care about archaeological remains. This concept transforms archaeological artifacts and features into "belongings" (Muntean et al. 2015, Schaepe et al. 2017; also see <http://www.digitalsqewlets.ca>) and can be taken forward through all these categories influencing professional behavior and practice.

Consent

"Consent" is another key point of ethics for archaeologists that can provide us with some reasonable guidelines. What is "harm" and "consent" in a world where landscape features—and potentially material cultural—are alive and maintain ancestral connections as elements of spirit? In light of Stó:lō indigeneity, the ontological binaries of living/non-living (or person/non-person) collapse. That worldview integrates the otherwise binary relationship between people and things, animate and inanimate. Consent in a Stó:lō cultural context applies broadly to both.

Respect

A primary principle within Stó:lō Nation's *Stó:lō Heritage Policy Manual* (Stó:lō Nation 2003) is "respect." Integrating a Stó:lō worldview and model of health affects an understanding of the scope of "respectful treatment"—commonly understood as a way of treating or thinking about something or someone with admiration; as being worthy of admiration because of good qualities; and to act in a way that shows awareness of someone's (extending to something's) rights and wishes.

Collaboration

Working together in partnership under a collaborative framework of inclusiveness emerged as the final guiding principle. This point arose through participating in the Intellectual Property Issues in Cultural Heritage project (see <https://www.sfu.ca/ipinch/>), as a broad-based collaborative project. Through this project, and general experience, the need for and benefits of collaboration became fundamentally understood as integral elements of public heritage (also see Silliman and Ferguson 2010).

THE LESSON OF TWO-ROW AND
ONE-ROW WAMPUM

Underlying public heritage definition, recognition, protection, and management are relationships between Indigenous people and the state. At the heart of this relationship lays the greatest repatriation effort in human history—the reconstitution of Indigenous governance from centuries of colonial dislocation and control. Aspects of governance include self-determination and sovereignty over a people's own identity, worldview, and cultural heritage. It is also connected to the management of land and resources. How can this be achieved? What kind of models of relationships can we look at to forge a new relationship? It is helpful to review historical views of models of relationships between Indigenous people and the state within the colonial context of Canada (Figure 3.6.7).

There are three primary actors to consider in this set of relations affecting public heritage: Indigenous people, colonial authorities, and land managers/land owners (Figure 3.6.8), the latter of which are sandwiched between the two main actors and their worldviews (i.e. Indigenous and colonial). The State, as the current embodiment

RELATIONAL THEORY & MODEL OF COMMUNITY

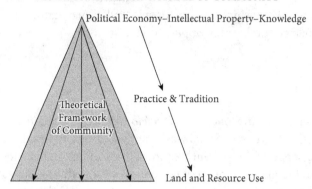

FIGURE 3.6.7. A theoretical framework of community, linked to political economy and world-view, practices and traditions, and land and resource use.

Actors in a Contemporary Field of Colonial Relations

I) **Indigenous Identity** – "If First Nations can't trust the government to act properly where a few hectares of trees are at issue, why should it trust it to respect the treaty process where the stakes are far higher -- *survival itself in the eyes of many aboriginal leaders*?"

- Stephen Hume (*Vancouver Sun*, 13 December 2003)

(III) **Land 'Managers'**– "Companies are looking for clarity around what areas of the province are absolutely open, or absolutely closed to mine development, which is where.. miners feel caught in the middle.. $400 billion worth of resource-related projects being proposed across Canada involve aboriginal interests."

- Derick Penner (*Vancouver Sun*, 12 November 2011)

(II) **Colonial Authority** - "We have no history of colonialism."

- Stephen Harper, Prime Minister, Canada (September 2010)

FIGURE 3.6.8. Actors in a contemporary field of colonial relations: three primary characters and agents affecting relations of public heritage.

of colonial power, includes a complex array of internal relations with underprivileged/ marginalized communities distinct from those of Indigenous peoples. Indigenous peoples originate *in situ* from a place and their knowledge, their intellectual properties, their ways, and their worldviews are inherent rights that originate from a place, often-times constituting interconnected relationships between peoples, places, and things and ultimately, an Indigenous paradigm, worldview, and values. Colonial intellectual knowledge is imported, imported rights into a place, imported from another place, occupying a conceptual vacant space in colonial doctrine and introduces foreign paradigms and values into a landscape (Figure 3.6.9). The fallacy of any such vacancy leads to our current problematic realities within these sets of relations. Scholarship exists on how such relations problematically play out through time as a factor of internalized colonialism within contemporary Indigenous worldviews, particularly in governance practices (e.g. Henders 2006, Young 2001, Young and Levy 2011).

Historically an initial framework for productive relationships between native peoples and outsiders comes from Iroquian contact with European settlers in the 1600s. One such Indigenous model is understood by some to have been woven into a belt of wampum beads—the Two-Row Wampum—c.1613 (Figure 3.6.10) (Gehring et al. 1987, Hau de no sau nee 1978, Otto 2013, Parmenter 2013, Venebles 2012). The Two-Row Wampum (Guswenta), a belt of woven wampum shell beads, serves as an Indigenous legal mechanism in which the belt's design set out a framework for relations between the Haudenosaunee (specifically the Mohawk of the Iroquois) and the Dutch government in what is now upstate New York. It is associated with the Tawagonshi Treaty. The belt, now maintained in Canada, simply has two horizontal purple-blue rows set against a white background. The two rows represent two canoes traveling parallel paths down the river of life, each maintaining their own laws, cultures, and beliefs—a model for living together under separate sovereignties. But history shows that after some time this model

The Heart of the Issue:
Political Economic Competition

 Two communities of Place, Power & Rights

(I) Indigenous Intellectual Properties & Inherent Rights
- Originating *in situ* from a place
- Constituting interconnected relations of people, places, things
- Aboriginal paradigm/values

(II) Colonialist Intellectual Property & Imported Rights
- Imported from another place
- Occupying a conceptual 'vacant space' (*Terra Nullius*) – *erasure/discovery*
- Foreign paradigm/values

FIGURE 3.6.9. A framework of Indigenous and Colonial political economies, intellectual properties, rights, and heritage communities.

RELATIONAL MODELS thru time

An Indigenous Framework – Two Rows:

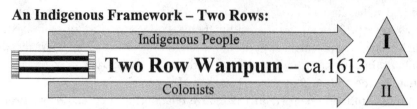

Haudenosaunee Iroquois and Dutch –
* Two Canoes & travelling Parallel Paths down the River of Life
    – each maintaining their own Laws, Culture and Beliefs
* Mutual Sovereignty; No Overlap

...IT DIDN'T WORK!

A Colonial Framework – One Row:

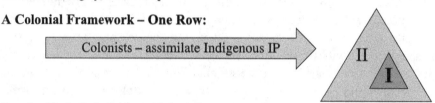

* Domination & Assimilation – 'Colonialism' - (term first used ca. 1853)
* Exclusive Unilateral Sovereignty; Uncontrolled Overlap

...IT DIDN'T WORK!

FIGURE 3.6.10. Historic Indigenous and colonial models of relations—Two-Row and One-Row models.

failed. There was disrespect of the rules and values of this framework by the colonial party, who figuratively steered their ship into the other. This collision of peoples saw the employment of the Doctrine of Discovery, colonial policies, and practices of extinguishment and assimilation aimed at subsuming Indigenous laws, culture, and beliefs (Hau de no sau nee 1978; see Deloria, Jr. 1969).

A second framework that was set in place in Canada in the eighteenth century, and more specifically in the mid-nineteenth century within British Columbia, can be conceived as a single row, colonial framework. Overcoming the two-row model results in a single one row of forced colonialization and assimilation of Indigenous peoples within a colonial society—domination over one by the other. It didn't work; that's been recognized. Public heritage in this context was historically influenced by colonial legislation and policy, such as played out in the British Commonwealth under the Civilization Act and subsequent Indian Act, forced assimilation and implementation of the Doctrine of Discovery. The Other, and their respective heritage, was ingested with the intent that they be destroyed. Under the influences of these colonial mechanisms the public heritage metamorphosed into one of an isolated and exclusive field of relations including tangible and intangible heritage.

A third model, that which is currently in place, is unclear—part status quo *Indian Act*, part programs and services contracted to First Nations and audited by the government,

CURRENT SITUATION:

- GAINING RECOGNITION and DEFINING RIGHTS thru Litigation, Negotiation, Direct Action, Consultation/Accommodation
- State power remains exclusive

...*HAS NOT WORKED!* Based on assessment of Indigenous standards of living and well-being.

A Legal Spectrum of Aboriginal Rights in Canada

Access/Use --- *Title*

(dependent on availability of resources Managed by others)

(only once been specifically Recognized – Tsilhqot'in v. BC 2014)

----------------*Management/Stewardship*-----

(a largely unexplored area & opportunity)

FIGURE 3.6.11. A representation of aboriginal rights along a spectrum ranging from access and use to title, with stewardship/management occupying a central but lesser known area of the legal landscape, based on current Canadian common law.

part land-claims negotiations and litigation, and part reconciliation-based (Figure 3.6.11). Mechanisms of the relationship include legislation, litigation, negotiation, direct action, and engagement/consultation. These mechanisms and the array of agreements that the governments are trying to reach with Indigenous peoples to work things out hasn't really worked. Clear evidence of this is quantified in the substantial imbalances between Indigenous and non-Indigenous rates of children in care, incarceration, unemployment, missing and murdered women, youth suicide, post-secondary enrollment, graduation, and other common measures of community health and well-being. It's a bit of a mess within this third model—today. This is substantially due to the fact of aboriginal sovereignty conceived of as secondary to the colonial State (Miller 2003). Numerous mechanisms have developed as a web of relations, tangled around the monolithic institution of centralized and consolidated State power.

Proposing a Three-row Model for Public Heritage

The legal spectrum of Indigenous rights is commonly understood to range from access and use (the right to access and use other peoples' resources and property; harvesting rights) to title (full ownership of the land and resources). Management is an area of relations, often overlooked in aboriginal law, which resides in-between harvesting (usufructory) rights and title (Supreme Court of Canada 2014). In between recognition of full ownership and rights to access and use another's property is a relationship to resources and environment forged in stewardship and management. I would therefore suggest that resource management, founded on collaborative planning and decision-making over the use of land and resources, may require a "three-row model," based on the co-occupation and sharing of place within a collective realm (Figure 3.6.12).

Currently, the exclusive authority to make decisions is commonly held within a singular governmental actor, such as a Minister (depending upon the governmental structure). Such centralization and monopolization of power is a current standard in the relationship between the State and Indigenous Peoples (Miller 2003). Our current messy existence remains a metamorphosed form of the failed two-row model. Exclusivity is maintained in respect of differing worldviews, customs, and beliefs, affecting values and understanding of place. Co-occupying and sharing place forges recognition of multiplicity and inclusivity in decision-making. This proposed field of relations is based on an intention of establishing a truer realm of public heritage, where we "overlay" (not exclude) Indigenous and colonial political economies and landscapes (cultural, economic, and so on). Integral to the third row are factors of definition and decision-making over the use of land and resources informing stewardship, caretaking, management. The distribution of authorities within this arena results from consensus-based, rather than democratic, processes and serves to equalize relations of power. The central row represents a place "with" each other; not over, through, around, or against the "other."

This model provides a controlled area, forum, field of play lacking in the historic models and relations of today. It, simply (recognizably over-simply), provides for the recognition and an equalization of power between colonially founded government

'THREE ROW' MODEL of RELATIONSHIPS

- Each maintains their own Laws, Culture & Beliefs (I & II) – i.e., exclusive IPs.
- Each shares in managing the land (III) – shared material economy/heritage managment.
- Set against a backdrop of mutual respect.

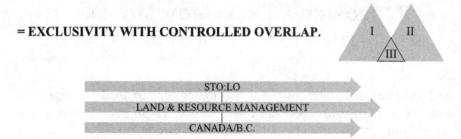

= EXCLUSIVITY WITH CONTROLLED OVERLAP.

FIGURE 3.6.12. A proposed "Three-Row" Model of "Public and Private" Relations—exclusivity with controlled overlap.

and Indigenous peoples with unique rights (as recognized within the *United Nations Declaration on the Rights of Indigenous Peoples*). These three rows are, like the original, set against a backdrop of mutual respect. This backdrop also incorporates principles and ethical guidelines forged from "boots on the ground" experience in public heritage, going beyond standard AAA/SAA party lines as presented above: do no harm, steward-ship, consent, respect (including recognition of worldviews), and collaboration.

Applied through Stó:lō mechanisms, the assertion of this formative model supports the achievement of three things—recognition of Stó:lō aboriginal title and rights; vis-ibility of the Stó:lō heritage landscape; and development of frameworks, models, and mechanisms for the collaborative management and decision-making over land and resources—intrinsically interconnected as fused elements of public heritage. Moving to the "three-row model" of collaborative management and shared decision-making can, could, and would support the development of a truly "public heritage" of shared, cross-cultural recognition and "cradling" of meaning within and between Indigenous and settler communities.

CONCLUSION: PUBLIC HERITAGE NEEDS A TRANSFORMED PUBLIC

Contemporary relations of public heritage playing out in this personal ethnography and cases situated within the Stó:lō Nation represent global questions, issues, challenges in this field of work. With global and national actions such as the ratification of the *United Nations Declaration on the Rights of Indigenous Peoples* (2007) and Canada's Truth and Reconciliation Commission (2015) recommendations and calls to action, State institutions and the general public are increasingly aware and involved in replacing or at least explicitly addressing colonialism and working toward decolonization. Academic institutions are one focus of indigenization. Public heritage is central to a field of rela-tions that presents a monstrous challenge requiring transformation to establish a "third row" of recognition, respect, understanding, appreciation, one-mindedness, helping es-tablish one "public" and a better way of doing things (Joe et al. 2007). Metamorphosis remains a backwater of colonialism and private heritage, erasure, invisibility, and resist-ance to inclusiveness. Transformation looms as our challenge, face of change, and vision of our future in achieving a new public and true public heritage.

NOTES

1. The content of this chapter is unconventionally a mix of spoken transcription and supple-
mental, written text. I include some references within my text; however most are included at
the end as supporting the content of this cumulative "presentation." I have added phonetic
pronunciations to all of the Halq'eméylem words used in this text.

2. American Anthropological Association, Archaeological Institute of America, British Columbia Association of Professional Archaeologists, Canadian Archaeological Association, International Committee on Archaeological Heritage Management, International Council on Monuments and Sites, Register of Professional Archaeologists, Society for American Archaeology, and the World Archaeological Congress.

References

American Anthropological Association. 2012. *Principles of Professional Responsibility*. <http://ethics.aaanet.org/ethics-statement-0-preamble/>.

Atalay, Sonya. 2006. "Indigenous Archaeology as Decolonizing Practice." *American Indian Quarterly* 30(3–4): 280–310.

Atalay, Sonya, Lee Rains Clauss, Randall H. McGuire, and John R. Welch, eds. 2014. *Transforming Archaeology: Activist Practices and Prospects*. Walnut Creek, CA: Left Coast Press.

Bartlett, C., Murdena Marshall, and Albert Marshall. 2012. *Journal of Environmental Studies and Sciences* 2(4): 331–340.

Basso, Keith H. 1996. *Wisdom Sits in Places*. Albuquerque: University of New Mexico Press.

Bourdieu, Pierre. 1977. *Outline of a Theory of Practice*. Cambridge: Cambridge University Press.

Bourdieu, Pierre. 1980. *The Logic of Practice*. Stanford: Stanford University Press.

Carlson, Keith Thor, David M. Schaepe, Albert 'Sonny' McHalsie, David Smith and Leanna Rhodes, eds. 2001. *A Stó:lō-Coast Salish Historical Atlas*. Vancouver, BC: Douglas-McIntyre and Stó:lō Heritage Trust.

Deloria, Vine, Jr. 1969. *Custer Died for your Sins: An Indian Manifesto*. Oklahoma City: University of Oklahoma Press.

Ferguson, T. J. 2009. "Improving the Quality of Archaeology in the United States through Consultation and Collaboration with Native Americans and Descendant Communities," in *Archaeology and Cultural Resource Management*, ed. Lynne Sebastian and William D. Lipe. Santa Fe, NM: School of Advanced Research, 169–193.

Ferris, Neal, and John R. Welch. 2015. "New Worlds: Ethics in Contemporary North American Archaeological Practice," in *Ethics and Archaeological Praxis*, ed. Cristobal Gnecco and Dorothy Lippert. New York: Springer, 69–92.

Gehring, Charles T., William Starna, and William Fenten. 1987. "The Tawagonshi Treaty of 1613: The Final Chapter." *New York History* 68(4): 373–393.

Hau de no sau nee. 1978. "A Basic Call to Consciousness: The Hau de no sau nee Address to the Western World Geneva, Switzerland, Autumn 1977." *Akwesasne Notes*, Mohawk Nation, via Roseveltown, NY.

Henders, Susan J. 2006. "Reimagining Minority and Aboriginal Self-Government: Visions from Buddhist and Aboriginal Philosophies," in *Human Rights in the Pacific Rim: Imagining a New Critical Discourse*, ed. Edmund Ryden and Barbara K Bundy. Taiwan: Fu Jen Catholic University Press, 167–194.

Joe, Herb, David M. Schaepe, and Albert "Sonny" McHalsie, executive producers. 2007. *T'xwelátse Is Finally Home*. Bear Image Productions. Chilliwack, BC: Stó:lō Nation. <https://www.srrmcentre.com/StoneTxweltase/1Home.html>.

Kafka, Franz. 1915. *Metamorphosis (Die Verwandlung)*. Leipzig: Kurt Wolff Verlag.

Kohn, Margaret. 2014. "Colonialism," in *The Stanford Encyclopedia of Philosophy*, ed. Edward N. Zalta. <https://plato.stanford.edu/archives/spr2014/entries/colonialism/>.

Lyons, Natasha. 2013. *Where the Wind Blows Us: Practicing Critical Community Archaeology in the Canadian North*. Tucson, AZ: University of Arizona Press.

McHalsie, Albert "Sonny." 2007. "We Have to Take Care of Everything That Belongs to Us," in *Be of Good Mind: Essays on the Coast Salish*, ed. B. G. Miller. Vancouver, British Columbia: University of British Columbia Press, 82–130.

McHalsie, Albert "Sonny", David M. Schaepe, and Keith Thor Carlson. 2001. "Making the World Right through the Transformations of Xexá:ls," in *A Stó:lō-Coast Salish Historical Atlas*, ed. K. T. Carlson, David M. Schaepe, Albert McHalsie, David Smith, and Leeanna Rhodes. Vancouver, BC: Douglas-McIntyre and Stó:lō Heritage Trust, 6–7.

McHalsie, Albert "Sonny", and David M. Schaepe. 2010. "Placing Archaeology in Sʼólh Téméxw." Unpublished poster presentation, Fraser Valley Archaeology Project Poster Session at the 72nd Annual Society for American Archaeology Conference, Vancouver, BC.

Miller, Bruce. 2003. *Invisible Indigenes: The Politics of Nonrecognition*. Lincoln: University of Nebraska Press.

Muntean, Reese, Kate Hennessy, Alissa Antile, Susan Rowley, Jordan Wilson, Brendan Matkin, Rachael Eckersley, Perry Tan, and Ron Wakkary. 2015. "ʔeləẃk̓ʷ—Belongings: Tangible Interactions with Intangible Heritage." *Journal of Science and Technology of the Arts* (CITAR Journal) 7(2): 59–69.

Nicholas, George P. 2006. "Decolonizing the Archaeological Landscape: The Practice and Politics of Archaeology in British Columbia." *American Indian Quarterly* 30(3–4): 350–380.

Nicholas, George P., and David M. Schaepe. 2008. "The IPinCH Project: Addressing Intellectual Properties Issues in BC Archaeology." Presentation at the British Columbia Archaeology Forum. Chilliwack, BC.

Otto, Paul. 2013. "Wampum, Tawagonshi, and the Two Row Belt." *Journal of Early American History* 3(1): 110–125.

Parmenter, Jon. 2013. "The Meaning of Kaswentha and the Two Row Wampum Belt in Haudenosaunee (Iroquois) History: Can Indigenous Oral Tradition Be Reconciled with the Documentary Record?" *Journal of Early American History* 3(1): 82–109.

Piccini, Angela, and David M. Schaepe. 2014. "The Messy Business of Archaeology as Participatory Local Knowledge: A Conversation between the Stó:lō Nation and Knowle West." *Canadian Journal of Archaeology* 2(38): 466–495.

Roseberry, William. 1988. "Political Economy." *Annual Review of Anthropology* 17: 161–185.

Sassaman, Kenneth. 2014. "Editor's Corner." *American Antiquity* 79(1): 3–4.

Schaepe, David M. 2003. "Developing a Comprehensive Heritage Management Plan." Presentation at the Union of BC Indian Chiefs—Land Claims Conference, Vancouver, BC.

Schaepe, David M. 2004. "The Cultural Landscape of Sʼólh Téméxw." Presentation at the American Association for the Advancement of Science, Seattle, WA.

Schaepe, David M. 2007. "Stó:lō Identity and the Cultural Landscape of Sʼólh Téméxw," in *Be of Good Mind: Essays on the Coast Salish*, ed. B. G. Miller. Vancouver, British Columbia: University of British Columbia Press, 243–259.

Schaepe, David M. 2008. "Archaeology and Heritage Management." Presentation at the In-Sight 10th Annual Aboriginal Land and Resource Management Conference, Vancouver, BC.

Schaepe, David M. 2009. "The Stó:lō, Sʼólh Téméxw, and Intellectual Property Issues in Cultural Heritage." Presentation at the Intellectual Property Issues in Cultural Heritage (IPinCH) Workshop, Burnaby, BC.

Schaepe, David M. 2011. "In the Face of Exploitation: Empowering Stó:lō Cultural Landscape Management and Heritage Preservation." Presentation at the American Anthropological Association 110th Annual Meeting, Montreal, QC, in "Reversing the Legacy of Colonialism in Heritage Research" (Session Organizer: Steven Loring).

Schaepe, David M. 2015. "Current Archaeological and Heritage Landscape Management Issues in S'ólh Téméxw." Presentation at the SFU Archaeology Forum / Intellectual Property Issues in Cultural Heritage (IPinCH), Burnaby, BC.

Schaepe, David, Karen Brady, Sue Formosa, and Stó:lō Advisory Committee. 2016. "S'ólh Téméxw Use Plan v1.0." Unpublished document on file at the Stó:lō Research and Resource Management Centre, Chilliwack, BC.

Schaepe David M., Bill Angelbeck, David Snook, and John R. Welch. 2017. "Archaeology as Therapy: Connecting Belongings, Knowledge, Time, Place and Well-Being." *Current Anthropology* 58(4): 502–533.

Schaepe, David M., and Ts'elxwéyeqw Tribe. 2017. *Being Ts'elxwéyeqw: Voices and History of the First Peoples Voices and History from the Chilliwack-Fraser Valley, British Columbia.* Vancouver: Harbour Press.

Silliman, Stephen, and T. J. Ferguson. 2010. "Consultation and Collaboration with Descendant Communities," in *Voices in American Archaeology*, ed. Wendy Ashmore, Dorothy T. Lippert, and Barbara J. Mills. Washington, DC: Society for American Archaeology, 48–72.

Society for American Archaeology. 2015. *Principles of Archaeological Ethics.* <http://www.saa.org/AbouttheSociety/PrinciplesofArchaeologicalEthics/tabid/203/Default.aspx>.

Stó:lō Nation. 2003. "Stó:lō Heritage Policy Manual, Version 1.1." Unpublished document on file in the Stó:lō Archives. Chilliwack, BC.

Stó:lō Research & Resource Management Centre/Stó:lō Nation and Sqewlets First Nation. 2017. *Sq'éwlets: A Stó:lō-Coast Salish Community in the Fraser River Valley.* <http://www.digitalsqewlets.ca>.

Supreme Court of Canada. 2014. *Tsilhqot'in Nation v. British Columbia* 2014 SCC 44. <https://scc-csc.lexum.com/scc-csc/scc-csc/en/item/14246/index.do>.

Truth and Reconciliation Commission of Canada. 2015. "Honouring the Truth, Reconciling for the Future: Summary of the Final Report of the Truth and Reconciliation Commission of Canada." Ottawa, ON: Truth and Reconciliation Commission of Canada. <http://www.trc.ca>.

United Nations. 2007. *United Nations Declaration on the Rights of Indigenous Peoples.* <https://www.un.org/development/desa/indigenouspeoples/declaration-on-the-rights-of-indigenous-peoples.html>.

Venebles, Robert. 2012. *An Analysis of the 1613 Tawagonshi Treaty.* <http://www.onondaganation.org/history/2012>.

Young, Iris Marion. 2001. "Pushing for Inclusion: Justice and the Politics of Difference," in *Theories of Democracy: A Reader*, ed. Ronald J. Terchek and Thomas C. Conte. Lanham, MD: Rowman & Littlefield Publishers, 268–278.

Young, Iris Marion, and Jacob Levy. 2011. *Colonialism and its Legacies.* Lanham, MD: Lexington Books.

Zedeno, Maria. 2000. "On What People Make of Places: A Behavioral Cartography," in *Social Theory in Archaeology*, ed. Michael B. Schiffer. Salt Lake City: University of Utah Press, 97–111.

PART IV

LIVING WITH CHANGE

THE SOCIAL SCIENCES

What Role in Conservation?

NED KAUFMAN

INTRODUCTION

CONSERVATION is losing touch with the sciences that describe human society and the environment (I shall call them social sciences for convenience). More troublingly, it is losing touch with the concrete realities those sciences describe, which are the same realities that shape conservation itself (Kaufman 2017 and forthcoming). Today's world is profoundly different from the one in which the rules of modern conservation were framed, yet conservation has not kept up with change: with the emergence of global warming, global migration, global finance, trade, and travel, widening economic in-equality, and so forth. Conservation must now reconnect with the world outside. The social sciences can help.

One of the many questions with which they can help concerns the nature and function of place, a concept central to conservation yet poorly defined. Why do places matter? What kinds of policies and programs will best protect them in our current world? In this chapter I shall focus on three disciplines that can help provide answers: environmental psychology, economics, and climate science. I have not chosen them for their superior explanatory power (some might turn to anthropology, cultural geography, political science, or sociology) but because they cover the range of conditions awaiting conservationists as they turn to the social sciences. They differ in scale, from that of the individual person (environmental psychology) through the social (economics) to the planetary (climate science). More importantly, they differ in usefulness. Where environmental psychology is essentially ready for adoption by conservationists, and climate science has become imperative, economics presents a more complex picture: orthodox economic thought is simply too discordant with what conservation science knows about the world to be useful, yet certain non-orthodox approaches are promising. The point is that the social sciences are less like a miracle drug to be gulped down by conservationists than a bowl of fruit to be carefully sorted through. While some of what nestles therein is both delicious and healthful, some is quite nasty and should be tossed out. If it helps solve a conservation problem, it is probably worth keeping; if it doesn't, the conservationist should probably continue rummaging.

Environmental Psychology

The concept of place is central to environmental psychology, as to conservation, yet the two disciplines see it differently. Environmental psychology studies how individuals relate emotionally, cognitively, and behaviorally to the world around them. Where conservation generally applies a lens of expert evaluation, psychology recognizes a deeper kind of person-place relationship, called *place attachment*, that draws on feelings rather than evaluation (Altman and Low 1992, esp. chapters by Hummon and Riley, Hidalgo and Hernández 2001, Manzo and Perkins 2006). To a notable degree, attachment to places resembles attachment to people. Both originate in the infant's attachment to its mother, who is initially both a person and a place (first a womb, then a bosom) (Gallagher 1993: 122–3). The capacity to form attachments to places, indeed to love them, is thus deeply rooted. Under normal circumstances, people do not talk much about their feelings for places and may actually be unaware of them; but when the bonds between person and place are threatened or destroyed, then the feelings surge to the fore, and love and dependence may be replaced by grief and disorientation (Fried 1963, Fullilove 1996 and 2005). Many factors can lead to the breaking of place bonds. While conservation typically lists destruction and disfigurement of buildings as leading threats, environmental psychology adds forced displacement (from war, civil discord, economic development, government planning, gentrification, disinvestment, or individual aging). Recently solastalgia, "the pain or sickness caused by the loss of, or inability to derive solace from, the present state of one's home environment" (Albrecht 2006: 35, Albrecht et al. 2007) has emerged as a widespread disruptor. Solastalgia is essentially disfigurement raised to an environmental scale, transforming a place so that it no longer feels like home. Energy development can cause solastalgia; increasingly climate change is doing so.

What factors makes people care for some places more than others? Not their objective merits, for researchers have found no correlation between place satisfaction and attachment: on the contrary, people often become emotionally attached to quite unsatisfactory places, and threats to the survival of those places may even strengthen their attachment (Anton and Lawrence 2016, Fried 1963, Hidalgo and Hernández 2001, Brown et al. 2003, Cuba and Hummon 1993, Devine-Wright 2009). This is partly because people's sense of their own identity gradually becomes entangled with their feelings for places, so that the loss of place (however imperfect or damaged) becomes also a loss of identity (Devine-Wright 2009, Korpela 1989, Proshansky et al. 1983, Twigger-Ross and Uzzell 1996).

People become attached to many kinds of places. Those associated with childhood, with significant later events or phases in life (either good or bad), and with the concept of home show up regularly in people's intimate atlases (Marcus 1992, Manzo 2005, Twigger-Ross and Uzzell 1996). Home in this sense may mean not only the dwelling but also the neighborhood, town, or region (Cuba and Hummon 1993, Després 1991, Fried 1963, Fullilove 1996 and 2005, Giuliani 1991, Manzo 2003, Sixsmith 1986): it is the zone or habitat within which much of ordinary life takes place. In terms of cultural conservation, it is where the heritage of home, family, sociability, religion, food, and more is nurtured.

At a more granular level, the list of places to which people typically become attached is as interesting for what it omits as for what it includes. Patriotic shrines, architectural monuments, and other staples of conservation practice do not appear very often. The places that do are mostly quite ordinary: community centers, playgrounds, gymnasia, shops, bars and restaurants, laundromats, and any number of nondescript houses and apartment buildings (Korpela 1989, Manzo 2005, Twigger-Ross and Uzzell 1996: for confirmation from other disciplines, see Hester 1985 and 1993). What makes these seemingly ordinary places important is personal connection rather than national narrative, lived experience rather than aesthetic salience, memory rather than historical documentation, attachment rather than evaluation. Though conservationists may be tempted to dismiss such places as "not heritage," they offer the most vital contact with lived heritage that many people will ever experience. And psychologists have repeatedly documented how devastating their loss can be (Fried 1963, Fullilove 1996 and 2005).

Conservationists may infer two crucial points from environmental psychology. First, that people's attachment to places and sense of heritage are broader than what conservation science posits. Second, that people's need for stability in the physical environment extends far beyond what conservation can provide through the protection of select monuments and sites. Thus environmental psychology points towards a more expansive form of conservation than any now on offer. Hugh Freeman, a psychologist working in the English Midlands in the 1970s, pointed this out many years ago. Shocked at how politicians and planners obliterated entire neighborhoods without the least concern for the psychological harm thereby inflicted, Freeman called for the "psychological conservation of the environment" (1984: 13), by which he meant conservation that would not stop at symbolic landmarks and listed buildings but would stabilize the patterns and textures of people's ordinary habitats, the streets and dwellings and shops and social spaces where they carried out most of their lives. Freeman's call, now backed up by more than four decades of additional research, continues to challenge conservation.

ECONOMICS

However psychologically rich, places must have a physical basis (generally on earth's surface). This means that nearly every *place* is also *property*: real estate. And this stirs up a conflict. Defined as *place*, the social value of a location lies in its capacity to support meanings and activities—its use value; defined as *property*, in its capacity to yield profits—its exchange value. This split identity is at the root of some of the gravest threats to cultural heritage: demolition, overdevelopment, disinvestment, gentrification, and much more. Clearly there is a need for economic explanation and, ultimately, reform.

Yet conservation's encounters with economics have been frustrating. It can be hard to tell whether economics in the sense of the economy (meaning patterns in the real world) or economics in the sense of a science of explanation is at fault, for economists often fail to distinguish between descriptive, normative, and ideological arguments. Then, too, it can be hard to separate what economic science actually says from what politicians and their clients and advisers *say* it says. These confusions signal the presence of a sort of hegemonic discourse which I shall call *orthodox economics*. Many conservationists try hard to master its language and adopt its values, but it never works. The discourse is simply too discordant.

Part of the problem is that orthodox economics has become blurred with economism, the reduction of social factors to economic factors and social values to economic values. Economism puts profits and economic growth ahead of sustainability, fairness, and quality of life. Pope Francis (a fine non-orthodox economist) has called economics "the art of achieving a fitting management of our common home, which is the world as a whole" (Pope Francis I 2013, par. 206), yet economism proposes just the opposite: that the world and society exist for the benefit of the economy. This view gains support from a curious creation of orthodox economics known as *homo economicus*, or economic man. Homo economicus always does what is economically best for himself, even if it means setting aside the claims of family, friends, and community (not to mention religion, culture, and aesthetics). Of course, actual people rarely behave like homo economicus: indeed to most people he is a monster. Yet to orthodox economics he represents the ideal of individual behavior and a model for social decision-making.

The ethical shortcomings of homo economicus are prejudicial to conservation at many points. They lead him to deprecate the expression of cultural identity, encourage the exploitation of heritage for tourism, elevate the interests of entrepreneurs over those of community and society at large, dismiss the whole subject of fairness or justice, and ignore the long-term value of conserving materials, energy, and familiar places. So discordant are the values of homo economicus with those of conservation that, unless conservationists are willing to abandon much of what they know to be true and believe to be right, it is hard to see how his guidance can be anything but so much mis-guidance.

Quite apart from its tendency to economism, orthodox economics has no way to deal with the phenomena of place which are central to conservation. Its concept of *land* is so broad as to include any natural resource whose supply is somehow limited: gold, timber, fresh water, radio frequencies, and even landing slots at airports. Land in this sense figures mainly as a factor of production, alongside labor, capital, and entrepreneurship, and is readily replaceable by any of them. Within this conceptual system, places in the sense that conservationists understand them—spatial units with unique characteristics and values—have no more than a tenuous existence, while places in the sense of environmental psychology have none at all. Of course one place may have a higher or lower monetary value than another, but any place is equivalent to (and exchangeable with) any other place of equal "value." The Taj Mahal can be replaced by two Eiffel Towers (each "worth" half as much), the Nasrallah family's neighborhood in Fes by the Nigrelli family's in Buenos Aires, a grizzly bear habitat by a monarch butterfly habitat.

Ignoring the impossibilities which lie at its core, many conservationists struggle to fit cultural heritage to the Procrustean bed of orthodox economics. They often start by translating units of heritage value into units of money. But what are the values to be translated? Because the real values of heritage (social usefulness and meaning, shared memory, cultural identity, tradition, enjoyment of the environment) are unquantifiable, analysts substitute visitation statistics, property tax revenues, or other proxies. Studies sampling people's willingness to pay to visit historic sites, or estimating the sites' contribution to tourism profits, or comparing costs to benefits proliferate and look responsible and even scientific: studies of the studies further elevate their respectability (de la Torre 2002, Getty Conservation Institute 1999, Mason 2005, Provins et. al. 2005, Throsby 2003). But to the extent that they claim (or are taken) to measure the value of heritage, they are simply misleading. They do not even capture the value of heritage *sites*, which are merely the tip of the iceberg.

Choosing money as a unit of measurement just makes the problem worse. For money is not neutral in the way of centimeters or kilograms: it represents its own value system. Financial writer Michael Lewis asserts, rather provocatively, that the chief role of money in the United States is to provide entertainment (1991: 114). But most people understand that money signifies political influence, cultural prestige, access to social networks, and, of course, a wealthy lifestyle. The point is that money means *something*. And since the 1980s it has increasingly come to mean what Lewis calls *the money culture*, a value system based on wealth, power, and display, condoning (even admiring) greed, and subsisting on financial manipulation and sometimes fraud. The money culture has had a huge impact on the economy, as finance has outstripped manufacturing as the dominant sector in advanced economies, and as assets have become more valuable for financial leverage than for producing goods. The money culture has even influenced conservation science, for it is no coincidence that monetary valuation studies became popular just as it was reshaping all of society in its image: indeed the proliferation of these studies is better understood as a symptom of the ascendancy of money than as an advance in the economic analysis of heritage.

An important attempt in the 1990s to calculate the economic value of ecosystem services (the benefits humans receive from nature) revealed another problem with economic analysis (Costanza et al. 1997). Totting everything up, the authors reached a very tentative total of about $33 trillion USD per year (nearly twice the world's entire annual GNP at the time). More compelling than their conclusion, however, was their caveat, which was that the entire exercise was flawed. Most ecosystem services never got into the money economy; if they did, they would upend the entire global price system, making all extrapolations from current pricing irrelevant. More importantly, since humans cannot live without certain ecosystem services, their economic value is infinite. The total monetary value of ecosystem services is therefore a meaningless concept: the most comprehensive recent study avoided even attempting an estimate (de Groot et al. 2012).

Though the services rendered by cultural heritage are not necessary to human life in the way of ecosystem services, they *are* essential to human civilization. Perhaps their total money value is infinite too, and calculating it another meaningless exercise.

If the ecosystem's infinite value taxes the analytic resources of orthodox economics, so does its non-infinite capacity to supply raw materials and energy and absorb wastes. Although the search for strategies to stay safely within ecological limits is central to today's conservation science, orthodox economics does not even acknowledge those limits. If we run out of one thing, it says, we will find another. Everything is fungible; innovation will solve all problems. Orthodox economics contemplates the destruction of the environment with equanimity because it "knows" that entrepreneurs will come up with some alternative.

At all of these points (and many more), orthodox economics either builds on premises that conservation science knows to be false or fails to answer questions it knows to be important. These are not minor faults: they pull the rug out from under most of the conclusions that follow, making orthodox economics a mode of analysis for conservation science to challenge, not to adopt. There is certainly a need for economic explanations of place and heritage, but it must be met through other forms of economic science. In fact, though an economics capable of explaining heritage and places and their conservation does not yet exist, many useful non-orthodox approaches flourish and deserve the attention of conservationists:

- *Behavioral economics* studies the behavior of actual human beings faced with economic decisions, drawing on psychology and often using experiments (Ariely 2010, Kahneman 2011). Dethroning homo economicus, it offers an account of economic behavior more nuanced and realistic than that of orthodox economics. Conservationists could use behavioral economics to study people's decision-making with regard to intangible cultural heritage, historic sites, domestic habitats, and indeed all kinds of heritage places. Complementing environmental psychology, it could provide a far more robust account than the brittle picture provided by monetary valuations, hedonic and willingness-to-pay studies, cost-benefit analyses, and other current techniques.
- *Human development economics* explores how economic resources can be deployed to improve the lives of the world's poor (Alkire 2010, Sen 2000 and 2003, Stiglitz et al. 2010, UNDP 1990 et seq.). Where orthodox development economics counts growth in GDP (gross domestic product) as evidence of improvement, human development economics constructs indices of human welfare based on quality-of-life factors like longevity, health, access to education, and political participation. Unlike orthodox economics, human development economics cares about economic justice. Its principles do not apply only to poor nations but provide a universal framework in which conservationists could assess the social values of heritage and compare the worth of different conservation programs and policies.

- The *Georgist school of economics* (named after Henry George, the American economist whose bestselling *Progress and Poverty* helped lay the groundwork for twentieth-century progressive movements) starts by asking why orthodox economic development always seems to bring poverty in its wake ([1879] 2005). George found the answer in land prices, and while many economists today dismiss his solutions, Georgist economics deserves the attention of conservationists for its sophisticated analysis of land and its focus on justice: it opens the way to an economic science of place (Gaffney 1962, 1994, 2001).

- *Common land economics* studies the behavior of land and other resources controlled by groups of people (perhaps Native tribes, villagers, or fishing cooperatives). Most English-language readers know of it, if at all, through Garrett Hardin's much-anthologized article, "The Tragedy of the Commons" (1968), which argued that common ownership of land inevitably led to overexploitation and environmental disaster. Hardin got it badly wrong: neither an ecologist nor an economist, he confused common land with open-access land, i.e. land open to unlimited exploitation by all. *Of course* such land will be exhausted. But common land is not open-access land; its managers can and do establish rules. And when open-minded economists study common land, they find that it can be a just and sustainable way to manage natural resources (Bardhan and Ray 2008, Bromley 1992, Dolšak and Ostrom 2003, Ostrom 1990 and 2012, Ostrom 2003, Poteete et al. 2010). For conservationists, the study of common land economics (and law) could loosen the rigid dichotomy of private and public land imposed by orthodox economics. In practical terms, that could lead to better protection of Indigenous heritage and more support for conservation trusts. Research into novel forms of shared ownership might even devise ways to vest place-rights in residents: that could finally make the psychological conservation of the environment achievable.

- *Ecological economics* builds on the sensible premise that the economy exists within the ecosystem, rather than above or apart from it (Costanza and Wainger 1991, Daly 1991 and 1996, Daly and Cobb 1989, Daly and Farley 2010, Sagoff 1988). Where orthodox economics imagines goods and income flowing around in a closed loop, ecological economics provides a realistic account of how the economy extracts energy and materials from the ecosystem and ejects waste products back into it. Because it recognizes the importance of ecological limits, it argues that limits must also be put on the size of the economy. So where orthodox economics promotes constant growth as a social norm, ecological economics calls for conservation of materials and energy. Like human development economics, it meets the Pope Francis test, bringing fundamental insights into how to manage the world which is our common home. Conservationists could use ecological economics to illuminate the value of conservation itself, not only of raw materials and energy but also of natural habitats and cultural places.

Although it is hardly possible to catalog the elements of an economic science of heritage and places and conservation that does not yet exist, these five non-orthodox approaches will surely contribute to its development.

Climate Science

A hundred and twenty years have passed since Swedish scientist Svante Arrhenius advanced the basic theory of climate change: that industrial processes central to the advanced economies were raising the concentration of carbon dioxide in the atmosphere, and that this would eventually heat it. It has been fifty years since scientists gained the tools to test his theory, and by thirty years ago they knew he was right—except that climate change was *already* happening. Today the effects of a warming atmosphere (and oceans) are felt around the planet; epic storms, killing heat waves, droughts, floods, melting ice caps and glaciers, rising sea levels, crop failures, and other unpleasant consequences have convinced growing numbers of the public that climate change is not only real but fearsome. A general grasp of the latest IPCC findings (IPCC) has become *de rigeur* for policy makers, including conservationists. Yet with proof of concept have come new evolutions of thought, as climate activists have learned to see a warming planet less as a pure problem of science and more as a problem of justice (Mary Robinson Foundation). This fusion has laid the groundwork for an emerging *social* science of climate, a nascent study of how climate changes affect human welfare and, conversely, how human activities change the climate. Conservation is deeply implicated in this.

From a scientific perspective, the remedy for climate change is straightforward: deeply and rapidly cut carbon dioxide and other greenhouse gas emissions. Climate science does not care where or by whom the cuts are made (though obviously the biggest cuts must come from the national economies and economic sectors where there is most to cut). The effort to reduce emissions, and thereby limit the heating process, constitutes the arm of climate policy known as *mitigation*: a second arm, known as *adaptation*, focuses on protecting civilization from the impacts of current and future heating. On the level of science, adaptation does not care who gets protected, or at whose expense.

Climate justice looks at the problem differently from either mitigation or adaptation: it is rapidly asserting itself as a third arm of climate policy. Unlike mitigation, justice *does* care where emissions come from, where cuts are made, and where the impacts of climate change are felt. Since the wealthy industrial nations have largely caused climate change (and have the resources to fight it), justice says they should bear the burden of quickly and drastically cutting their emissions; conversely, since the poorer and less developed nations did little to cause the problem (and lack the economic resources to fix it), justice says they should not be held responsible for deep and rapid emissions cuts: on the contrary, their governments are morally responsible for lifting up their citizens' living standards, perhaps even if that means *increasing* emissions. As for adaptation, climate justice *does* care who gets protected and at whose expense. Science predicts that the most harmful impacts will fall on poorer and less developed nations; justice says the richer nations should help protect them. The sharply contested issue of how much the richer nations owe to cover the *loss and damage* caused by their actions has emerged as an important dimension of climate justice and of climate policy.

In place of the global problem depicted by science, then, the lens of justice reveals a deeply divided world, and the divisions challenge conservation policy at many points. Under adaptation, people look to conservation to protect cultural heritage—but what heritage, and where? There is little doubt that the world's leading conservation groups will muster the resources to protect many great monuments in the wealthy nations, and some in the poorer nations as well. But climate change also imperils the living cultural heritage of coastlines, high deserts, and tundra—especially in the poorer nations. Who should safeguard this heritage? Justice points to the wealthy nations. Yet when the Inuit people, whose entire heritage and way of life are threatened by climate change, went to court seeking help from the United States government, the request was refused (Revkin 2006, Watt-Cloutier 2005); and although groups like ICOMOS show some interest in preserving the Arctic heritage of European explorers, so far as I know no nongovernmental conservation group has come forward to help the Inuit protect their own. Should such assistance should be regarded as a matter of charity (and therefore optional), or as part of the national debt due for loss and damage? The question deserves debate.

Global divisions also shape conservation's responsibilities for mitigation. These basically center on buildings, which produce about a third of global emissions from energy (more in the developed economies, and much more in cities). So large is the building sector's contribution, and so easy to cut, that the United Nations Environmental Programme has flagged it as the single most promising source of emissions reductions (UNEP 2009, 9). This has created an enormous (and so far unrealized) opportunity for conservation, but a crucial question must first be answered. The central issue is not, as many people think, whether older buildings are inherently inefficient (they are not). More important is the question of process: should priority be given to cutting emissions from existing buildings or to constructing efficient new ones: that is, to green *retrofit* or green *building*?

For answers, conservation must turn to climate science. And science says: it depends. In much of the developing world, populations are projected to grow and urbanize, living standards to rise—and the building stock to balloon. Green building will be essential to controlling emissions: conversely, green retrofit can play no more than a supporting role as the proportion of the total building stock represented by older buildings shrinks. In the developed economies the situation is precisely the reverse. Living standards are already high and populations are not projected to grow much (in some places they are shrinking, leaving stocks of surplus buildings). The huge stock of existing buildings can serve most of society's needs for many years; and, if demolitions and new construction are held to a minimum, existing buildings will remain a substantial proportion of total building stock. In this scenario, improving the efficiency of new buildings will not reduce total emissions very much. Conversely, retrofitting the existing building stock will reduce it significantly. Of course, a high rate of demolition and replacement (for example, for new green buildings) would invalidate the equations, but such a policy would be a serious mistake. All new construction (even of green buildings) releases an immediate burst of carbon, pushing emissions *up* in the short term, just when it is crucial to push them down. While decades of efficient operation will eventually result in a net reduction of emissions, we cannot wait that long. Though green retrofit cannot always deliver the deep energy cuts promised by new green construction, it uses so much less energy up front that it can realize reductions twenty-five, fifty, or even seventy-five years ahead of new buildings (Empty Homes Agency 2008, NTHP 2011).

In the developed economies, then, science points to conservation as the solution, but to a kind of conservation that does not yet exist, for science tells us that nothing short of protecting millions of buildings will have a meaningful impact on the climate. To succeed, then, a green retrofit policy will have to protect not merely the world's cultural gems but also the ordinary environment of neighborhoods and cities. It will, in other words, have to look very much like Freeman's psychological conservation of the environment. Of course, protection will not be enough: it will also have to upgrade the energy performance of those millions of buildings. Another challenge to conservation practice.

Beyond putting building conservation in a new light, climate science reveals a surprising new role for place conservation. For even though climate change is global, the infrastructure needed to turn fossil fuels into energy (and ultimately carbon emissions) is local. Each well, mine, drilling pad, power plant, transmission line, access road, pipeline, compressor station, storage tank, rail line, transfer station, terminal, and waste dump must go somewhere. And all over the world, climate activists are discovering that mobilizing to block these projects can be an effective strategy for limiting future emissions: more effective in many cases than national legislation (Klein 2014). Cultural conservationists and Indigenous land groups have formed unprecedented coalitions with climate activists: together they have moved the conservation of place into the forefront of climate strategy.

CONCLUSION

Conservation cannot meet the challenges of the contemporary world by refining its own codes and criteria, rules that were first drafted for a very different world. This is one of those times when conservation must reorient itself to external conditions, of which climate change is only the most obviously challenging. But how to understand conditions which lie far outside conservation's ken? A vital conservation practice must search outside itself, by turning to the social and environmental sciences that describe today's world. Not blindly, but guided by the light of its own vision, and with humility tempered by confidence in its own knowledge.

REFERENCES

Albrecht, Glenn. 2006. "Solastalgia." *Alternatives Journal* 32(4/5): 95–98.

Albrecht, Glenn, Gina-Maree Sartore, Linda Connor, Nick Higginbotham, Sonia Freeman, Brien Kelly, et al. 2007. "Solastalgia: The Distress Caused by Environmental Change." *Australian Psychiatry* 15, supplement: 95–99.

Alkire, Sabine. 2010. *Human Development: Definitions, Critiques, and Related Concepts.* New York: United Nations Development Programme.

Altman, Irwin, and Setha M. Low, eds. 1992. *Place Attachment.* New York: Plenum Press.

Anton, Charis E., and Carmen Lawrence. 2016. "The Relationship between Place Attachment, the Theory of Planned Behaviour and Residents' Response to Place Change." *Journal of Environmental Psychology* 47: 145–154.

Ariely, Dan. 2010. *Predictably Irrational: The Hidden Forces That Shape Our Decisions.* New York: Harper Perennial.

Bardhan, Pranab, and Isha Ray, eds. 2008. *The Contested Commons: Conversations between Economists and Anthropologists.* Malden, MA and Oxford: Blackwell.

Bromley, Daniel, ed. 1992. *Making the Commons Work: Theory, Practice, and Policy.* San Francisco: ICS Press.

Brown, Barbara, Douglas D. Perkins, and Graham Brown. 2003. "Place Attachment in a Revitalizing Neighborhood: Individual and Block Levels of Analysis." *Journal of Environmental Psychology* 23: 259–271.

Costanza, Robert, Ralph D'Arge, Rudolf de Groot, Stephen Farber, Monica Grasso, Bruce Hannon, et al. 1997. "The Value of the World's Ecosystem Services and Natural Capital." *Nature* 387: 253–260.

Costanza, Robert, and Lisa Wainger, eds. 1991. *Ecological Economics: The Science and Management of Sustainability.* New York: Columbia University Press.

Cuba, Lee, and David M. Hummon. 1993. "A Place to Call Home: Identification with Dwelling, Community and Region." *Sociological Quarterly* 34: 111–131.

Daly, Herman E. 1991. *Steady-State Economics.* 2nd edn. Washington, DC: Island Press.

Daly, Herman E. 1996. *Beyond Growth: The Economics of Sustainable Development.* Boston: Beacon Press.

Daly, Herman E., and John B. Cobb, Jr. 1989. *For the Common Good: Redirecting the Economy toward Community, the Environment, and a Sustainable Future.* Boston: Beacon Press.

Daly, Herman E., and Joshua C. Farley. 2010. *Ecological Economics: Principles and Applications.* Washington, DC: Island Press.

de Groot, Rudolf, Luke Brander, Sander van der Ploeg, Robert Costanza, Florence Bernard, Leon Braat, et al. 2012. "Global Estimates of the Value of Ecosystems and their Services in Monetary Units." *Ecosystem Services* 1(1): 50–61.

de la Torre, Marta, ed. 2002. *Assessing the Values of Cultural Heritage: Research Report.* Los Angeles: Getty Conservation Institute.

Després, Carole. 1991. "The Meaning of Home: Literature Review and Directions for Future Research and Theoretical Development." *Journal of Architectural and Planning Research* 8(2): 96–115.

Devine-Wright, P. 2009. "Rethinking NIMBYism: The Role of Place Attachment and Place Identity in Explaining Place-Protective Action." *Journal of Community Applied Sociology* 19(6): 426–441.

Dolšak, Nives, and Elinor Ostrom, eds. 2003. *The Commons in the New Millennium: Challenges and Adaptation.* Cambridge, MA: MIT.

Empty Homes Agency. 2008. *New Tricks with Old Bricks: How Reusing Old Buildings Can Cut Carbon Emissions.* London: Empty Homes Agency.

Freeman, Hugh L. 1984. "Introduction," in *Mental Health and the Environment*, ed. Hugh L. Freeman. London and New York: Churchill Livingstone.

Fried, Marc. 1963. "Grieving for a Lost Home," in *The Urban Condition: People and Policy in the Metropolis*, ed. Leonard J. Duhl. New York: Basic Books, 151–171.

Fullilove, Mindy Thompson. 1996. "Psychiatric Implications of Displacement: Contributions from the Psychology of Place." *American Journal of Psychiatry* 153(12): 1516–1523.

Fullilove, Mindy Thompson. 2005. *Root Shock: How Tearing Up City Neighborhoods Hurts America, and What We Can Do about It*. New York: One World/Ballantine Books.

Gaffney, M. Mason. 1962. "Land and Rent in Welfare Economics," in *Land Economics Research*, ed. Marion Clawson, Marshall Harriss, and Joseph Ackerman. Baltimore: The Johns Hopkins University Press, 141–167.

Gaffney, M. Mason. 1994. "Land as a Distinctive Factor of Production," in *Land and Taxation*, ed. Nicolaus Tideman. London: Shepheard-Walwyn Ltd., 39–102.

Gaffney, M. Mason. 2001. "The Role of Ground Rent in Urban Decay and Revival: How to Revitalize a Failing City." *Journal of Economics and Sociology* 60: 55–84.

Gallagher, Winifred. 1993. *The Power of Place: How our Surroundings Shape our Thoughts, Emotions, and Actions*. New York: Poseidon Press.

George, Henry. [1879] 2005. *Progress and Poverty: An Inquiry into the Cause of Industrial Depressions and of Increase of Want*. New York: Cosimo.

Getty Conservation Institute. 1999. *Economics and Heritage Conservation: A Meeting Organized by the Getty Conservation Institute, December, 1998*. Los Angeles: J. Paul Getty Trust.

Giuliani, M. Vittoria. 1991. "Toward an Analysis of Mental Representations of Attachment to the Home." *Journal of Architectural and Planning Research* 8: 133–146.

Hardin, Garrett. 1968. "The Tragedy of the Commons." *Science* 162: 1243–1248.

Hester, Randolph T. 1985. "Subconscious Landscapes of the Heart." *Places* 2(3): 10–22.

Hester, Randolph T. 1993. "Sacred Structures and Everyday Life: A Return to Manteo, North Carolina," in *Dwelling, Seeing and Designing: Toward a Phenomenological Ecology*, ed. David Seamon. Albany, NY: SUNY Press, 171–197.

Hidalgo, M. Carmen, and Bernardo Hernández. 2001. "Place Attachment: Conceptual and Empirical Questions." *Journal of Environmental Psychology* 21: 273–281.

Hummon, David M. 1992. "Community Attachment: Local Sentiment and Sense of Place," in Altman and Low (eds) 1992, 253–278.

IPCC (Intergovernmental Panel on Climate Change), <http://www.ipcc.ch>.

Kahneman, Daniel. 2011. *Thinking Fast and Slow*. New York: Farrar, Straus, and Giroux.

Kaufman, Ned. 2017. "Perspectives from the Field: Non-Disruption and Non-Emissions as Cultural Resources." *Environmental Practice* 18(3): 219–221.

Kaufman, Ned. 2019. "Resistance to Research, Diagnosis and Treatment of a Disciplinary Ailment," in *Human-Centered Built Environment Heritage Preservation: Theory and Evidence-Based Practice*, ed. Jeremy C. Wells and Barry Stiefel. New York: Routledge.

Klein, Naomi. 2014. *This Changes Everything: Capitalism vs. the Climate*. New York: Simon and Schuster.

Korpela, Kalevi Mikael. 1989. "Place-Identity as a Product of Environmental Self-Regulation." *Journal of Environmental Psychology* 9: 241–256.

Lewis, Michael. 1991. *The Money Culture*. London: Hodder and Stoughton.

Manzo, Lynne C. 2003. "Beyond House and Haven: Toward a Revisioning of Emotional Relationships with Places." *Journal of Environmmental Psychology* 23(1): 47–61.

Manzo, Lynne C. 2005. "For Better or Worse: Exploring Multiple Dimensions of Place Meaning." *Journal of Environmental Psychology* 25: 67–86.

Manzo, Lynne C., and D. D. Perkins. 2006. "Finding Common Ground: The Importance of Place Attachment to Community Participation and Planning." *Journal of Planning Literature* 20(4): 335–350.

Marcus, Clare Cooper. 1992. "Environmental Memories," in Altman and Low (eds) 1992, 87–112.

Mary Robinson Foundation. "Principles of Climate Justice." <http://www.mrfcj.org/principles-of-climate-justice/>.

Mason, Randall. 2005. *Economics and Historic Preservation: A Guide and Review of the Literature*. Washington, DC: Brookings Institution.

NTHP (National Trust for Historic Preservation). 2011. *The Greenest Building: Quantifying the Environmental Value of Building Reuse*. Washington, DC: National Trust for Historic Preservation.

Ostrom, Elinor. 1990. *Governing the Commons: The Evolution of Institutions for Collective Action*. Cambridge: Cambridge University Press.

Ostrom, Elinor, ed. 2003. *The Drama of the Commons*. Washington, DC: National Academy Press.

Ostrom, Elinor. 2012. *The Future of the Commons*. London: Institute of Economic Affairs.

Pope Francis I. 2013. *Apostolic Exhortation Evangelii Gaudium of the Holy Father Francis to the Bishops, Clergy, Consecrated Persons and the Lay Faithful on the Proclamation of the Gospel in Today's World*. Vatican City: Vatican Press.

Poteete, Amy R., Marco Janssen, and Elinor Ostrom, eds. 2010. *Working Together: Collective Action, the Commons, and Multiple Methods in Practice*. Princeton, NJ: Princeton University Press.

Proshansky, Harold M., Abbe Fabian, and Robert Kaminoff. 1983. "Place-Identity: Physical World Socialization of the Self." *Journal of Environmental Psychology* 3(1): 57–83.

Provins, Allan, David Pearce, Ece Ozdemiroglu, Susana Mourato, and Sian Morse-Jones. 2005. "Valuation of the Historic Environment: The Scope for Using Economic Valuation Evidence in the Approaisal of Heritage-Related Projects." *Progress in Planning* 69(4): 131–175.

Revkin, Andrew G. 2006. "Inuit Climate Change Petition Rejected." *New York Times— Americas*. December 16: <http://www.nytimes.com/2006/12/16/world/americas/16briefs-inuitcomplaint.html?_r=0>.

Riley, Robert B. 1992. "Attachment to the Ordinary Landscape," in Altman and Low (eds) 1992, 13–36.

Sagoff, Mark. 1988. *The Economy of the Earth: Philosophy, Law, and the Environment*. Cambridge: Cambridge University Press.

Sen, Amartya. 2000. *Development as Freedom*. New York: Anchor Books.

Sen, Amartya. 2003. "Development as Capability Expansion," in *Readings in Human Development*, ed. S. Fukuda-Parr. New Delhi and New York: Oxford University Press, 41–58.

Sixsmith, J. 1986. "The Meaning of Home: An Exploratory Study of Environmental Experience." *Journal of Environmental Psychology* 6: 281–298.

Stiglitz, Joseph E., Amartya Sen, and Jean-Paul Fitoussi. 2010. *Mismeasuring our Lives: Why GDP Doesn't Add Up*. New York and London: The New Press.

Throsby, David. 2003. "Determining the Value of Cultural Goods: How Much (or How Little) Does Contingent Valuation Tell Us?" *Journal of Cultural Economics* 27: 275–285.

Twigger-Ross, Clare L., and David L. Uzzell. 1996. "Place and Identity Processes." *Journal of Environmmental Psychology* 16: 205–220.

UNDP (United Nations Development Programme). 1990 et seq. *Human Development Reports.* New York: United Nations Development Programme.

UNEP (United Nations Environment Programme). 2009. *Buildings and Climate Change: Summary for Decision-Makers.* Paris: UNEP.

Watt-Cloutier, Sheila (with support of Inuit Circumpolar Conference). 2005. *Petition to the Inter American Commission on Human Rights Seeking Relief from Violations Resulting from Global Warming Caused by Acts and Omissions of the United States.* December 7.

PEOPLE IN PLACE
Local Planning to Preserve Diverse Cultures

JAMES MICHAEL BUCKLEY

DESPITE the heterogeneity of America's cities, public heritage practice in the United States has largely focused on preservation of the physical landscape of the European-based majority culture. As the nation's urban areas continue to become more culturally diverse, preservationists have begun to explore new approaches that incorporate aspects of community development planning to serve the needs of urban minority populations. Because much of America's public heritage activity takes place through the regulatory controls of land use planning, a key question is whether preservationists can develop new tools that both protect minority cultures and enhance the conditions of the people who practice them.

CULTIVATING DIVERSITY IN US PRESERVATION

Early preservation of America's architectural legacy focused on saving prominent symbols of an imagined nationalist culture, such as George Washington's estate at Mt. Vernon and the remains of the colonial settlement at Williamsburg, Virginia, in the 1930s. Even as millions of culturally diverse immigrants poured into US cities to operate the nation's thriving industrial economy in the late nineteenth and early twentieth centuries, cultural heritage activities remained focused primarily on the Anglo traditions of the colonial and early republican era. Charitable organizations like the Society for Preservation of New England Antiquities in Boston and the Society for the Preservation of Old Buildings in Charleston, South Carolina, fostered the role of preservationists as curators of fine architecture more than keepers of diverse culture (Stipe 2003, Lee 2003 and 2004, Page and Mason 2004).

In the mid-twentieth century, preservationists opposed the loss of historic fabric under postwar urban renewal efforts, but in doing so they advocated for preserving the built environment without focusing on the fate of the displaced minority populations who occupied urban cores (Tomlin 2015). The 1966 National Historic Preservation Act (NHPA) introduced cultural resource management practices that have largely continued the field's curatorial focus on the authenticity of building fabric remaining from the original builders (Mason 2004, Bluestone 2016). As a result, efforts to understand and celebrate the history of populations defined by differences in race, gender, ethnicity, and sexual preference have generally taken a back seat to conservation of the landscape of the majority culture (Fitch 1982, Murtagh 1988, Stipe 2003, Ryberg and Kinahan 2014, Minner 2016).

A number of professional and academic efforts broke the mold in the 1990s. Dolores Hayden, for example, an architecture scholar at UCLA, argued that race and gender had become increasingly important in the writing of urban history in recent years and, as a result, the "politics of identity . . . are an inescapable and important aspect of dealing with the urban built environment" (Hayden 1995: 7). She promoted a "politically conscious approach to urban preservation" that "must go beyond the techniques of traditional preservation (making preserved structures into museums or attractive commercial real estate) to reach broader audiences. It must emphasize public processes and public memory" (Hayden 1995: 11).

Hayden's nonprofit group Power of Place designed several projects based on this approach, including Biddy Mason Park in central Los Angeles, a public art project completed in 1989 that resurrected the life of a nineteenth-century African-American community midwife and former slave on the site of her former house. The project demonstrated how heritage programs might give voice to the experience of minority populations in the urban landscape, even though no tangible evidence of Mason's existence remained.

Interest in preserving a broader range of American cultures increased around this time at both the national and local level. In New York City, controversies over the Audubon Ballroom, site of Malcom X's assassination, and the inappropriate handling of the African Burying Ground near City Hall during new building construction sparked the interest of African-Americans in better understanding and treatment of the city's extensive black history (Kaufman 2009a). In California, the long, troubled history of Asian American presence within the majority culture spawned important site recognitions, including Federal historic designations of the Japanese-American internment camp at Manzanar (1985) and the Angel Island Immigration Station (1997). With support from the National Park Service, the state of California published "Five Views: An Ethnic Historic Site Survey for California" in 1988, which attempted to introduce an official method for interpreting public heritage sites in a broader cultural context (California Department of Parks and Recreation 1988).

Following the larger political trends toward identity politics in the United States during this period, the heritage profession sponsored a number of gatherings and studies that addressed the field's "diversity gap." The National Park Service developed a Cultural Resources Diversity Initiative in 1998 and commissioned a cultural heritage needs assessment in 2002 (Kaufman 2009c). The 2006 Preserve America Summit, which was held by the US Advisory Council of Historic Preservation to celebrate the fortieth anniversary of the NHPA, included a panel on "Involving All Cultures," and the National Park Service under the Obama administration promulgated a series of his-toric context statements intended to facilitate designation of sites associated with the historical cultures of women, African-Americans, Latinos, and LGBTQ populations (Hutt 2007).

Tangible and Intangible Heritage Preservation in San Francisco

By the turn of the twenty-first century, it was clear that the formative 1966 NHPA leg-islation did not preclude the preservation apparatus from considering the cultural re-sources of urban minorities, but that doing so would take a concerted effort. One reason preservationists have begun to examine diverse heritage more fully is the recent "return to the city" trend among middle- and upper-income households (Fishman 2005, Hyra 2015). As wealthier populations seek out homes and business opportunities in areas that have been occupied for decades by low-income and minority communities, concerns about gentrification-driven displacement have cast an ever-stronger shadow over efforts to preserve historic urban neighborhoods (Leichenko et al. 2001, Freeman 2005, Talen et al. 2015, Tissot 2015, McCabe and Ellen 2016).

San Francisco has served as an epicenter of cultural preservation and planning issues since the turn of the twenty-first century. Known as a community of diverse cultures from its early Gold Rush days, the city's variety of ethnic traditions and alter-native lifestyles has come under threat as the financial success of Silicon Valley's tech-nology industry has attracted overwhelming new development. Long-term minority communities, from Latinos in the Mission District to residents of Chinatown, found themselves fighting against constantly increasing property values and threats to de-molish community landmarks for dense new commercial and residential projects (Buckley and Graves 2016).

In response to development pressures, advocates for both historic preservation and urban planning began to join forces to protect the city's diverse cultural groups, starting with the historic Japantown community. These advocates quickly realized, however, that heritage concerns in minority communities might require a re-thinking of the typical historic designation process. Like most American cities, San Francisco both initiates nominations of historic resources as local landmarks, with protections from demoli-tion or alteration through local land use law, and nominates sites to be considered by the National Park Service for inclusion on the National Register of Historic Places, which offers greater visibility but few controls over what happens to the property (Stipe 2003). Both types of designation rely on the federal criteria laid out under the NHPA, which have in the past been interpreted as favoring buildings and other physical structures over broader historical meaning because of the requirement that sites retain proper "integrity" of their original building fabric (Howett 2000, Kaufman 2009b, National Park Service 1997).

When private redevelopment threatened San Francisco's Japan Center mall, which housed numerous locally owned ethnic businesses, the city worked with the community to develop a heritage conservation plan known as the Japantown Cultural Heritage and Economic Sustainability Strategy (JCHESS) (San Francisco Planning Department 2013). One of the first steps in this planning process was to inventory the broad array of places in the district that community members felt convey cultural meaning, but this list went beyond just physical structures to include activities, businesses, and cultural organizations as well. By mapping and documenting the presence of both tangible and intangible resources, many of which had never before been considered worthy of either local or federal historic designation, residents felt they could harness future development in ways that would protect and even enhance traditional activities, from the annual Cherry Blossom Festival to the San Francisco Taiko Dojo drum group. The JCHESS plan included additional measures typical of planning for historic neighborhoods, including urban design and land use regulations, but the major innovation for heritage conservation was inclusion of the cultural resource inventory in the community plan. This inventory serves as a proactive measure to assure that future actors, both public and private sector, will have an understanding of community traditions and be aware of local expectations and needs before taking any major actions.

The city's planning department soon brought this concept to other non-majority cultural groups in different parts of the city. In the South of Market (SoMa) community, the city started a new planning process to deal with the significant changes occurring as social media companies made this area their headquarters (Western SoMa Citizens 2011). San Francisco's Filipino community had survived earlier urban renewal activities in this neighborhood and used the opportunity of a new plan to lay claim to both structures and spaces that held meaning for the community. The physical sites of Catholic churches, nonprofit service agencies, and Filipino businesses joined the locations of the annual Patrol Lantern Festival and the 1888 visit of a Filipino national hero on a list of important "Features and Individual Assets" (San Francisco Planning Department 2011). The new plan proposed the establishment of a Cultural Heritage District that would require future planning decisions to consider protection and enhancement of these places. While physical structures or activities would not be designated as local landmarks or specifically protected by zoning or other land use controls, the draft legislation anticipated that development bonuses like extra height or bulk would be offered to new projects that incorporated traditional culture sites into their proposals.

The Western SoMa Community Plan also explored the possibility of preserving and promoting the neighborhood's historical gay and lesbian culture through a similar heritage district. Starting in the 1970s, San Francisco's expanding leather scene found a safe environment in the area's industrial warehouses and alleyways, culminating in the annual Folsom Street Fair that now attracts hundreds of thousands of fetish enthusiasts and spectators. The final version of the community plan included a list of places identified with LGBTQ history, including gathering places like bars and bathhouses, leather costume shops, cruising areas, and the headquarters of a national gay rights organization. Like the Filipino district, the proposal does not call for local landmark protection that would prevent alteration of these sites but anticipates that zoning and tax-related incentives would encourage new development to incorporate these legacy assets within project plans.

Both of these cultural heritage districts have faced challenges in implementation since legislative approval of the overall Western SoMa community plan in 2013. The legal standing for each would be established through a Special Use District within the city's Zoning Code, but the planning department is unsure how to incorporate these new "soft" controls over heritage-related use into the well-established system of land use regulation. "Part of the problem is we haven't decided what 'it' is yet, whether it is a district designation or a program to help businesses or whether it is ultimately some combination of those mechanisms," said the city's planning director John Rahaim. "This is outside our typical land use controls" (Bajko 2016). The city officially approved the Filipino cultural heritage district in 2016 and a community process is underway to determine the best approach for implementation (San Francisco Planning Department 2016a). In the meantime, the urgency of the community preservation issue was demonstrated by the potential loss of the Gran Oriente Residential Hotel, a long-time low-income housing resource for Filipinos and others in the neighborhood. The owners listed the property for sale, but before it could be sold for other uses or even demolition, the city had put the property on its list for landmark status as a result of the Filipino Heritage District discussion and is now looking at acquisition of the property (Balitang America 2016, Socketsite web page 2016).

The effort to develop an LGBTQ heritage district in the Western SOMA community plan instigated a larger conversation about identifying and preserving such resources throughout San Francisco. As a result, in 2013 the city sponsored preparation of a citywide context statement for LGBTQ history (Graves and Watson 2016a,b). This document explores a number of themes, from early influences on LGBTQ identities through the later gay liberation movement and the AIDS Epidemic, in order to provide a broad foundation for recognizing and interpreting individual sites as local landmarks or National Register listings.[1] The city's Board of Supervisors approved the context statement in 2015 and the following year launched a working group to implement the strategies contained in the document through a Cultural Heritage Strategy (San Francisco Planning Department 2016b).

San Francisco's LGBTQ context statement notes that, as for many populations outside the dominant culture, the requirements of federal historic preservation policy for nomination of sites to the National Register have put identification of LGBTQ historic sites at a disadvantage. The emphasis on *integrity*, defined as "the authenticity of a property's historic identity, evidenced by the survival of physical characteristics that existed during the property's historic or prehistoric period," is problematic for populations whose actions may be considered socially improper or even criminalized

(National Park Service 2002). "Because so many aspects of LGBTQ history were intentionally buried or hidden," notes the context statement, "the luxuries of physical visibility and longevity-in-place were not available until relatively recently" (Graves and Watson 2016a: 353). Many LGBTQ sites are part of hidden histories and have therefore been more susceptible to subsequent alteration, and the report recommends that evaluation of these resources should emphasize more intangible aspects within the officially defined concept of integrity, including location, association, and feeling, over physical criteria like design, setting, materials, and workmanship. The effort to recognize LGBTQ history in San Francisco demonstrates that working with the culture of marginalized people requires US preservationists to stretch the traditional definitions of what qualifies as official heritage to include sites that are less pristine or have less remaining physical material than typical designations. In this case, the guidelines have proven flexible enough to accommodate the experience of communities that operate at the edge of social awareness, so that, as the context statement authors point out, even "properties no longer extant or that have undergone physical change can still retain powerful meaning for communities and remain important cultural sites" (Graves and Watson 2016b: 26).

Soon after the LGBTQ historic context statement was approved, a controversy broke out over a development project in the city's Tenderloin neighborhood that some felt threatened important historic LGBTQ resources. The project site was in an area that had served San Francisco's transgender community for decades; an important event in trans rights activism occurred nearby when trans patrons of a nearby 24-hour restaurant fought back against police harassment in the Compton's Cafeteria riot of 1966 (Stryker 2008). The citywide context statement helped publicize the importance of this area to trans history, and community members pointed out that the new development would demolish several of the bars that had historically supported trans social life. Local leaders negotiated a compromise that will initiate the nation's first local transgender cultural district near the site of the controversial project, a perfect example of how the historic context statement laid the groundwork for maintaining awareness of diverse cultural histories in San Francisco (Bajko 2017).

A key player in the development of San Francisco's preservation diversity programs has been the city's advocacy organization, San Francisco Heritage. This group organized a citywide conference on heritage diversity in 2013 and produced a policy paper on approaches to preservation of minority cultures that drew on practices around the world (San Francisco Heritage 2014). One of the most successful outcomes of this effort has been the Legacy Business Registry, an opportunity for small businesses and nonprofit organizations to receive recognition and financial assistance (City of San Francisco 2016). The Mayor or a member of the Board of Supervisors can nominate to the Registry a business that has been operating continuously for thirty or more years and has made a significant impact on the history or culture of their neighborhood, which makes both the business and its landlord eligible for grants that help the business stay in place despite rising rental costs. The program serves all of the city's cultural communities, from the famous Caffe Trieste in North Beach and Acción Latina in the Mission to Sam Wo's

Restaurant in Chinatown and Sam Jordan's Bar in the largely African American Bayview neighborhood.

New Directions in Public Heritage Planning: Place as Art

San Francisco is one of many US cities where preservationists and planners are starting to employ the heritage of diverse populations as part of their community development planning efforts. Marginalized populations are using their history to protect and enhance their ways of life through new housing, commercial revitalization, and even heritage tourism (Rios 2013, MIG, Inc. 2015, Weed 2016, Inwood 2010, Eskew 2009). Whether it is in hyper-active real estate markets in booming cities or in decaying industrial cities, members of minority cultures are incorporating heritage preservation into plans for community improvement (Hurley 2010).

One of the ways public heritage intersects with contemporary American city planning is the idea of "place-making" (Markusen and Gadwa 2010, Fleming 2007, Florida 2002, Ryberg and Kinahan 2014). Planners seeking to capture high value "creative" industries are using the design of unique spaces like parks, markets, and artists' space to create a distinctive urban character that can in turn attract businesses and new residents. While planners have primarily used place-making as a tool for commercial economic development, some individual artists and communities have asked how place-making that uses the historic environment occupied by marginalized populations might create a space for conveying their concerns in ways that traditional interpretations have not—that is, using the locations where minority culture is produced to strengthen community bonds and make a stand against displacement. Veteran arts administrator Robert Bedoya suggests that place-making "enacts identity and activities that allow personal memories, cultural histories, imagination, and feelings to enliven the sense of 'belonging' through human and spatial relationships" (Bedoya 2013). This sense of belonging is heightened through an expression of historical connections and relationships, including those of ethnicity, class, race, and gender; as a result, place-making projects are often linked to local histories.[2]

Several African-American artists, for example, have pursued an aesthetic approach to public heritage that is deeply embedded in the physical and social fabric of their cultural communities. Through what is being termed "socially engaged art," they have used the physical landscape of historic black neighborhoods as a medium for expressing their sense of the experience of living in these communities (Thompson 2010, Thompson 2012, Burton 2016). Since the late 1980s, Tyree Guyton has taken the run-down block in East Detroit where he grew up and scattered found objects of art around, on, and inside the dilapidated historic houses that remain in place (Che 2007). Theaster Gates has acquired several historic structures on Chicago's South Side and repurposed them as symbols of black life in the United States, including a vacant 1920s banking hall that now houses a vast library of books from a closed store, the inventory of music from a closed soul music record store, and an archive of the black magazines *Jet* and *Ebony* (Austen 2013, Reinhardt 2015).

Project Row Houses (PRH) in Houston, Texas, is a prime example of how an artist can use a minority community's historic landscape as a canvas to provide an aesthetic expression of cultural experience, while at the same time planning for positive change for the existing population (Kimmelman 2006, Thompson 2010, Burton 2016). In 1993, Rick Lowe worked with a group of fellow artists to acquire and transform a series of twenty-two abandoned "shotgun" row houses in the historically black Third Ward neighborhood into a combination of spaces that house art exhibitions and community-serving services. Shotgun houses are common in many southern US urban neighborhoods and vernacular architecture historians trace this residential form back through its roots in the Caribbean and Africa; as a result, the shotgun house serves as a cultural artifact of American black heritage traced back to its source (Vlach 1976, Tucker 1995, Edwards 2009). Lowe's mentor at nearby Texas Southern University, the artist Joseph Biggers, seized on the shotgun house as a cultural symbol in a series of works; Lowe combined this influence with that of Joseph Beuys' ideas from the 1970s about "social sculpture"—art that invites observers to be part of the aesthetic expression—in his inclusion of art exhibit space at Project Row Houses (Wardlaw 1995, Theisen 2010). Artists, many of them minority, have contributed to nearly fifty rounds of exhibitions in the cozy spaces of the shotgun houses, while PRH has also sponsored newly constructed affordable housing and programs to serve the neighborhood's low-income population.

While PRH's refurbished historic homes have contributed to the stabilization of the economically depressed Third Ward, this historic neighborhood faces new pressures. Developers seeking to satisfy the housing demands of office workers in the adjacent downtown district have bought up a number of the neighborhood's many vacant properties to replace the old shotgun rows with a modern version of row houses—dense three-story condominium units that take up most of the lot. In response to the displacement of existing residents and destruction of the historic character of the neighborhood, Lowe and other community leaders helped organize a neighborhood-based community planning organization—the Emancipation Economic Development Council (EEDC)—to consider ways the community could maintain its historic fabric and use it to create an improved future. The EEDC's mission is to "inspire hope and contribute to the revitalization and preservation of the Third Ward"; its vision is to plan for "a community where people live, work and thrive in a historically and culturally rich African-American neighborhood." This suggests a different approach to public heritage, one that seeks to revitalize a minority neighborhood in ways that are as sensitive to the historic social fabric as they are to the physical. In contrast to much inner-city preservation work in the United States, PRH's promotion of black experience is intended to keep the historic character of the community intact while avoiding displacement of existing residents.

"The new social relations envisioned and enacted through the actions of Project Row Houses were based on finding value in under-valued things," observes sociologist George Lipsitz. "This sensibility also honed and sharpened the community's ability to find value in undervalued people" (Lipsitz 2016). The importance of the shotgun house, under-valued in traditional heritage approaches, was appreciated by people whose own history was connected to these structures. The exhibitions inside those structures, like the work of Theaster Gates and Tyree Guyton, reflect an understanding that heritage has an immaterial aspect, a layer of meaning that is not tangible but that can nonetheless be conveyed and comprehended. "The residents of Black Metropolis are not just objects of history or of socioeconomic circumstances," write a group of sociologists describing the vernacular "place-making" efforts of Chicago's African-Americans, "they are also subjects that fashion places by inscribing them with their own interpretations, meanings, and cultural significance" (Hunter et al. 2016).

CONCLUSION

Fifteen years ago, NPS historian Antoinette Lee suggested that "the larger question facing the historic preservation field is the long-term effect of this emphasis on diversity. Will it lead to greater appreciation and acceptance of diverse groups, or will it lead to resentments and alienation?" (Lee 2003). In 2012, she replied to her question, saying that, "the subject of diversity is no longer an edgy topic in the historic preservation field. It is part of the mainstream of historic preservation goals and objectives as well as projects and programs" (Lee 2012: 21).

While diversity concerns are indeed no longer "edgy" for US preservationists, the programs in San Francisco and Houston still represent an exception to general practice, which remains oriented to traditional designation processes that often exclude groups that lie outside of the dominant culture (Buckley and Graves 2016). The field of preservation missed much of the move toward inclusion made by allied fields like public archaeology and public folklore, and it is still criticized for its focus on material fabric rather than the lived experience of America's diverse citizens (Merriman 2004, Baron and Spitzer 2007, Page 2016). American life in the first quarter of the twenty-first century continues to involve prominent questions of identity by race, ethnicity, gender, and class, and contemporary contestations such as the Black Lives Matter movement, immigration reform policies, the fight for gay marriage, and support for trans rights make understanding of the nation's pluralistic roots even more critical. The efforts in San Francisco, Houston, and elsewhere offer useful examples of the ways in which American practitioners of public heritage might develop new tools to celebrate and protect social traditions that don't fit within mainstream culture (Page and Miller 2016). The greater collaboration of public heritage with the practice of community planning may eventually help preservationists serve the wide range of cultures that characterize the United States and pave the way for greater social integration.

NOTES

1. Los Angeles's Office of Historic Resources commissioned a similar document, "Survey LA: LGBT Historic Context Statement," completed by GPA Consulting in September 2014 and accessible online at: <http://preservation.lacity.org/sites/default/files/LGBT%20 Historic%20Context%209-14.pdf>.
2. See, for example, Partnership for Public Spaces Historic Preservation web archive: <https:// www.pps.org/blog/category/blog-categories/historic-preservation/>.

REFERENCES

Austen, Ben. 2013. "Chicago's Opportunity Artist." *New York Times*, October 20, 2013; Rebuild Foundation website: <https://rebuild-foundation.org>.

Bajko, Matthew S. 2016. "Work on stalled LGBTQ district expected in 2017." *Bay Area Reporter*, July 28, 2016: <http://www.ebar.com/news/article.php?sec=news&article=71756>.

Bajko, Matthew S. 2017. "SF leaders back LGBT history projects." *Bay Area Reporter*, February 2, 2017: <http://www.ebar.com/news/article.php?sec=news&article=72299>.

Balitang America. 2016. "City Official Helps Keep Filipino Landmark In San Francisco," Balitang America website, Henni Espinosa, September 8, 2016: <http://www. balitangamerica.tv/city-official-helps-keep-filipino-landmark-in-san-francisco/>.

Baron, Robert, and Nick Spitzer, eds. 2007. *Public Folklore*. Oxford, MS: University of Mississippi.

Bedoya, Roberto. 2013. "Placemaking and the Politics of Belonging and Dis-belonging." *GIA Reader* 24(1): <http://www.giarts.org/article/placemaking-and-politics-belonging-and-dis-belonging>.

Bluestone, Daniel. 2016. "Dislodging the Curatorial," in *Bending the Curve: 50 Ideas for the Next 50 Years of Historic Preservation in the United States*, ed. Max Page and Marla R. Miller. Amherst, MA: University of Massachusetts.

Buckley, James Michael, and Donna Graves. 2016. "Tangible Benefits from Intangible Resources: Using Social and Cultural History to Plan Neighborhood Futures." *Journal of the American Planning Association* 82(2): 152–156.

Burton, Johanna, ed. 2016. *Public Servants: Art and the Crisis of the Common Good*. Cambridge, MA: MIT.

California Department of Parks and Recreation. 1988. "FIVE VIEWS: An Ethnic Historic Site Survey for California." Sacramento: California Department of Parks and Recreation.

Che, Deborah. 2007. "Connecting the Dots to Urban Revitalization with the Heidelberg Project." *Material Culture* 39(1): 33–49.

City of San Francisco. 2016. Legacy Business Program description: <http://sfosb.org/legacy-business/apply>.

Edwards, Jay D. 2009. "Shotgun: The Most Contested House in America." *Buildings & Landscapes* 16(1): 62–96.

Eskew, Glenn T. 2009. "Exploring Civil Rights Heritage Tourism and Historic Preservation as Revitalization Tools," in *Past Trends and Future Prospects of the American City: The Dynamics of Atlanta*, ed. David. L. Sjoquist. Lanham, MD: Lexington.

Fishman, Robert. 2005. "Longer View: The Fifth Migration." *Journal of the American Planning Association* 71(4): 357–366.

Fitch, James Marston. 1982. *Historic Preservation: Curatorial Management of the Built World*. New York: McGraw-Hill.

Fleming, Ronald Lee. 2007. *The Art of Placemaking: Interpreting Community Through Public Art and Urban Design*. London: Merrell.

Florida, Richard. 2002. *The Rise of the Creative Class*. New York: Basic Books.

Freeman, Lance. 2005. "Displacement or Succession? Residential Mobility in Gentrifying Neighborhoods." *Urban Affairs Review* 40(4): 463–491.

Graves, Donna J., and Shayne E. Watson. 2016a. "Citywide Historic Context Statement for LGBTQ History in San Francisco." San Francisco: City of San Francisco.

Graves, Donna J., and Shayne E. Watson. 2016b. "San Francisco: Placing LGBTQ Histories in the City by the Bay," in *LGBTQ America: A Theme Study of Lesbian, Gay, Bisexual, Transgender, and Queer History*, ed. Megan E. Springate. Washington, DC: National Park Service, 25–27.

Hayden, Dolores. 1995. *The Power of Place: Urban Landscapes as Public History*. Cambridge, MA: MIT.

Howett, Catherine. 2000. "Integrity as a Value in Cultural Landscape Preservation," in *Preserving Cultural Landscapes in America*, ed. A. R. Alanen and R. Z. Melnick. Baltimore, MD: Johns Hopkins University Press, 186–208.

Hunter, Marcus Anthony, et al. 2016. "Black Placemaking: Celebration, Play, and Poetry." *Theory, Culture & Society* 33(7–8): 34.

Hurley, Andrew. 2010. *Beyond Preservation: Using Public History to Revitalize Inner Cities*. Philadelphia, PA: Temple University.

Hutt, Sherry, et al. 2007. "Involving All Cultures: Preserve America Summit Issue Areas Panel Report." Washington, DC: Advisory Council on Historic Preservation.

Hyra, Derek. 2015. "The Back-to-the-City Movement: Neighbourhood Redevelopment and Processes of Political and Cultural Displacement." *Urban Affairs* 52(10): 1753–1773.

Inwood, Joshua F. J. 2010. "Sweet Auburn: Constructing Atlanta's Auburn Avenue as a Heritage Tourist Destination." *Urban Geography* 31(5): 573–594.

Kaufman, Ned. 2009a. "Heritage and the Cultural Politics of Preservation: The African Burial Ground and the Audubon Ballroom," in *Race, Place, and Story: Essays on the Past and Future of Historic Preservation*. New York: Routledge, 296–308.

Kaufman, Ned. 2009b. "A Plan to Save New York's Places of History and Tradition," in *Race, Place, and Story: Essays on the Past and Future of Historic Preservation*. New York: Routledge, 230–295.

Kaufman, Ned. 2009c. "Eliminating the Diversity Deficit," in *Place, Race, and Story: Essays on the Past and Future of Historic Preservation*. New York: Routledge, 75–138.

Kimmelman, Michael. 2006. "In Houston, Art Is Where the Home Is." *New York Times*, October 17, 2006.

Lee, Antoinette. 2003. "The Social and Ethnic Dimensions of Historic Preservation," in *A Richer Heritage: Historic Preservation in the Twenty-First Century*, ed. Robert E. Stipe. Chapel Hill, NC: University of North Carolina.

Lee, Antoinette. 2004. "From Historic Architecture to Cultural Heritage: A Journey Through Diversity, Identity, and Community." *Future Anterior: Journal of Historic Preservation, History, Theory, and Criticism* 1(2): 14–23.

Lee, Toni. 2012. "Cultural Diversity in Historic Preservation: Where We Have Been, Where We Are Going." *Forum Journal* 27(1): 20–34.

Leichenko, Robin M., N. Edward Coulson, and David Listokin. 2001. "Historic Preservation and Residential Property Values: An Analysis of Texas Cities." *Urban Studies* 38(11): 1973–1987.

Lipsitz, George. 2016. "'Time Has Come Today': Why Sociology Matters Now." *Michigan Sociological Review* 30: 12.

Markusen, Ann, and Anne Gadwa. 2010. "Creative Placemaking." Washington, DC: The Mayors' Institute on City Design: <https://www.arts.gov/sites/default/files/Creative Placemaking-Paper.pdf>.

Mason, Randy. 2004. "Historic Preservation, Public Memory, and the Making of Modern New York," in *Giving Preservation a History: Histories of Historic Preservation in the United States*, ed. Max Page and Randy Mason. New York: Routledge.

McCabe, Brian J., and Ingrid Gould Ellen. 2016. "Does Preservation Accelerate Neighborhood Change? Examining the Impact of Historic Preservation in New York City." *Journal of the American Planning Association* 82(2): 134–146.

Merriman, Nick, ed. 2004. *Public Archaeology*. New York: Routledge.

MIG, Inc. 2015. "Barrio Logan Community Plan and Local Coastal Program": <http://sdchamber.org/wp-content/uploads/2015/08/bl_cpu_full_w_historic_res_091913.pdf>.

Minner, Jennifer. 2016. "Revealing Synergies, Tensions, and Silences between Preservation and Planning." *Journal of the American Planning Association* 82(2): 72–87.

Murtagh, William J. 1988. *Keeping Time: The History and Theory of Preservation in America*. Pittstown, NJ: Main Street Press.

National Park Service. 1997. *National Register Bulletin: How to Apply the National Register Criteria for Evaluation*. Washington, DC: US Department of Interior.

National Park Service. 2002. *National Register Bulletin: How to Complete the National Register Form*. Washington, DC: US Department of Interior.

Page, Max. 2016. *Why Preservation Matters*. New Haven, CT: Yale.

Page, Max, and Randy Mason, eds. 2004. *Giving Preservation a History: Histories of Historic Preservation in the United States*. New York: Routledge.

Page, Max, and Marla R. Miller. 2016. *Bending the Curve: 50 Ideas for the Next 50 Years of Historic Preservation in the United States*. Amherst, MA: University of Massachusetts.

Reinhardt, Kathleen. 2015. "Theaster Gates's Dorchester Projects in Chicago." *Journal of Urban History* 41(2): 193–206.

Rios, Michael. 2013. "From a Neighborhood of Strangers to a Community of Fate: The Village at Market Creek Plaza," in *Transcultural Cities: Border Crossing and Placemaking*, ed. Jeffrey Hou. New York: Routledge.

Ryberg-Webster, Stephanie, and K. L. Kinahan. 2014. "Historic Preservation and Urban Revitalization in the Twenty-First Century." *Journal of Planning Literature* 29(2): 119–139.

San Francisco Heritage. 2014. "Sustaining San Francisco's Living History: Strategies for Conserving Cultural Heritage Assets." San Francisco: San Francisco Heritage: <https://www.sfheritage.org/cultural-heritage/>.

San Francisco Planning Department. 2011. "Recognizing, Protecting and Memorializing South of Market Filipino Social Heritage Neighborhood Resources": <http://commissions.sfplanning.org/soma/DRAFT%20SoMa%20Philippines%20SUD_PAL%206_11.pdf>.

San Francisco Planning Department. 2013. "Japantown Cultural Heritage and Economic Sustainability Strategy (JCHESS)": <http://www.sf-planning.org/ftp/files/plans-and-programs/in-your-neighborhood/japantown/JCHESS_FinalDraft_07-10-13.pdf>.

San Francisco Planning Department and SoMa Pilipinas Working Group. 2016a. "SoMa PILIPINAS Progress Report: Filipino Cultural Heritage District Community Planning Process": <http://commissions.sfplanning.org/cpcpackets/2016-008314CWP.pdf>.

San Francisco Planning Department. 2016b. "Citywide LGBTQ Cultural Heritage Strategy": <http://sf-planning.org/LGBTQStrategy>.

Socketsitewebpage.2016."HistoricSouthParkResidentialHotelontheMarketfor$3.2M."April18, 2016: <http://www.socketsite.com/archives/2016/04/historic-south-park-residential-hotel-on-the-market-for-3-2-million.html>.

Stipe, Robert E. 2003. "Prologue" and "Some Preservation Fundamentals," in *A Richer Heritage: Historic Preservation in The Twenty-First Century*, ed. Robert E. Stipe. Chapel Hill, NC: University of North Carolina.

Stryker, Susan. 2008. "Transgender History, Homonormativity, and Disciplinarity." *Radical History Review* 100: 144–157.

Talen, Emily, S. Menozzi, and C. Schaefer. 2015. "What Is a 'Great Neighborhood'? An Analysis of APA's Top-Rated Places." *Journal of the American Planning Association* 81(2): 121–141.

Theisen, Ollie Jensen. 2010. *Walls that Speak: The Murals of John Thomas Biggers*. Denton, TX: University of North Texas.

Thompson, Nato. 2010. "Socially Engaged Contemporary Art: Tactical and Strategic Manifestations." Washington, DC: Animating Democracy: <http://landscape.animatingdemocracy.org/sites/default/files/NThompson%20Trend%20Paper.pdf>.

Thompson, Nato, ed. 2012. *Living as Form: Socially Engaged Art from 1991–2011*. New York: Creative Time.

Tissot, Sylvie. 2015. *Good Neighbors: Gentrifying Diversity in Boston's South End*. New York: Verso.

Tomlin, Michael A. 2015. *Historic Preservation: Caring for our Expanding Legacy*. New York: Springer.

Tucker, Sheryl G. 1995. "Reinnovating the African-American Shotgun House." *Places* 10(1): 64–71.

Vlach, John Michael. 1976. "The Shotgun House: An African Architectural Legacy. Part I and Part II." *Pioneer America* 8(1): 47–56.

Wardlaw, Alvia J. 1995. *The Art of John Biggers: View from the Upper Room*. Houston: Museum of Fine Arts.

Weed, Julie. 2016. "Civil Rights History Finds Heightened Relevance in a Troubled Present." *New York Times*, October 17, 2016: <https://www.nytimes.com/2016/10/18/business/civil-rights-history-finds-heightened-relevance-in-a-troubled-present.html?_r=0>.

Western SoMa Citizens Planning Task Force. 2011. <http://sf-planning.org/western-soma>.

CHAPTER 4.3

....

HERITAGE AS AN ELEMENT
OF THE SCENESCAPE

....

MARTHA FRISH OKABE, DANIEL SILVER, AND
TERRY NICHOLS CLARK

SCENESCAPES (Silver and Clark 2016) advanced a general approach to culture and place, the "scenes approach." A central thrust is to conceptualize environment and action scenically. We often speak of nature in such terms: in taking the scenic route, we linger on the sights and sounds along the way. The view of a mountain or sunset is a distinctly aesthetic phenomenon.

The scenes approach extends this perspective to social life and the built environment. This has great relevance to cultural heritage protection, management, and promotion. It points to not just one heritage structure like a house in isolation, but stresses how the house is part of a scene surrounding it. "Neighborhood" or "place" are classic labels here, but the scenes approach adds more specificity. We build on hundreds of components that distinguish neighborhoods. Businesses and institutions (e.g. tattoo parlors, churches, restaurants), people (e.g. artists, old-timers), practices (e.g. worshiping, conversing, performing) join to produce areas with distinct aesthetics—hip, edgy, refined, glamorous, rustic, charming, and the like. These aesthetic qualities make it possible to move about a city scenically, taking the scenic route to discover the styles of life each has to offer.

Far from denying the relevance of economic and political concerns, the scenes approach suggests mutual feedback-feedforward processes. Local scenes can be targets of economic development proposals and focal points of economic activity. They can draw the politically like-minded together, and become intense objects of political controversy, for and against. They shape neighborhoods and cities by attracting and sustaining residents; yet they evolve as tastes change.

Scenescapes elaborates and illustrates these claims in detail, in conversation with the relevant social science components of economic growth, residential communities, and politics. Despite its apparent relevance, we have not previously examined heritage seriously as an element of the scenescape. Heritage clearly helps define the character of a scene, and heritage designations are clearly efforts to intervene on and regulate the scenery of life, with consequences for the overall scenes that coalesce around them.

The main reasons for this oversight are threefold: time, disciplinary blinders, and limited expertise. We are thus extremely grateful to the editors for giving us the opportunity to think through how to approach heritage from a scenes perspective and in an inter-disciplinary context. The three of us have collaborated for over a year on exploring ways to join scenes themes with heritage more concretely. This chapter is a first report.

Nevertheless, this chapter should be read as a provisional experiment: a first effort to extend scenes thinking to heritage (and vice versa) that we offer as an invitation for critical dialogue and collaboration. While we believe many of these insights extend to rural and even wilderness areas, here we highlight more urban contexts. In this way we build on and extend the important recent effort of Ryberg-Webster and Kinahan (2014) to build bridges between heritage and urban research.

We proceed in three major sections. First, we articulate some general ideas that inform scenes thinking. Second, we speculate how these ideas may be relevant for understanding heritage. Third, we discuss some potential lines of analysis for studying heritage as part of a scenescape. We often refer to other work that elaborates these ideas.

SCENES THINKING: SOME GENERAL IDEAS

What are some key ideas of scenes thinking in general? These are not comprehensive, but to give a general flavor. More detail is in Silver and Clark (2016) and available online (<http://scenescapes.weebly.com>). Four key principles are holism, multi-dimensionality, context, and feedback.

Holism

Consider John Dewey's description of various ways of experiencing New York City from a ferry (Dewey 1934: 141). Some regard the ferry as a "trip to get them where they want to be." Others let their "thoughts roam to the congestion of a great industrial and commercial center" and draw conclusions about "the chaos of a society organized on the basis of conflict rather than cooperation." Still others approach the city "esthetically, as a painter might . . . The scene formed by the buildings may be looked at as colored and lighted volumes in relation to one another, to the sky and the river." Encountered in this manner, the scene presents itself as a "perceptual whole, constituted by related parts. No one single figure, aspect, or quality is picked out as a means to some further external result which is desired, nor as a sign of an inference."

Dewey nicely captures the holistic nature of scenes thinking. To perceive the situation as a scene involves taking it up as a painter or poet might. Whether an ensemble of buildings is a consistent, restrained Classical Revival row of townhouses in New York or a more riotous block of rambling Queen Anne houses in Chicago helps define distinctive aesthetic environments in each place. The built environment is a key part of the ensemble, whether it is the glass and steel skyscrapers or "huge, communal edifices of stone and adobe" of the Indian pueblos of Taos, New Mexico (Morrison 1952). The buildings and their history create a specific tangible envelope in which particular "scenes" happen.

We approach buildings, people, and practices not atomistically but in how they interface with one another to support qualities of experience that pervade the situation. Skyscrapers, power lunches, busy suited executives, and flashing stock tickers join to fill downtowns with a distinct energy, urgency, ambition, and power. Tree-lined streets, neatly cut grass, colorful playgrounds, and children's laughter produce a different atmosphere, a Disney Heaven of safety, neighborliness, and parental warmth. Whether as dreams for some and nightmares for others, no single component alone defines the qualities that suffuse a scene.

Multi-dimensionality

If scenes are suffused by holistic qualities, they are nevertheless complex wholes. A classic example is bohemia. The term "bohemia" denotes an overall style of experience that pervades certain areas, for instance mid-nineteenth-century Montmartre, early twentieth-century Greenwich Village, or late twentieth-century Wicker Park. Yet this overall bohemian ambiance can be more precisely described as a complex mix of multiple dimensions: a transgressive style of appearance; a valorization of personal self-expression; a fascination with the marginal.[1] These contrast and often conflict with the legitimacy of such competing values as tradition and efficiency, and the authenticity of reason.

The scenes perspective takes these sorts of insights and expands them into a more general matrix for specifying the distinct character of a scene as a complex of multiple dimensions. We organize this matrix into three major dimensions: theatricality, authenticity, and legitimacy. Each highlights a form of qualitative experience a scene can evoke, which in turn manifests in specific ways. Theatricality highlights styles of appearance—ways of seeing and being seen, for instance—glamorously, transgressively, or exhibitionistically. Authenticity highlights sources of identity a scene may evince (or attack)—ways of being genuine or phony, for instance, local, ethnic, or corporate authenticity. Legitimacy features normative authorities for action a scene may valorize (or resist)—such as tradition, utilitarian efficiency, the charismatic individual, or personal spontaneity.

Tables 4.3.1 and 4.3.2 summarize the dimensions of theatricality, authenticity, and legitimacy we use to specify the character of scenes. These dimensions are not exhaustive. But they do provide a fruitfully generative matrix in which any specific scene can be located and compared to many others in terms of the mix of qualities they evoke. The larger point is that there is no single quality that defines all scenes, and that all qualities must be qualified: there is no "authenticity" in itself, only specific forms, which combine and clash in various ways.

Table 4.3.1. Analytical Components of Scenes I: Theatricality, Authenticity, Legitimacy.

Theatricality	Authenticity	Legitimacy
Mutual self-display	Discovering the real thing	Acting on moral bases
Seeing and being seen	Touching ground	Listening to duty
Appropriate vs. Inappropriate	Genuine vs. Phony	Right vs. Wrong
Appearance	Identity	Intentions to act
Performing	Rooting	Evaluating

Table 4.3.2. Analytical Dimensions of Scenes II: Dimensions of Theatricality, Authenticity, and Legitimacy.

Theatricality	
Exhibitionistic	Reserved
Glamorous	Ordinary
Neighborly	Distant
Transgressive	Conformist
Formal	Informal
Legitimacy	
Traditional	Novel
Charismatic	Routine
Utilitarian	Unproductive
Egalitarian	Particularist
Self-Expressive	Scripted
Authenticity	
Local	Global
State	Anti-State
Ethnic	Non-Ethnic
Corporate	Independent
Natural	Artificial
Rational	Irrational

Context

Because scenes are multi-dimensional complexes, their dimensional configurations can vary by context. Consider bohemia once again. While some emphasis on transgression cuts across most bohemias, specific bohemian scenes might emphasize one set of values more than others. In one, resisting corporateness can be paramount; in others, personal creativity or sense of humor can prevail. One recent Twitter post by Ariel Dumas (@ArielDumas, March 21, 2017) captioned "There are no rules anymore," contrasting the name of a store with its merchandise (Figure 4.3.1), serves as an example. The "same" scene acquires different meanings in different contexts as the dimensional mix shifts.

Sensitivity to context means being attentive to how similar processes unfold in different situations. For example, in *Scenescapes* we show how "charisma" takes on different meanings in Chicago, New York, and Los Angeles scenes (Figure 4.3.2). In the

FIGURE 4.3.1 Twitter post, captioned "There are no rules anymore."

Source: Ariel Dumas (@ArielDumas), <https://twitter.com/ArielDumas/status/844336929118310402>.

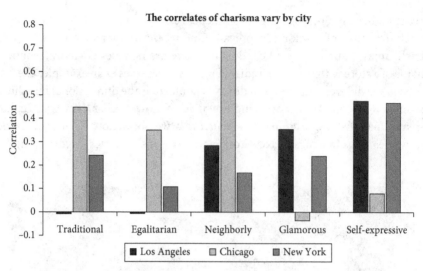

FIGURE 4.3.2 Pearson correlations of charismatic scenes with five other dimensions of scenes, within New York, Chicago, and Los Angeles. These combine data for hundreds of individual amenities like cafes and churches for all US zip codes. Details in Silver and Clark 2016.

latter two cities, charisma appears more in scenes that highlight personal expression and glamorous self-display: scenes of movie stars and fashion icons. In Chicago scenes, by contrast, charisma is more often joined with a sense of neighborliness and the authority of tradition: the parish priest, the fiery pastor, and the ward boss are more iconic. Thus the distinct flavor of a concrete scene emerges in a dynamic process as specific dimensions (such as charisma, glamor, and self-expression) fuse into context-specific configurations.

These examples illustrate how we use general dimensions like charisma but add more concrete meaning by combining general components in locally distinctive ways. We have implemented these by linking with past histories of specific sites like Greenwich Village, in ethnographic study of one neighborhood like Wicker Park in Chicago, by assembling thousands of indicators for every US zip code and similar units in other countries from Korea to France, Spain, and more. The scenes approach links easily with these multiple methods by pointing to specifics (like tattoo parlors and cafes) that in turn generate the more abstract (like bohemia). The links facilitate comparison and more general inter-pretation of each building with its unique components. These take on more power by identifying social and political specifics such as patriotism rising or being challenged (as in protest parades of new social movements), or how the legacy of the counterculture persists in some neighborhoods more than others (captured by bohemian indicators like cafes or tattoo parlors that spread from Greenwich Village across thousands of zip codes).

Feedback

Scenes are multi-dimensional complexes that are themselves one dimension of a broader constellation of processes that shape the fate and fortunes of any given place.

When we encounter an area scenically, we tune into the experiences it has to offer, and respond with corresponding judgments—delight, aversion, intrigue, indifference, and the like. But this is not the only way to engage with a place: the same place that supports a scene can also be an opportunity for work and investment, a habitat for residence and community, a base for political mobilization and target of political conflict. Each implies corresponding policy decisions that can be subtly inferred from precise data, or made more casually.

Scenic qualities can feed into all of these other processes: in choosing where to live, where to invest, and how to gather political support. *Scenescapes* organizes diverse evidence for these complex interactions. For instance, we show how scenes that evoke personal self-expression and glamorous theatricality tend to exhibit relatively high levels of economic growth—even controlling for numerous other factors that spark growth. We also show that the local economic impact of technology clusters is enhanced in self-expressive scenes, and that residential patterns follow scene patterns (and as Silver 2017 shows, vice versa) (Figure 4.3.3).

Additionally, through case studies of Toronto and Chicago neighborhoods, we show how participants attempt to channel scenes policies: developers see investment opportunities; politicians and movement activists seek to mobilize support; artists and other scene-makers add excitement and buzz with posters, slogans, websites, and social media—to rechannel money, influence, and power toward different ends. Silver and Clark 2013 elaborates such details of dynamic and conflictual processes flowing through scenes.

These various examples all illustrate how the scenes approach does not seek to replace past interpretative approaches, but complements and extends them by adding holism, multidimensionality, context, and feedback.

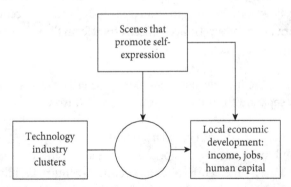

FIGURE 4.3.3 Diagram illustrating the interactive approach to scenes analysis in examining how a self-expressive scene enhances the impact of technology clusters on the local economy. This figure illustrates the following: (1) A multicausal approach of joining tech clusters and self-expressive scenes, and various other core variables (e.g. rent, education, race, artist clusters, population, crime rates, party voting), not displayed. The direct effects of both follow two paths, extending from the self-expression and tech cluster boxes, respectively. (2) The third path leads into the circle. It designates the interaction or mediated effect, which occurs when tech clusters combine with self-expressive scenes.

EXTENDING SCENES THINKING TO HERITAGE

This section extends these general principles of thinking scenically to suggestions for how to study heritage as an element of the scenescape.

Holism

The first suggestion is to consider heritage not only "in itself" but rather "for the scene"— in terms of the overall series of experiences of which it is a part. This can mean paying attention to things that might often seem unimportant or inessential to a building considered in isolation, by asking questions such as:

- What activities do heritage spaces support, within and around them?
- What sorts of shops or restaurants are nearby?
- Do they harmonize or clash with one another?
- What sort of street life animates the surrounding area?
- Do people tend to mill around out front or enter and exit quickly? By car or on foot?
- How do traditional natural elements like waterfalls or beaches complement man-made structures?
- Are directions/signs to find the site, visiting hours, and accommodations like parking, toilets, gas stations, and restaurants accessible so visitors are not inconvenienced by these?
- How does the heritage of an area impact the experience of other things in the area? For instance, how does the juxtaposition of an early twentieth- century bank façade with a modern glass and steel office building transform the way we encounter both? See Figure 4.3.4 for an example.

Such questions may seem irrelevant when considering heritage spaces atomistically, unto themselves, separate from their surroundings. But from a holistic point of view one understands any entity (person, building, organization, neighborhood, and so on) through its dynamic interface with its environment.

To begin to think more concretely about heritage scenically, consider the matter as a painter might.[2] Take a nineteenth- or early twentieth-century building, and consider the many ways you might paint the scene of which it is a part. Imagine a scene in which the historic building is central, and all else orbits around it. Imagine the same scene, but without that building—what would be missing, or transformed? Now put that building at the periphery, and make the hot dog stand or parking lot the centerpiece. Consider the building without its characteristic activities, or with new or different ones. How does the overall scene of which it is a part change?

FIGURE 4.3.4 Italian American bank (built 1907) as base for 456 Montgomery Plaza, San Francisco, CA.

Photo: Alvis Hendley, NoeHill.

As you run components and contexts through multiple permutations, each becomes more clearly delineated. The overall qualities of the scene and the specific contribution of the historic fabric emerge more forcefully. These sorts of experiments can be pursued imaginatively or photographically, but also through various statistical and simulation techniques for examining the interaction of object and environment across situations.

Multi-dimensionality

Recognizing multi-dimensionality helps to elaborate more precisely the many ways that heritage can contribute to a scene. For example, it is common to refer to heritage as producing a sense of authenticity, despite the challenge in elaborating what an unqualified notion of authenticity consists in. Simply qualifying the term gives it more concrete and determinate significance. Does heritage aim to preserve scenes of ethnic or local authenticity against homogeny; a sense of a nation's distinct identity against global norms; or even the association of a distinct brand with an area's historic identity?

At the same time, multi-dimensionality can take us beyond narrow adherence to authenticity as the sole source of value heritage might bring to a scene. Multiple interacting values can be at work. For example, preserving a historic façade within a modern building (as at the Royal Ontario Museum in Toronto, shown in Figure 4.3.5) situates the past as part of a fluid process of re-interpretation and sometimes clashing styles.

Those who seek to preserve not simply a building but its "associational and contextual" value as part of a distinctive, counter-cultural music scene (Ross 2017) may even treat transgressiveness as a form of heritage. Other ways may invoke more strict traditionalism: an unchanging scene fixed for all time to preserve a memory.

Heritage may even be invoked in an anti-traditionalist manner. For example, buildings themselves may be treated as possessing minimal distinctive value because they can be reconstructed/rebuilt in a traditional way to match any particular historical era. This is a view attributed by some observers to at least some contemporary Chinese practices, in which the power of the state is paramount (Zhang 2014). By contrast, much American and European practice assumes that both the method of construction and the intellectual philosophy behind it are of value and worthy of preservation. Thus, the emphasis on the aesthetic and philosophical value of architectural style and the maintenance of its integrity is not globally shared. Noting and helping elaborate these

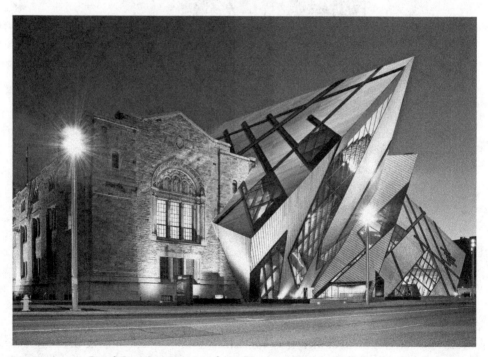

FIGURE 4.3.5 Royal Ontario Museum of Art (Toronto, Canada, built 1914), with the Michael Lee-Chin Crystal, designed by Studio Daniel Libeskind (2007).

Photo: Elliot Lewis Photography, 2011.

disparities in criteria of assessment is a contribution that scenes analysis can add to written or tour-guide comments about a particular historic site. Acknowledging such multiple perspectives helps sidestep conflicts over what is the "correct" historical interpretation, such as of Civil War statues in the US South, Protestant and Catholic sites in Prague or Northern Ireland, or former Soviet landmarks in Eastern Europe. All have experienced forcible removal and restoration of emotionally charged items.

Beyond the specific examples, one could use the multi-dimensional framework of the scenes perspective to situate various approaches to heritage in a complex continuum of a variety of values.

Context

An implication of the foregoing is that there is no single or universal meaning of "heritage." What it means to "appeal to heritage" to preserve or create a scene will vary by context. For example, national context may matter: to appeal to "national heritage" in sustaining a scene in the United States is to do so in a distinct context, one that—speaking very broadly—tends to prize the preservation of an original founding moment. By contrast "national heritage" in China may carry quite different implications.

These differences have deep historical roots that define conventions according to which the value of heritage for a scene is upheld. Part of what it means to elaborate the nature of a context is to trace this history. For example, the strong traditionalism in much US heritage thinking grows out of the fact that historic preservation in the United States began as a specifically patriotic, cultural concern. In 1853, Ann Pamela Cunningham founded the Mt. Vernon Ladies' Association to protect and preserve the Mansion, grounds, outbuildings, and legacy of George Washington. Today, the Mt. Vernon Ladies' Association remains the owner and operator of this estate, and has pioneered many important historic preservation concepts including the restoration and interpretation of the estate's outbuildings, relying on scientific analyses to determine paint colors and embracing archaeological research as a primary source for learning about the past (Tomlan 2015: 7–8).

Over time, the emphasis on the founding events of this country exemplified at Mt. Vernon evolved into a more broadly based cultural effort. This philosophy was codified in the National Historic Preservation Act of 1966, which established criteria for recognizing buildings as having aesthetic, historical, or cultural value, which emphasized history, great figures from the past, and styles from distinct periods. These criteria provided an official definition of "ethical heritage practice" in the United States.

Since 1966, the professional field of historic preservation has evolved and its practice has been influenced by other professions and issues. These include legal requirements and economic constraints. Yet the strong emphasis on tradition remains central. On the fiftieth anniversary of the passage of the National Historic Preservation Act (NHPA), President Obama issued a statement emphasizing the Federal government's long-standing interest in architectural history, which read in part:

America's history is rooted in places—from rolling hills to vast plains to coastlines along the sea—that reflect the diversity of our people and the beliefs that have shaped our Nation. [The NHPA gave] life to the cultural foundations of our country and [enables] our people to gain insights into generations before them. The Act helps Americans serve as stewards of their history and preserve vital places in their communities. In marking this special milestone, we are reminded that though our journey to live up to our highest ideals remains incomplete, we can always look to the lessons of history as we chart our course.

(Obama 2016)

Yet context itself is contextual. For example, "China" and the "United States" are large, multi-faceted entities that cannot be reduced to a single "culture." Parts of California are in some dimensions more similar to parts of Texas than they are to the rest of California—for instance, the alternative cultural scenes of the Bay Area and Austin. To appeal to the importance of "cultural heritage" in preserving these sorts of scenes may not carry great weight set against a backdrop where "keeping Austin weird" resonates. But elsewhere—perhaps just a hundred miles away—the same appeal may fall flat. Thus, to examine how heritage appeals operate in practice requires situating them both in reference to the scene they seek to sustain and in the context of the local audience to which they are made.

Where and how these boundaries are drawn differs if one respects or rejects the "New West" rewriting of US history, with its stress on Native Americans, race, gender roles, and other themes that emerged as salient in 1970s America. Recognizing the importance of clarifying these criteria, for visitors and professionals, rather than seeking a single "correct" answer, flows naturally from scenic thinking. The Museum of the City of New Orleans has been a model featuring competing interpretations of the past, such as showing letters from visitors in the early nineteenth century who lamented that the main concerns of residents seemed to be horseback riding, dancing, and party conversation, not working, while later items showed city council members being murdered by Klansmen, then retribution from "rootless carpet baggers," and so forth. Faulkner novels resonate with such conflicting and impassioned themes and counter themes. Indeed, the William Faulkner House in New Orleans has long been staffed by guides who can knowledgably discuss all manner of historical and literary themes, conflicts and counter-interpretations, and visibly enjoy doing so with visitors. Some sites are "Made for Children," others appeal to different subsets of visitors. Where and how to incorporate such diversity with congeniality and grace is a challenge to all.

Feedback

Attention to feedback provides a major source of analytical leverage for joining scenes, heritage, and other processes that may affect local area development. There are many potential directions to pursue. One could integrate heritage into the interactive models developed in *Scenescapes*. For instance, we could examine not only whether the presence of heritage buildings sparks economic growth (cf. Mason 2005) or shapes residential patterns and tourism (Nasser 2003), but if and how these shift depending on the scene. Perhaps areas with heritage designations *and* scenes that prize self-expression or local authenticity attract different groups and spark growth at different rates. Similarly, we have found that individuals who reside in scenes that invoke tradition, local authenticity, and neighborliness are more likely to have conservative political attitudes (Miller and Silver 2015). Does the presence of heritage designations enhance or moderate this connection?

Another way to examine feedback is through studying the interplay of heritage, scenes, and the complex, conflictual, dynamic array of resources, groups, and actors outlined in Silver and Clark 2013 (and ch. 6 of *Scenescapes*; see also Silver 2013). From this vantage point, "heritage" can be a symbolic tool—sometimes a weapon—wielded in the course of local debates about the character of a place (Ryberg-Webster and Kinahan 2014 review key case studies joining heritage and urban politics, such as Reichl 1997, Newman 2001, and Zhang 2011).

There are multiple analytical questions as to when, who, how, and how successfully this tool is utilized. For example:

- *When and why do some groups seek heritage designation to preserve the character of a scene they value, but others not?* Ross 2017 takes an important step in this direction, examining how local activism led some Toronto music venues to receive heritage designation, others not. Pushing this line of research further could involve comparative study of heritage planning documents not only as neutral records but also as outcomes of significant community pressure and input.
- *Which types of scenes are more likely to support successful efforts at heritage advocacy, and how does this vary by context?* For example, when the scene is in a residential community or a tourist area, advocated for on the basis of economic value or community benefits, by broad coalitions or narrow interest groups, in a growth or anti-growth political culture?
- *When and why do specific dimensions of scenes become targets of heritage activism, such as maintaining local authenticity, a spirit of transgression, an ethnic culture, a creative sensibility, or any other scene dimension?* Comparative case studies of local political controversies over heritage designation could examine when, and why various groups appeal to the value of heritage for a scene in general, but also for sustaining specific scenic qualities.

There have been many case studies produced by the National Trust for Historic Preservation, state and local preservation organizations and major media publications, and scholars; these present opportunities for creative further research. The scenes perspective provides neither answers nor advocacy for these and similar questions, but it offers a language and analytical framework to pursue them more deeply and more subtly.

These are likely additions for future agendas as citizens the world over are better educated and seek more complex, engaging, and challenging experiences as they visit historic sites.

INTEGRATING HERITAGE INTO SCENES RESEARCH, AND VICE VERSA: METHODS AND DATA

Pursuing these suggestions in detail is a large and challenging project. Many methods and data sources are possible, traditional and novel.

Traditional methods such as ethnographic case studies, archival research, interviews, and surveys are extremely important for pursuing linkages between scenes and heritage. Adopting a scenes approach simply focuses attention to perhaps understudied aspects. The multi-dimensional framework can clue the analysis in to issues that go beyond generic "authenticity" or "associational context," and help elaborate the more specific values heritage activists might seek to preserve. It can also be used to identify and sidestep conflicts among visitors or sponsors with competing agendas.

Other promising approaches utilize "big data." When and why do some groups seek heritage designation to preserve the character of a scene they value, but others not? Much of our quantitative research on scenes builds scenes metrics from digital directories that provide localized information about hundreds of organizational types, such as tattoo parlors, art galleries, restaurants, churches, and more. Merging these metrics with National Register and local heritage inventories, as well as interviews and local histories, provides an exciting opportunity to study interaction of scene and heritage across contexts. We have merged some of these data and can share parts of them with others. Social media data from sources such as Facebook, Twitter, or Instagram provide comments on specific sites and what types of photos visitors took. These provide insight into the varieties of "buzz" that various heritage sites generate, and how these shift across scenes. New visual pattern recognition techniques can discern the visual styles of the buildings and street life of scenes, which may or may not include designated historic districts. Programs now can code street façades from a dozen or more cities more precisely than most human experts.

But these are complex and ambitious. Readers sensitive to heritage can simply add some core concepts about scenes thinking introduced in this chapter in revisiting a favorite site and seeking to enrich the site for oneself and others by digging a bit more deeply into how it works as a part of a heritage scene. Give it a try: consider leading three tours with three sets of highly disparate visitors and consider how to engage each of them at the same site.

CONCLUSION

The main goal of this brief chapter has been to articulate some general suggestions for integrating heritage into scenes thinking and to illustrate the sorts of analytical questions this synthesis helps pose. Scenes thinking is holistic, multi-dimensional, contextual, and sensitive to multiple feedback processes. Extending these principles to the study of heritage offers exciting and challenging opportunities to pose new questions and to question familiar answers.

NOTES

1. *Scenescapes* (ch. 2) elaborates this analysis, grounded in literary and sociological descriptions of bohemian life.
2. Rudolf Arnheim (1969: 45) describes this attitude well: "The changing appearance of a landscape or building in the morning, the evening, under electric light, with different weather and in different seasons offers two advantages. It presents an extraordinary richness of sight, and it tests the nature of the object by exposing it to varying conditions. A person perceived as the dominant figure in his home, surrounded by subordinate furniture, offers an aspect of the human kind quite different form the small creatures crawling at the bottom of a city street."

REFERENCES

Arnheim, R. 1969. *Visual Thinking*. Berkeley and Los Angeles: University of California Press.

Dewey, John. 1934. *Art as Experience*. New York: Penguin.

Mason, Randall. 2005. *Economics and Historic Preservation: A Guide and Review of the Literature*. Washington, DC: Brookings Institution, Metropolitan Policy Program.

Miller, Diana L., and Daniel Silver. 2015. "Cultural Scenes and Contextual Effects on Political Attitudes." *European Journal of Cultural and Political Sociology* 2(3–4): 241–266.

Morrison, Hugh. 1952. *Early American Architecture from the First Colonial Settlements to the National Period*. New York: Oxford University Press.

Nasser, Noha. 2003. "Planning for Urban Heritage Places: Reconciling Conservation, Tourism, and Sustainable Development." *Journal of Planning Literature* 17(4): 467–479.

Newman, Harvey K. 2001. "Historic Preservation Policy and Regime Politics in Atlanta." *Journal of Urban Affairs* 23(1): 71–86.

Obama, Barack. 2016. "Presidential Statement on the 50th Anniversary of the National Historic Preservation Act, October 14. <http://www.preserveamerica.gov/docs/presidentobamapreserve.pdf>.

Reichl, Alexander J. 1997. "Historic Preservation and Progrowth Politics in U.S. Cities." *Urban Affairs Review* 32(4): 513–535.

Ross, S. G. 2017. "Development versus Preservation Interests in the Making of a Music City: A Case Study of Select Iconic Toronto Music Venues and the Treatment of Their Intangible Cultural Heritage Value." *International Journal of Cultural Property* 24(1): 31–56.

Ryberg-Webster, S., and K. L. Kinahan. 2014. "Historic Preservation and Urban Revitalization in the Twenty-First Century." *CPL bibliography* 29(2): 119–139.

Silver, D. 2017. "Some Scenes of Urban Life," in *The Sage Handbook of New Urban Studies*, ed. John Hannigan and Greg Richards. Thousand Oaks: Sage, 408–429.

Silver, D., and T. N. Clark. 2013. "Buzz as an Urban Resource." *Canadian Journal of Sociology* 38(1): 1–32.

Silver, D. A., and T. N. Clark. 2016. *Scenescapes: How qualities of place shape social life.* Chicago: University of Chicago Press.

Tomlan, Michael A. 2015. *Historic Preservation: Caring for Our Expanding Legacy.* New York: Springer.

Zhang, Yue. 2011. "Boundaries of Power: Politics of Urban Preservation in Two Chicago Neighborhoods." *Urban Affairs Review* 47(4): 511–540.

Zhang, Yue. 2014. *The Fragmented Politics of Urban Preservation: Beijing, Chicago, and Paris.* Minnesota: University of Minnesota Press.

CHAPTER 4.4

....

CONTESTING THE AESTHETIC CONSTRUCTION OF COMMUNITY

The New Suburban Landscape

....

DENISE LAWRENCE-ZÚÑIGA

HERITAGE of place is often promoted by cities and states as a genuine representation of their history, as a way to construct and project a cultural identity, and as a branding exercise to foster tourism and business. It is frequently envisioned in the physical preservation of architecture or conservation of landscape as a means to re-capture the original material qualities of the past with the intention of evoking historical meanings. In protecting iconic buildings and monuments, heritage preservation rescues symbols of meaning that appear to be more firmly rooted in an unchanging past than in the ever-shifting present, and uses these as core constituents to construct the uniqueness of a place. The public, however, may not be universally sympathetic to arguments favoring a historic aesthetic, especially when alternative and contrasting aesthetic and functional values—modernist or ethnic—are possible. Thus, at the center of place-making are conflicts about the contested aesthetic construction of community.

Efforts to preserve historic landscapes have traditionally focused on urban monuments and civic cores, though increasingly the residents of "older" suburban neighborhoods have begun clamoring for protections for their homes. Residents may initially focus protection interests on the material details of their own houses, but then extend those sentiments to the neighborhood context in order to create a broader historic landscape in which to live. Establishing protections for residential heritage by circumscribing the range of aesthetic possibilities in remodeling brings issues of place aesthetics closer to people's everyday lives. They may also encourage or challenge relationships between and among neighbors. The residential preservation project, because it requires the participation of like-minded homeowners, is not a solitary endeavor. Collective efforts required to restore a neighborhood may involve forming advocacy organizations to advance protections or educational projects. They may also involve city staff in assisting with writing legislation and enforcing protections, and other sympathetic groups such as local history societies to promote education. Heritage preservation can be a very large cultural project.

By the same token, preservation efforts may raise concerns among some citizens who feel personally threatened by aesthetic ideas that conflict with their own, or the prospect of having their preferences controlled by the neighborhood or local government. While the preserved past represents and reinforces a certain reassuring sense of historic authenticity for some, it doesn't for everyone. Older deteriorated neighborhoods are known to supply affordable housing to a wide spectrum of residents: renters as well as owners, older people as well as younger ones, poorer and wealthier households, and long-term residents and recent arrivals (Wyly and Hammel 2005). By contrast, developers and private buyers see in these neighborhoods economic opportunities for demolishing and rebuilding, or "flipping" houses to make a profit. Affordability makes these sites ripe for gentrification where new arrivals or "pioneers" displace existing residents as they restore houses according to their aesthetic preferences and make real estate values rise (Smith 1996). Although the economics of residential restoration play a key role, the question of which aesthetic preference should dominate remains. The neighborhood thus becomes the setting for resolving conflicts about these disruptive aesthetic preferences.

FRAMING THE ARGUMENT

Focusing on the aesthetic qualities of historic preservation projects raises issues about the construction of personal identity and lifestyle. Studies of place attachment reveal that people's emotional ties to a locale are a product of their identification with the community as defined by its physical qualities and social characteristics (Hummon 1992: 260, Zukin 1982, Butler 1997). The physical character of a place acts as a key symbol capable of evoking a sense of another time or place. Urban design may deliberately use "scenographic tableaux" to materially represent collective memory, obliquely referencing history while offering escape and a re-centering of life in a globalizing world (Boyer 1992: 192). Gestures to re-center life increasingly motivate heritage-style development projects in the neoliberal city (McGuigan, this volume), but also in suburban neighborhoods.

Residents of many small towns and neighborhoods embrace preserving cultural and environmental features as a way to create a meaningful community identity (Dorst 1989; Mulligan, this volume). These communities, however, are not necessarily socially homogeneous, and arguments over heritage expressions and practices may reveal deep divisions by class and ethnicity. While legal protections can ensure that a landscape acquires an exclusive aura as a positional good, conflicts over landscape restoration reveal the aesthetics of class distinction (Duncan and Duncan 2001: 390). Engaging in preservation and conservation practices provides an avenue for participating in and experiencing the reconstruction and reproduction of history through place making; however, it is an exclusionary act. To restore a house to its original qualities suggests a preference for historic aesthetic principles; to require that kind of restoration essentially excludes any other set of aesthetic tastes. This is especially true where social divisions organize homeowners for advocacy but alienate them against others who have alternative values.

Individual residents who themselves advocate for historic preservation laws in their communities, often become motivated by restoring their own houses. Discovering the identities of the original designers and owners stimulates their interest in history, which animates restoration and the production of a moral domestic landscape (Lawrence-Zúñiga 2010). Some homeowners say they listen to "what the house tells them to do" as a preservation strategy. "Listening" establishes links to the people who first created the material qualities of the house and enables the recognition of their agency that gives meaning to life in a historic structure (Gell 1998, Miller 1995). Homeowners motivated to conserve the original character of home easily extend concern to their neighborhood through civic means. Cities that adopt historic preservation legislation or other protections use graphic codes to describe the appropriate house forms homeowners are expected to model in their projects. Ghertner (2010), working in Delhi, suggests that these measures constitute a form of "aesthetic governmentality," a neoliberal governmental policy that uses visual techniques to draw an applicant into a photographed scene as a means to change their inter-subjective experiential knowledge of space. The goal of these regulations is to have homeowners take responsibility for their aesthetic choices, to change the way they perceive space and their place in it, and to foster a new set of aesthetic values. The goal of government policy is to gain compliance in the production of the historic landscape (Lawrence-Zúñiga 2015).

Historic Preservation Professionalism

The organization of historic preservation as a professional practice and homeowner vocation participates in the construction of a cosmology around the value of material or built forms. These cosmologies include beliefs and practices that emphasize the historic worthiness of materials for conservation or preservation. In American practice, legislation codifies these understandings according to two distinct attributes, the *significance* of the object for preservation, and its *integrity*. Significance addresses the historical importance of the object—its association with historic persons or events, or its capacity to represent a classic style or provide materials for research—while integrity refers to its capacity to be recognized as "historic" or original. Although older objects may survive untouched over time, more likely these objects are altered as different owners and occupants come into contact with them, which then renders them less and less capable of communicating historic significance. These issues are at the center of professional concerns with historic preservation. Federal, state, and local laws are codified around these notions, although actual local interpretations of significance and integrity vary quite a lot (Tyler 2000). For instance, local preservation laws may emphasize the importance of local history, while state laws are more concerned with geographically broader concerns. Moreover, historic preservation laws protect individual buildings by landmarking, but may also recognize collections of buildings in landmarked districts. Again, the variation in appropriating measures and the strictness of interpretation differs greatly from one city to another.

Although not every resident recognizes the unique historical significance of their home, its integrity, which makes protection possible, relies on the capacity of its material properties to signify its originality and age. In endeavoring to restore their own houses homeowners engage in frequent and often quite intense practices to recover the original material qualities, alternating between searching for agency in the materials they seek to restore and justifying their work by citing the cosmology of historic preservation. To approximate the restoration of the original requires them to become acquainted with the design intentions of previous builders or owners who built the house, as well as with the materials and methods of construction, design conventions, and functional expectations from earlier decades. They hire contractors who specialize in working with older homes or learn how to do the work themselves. In the process, many homeowners construct new identities and lifestyles around their restoration practices, becoming experts in Arts and Crafts or other historical styles, locating vendors for services and products, and participating in educational outreach through their local preservation organization. Homeowners who adhere strongly, and often literally, to a strict interpretation of preservation values call themselves "purists" (Lawrence-Zúñiga 2014, 2016).

Education is embraced as one of the key issues motivating preservation homeowners, because older neighbors and new home purchasers often lack the basic understanding of the meaning of "integrity" in remodeling their houses. Older houses have features that make contemporary lifestyles difficult, but "purist" owners are committed to finding ways to remodel without destroying the integrity of the house—both inside and out. Conflicts between and among homeowners in historic neighborhoods are often negotiated locally through informal contacts, but frequently enough such conflicts rise to the city level when a homeowner applies for a permit to renovate a house or to demolish and build a new house. In addition to issuing landmark status for individual structures and neighborhoods, preservation laws require a "certificate of appropriateness" from the historic preservation commission before a homeowner can apply for building and zoning permits. Some meetings of the preservation commission, design review board, or city council become openly contentious when disagreeing parties air their differences.

The research on which this chapter is based was conducted over a ten-year period, from 2006–16, in five California cities including Pasadena, Monrovia, Ontario, Riverside, and Alhambra (Figure 4.4.1). Data were gathered from in-depth interviews with over fifty homeowners, nine city officials and other public officials, and leaders of twelve civic and non-profit organizations. In addition, data were collected from

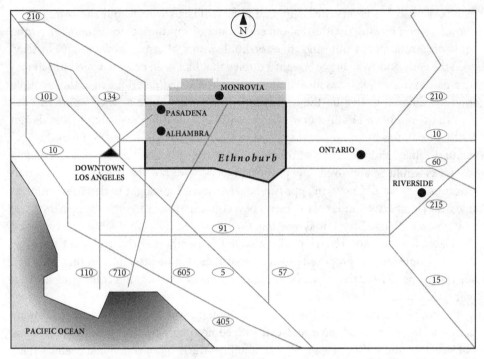

FIGURE 4.4.1 Map of southern California region showing the location of the five cities and the Asian settlement area known as the "ethnoburb."

Map by Nadim Itani.

observations of multiple civic meetings, local preservation group functions, and home tours and consultations with municipal archives (Lawrence-Zúñiga 2016).

NEW NEIGHBORS AND HISTORIC HOUSES IN MONROVIA

Communities with older houses attract a wide variety of people looking to buy appealing homes at affordable prices. Monrovia is one of those communities. It boasts an inventory of older Victorian, Craftsman, and Revival-styled homes, as well as many postwar contemporary styles. Monrovia has historic preservation legislation with many landmarked houses but only one district, and a commission that reviews applications for certificates of appropriateness and land marking status for houses appearing in a historic inventory. It also has a community-wide organization, Monrovia Old House Preservation Group (MOHPG), that holds home tours each year and provides educational and cultural services to the public. MOHPG members participate in city-wide preservation efforts by providing a majority of board members on the historic preservation commission.

Monrovia also has a very well-regarded local historian with whom the commission consults when making decisions about certificates of appropriateness. There is a strong sense of community identity and cohesion built around Monrovia's own unique history.

In the early 2000s, a couple bought a duplex that had been designed and built in 1913 by a pair of highly regarded local builders. The house had deteriorated and the couple found it difficult to live in; they complained of mice and fleas. They wanted to demolish the house and build a new one in its place, and so hired an architect to design for them a Tudor-styled house. They were aware of the city's fondness for historic architectural values, and thought that the new Tudor-styled house, because it was a historical style, would be approved. The proposal was reviewed by the Historic Preservation Commission, but did not win approval largely because it sought to demolish an original historic structure and replace it with new construction. Although the owners of the house never attended the initial meeting, they appealed the commission's decision and then attended the second hearing. Many MOHPG members also attended the meeting. In fact, people said the proposed project had attracted more local interest than they had seen in the past. The meeting was contentious as it revolved around conflicting ideas of what is historic.

The couple explained that the house they bought was old and used up, had many deficiencies, and needed to be replaced with something new. This proclamation drew out people in the audience who talked about how the neighborhood had been used for film shoots and had value because the original character of the neighborhood was still intact. Individuals testified that they too had encountered problems with mice and fleas and could recommend exterminators to help them deal with those problems. Still others characterized their proposal to eliminate an original structure as "molestation." Near the end of the meeting one person encapsulated the sentiments of the preservationist homeowners by saying, "If you do not want to preserve the house, you should leave. You could come back, of course, if you committed to preserving the old house." The owners thanked the residents for their advice and said that they would stay in Monrovia to restore the old house, but within a year they had sold it and moved on.

PRESERVATION ELITES IN RIVERSIDE

In the city of Riverside, one particularly large historic area, divided into a historic district and historic conservation area, has long been the locus of conflicts among the neighbors over remodeling ideas. The area has a history of its own. Riverside was one of the earliest adopters of historic preservation legislation in the state of California in 1969, but not surprisingly it also encountered residents' initial resistance to preservation. In early surveys undertaken by the municipal museum's Cultural Heritage Board, the older homes in this and four other subdivisions were described as having historic value. Thus, the Board made proposals to the residents of each area to form a district where laws to protect the material conditions of the houses from modernization or other transformations could be enacted. Residents in many areas declined the proposed protections because they did not want the government telling them what they could and could not do to their houses. Eventually, attitudes began to change when they realized that the laws would protect the value of their homes when new owners moved into the neighborhood and wanted to alter their houses, or when real estate conditions might change.

In the large Oak Streets conservation area, residents in several streets eventually organized themselves to accept the designation as a historic district and form a neighborhood association, but they resisted inviting the households outside their immediate neighborhood to join them. Thus, two distinct historic areas were created and continue to this day, although both are subject to the same preservation reviews. The city has recently encouraged them to merge because in their eyes they are virtually the same in terms of historic value. But residents of the historic district have refused because they consider the houses in the conservation area to be of lesser quality and value than their own. Residents of the official "historic" district also believe the neighboring conservation area is a lower socioeconomic zone where owners have lower incomes and more crime. The current neighborhood association spends resources trying to track "crime" in the neighborhood—actually, these consist of simply posting on the neighborhood website residents' reports about suspicious activity such as black or brown people walking down alleyways.

Unlike Monrovia, historic preservation concerns are not very intense in driving homeowners' own restorations, but seem to get activated when neighbors remodel. Neighbors monitor the home improvements of others to make sure they conform to their understanding of the laws and regulations concerning "design." When a neighbor requests permission to build something substantial, and which can be interpreted as a possible threat to the neighbors, a hearing is held at the Cultural Heritage Board. Approvals for remodeling are usually unremarkable; however, sometimes neighbors can oppose even "reasonable" interpretations of the preservation code. One couple who had bought a house in 1991 sought to remodel their house by adding a second story, stepped back from the front façade, to accommodate their two teenage children. They hired an architect to design the addition and submitted it to the Cultural Heritage Board. The board's decision was mixed, but a majority approved of and permitted the design. Unfortunately, the neighbor who lived across the street strongly objected to the proposed remodel, arguing that adding a second story conflicted with the "original" design of the house under preservation regulations. The neighbor protested and appealed the board's decision, taking the case to the city council.

In preparation for the appeal, the couple researched the number of houses with second stories in the district, and sought signatures of support from the majority of their neighbors. When the appeal was heard, a city council committee said the couple should have gotten the neighbors' approval before starting; it ignored the signatures they had gathered and presented. The neighbor who protested the addition was a long-term resident of the city and historic district, and had previously worked as a staff member for the city council. She also had gotten support from one other neighbor, but made sure that her friends on the city council were sympathetic to her cause. In the final decision, the project was denied, in large part because the two neighbors opposed the project. The couple lamented the fact that they had taken extra measures to make sure their design was appropriate to fit the character of the house and neighborhood. But they said that nowhere in the regulations governing house remodeling had the city stated that neighbors had to approve the proposed design in advance. In the end, the children grew up and moved out, and the couple never did change their house.

Although the conflicts over house design in Monrovia and Riverside were similar, they represent two different outcomes for historic preservation. Monrovia is a city that had been troubled in the postwar period by "white flight" as residents moved to newer suburbs. The housing stock deteriorated and the city experienced an increase in gangs, drugs, and crime. In the 1970s when people began to rediscover the city and its older housing, they initiated restoration practices, created a historic preservation organization, and moved to pass protection laws. Since that time, Monrovia has become a highly desirable community for preservation. As more and more residents have been attracted to Monrovia for its affordable home prices, it has gentrified. Thus, the actions of the city's Historic Preservation Commission and its community organization have been important for protecting its valued resources. Preservation homeowners play an active role in guarding against the destruction of historic resources.

In the case of Riverside, however, gentrification never occurred, at least not in this area of the city. Rather, elites, once they overcame their initial resistance to preservation restrictions, used historic preservation laws strategically to reinforce their own position by excluding new neighbors and teaching them to conform to elite aesthetic values. The preservation of their elite status in the city, rather than promoting historic preservation values, is their most important goal. In the Oak Streets neighborhood, the "historic district" refuses to merge with the conservation area in order to maintain its aura and distinction as a positional good. In the conflict over the remodel, proposals to add a second story are common for older houses with limited space and in other cities they usually win approval with a good design that does not overwhelm the original house. Even though the proposed project was located in the original historic district where the desire to preserve the historic character is presumably most intense, preservation restrictions were used instead to signal the asymmetrical status and power relations between a long-term resident and newcomer.

Chinese Mansions in Alhambra

The city of Alhambra attracts newly arriving Chinese immigrants from Taiwan, Hong Kong, the Chinese Mainland, and Southeast Asia and has become the center for finance, insurance, and real estate (FIRE) for the sprawling local ethnic community. Alhambra and its surrounding cities also comprise what is known as the larger southern California

Chinese ethnoburb, multiethnic cities where no one ethnicity predominates (Li 2009), a phenomenon that has become more widespread since the 1990s. In spite of having a large number of older houses that remain affordable, Alhambra has never passed historic preservation legislation. Rather, in 2009 it adopted Residential Design Guidelines to provide somewhat weaker protections for homes and neighborhoods. Alhambra has become the site of highly contested aesthetic values that pitch two competing visions for the city—historic preservation or Asian mansionization.

Much of the advocacy for the protection of historic homes has come from the Alhambra Preservation Group (APG), founded in 2003. Their community activism has focused on citizen education and the election of sympathetic city council members. According to members of the APG, members and associates of the business-oriented Chamber of Commerce have dominated local politics by promoting their recommended candidates for council offices. In fact, preservation advocates argue that the city's same developer-politicians who have personally enriched themselves in development schemes now also support the new Chinese bankers and investors, and have been supporting real estate investors and developers that have been converting older homes to rental apartments or building additional units on residential lots.

Although Alhambra lacks preservation legislation, the city employs an architect and has a Design Review Board to review and grant permission for different architectural projects. The Design Review Board (DRB) is comprised of five members, four of whom are immigrants of Asian descent and are licensed to practice as real estate development or design professionals. The board meets at least once a month and considers applications to change signage or exterior remodeling. Homeowners or their representatives who appear before the board include whites, Latinos, and Asians, although recently there has been an increase in Chinese.

Alhambra is one of several southern California cities made popular for the purchase and sale of remodeled older houses to overseas buyers living in China. Transnational real estate representatives directly market houses to Chinese nationals, to their tastes and requirements, and provide buyers a means to invest their money and relocate their families outside China. Local immigrant Chinese contractors and realtors collaborate with co-ethnic buyers who envision developing a property for a quick sale, but many of the design and construction "professionals" do not have much understanding of how regulations work to ensure designs conform to local or professional standards. Moreover, many immigrants, not just the Chinese, are not particularly interested in preserving someone else's history. They tend to see the older bungalows as old and worn out, and in need of replacement. The Design Review Board acts as a vehicle to ensure compliance to local standards, but their decisions are suggestions rather than the legally binding requirements of historic preservation laws.

Although whites, Latinos, and Asians all make applications for permits to remodel their houses, Asians tend to dominate with more than half of the petitions. Asians also tend to be more affluent than Latinos and propose much more elaborate remodels (Li

2009: 139). With each proposal, the homeowner submits a drawing of the intended design along with paperwork outlining the work to be done. The staff architect reviews the proposal and writes a brief report recommending approval or requiring more refinement. These reports are the basis for hearings in the DRB. The applicants—owners and/or contractors—are expected to be present so that the details of the proposal can be discussed. Often, the DRB makes suggestions and corrections the applicant does not understand, but this is not for linguistic reasons—it is cultural. For instance, concerns about stylistic integrity—that the elements of a Craftsman style are consistent throughout the design proposal—are often discussed. These are often matters of education or practical experience, which applicants may lack. More often applicant preferences are cultural and are shared with local and international co-ethnic Chinese. It is fairly clear from DRB meetings that applicants rarely consult the Residential Design Guidelines.

One local immigrant Chinese contractor, Mr. Lim (a pseudonym), who returned repeatedly to the DRB with a series of proposals for different houses, had become really stuck on one of them. Initially he proposed to convert the bungalow to a Mediterranean Revival style, but returned during the next month to proclaim that the house should be a Craftsman. Each time the DRB tried to help him work out the stylistic details, while noting that he failed to grasp the subtle nuances of American home design. Finally, during the following month he returned again saying he had changed his mind, because his client—the owner—preferred a large Mediterranean Revival house—a mansion. The Craftsman style would be difficult to enlarge to accommodate a mansion, and his client really did not like the style. Instead, the client had embraced a stucco "Asian Mediterranean" style, which could be seen in nearby ethnoburb communities from Alhambra to Arcadia. The scale of the house would dwarf the neighboring houses, but as one Asian applicant proclaimed, in a very short time these mansions would dominate and differences in scale would disappear.

Members of the APG are active participants in the DRB hearings, which they attend to comment on design proposals. According to DRB members, they help facilitate a deeper historical understanding of the houses under consideration. For instance, some APG members take pictures of the houses and research their histories to present at the hearings. Board members appreciate their efforts, often referencing and incorporating those facts in their decisions. In the case of Mr. Lim's proposal to convert a small bungalow to a large Asian-Mediterranean mansion, APG members presented historical facts about the house and house style, arguing that its scale was an integral part of the neighborhood, and that the current façade should be preserved in any kind of renovation. Referring to the Residential Design Guidelines to legitimize their decision, the DRB ruled that Mr. Lim's remodeling proposal should be limited to the size and style that conformed to the existing context of the neighborhood. Notably, Mr. Lim was unaware of the design guidelines, but was also unaware of their purpose to act as a "cultural test" in getting authorities to grant required permissions (Ong 1996). The large gap in knowledge and expectations between the city and its new immigrants has made bridging the cultural chasm between them more challenging.

CONCLUSION

The three cases outlined here suggest that historic preservation sentiments and visions of community are often contested in the civic sphere as alternative aesthetic views are put forward and debated. Many homeowners still resist having any kind of government control over the aesthetic and material conditions of their properties. Initially people in Riverside resented the intrusion of government processes in what they consider their private lives and especially in regards to their private property, even though government regulations already control a good deal of domestic life. Witness for example the controls on the number of dogs or cats a homeowner can have, the delivery of television and cable services or water and electric utilities, or restrictions placed on permitted uses of residential front yards, all of which exemplify local government interventions to ostensibly protect health and safety. Why these restrictions are considered legitimate, but aesthetic controls are not, is not exactly clear. Indeed, some people seek out gated residential complexes where aesthetic controls exist because, they say, they want a predictable environment in which to live.

For many homeowners, the historic preservation vision presents few problems or impediments that would obstruct their desires to remodel their houses. In fact, they find it comforting to know that government regulations prevent their neighbors from redesigning their house in a radically different style or scale. In Monrovia, historic preservation-oriented sentiments were expressed as a kind of "purist" aesthetic position, as homeowners struggled over the meaning of "history." Local decisions concluded that history really was about the actual facts of Monrovia's builders rather than the proposal for a new house built in a historic style. In Riverside, by contrast, some neighbors promoted an elitist interpretation of historic preservation, by which they asserted their own power over aesthetic decisions based on who was there first. This conflict suggests the length of residency in the neighborhood should confer greater rights and knowledge in resolving aesthetic issues.

These two communities use preservation laws to control and regulate who builds what in their neighborhoods, and to determine the aesthetic shape of the landscape. Each dispute over the meaning of the "history" that will be preserved reflects a concern with social standing and status, and the arguments people advance strive to indicate their morally superior standing. In Monrovia, homeowners assert that their historic landscape will be destroyed by the demolition of original houses and rebuilding efforts of their new neighbors. They cling to the sense of a moral community that historic preservation laws and practices have helped them create; a community landscape that they love and that is popular with the film industry. In Riverside, however, the meaning of the historic preservation has more to do with who has the "better" knowledge and understanding. The neighbors who contested the couple's design proposal asserted that their longer residence in the neighborhood gave them a more perfect understanding of what was "historic," even if the principle of their opposition was not specifically identified in the design guidelines. They "knew" because they had lived there longer.

In Alhambra, without any historic preservation laws and regulations, residents took opposing sides to contest the visual character of competing neighborhood landscapes. While local historic preservation advocates work hard to promote values to protect traditional neighborhoods, transnational immigrants have asserted an alternative vision based on an immigrant ideal. Competing aesthetic values opens a debate about what group Alhambra belongs. With the influx of transnational capital and affluent buyers brings the capacity to erect mansions in the spaces that humble bungalows once occupied. In a competitive drive to replicate the new mansions found in other local communities, Chinese immigrants seek to create an entire regional landscape based on their aesthetic ideal. To them the historic values promoted by preservationists have little or no appeal because, in large part, they do not represent "their" history.

The growing popularity of historic preservation laws and residential design guidelines indicates that battles over the appearance of local community landscapes are becoming more common. Residents in these communities, however, are not always in universal agreement when it concerns historic preservation or other aesthetic codes. And it seems very difficult to secure the agreement or compliance of homeowners with required preservationist preferences, especially if they disagree. By living in old houses, household members may experience their material agency, and find it reinforces or, alternatively, undermines domestic meanings. Reciprocal relations established by inhabitants with the design of their homes are personal and emotional, and intimately tied to the construction of identity and lifestyle. The aesthetic values embedded in home design may also be aspirational for household members; they express the occupants' desires and expectations of what they hold to be of value. They convey respect and appreciation for conserving abstract historic values as a noble endeavor, beyond just the construction of personal identity, and demonstrate a commitment to civic responsibility. Preservation homeowners' experiences, then, are as much about contemporary local power struggles as they are about projecting a historically authentic vision of the moral landscape of their community.

REFERENCES

Boyer, M. Christine. 1992. "Cities for Sale: Merchandising History at South Street Seaport," in *Variations on a Theme Park: The New American City and the End of Public Space*, ed. Michael Sorkin. New York: Hill and Wang, 181–204.

Butler, Tim. 1997. *Gentrification and the Middle Classes*. Aldershot: Ashgate.

Dorst, John D. 1989. *The Written Suburb: An American Site, An Ethnographic Dilemma*. Philadelphia: University of Pennsylvania Press.

Duncan, James, and Nancy Duncan. 2001. "Aestheticization of the Politics of Landscape Preservation." *Annals of the Association of American Geographers* 91(2): 387–409.

Gell, Alfred. 1998. *Art and Agency: An Anthropological Theory*. Oxford: Clarendon Press.

Ghertner, D. Asher. 2010. "Calculating without Numbers: Aesthetic Governmentality in Delhi's Slums." *Economy and Society* 39(2): 185–217.

Hummon, David. 1992. "Community Attachment: Local Sentiment and Sense of Place," in *Place Attachment*, ed. Irwin Altman and Setha Low. New York: Plenum Press, 253–278.

Lawrence-Zúñiga, Denise. 2010. "Cosmologies of Bungalow Preservation: Identity, Lifestyle and Civic Virtue." *City and Society* 22(2): 211–236.

Lawrence-Zúñiga, Denise. 2014. "Bungalows and Mansions: White Suburbs, Immigrant Aspirations, and Aesthetic Governmentality." *Anthropological Quarterly* 87(3): 819–854.

Lawrence-Zúñiga, Denise. 2015. "Residential Design Guidelines, Aesthetic Governmentality and Contested Notion of Southern California Suburban Places." *Economic Anthropology* 2: 120–144.

Lawrence-Zúñiga, Denise. 2016. *Protecting Suburban America Gentrification, Advocacy and the Historic Imaginary*. London: Bloomsbury.

Li, Wei. 2009. *Ethnoburb: The New Ethnic Community in Urban America*. Honolulu: University of Hawai'i Press.

Miller, Daniel. 1995. "Consumption Studies as the Transformation of Anthropology," in *Acknowledging Consumption: A Review of New Studies*, ed. Daniel Miller. London: Routledge, 264–295.

Ong, Aihwa. 1996. "Cultural Citizenship as Subject-Making: Immigrants Negotiate Racial and Cultural Boundaries in the United States." *Current Anthropology* 37(5): 737–751.

Smith, Neil. 1996. *The New Urban Frontier: Gentrification and the Revanchist City*. London: Routledge.

Tyler, Norman. 2000. *Historic Preservation: An Introduction to its History, Principles, and Practice*. New York: W. W. Norton and Co.

Wyly, Elvin, and Daniel Hammel. 2005. "Mapping Neo-Liberal American Urbanism," in *Gentrification in a Global Context: The New Urban Colonialism*, ed. Rowland Atkinson and Gary Bridge. London: Routledge, 18–38.

Zukin, Sharon. 1982. *Loft Living: Culture and Capital in Urban Change*. Baltimore: Johns Hopkins University Press.

CHAPTER 4.5

....

AGRICULTURAL HERITAGE AND CONSERVATION BEYOND THE ANTHROPOCENE

....

DANIEL NILES

Great Nature, ever young, yet full of eld,
Still moving, yet unmoved from her sted,
Unseene of any, yet of all beheld
            Edmund Spencer, *Mutabilitie Cantos*

Nature was dead, but complexity remained.
                        Nicolescu 2002: 60

THIS chapter explores the contemporary significance of agricultural heritage, a concept in which the largely cultural and societal concerns for heritage preservation are mixed with those related to nature conservation and the development of agriculture. As described below, both heritage preservation and nature conservation cast mutually constitutive and relatively fixed ideas of past nature and culture into present and future. Agriculture, too, arrives heavily burdened with meaning, as historically and materially it is "Exhibit A" in the powerful modern narrative of "Culture" gradually rising over "Nature," of human sophistication (intellectual, technological, and institutional) reflected in the societal ability to control nature and manage its native complexity. As an earlier, lesser-developed expression of this societal and technological ability (cf. Stengers 2000: 151–152), agricultural heritage is almost automatically cast as a relic of the past ways of traditional peoples and their less efficient, less useful, pre-modern natures. In the context of contemporary concern for the agricultural sustainability in the Earth System, therefore, agricultural heritage too easily appears as a "boutique" agriculture largely irrelevant to the pressing environmental challenges of the day.

If agricultural heritage is still a handy term to describe long-standing cultural-agroecologies, some of which have persisted for thousands of years (and which incorporate knowledge and practices of even more distant origin), is such environmental experience not of greater significance to the world today?[1] While the ecological value of agricultural heritage sites is indeed gaining attention, the value of their associated cultural practices is still largely unrecognized. This chapter suggests that agricultural heritage represents one of humankind's richest bodies of environmental experience and most successful manners of conveying knowledge through time. Greater attention to the knowledge dimensions of agricultural heritage sheds light not only on sets of agroecological practices, but on the epistemic and ontological fields in which such practices are sensible. Agricultural heritage, that is, provides material examples of alternative knowledge of nature itself. It is of practical and heuristic relevance to contemporary understanding of the Anthropocene.

Holocene, Earth System, and Anthropocene

Heritage is tinged with nostalgia. It calls out to the way things used to be. While heritage preservation may be a global phenomenon defined and propelled by prestigious international and public agencies (cf. Lowenthal 2004, Harrison 2013), its expressions are often decidedly provincial. Its curated images of former times and ways are inevitably tethered to assumed and unspoken loyalties. Heritage operates block-by-block.

The concept of nature conservation (hereafter referred to as "conservation"), meanwhile, tends to range more freely. It is more closely linked to the overarching societal concerns of our time—to contemporary environmental change, economic and societal development, poverty, natural resources, intergenerational equity, and the rights of animals, among others. Conservation orbits the notoriously complex concept of *nature*, the ultimate referent of the objective reality of the world, and given present environmental challenges, a central problematic in the world today. Concerned for the future, conservationism is generally inspired by and modeled after imagined past states of nature—typically those more fecund, balanced, and benign than found today—even if it is ambivalent about the related societal agencies and orders of those former times. The modern conservationist imaginary is not only inspired by past natures that seem of special value today, however. In order to appear as a legitimate technique for the management of nature, conservation must also appear to faithfully express nature's *real order*. It must define the natural phenomena that exist, the ways in which they act individually and in relation to one another, and the ways in which they can be properly evaluated and monitored, no matter where they are found. In short, conservation requires *Science*, a body of knowledge whose universal ability to describe the formal properties of the material world is based on its "cunning" ability to declare its observations as "spontaneous self-evidence . . . above all because the undeniable character of those self-evidences stems from the fact that they are said to be founded upon nature" (Descola 2013, 199).[2] In defining and defending what is literally given as "natural," conservation appears to be essentially empty of social ambition or artifice.[3] Like any other method developed by humankind, however, it is instead linked fast to social imaginaries and institutions (Lemonnier 2002, 2016).

Conservation is an ontological and epistemic project. It is not just a defensive technique or alternative to business-as-usual scenarios, but a primary method by which humans define and seek to enable particular forms of nature. As such, it has been extremely effective in the world. Approximately 14 percent of the total terrestrial surface is currently under some form of conservation management (World Bank 2017), and by 2020 the Convention on Biological Diversity Aichi Biodiversity Target 11 seeks to increase total terrestrial and coastal and marine conservation areas to 17 percent and 10 percent, respectively (CBD 2017). Such goals are inseparable from historically specific societal experience and imaginaries—which themselves can be linked to particular (often colonial or post-colonial) sources and kinds of power (Martinez-Alier 2002, Vogel 2015). The legitimacy and authority of many global conservation goals—even such apparently beneficial practices as carbon sequestration—is still contested (cf. Lahsen 2009, Minteer and Pyne 2015, Wuerthner et al. 2014), in some cases because in institutional terms global conservation goals also presume, or at least postulate, some authoritative approach to coordinated Earth governance.[4]

As a highly institutionalized approach for the management of nature, conservation can be seen as a constitutive, rather than contrary, element of the concept of the Anthropocene—the protean proposition that humankind has become an actor of geological proportion and significance (Hamilton et al. 2015, Schwägerl 2014). As an idea, the "Anthropocene" was initially coined to summarize an emerging understanding of humankind's ever-increasing impact on the biosphere (e.g. Vituosek et al. 1986, 1997, Turner et al. 1990), but the idea that the Earth is now within a "geology of mankind" (Crutzen 2002), or "age of humanity" (Future Earth 2016) has proven extremely provocative.

In relation to agricultural heritage, at least, one interesting and perhaps positive dimension of the Anthropocene concept is that it proposes the end of the Holocene and its defining characteristic, the idea of a stable, law-bound, predictable, and so hospitable nature. The idealized "cohesion of a perfectly unified world in a rational space" (Descola 2014: 59), Renee Descartes's *res extensa*, has been embedded in the scientific mind since the seventeenth century; it is a key image of modernity itself. The advance of the human species has always appeared as perfectly logical and rational in light of its special understanding of the laws of nature.

The story of human evolution in the Holocene has been accordingly *Holocentric*. In the conventional historical view, while earlier Earth environments were unduly harsh and unpredictable (and humankind correspondingly savage), Holocene climate was warmer, wetter, and generally more stable and benign. Holocene nature enabled humankind's greatest achievements, including domestication of plants and animals, agriculture, settlement, technology, urbanization, art, philosophy, science, and civilization. Running through and linking this progressive sequence is a view of humankind as a great *transformer-* and *controller-of-nature*, a view "embedded in a grand narrative of the human transcendence of nature, in which the domestication of plants and animals figures as the counterpart of the self-domestication of humanity in the process of civilisation" (Ingold 2000: 77).[5] In the history of agriculture no less than that of the human species as a whole, cultural advance has been understood as a process achieved through *control of nature*, in which a greater degree of control is equivalent to a higher level of civilization, and *vice versa*. In Earth history, *Homo sapiens* has been the exceptional species and Holocene nature has been its greatest stage.

The Anthropocene concept—especially the connotation that humanity has become "too big for nature" (Ellis 2015)—is now settling into the contemporary scientific mind as powerfully as did the Holocene in former times. Interestingly, its currency even before being officially endorsed by the International Commission on Stratigraphy is not primarily based on any nominally objective indicator, but instead reflects widespread acceptance of the view of Earth as Earth System (Bonneuil and Fressoz 2015). In this view, greatly elaborated in recent decades,[6] Earth is the ultimate complex system, comprised of flows of matter and energy cycling in immense feedback loops in which humankind is entangled and now has the power to alter (Steffen et al. 2004). In the research fields related to contemporary global environmental change, the "Earth-as-system" model is so pervasive as to constitute an episteme. For decades, systems concepts and models have been applied to human beings and communities as readily as they were to organisms and ecosystems (e.g. Odum 1953, Vayda 1969, Orlove 1980, Moran 1990, Scheffer 2009); they still color the major conceptual categories within the science of "social-ecological systems" (cf. Uhrqvist 2014, Bonneuil and Fressoz 2015, Hamilton 2015).[7] The Earth System imaginary is all but inseparable from contemporary understandings of climate change defined by the UN Intergovernmental Panel on Climate Change. It is fundamental to sustainability science in general (Kates et al. 2001), and to related discussions of conservation and sustainable agriculture.

NATURE IN THE EARTH SYSTEM

The global science and sustainability discourse in which the concept of Earth System figures so prominently has had special effect on conservation and agriculture. In more Holocentric times, it was possible in a way much more difficult at present to pursue conservation goals essentially through endeavors to protect nature from the common patterns of socioeconomic development. In most cases this was conservation through the creation of parks and preserves, of bounded territories in which expressions of endogenous nature could continue largely undisturbed. The human role in these "temples to nature" was to serve as guardian and respectful observer, rather than direct participant. This orientation and imaginary has remained remarkably current in conservation discourse despite substantial commentaries offered by Cronon (1995), and Martinez-Alier (2002), among others, regarding the cultural and historical role of the human even in idealized "pristine" natural zones.

While the perceived need to "defend" nature persists in conservation institutions and nature writing (e.g. Minteer and Pyne 2015), in many ways the role of conservation has shifted dramatically as humankind's impact on the biosphere has become ever more apparent to the ecological mode of analysis (Steffen et al. 2004). For one, conservation zones often include areas of human habitation and there is increasing acceptance that some human activities can be compatible with ecological conservation goals (Mascia et al. 2003, Sandbrook et al. 2013, IUCN 2014; 2018). Perhaps more significantly, conservation values are increasingly described in terms of their functional contributions to the Earth System. The rising currency in recent decades of the concept of "ecosystem services" (codified in 2012 at the international level in the Intergovernmental Panel on Biodiversity and Ecosystem Services [IPBES]), reflects broad recognition of the extent to which human populations are inextricably mixed into the biogeochemical "flows" that constitute life in the biosphere. It is telling that one of the grand challenges and motivations for the IPBES was to provide analytical tools and data linking biodiversity and ecosystem services to human wellbeing (see e.g. <http://www.ipbes.net>). The UN Sustainable Development Goals (SDGs) express a similar conceptual evolution, as many of the goals directly related to human well-being and development are at long last nearly inseparable from those concerning environmental quality or ecological integrity (SDG 2016). Re-conceptualized as bundles of ecosystem services and natural assets vital to humankind, nature is *everywhere*; its "conservation" within the Earth System is no longer a sectoral concern, but has finally become a *de facto* global ecological, financial, and very Anthropocene Epoch goal.

A similar conceptual shift is notable in the study of agriculture. At the crucible of population and resource debates since Malthus (1926), and long a central subject in investigation of human impacts on local and regional environments (e.g. Denevan 2001, Whitmore and Turner 2002, Balée 2013, Sauer 1952, Crosby 2004), agriculture occupies an outsize presence in the story of humankind's arrival at the door of the Anthropocene. Population, urbanization, consumption of fossil fuels, deforestation and land conversion, species extinction, pollution of multiple kinds, dietary transition, public health, and so on: agriculture has become implicated in them all, leading what were once relatively particular and sectoral concerns into dialogue with those of global ecology and sustainability.

The problem of *global agricultural sustainability*—construed as a balance between global population growth, global demand for food, and agriculture's aggregate impact on the biosphere—was perhaps most authoritatively and influentially defined in 1999 at a colloquium convened by the United States National Academy of Sciences (NAS) (Fedoroff and Cohen 1999, Dyson 1999, Alexandratos 1999). A key assessment emerging from the NAS colloquium was the need to double world food production by 2050 in order to meet expected increases in global demand, while also significantly reducing the environmental impact of total agricultural production on the Earth System (Cassman 1999, Tilman 1999, Tilman et al. 2002). In terms of agricultural dynamics, this assessment bolstered belief in the need for ever greater levels of agroecological control, often through the development of high-tech systems (or "precision agriculture") to intensify production on "best" lands (Conway 1999). The imaginary has achieved the status of "orthodoxy" (Niles 2009) in relation to economic development, rural poverty, landscape "services," biogeochemical phenomena in general, as well as the features of what is considered to be "climate smart" agriculture (Green et al. 2005, Waggoner 1994, Perfecto and Vandermeer 2010, Fedoroff et al. 2010, Monsanto 2016, WBCSD 2017).

In sum, the goals for nature conservation and future agriculture are increasingly defined by utilitarian and instrumental assessments of global ecological flows, ecosystem services, and natural assets of the Earth System. In this plot, the Anthropocene is the *deus ex machina*; its arrival raises the stakes immeasurably, as in highlighting the significance of human action to (and understanding of) the Earth System, it self-evidently and compellingly extends humankind's special status and responsibility for nature. Almost axiomatically, the Anthropocene concept lends support to the potent idea that humankind is now, and shall likely remain, as dependent on modern technological systems as it is on nature itself (Haff 2013, 2014; see also Niles nd.), legitimizing the search for a next generation of global Earth System technologies by which humankind can finally properly manage the biosphere (Nordhaus et al. 2015).

Paradoxically, at the same time that it appears to oblige a final, "sustainable" level of human control, the Anthropocene is profoundly unsettling (cf. Latour 2014). *Enlivened* by human agency, the nature of the Anthropocene threatens to change beyond known patterns of natural variability and predictability (Rockström et al. 2009); in the face of the possibility of "runaway" or "cascading" climate change, the ideal of technological control is less and less tenable just as it appears more and more necessary. This dynamic Anthropocene nature in which humankind is always already present foists a deeply unsettling epistemological dilemma upon the systems imaginary and the scientific mode in which it is based: unpredictability at all scales, the fragmentation of the *res extensa*.

AGRICULTURAL HERITAGE: PAST AS PRESENT

In the context of the grand concerns just described—the preservation of the Earth's very "life support system"—agricultural heritage might seem a distracting indulgence based in nostalgic attachment to past life-ways and ecologies. Nevertheless, agricultural heritage has recently been recognized at the international level in the form of the Globally

Important Agricultural Heritage Systems (GIAHS) Programme, formally established in 2015 by the Food and Agriculture Organization (FAO) of the United Nations.[8] For reasons related to the institutional processes of the FAO, by that time nearly two dozen sites had been recognized by the GIAHS Secretariat in Rome. The sites vary considerably in nearly every detail—they range from upland tea orchards to elaborate paddy-rice complexes to age-old agropastoral practices—each one of which deserves much richer discussion than can be granted here (but see Koohafkan and Altieri 2016). Despite their variety, however, all GIAHS sites are supposed to demonstrate historical links between local livelihood, food security, traditional knowledge, cultural values, agrobiodiversity, landscape form, and local ecology. As sites they can be seen as "wholes"—cultural-ecological complexes completely embedded in place—whose significance as examples of long-standing patterns of human-environmental interaction and deep wells of environmental experience has not yet received full consideration.

The *expressly ecological* values of agricultural heritage sites, however, are ever more apparent and relevant to contemporary ecological, agroecological, and socialecological science. Min et al. (2016) reference an impressive body of research conducted largely in GIAHS sites in China (including also China's national agricultural heritage [NIAHS] sites, of which there are sixty-two). The genetic diversity, especially agrobiodiversity, found in such sites is one of their key qualities and begs special attention. Over the long term, high rates of biodiversity are associated with careful use and management of local hydrology, maintenance and improvement of soil fertility, and control of pests, weeds, and pathogens—all phenomena long of interest to agroecologists (Altieri 1987; Gliessman 1998; Mendez et al. 2016). In historical view, the relation between agrobiodiversity to surrounding biodiversity raises interesting questions regarding interactions between domesticated plant species and their wild relatives (Hunter and Heywood 2011), and patterns of landscape-level people–plant interactions that distinguish domesticated, semi-domesticated, and wild species (Matthews 2014).

The lessons of agricultural heritage can also be brought to bear on the science of socioecological complexity, as persistence of high rates of biodiversity in zones of long-term human habitation, for example, does not point to principles of simplification and control, as is commonly believed, but rather to patterns of multi-species interaction and network structure (Vandermeer and Perfecto 2015: 99; see also Niles and Abe 2015, Tsing 2015). Similarly, agricultural heritage zones are relevant to empirical study of interactions between different components of the hydrosphere, atmosphere, and lithosphere. The ways in which such interactions are perceived and amplified in local contexts speaks also to long-standing spatial and temporal sensibilities that can inform theoretical re-conceptualization of "system" identity and behavior, including non-linear processes such as emergence and transformation.

Agricultural heritage sites provide rich contexts in which to study the relationships between the proper "agricultural" features of a place (e.g. the fixed fields and principal products) and surrounding ecologies and landscapes. Sites often include nearby forests (or other "secondary" zones) in which long-standing patterns of human activity may have had significant but easily overlooked impacts. In deeper historical view secondary practices and places may even point to the structural origins of the "principal" agricultural features or practices, and so to the origins of domestication in an area. As with investigation of the links between domesticated species and their wild relatives, this line of inquiry returns to intriguing but relatively unexplored historical questions of continuities in people-plant interactions among non-agricultural and agricultural peoples (cf. Gremillion 1997). It also asks of underlying continuities in the environmental experience of later Pleistocene and early Holocene peoples, especially in regions that were ice-free in the last glacial period.

In sum, the diverse ecological values of agricultural heritage come gradually into view as environmental science advances. Are these values not originally present by a different logic, however, one based in a people's body of deep historical—yet flexible and evolving—experience in particular places, yet largely invisible from a conventional conservationist perspective?[9] If so, the relation of what is now most readily understood as "ecological" to cultural knowledge and practice presents another fascinating research frontier. In some ways, the "cultural" dimensions of agricultural heritage are most readily apparent and sensible; it is difficult to fundamentally dissociate food culture from agricultural practices and seasonal cycles, for example, or to draw clear lines between local rituals and institutions, cosmologies, and collective sense of self.[10] In this light, it is clear that the cultural dimensions of agricultural heritage are often as explicitly related to specific environmental phenomena as they are to a particular environmental ethos (though the latter is again often considered as a purely "cultural" phenomenon).

At the same time, the cultural knowledge and practice embedded in agricultural heritage is environmental in an additional sense, in that it also refers to particular perceptions of the agencies, properties, and relationships that extend from what Philippe Descola (2015) described as a people's "ontological sifting of the qualities of the world." According to Descola, human action in particular places is gradually stabilized through "communities of practice" in which

> specific schemes of action and thought emerge, which imbibe life we lead in common with an observable coherence. We can see these operations as a sort of *ontological sifting* of the qualities of the world that impinges upon many aspects of human experience: the *sorting of existing things into categories*; the type of *agency* with which these existing things are credited, and the nature of the *relations* they maintain; the way in which collectives are *constituted* and in which they *interact* with other collectives; the *definition* of what an agent and a patient is, *of how a legitimate or effective action can be deployed*; the conditions under which *a proposition can be held to be true and knowledge to be authentic*; the types of *metaphysical and epistemological problems* that humans are confronted with and the *procedures to solve them*. All these basic features of human existence, along with many others, are instituted according to distinct *modalities*.

> (Descola 2015, emphasis added)

For the purposes of this discussion, Descola points out that the knowledge and practices that maintain longstanding agroecological complexes refer explicitly and implicitly to *what is and can be known*, to the nature of reality, or what by extreme cunning is often named as Nature itself.

This epistemological dimension of agricultural heritage deserves greater attention in itself and in relation to the ecological values now of interest to normal science (Niles and Roth 2016). Knowledge—or what Renn and Laubichler (2015) designate as "encoded experience"—should be seen as a key dynamic element in the persistence of agroecological complexes. If so, the processes by which this experience is conveyed through generations are extremely relevant to comprehension of agricultural heritage as a dynamic phenomenon. Developing this understanding of the evolution of knowledge is a profound challenge, however, as knowledge frameworks vary greatly in form and structure and the knowledge they convey also takes many different forms. In the study of knowledge and cultural evolution described by Renn (2015), knowledge is understood to take immaterial form, such as institutions, that can have important regulative functions in cultural and societal evolution (i.e. that significantly affect family structure, distribution of wealth or land relationships of a societal group).

Renn (2015: 41) also notes:

> "[k]nowledge is not, however, just a mental structure. It also involves material and social dimensions that play a crucial role in determining what actions are possible and legitimate in a given historical situation. Knowledge may be shared within a group or a society. Material artifacts and external representations, such as instruments or texts, may be used in learning processes organized by societal institutions. In this way, individuals can appropriate the shared knowledge. The social and material dimensions of knowledge are hence critical for understanding its transmission from generation to generation."

This passage is of particular relevance to agricultural heritage as it points to the role of *material culture* in conveying knowledge through time. Cultural artifacts are direct expressions of shared knowledge—how to cook or weave, for example, or where to find a particular plant or animal. They are also at the same time linked into "currents of social activity" (Ingold 2000: 346) and wider systems of thought and action (Lemonnier 2016, van der Leeuw 2002). That is, they express a people's "ontological siftings": perceptions of how to live amidst the relevant agencies, relationships, interactions, and so on. Cultural artifacts are in this sense embedded in ethical contexts, as they reflect a people's sense of their proper place in the order of the wider world.

The knowledge embedded within material culture therefore plays a multi-dimensional role in cultural persistence, as "the material culture itself becomes a crucial factor in the evolution of institutions and knowledge" (Renn 2015: 42). In agricultural heritage sites, we can see how varied are the material and immaterial forms in which knowledge is present and conveyed to successive generations (Niles 2017). In addition to the typical objects of interest to material culture studies, the biocultural elements of an agricultural heritage site, such as seeds, agrobiodiversity in general, and even in some degree the wider ecological communities or networks of which they are a part, must also be considered as part of the wider knowledge system (cf. Kohn 2013). Together, over the long term, material and immaterial forms of knowledge create the agricultural heritage context. The mental and material evolve together (Renn and Laubichler 2015; Laubichler and Renn 2015).

Agricultural heritage, in this light, remains one of humankind's most successful forms of knowledge of the natural world. It has persisted only because it has remained socially sensible, vialbe and adaptable, enabling cultural continuity in the midst of Earth environments that often undergo dramatic change. It should draw special attention to the particular understandings of nature it involves in different circumstances, and to the full range of mental and material forms through which these understandings are understood to be present.

AGRICULTURAL HERITAGE BEYOND THE ANTHROPOCENE

Even when recognized by international institutions such as the FAO, agricultural heritage is nearly a toothless mechanism and seemingly of little significance to the challenges of the contemporary environment. It nevertheless provides an important mode through which approaches to conservation and agricultural sustainability can be reconsidered. Agricultural heritage sites provide examples of humankind's knowledge of how to focus native ecological potential in order to obtain favored foods and materials. In cultural and ecological perspective, persistence of agricultural heritage is evidence of dynamic co-evolutionary fields of interaction, rather than of relatively fixed "traditional" ones. In this sense, no agriculture can survive as heritage, but only as a continuously evolving way of living amidst nature. As a field of experience, moreover, agricultural heritage can still inform imaginaries of the future, as it is based in real material and cultural contexts in which the inherent "horizon of possibilities . . . is larger than anticipated by any given set of actors" (Renn and Laubichler 2015: 42).

In this sense, perhaps it is for the best if the threat of the Anthropocene finally cracks the illusion of human salvation through control of nature. Other sources of environmental knowledge exist. In times beyond the Anthropocene agricultural heritage provides an example of human experience of nature in which we can see the possibility of conservation as an active human endeavor, heritage as a living present, and dynamic nature as ontological opportunity rather than existential threat.

ACKNOWLEDGMENTS

The author gratefully acknowledges intellectual and material support of the FEAST Project (No. 14200116) (<http://www.chikyu.ac.jp/rihn_e/project/2016-01.html>) and Small Scale

Economies Project (No. 14200084) (<http://www.chikyu.ac.jp/fooddiversity/en/>) of the Research Institute for Humanity and Nature (Kyoto, Japan) and Department I (Structural Changes in the Systems of Knowledge) at the Max Planck Institute for the History of Science (Berlin, Germany).

Notes

1. Here I treat designated agricultural heritage sites as emblematic of a wider agricultural heritage experience, and use the two terms fairly interchangeably, as properly designated agricultural heritage sites are relatively few and recent, while the environmental experience they indicate is still widely present in the world today.

2. The next sentence continues: "This is an irrefutable argument when it comes to disqualifying rival ontologies." The same idea is presented by Merleau-Ponty: "It is not scientific discoveries that brought about a change in the idea of Nature. Rather, it is the change in the idea of Nature that has made those discoveries possible" (cited in Descola 2014: 68; also see Westling 2014).

3. Demonstrated, for example, at the 2017 March for Science in Washington, DC, at which scientists displayed hand-painted signs declaring "SCIENCE REVEALS REALITY," "SCIENCE HAS NO AGENDA," and simply "TRUTH" (see <http://www.satellites.marchforscience.com>).

4. It is not difficult to imagine that in the future conservation could center on stewardship of nutrient cycles or other ecosystem services (as discussed briefly below), rather than bounded territories. Conservation would be achieved by facilitating biogeochemical "rights of passage," so speaking to a new recognition of the agencies of nature, what Isabelle Stengers (2010) and Bruno Latour (2014) discuss in greater depth as "cosmopolitics."

5. In his expansive survey of the concepts of nature and culture, Philippe Descola also warns of ethnocentrism within the idea of the Neolithic revolution and the related fact that "the values and meanings attached to the opposition between wild and domesticated belong to one particular historical trajectory" (Descola 2013: 52).

6. See Future Earth (<http://www.futureearth.org>); also the review of Mooney, Duraiappah, and Larigauderie (2013).

7. The 2017 Future Earth PEGASuS Biodiversity and Natural Assets (see Future Earth 2017) call for research proposals gives an example of the highly coded areas of research presently considered relevant:

   Proposals should address some or all of the following thematic areas: (1) biodiversity valuation, ecosystem functions, ecosystem services, requisite socioeconomic transformations, and the sustainable consumption and production of natural resources; (2) biodiversity indicators, scenario planning and prediction, risk analysis, identification of tipping points and/or feedbacks between socioeconomic, biodiversity, and ecosystem dynamics. Preference will be given to research projects that show significant potential to advance the science and capacity needed to predict and effectively respond to the scale, pace, and impact of global change.

8. On GIAHS, see basic information available at <http//www.fao.org/giahs/en/> as well as Altieri and Koohafkan (nd); Koohafkan and Altieri (2011); Min et al. (2016); Niles and Roth (2016). I was a member of the GIAHS Scientific Advisory Committee from 2012 until it was dissolved in early 2015.

9. This is a research frontier that extends from a considerable body of cultural ecological research into the significance of land practices of traditional peoples to even the most "authentic" natural landscapes, such as the vast Amazon forest. See Denevan (2001), Balée (2013), and Raffles and Winkerprins (2003) for a small sample. Related studies also emphasize "surrounding" cultural practices within traditional agroecologies (e.g. Netting 1993, Brookfield 2001).

10. For a particularly impressive example of the ways in which agricultural phenomena, in this case the cultivation of maize, are essential to the cosmological, religious, and political order of a time and place, see Enrique Florescano (2004).

REFERENCES

Alexandratos, N. 1999. "World Food and Agriculture: Outlook for the Medium and Longer Term." *Proceedings of the National Academy of Sciences* 96(11): 5908–5914.

Altieri, M. A. 1987. *Agroecology: The Scientific Basis of Sustainable Agriculture*. Boulder, CO: Westview Press.

Altieri, M. A., and P. Koohafkan. nd. "Globally Important Ingenious Agricultural Heritage Systems (GIAHS): Extent, Significance, and Implications for Development." <http://www.fao.org/docrep/015/ap021e/ap021e.pdf> [accessed March 31, 2017].

Balée, William. 2013. *Cultural Forests of the Amazon: A Historical Ecology of People and their Landscapes*. Tuscaloosa: University of Alabama Press.

Bonneuil, Christophe, and Jean-Baptiste Fressoz. 2015. *The Shock of the Anthropocene: The Earth, History, and Us*. London: Verso.

Brookfield, Harold 2001. *Exploring Agrodiversity*. New York: Columbia University Press.

Cassman, K. G. 1999. "Ecologial Intensification of Cereal Production Systems: Yield Potential, Soil Quality, and Precision Agriculture." *Proceedings, National Academy of Sciences* 96: 5952–5959.

Convention on Biological Diversity. 2017. Target 11. <https://www.cbd.int/sp/targets/rationale/target-11/> [accessed July 1, 2017].

Conway, Gordon. 1999. *The Doubly Green Revolution: Food for All in the Twenty-First Century*. Ithaca: Cornell University Press.

Cronon, William. 1995. "The Trouble with Wilderness: Or, Getting Back to the Wrong Nature," in *Uncommon Ground: Rethinking the Human Place in Nature*, ed. William Cronon. New York: W. W. Norton and Co., 69–90.

Crosby, Alfred W. 2004 [1986]. *Ecological Imperialism: The Biological Expansion of Europe, 900–1900*. Cambridge: Cambridge University Press.

Crutzen, Paul. 2002. "Geology of Mankind." *Nature* 415: 23.

Denevan, William M. 2001. *Cultivated Landscapes of Native Amazonia and the Andes*. Oxford Geographical and Environmental Studies. Oxford: Oxford University Press.

Descola, Philippe. 2013. *Beyond Nature and Culture*. Chicago: University of Chicago.

Descola, Philippe. 2015. "Prof. Philippe Descola: Winner of the 2012 CNRS Golden Medal." College de France newsletter 7: 22–24.

Dyson, Tim. 1999. "World Food Trends and Prospects to 2025." *Proceedings of the National Academy of Sciences* 96(11): 5929–5936.

Ellis, Earle. 2015. "Too Big for Nature," in *After Preservation: Saving American Nature in the Age of Humans*, ed. Ben A. Minteer and Steven J. Pyne. Chicago: University of Chicago Press, 24–31.

Fedoroff, Nina, and Joel. E. Cohen. 1999. "Plants and Population: Is There Time?" *Proceedings of the National Academy of Sciences* 96: 5903–5907.

Fedoroff, N. V., D. S. Battisti, R. N. Beachy, P. J. M. Cooper, D. A. Fischoff, C. N. Hodges, et al. 2010. "Radically Rethinking Agriculture for the 21st Century." *Science* 327: 833–834.

Florescano, Enrique. 2004. *Quetzalcóatl y los Mitos Fundadores de Mesoamérica.* Satillana Ediciones Generales. Taurus: Mexico.

Future Earth. 2016. "Anthropocene: Innovation in the Human Age." Issue 1, October. <http://www.anthropocenemagazine.org> [accessed 1 June 2017].

Future Earth. 2017. "PEGASuS Biodiversity and Natural Assets: Request for Proposals." Research call available at: <https://higherlogicdownload.s3.amazonaws.com/FUTUREEARTH/332ef4c9-88f9-46d7-9d10-6e3d91b8dff8/UploadedImages/Files/PEGASuS%20I%20-%20RFP%20FINAL%20(2).pdf> [accessed May 18, 2017].

Gliessman, Stephen R. 1998. *Agroecology: Ecological Processes in Sustainable Agriculture.* Ann Arbor, MI: Ann Arbor Press.

Green, R. E., S. J. Cornell, J. P. W. Scharlemann, and A. Balmford. 2005. "Farming and the Fate of Wild Nature." *Science* 307: 550–555.

Gremillion, Kristen J. 1997. *People, Plants, and Landscapes: Studies in Paleoethnobotany.* Tuscaloosa: The University of Alabama Press.

Haff, Peter K. 2013. "Technology as a Geological Phenomenon: Implications for Human Well-Being," in *A Stratigraphical Basis for the Anthropocene*, ed. Colin Neil Waters, Jan Zalasiewicz, Mark Williams, Michael A. Ellis, and Andrea Snelling. Geological Society London, Special Publication 395.

Haff, Peter K. 2014. "Humans and Technology in the Anthropocene: Six Rules." *The Anthropocene Review* 1(2): 126–136.

Hamilton, Clive. 2015. "Getting the Anthropocene So Wrong." *The Anthropocene Review* 2(2): 102–107.

Hamilton, Clive, Francois Gemmene, and Christophe Bonneuil. 2015. *The Anthropocene and the Global Environmental Crisis: Rethinking Modernity in a New Epoch.* Oxon: Routledge.

Harrison, Rodney. 2013. *Heritage: Critical Approaches.* New York: Routledge.

Hunter, Danny, and Vernon Heywood. 2011. *Wild Crop Relatives: A Manual of In Situ Conservation.* London: Earthscan.

Ingold, Tim. 2000. *The Perception of the Environment: Essays on Livelihood, Dwelling and Skill.* London: Routledge.

IUCN 2014. *The Promise of Sydney.* World Parks Congress Sydney 2014. <http://worldparkscongress.org/about/promise_of_sydney.html> [last accessed February 26, 2018].

IUCN 2018. *Protected Area Categories.* < https://www.iucn.org/theme/protected-areas/about/protected-area-categories/> [accessed February 26, 2018].

Kates, Robert W., William C. Clark, R. Corell, J. M. Hall, C. C. Jaeger, I. Lowe, et al. 2001. "Sustainability Science." *Science* 292(5517): 641–642.

Kohn, Eduardo. 2013. *How Forests Think: Toward an Anthropology Beyond the Human.* Berkeley: University of California Press.

Koohafkan, Parviz, and Miguel A. Altieri. 2011. *Globally Important Agricultural Heritage Systems: A Legacy for the Future.* FAO: Rome.

Koohafkan, Parviz, and Miguel A. Altieri. 2016. *Forgotten Agricultural Heritage: Reconnecting Food Systems and Sustainable Development.* Oxon: Routledge.

Lahsen, Myanna. 2009. "A Science-Policy Interface in the Global South: The Politics of Carbon Sinks and Science in Brazil." *Climatic Change* 97(3): 339–372.

Latour, Bruno. 2014. "Agency at the Time of the Anthropocene." *New Literary History* 45(1): 1–8.

Laubichler, Manfred D. and Jurgen Renn. 2015. "Extended Evolution: A Conceptual Framework for Integrating Regulatory Networks and Niche Construction" *Extended Evolution*, Manfred D. Laubichler and Jurgen Renn, Preprint 471, Max Planck Institute for the History of Science, 1–36.

Lemonnier, Pierre. 2002 [1993]. "Introduction," in *Technological Choices: Transformation in Material Cultures since the Neolithic*, ed. Pierre Lemonnier. London: Routledge, 1–35.

Lemonnier, Pierre. 2016 [2012]. *Mundane Objects: Materiality and Non-Verbal Communication*. Routledge: London.

Lowenthal, David. 2004. *The Heritage Crusade and the Spoils of History*. Cambridge: Cambridge University Press.

Malthus, Thomas R. 1926 [1798]. *First Essay on Population*. London: MacMillan and Co., Ltd.

Martinez-Alier, Joan. 2002. *The Environmentalism of the Poor: A Study of Ecological Conflicts and Valuation*. Cheltenham: Edward Elgar Publishing Limited.

Mascia, M. B., J. P. Brosius, T. A. Dobson, B. C. Forbes, L. Horowitz, M. A. McKean, et al. 2003. "Conservation and the Social Sciences." *Conservation Biology* 17(3): 649–650.

Matthews, Peter J. 2014. *On the Trail of Taro: An Exploration of Natural and Cultural History*. Osaka: National Museum of Ethnology.

Mendez, V. E., C. M. Bacon, R. Cohen, S. T. Gliessman. 2016. *Agroecology: A Transdisciplinary, Participatory and Action-oriented Approach*. CRC Press: Boca Raton.

Min W., Y. Zhang, W. Jiao, and X. Sun. 2016. "Responding to Common Questions on the Conservation of Agricultural Heritage Systems in China." *Journal of Geographical Sciences* 26(7): 969–982.

Minteer, Ben A., and Steven. J. Pyne. 2015. *After Preservation: Saving American Nature in the Age of Humans*. Chicago: University of Chicago Press.

Monsanto. 2016. "Growing Better Together: Monsanto 2016 Sustainability Report." <https://monsanto.com/app/uploads/2017/05/2016-sustainability-report-2.pdf> [accessed July 4, 2017].

Mooney Harold A., Anantha Duraiappah, and Anne Larigauderie. 2013. "Evolution of Natural and Social Science Interactions in Global Change Research Programs." *Proceedings, National Academy of Sciences* 110(1): 3665–3672.

Moran, Eduardo. 1990. *The Ecosystem Approach in Anthropology*. Ann Arbor: University of Michigan Press.

Netting, Robert McC. 1993. *Smallholders, Householders: Farm Families and the Ecology of Intensive, Sustainable Agriculture*. Stanford: Stanford University Press.

Nicolescu, Basarab. 2002. *Manifesto of Transdisciplinarity*. Binghamton: SUNY Press.

Niles, Daniel. 2009. "Moving beyond the Orthodoxies in 'Sustainable Agriculture.'" *Bulletin of the National Museum of Ethnology* 33(3): 421–452.

Niles, Daniel. 2017. "The Charcoal Forest: Ecology, Aesthetics, and the Anthropocene." Preprint available at <https://osf.io/preprints/socarxiv/hk5g8/>.

Niles, Daniel. nd. "Sputnik of our Time." <http://www.anthropocene-curriculum.org/pages/root/campus-2016/co-evolutionary-perspectives-on-the-technosphere/> [accessed June 1, 2017].

Niles, Daniel, and Ken-Ichi Abe. 2015. Humanity and Nature in the Japanese Archipelago. Kyoto: Research Institute for Humanity and Nature.

Niles, Daniel, and Robin Roth. 2016. "Conservation of Traditional Agriculture as Living Knowledge Systems, Not Cultural Relics." *Journal of Resources and Ecology* 7(3): 231–236.

Nordhaus, Ted, Michael Shellenberger, and Jenna Mukuno. 2015. "Ecomodernism and the Anthropocene: Humanity as a Force for Good." *The Breakthrough Journal*. <https://thebreakthrough.org/index.php/journal/past-issues/issue-5/ecomodernism-and-the-anthropocene> [accessed June 15, 2016].

Odum, E. P. 1953. *Fundamentals of Ecology*. Philadelphia: Saunders.

Orlove, B. S. 1980. "Ecological Anthropology." *Annual Review of Anthropology* 9: 235–273.

Perfecto, Ivette, and Jan Vandermeer. 2010. "The Agroecological Matric as Alternative to the Land Sparing/Agricultural Intensification Model." *Proceedings of the National Academy of Sciences* 107(13): 5786–5791.

Raffles, Hugh, and Annette M. G. A. Winklerprins. 2003. "Further Reflections on Amazonian Environmental History: Transformations of Rivers and Streams." *Latin American Research Review* 38(3): 165–184.

Renn, Jürgen. 2015. "From the History of Science to the History of Knowledge—and Back." *Centaurus* 75: 37–53.

Renn, Jürgen, and Manfred D. Laubichler. 2015. "Extended Evolution and the History of Knowledge," in *Extended Evolution*, Manfred D. Laubichler and Jurgen Renn, Preprint 471, Max Planck Institute for the History of Science, 37–64.

Rockström, J., W. Steffen, K. Noone, Å Persson, F. Stuart Chapin, E. F. Lambin, et al. 2009. "A Safe Operating Space for Humanity." *Nature* 461: 472–475.

Sandbrook, C. W. M. Adams, B. Buscher, and B. Vira. 2013. "Social Research and Biodiversity Conservation." *Conservation Biology* 27(5): 1487–1490.

Sauer, Carl O. 1952. *Agricultural Origins and Dispersals*. New York: The American Geographical Society.

Scheffer, Martin. 2009. *Critical Transitions in Nature and Society*. Princeton: University of Princeton Press.

Schwägerl, Christian. 2014. *The Anthropocene: The Human Era and How It Shapes our Planet*. Santa Fe: Synergetic Press.

Steffen, W., A. Sanderson, P. D. Tyson, J. Jager, P. A. Matson, B. Moore II, et al. 2004. *Global Change and the Earth System: A Planet Under Pressure*. Springer: New York.

Stengers, Isabelle. 2000. *The Invention of Modern Science*. Minneapolis: University of Minnesota Press.

Stengers, Isabelle. 2010. *Cosmopolitics I*. Minneapolis: University of Minnesota Press.

Sustainable Development Goals. 2016. "Sustainable Development Knowledge Platform." <https://sustainabledevelopment.un.org/?menu=1300> [accessed June 15, 2016].

Tilman, David. 1999. "Global Environmental Impacts of Agricultural Expansion: The Need for Sustainable and Efficient Practices." *Proceedings of the National Academy of Sciences* 96(11): 5995–6000.

Tilman, David, Kenneth G. Cassman, Pamela A. Matson, et al. 2002. "Agricultural Sustainability and Intensive Production Practices." *Nature* 418: 671–677.

Tsing, Anna Lowenhaupt. 2015. *The Mushroom at the End of the World: On the Possibility of Life in Capitalist Ruins*. Princeton: Princeton University Press.

Turner, Billie Lee, II, William C. Clark, Robert W. Kates, J. F. Richards, J. T. Mathews, and William B. Meyer. 1990. *The Earth as Transformed by Human Action: Global and Regional Changes in the Biosphere over the Past 300 Years*. Cambridge: Cambridge University Press.

Uhrqvist, Ola. 2014. *Seeing and Knowing the Earth as a System: An Effective History of Global Environmental Change Research as Scientific and Political Practice*. Linköping Studies in Arts and Sciences No. 631. Linköping University.

Vandermeer, Jan, and Ivette Perfecto. 2015. "Complexity in Tradition and Science: Intersecting Theoretical Frameworks in Agroecological Research," in *Agroecology: A Transdisciplinary, Participatory and Action-oriented Approach*, ed. V. E. Mendez, C. M. Bacon, R. Cohen, and S. R. Gliessman. Boca Raton: CRC Press, 76–89.

van der Leeuw, S. 2002 [1993]. "Giving the Potter a Choice: Conceptual Aspects of Pottery Techniques," in *Technological Choices: Transformation in Material Cultures since the Neolithic*, ed. Pierre Lemonnier. London: Routledge, 238–288.

Vayda, A. P. 1969. *Environment and Cultural Behavior: Ecological Studies in Cultural Anthropology*. Austin: University of Texas Press.

Vituosek, P. M., P. R. Ehrlich, A. H. Ehrlich, and P. A. Matson. 1986. "Human Appropriation of the Products of Photosynthesis." *BioScience* 36(6): 368–373.

Vituosek P. M., H. A. Mooney, J. Lubchenco, and J. M. Melillo. 1997. "Human Domination of Earth's Ecosystems." *Science* 277(5325): 494–499.

Vogel, Stephen. 2015. *Thinking Like a Mall: Environmental Philosophy after the End of Nature*. Cambridge: MIT.

Waggoner, P. E. 1994. "How Much Land Can Ten Billion People Spare for Nature?" Task Force Report. Council for Agricultural Science and Technology No. 121, Report 0194–4088. Ames, IA: Council for Agricultural Science and Technology.

Westling, Doris. 2014. *The Logos of the Living World: Merleau-Ponty, Animals, and Language*. New York: Fordham University Press.

Whitmore, T. M., and B. L. Turner, II. 2002. *Cultivated Landscapes of Middle America on the Eve of Conquest*. Oxford Geographical and Environmental Studies. Oxford: Oxford University Press.

World Bank 2017. "Terrestrial Protected Areas." <http://data.worldbank.org/indicator/ER.LND.PTLD.ZS> [accessed July 1, 2017].

World Business Council for Sustainable Development (WCBSD). 2017. "Climate Smart Agriculture." <http://www.wbcsd.org/Projects/Climate-Smart-Agriculture> [accessed June 15, 2017].

Wuerthner, G., E. Crist, and T. Butler. 2014. *Keeping the Wild: Against the Domestication of Earth*. Washington: Island Press.

CHAPTER 4.6

....

PUBLIC HERITAGE IN THE SYMBIOCENE

....

GLENN A. ALBRECHT

INTRODUCTION

THE Anthropocene shows no sign of imminent collapse. As a human artifact at global scale, the leviathan we know as the Anthropocene is now predominantly controlled by those who seem to have little interest in heritage as exemplifying the cumulative memory of communities of the valued historic past. The past, as represented by valued built and natural heritage sites, is to be bulldozed or re-purposed to make way for a future that entrenches, even deeper, anything that gets in the way of further industrial and technological domination of cultural and natural landscapes. In the domain of natural heritage, we are seeing the gradual erosion of biota and biodiversity to such an extent that many scholars refer to the era we are in as "The Sixth Extinction" (Kolbert 2014).

The extinction of cultural diversity is running in parallel with the loss of natural diversity. We are rapidly losing languages and distinctive human cultures over the remainder of the undeveloped parts of the globe (Maffi and Woodley 2010). In some respects, it is not hyperbole to speculate on a future where only one type of culture and its values dominate the Earth. Such a conclusion should come as no surprise, since, in our past, the many ways of being human sat within distinctive bioregions and biomes all over the habitable parts of the planet. However, under global development pressures and the homogenizing power of capitalism and its universal forms of design, architecture, planning, management, and technology, both the distinctiveness of place and the human culture that once inhabited that place have been obliterated or are in the process of being metastasized by "progress." Those sensitive to the scope and scale of such losses feel a deep emotional distress.

My work on solastalgia (Albrecht 2005) as the lived experience of negative environmental change has relevance here. There are large emotional and psychological costs associated with the loss and degradation of valued and indeed loved natural and social heritage. If we are to challenge and resist this process, then it will entail challenging the globalized Anthropocene at its foundations. While admittedly an optimistic view in the light of the current political ascendency of champions of the Anthropocene, I wish to forward its opposite world-view, that which I call the Symbiocene (Albrecht 2011b, 2014, 2016b). I argue that the Symbiocene, as a period in the history of humanity of this Earth, will be characterized by human intelligence that replicates the symbiotic and mutually reinforcing life-reproducing forms and processes found in living systems. That intelligence will then oversee the creation of the built environment and its commodities in such a way as to satisfy the key foundational principles of the Symbiocene.

The Symbiocene will be an era identified by a positive affirmation of the value of life and the love of life. Here, a role for public heritage will be to help us cultivate and nurture values that support life in general and human life in particular. As the re-unification of human culture with nature takes place, heritage will play an invaluable educative role showing what went wrong in the Anthropocene and what in the past exemplified the proto-Symbiocene. Symbiocene heritage will be an elusive and ephemeral experience, because, once it is in place, the full reunification of human praxis with life support systems will mean there will be almost no distinctive signature left on Earth that could be highlighted as "human heritage." Heritage as something that defies the "beauty of decay" will be a deliberate act of creation whose purpose will be primarily educative.

The Anthropocene and Heritage

The most powerfully transformative period within the geological era known as "the Anthropocene" (Crutzen and Stoermer 2000) largely coincides with my lifetime. I am a baby boomer born in Perth, Western Australia, in 1953. As I have matured during my time on Earth, the biophysical world I experienced as a child has almost disappeared. In Perth, only remnants of it survive and even they are under constant threat from further development. The institutional structures of my adulthood and working life are locked into a "permanent strategic revolution," while the world I inhabit now as a retired "farmosopher" (philosophical farmer) seems to be on the brink of a global eco-climatic-nuclear collapse. It is hard to be "on the land," trying to grow food with a limited water supply, in summer temperatures that are now regularly over 38 degrees Celsius. My current home in New South Wales (NSW) is on the verge of becoming uninhabitable as we endured a record-breaking 47 degrees Celsius day in the summer of 2017.

Bleak forecasts of a possible seven-degree Celsius rise in global temperature within one lifetime from now (Friedrich et al. 2016) are enough to stop me sleeping at night. A four-degree rise is enough to wipe out most complex life on Earth, including human life. As such, we are no longer talking about climate change, since, as the sceptics and denialists constantly point out, the climate has always changed . . . we are more precisely talking about "climate calescence" or, by definition, an increasingly warm climate (Albrecht 2017).

The concept of the Anthropocene is so arresting because it conveys a strong impression of human domination of the planet. All of the major planetary-scale biogeochemical cycles are now seriously affected by human action with, for example, climate calamity the direct result of human disruption of the carbon cycle balance. The pervasive presence of radio nucleotides and persistent plastics worldwide in sediments and the guts of animals are also presented as signs of the existence of the Anthropocene. As humans have greater impacts, the question of balance becomes even more critical. After some ten thousand years of relative Holocene harmony, the patterns and rhythms in nature (as studied by phenology) are now breaking down and failing those species that are highly dependent on them. The replacement of the Holocene by the Anthropocene will have major implications for species health and survival (Albrecht 2011a, McMichael et al. 2017).

Unfortunately, for humans, we are one such species as, in order to feed ourselves, even with the might of global agribusiness, we still need seasonal regularity with rainfall and weather favorable for good crops and healthy stock. All over the world we are seeing how erratic weather in the form of drought, floods and intense rain, destructive storms and super typhoons (aka hurricanes and cyclones), and extreme high temperatures negate all our technological advances and, in some instances already, reduce the total harvest in crops such as wheat in Australia (Hochman et al. 2017). There can be no "good Anthropocene" in the future. Humans, despite their hubris, are not "in charge" of nature and earth-systems. We have put the human project we currently call "civilization" at risk because the forces of nature will counter our hubris and titanism. As the Gaians constantly point out, life on Earth will continue; however, it will be the current form of human civilization that will fail at the end of the bad Anthropocene.

The Anthropocene also strikes me as an important concept precisely because it is so at odds with how life has evolved on this planet. Once I understood the full implications of being in the Anthropocene, I instantly wanted out. It was a gut feeling, almost like the onset of acute food poisoning . . . I wanted out of it and it out of me. The last time I had felt such a gut-wrenching feeling was when I was confronted by large-scale open pit coal mining in the Hunter Valley of NSW. I had been researching the journey of John and Elizabeth Gould, the British ornithologists and artists, into the Hunter Valley in 1839–40. They both gave graphic descriptions of the beauty of the Valley and its natural productions. Others, also taken by its great beauty, had called this valley, "the Tuscany of the South."

On one journey from the coast of NSW into the Upper Hunter Valley, I came by car over a rise to see below me hundreds of square kilometers of open-cut black coal mines feeding two large power stations and a rail system to take coal to the port of Newcastle for export by ship. I stopped the car and got out to have an unmediated, un-air-conditioned experience of what lay before me. The air was thick with dust and there was the smell of raw coal in the air. You could hear the monstrous draglines and dump trucks hard at work in the mine sites. Great, long, diesel-powered trains belched and snaked their way through the valley as they transported the coal. The power stations ejected huge amounts of steam from their cooling towers, creating their own dust-colored clouds over the valley. Carbon dioxide and dozens of toxic but invisible fumes left the giant chimney stacks in amounts measurable in thousands of tons per annum. Creeks and the Hunter River itself were being seriously degraded by coal dust and the products of disturbed land and erosive forces. The industrial landscape below me was the very opposite of the undulating hills of Tuscany. One local Mayor claimed that his local government area was being turned into "a moonscape" while other citizens objected in vain to the insults and damage being caused by multinational mining corporations.

The colonial people of the Hunter Valley had a history of coal mining but the old underground workings were nothing compared to the gaping open-cut wounds to the land inflicted by the new forms of mining. In extracting coal, the new leviathans were obliterating the strata of history in this part of the world and terraforming the landscape into massive flat-top spoil hills and deep voids full of toxic water. The natural history was being blown-up for the coal, the remaining "solid" Indigenous history of the Wonnarua people was being pulverized by the massive machinery and the colonial history (including whole villages) was being swallowed by an industry with no limits to its appetite. Here was a case study in the loss of heritage par excellence. Natural and human heritage were being sacrificed for a locally polluting and global climate-changing source of energy.

Coal was a vital source of power at the beginning of the industrial revolution in England, and today, coal from the Hunter Valley in NSW is driving the new globalized industrial revolution in places like China, India, Japan, and Korea. If you want to see the Anthropocene in action, then right here in the Upper Hunter Valley is your place to go. However, for some strange reason, most tourists bypass the mined areas and the power stations and head for other parts of the valley where more pleasurable pursuits are to be found. Located on the edge of the mines and coal leases are green rural idylls in the form of thoroughbred horse studs and premium quality vineyards. The juxtaposition could not be any greater. Already some of the vineyards have given way to the mines. The horse studs remain, for the moment, but one industry has to go . . . they cannot co-exist.

The Hunter Valley of NSW Australia provides us with a snapshot of what is going on over the whole world. Development via the use of massively transformative technologies is driving change at a pace and scale never before seen in human history. In turn, this rapid change suits some who benefit economically from the transformation and hurts others who are victims in its path. The "hurt" that some feel is a deep and heart-felt distress at the loss of home as a place of solace and comfort.

Magnified to the global scale, our home, the Earth, is also a place under stress and duress. Earth citizens can now feel something similar to the distressed citizens of the Hunter Valley as the Anthropocene churns its way into every sector of the globe.

SOLASTALGIA

Out of the feeling that there was something seriously wrong with this state of affairs I began to think about what happens when a place and its people are violated by desolating material forces beyond their control. In particular, I wondered what the emotional impact of the psychological desolation of the Hunter Valley was having on its inhabitants. Did they feel much the same as I did? Was I just an unusual "ultra-sensitive," bird-loving, atavistic aesthete? In 2003 I created a new concept to describe this feeling of desolation and I soon realized that it was able to be understood and shared by those for whom I was concerned. "Solastalgia," or the lived experience of negative environmental change, was about to become a new concept on the fields of place identity and human mental health (Albrecht 2005).

I have published elsewhere on the concept of solastalgia (Albrecht et al. 2007, 2012a, 2012b) but for consistency the definition of solastalgia has always been:

> the pain or distress caused by the loss of, or inability to derive, solace connected to the negatively perceived state of one's home environment. Solastalgia exists when there is the lived experience of the physical desolation of home.
>
> (Albrecht et al. 2007: 96)

I have always tied the definition of the emplaced, existential feeling of solastalgia to the state of the biophysical environment and, in the case of the Upper Hunter, the clearly defined biophysical entity was the valley, its river, and the landscape contained within it. However, even in the first published essay on solastalgia, I was aware that "the environment" was a broad concept:

> The factors that cause solastalgia can be both natural and artificial. Drought, fire and flood can cause solastalgia, as can war, terrorism, land clearing, mining, rapid institutional change and the gentrification of older parts of cities. I claim that the concept has universal relevance in any context where there is the direct experience of transformation or destruction of the physical environment (home) by forces that undermine a personal and community sense of identity and control. Loss of place leads to loss of sense of place experienced as the condition of solastalgia.
>
> (Albrecht 2005: 46)

Solastalgia promoted by change to the built environment has never been a major focus of my work since the most obvious impact of mining is on natural and rural landscapes (National Parks, private uncleared land and its native vegetation, and improved pasture and cropping land). However, I was aware of heritage issues with respect to the loss of long-standing villages, convict history and its buildings, colonial homesteads and Indigenous contexts. To some extent they were already covered under the formal Environmental Impact Assessment (EIA) concept of heritage and were considered in the social impact component (SIA) of EIA development proposals.

However, as I became more aware of just how little heritage mattered when final decisions were being made to give mines the go-ahead, I realized that solastalgia applied as much to the built environment as it did to the natural environment. Further, the SIA process, as practiced in NSW, did not even ask questions about a human sense of place, or history and social cohesion. There were mandatory questions of conventionally de-fined heritage, but they too were hardly ever permitted to be elevated above economic considerations when determining the outcome of a development application.

Solastalgia went to the NSW Land and Environment Court (NSW L&EC) in 2013 (McManus et al. 2014, Kennedy 2016). I was asked to help a soliphilia-driven commu-nity group, the Bulga Milbrodale Progress Association that was fighting the expansion of an already large open-cut coal mine promoted by both the coal industry and the State Government. I call them "soliphilia-driven" because they were a disparate group of people united in their belief that their love of the places, Bulga and Milbrodale, were worth defending. They met my definition of soliphilia as an affiliation of people who love their place and the solidarity needed between them to be responsible for that place and the unity of interrelated interests within it (Albrecht 2012b). They, like me, had a be-lief that solastalgic distress could be overcome only when a sufficient number of us act in solidarity to defeat the forces of desolation. The politics of love of place could defeat the politics of its destruction.

I was an expert witness for the community group and my job was to convince a judge that issues like sense of place matter and that they cannot simply be dismissed because they are not assessable in dollar terms. I presented testimony from people in the affected community about the impact of the existing mine and how those impacts would be made intolerable should the mine be expanded. I explained that, in essence, solastalgia meant the personal and community distress associated with a loss of sense of place. The judge agreed with me. He concluded:

> In relation to social impacts, I find that the Project's impacts in terms of noise, dust and visual impacts and the adverse change in the composition of the community by reason of the acquisition of noise and air quality affected properties, are likely to cause adverse social impacts on individuals and the community of Bulga. The Project's impacts would exacerbate the loss of sense of place, and materially and ad-versely change the sense of community, of the residents of Bulga and the surrounding countryside.
>
> (NSW L&EC 2013)

The people of the community of Bulga thus won a significant victory in the NSW L&EC and followed up with a victory in the NSW Supreme Court when the propo-nent and the State appealed the refusal to expand the mine. It would have been an on-going important legal precedent (Kennedy 2016); at that point, however, the mining industry and the State government decided to change the law in NSW so that economic considerations would trump all social and environmental factors when making signif-icant development decisions. When that law was promulgated, the proponent simply put a slightly modified "new" application in for approval and, of course, the planning authorities were obliged, under the new law, to approve it. So, Bulga and its people lost and Rio Tinto and the State Government won! The Anthropocene had triumphed yet again.

If heritage is defined as "those valuable features of our environment which we seek to conserve from the ravages of development and decay" (Davison 1991) then quite clearly heritage in the Upper Hunter was/is being lost. The Planning and Assessment Commission, the body charged by law to make the final decision, at one stage even suggested that, since the mine was coming so close to the village of Bulga, Bulga would have to be relocated or else it would suffer irreparable damage. That has not occurred, so the historic village of Bulga (as have many others) will be sacrificed for the coal industry. Along with the village, another aspect of Colonial heritage identified as important in the area to be affected by the mine is a section of "The Great North Road" which was constructed between 1826 and 1836 using convict labor. It lies in the path of the mine extension so it too has to go. The Indigenous heritage issues are complex but there is some evidence that the mine extension will obliterate a ceremonial area, and the whole area has been deemed by local Indigenous people to be a spiritual and physical pathway (songline) to important sacred sites in the region. In any case, an application by a developer for the destruction of Aboriginal heritage and evidence of culture is almost always approved by the NSW government (The Greens 2015).

I do not need to go into detail to mount the case that, subject to open-cut mining, the biophysical environment will be transformed by land-clearing, blasting, massive machinery, terraforming, coal extraction, and transport. The mine at Bulga will leave a desolated landscape with a final void of almost 1000 hectares which will be over 300 meters in depth. Just in case you might have thought such a void could be a landscape asset, especially when it fills with water, it will not. The water will be off-limits because it will be highly saline and full of toxic metals.

The conclusion, from where I sit in NSW, is that, like so many other once valued aspects of culture and the environment, heritage, even as manifest in shifting baselines of value in the Upper Hunter, has become a victim of the Anthropocene. There will be very few traces left of the older strata of human culture and the landscape will become unrecognizable. Biodiversity as heritage has also been sacrificed. Indeed, this whole area is a heritage sacrifice zone[1] where soliphilia was not sufficient to save heritage and an endemic sense of place.

As an interim measure, with my human geographer colleague Phil McManus, we have suggested how to improve impact assessment so that "psychoterratic geographies," or the emotional and psychological aspects of the heritage/development dialectic, can be incorporated into EIA and SIA. We concluded:

> In this article we examined the issue of a proposed coal mine in the Upper Hunter region of NSW from the perspective of an emergent psychoterratic geography, thereby offering a much-needed conceptual framework and vocabulary for incorporating feelings of strong emotional attachment to place, concerns about potential threats to much-loved places, and the feelings of desolation experienced by those residing in a place that has been significantly, and negatively, changed.
>
> (McManus et al. 2014: 64)

The more inclusive approach I have in mind here has been well expressed by Rodney Harrison's notion of "dialogical heritage" (Harrison 2013). What I call "psychoterratic" (psyche–earth) relationships can be teased out and defended at a local level where citizens have the opportunity to be directly involved in the assessment and decision-making processes, including when community concerns determine that development is prohibited. However, despite the obvious appeal of dialogical approaches to heritage, the Hunter Valley case study suggests that, when push comes to shove, the community and their concerns about heritage will be marginalized.

The Symbiocene and Heritage

I see no real future for heritage of any type in the final stages of the Anthropocene. Even our best soliphilic efforts will be defeated by powerful forces. As public spaces and their objects are privatized, as public service is cut back, and as valued spaces are compromised to be "commercially viable," the past as heritage will vanish. A new meme, one powerful and attractive enough to appeal to disillusioned Anthropocene people where they can clearly see a positive role for themselves, is urgently needed. For this reason, I have created the concept of the Symbiocene (Albrecht 2011b, 2014, 2016a). The concept is derived from the term "symbiosis" which itself is derived from the Greek *sumbiosis* (companionship)—and which shares a root with *sumbion* (to live together), *sumbios* (living together), and *bios* (life)—and *cene* (new), as in a new era. However, the conceptual foundation for this concept lies within ecological science.

In almost every area of ecologically relevant science, we are discovering that two of the foundational rules of nature and life are interconnectedness and "balance," as understood as dynamic equilibrium or homeostasis. The importance of the degree of interconnectedness has been provided for us in the field of mycology. In plant science, in particular, we have seen huge advances in the understanding of the relationships between fungi and roots. We have only recently discovered the immense mutually beneficial associations of macrofungi with flowering plants in complex positive metabolic symbiotic relationship to each other in ecosystems all over the world. These positive relationships help to maximize benefits for the life-chances of whole species. In essence, there is a form of "natural justice" that prevails. From Simard's work we now know that, for example, health in all forest ecosystems is regulated by what are called "mother trees" that control fungal networks that in turn interconnect trees of varying ages (Simard et al. 2015). The control system also regulates nutrient flows to trees, such as to the very young, that need them most. There has also been discovered a role in the transfer of information and energy from dying species to those that might continue to thrive, thus maintaining homeostasis and balance in "the forest" (see Frazer 2015). As Suzanne Simard has put it:

We have learned that mother trees recognise and talk with their kin, shaping future generations. In addition, injured trees pass their legacies on to their neighbors,
affecting gene regulation, defence chemistry, and resilience in the forest community.
These discoveries have transformed our understanding of trees from competitive
crusaders of the self to members of a connected, relating, communicating system.

(Simard, in Wohlleben 2016)

Given that forest ecosystems are foundational for most life on Earth, including
humans, the so-called "wood-wide-web" also represents a revolution in understanding
the total flow of life and these insights must be incorporated into our culture as well as
our technologies. As a consequence of my understanding of this post-Spencerian view
of life, I argue that the Symbiocene, as a period in the history of humanity on this Earth,
will be characterized by human intelligence that replicates, within all human artifacts,
the symbiotic and mutually reinforcing life-reproducing forms and processes found
in the living systems of nature. "Symbiotechnologies," for example, will put humans
back into nature as their alienating and despotic counterparts in the Anthropocene are
dismantled. What will need to be replicated in human systems are the life-principles
that make life possible, to flourish and be restorative. Just some of these Symbiocene life-
principles include:

- full and benign recyclability and biodegradability of all inputs and outputs;
- safe and socially just forms of clean, renewable energy;
- full and harmonious integration of human systems with biogeochemical systems at
  all scales;
- the elimination of toxic waste in all aspects of production, consumption, and
  enterprise;
- all species, great and small, having their life-interests and kinship taken into
  account;
- evidence of a harmony or balance of interests where conflict and cooperation are
  mutually inclusive.

None of these Symbiocene processes is difficult to achieve even given the current state
of human science, knowledge, and technology. If we put real effort into Symbiocene
science, citizen science, Indigenous knowledge, and technology and use the very best of
biomimicry (organic form) and symbiomimicry (organic process) (Albrecht 2015), we
could get well into Symbiocene living in decades.

What is interesting for the concept of heritage is that, if the Symbiocene is embraced,
there will be very little in the way of heritage left behind by its presence. In the proto-
Symbiocene cultures of the Earth, such as the Australian Aboriginal people, there are
so few precious long-term "concrete" remains of their presence because they lived in
a way that satisfied all the above Symbiocene principles. They used organic materials,
recycled everything, built from substances that naturally biodegrade and died
leaving their bones and teeth as material evidence of their occupation of continental

Australia. They also left artworks that have persisted for thousands of years; however, to remain vital and part of a living culture, these artworks such as rock engravings had to be re-pecked by stone implements each generation so as to revive and polish their meaning within culture. Without such re-touching, the current generations lose all sense of the meaning of the "art" and its connections to culture. Without the active involvement of people, these important forms of cultural knowledge become merely "art" or "dead" heritage.

Above all, where evidence of the past seemed inconvenient or an embarrassment to the prevailing culture, these things and places must be preserved or even reconstructed as proto-Symbiocene heritage. In Australia, the colonial assumption of *terra nullius* or "land belonging to no one" was directly contradicted by the existence of stone houses and large engineering works made by Aboriginal people. They were removed from the landscape by those who wanted to appropriate their land (Pascoe 2014). With the support and permission of Indigenous people, such "heritage crimes" (Hutchings and La Salle 2017) can be redressed as a meaningful part of restorative justice.

The remains of pre-industrial cultures are significant because they show that it was possible to be human without violating the Symbiocene principles. Part of their educative role as "heritage" is to demonstrate that human energy and intelligence can be applied to that which is already part of the fabric of life to meet human needs. That process went on for 300,000 years (*Homo sapiens sapiens*) before the industrial revolution so it is vital that sumbiophilia, or the love of living together (Albrecht 2016a), produces a continuous tradition and be acknowledged and protected for all humanity.

The heritage elements of the industrial revolution onwards tell a different story and it is one about the gradual then rapid technological and cultural pivot humans undertook towards the full Anthropocene. The coal and steam revolution becomes a series of steps from Stephenson's Rocket to the world's largest coal-fired power plants, illustrating how humans achieved anthropogenic global climate calescence (hot change), globalized toxic pollution, and precipitated events like the sixth extinction in the space of only three hundred years and most rapidly in the last sixty-four years.

Elements of the industrial revolution that put us on the path towards the Symbiocene also become important examples of heritage. The earliest wind turbines, the first solar cells, prototype electric vehicles, and the places where they were invented and built become key items of heritage. These transition technologies should be celebrated despite the fact that they were made of some toxic and non-biodegradable materials and used non-sustainable forms of energy.

Conclusion

In the Symbiocene, heritage will tell us a story about where we have come from, where we went wrong and how we got back on track again. The Anthropocene takes us into the age of solastalgia and, as a consequence, cultural heritage loss is most likely to be experienced as negative environmental change. As the cultural landscape is homogenized, people will become alienated from their own cultural history and will likely suffer solastalgia (and worse). As Robert Macfarlane has put it:

> Solastalgia speaks of a modern uncanny, in which a familiar place is rendered unrecognisable by climate change or corporate action: the home become suddenly unhomely around its inhabitants.

(Macfarlane 2016)

That lived experience of home-heritage distress will be hopefully short-lived as people look for new ways to make connections within a dynamic conception of place. I believe the Symbiocene will arise out of mass soliphilia as people recover their "humans-as-part-of-nature" heritage from those who wish to deny it. Out of the creativity of the Symbiocene will arise new ways of living with new forms of design, architecture, engineering, and art. There will have to be a new politics that represents a dynamic, vibrant and inclusive decision-making process I call Sumbiocracy (Albrecht 2016a). With all that will come a revival of the importance of heritage and history and the commitment and expertise to tell the new story about the end of the Anthropocene and the start of the Symbiocene.

As argued above, heritage in the active Symbiocene will be always educative. We will keep examples of Anthropocene heritage to show present and future generations precisely how such artifacts violated Symbiocene principles. Despite their design and manufacture to be completely recyclable and part of a fully restorative economy, Symbiocene heritage will tell the story of how we replaced Anthropocene "heritage" with new creations that preserved their function, but revolutionized their form and process. However, we will actually want most of our objects, buildings, and artifacts to ultimately disappear with "the beauty of decay" . . . as everything should. Those artifacts that we wish to preserve will be by acts of choice to display how the Symbiocene is deliberately made to be completely recycled back into life. The conclusive evidence that we are in the Symbiocene will be the failure to find a distinctively human presence located in the most recent layers of the Earth. Hence, in the Symbiocene, our heritage will be . . . the whole Earth.

NOTE

1. Indeed, anthropogenic pressure is having an increasingly negative impact on existing remnant natural heritage worldwide with even designated Natural World Heritage Sites (NWHS) under stress with the conclusion of a recently published study suggesting that "many NWHS are rapidly deteriorating and are more threatened than previously thought" (Allan et al. 2017).

REFERENCES

Albrecht, Glenn A. 2005. "Solastalgia: A New Concept in Human Health and Identity." *PAN (Philosophy Activism Nature)* (3): 41–55.

Albrecht, Glenn A. 2011a. "Chronic Environmental Change and Mental Health," in *Climate Change and Human Well-Being: Global Challenges and Opportunities*, ed. Inka Weissbecker. New York: Springer SBM, 43–56.

Albrecht, Glenn A. 2011b. "Symbiocene: Healthearth." <http://healthearth.blogspot.com.au/2011/05/symbiocene.html>.

Albrecht, Glenn A. 2012a. "The Age of Solastalgia." <https://theconversation.com/the-age-of-solastalgia-8337>.

Albrecht, Glenn A. 2012b. "Psychoterratic Conditions in a Scientific and Technological World," in *Ecopsychology: Science, Totems and the Technological Species*, ed. Peter H. Kahn and Patricia H. Hasbach. Cambridge, MA: MIT Press, 241–264.

Albrecht, Glenn A. 2014. "Ecopsychology in 'The Symbiocene.'" *Ecopsychology* 6(1): 58–9. DOI: 10.1089/eco.2013.0091.

Albrecht, Glenn A. 2015. "Symbiomimicry." Psychoterratica, Wordpress: <https://glennaalbrecht.wordpress.com/2015/04/17/symbiomimicry/>.

Albrecht, Glenn A. 2016a. "Sumbiophilia." <https://glennaalbrecht.wordpress.com/2016/02/28/sumbiophilia-2/>.

Albrecht, Glenn A. 2016b. "Exiting the Anthropocene and Entering the Symbiocene." *Minding Nature* 9(2): 12–16. <https://www.humansandnature.org/filebin/pdf/minding_nature/may_2016/Minding-Nature-v9n2-May-2016.pdf>.

Albrecht, Glenn A. 2017. "Climate Calescence." <https://glennaalbrecht.wordpress.com/2017/01/30/climate-calescence/>.

Albrecht, Glenn, Gina-Maree Sartore, Linda Connor, Nick Higginbotham, Sonia Freeman, Brian Kelly, et al. 2007. "Solastalgia: The Distress Caused by Environmental Change." *Australasian Psychiatry* 15, Special Supplement: 95–98.

Allan, James R., Oscar Venter, Sean Maxwell, Bastian Bertzky, Kendall Jones, Yichuan Shi, and James E. M. Watson. 2017. "Recent Increases in Human Pressure and Forest Loss Threaten Many Natural World Heritage Sites." *Biological Conservation* 206: 47–55.

Crutzen, Paul J., and Eugene F. Stoermer. 2000. "The 'Anthropocene.'" *International Geosphere-Biosphere Program Newsletter* 41: 17–18.

Davison, Graeme. 1991. "The Meanings of Heritage," in *Heritage Handbook*, ed. Graeme Davison and Chris McConville. Sydney: Allen and Unwin, 1–13.

Frazer, Jennifer. 2015. "Dying Trees Can Send Food to Neighbors of Different Species." *Scientific American*, May 9. <http://blogs.scientificamerican.com/artful-amoeba/dying-trees-can-send-food-to-neighbors-of-different-species>.

Friedrich, Tobias, Axel Timmermann, Michelle Tigchelaar, Oliver Elison Timm, and Andrey Ganopolski. 2016. "Nonlinear Climate Sensitivity and its Implications for Future Greenhouse Warming." *Science Advances* 2(11): e1501923. DOI: 10.1126/sciadv.1501923. <http://advances.sciencemag.org/content/2/11/e1501923>.

Harrison, Rodney. 2013. *Heritage: Critical Approaches*. Milton Park: Routledge.

Hochman, Zvi, David Gobbett, and Heidi Horan. 2017. "Changing Climate Has Stalled Australian Wheat Yields: Study." *The Conversation*, January 25. <https://theconversation.com/changing-climate-has-stalled-australian-wheat-yields-study-71411>.

Hutchings, R. M., and M. La Salle. 2017. "Archaeology as State Heritage Crime." *Archaeologies: Journal of the World Archaeological Congress*, published online March 18. DOI: 10.1007/s11759-017-9308-8.

Kennedy, Amanda. 2016. "A Case of Place: Solastalgia Comes before the Court." *PAN (Philosophy Activism Nature)* 12: 23–33.

Kolbert, Elizabeth. 2014. *The Sixth Extinction: An Unnatural History*. New York: Henry Holt & Company.

MacFarlane, Robert. 2016. "Generation Anthropocene: How Humans Have Altered the Planet Forever." <https://www.theguardian.com/books/2016/apr/01/generation-anthropocene-altered-planet-for-ever>.

Maffi, Luisa, and Ellen Woodley. 2010. *Biocultural Diversity Conservation: A Global Sourcebook*. Washington, DC: Earthscan.

McManus, Phil, Glenn A. Albrecht, and Raewyn Graham. 2014. "Psychoterratic Geographies of the Upper Hunter Region, Australia." *Geoforum* 51: 58–65.

McMichael, Anthony, Alastair Woodward, and Cameron Muir. 2017. *Climate Change and the Health of Nations: Famines, Fevers, and the Fate of Populations*. Oxford: Oxford University Press.

Maffi, Luisa, and Ellen Woodley. 2010. *Biocultural Diversity Conservation: A Global Sourcebook*. Washington, DC: Earthscan.

NSW Land and Environment Court. 2013. "Bulga Milbrodale Progress Association Inc v Minister for Planning and Infrastructure and Warkworth Mining Limited." NSWLEC 48. <https://www.caselaw.nsw.gov.au/decision/54a6399430004de94513da836>.

Pascoe, Bruce. 2014. *Dark Emu: Black Seeds: Agriculture or Accident?* Broome: Magabala Books.

Simard, Suzanne. 2016. "Note from a Forest Scientist," in *The Hidden Life of Trees*, ed. Peter Wohlleben. Vancouver: Greystone Books, 247–250.

Simard, Suzanne, Amanda Asay, Kevin Beiler, Marcus Bingham, Julie Deslippe, Xinhua He, et al. 2015. "Resource Transfer between Plants through Ectomycorrhizal Networks," in *Mycorrhizal Networks*, ed. Thomas R. Horton. Dordrecht: Springer. <https://www.researchgate.net/publication/272567309_Resource_transfer_between_plants_through_ectomycorrhizal_fungal_networks>.

The Greens. 2015. "Aboriginal Heritage—100% Destruction Rate from NSW Government." <http://davidshoebridge.org.au/2015/03/25/aboriginal-heritage-100-destruction-rate-from-nsw-government/>.

PART V

HERITAGE, MEMORY,
AND WELL-BEING

MAPPING AUTHENTICITY

Cognition and Emotion in Public Heritage

STEVEN J. MOCK

THE COMPLEXITIES OF PUBLIC HERITAGE

As with any inherently interdisciplinary subject, the study of heritage is characterized by seemingly intractable debates deriving from the various levels of analysis from which the topic must be approached. Is heritage ultimately about the past, or about present-day ways of engaging with the past? Is it a top-down phenomenon, an elite-driven authorized discourse forged primarily at the level of the nation-state and wedded to the norms of capitalist modernity? Or bottom-up, generated as much by the audiences that consume it, and subject to a multiplicity of interpretation according to variations of class, ethnicity, indigeneity, gender, and locality? And is it primarily about things, objects and sites of a monumental nature? Or is it about processes; stories, rituals, and intangible emotional connections drawn between people, place, community, and history?

Weaved through these debates is the notion of authenticity. While the criteria defining this term may vary between disciplines, it is generally understood as a signifier of legitimacy to heritage. For an object, material or intangible, to be deemed authentic is to say that it genuinely belongs to the heritage tradition with which it is associated. But from whence comes this sense of legitimacy? Is it entirely subjective or can it be operationalized and measured? To experts charged with the preservation and maintenance of public heritage—historians and archaeologists, as well as practitioners involved in the tourism industry, monument or site management, or the preservation and curation of artifacts—authenticity is primarily a factor of antiquity, or at least veracity; that a thing is what and from when it purports to be. But to those approaching the matter from a critical perspective, whose focus of study is more the custodians and consumers of heritage rather than the objects and histories themselves, authenticity is more a question of why an object, once genuine, comes to be valued (Silverman 2015: 69). While veracity, or at least the perception of it, clearly contributes to an object's value as heritage, it is not sufficient and may not even be necessary. Once established, the question remains why a given age or origin confers authenticity where a different narrative would deny it. Such explanation delves into the relationship of the object to systems of meaning, memory, power, and identity, carrying us into an entirely different theoretical register implicating disciplines as diverse as sociology, psychology, and anthropology.

Authenticity attaches to objects that successfully reinforce the link between the individual, the community, and that community's history. By revering the same object in unison, linked to a sense of shared narrative and common emotional response, members of a community experience and reaffirm connection to one another that maintains the cohesion of the group. To fulfill this function, the object must therefore substantiate a link to the past, while at the same time conforming to and reaffirming norms and patterns recognizable to the present-day community. What happens, then, when these goals come into conflict? At the psychological level, an artifact, practice, text, or site is authentic to the extent that it can be verified as belonging to, and therefore reinforcing the individual's link to a continuous collective project greater and more durable than her own mortal existence. But at the level of social communication, the discourses attached to these artifacts, practices, texts, and sites must remain fluid, able to reinforce shifting norms characteristic of the modern dynamic society recognizable to the individual in the present—norms often palpably different from those reflected in the past which these objects reference.

Laurajane Smith argues that debates between disciplines as to whether heritage is about the past or present, the tangible or intangible, object or process are irresolvable precisely because they reflect this tension, inherent to the very concept of heritage which by its nature must emerge from interaction between material objects and the conceptual discourses attached to them (Smith 2006: 74–7). While the mind craves the convincing authority, permanence, and uniformity suggested by the materiality of the singular physical object, the social order on which the individual relies for well-being requires that the same object be flexible to a multiplicity of interpretations, authoritative and subversive, personal, communal, and national. Public heritage serves its function of reifying imagined community and affirming identity only by containing the dissonance that inevitably results from this inherent duality; the fact that it is "simultaneously about change and continuity" (Smith 2006: 83). Authenticity is therefore most likely to attach to those objects best able to negotiate this conflict through their ability to channel contradictory forces, with the physicality of the tangible providing a psychological link to a verifiable past and the stable, immutable collective identity it represents; while associated discourses reinforce present-day norms amenable to the cohesion of a modern, dynamic, diverse society.

Operationalizing authenticity as a tractable property therefore requires a method capable of tracking interactions between stable physical objects and dynamic cognitive/social processes, between empirically valid constructions of the past and intersubjective constructions of the present. The best approach, then, is one that frames authenticity as an emergent product of interaction between systems that operate on multiple levels of analysis: individual minds, networks of social communication, and material objects of the natural and human environment, both past and present.

COGNITIVE-AFFECTIVE MAPPING

The Ideological Conflict Project, based at the Balsillie School for International Affairs, has developed a suite of methods for understanding beliefs, belief change, and the impact of beliefs on political behavior, by linking the cognitive and social sciences through the framework of complexity theory, a body of concepts that explain how interaction between densely connected systems, often operating at different levels of analysis, generate emergent properties and behaviors (Mock and Homer-Dixon 2015). Among these new methods, Cognitive-Affective Mapping is used to graphically depict the content of belief systems in a way that reflects the functioning of neural networks, where the activation of one concept leads to the activation of another according to a characteristic pattern.[1] The products of this method—cognitive-affective maps (CAMs for short)—represent an individual's beliefs about a particular subject using shapes to represent distinct concepts and lines to represent relations between concepts. Ovals represent emotionally positive elements, hexagons emotionally negative ones, and rectangles represent elements that are emotionally neutral.[2] A superimposed oval and hexagon indicates ambivalence, a single element that can have either positive or negative emotional valence depending on context. The thickness of the shapes' lines represents the relative strength of the positive or negative valences associated with them. Links between shapes depict relations between elements: the activation of one tends to trigger the activation of the other. Solid lines represent relations between elements that are emotionally compatible or mutually supportive (if you like one you also like the other). Dashed lines represent relations between elements that are emotionally incompatible or opposed. The thickness of links indicates the strength of the emotional connection between two elements.

The product amounts to a network of interconnected elements, as illustrated in Figure 5.1.1.

There are five steps to constructing a CAM:

(1) Identify the main concepts of the subject being modeled concerning the issue in question.
(2) Identify these concepts as emotionally positive, negative, neutral, or ambivalent and represent them accordingly with ovals, hexagons, rectangles, or ovals within hexagons, respectively.
(3) Identify relations of compatibility (solid lines) or incompatibility (dashed lines) between concepts and the relative strength of these relations.
(4) Arrange the concepts and their relations to minimize crossing links. Doing so maximizes graph modularity (clustering closely related concepts) and helps identify highly connected concepts or "hubs."

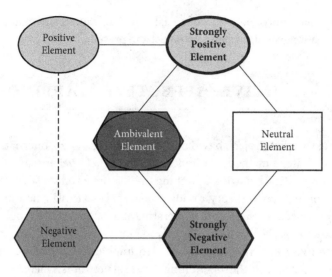

FIGURE 5.1.1 Basic cognitive-affective map (<http://cogsci.uwaterloo.ca/empathica.html>).

(5) Finally, confirm the validity of the resulting map, by either:
   (a) showing it to the subject to see if it accurately captures his or her understanding of the issue (because the method is easy to grasp, a subject can
   quickly understand and if necessary correct CAMs representing his or her
   viewpoint);
   (b) showing it to other people familiar with the subject's views on the issue in
   question; or,
   (c) assessing it against interview, survey, or textual data that reveal the subject's
   beliefs and emotional attitudes that had not been used previously to develop
   the CAM.

Before starting, a person constructing a CAM must have some prior body of evidence
from which inferences about the subject's beliefs and emotions can be drawn. This evidence might initially be no more than personal experience with the subject that allows
the development of a provisional hypothesis about the subject's beliefs. But one of the
benefits of this method is that it allows for input from a convergence of varied empirical sources. Maps could be drawn from analysis of texts, from survey or interview data,
even by subjects of study themselves, or through a combination of such sources.

The benefit of this method to the study of heritage is that it enables us to treat tangible and intangible objects equally as units of data that can interact. Physical objects in
and of themselves cannot become elements of heritage until they are represented in the
mind. Myths, memories, values, and emotional associations are also ultimately brain
processes, similarly tractable as objects in nature rather than ephemeral abstractions.
Objects in a CAM can thus include artifacts, monuments, historical events, characters
in a story, political principles, ritual practices, or even tastes, sounds, and smells, as all
function and interact similarly in a belief system as mental representations. Each object
and link amounts to a specific claim testable against a body of empirical evidence.

Grounded as it is in the cognitive sciences, CAM is predicated on at least a quali-fied methodological individualism. Essential to any conceptual system is the involve-ment of at least one human mind capable of forming concepts. This, however, does not confine the method to the individual level of analysis. It can account for the fact that mental representations and systems of mental representations inevitably form under the influence of the material and social environment. While in principle a CAM is always a depiction of concepts within the mind of an individual, this can be a hypo-thetical individual or prototypical group member. And one can draw CAMs depicting sub-networks of mental representations that are communicated, complete with their emotional loading, to members of a given group or shared between those impacted by a common natural or cultural landscape, thereby offering empirical substance to notions of collective memory (Milkoreit and Mock 2014).

Admittedly, a fair amount of information is obscured by this method. Breaking down mental representations to individual words or phrases vastly oversimplifies both their semantic and neurological content. While CAM may be based on the pattern of a neural network, it is not a neural network; each object in a CAM stands in itself for a com-plex network of neural firings, while attributing to each object only positive, negative, or neutral valence also misses varieties of emotion. This method alone cannot draw out the often significant differences between the positive emotions of, for example, happiness, pride, exuberance, contentment, arousal, etc., or the negative emotions of anger, hate, jealousy, disgust, frustration, and so on. But any modeling language is by nature reduc-tionist, providing tools to zero in on a limited set of factors to draw out a limited set of connections in the interests of a limited argument. While the reduction of mental representations to single words or phrases has the potential to oversimplify, it also provides a means by which the hidden complexity of composite beliefs can be depicted and unpacked. At the cost of representing the nuances of emotion, what CAM can illus-trate are patterns of emotional coherence, and the importance of such coherence to the functioning and stability of a belief system.

Coherence is the central process for problem solving or decision making in a net-work of mental representations (Thagard 2000). Cognitive change requires changes to several nodes and links simultaneously, thereby restructuring the network in a manner that maintains coherence at the system level. Most significantly, CAM highlights the centrality of emotion to any rational decision process, recognizing the inexorable link between cognition and emotion established in current cogni-tive science research (Damasio 1995, Thagard 2006, Vohs et al. 2007) and increas-ingly recognized in the study of public heritage as well (see Smith and Campbell 2016). The network represented by a CAM is formed primarily through emotional rather than logical or semantic associations, in recognition of the fact that mental representations, once formed, are rarely value-neutral. Each comes with a distinct bodily response, which helps associate them with other concepts that trigger related bodily responses.

Representing heritage in the form of a CAM, as a composite system of emotion-ally loaded mental representations, offers a means to track the internal logic behind a given object's perceived authenticity. If the subjective property of authenticity can be measured, it is ultimately as a form of emotional valuation, requiring a method that approaches emotion as empirically tractable. Tracing both the emotional valuation of concepts and the felt connections between concepts allows us to locate and measure the significance not just of "energized" concepts that explicitly feature in heritage discourse in emotionally charged terms, but the underlying value of "banal" concepts as well; objects that reinforce connection between the individual and community simply by the way in which they blend into and shape the language of everyday life (Billig 1995). Objects become important not just for their own intrinsic valuation, but also when they are needed to maintain coherence in the face of the contradictory forces inherent to any heritage narrative. A seemingly banal concept may nonetheless be important as a hub connecting multiple highly charged concepts, or as a bridge providing a semantic link between networks of concepts crucial for holding the structure of the overall belief system together. This can explain why certain concepts that seem to play only a minor role in a given heritage discourse become emotionally charged when their authenticity is challenged.

In summary, CAM provides a means to model heritage in a way that integrates the tangible and the intangible, object and process, the discursive and the affective, the social and the individual. It can be used to track the complex interplay within the individual mind of both official and alternative discourses at the nation-state, group and local levels.

Example 1: National Heritage Illustrated

To illustrate how this method might be used to visually depict the structure of a national heritage, consider Figure 5.1.2 below, a rudimentary cognitive-affective map of the concept of "Switzerland".

These are the concepts and connections generally understood as belonging to and to some extent defining what "Switzerland" is as a unique system of values and beliefs. Of course, it is dramatically oversimplified for the purpose of the illustration. A thoroughly researched CAM depicting any conceptual system as multi-faceted as a national identity will be more than a single hub connected to positively associated nodes, but rather will involve intricate networks of interaction along with negative associations—those things that the nation *is not* in addition to what it *is*. But this simplified CAM suggests a framework for how a national heritage might be depicted, with the nation serving as the link connecting a wide range of otherwise disparate concepts: principles for establishing group boundaries (language, ethnicity, territory), in-group organization (federalism, democracy), inter-group relations (neutrality); founding myths (Rutli Oath), symbols and stories (Wilhelm Tell), territory and physical objects (Alps), cultural traits, even seemingly superficial associations like characteristic foods.

To illustrate how the method might be used to track the significance of a particular heritage object, consider how the following CAM is used to represent the relationship between the nation and characteristic elements of its natural landscape. One begins with

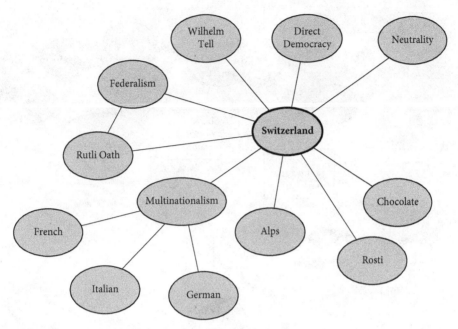

FIGURE 5.1.2 Simplified representation of Switzerland.

a territorial symbol associated with the nation—in this case, the Alps—placed at the center of the map, and from there extrapolates the cognitive and emotional associations that this concept reinforces between other concepts pivotal to the stability of the nation's distinct social system and its self-understanding as a durable immortality project.

The CAM in Figure 5.1.3 represents the cognitive-emotional process by which the tangible concept of the Alps comes to serve as a bridge between the nation and various intangible myths and organizational principles associated with the national identity. The pillars of a distinct Swiss national identity are widely acknowledged as including the notions of multinationalism, neutrality, federalism, and direct democracy (see, for example, Skenderovic 2009: 47). The concept of multinationalism, crucial to the cohesion of the modern Swiss nation, would appear, on the surface, contradictory to the notion of a shared national character, just as crucial to the sense of a historically durable collective identity sufficient to provide the individual with an existential sense of belonging to a common "immortality project." The alpine landscape can be pointed to by members of all sub-groups within the nation as a common and distinctly Swiss experience, as well as the backdrop to events and stories set in the distant past and formative of a shared political project in the present. The landscape could also be said to forge elements of a shared national character, through the isolation it historically provided to culturally distinct communities, enabling their autonomy, shared sense of aloofness from wider European affairs, and consequent ethic of neutrality.

This demonstrates how CAM offers a ready means to visually track the process of how a physical object such as an artifact, monument, or landscape comes to be imbued

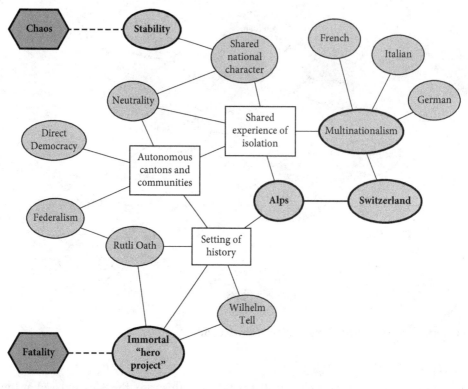

FIGURE 5.1.3 Switzerland with the Alps.

with the status of an authentic signifier of national community. Anyone can see a mountain and form an abstract representation of that mountain in their mind. But it takes the internalization of a particular pattern of associations to know that a mountain is the Matterhorn, and it takes the internalization of a characteristic pattern of values associated with a particular construct of identity in order to respond emotionally to the Matterhorn as a national symbol.

Example 2: Heritage in Conflict

To illustrate how CAM could be used to improve understanding of heritage objects whose authenticity is contested between groups in conflict, let's apply the method to an object widely considered to be at the fulcrum of the long-standing conflict for territorial sovereignty between Israel and the Palestinians: Jerusalem, specifically the Temple Mount complex known to Jews as Har HaBayit and to Muslims as the Haram 'al-Sharif. This precinct, often placed at the center of the world in medieval maps, has foundational status to the three Western monotheistic religions, traditionally believed to be the place where Abraham attempted to sacrifice his son (Isaac to Jews and Christians, Ishmael to Muslims) before his hand was stayed by God. It is understood to have been the location of the First and Second Temples, the ritual and political center of ancient Judea. But it is also designated as the spot from which Mohammed embarked on his "Night Journey" to heaven as described in the Qur'an (Sura 17), giving Jerusalem the status of the third holiest place in Islam after Mecca and Medina. The Haram has remained under formal Muslim religious authority since it was conquered by Caliph Omar in 640 CE, with only a brief interruption at the time of the Crusades, through subsequent periods of Ottoman, British, and Jordanian rule. It continues to be administered by the Muslim Waqf (religious trust) which controls entry and determines rules of conduct, though in practice this authority is at the sufferance of Israeli authorities since the annexation of the surrounding area of Jerusalem by Israel after the 1967 Six-Day War. Prayer is conducted by Jews in front of the exposed section of the Western Wall, part of the retaining wall of the complex which contains original stones from the Second Temple period. After the Temple's destruction by the Romans in 70 CE, the Western Wall developed the status of a Jewish holy place and, since its capture in 1967, has become Israel's most important national shrine.

On the surface, conflict over possession of this site would appear to be irreconcilable: two sides claim sovereignty over the same location to which both attribute religious and national significance. This assumption has, at times, caused the contending sides to misread each other's intentions, leading to violence and hindering resolution of the dispute. In the 1920s, efforts to introduce seemingly innocuous elements into Jewish worship at the Western Wall—candles, benches, and dividers separating men and women—were vigorously opposed by Arab nationalist leaders leading to a series of demonstrations and counter-demonstrations, culminating in the riots of 1929 that appeared to end any hope of Arab–Jewish reconciliation under the British Mandate (Friedland and Hecht 1991, Wasserstein 2001). In 1996, the opening by Israeli authorities of a second entrance to a tunnel allowing tourists and worshippers access to excavations along the northern continuation of the Western Wall sparked violent protests that left eighty Palestinians and fifteen Israelis dead (Enderlin 2003). And in September 2000, Ariel Sharon visited the Haram in his capacity as leader of the Likud party, again sparking violence that led to the breakdown of peace talks (Enderlin 2003). Five months later, he was elected Prime Minister and the Palestinians were in the midst of their "Second Intifada," tellingly referred to as the "Al-Aqsa Intifada" for the site where it began and the shrine that was perceived as being defended. In each of these cases, violence resulted from initially minor provocations triggering fears that Jews aimed to assert more far-reaching claims against Palestinian sovereignty over a site significant to the identities of both groups.

UNESCO has since intervened in its capacity as the international agency tasked with identifying and ensuring the preservation of World Heritage sites. In October 2016 it passed an extensive resolution authorizing a series of efforts by the Waqf to administer, maintain, and renovate the site while condemning comparable efforts by Israeli authorities in those areas under which they claim jurisdiction.[3] As this resolution referred to the site and its component parts exclusively by their Arabic names—including the Al-Buraq Plaza, referred to as the "Western Wall" only in scare-quotes—it was widely read by Israeli Jews as denying the legitimacy of the site's connection to Jewish heritage.[4] In May 2017 UNESCO passed a somewhat softer resolution that did not specifically mention the Haram.[5] But as it condemned Israeli excavation efforts throughout the Old City, it was interpreted by the Israeli government as going even further and opposing the legitimacy of Israel's connection to and consequent claim over any parts of the city occupied in 1967.

On the surface, UNESCO's position is easily comprehensible. If their goal was to endorse Palestinian heritage claims over the site, denying the legitimacy of Jewish counterclaims over the same site would appear to follow.[6] The assumption that the Jewish national movement, historically not shy about aggressive assertions of national sovereignty, would seek jurisdiction over Judaism's holiest site is predictable. And as two groups cannot simultaneously enjoy exclusive sovereignty over the same site, the legitimacy of such a claim by one logically necessitates the rejection of a competing claim by the other.

UNESCO's perception of Israeli attitudes to the Temple Mount might be depicted in the following CAM (Figure 5.1.4).

If one starts from an unconditionally positive emotional attachment to the image of the Temple, as both a religious object and as the political center of the ancient Judean state, the historical destruction of this state and the object at its center will be

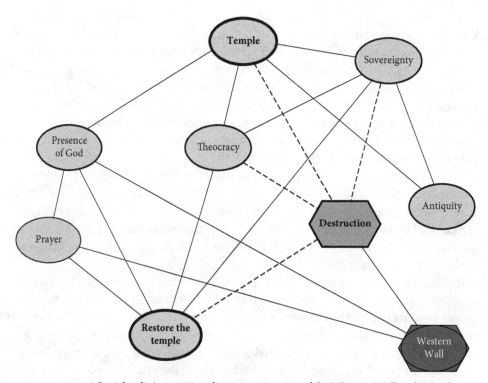

FIGURE 5.1.4 A Jewish religious nationalist representation of the Western Wall and Temple.

experienced as an unambiguous negative. The nationalist will seek to transcend this destruction through a return to sovereignty as it was enjoyed in antiquity. This act would be symbolized by reclaiming the site of the Temple and effecting its restoration, an outcome with a strongly positive emotional value. The Western Wall, within this framework, is little more than a temporary substitute, a mere fragment of the Temple itself, which is the true locus of symbolic power. It may provoke positive emotions as a site of religious significance and character, but the activist nationalist ethic would be expected to react negatively to the passive acceptance of destruction that attachment to this relic implies.

The reality, however, is that though there may be some in Israeli political culture who hold attitudes accurately represented by this CAM, they are a minority: those who combine strict adherence to Jewish religious tradition with the active pursuit of claims of collective self-determination associated with modern nationalism. And while such religious nationalists have exerted disproportionate influence over certain aspects of Israeli political culture—most notably at the forefront of the movement to expand Jewish settlements in the occupied territories—their position on the Temple Mount garners remarkably little public support, even over demands as modest as the right to pray at the site. Small groups of activists have been responsible for flamboyant attempts to challenge exclusive Muslim authority over the Haram; a development that the October 2016 UNESCO resolution notes with alarm, even implying that they are abetted by and ultimately serve the interests of the state. In fact, the decision in 1967 to turn the site over to the Waqf has been upheld by every Israeli government since, engendering little in the way of mass opposition.

This is because the mainstream of Israeli national-political culture tends to hold more ambivalent sentiments toward the historical image of the Temple (for reasons examined more extensively in Mock 2011). While they might recognize it as a symbol connecting their nation to an ancient and durable history, their modern national identity also includes principles such as democracy and secularism inimical to the sort of theocratic system that this history reflects. The beliefs of this mainstream are better represented by the following CAM (Figure 5.1.5).

To a modern secular nationalist movement, the people or culture must be the font of ultimate political authority, not the deity or faith as is the case for religious nationalism. The mainstream of modern Jewish nationalism or Zionism falls into this former category, despite its being the national movement of a people distinguished by an eponymous religion. Belief in God and participation in religious ritual are personal options, and feelings toward the image of the Temple are in fact ambivalent. The Temple provides a link to antiquity and a sense of a glorious and continuous national history, yet it also represents an antiquated theocratic social system most Israelis would reject. Its destruction, representing both the end of Jewish self-rule in antiquity and the end of the theocratic system, therefore also evokes both positive and negative associations. Whereas religious nationalists experience both as negative, mainstream nationalists experience the historical end of Jewish self-rule as negative but the end of theocracy as positive. Someone operating in this conceptual system would have a negative emotional response

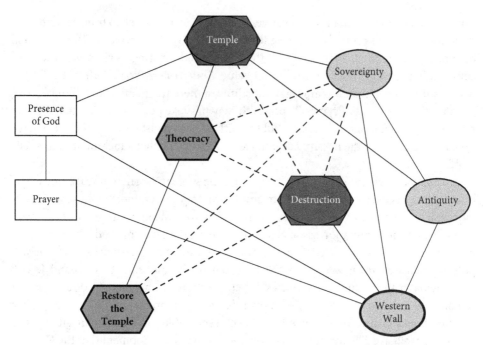

FIGURE 5.1.5 A mainstream Israeli's representation of the Western Wall and Temple.

to the prospect of the Temple's restoration, because it would represent a reversion to a regressive society. This is how the Western Wall comes to take on a more dominant role in Israeli national ideology as a public heritage site. It evokes strong positive emotions through its association with positive aspects of the Temple—its link to antiquity and an earlier period of Jewish sovereignty—while at the same time re-enacting the destruction of the object at the center of the regressive social system that prevailed during that period, allowing for the emergence of the modern nation with which the individual seeks continued identification.

If, indeed, this were a zero-sum conflict for sovereignty over the same object, then UNESCO's stance predicated on acknowledging the claims of one side and rejecting those of the other might be sensible. If the authenticity of Jewish heritage claims to the site could be plausibly denied, its significance to Jews would be invalidated and any claims to sovereignty on such grounds rendered moot. However, unpacking the complexity and multiplicity of Israeli Jewish attitudes toward the object using CAM reveals a visually tractable explanation as to why this strategy not only does not work, but also serves to exacerbate the problem. The only path of positive emotion emanating from the image of the Temple for the political mainstream is through the connection substantiated between the modern nation and a durable ancient history. Challenging the authenticity of that connection is therefore the surest way to evoke a defensive reaction that would justify the assertion of claims to sovereignty that are otherwise not desired but perceived as necessary to defend that historical connection. On the other hand, given a secure sense that the Jewish history of the object was acknowledged as consensus, with safeguards in place to protect it, most Jewish Israelis, outside of a religious-nationalist fringe, would be left with no further felt reason to object to continued Muslim-Palestinian custodianship over the site.

Particularly harmful is the way the October 2016 resolution explicitly treats the vicinity of the Western Wall as continuous with the rest of the Haram and subject to the same claims. The CAM in Figure 5.1.5 shows how the Western Wall comes to take the place of the Temple as an alternative emotional locus of Jewish national, if not religious identity, insofar as it absorbs positive emotions relating to Jewish historical and religious continuity as well as national sacrifice with few of the negative connotations of resurgent theocracy. Denial of this object's special status is therefore felt as a denial of the nation's link with its history, and therefore the legitimacy and cohesion of the nation itself. In effect, the symbol of the Western Wall functions as a conceptual safety valve, drawing in to itself emotional associations otherwise *not* directed at the Temple Mount as a whole. Insisting that it be defined as continuous with the area in dispute ensures that this dispute will retain existential significance for a larger cross-section of the national group, rather than just for a small religious-nationalist minority.

Of course, representing the conflict in such binary terms has the effect of oversimplifying a dispute that in practice has more than two sides. What we offer here is a contrast of CAMs reflecting the beliefs of only two sub-sets of one national group; or, framed differently, a contrast between an outsider's perception of the shared beliefs of a national group, and an alternative theory of the actual beliefs of that group. A more thorough examination of the case could employ CAM to map the beliefs, and perceptions of others' beliefs, held by a multiplicity of groups that relate in varying ways to the Temple Mount and the Western Wall at various levels of abstraction—from the broadly shared beliefs of national groups (Israelis, Palestinians) or religious traditions (Islam, Judaism, Christianity), to the particular beliefs characteristic of various sub-groups or institutions (the Palestinian Authority, The Jerusalem Waqf; the Temple Mount Faithful or Women of the Wall), to the specific beliefs of individual leaders—contrasting these to highlight multiple points of difference and potential miscommunication between any set of contending pairs. Nevertheless, it is hoped that the example of one such contrast at least demonstrates how CAM can be used to draw out nuances of how the same physical object can evoke different meanings and emotional import for different groups, revealing avenues for conflict resolution that are not visible when the dispute is framed as a zero-sum competition for the object's possession.

CONCLUSION

Contradictions are inherent to the very concept of heritage, a field of human experience that emerges through interaction between past and present, between continuity and change, between the material and the intangible, between the individual and the community. Objects of a given heritage will therefore be felt authentic to the extent that they are able to comfortably embody and potentially resolve this system of contradictions, thereby effecting the reification of the imagined community that the individual relies on for ultimate meaning and social stability. A method capable of revealing the source of an object's perceived authenticity must therefore be capable of framing this property as the emergent product of dense interaction between systems at different levels of analysis: the individual mind, systems of social communication, and systems of the natural-material environment.

Cognitive-affective mapping allows us to locate objects of radically different natures—tangible and intangible, material, performative, discursive, and affective—where they meet and interact on common ground: as mental representations; tangible brain processes that are tractable at least in principle, even if our knowledge of their composition and function is still developing. It can illuminate how a given object connects the individual to intangible values that function to provide a sense of belonging to the group while reinforcing principles that maintain social cohesion. Particularly in conflict situations, CAM offers a fast and easy means to explain how heritage objects acquire existential significance to members of a given group otherwise difficult for outsiders to that group to fathom. It can also show how objects are experienced and understood differently by different groups, sub-groups, and individuals within a group, thereby highlighting points of misunderstanding and potentially revealing creative avenues for conflict resolution.

The emotions aroused by heritage objects are not just given irrational attachments. There is a logic and pattern to them that can be discerned, mapped, and predicted. Treating emotional valuations attached to heritage objects as products of the mind prevents us from dismissing them as irrational and therefore unfathomable factors. They can be understood, given the right tools.

Notes

1. For more on the method, see P. Thagard (2010) "EMPATHICA: A Computer Support System with Visual Representations for Cognitive-affective Mapping," in *Proceedings of the Workshop on Visual Reasoning and Representation*, Menlo Park, CA: AAAI Press, 79–81; and Thomas Homer-Dixon, Manjana Milkoreit, Steven J. Mock, Tobias Schröder, Paul Thagard 2014. *The Conceptual Structure of Social Disputes: Cognitive-Affective Maps as a Tool for Conflict Analysis and Resolution*, SAGE Open: <https://doi.org/10.1177/2158244014526210>.
2. Where color is available, positive objects are rendered green (go), negative ones red (stop), neutral ones yellow, and ambivalent objects purple.
3. <http://www.haaretz.com/israel-news/1.747982>; October 18, 2016.
4. <http://www.haaretz.com/israel-news/1.747314>; October 13, 2016.
5. <http://www.haaretz.com/israel-news/1.786832>; May 3, 2017.
6. Though, to be fair, the position of the whole of the organization cannot be discerned from these two resolutions alone, and the Director-General of UNESCO has explicitly rejected the claim that her organization denies the Jewish historical connection to Jerusalem or to the sites in question: <http://www.jpost.com/Christian-News/There-is-no-denying-Jewish-ties-to-Jerusalem-UNESCO-head-says-486136>.

REFERENCES

Billig, Michael. 1995. *Banal Nationalism*. London: Sage Publications.

Damasio, Antonio R. 1995. *Descartes' Error: Emotion, Reason, and the Human Brain*. New York: Harper Perennial.

Enderlin, Charles. 2003. *Shattered Dreams: The Failure of the Peace Process in the Middle East, 1995–2002*. Translated by S. Fairfield. New York: Other Press.

Friedland, Roger, and Richard D. Hecht. 1991. "The Politics of Sacred Place: Jerusalem's Temple Mount," in *Sacred Places and Profane Spaces: Essays in the Geographies of Judaism, Christianity and Islam*, ed. Jamie Scott and Paul Simpson-Housley. Westport: Greenwood Press, 21–61.

Milkoreit, Manjana, and Steven Mock. 2014. "The Networked Mind: Collective Identities as the Key to Understanding Conflict," in *Networks and Network Analysis for Defense and Security*, ed. Anthony J. Masys. Cham: Springer, 161–188.

Mock, Steven J. 2011. *Symbols of Defeat in the Construction of National Identity*. New York: Cambridge University Press.

Mock, Steven, and Thomas Homer-Dixon. 2015. *The Ideological Conflict Project: Theoretical and Methodological Foundations*. CIGI Papers no. 74: <https://www.cigionline.org/sites/default/files/cigi_paper_74_web_0.pdf>.

Silverman, Helaine. 2015. "Heritage and Authenticity," in *The Palgrave Handbook of Contemporary Heritage Research*, ed. Emma Waterton and Steve Watson. Basingstoke: Palgrave MacMillan, 69–88.

Skenderovic, Damir. 2009. *The Radical Right in Switzerland: Continuity and Change, 1945–2000*. New York and Oxford: Berghahn Books.

Smith, Laurajane. 2006. *Uses of Heritage*. London: Routledge.

Smith, Laurajane, and Gary Campbell. 2016. "The Elephant in the Room: Heritage, Affect, and Emotion," in *A Companion to Heritage Studies*, ed. William Logan, Máiréad Nic Craith, and Ullrich Kockel. Oxford: Wiley Blackwell, 443–460.

Thagard, Paul. 2000. *Coherence in Thought and Action: Life and Mind*. Cambridge, MA: MIT.

Thagard, Paul. 2006. *Hot Thought: Mechanisms and Applications of Emotional Cognition*. Cambridge, MA: MIT.

Vohs, Kathleen D., Roy F. Baumeister, and Geroge Loewenstein, eds. 2007. *Do Emotions Help Or Hurt Decision Making?: A Hedgefoxian Perspective*. New York: Russell Sage Foundation.

Wasserstein, Bernard. 2001. *Divided Jerusalem: The Struggle for the Holy City*. New Haven: Yale University Press.

CHAPTER 5.2

UNDERSTANDING WELL-BEING

A Mechanism for Measuring the Impact of Heritage Practice on Well-Being

FAYE SAYER

BACKGROUND

WELL-BEING is difficult to accurately define due in part to its intangible nature (Griffin 1988). For the purposes of this chapter, well-being is defined as a facet of an individual's overall self perception, attributed to a combination of physical, social, and psychological variables (Dodge, Daly, Huyton, and Sanders 2012). Positive well-being is consistent with the concepts of "happiness" and mental good health; as such a person could be deemed to have positive well-being if they have positive perceptions of themselves and the surrounding environment (Lyubomirsky, Sheldon, and Schkade 2005). Well-being is associated with physical health and quality of life, and often used interchangeably with happiness, which is associated with good mental health, personal satisfaction, and positive emotional states (Griffin 1988, Seligman 2011, McNaught and Knight 2011, Seligman 2011). Positive well-being has been linked to high levels of personal happiness (McNaught and Knight 2011, Seligman 2011) and is identified and measured through various quantitative variables, for example, job satisfaction or the perception that life is meaningful and worthwhile (Lyubomirsky, Sheldon, and Schkade 2005). As such, an individual giving a score of 10 out of 10 for job satisfaction could be inferred to have high levels of personal well-being.

Improving well-being has become a political goal for many international and national organizations and governments. For example, the United Nations has investigated well-being on a global scale and the UK Government's Office of National Statistics has attempted to capture, measure, and note changes in society's well-being, which it has measured through positive and negative associations across categories such as satisfaction, worthwhileness, personal happiness, and anxiety (Office for National Statistics 2013). In these and other contexts, well-being has become a hallmark of a "healthy" society's development.

Mirroring a trend from many countries around the world, including Bhutan, the United States, and Poland, the UK government commissioned a national survey to measure well-being (Office for National Statistics 2013). The Office for National Statistics (ONS) well-being survey measured changes in UK population over a three-year period. This survey was based on both objective and subjective measures, which consisted of forty-one headline measures in ten domains, including: health, where we live, what we do, and our relationships (Evans, Macrory, and Randall 2015: 1). This aimed to chart how lives had improved, deteriorated, or remained static over time (Evans et al. 2015: 2). The questions for this study were, in part, based on those from the Health Questionnaire (Beaumont and Lofts 2013: 1, Goldberg and Hillier 1979). The ONS survey was based on an 11-point Likert scale (ranging 0–10). This scale was uniformly selected for all the questions in the ONS survey to enable comparison and analysis across different sections, to produce more consistent responses, and because it is considered a simple method for the respondent.

In 2008, the New Economics Foundation, supported by the UK government, qualitatively researched what made people happy and produced five evidence-based actions for achieving well-being (Aked, Marks, Cordon, and Thompson 2008). Paraphrased, these were:

1. making or strengthening social connections;
2. engaging in physical activity;
3. being curious and aware of surroundings;
4. learning new things;
5. volunteering or contributing to one's local community.

Projects that offer participants the attributes listed above are therefore likely to result in increased well-being. In particular, I have suggested that personal involvement in community projects, specifically archaeological excavations, that proactively engage individuals with their heritage, whilst also connecting people and helping them to learn, had the potential to improve participant well-being (Sayer 2015). These benefits to be derived from heritage projects have previously been identified by multiple sources (i.e. Darvill 1995, Holtorf 2005, Renfrew 2006), typically without the support of either quantitative or qualitative evidence. More recently, limited research has been undertaken that begins to effectively test these assertions, suggesting that it is possible to gather demonstrable evidence that heritage does have a beneficial social role (Simpson and Williams 2008, Kiddey and Schofield 2011, McGhee 2012, Nissinaha and Soininen 2014, Sayer and Sayer 2016, Nimenko and Simpson 2014, Finnegan 2016, Kindleysides and Biglands 2015).

The Value of the Humanistic Approach to Studying Well-being in Heritage

The humanistic paradigm proposes that individuals can alter the conditions of their existence, such as feelings of happiness, through action (Hamilakis and Efthimis 2013). The application of this humanist approach to heritage practice considers the socio-situational frameworks in which heritage projects operate, allowing us to better understand heritage's role and value within its community setting. Through this lens, heritage projects are viewed as a social practice, which can reflect and contribute to a community's image of itself (English Heritage 2000, 2006, Thomas 2004: 195). Heritage has become regarded as a social activity, in which societal and cultural boundaries are overcome and community relationships and collective partnerships are formed (Hamilakis and Efthimis 2013: 181). This rethinking of heritage processes and values has led to suppositions that active participation in heritage can influence personal and community well-being, offering individuals opportunities to participate in collective action. This viewpoint has encouraged heritage professionals to engage with other disciplines, such as arts and public health, which have developed longstanding experience with engagement techniques to provide wider benefits and value for communities and individuals, including mental health services and greater inclusion of marginalized or minority communities (Fujiwara, Cornwall, and Dolan 2014, English Heritage 2006, 2014).

The wider impacts of heritage activity on an engaged community has been researched and discussed by a number of professionals and academics (e.g. Thomas 2004: 1, Lipe 1984, 2007, Darvill 1995, Holtorf 2005, Ascherson 2000, Simpson and Williams 2008, Simpson 2010, Cunliffe 1981, Hodder 2000, Kiddey and Schofield 2011, Renfrew 2006, Smith 2004, McGhee 2012, Nissinaha and Soininen 2014). Indeed, research into the social values of heritage reflects changing approaches to value analysis within the sector, with many ideas based on the concept of value systems, in which different values form networks that interact and impact on each other. As such, the past is perceived as active in the present, impacting on both current and future individual and community values (Simpson 2010). The concept of interrelating value networks has enabled heritage professionals to focus on practice that has societal impact (Kiddey and Schofield 2011, Simpson and Williams 2008, Simpson 2010, Smith 2004, Nissinaho and Soininen 2014, McGhee 2012).

Recent ethnographically situated heritage research, specifically that involving community heritage projects including the Turbo Island Project, Oakington "Bones without Barriers," and Ministry of Defence, Defence Archaeology Group, have provided qualitative evidence of the social well-being impacts of heritage projects on the public (Kiddey and Schofield 2011, Sayer and Sayer 2016, Nimenko and Simpson 2014, Finnegan 2016, Kindleysides and Biglands 2015, Belford 2011). These positive social impacts included those directly linked to well-being such as:

- building confidence;
- team-working;

- forming relationships and making friends and breaking down barriers;
- reintegration of disparate groups back into society;
- reducing anti-social behavior;
- improving communication skills;
- developing a feeling of ownership;
- developing a sense of community.

Darvill (1995) identified the role of heritage in helping to create well-being, specifically through its ability to generate a sense of belonging and to connect people to the present by using the past, with heritage projects and sites acting as mechanisms for personal and communal interaction with one another and with their environment. Museums and galleries have long engaged in discourse relating to well-being, providing both quantitative and qualitative evaluative evidence and outlining methodologies to inform future practice (Thomson et al. 2012, Smiraglia 2015, Chatterjee and Camic 2015, Kindleysides and Binglands 2015). Yet the role of heritage in supporting individual and community well-being, for example community archaeology excavations, has in the majority of cases only been considered through qualitative surveys and individual case studies rather than wider studies utilizing mixed methods (McGhee 2012, Atalay 2007, Simpson 2010, Belford 2011). As such, the potential of heritage as a social practice that impacts upon "public health" and well-being is not being consistently evaluated, and methods and strategies for best practice have not yet been effectively developed.

However, the potential impact that heritage can have on personal and communal well-being has inspired new approaches in the design of recent heritage projects. For example, the Human Henge project utilizes the historical landscapes at Stonehenge as a backdrop to support mental health (<http://www.humanhenge.org>). The Human Henge project is funded by HLF, Aylesbury Area Board, and English Heritage and is a partnership project between public health, heritage organizations, and universities, including: the Restoration Trust, Richmond Fellowship, English Heritage, and Bournemouth University. This project demonstrates that adapting and applying public health perspectives and collaborating with a team of multi-disciplinary professionals holds the key to better understanding the role heritage has in improving well-being and tackling mental health issues (Chatterjee and Camic 2015).

Existing Methods

Qualitative

Studies of social values initially focused on using qualitative social science methods to understand the complexities and intangibility of values (Jones 2004, Simpson 2010). Early on, researchers believed that quantitative data would not provide evidence of values; as such, quantitative methods such as demographic analysis, visitor numbers, and close question surveys were not used to assist in understanding personal and social values (Merriman 2004, Jones 2004, Simpson 2010, Whelan 2015). Instead, qualitative studies used interviews, open questions, and conversational and behavioral analysis to assess the myriad social benefits of heritage. Research frequently relied on the thematic analysis of answers based on constructivist theories and attempted to find patterns for changes in social values based on engagement with heritage (Jones 2004, Simpson 2010, Avrami, Mason, and La Torre 2000, Nissinaho and Soininen 2014, McGhee 2012).

Qualitative data from conversations, log books, open-ended questions, personal reflections, and behavioral analysis can provide data for understanding key changes to individual mental health brought about by participation in specific heritage activities (Kindleysides and Biglands 2015, Finnegan 2016). Qualitative studies have enabled the identification of thematic patterns of behavior and changes to individual and community social values that can be linked to well-being (Kindleysides and Biglands 2015, Sayer and Sayer 2016, Nimenko and Simpson 2014). Studies of heritage and well-being using qualitative evaluation methods, including those by Kindleysides and Biglands at Beamish Museum, The Living Museum of the North, and by Finnegan at the Ministry of Defence as part of Operation Nightingale, an initiative to help rehabilitate injured soldiers through involving them in archaeological investigation, indicate that heritage can indeed play a role in improving well-being (Kindleysides and Biglands 2015, Finnegan 2016).

Quantitative

Recently, heritage professionals and academics have recognized that relying upon qualitative data alone is problematic. Qualitative data are not easily amenable to statistical analysis, which can hinder more finely grained analyses of the social and personal impacts of involvement in heritage activity (Merriman 2004, Thomson et al. 2012). As a result, heritage evaluation has begun to utilize quantitative methods that are accepted and approved by government agencies and health care professionals, enabling heritage researchers to incorporate pre-existing evaluative frameworks and therefore potentially influence policy relating to well-being (Chatterjee and Camic 2015).

The museum sector has led the way in implementing formal quantitative public health–based evaluative methods to assess the impact of heritage outreach on well-being (Thomson et al. 2011, 2012, <http://www.happiermuseumproject.org>, Thomson and Chatterjee 2014, Chatterjee and Camic 2015). Researchers at University College London (UCL) investigated the impact on hospital patients of handling archaeological and historical objects (Thomson et al. 2012, Thomson and Chatterjee 2014). This study used quantitative methods from public health studies, including the visual analogue scale (VAS, EuroQol Group 1990) and the positive and negative effect schedule (PANAS, Watson, Clark, and Tellegen 1988), to analyze changes in well-being over time. Results highlighted that practical engagement with heritage had positive impacts on well-being. These studies and the subsequent UCL's Museum Well-being Measures Toolkit provide guidelines and strategies that the wider heritage sector should adapt to assess the impact of their projects on participant well-being (Thomson and Chatterjee 2013, Chatterjee and Camic 2015). Furthermore, these evaluation methods enable the surveys to be modified so as to be age-specific and contextual, providing tangible results of project impact.

PANAS measures positive and negative moods through words, which are linked to positive and negative emotions, measured by individual choice against a 1–5 Likert scale (Watson, Clark, and Tellegen 1988): the participant chooses a number from one to five for each emotive word on the list (1 = not at all, 5 = extremely). Positive words included attentive, interested, alert, excited, enthusiastic, strong, inspired, active, proud, determined. Negative words included distressed, jittery, guilty, afraid, irritable, ashamed, scared, hostile, nervous, and upset. Positive and negative emotions are scored; if a participant scores a low score on positive words and a high score on negative words, they are deemed to be unhappy. An increase in positive word scores over the course of a project indicates increased well-being. Changing patterns in positive and negative word associations are quickly highlighted, thus assisting in impact analysis at each stage of the project.

MVAS utilizes modified elements of the Visual Analogue Scale (VAS), the General Health Questionnaire (GHQ), the ONS well-being Survey, and the Warwick–Edinburgh mental well-being scale (EuroQol Group 1990, Evans, Macrory, and Randall 2015, Goldberg and Hillier 1979, Tennant, Hiller, Fishwick, Platt, Joseph, Weich, Parkinson, Secker, and Stewart-Brown 2007). For participant understanding and ease a simplified 1–10 Likert-type scale is suggested. The questions were modified to incorporate the aforementioned New Economic Foundation five evidence-based actions for well-being (Aked, Marks, Cordon, and Thompson 2008). For example:

- Thinking about yourself, how interested are you in the world around you?
- Thinking about your own life, at present how connected do you feel to people around you?
- When considering your personal happiness, at the moment how happy would you rate yourself?
- Thinking about your own life and personal circumstances, how satisfied are you with your life as a whole?

High scores in each of these categories would be associated with high levels of personal happiness. Consequently, an increase in score during the project could be linked to increased well-being. If a pattern of increased well-being emerges from participants during the lifespan of a project, this could be attributed to participation in heritage activities.

Mixed Method

A mixed-method approach to evaluation involves combining quantitative and qualitative approaches to collect multiple data sets, such as PANAS, VAS, conversational data, open-ended question surveys, interview data, and behavioral analysis data (Nimenko and Simpson 2014, Sayer and Sayer 2016). This approach provides data patterns that map how specific heritage practices and methods are associated with specific behavioral changes, which can be linked to personal and community well-being. This mixed-method evaluation approach enables heritage professionals to understand not only the "impact" heritage has on well-being, but the actions required to create this impact (Sayer and Sayer 2016).

The mixed-method approach has helped to understand how heritage can change complex social dynamics and how these dynamics are linked to positive changes in well-being (Nimenko and Simpson 2014, Finnegan 2016, Kindleysides and Biglands 2015, Sayer and Sayer 2016). This has shed light on the complex social relationships that community members have with themselves and their past, and how heritage practice can help individuals reconnect with their own physical and social identity, and resultantly impact on their personal well-being. For example a study by Sayer and Sayer (2016: 158) demonstrated that personal involvement in the community heritage project "Bones without Barriers," which enabled the public to view the excavation of Anglo-Saxon human remains, helped participants deal with death, and relationships with the dead.

Changing Impacts Over Time

My own research into well-being and heritage applied MVAS and PANAS to a variety of heritage projects involving both adults and children (Sayer 2015). The first of these studies was on 170 individuals participating in six student- and community-oriented UK and US archaeological excavations from a range of archaeological time periods, including prehistoric, Roman, Anglo-Saxon, and post-Modern sites (Sayer 2015: 257). Participants of case-study excavations were asked to complete PANAS and MVAS surveys on three separate occasions during each project, week one, week two, and week three.

For the analysis, MVAS and PANAS data were divided into two groups of students and community participants to enable a comparison in results. Statistical analysis of the MVAS and PANAS results included comparing the percentage difference between mean results from week 1 and week 3, and looking for overarching data patterns. Participants were excluded from the analysis if one score was missing; thus, the number of participants was significantly reduced from 170 to 92.

Statistical significance was determined through standard deviation; for example, lower variability between results was deemed to illustrate patterns of behavior. Significance tests, such as the Wilcoxon paired sample significance test, were applied on participant scores from week 1 and week 3 (< p value) to test for improvement in well-being over time. Results were deemed statistically significant below .025 (2.5%). The Wilcoxon test was used on pairs of data from two related data-sets (for example data from week 1 and week 3). A dependent variable was measured at a continuous level; for example, MVAS 1–10-point scale and PANAS 5-point scale.

Mean MVAS results from week 1 to week 3 indicate a percentage improvement for all participants across all measured factors of 5.85%. Connectedness increased the most at 7.76% (+ .55) and interest had increased the least at 3.56% (+ .22), happiness improved by 5.28% (+ .52), and satisfaction by 5.76% (+ .36) (Sayer 2016: 253). These results suggest that overall improvement in well-being was low, yet the Wilcoxon test indicated that the changes in connectedness (.001) and happiness (.017) were significant (Sayer 2016: 253).

Analysis of mean scores showed patterns in results; the average mean score for week 3 was consistently higher and variability was reduced for all four aspects of MVAS, with interest having the greatest reduction in variability (– .42) (Sayer 2016: 253). Comparison of the MVAS data from community and student projects, specifically week 1 and week 3 mean results, highlighted differences between participants' results. The Wilcoxon test illustrated that both the student and community groups experienced statistically identical, significant changes in connectedness (.003), and that the community groups underwent significant changes to happiness (.038) and satisfaction (.0011) (Sayer 2016: 254).

The percentage change in average mean scores indicated that participants of the community projects gave higher ratings (percentage rises) for all four criteria, i.e. they appeared more interested, connected, satisfied, and happier than those participants involved in student excavations. The largest percentage rises for community participants were for satisfaction (11.0%) and connectivity (10.1%). The largest percentage increases for the student projects were for connectivity (6.8%) and happiness (4.4%), with a slight decrease in satisfaction (2.2%) (Figure 5.2.1) (Sayer 2016: 254).

Mean PANAS results for positive affects indicated that "proud" 8.3% (+ .51) and "strong" 7.2% (+ .40) increased the most. Standard deviation highlighted that strength

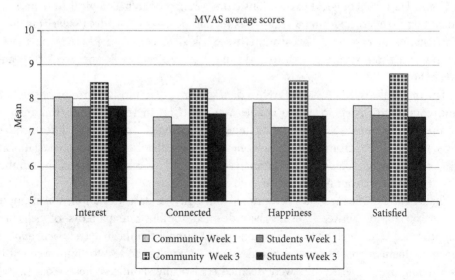

FIGURE 5.2.1. Community and student changes in average scores for MVAS.

(– .23), pride (– .20), and inspiration (– .16) had less variability at the end of the project suggesting statistically significant changes in these affects (Sayer 2016: 254). The results indicated a slight decrease in interest (– .04), excitement (– .21), enthusiasm (– .14), and activity (– .90) (Sayer 2016: 254). The Wilcoxon test suggested increased strength (.004) and decreased enthusiasm was a statistically significant change from week 1 to 3 (Sayer 2016: 254). Mean results for negative affects indicated that irritability increased the most (+ .16), whilst nervousness decreased the most (– .18). Standard deviation indicated that jittery (.28), upset (.26), guilty (– .19) and irritable (.19) were less variable at the end of the project than at the beginning (Sayer 2016: 255). Mean results for negative affects indicate low scores throughout the testing and the Wilcoxon test highlighted that these changes in negative affects were statistically insignificant in all but two factors; nervousness, which decreased by 13.5% (.030), and guilt, which decreased by 15.3% (.041).

Comparison between community and student projects demonstrated significant differences in participants' mean PANAS results. Positive affect results for community groups indicate that the only statistically significant change was participants' feelings of strength (.011), which increased by 13%. Amongst student groups the only statistically significant result was pride (.016), which increased by 19%; negative changes in interest (.003), excitement (.009), and enthusiasm (.002) were also statistically significant (Figure 5.2.2). These negative affects highlighted disparities between the different groups; participants in community projects only experienced significant reductions in irritability of – 27% (.17), whilst those involved in student projects experienced significant increases in irritability (.001), hostility (.87), and distress (.018), and a positive reduction in nervousness by 28% (.001) (Figures 5.2.2 and 5.2.3).

This case study highlighted significant changes in well-being over a three-week period. The MVAS and PANAS surveys indicated that individuals participating in

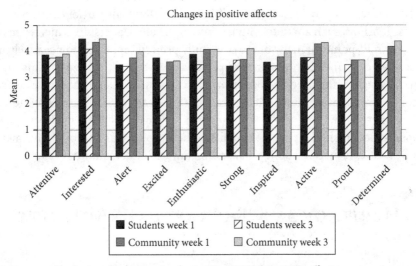

FIGURE 5.2.2. Student and community changes in PANAS positive affects.

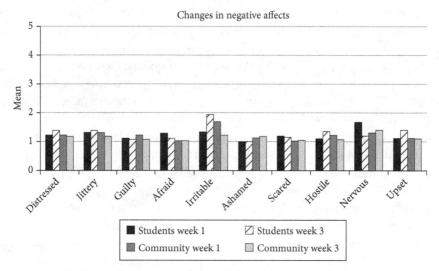

FIGURE 5.2.3. Student and community changes in PANAS negative affects.

community archaeology projects experienced the greatest increase in well-being, as compared to participants involved in student training excavations. For example, in the MVAS survey, the combination of minor increases in the mean scores for interest, connectivity, and happiness and a decrease in satisfaction could suggest that participants of student field projects experienced minimal changes in well-being. MVAS indicators for participants of community projects recorded increased mean scores for all the well-being criteria, contrastingly suggesting that volunteer participation in a community project indeed has a positive effect on well-being.

A decrease in well-being scores during the mid-points of each project, alongside an increase in PANAS negative effects and decrease in MVAS interest score, suggests that social dynamics can play a role in the well-being of individuals participating in heritage projects. Tensions, such as issues with team-working and leadership, which were noted during the mid-points of many of the case study projects, appeared to negatively influence feelings of connectivity and in turn personal well-being (Sayer 2015). This suggests that well-being is influenced by both external factors such as personal choice and social and contextual dynamics and heritage practice (Smith 2004, Smith and Waterton 2012, Sayer 2015: 257). This case study indicates that heritage professionals can implement methods to document the positive benefits of their projects, and through this methodology provide evidence that policy makers and funders understand and value.

HERITAGE AS A THERAPEUTIC ACTIVITY

The second well-being study by Sayer and Walling involved 160 primary and secondary school children who engaged in a range of heritage activities on the Heritage Lottery

Funded project "Bones without Barriers," Cambridgeshire (UK) (Sayer and Walling 2014). Participants were from two schools, Trinity School, a special school for children with social, emotional, and behavioral difficulties aged 13–16, and Oakington Primary School, children aged 5–12. The "Bones without Barriers" project aimed to engage young people in a range of archaeologically related activities, including excavation, test pitting, finds recording, and experimental archaeology. A broad spectrum of cross-curricular heritage activities sought to encourage active participation with all aspects of archaeological excavation. This project sought to support students with diverse learning, behavioral, and social needs, and to study the educational and social benefits experienced by the participants.

In this study, the project team used MVAS to collect quantitative and qualitative data from a range of children participating in four different heritage activities, which included test pitting, festival day activities, visiting an archaeological site, and visiting a museum (Sayer and Walling 2014). The MVAS questionnaire was modified to be appropriate for this demographic; children were asked to give 1–10 Likert-scale answers represented by happy and sad faces for seven questions, after each activity (Table 5.2.1). This data was simply used to compare mean scores, as only one exit data set per activity was collected. This exit data approach was chosen due to access issues with children prior to project, confidentiality requirements, and the short time-span of the specific activities; most were limited to one day. As such these results are limited to understanding the different potential impacts of specific heritage-related activities on well-being, rather than changes in well-being over time.

Trinity participants gave the project an overall low mean score (5.7), whilst Oakington primary school participants gave the project a high mean score (8.5). Specifically, participants from Oakington primary school gave high mean scores for happiness (9.2), learning new things (8.1), learning more (8.8), and knowledge (8.6).

The quantitative and qualitative evidence suggested that "proactive activities," such as test pitting, re-enactment, and experimental archaeology (including cooking, pottery, and boat making), were the most successful in developing a sense of well-being. A comparison between heritage activities mean scores indicated that test pitting received the highest mean scores in all categories bar happiness (6); this included learning (8.3), wanting to learn more (9.7), making friends (7.7), knowledge (8), confidence (8.3), and doing more archaeology (9.3). The festival day also received high scores, including the highest score for happiness (7). Low mean scores were received for the visits to living museums and museums, below 5 for all categories barring happiness.

Overall results suggest that primary school children from Oakington primary school received greater benefits to well-being from the project than Trinity secondary school children. The differences between Oakington and Trinity in heritage activities well-being scores could, in part, be related to age differences between the groups, suggesting that heritage activities had a greater impact on the well-being of children aged 5–10 than children aged 13–16. Yet this difference in mean well-being scores could also be attributed to the social, behavioral, and learning difficulties of the students from Trinity school, highlighting the complexities of developing projects that seek to improve well-being of participants with special educational needs.

This study indicated test pitting and the festival day had the most positive impact on personal well-being amongst the majority of both Trinity and Oakington primary school children (Figure 5.2.1). Mean results for visits to museums and archaeological sites suggest these activities had the least positive impact on children's well-being. As such, activities that involved physical participation in archaeology and heritage, such as test pitting and the festival, which included excavation, experimental boat and house building, cooking, and re-enactment, had greatest impact on mean well-being for both Trinity and Oakington primary school children. Test pitting and the festival encouraged ownership of heritage; for example the test pits for both schools were situated within the children's school grounds and small class groups were given their own test pit to excavate and record. The festival day was prepared for and planned by the children, with art displays and food preparation work undertaken in the weeks leading up to the festival, and parents invited along to celebrate the achievements of the children.

Table 5.2.1. Mean MVAS results from children involved in "Bones without Barriers."

Question	Museum Visit	Oakington Festival Day	Living Museum Visit	Test Pitting
How happy did the visit make you?	5.5	7	6.7	6
Did you learn many new things today?	3.7	7.3	6.7	8.3
How much has the visit today made you want to learn more?	3.8	6.5	5.7	9.7
How much did the visit today help you make friends?	3.3	4.5	0.7	7.7
How much did the visit today help your knowledge of the Anglo-Saxon period?	4	7	7	8
How much did the visit today help your confidence?	3.2	6	4	8.3
How much would you like to do another archaeology visit?	5.8	7	3.7	9.3

This case study indicates that engagement in "hands on" and participatory heritage activities can positively impact on children's well-being. Yet, it also highlights the difficulties of developing heritage projects that aim to positively affect children's well-being; and specifically projects for children with specific social, behavioral, or learning requirements. This case study suggests that it is vital, when developing heritage projects that seek to improve children's well-being, to include a range of multi-disciplinary professionals, including educational and behavioral psychologists, alongside teachers and parents. This consultative and collaborative approach can support heritage professionals to develop projects that have positive impacts on well-being to a broader spectrum of children, including those with mental health issues.

Conclusions

The mixed-method evaluative approach is not without flaws; for example PANAS and MVAS are complex evaluation methods designed by health care professionals, psychologists, economists, and social scientists (Whelan 2015: 201, Sayer 2015). Their application to heritage projects requires new research skills to develop effective surveys for statistical analysis within specific cultural contexts, and to follow the relevant ethics for human subject research. The application of these surveys in the field requires professional training and external support in the application of statistical analytic techniques, such as the Wilcoxon paired sample significance test (Sayer 2015: 253). Surveys need to be adapted to work within a heritage context and to be demographically relevant, for example adapting the MVAS survey to be appropriate for the emotional intelligence of children or not using the PANAS survey with children. Understanding ethical, social, and cultural contexts is essential and questions must therefore be tailored accordingly. Simplifying the PANAS words and changing the scale for MVAS can help support the participation of people with different levels of emotional intelligence in the surveys. As demonstrated by the first case study, the need to exclude incomplete survey data for statistical analysis requires the researcher to increase the numbers of participants accordingly. It is also essential that individual participants and their data are consistently coded and collected between weeks 1–3, something which can be achieved through providing participants with anonymous number codes to add to their MVAS and PANAS questionnaires as required by Institutional Review Boards (IRB). These potential issues must be tackled appropriately and through researcher training before engaging in project well-being evaluation (Whelan 2015, Sayer 2015).

A holistic approach should be considered best practice when planning heritage projects that aim to influence well-being. Case study projects indicate that the methods that heritage projects use should be aligned with the NEF's five key factors to well-being (Aked, Marks, Cordon, and Thompson 2008). As such, the case studies presented in this chapter suggest specific characteristics should be included when designing heritage projects to support the development of community and personal well-being (Sayer 2015: 258). These are:

- community centered;
- contextually specific;
- demographically diverse;
- providing freedom and choice;
- encouraging ownership;
- providing physical activities.

These case studies have indicated that heritage can improve public well-being and mental health. However, the heritage sector is methodologically lagging behind other cultural industries, and often fails to provide evidence of impact on well-being. This must be addressed if heritage is to maximize its impact on public health policy and compete with other cultural industries, including theater and literature. Proactively demonstrating the global potential of heritage to support international health and well-being agendas will open heritage up to a new wave of partners, funders, and participants. Proving the societal value of heritage is critical to its future.

REFERENCES

Aked, Jody, Nic Marks, Cor Cordon, and Sam Thompson. 2008. "Five Ways to Wellbeing: A Report Presented to the Foresight Project on Communicating the Evidence Base for Improving People's Well-Being." Centre for Wellbeing, The New Economics Foundation. Retrieved from: <http://b.3cdn.net/nefoundation/8984c5089d5c2285ee_t4m6bhqq5.pdf>.

Ascherson, Neil. 2000. "Editorial." *Public Archaeology* 1(1): 1–4.

Atalay, Sonya. 2007. "Global Application of Indigenous Archaeology: Community Based Participatory Research in Turkey." *Archaeologies* 249(3): 249–270.

Avrami, Erica, Randall Mason, and Marta De la Torre. 2000. "Values and Heritage Conservation: Research Report." Los Angeles: The Getty Conservation Institute.

Beaumont, J., and H. Lofts. 2013. "Measuring National Wellbeing—Health 2013." Office for National Statistics. Retrieved from: <http://www.ons.gov.uk/ons/dcp171766_310300.pdf>.

Belford, Paul. 2011. "Archaeology, Community and Identity in a New English Town." *The Historic Environment* 2(1): 46–67.

Chatterjee, Helan, and Paul Camic. 2015. "The Health and Well-Being Potential of Museums and Art Galleries." *Arts and Health* 7(3): 183–186.

Cunliffe, Barry. 1981. "Introduction: The Public Face of the Past," in *Antiquity and Man: Essays in Honour of Glyn Daniel*, ed. John Evans, Barry Cunliffe, and Colin Renfrew. London: Thames and Hudson, 192–194.

Darvill, Tim. 1995. "Value Systems in Archaeology," in *Managing Archaeology*, ed. Malcolm Cooper, Anthony Firth, John Carman, and David Wheatley. London: Routledge, 40–50.

Dodge, Rachel, Annette Daly, Jan Huyton, and Lalage Sanders. 2012. "The Challenge of Defining Wellbeing." *International Journal of Wellbeing* 2(3): 222–235.

English Heritage. 2000. "Power of Place: The Future of the Historic Environment." London: English Heritage for the Historic Environment Steering Group.

English Heritage. 2006. "Heritage Counts: The State of England's Historic Environment 2006." London: English Heritage.

English Heritage. 2014. "Heritage Counts: England 2014." London: English Heritage.

EuroQol Group. 1990. "EuroQol: A New Facility for the Measurement of Health-Related Quality of Life." *Health Policy* 16(3): 199–208.

Evans, Joanne, Ian Macrory, and Chris Randall. 2015. "Measuring National Wellbeing: Life in the UK, 2015." Office for National Statistics. Retrieved from: <http://www.ons.gov.uk/ons/dcp171766_398059.pdf>.

Finnegan, Alan. 2016. "The Biopsychosocial Benefits and Shortfalls for Armed Forces Veterans Engaged in Archaeological Activities." *Nurse Education Today* 47: 15–22.

Fujiwara, Daniel, Thomas Cornwall, and Paul Dolan. 2014. "Heritage and Wellbeing." London: English Heritage. Retrieved from: <https://www.hc.english-heritage.org.uk/context/pub/2014/heritage-wellbeing.pdf>.

Goldberg, David, and Valerie Hillier. 1979. "A Scaled Version of the General Health Questionnaire." *Psychological Medicine* 9(1): 139–145.

Griffin, J. 1988. "Well-Being: Its Meaning, Measurement and Moral Importance." Wotton-Under-Edge: Clarendon Press.

Hamilakis, Yannis, and Theou Efthimis. 2013. "Enacted Multi-Temporality: The Archaeological Sites as a Shared Performative Space," in *Reclaiming Archaeology: Beyond the Tropes of Modernity*, ed. Alfredo Gonzalez-Ruibal. London: Routledge, 181–194.

Hodder, Ian. 2000. *Towards Reflexive Method in Archaeology: The Example at Çatalhöyük*. Cambridge: McDonald Institute for Archaeological Research, University of Cambridge.

Holtorf, Cornellus. 2005. *From Stonehenge to Las Vegas: Archaeology as Popular Culture*. Oxford: Altamira Press.

Human Henge Project. <http://humanhenge.org>.

Jones, Sian. 2004. *Early Medieval Sculpture and the Productions of Meaning, Values and Place: The Case of Hilton of Cadboll*. Edinburgh: Historic Scotland.

Kiddey, Rachel, and John Schofield. 2011. "Embrace the Margins: Adventures in Archaeology and Homelessness." *Public Archaeology* 10(1): 4–22.

Kindleysides, Michelle, and Emma Biglands. 2015. " 'Thinking outside the Box, and Making It Too': Piloting an Occupational Therapy Group at an Open-Air Museum." *Arts and Health* 7(3): 271–278.

Lipe, William. 1984. "Value and Meaning in Cultural Resources," in *Approaches to the Archaeological Heritage: A Comparative Study of World Cultural Resource Management Systems*, ed. Henry Cleere. Cambridge: Cambridge University Press, 1–11.

Lipe, William. 2007. "Value and Meaning in Cultural Resources," in *Cultural Heritage: Critical Concepts in Media and Cultural Studies*, ed. Laura Jane Smith. Vol. 1. London: Routledge, 286–306.

Lyubomirsky, Sonja, Kennon Sheldon, and David Schkade. 2005. "Pursuing Happiness: The Architecture of Sustainable Change." *Review of General Psychology* 9(2): 111–131.

McGhee, Fred L. 2012. "Participatory Action Research and Archaeology," in *The Oxford Handbook of Public Archaeology*, ed. Robin Skeates, Carol McDavid, and John Carman. Oxford: Oxford University Press, 213–229. DOI: 10.1093/oxfordhb/9780199237821.013.0012.

McNaught, Allan, and Anneyce Knight. 2011. *Understanding Wellbeing: An Introduction for Students and Practitioners of Health and Social Care*. Oxford: Lantern Publishing.

Merriman, Nick. 2004. "Introduction: Diversity and Dissonance in Public Archaeology," in *Public Archaeology*, ed. Nick Merriman. London: Routledge, 1–18.

Nimenko, Wasyl, and Robin Simpson. 2014. "Rear Operations Group Medicine: A Pilot Study of Psychological Decompression in a Rear Operations Group during Operation HERRICK 14." *Journal of the Royal Army Medical Corps* 160(4): 295–297.

Nissinaho, Aino, and Tuija-Liisa Soininen. 2014. "Adopt a Monument: Social Meaning from Community Archaeology," in *Public Participation in Archaeology*, ed. Suzie Thomas and Joanne Lea. Woodbridge: The Boydell Press, 175–182.

Office of National Statistics. 2013. "Personal Wellbeing-Across the UK." Retrieved from: <http://www.ons.gov.uk/ons/dcp171778_328486.pdf>.

Renfrew, Colin. 2006. *Figuring It Out: What Are We? Where Do We Come From?* London: Thames and Hudson.

Sayer, Faye, and Amy Walling. 2014. "Bones without Barriers Report." Unpublished, Heritage Lottery Fund Report.

Sayer, Faye. 2014. "Politics and the Development of Community Archaeology in the UK." *The Historic Environment* 5(1): 55–73.

Sayer, Faye. 2015. "Can Digging Make You Happy? Archaeological Excavations, Happiness and Heritage." *Arts and Health* 7(3): 247–260.

Sayer, Faye, and Duncan Sayer. 2016. "Bones without Barriers: The Social Impact of Digging the Dead," in *Archaeologists of the Dead: Mortuary Archaeology in Contemporary Society*, ed. Howard Williams and Melanie Giles. Oxford: Oxford University Press, 139–165.

Seligman, Martin. 2011. *Flourish*. New York: Simon and Schuster.

Simpson, Faye. 2010. *The Values of Community Archaeology: A Comparative Assessment between the UK and US*. Oxford: Oxbow, British Archaeological Review.

Simpson, Faye, and Howard Williams. 2008. "Evaluating Community Archaeology in the UK." *Public Archaeology* 7(2): 69–90.

Smiraglia, Christina. 2015. "Museum Programming and Mood: Participant Responses to an Object-Based Reminiscence Outreach Program in Retirement Communities." *Arts and Health* 7(3): 187–201.

Smith, Laurajane. 2004. *Archaeological Theory and the Politics of Cultural Heritage*. London: Routledge.

Smith, Laurajane, and Emma Waterton. 2012. "Constrained by Commonsense: The Authorized Heritage Discourse in Contemporary Debates," in *The Oxford Handbook of Public Archaeology*, ed. Robin Skeates, Carol McDavid, and John Carman. Oxford: Oxford University Press, 154–171. DOI: 10.1093/oxfordhb/9780199237821.013.0009.

Tennant, Ruth, Louise Hiller, Ruth Fishwick, Stephen Platt, Stephen Joseph, Scott Weich, Jane Parkinson, Jenny Secker, and Sarah Stewart-Brown. 2007. "The Warwick-Edinburgh Mental Well-Being Scale (WEMWBS): Development and UK Validation." *Health and Quality of Life Outcomes* 5(1): 63.

The EuroQol Group. 1990. "EuroQol: A New Facility for the Measurement of Health-Related Quality of Life." *Health Policy* 16: 199–208.

Thomas, Julian. 2004. *Archaeology and Modernity*. London: Routledge.

Thomson, Linda, and Helen Chatterjee. 2013. "UCL Museums Wellbeing Measures Toolkit." Retrieved from: <http://www.ucl.ac.uk/museums/research/touch/museumwellbeingmeasures/wellbeing-measures/UCL_Museum_Wellbeing_Measures_Toolkit_Sept2013.pdf>.

Thomson, Linda, and Helen Chatterjee. 2014. "Assessing Wellbeing Outcomes for Arts and Heritage Activities: Development of a Museum Wellbeing Measures Toolkit." *Journal of Applied Arts & Health* 5(1): 29–50.

Thomson, Linda, Eric Ander, Usha Menon, Anne Lanceley, and Helan Chatterjee. 2011. "Evaluating the Therapeutic Effects of Museum Object Handling with Hospital Patients: A Review of Initial Trial of Wellbeing Measures." *Journal of Applied Arts and Health* 2(1): 37–56.

Thomson, Linda, Eric Ander, Usha Menon, Anne Lanceley, and Helan Chatterjee. 2012. "Quantitative Evidence for Welling Benefits from a Heritage-in-Heath Intervention with Hospital Patients." I*nternational Journal of Art Therapy* 17(2): 63–79.

Watson, David, Lee Clark, and Auke Tellegen. 1988. "Development and Validation of Brief Measures of Positive and Negative Affect: The PANAS Scale." *Journal of Personality and Social Psychology* 54(6): 1063–70.

Whelan, Gayle. 2015. "Understanding the Social Value and Well-Being Benefits Created by Museums: A Case for Social Return on Investment Methodology." *Arts and Health* 7(3): 216–230.

....

EFFECTS OF CONVERSATIONS WITH SITES OF PUBLIC HERITAGE ON COLLECTIVE MEMORY

....

MARTIN M. FAGIN

HUMAN beings are social animals, and they are so by necessity. We would not have survived very long as a species, let alone become the dominant force on the planet, if we all behaved like disparate individuals and had not integrated into collective societies. One of the driving forces allowing us to form social groups is our ability to form and maintain collective representations that "exist" over time (Hirst 2010). Similar to the role autobiographical memory plays for the individual, a group's public cultural heritage allows the group to be thought of as relatively stable, and therefore to persist in the face of historical change.

Herein public heritage is defined, similar to Assmann (1995), as the total body of shared knowledge, including texts, images, commemorations, rituals, and the like, that serves to stabilize and define that society's image by successfully permeating its collective consciousness. Of course, not all cultural artifacts will have an impact on public heritage at any particular time. That said, those artifacts that convey messages that are successfully received by the individuals that make up a given collective, and are assimilated into a group's collective memory, and therefore identity, are most likely to be propagated forward, and influence representations of that collective's public heritage.

In the attempt to concretely define public heritage, the distinct, yet significantly, and reciprocally, related concepts of collective memory, and the sense of collective identity they instantiate at any given moment, are also activated. Herein *collective memory* refers to shared representations of the past that group members hold that have a bearing on that group's collective identity (Hirst 2010). Just as episodic memories are distinguished from autobiographic by the relevance the memory has to the conception of self, so too are shared memories distinguished from collective memories by the relevance the memory has to the conception of the collective. Thus, they are not simply the aggregate of shared knowledge, but that shared knowledge that creates a sense of group entitativity or *collective identity*.

Although these are distinct concepts, one cannot effectively account for one without accounting for the others. Therefore, collective memory is a part of our public heritage, exerts influence over it, and is also affected by it. Further, artifacts that embody public heritage are often commemorations of important events or ideals already present in collective memory. This relationship is fluid and reciprocal, and can lead to the formation, maintenance, change, and/or propagation of collective memories, and different interpretations and/or levels of influence for a particular artifact, at any given time. This, then, influences what instantiation of collective identity becomes activated, which can be used to serve the identity needs of the moment. Therefore, by creating and cultivating public heritage, a group can achieve a greater measure of social cohesion through the reciprocal connections public heritage has with collective memory and identity. Given the clear adaptive advantage social cohesion normally bestows on members of a collective, and the role public heritage plays in this process, the drive to create and maintain sites of public heritage must be adaptive as well. Thus, it is of crucial importance that we understand how, and under what circumstances, collective representations of heritage are formed, influenced, and propagated over time, largely by determining what pieces of our collectively shared past are more or less accessible to mind, and the form that information takes.

This chapter will focus on empirical evidence that suggests that the inclusion or exclusion of a certain place, event, or relic in a collective narrative at any given time is closely connected with the functional role that the specific cultural element plays in shaping collective identity, not its historical accuracy or the validity of its underlying message. Specifically, this chapter will focus on the role that conversational dynamics play in the formation of collective memories. If we conceive of conversations as not only happening between multiple physically co-present individuals, but also, as between individuals and all manner of distributed cognitive structures in their environments (e.g. monuments, written works, video archives), understanding conversations' effect on collective memory becomes even more important. In fact, one can even conceive of our internal monologues (i.e. conscious thoughts) about our identity and place in history as a conversation—with oneself, or with a virtual audience (Fagin et al. 2015). If conceived of this way, the extended interactional dynamics of conversational remembering are of paramount importance to public heritage. Thus, the focus of this chapter will be how this historical, archaeological, and memory-based information is received, influenced, and propagated through conversations with sites of public heritage using distributed cognitive processes that reliably interact with our sociocognitive mechanisms to create a shared representation of the past.

THE DISTRIBUTED NATURE OF COGNITION

Researchers have long understood that human memory could not be completely dissociated from the environment within which it takes place. Bartlett (1932) showed that memory is actively reconstructed using schemas, which are based on socially learned attitudes and beliefs about what was most likely to have happened in a given situation. Even earlier, Halbwachs (1925) believed that the workings of memory cannot be disentangled from the others we remember with, or the structural scaffolding provided by a given social environment. Even Ebbinghaus (1964), who was largely concerned with dissociating the mind from its environment so as to get at the raw materials of memory, acknowledges in this approach the social and distributed nature of cognition. His error was to struggle against those social influences that are just as much a part of cognition as that which is located beneath the surface of our skin.

Ebbinghaus's error has started to be reversed in the interdisciplinary study of *distributed cognition*. Philosophers such as Clark and Chalmers (1998) and cognitive neuroscientists such as Donald (2001) have shown that the mind cannot be thought of as completely localized within the brain, or even within the body, but must extend out into the environment that interacts with, supports, and largely determines what information is most available to mind. Examples such as Bateson's (1979) blind man navigating through the use of his cane, Hutchins's (1995) pilots and their "speed cards" that help them land successfully, or the proverbial string around the finger as a memory aid are but a few that highlight the important role that external structures play in helping us distribute the burdens placed on us by cognition. The implication inherent in the need to distribute cognition, and therefore acts of remembering, is that by doing so we are enhancing our mnemonic capabilities.

There is a clear link between our need to distribute cognition and the formation of public heritage, which then reciprocally interact with our collective memories to affect our collective identity. Given our biological mnemonic limitations, and therefore our need to distribute cognition, the artifacts of public heritage serve as helpful mnemonic devices. And it is our need to distribute cognition that leads to the public display of heritage to begin with, and therefore allows for the influence public heritage has on collective memory formation and collective identity instantiation, and the propagation of this information.

DISTRIBUTED CONVERSATIONAL REMEMBERING

One of the social means by which we distribute the process of remembering is conversation. The uniquely human activity of conversing about shared bodies of knowledge and past events allows us to not only distribute the cognitive burden of remembering, but to socially share our knowledge base. Given that research has shown that when humans discuss a familiar topic they most often converse about shared bodies of knowledge (Wittenbaum and Park 2001), conversations seem the perfect sociocognitive mechanism to support the formation(s), maintenance, and propagation of heritage, largely through the cultivation of collective memories.

The memories participants' hold prior to a conversation is not the same as the memories they hold after the conversation. Importantly, they not only change, but change in ways that promote the formation of collective memories. Here we are not particularly concerned with the imparting of new information. For example, when a visitor descends the steps of the 9/11 Memorial, they likely already know a great deal about the 9/11 attacks. The question for us is how the memorial, or any conversation writ large, changes pre-existing memories. One might ask the question in terms of how speakers reshape their own and their audience's memories, but in order to underscore that this reshaping promotes the formation and/or evolution of a collective memory, one must also recognize that the influences are distributed—that is, between speakers and themselves and between speaker and listeners. Importantly, since conversations need not be between two or more physically co-present people, but can be between people and all manner of public heritage artifacts, this means that "speakers," depending on the particular site of public heritage, can be any combination of artists, artifacts, curators, tour guides, moneyed interests, and so on.

The effects of distributed acts of conversational remembering have often been conceived of as either benefits or costs (for a review, see Hirst and Echterhoff 2012). Our focus here is not on benefits or costs, per se, but on how what is or isn't said in a conversation leads to additions and subtractions from a collective narrative due to the interactional relationship between sites of public heritage, collective memory, and collective identity. These additions and subtractions are not necessarily permanent, especially given the ever changing reciprocal relationship between public heritage, collective memory, and collective identity, but more so take the form of increased or decreased accessibility to certain pieces of relevant information. But, regardless of additions or subtractions, the important point is that the result is often the formation of a collective memory, which can serve as the foundation for a collective heritage. Next, we will briefly review two important phenomena that lead to additions and subtractions from a collective narrative, and then turn our focus to the extended interactional dynamics that govern their reception and propagation.

Additions to Collective Memory Due to Social Contagion

Conversations provide an opportunity for mnemonic convergence, but the shared representation need not be valid. Social contagion of memory (SC) occurs when information from an external source is mistakenly incorporated into one's own memory. This can have benefits when the information is corrective in nature, but our interest here is in the effects of misinformation.

Psychologists have long recognized that one person can implant a memory into another. This can happen through the use of cultural artifacts (e.g. photographs), through more mediated forms of communication (e.g. written text, online interactions), as well as face-to-face interactions (Loftus 2005), all of which are important potential forms of information reception that would result from conversations with sites of public heritage. SC is the result of source monitoring errors, where one confuses the post-event information with their memory of the original event (Johnson et al. 1993). Thus, no matter the specific conversational format, SC can lead to shared representations of the past, and influence our collective memory. For example, the myth of George Washington and his cherry tree meant to embody his high moral standards and un-wavering honesty has been fully integrated into American's collective consciousness, but has since been proven false, and traced back to misinformation that was implanted by one of Washington's first biographers Mason Weems in 1800. This misinformation was then legitimized and propagated forward decades later by William McGuffy who included it in a series of school textbooks that remained in use for almost one hundred years (Richardson 2017). This is just one example among unknown and countless others that shows the important role that conversations with public heritage artifacts can play in the formation, influence, and propagation of the collective memories by causing SC.

Subtractions from Collective Memory Due to Retrieval-Induced Forgetting

When we consider the impacts of conversational remembering on what pieces of shared information are more or less accessible to mind, retrieval-induced forgetting (RIF) figures prominently. The phenomenon of RIF was first studied with respect to the rememberers themselves. Research showed that selectively recalled previously encoded information is not only reinforced, but that which is related to what was selectively rehearsed become least accessible to the individual, even when compared to unrelated unpracticed information (Anderson et al. 1994). But, the RIF paradigm has little to do with acts of communication, except potential effects on the speaker in a conversation. Hirst and colleagues extended the phenomenon of RIF to communicative settings and examined the effect of selective retelling not just on the source of a communication, but also on recipients. They not only established that RIF could be found in conversations, but, critically, they also observed RIF in listeners, so-called *socially shared retrieval-induced forgetting* (SSRIF). Thus, SSRIF can, and does, support the creation of collective memory between speakers and listeners by increasing the probability that individuals have access to more shared representations of the past after a conversation than they did before it.

SSRIF is believed to occur because attendees to a communication concurrently, albeit covertly, retrieve along with the communicator. As a result, the attendees find themselves in situations similar to that of communicators, retrieving some memories while leaving others unmentioned, leaving them susceptible to SSRIF. For the communicator retrieval is mandatory: one cannot discuss a shared past without successfully retrieving the information first. For the recipient of a communication, retrieval is optional. Thus, for a site of public heritage to induce SSRIF in those it communicates with, the recipients must put in enough effort to retrieve along the lines communicated by the site. Otherwise, mnemonic convergence between the site's message and the recipients is unlikely to be increased.

Of crucial importance to our discussion here: first, SSRIF has been shown for not only face-to-face interactions, but through mediated forms of communication as well (e.g. written text, video lectures) (Fagin and Hirst 2015). Second, SSRIF has been shown to serve as a facilitatory mechanism in the formation of collective memory (Stone et al. 2014). Third, SSRIF has also been shown to propagate through multiple conversational interactions (1–60), and lead to mnemonic convergence in larger groups, though it was more likely to propagate in homogeneous groups of up to fifty people (Coman and Hirst 2012; Coman et al. 2012). Fourth, although earlier studies suggested RIF lasted only a brief time, more recent evidence suggests that it can last for a week, a month, or even longer (Fagin et al. 2017). Given its transactive nature, durability, ability to be received through mediated formats (think sites of public heritage), and ability to shape collective memory SSRIF is a sociocognitive mechanism well suited to help form, influence, and propagate the collective memories that make up our sense of collective identity, and give us a collective heritage. This is illustrated well by the recent removal of the last Confederate monuments from New Orleans, which were attempts to influence collective memory formation, evolution, and propagation by selectively practicing a sanitized and fictionalized history of Confederate ideals, while remaining silent about the humanitarian atrocities committed in their name. Over time, "conversations" with these sites of public heritage would lead to increased access to this glorified Confederacy, and decreased access to the horrific truth.

THE EXTENDED INTERACTIONAL DYNAMICS OF CONVERSATIONS

The potential influences of distributed conversational remembering are made possible by the "imperfect" nature of human memory. If our memories were not so malleable, conversations with other agents and artifacts in our environment would have little functional impact, and originally discrepant renderings of the past would remain that way, and not coalesce into a shared one. But, will these potential influences on memory always be operative, or are there extended interactional dynamics that govern the effects of conversational remembering? A variety of influences, both cognitive and social, reliably affect the impact that information has on subsequent recall (Fagin et al. 2013). Given our focus on the social nature of conversational remembering, here we focus on the more social influences as they relate to SC and SSRIF.

Motivational Influences and Mnemonic Convergence

The cognitive resources the recipient of a communication puts into the interaction moderates the effects of both SC and SSRIF. In the case of SC, increased effort on the part of the listener normally leads to a reduced impact of the post-event misinformation. In the case of SSRIF, increased effort on the part of the listener normally leads to an increased influence of the speaker on their memory. As for the speaker, effort factors in less, but other socially driven motivators, such as the desire to connect with your audience, can influence both speaker and listener. Thus, if we are to understand how and when conversations with sites of public heritage affect mnemonic convergence, these motivational factors must be explicated. Building on the foundational work on shared reality of Echterhoff, Higgins, and colleagues, here we focus on two motives affecting the impact of conversations with sites of public heritage on collective memory: Epistemic and relational (Echterhoff et al. 2009a).

Epistemic Motives

Epistemic motives refer to the need to achieve a valid and reliable understanding of the world.[1] When viewed in the context of conversational remembering, epistemic motives reflect the need to ensure that what the speaker says is accurate. One way a listener could make this assessment is by concurrently retrieving with the speaker. Thus, to the extent that listeners are guided by epistemic motives, they should be more willing to make the effort to engage in concurrent retrieval if they mistrust the speaker and/or their memory, and less likely to make the effort to concurrently retrieve if they trust the speaker and/or their memory. If epistemic motives reliably influence conversational remembering, then differences in susceptibility to SC and SSRIF should be apparent.

Epistemic motives boil down to trust. If you trust your source then there is no need to waste precious cognitive resources to fact check them, or to source monitor following the interaction. You simply trust them, which then leaves one more susceptible to SC. For example, research on SC has used the trust we have in our parents (Mazzoni et al. 2010), friends, and significant others to induce false memories. We also tend to trust others' memory over our own if they have power in numbers, which makes sense given our propensity to conform to the group consensus. Just as power in numbers can induce SC, so can the power dynamics between individuals: When the speaker has more of it, SC is found in the listener. Given that we normally trust those in positions of authority, this finding seems epistemically motivated as well. Similarly, we tend to trust the narrator of a story (after all, why tell the story if you don't know what happened?), who has been shown to induce SC in multiple listeners. Turning the notion of trust on its head, when prewarned not to trust the source of information listeners can avoid SC effects altogether.

The above findings have clear relevance to the influence conversations with sites of public heritage have. For example, other people, not only artifacts, can serve as sites of public heritage. Thus, the trust we have for loved ones can easily lead to SC of collective memory for important events related to collective identity (e.g. who assassinated JFK). As for our propensity to conform to the group consensus, one could converse with multiple sources that all endorse the same misinformation and fall prey to SC (e.g. textbooks that say Columbus discovered the Americas, even though he landed in the Caribbean).

412   MARTIN M. FAGIN

An example of SC of collective memory from authority figures is well demonstrated by President Trump's false claim during a speech of a terrorist attack that occurred in Sweden (a non-existent attack), which permeated the collective memory of his supporters (Chan 2017). Narrators of stories are operative at almost all levels of sites of public heritage (e.g. the artist(s), tour guides, curators), and can easily induce SC in their listeners. Thus, epistemic motives clearly influence conversations between sites of public heritage and their visitors, and can lead to SC, but what about SSRIF?

Remember that for SSRIF, unlike SC, more effort on the part of the listener, which leads them to concurrently retrieve along with the speaker, leads to increased mnemonic convergence. For example, when told to monitor the speaker's selective retrieval for accuracy (as opposed to fluidity), SSRIF is only found in the accuracy condition. Similarly, when the speaker is identified as an expert SSRIF is less likely (although SC is more likely), but when the speaker is identified as untrustworthy SSRIF is more likely, exactly what one would expect when epistemic motives are operative. Similar results have been found in a large body of research. How is this relevant to sites of public heritage? Imagine an American tourist visiting the Russian Cold War museum in Moscow. The American will likely have less trust in the information communicated by this site, leading to increased attention to what is said, and more SSRIF. Thus, clearly, epistemic motives are operative in both SSRIF and SC, and produce the opposite effects on mnemonic convergence: When we trust the source of a communication, whether the source be physically embodied or a cultural artifact, SC can lead to increased mnemonic convergence, when we mistrust the source of information, SSRIF can lead to increased mnemonic convergence. Regardless, one cannot avoid the formative effects of distributed conversational remembering with sites of public heritage on collective memory.

Relational Motives

Epistemic motives are not the only moderators related to conversational remembering to consider. Relational motives move people to affiliate and feel connected to others. In doing so, they can shape the way and what people remember. Though the extant research on SC has been less focused on relational motives, a few observations can still be made. As mentioned above, SC has employed participants' parents, friends, and significant others to induce false memories. Although this can be attributed to trust, as done above, it could also be attributed to relational motives: since the listener and speaker share the same in-group (e.g. family), and therefore desire to, or are required to, create a shared reality together, the speaker influences the listener. So, when that same American tourist now visits The Cold War Museum in Virginia, they are much more likely to fall prey to SC than SSRIF. In other words, they are more likely to make incorrect additions to their collective memory than to subtract relevant information from it, due to the desire to connect with the message of the in-group site of public heritage. Further, in a twist on *audience tuning*, where a speaker will present ambiguous information to listeners in line with what listeners want to hear: when a speaker desired to create a shared reality with their audience, their audience tuned message shows a contagion effect on their own memory (*saying-is-believing effect*) (Echterhoff et al. 2009b). For example, a tour guide might tune their message based on the nationality of a visiting group. If the tour guide desires to create a shared reality with this group, they will contaminate their own memory for the information they provide, which may spill over into future presentations. Thus, relational motives affect whether conversations with sites of public heritage will lead to SC of collective memory as well.

Given that relational motives are likely to lead to increased attention, they presumably can lead people to make the effort to recount with others a shared past. Research on SSRIF and relational motives has mostly used in-group/out-group dynamics to investigate the contributions of relational motives in mnemonic convergence. For example, Coman and Hirst (2015) had participants listen while a speaker recalled previously studied materials. If the speaker was identified as a fellow Princeton student, SSRIF was found in listeners. If they were identified as a Yale student, it was not. Further, if the fact that both speaker and listener were students was accentuated, SSRIF was again found. These findings suggest that when listeners are relationally motivated to concurrently retrieve along with the speaker, SSRIF is found. This study also highlights that we are a collection of various identities, which each have their own (sometimes overlapping) reservoir of collective memories. In order to know how conversing with a site of public heritage will affect us, we must also know which identity is most activated. For example, a German Jew visiting the Auschwitz Memorial will have their collective memories differentially affected depending on whether their German or Jewish identities are more activated. Thus, how a site of public heritage and/or its message is framed can have a significant influence on how that message is received, and its potential impact on collective memory formation, maintenance, and propagation.

Stone et al. (2014) investigated the role of relational motives in SSRIF by measuring the effects of a yearly address given by the king of Belgium. The king gives his speech in the two dominant languages of Belgium: French and Flemish, but is himself more associated with the French-speaking Belgians. Results showed that attending to the king's speech led to SSRIF, but only in French-speaking participants. Why? Because the French-speaking Belgians have more of a desire to create a shared reality with their French-speaking king. This has clear implications for politically or nationally relevant cultural artifacts: when you embrace the source of, and/or ideals communicated by, said artifact your accessibility to that information is increased, and your accessibility to related, but unmentioned, information will be reduced.

Fagin and Hirst (2015) investigated the minimum level of *social presence* a speaker must embody to induce relationally motivated concurrent retrieval, and therefore SSRIF, in the listeners of mediated forms of communication (e.g. text, audio, video). Results showed that a visual representation of the source (e.g. photo and text), or the personalization of a message without a visual representation (e.g. first-person audio) are the minimal requirements needed to induce concurrent retrieval in the listener in the absence of epistemic motives. These findings are of high import to sites of public heritage. For example, if a written work is to have the most impact on mnemonic convergence, then a visual representation of the author should be provided. If a memorial or museum wants to have an increased impact, include audio/video archives with first-person accounts. Taken together, these findings demonstrate the importance of relational motives in developing mnemonic convergence between speakers and listeners, and therefore the role they play in the formation of collective memory through interactions with sites of public heritage.

General Discussion

Although we are only recently starting to explicitly understand the role that the shaping and propagation of collective representations of the past plays in the formation of collective identity, human beings' unique drive to immortalize the important lessons we have learned shows we've had, for perhaps as long as civilization itself, at least an implicit understanding of the importance of maintaining vital collective representations over time. From cave paintings to the oral tradition, to film, blogs, and everything in between, we have sought to pass on our cultural heritage not only to those surrounding us presently, but to future listeners as well. And, these sites of public heritage have affected the content of our collective memories, and therefore our collective identities and ability to create social cohesion.

Importantly, in all cases of the sharing and propagating of cultural heritage, we must distribute the cognitive burdens of this task. Therefore, heritage and its propagation are inherently social endeavors that require us to go beyond our physiological short-comings and to use all the tools and materials available to us, whether that be other people, or cultural artifacts. If it were not for the need to distribute cognition, cultural heritage would never be made public, and would never be capable of being propagated forward through time and space. One of the main vehicles by which we create, influence, and propagate our public heritage is conversational remembering. Through distributing our mnemonic burdens conversationally, we increase the likelihood of mnemonic convergence onto a shared representation of a collective past, and therefore acquire the basic building blocks of collective identity, and public heritage.

But, with the need to distribute cognition conversationally comes not only benefits, but also costs. Whether we should see the overall impact of our need to distribute cognition conversationally as truly being a negative, or a cost, remains to be seen. On an "individual" level, or in specific instances, these costs can be very real, such as in false eyewitness memories or false "recovered" memories of childhood trauma (Fagin et al. 2013). Taking the larger scale perspective though, what seems a deficit of the individual is a strength of the collective, which then supports said individuals. That's not to suggest that larger scale social cohesion doesn't have potential costs, which has been well demonstrated by examples of nationalism run amuck (e.g. Nazi Germany), or the type of in-group/out-group bias that leads to acts of dehumanization, slavery, and the like. Still, the argument made here is that the adaptive benefits of fostering social cohesion through the cultivation of collective memories, and therefore collective identities, far outweighs the costs. For animals as physically frail as humans, the alternative would be to simply not exist, which would be the greatest cost of all. We would not have survived very long as a species, and certainly not accomplished all that we have, without the ability to foster social cohesion through the formation, maintenance, and propagation of collective memories, and therefore collective identities, aided by conversations with sites of public heritage. Thus, the "imperfect" nature of our memory perhaps functions just as it evolved to do, by serving the adaptive function of creating, however imperfect they may be, the collective memories that hold our various collective identities together.

But the way our cultural heritage is being commemorated and archived today is changing in ways that will have an effect on what information gets into our collective memories, how long it will remain there, and how many individuals it can impact. Although books, monuments, and the like will continue to be forces in the preservation of cultural heritage, more mediated forms that mimic direct in-person communications, or at least utilize a real-time interactive element, are being used (e.g. virtual reality, holograms, 3D printing) (Antlej et al. 2011, Lind et al. 2013, Sarakinos et al. 2013). For example, one can now take hundreds of virtual reality tours of museums like the Louvre or sites of antiquity like Sicily's Valle Dei Templi, or even interact with a holographic Abraham Lincoln. Therefore, further elucidating the extended interactional dynamics that govern the way distributed acts of conversational remembering with sites of public heritage influence the formation, maintenance, and propagation of collective memories, and therefore collective identities, remains crucial, as they will determine instantiations of collective identity, and how best information can be shared within, and between, distinct groups.

Here we focused on the effects of distributed conversational remembering on what information is more or less accessible to individuals, and therefore the collectives they make up, and the motivational factors that moderate its influence on collective memory. Regardless of whether future research focuses on more mediated forms of communication with sites of public heritage, how mediated "conversations" with sites of public heritage affect subsequent conversations, or how distinct cultural groups converse with, and affect, each other using sites of public heritage, the role of the extended interactional dynamics that govern this process will continue to figure prominently.

ACKNOWLEDGMENTS

I'd like to gratefully acknowledge the support and mentorship of Dr. William Hirst. Without the countless conversations with him, leading to the formation of collective memories between us, little of the work herein would have been possible.

NOTE

1. For a more thorough review of research findings related to epistemic motives influence over the formation of collective memory than possible here, see Hirst and Echterhoff (2012). All studies reviewed in this section without an in-text citation are thoroughly documented there.

REFERENCES

Anderson, Michael C., Robert A. Bjork, and Elizabeth L. Bjork. 1994. "Remembering Can Cause Forgetting: Retrieval Dynamics in Long-Term memory." *Journal of Experimental Psychology: Learning, Memory, and Cognition* 20(5): 1063.

Antlej, Kaja, Miran Eric, Mojca Šavnik, Bernarda Županek, Janja Slabe, and Borut Battestin. 2011. "Combining 3D Technologies in the Field of Cultural Heritage: Three Case Studies." *VAST Conference 2011, International Symposium on Virtual Reality, Archaeology and Cultural Heritage, Short and Project Paper Proceedings*, 1–4.

Assmann, Jan. 1995. "Collective Memory and Cultural Identity." *New German Critique* 65: 125–133.

Bartlett, Frederic Charles. 1932. "Remembering: A Study in Experimental and Social Psychology." New York: Cambridge University Press.

Bateson, Gregory. 1979. "Mind and Nature: A Necessary Unity (Advances in Systems Theory, Complexity, and the Human Sciences)." New York: Hampton Press.

Chan, Sewell. 2017. "'Last Night in Sweden'? Trump's Remark Baffles a Nation." *New York Times*, February 19, 2017.

Clark, Andy, and David Chalmers. 1998. "The Extended Mind." *Analysis*: 7–19.

Coman, Alin, and William Hirst. 2012. "Cognition through a Social Network: The Propagation of Induced Forgetting and Practice Effects." *Journal of Experimental Psychology: General* 141(2): 321.

Coman, Alin, and William Hirst. 2015. "Social Identity and Socially Shared Retrieval-Induced Forgetting: The Effects of Group Membership." *Journal of Experimental Psychology: General* 144(4): 717.

Coman, Alin, Andreas Kolling, Michael Lewis, and William Hirst. 2012. "Mnemonic Convergence: From Empirical Data to Large-Scale Dynamics." *International Conference on Social Computing, Behavioral-Cultural Modeling, and Prediction.* Berlin and Heidelberg: Springer, 256–265.

Donald, Merlin. 2001. *A Mind So Rare: The Evolution of Human Consciousness.* New York: W. W. Norton and Company.

Ebbinghaus, Hermann. [1913] 1964. "On Memory." Translated by H. A. Ruger and C. E. Bussenius. New York: Teachers' College.

Echterhoff, Gerald, E. Tory Higgins, and John M. Levine. 2009a. "Shared Reality Experiencing Commonality with Others' Inner States about the World." *Perspectives on Psychological Science* 4(5): 496–521.

Echterhoff, Gerald, Sonja Lang, Nicole Krämer, and E. Tory Higgins. 2009b. "Audience-Tuning Effects on Memory: The Role of Audience Status in Sharing Reality." *Social Psychology* 40(3): 150–163.

Fagin, Martin M., Travis G. Cyr, and William Hirst. 2015. "The Effects of Communicative Source and Dynamics on the Maintenance and Accessibility of Longer-Term Memories: Applications to Sexual Abuse and its Public Disclosure." *Applied Cognitive Psychology* 29(6): 808–819.

Fagin, Martin M., and William Hirst. 2015. "Fostering Mnemonic Convergence: The Role of Relational Motives and Social Presence In Eliciting Socially Shared Retrieval-Induced Forgetting." Manuscript in preparation.

Fagin, Martin M., Robert Meksin, and William Hirst. 2017. "Durability of Retrieval-Induced Forgetting: Effects of Distributed and Massed Practice." Manuscript submitted.

Fagin, Martin M., Jeremy K. Yamashiro, and William C. Hirst. 2013. "The Adaptive Function of Distributed Remembering: Contributions to the Formation of Collective Memory." *Review of Philosophy and Psychology* 4(1): 91–106.

Halbwachs, Maurice. 1925. "Les cadres sociaux de la mémoire." Paris: Les Presses universitaires de France.

Hirst, William. 2010. "A Virtue of Memory: The Contribution of Mnemonic Malleability to Collective Memory," in *The Cognitive Neuroscience of the Mind: A Tribute to Michael S. Gazzaniga*, ed. Patricia A. Reuter-Lorenz et al. Cambridge, MA: MIT, 139–154.

Hirst, William, and Gerald Echterhoff. 2012. "Remembering in Conversations: The Social Sharing and Reshaping of Memories." *Annual Review of Psychology* 63: 55–79.

Hutchins, Edwin. 1995. *Cognition in the Wild*. Cambridge, MA: MIT.

Johnson, Marcia K., Shahin Hashtroudi, and D. Stephen Lindsay. 1993. "Source Monitoring." *Psychological Bulletin* 114(1): 3.

Lind, Laura H., Michael F. Schober, Frederick G. Conrad, and Heidi Reichert. 2013. "Why Do Survey Respondents Disclose More When Computers Ask the Questions?" *Public Opinion Quarterly* 77(4): 888–935.

Loftus, Elizabeth F. 2005. "Planting Misinformation in the Human Mind: A 30-Year Investigation of the Malleability of Memory." *Learning & Memory* 12(4): 361–366.

Mazzoni, Giuliana, Alan Scoboria, and Lucy Harvey. 2010. "Nonbelieved Memories." *Psychological Science* 21(9): 1334–1340.

Richardson, Jay. 2017. "Cherry Tree Myth." *The Digital Encyclopedia of George Washington*. <http://www.mountvernon.org/digital-encyclopedia/article/cherry-tree-myth/> [accessed June 18, 2017].

Sarakinos, A., A. Lembessis, and N. Zervos. 2013. "A Transportable System for the In Situ Recording of Color Denisyuk Holograms of Greek Cultural Heritage Artifacts in Silver Halide Panchromatic Emulsions and an Optimized Illuminating Device for the Finished Holograms." *Journal of Physics: Conference Series*, vol. 415(1). Bristol: IOP Publishing, 012024.

Stone, C. B., O. Luminet, O. Klein, L. Licata, and W. Hirst. 2014. "Socially Shared Retrieval-Induced Forgetting of 'Collective' Memories: The Mnemonic Consequences of Attending to the Belgian King's 2012 Summer Speech." Manuscript in preparation.

Wittenbaum, Gwen M., and Ernest S. Park. 2001. "The Collective Preference for Shared Information." *Current Directions in Psychological Science* 10(2): 70–73.

CHAPTER 5.4

INTERGENERATIONAL LEARNING

A Tool for Building and Transforming Cultural Heritage

GIULIA CORTELLESI, JESSICA HARPLEY,
AND MARGARET KERNAN

YOUNG AND OLD TOGETHER

THE modern world is one of mass migration, social change, and changing family structures. These changes affect the shape of societies and communities, as well as the identities and growth of individuals. In response to the ever-shifting cultural landscape, intergenerational learning projects in countries across the world have sought to bring disparate populations together, find value in cultural diversity and aging populations, and preserve the cultural heritage of individuals and communities.

This chapter reflects on the link between intergenerational learning and cultural heritage, based on the knowledge and insights of the ongoing Together Old and Young (TOY) Programme [<http://www.toyproject.net/>], the goal of which is to promote intergenerational learning and create new possibilities for older adults and young children to learn together and benefit from each other's company. TOY responds to three key societal concerns. The first is age segregation, in societies that often isolate age groups into same-age institutions (such as pre-schools and care homes); the second is the need for better age integration, in response to a global aging population; and the third is the need for social cohesion and solidarity in culturally diverse societies. This last point is of particular importance in multicultural societies, to encourage the conservation and expression of rich cultural backgrounds.

The TOY Programme originated in the EU-funded TOY Project (2012–14) which took place in seven countries: Ireland, Italy, Slovenia, Spain, the Netherlands, Poland, and

Portugal. The TOY Project was unique amongst European intergenerational learning projects with its explicit focus on children in the early childhood years (o to 8 years). In collaboration with universities, NGOs, and municipalities members of the TOY consortium researched, documented, and supported learning initiatives involving young children and older adults in Europe. The research methodology employed include case study analysis, observation, interviews, and focus groups analysis. These initiatives took place in libraries, arts and cultural centers, community gardens, pre-schools, and schools. The TOY project integrates perspectives from many disciplines, including pedagogical communities, developmental psychology, gerontology, social policy, and cultural anthropology, in order to better understand the learning relations between generations and benefits to young, old, and communities. Many of the supported initiatives tackled cultural heritage and its transmission from one generation to the next, showing also the power intergenerational learning can have in transforming and renegotiating culture and collective memories, so that new members of the community can also develop a sense of belonging.

The present chapter builds on an earlier article in which it was argued that interactions between young children and older people can develop solidarity, social cohesion, and intercultural understanding (Cortellesi and Kernan 2016). The current chapter discusses first how intergenerational programs foster cultural transmission and transformation, and the impact of this on well-being, and second how IGL processes can support the integration and social inclusion of marginalized groups in society, such as young children and older adults with a history of migration, or belonging to ethnic minorities. It explores how intergenerational learning happening in formal, non-formal, and informal spaces in communities around the globe can and does contribute to cultural conservation, but also how it initiates cultural transformation. To begin, a review will be presented of the key concepts central to the current thesis, including intergenerational learning, cultural transformation, and intangible cultural heritage.

Specifically, in this chapter, the following questions are addressed:

1. How does the maintenance, transmission, and transformation of cultural heritage affect the health and well-being of children, older adults, and communities?
2. What role does IGL have in this process?
3. How can IGL encourage social cohesion in diverse communities?
4. How does cultural transmission and transformation relate to the integration of marginalized communities in practice?

Defining Intergenerational Learning

Intergenerational learning or IGL is interpreted differently by many authors (Bottery 2016, Franz and Scheunpflug 2016). In summary, it is the oldest method of learning, whereby knowledge, skills, values, and norms are transmitted between generations, typically through the family (Hoff 2007), and involves learning that takes place naturally as part of day-to-day social activity. A newer model of intergenerational learning—extrafamilial intergenerational learning—facilitates wider social groups outside the family to contribute to the socialization of the young, and focuses on relationships (Kaplan 2002, Newman and Hatton-Yeo 2008, Vanderbeck and Worth 2015). The working definition of IGL utilized throughout the TOY program is "Intergenerational learning involves different age groups learning together, learning from each other and learning about each other in a range of settings."

The TOY approach identifies five goals of IGL specifically involving young children and older adults: (1) building and sustaining relationships; (2) enhancing social cohesion in the community; (3) facilitating older people as guardians of knowledge; (4) recognizing the roles of grandparents in young children's lives; (5) enriching the learning processes of both children and older adults. The overarching goal, integrating all five sub-goals, is improved health and well-being of both generations and of communities in general.

Growing interest in IGL stems from both new societal concerns and opportunities, and new understandings of the processes and participation involved in education and learning. This includes the notions of lifelong and lifewide learning, combined with the need to respond positively to the growing separation of generations due to urbanization, migration, family breakdown, and an increasing spread of extended networks of families across communities and continents. At a broader level, demographic change, particularly the phenomenon of aging populations, but also expanding and shrinking populations, has been a key influence in the advocacy of many intergenerational (IG) projects.

INTERGENERATIONAL LEARNING AS A CATALYST FOR HERITAGE CONSERVATION AND CULTURAL TRANSFORMATION

Many social science disciplines extensively explore cultural transmission because it is useful for explaining cultural stability and cultural change (Schönpflug 2009). Intergenerational cultural transmission refers to the transmission of cultural ideas (e.g. values, beliefs, knowledge, practices) from one generation to the next, and is a selective process during which the older generation (parents, grandparents, or elderly in the community) decides consciously and unconsciously which cultural ideas to transmit to the young generation (Tam 2015). The process by which intergenerational learning fosters cultural transmission varies across the globe and different enculturation regimes and social exchange systems shape these processes, putting the emphasis on some members of the family more than others, or on specific members of the community (Nsamenang 2012).

The understanding of "culture" presented here, and assumed through the TOY Project, is based on the cultural anthropological definition of this concept developed by Clifford Geertz: a web of meanings that are constantly transmitted, shared, transformed, and reinterpreted by a group of people over time (Geertz 1973). Anthropology has studied intergenerational transmission of material and immaterial culture and cultural heritage for decades (Mannheim 1927, cited in Pickering and Keightley 2013). Cultural transmission happens through collective memory, which develops from individuals who create their own narrations, reinterpreting, translating, negotiating, and constructing memories in and over time (Pickering and Keightley 2013).

Cultural transformation is central to the field of cultural heritage, though it is acknowledged that definitions of cultural heritage are much debated and in continuous transformation, due to the changing nature of all ideas and concepts used by people (Konsa 2013). Cultural heritage is influenced by historical, political, and social conditions, and refers to a purportedly shared past; it bears directly upon the experiences of the present and the expectations of the future (Konsa 2013, Han and Antrosio 2016). In the *Oxford Handbook of Culture and Psychology*, cultural transformation between generations is discussed as a form of social evolution, ensuring the survival of not only children, but also individual culture (Nsamenang 2012). In this way, cultural heritage is preserved and sometimes imagined and constructed by communities as a resource for the diverse wants and needs of members of a community.

Approaching intergenerational learning from a cultural anthropological perspective, it is crucial to consider how childhood and old age produce their own cultures and how they shape the culture of other generations (Danely 2013: 1, Hirschfeld 2002). In other words, it is necessary to recognize how each generation's body of cultural heritage, knowledge, and related values differs from that of both earlier and later generations (Strom and Strom 2011). By doing so, it is possible to pose the following question: how is cultural heritage interpreted, transmitted, preserved, and transformed in the interaction between generations and their cultures?

Intergenerational learning is often seen as a one-directional process from the older generations to the young ones, but central to the thesis presented in this chapter is the idea that IGL is bi-directional or multidirectional. Based on the evidence from the TOY research, it is argued that cultural transmission through intergenerational learning experiences is not only vertical, oblique, and horizontal (Cavalli-Sforza and Feldman 1981), but is also influenced by children—including very young children—who transmit cultural ideas to older generations and contribute to the transformation of cultural landscapes, together with older members of their communities.

In this chapter, we demonstrate how non-familial intergenerational learning activities contribute to the preservation of cultural heritage, impacting the well-being of individuals and communities by developing shared interpretations of the past, the present, and the future. Of particular importance here is the preservation of intangible cultural heritage, which encompasses a full range of ideas, memories, languages, dances, songs, recipes, and many other elements of who we are and how we identify ourselves

(UNESCO, 2003). It also encompasses the contemporary activities, meanings, values, and behaviors that are drawn from these to create visions of the present and the future.

Cultural Heritage, IGL, and Individual and Community Well-Being

The maintenance, transmission, and transformation of cultural heritage affects health and well-being, both on an individual and community level. For the individual, cultural heritage encourages the formation of an identity and sense of self, from micro-culture sources (e.g. regional and communal) and macro-culture sources (e.g. state and transnational) (Konsa 2013). Furthermore, the sharing of culture can encourage skill development and re-engage individuals with their past. On a community level, IGL can develop a positive and integrative society, and decrease marginalization of communities or populations. As previously stated, the overarching goal of the TOY program is to improve the well-being of the old, the young, and the communities involved. The following section will illustrate how IG programs can have such an effect, first on an individual level, and then on a community level.

Developmental Well-Being

For children and young people, the ability to engage in meaningful relationships with the older generation provides access to a sustained cultural heritage. Older adults are seen as "models" of culture (Acerbi, Ghirlanda, and Enquist 2012), given that each person is born devoid of cultural identity, and acquires their personal culture across the lifespan. Thus, older generations can be "suppliers" of cultural traits. It is important to note that, as much as rich and valuable aspects of a person's cultural identity can be shared, so too can prejudices, social hierarchies, and cultural norms that are not conducive to positive relationships and participant well-being. However, children, especially the very young, can benefit from access to the beauty, creativity, and variety of a distinct cultural heritage (Acerbi and Parisi 2006), and in turn can influence the transformation of such cultural traits in a reciprocal relationship, as theorized in the preceding section.

This two-directional partnership provides children with a feeling of autonomy and power that is not often afforded them; increased public perceptions of children as vulnerable, and an increase in risk aversive cultures in first-world countries, has limited children's capacities to explore, direct, and lead in day-to-day life (Phillips and Tossa 2016). Leadership and autonomy are necessary skills for a positive transition into adulthood, and thus should be fostered in younger generations (Arnett 2000, Lopez and Snyder 2011). Reciprocal intergenerational relationships provide young children with the opportunity to develop these skills. For example, a neighborhood walking project piloted in Brisbane, Australia, and now being applied in Thailand, encouraged children to design and lead groups of adults on walks through public spaces. Children were seen to competently manage the responsibility of planning and conducting guided tours of public spaces for an adult audience, and audience members "witnessed capabilities of children that are rarely recognised" (Phillips and Tossa 2015: 26). IGL projects commonly report benefits for children's self-confidence and personal agency (Dumbrajs 2012, Hickey and Phillips 2013). Thus, there are many benefits for the developmental well-being of young children involved in IGL projects.

For older generations, the benefits of IGL projects relate to anthropologist Jordan Lewis's (2013) definition of aging well, which includes four elements: emotional well-being, community engagement, physical health, and spirituality. Successful aging is linked to IG contact in TOY with respect to the following dimensions: being and feeling mentally and physically active and useful; being and feeling valued; being and feeling able to contribute; having fun and bringing fun; developing self-confidence and esteem; taking care and being part of the future of their communities. Intergenerational initiatives increase feelings of self-worth for older adults (Dumbrajs 2012), as well as feelings of generativity and engagement (Andreoletti and Howard 2016). Interestingly, several projects have also highlighted the protective abilities of intergenerational interactions to encourage memory recall in older people experiencing troubles with memory loss and degrees of dementia (Nilsson and Herrman 2016).

One project funded by the Swedish Arts Council, and focusing on the revival of traditional cultural songs, utilized music and group singing as an intergenerational activity between pensioners and pre-schoolers (Nilsson and Herrman 2016). In an ongoing evaluation of the project, a multidisciplinary team discussed the importance of sensory stimulation for the vitality of aged persons, and that positive interactive experiences such as music making with young children provide a buffer for negative thoughts and feelings of pain. Additionally, hearing children's voices and traditional cultural songs elicited remembering in older individuals, and provided an opportunity to pass on intangible cultural heritage to younger generations. Staff reported that "older people with memory loss and a limited ability to communicate verbally can suddenly start singing songs correctly" (Nilsson and Herrman 2016: 193).

Similarly, an IGL project conducted in Helsinki, Finland, focused on the reciprocal transmission of culture between old and young, and encouraged fluid and self-directed partnerships between the generations, based around shared stories, experiences, and hobbies (Dumbrajs 2012). Through the shared expression of culture with younger generations, pensioners were able to re-engage with past passions and hobbies. Sharing stories not only encouraged memory recall, but also encouraged old people to talk more, providing protective factors against the effects of aging. In summary, intergenerational activities focusing on the sharing of cultural heritage benefits both the transmission of heritage to younger generations, as well as the mental, emotional, and physical well-being of both generations.

Social and Community Well-Being

Influenced by the work of Bandura (1977), Smith et al (2008) proposed that because human behavior is influenced by social learning, understanding cultural transmission is key to understanding human behavior. From this framework, exposure to social groups that are often isolated from one another can have positive impacts on the perspectives and "otherness" related to those groups. In a modern society, where old and young populations are becoming steadily more separated, and often isolated to same age institutions and spaces (e.g. school or retirement home), it becomes easy to adopt misplaced conceptions about oldness or childhood. Childhood has often been identified as an age of spontaneity and immaturity, while oldness can be related to a lack of generativity. Intergenerational activities can question both these assumptions, providing young children and older people the opportunity to express and experience different selves, to be active learners at any age and to build connections instead of disjunctions (Wentzell 2013).

Elaborating on the cautionary note of the previous section, it is important to recognize that, for some intergenerational relationships, disjunctions are difficult to overcome. One intergenerational gardening and story-sharing project in Delaware, United States, reflected on the difficulties of navigating hierarchical age and gender norms of older Vietnamese males in intergenerational relationships (Yoshida, Henkin, and Lehrman 2013). The project linked migrant Vietnamese elders with first-generation American children with a migrant history, in an effort to encourage social cohesion and bi-directional learning between young and old. Despite an overarching positive impact of the project on perspectives of both cultures and generations, and increased feelings of empathy and understanding towards the other, staff and members reported a challenge in connecting with some of the elders on a deeper level. This was in large part due to a reflection of societal norms from the Vietnamese culture, which often positions male elders in the highest position in the community. Thus, some members projected this cultural norm onto the staff and volunteers, the majority of whom were young females. This had a decisive impact on the nature of the relationship, as staff reported a more unidirectional relationship, with older members taking the role of teachers, and children the role of learners.

Although there is a risk of transmitting such maladaptive traits and norms in these projects, intergenerational learning can also challenge negative views of others, by providing a platform for co-creating of a new social understanding or acceptance. The opportunity to overcome negative views about older people was a common goal of IG activities researched as part of the TOY project (TOY Project Consortium 2013b). Positive, transactional relationships between young and old can combat negative associations that children may have towards old age (including death, illness, shaking hands, retirement, forgetting). Similarly, seniors also mentioned that the stereotypical views they had about children were challenged. Mia, a 94-year-old woman from an intergenerational project in the Netherlands, which was one of the case studies in TOY, described it as follows:

> When you have contact with one another you become more comfortable with one another . . . the contact helps [older people] to become more tolerant of young children. There are elderly people who think young children just make a lot of noise, who find them difficult.
>
> (TOY Project Consortium 2013c)

Both groups had to adapt to and learn how to interact with the "other," and adapt to different personalities outside the family. Additionally, children and adults working together in meaningful exchanges learn to adapt to the perspectives of the other, reinterpreting, reimagining, and co-constructing knowledge together (TOY Project Consortium 2013a, Phillips and Tossa 2015). This process was illustrated in the afore-mentioned neighborhood walk project in Thailand, which cultivated adult "re-sensing, re-thinking and re-imagining of children, childhood, and space." Adults involved in the walk spoke of "a desire to understand children and the neighbourhood differently," reflecting the nature of exposure and interaction as a powerful tool for encouraging new perspectives and disbanding negative stereotypes (Phillips and Tossa 2015: 26).

In summary, intergenerational learning can help overcome stereotypes and at the same time fosters cultural transmission and the co-creation of original cultural landscapes, over which community members with different backgrounds can embrace a shared ownership. This process encourages a cohesive society built on an intercultural understanding and a shared sense of belonging, for the well-being of entire communities.

CONTRIBUTION OF IGL TO SOCIAL COHESION IN DIVERSE COMMUNITIES

As outlined in the previous section of this chapter, the findings of the TOY Project as well as research conducted by many scholars demonstrates that social engagement between generations is a key factor in the well-being of all, as well as a catalyst in the creation of a shared cross-generational heritage and culture. In this section, it is argued that intergenerational learning can also decrease the marginalization of young children and older people, especially those living in difficult circumstances. The TOY Project has specifically targeted groups such as migrants, refugees, and Roma communities, with the goal of making contributions to bridging the existent gap between different social groups in society.

Among the demographic and social changes already referred to in the introduction of this chapter, inequality is also a growing phenomenon across the globe and characterizes the so-called privileged Western societies (Pearson et al. 2008, Fitz 2015). The number of people who leave, or are forced to leave, their homes and countries of origin due to the impacts of increasing inequalities is growing. Societies are becoming more diverse, and policies to promote multiculturalism and integration are showing their limitations and are often failing (Castles 2004). In addition to inequality, social isolation plays a detrimental role in communities with a migrant (family) background, which have less capacity to network with others, and to build relationships between themselves and with institutions (Pauw 2016). Thus, in addition to changes in population demographics and the growing separation of families and ages, an increase in cultural diversity world-wide calls for the kind of multicultural cohesion that IGL programs have been shown to foster.

This underlines just how important dialogue and solidarity between generations and communities from diverse social and cultural backgrounds is, and how important it is to look for similarities instead of systematically denying or disregarding "the unknown other," either young or old or socio-culturally different. Facilitating intergenerational learning between young and old provides a valuable way forward. How does it work in practice?

As far back as the late 1980s, intergenerational programs were considered effective interventions to decrease acculturation stress among immigrant adolescents and their parents, and to promote the transmission of local cultural values, beliefs, and practices to new migrant families (Bacallao and Smokowski 2017, Este and Van Ngo 2011, Skilton-Sylvester and Garcia 1999). Since then, many projects have utilized older generations as cultural models or mentors for young people. In Kaplan's well-known publication for UNESCO, the author highlights several models that provide immigrant children and youth with the support of local older adults to improve their language skills and their understanding of the hosting culture (Kaplan 2002). However, it is arguable that such programs focused mainly on the assimilation and acculturation of migrant youth to the hosting culture, underestimating the role of the migrant's cultural heritage in the con-struction of individual and group identities and their interaction with the new cultural environment. More recent programs and approaches to IGL in cross-cultural situations seem to be more aware of the problems of acculturation and assimilation with regards to cultural transmission and public heritage. They support the recognition of the heritage of every group involved, the conflicts that can arise, and the contribution that IGL activ-ities can make to create a bridge between cultures and identities to build a shared sense of belonging.

An example of this approach can be found in a program where older adults filled the role of "grandparents," for example in situations where biological grandparents had remained in the home country (Ward 2000). This concept was developed as part of the TOY project, and is referred to as "social grandparenting" (TOY 2013b). It recognizes the importance of the role of grandparents in the healthy psychosocial and affective de-velopment of children (Nicholson and Zeece 2008). When grandparents are not avail-able, IGL programs can provide a platform for other older adults to play this role, if enough space and time is given to both young and old to develop a relationship through play, exploration, sharing of values, and transfer and transformation of knowledge and heritage.

This is the case in a project implemented in Sicily (Italy) in 2010, where second-generation migrant children "adopted" a grandparent from the local community and initiated an intercultural trajectory together (Redattore Sociale 2010). Three elements composed this trajectory: the joint visit to the cultural sites of the town of Termini Imerese, guided by official guides and with insights from the "adopted grandparents"; the organization of a joint play session for young and old, with games from different generations and culture; and, finally, a storytelling session during which young and old could tell their experiences, memories, feelings, and emotions. The aim of this project was to strengthen the ties between families with a migrant background and local older adults, in order to foster intercultural dialogue and build a generational alliance based on mutual solidarity and shared ownership of the local community and cultural heritage. Second-generation children with a migrant background are already engaged in a long journey to find their own position between the value demands of their country and the country of their parents and research shows that intergenerational learning activities that incorporate an intercultural approach can support their journey from an early age.

As part of the TOY project, similar intergenerational initiatives have been documented, and findings suggest that they contributed to a better understanding of the lives of families with a migrant background. Initiatives included home visits of senior volunteers to read stories to children in the Netherlands, listening to children with a migrant background about their home lives as a volunteer in a library in Italy, or working with children from play-centers with predominantly migrant (family) backgrounds in Spain (TOY Project Consortium 2013c, TOY Project Consortium 2014). Intergenerational activities can also be applied in reverse; to those members of the family "left behind" due to emigration of family members. This became the rationale for intergenerational activities, for example in Portugal, where children with and without a migrant background visit, and exchange letters with seniors in a care home for older people (TOY Project Consortium 2013c).

Intergenerational programs that aim to promote cross-generational interaction within migrant families and communities offer another perspective in this discussion. These programs allow immigrant and refugee elders to transmit their cultural heritage and experiences to younger generations and help them maintain a sense of purpose through sharing their cultural knowledge. A project supported by the Temple University Intergenerational Centre in the United States—already mentioned in the previous section of this chapter—shows how intergenerational activities can have a positive impact in promoting understanding and solving generational conflicts between Mexican–American or Vietnamese children and their grandparents, who are concerned about the acculturation of their grandchildren (Yoshida, Henkin, and Lehrman 2013), although not without challenges.

In the European context, the TOY Project has been reconceptualized as TOY for Inclusion[1] to specifically work with children of Roma background who are often victims to double discrimination: as an ethnic minority and as children. To date there has been little research on the convergence of the principles shared by age-friendly, child-friendly, and intercultural cities and communities (Biggs and Carr. 2015), three well-known but separate initiatives promoted to respectively tackle age-segregation and ageism (WHO[2]), accessibility of urban spaces to children (UNICEF[3]), and intercultural contact in urban spaces (Council of Europe[4]). The TOY for Inclusion project attempts to address this gap in the literature and aims to improve the transition experience of Roma children to schools by offering an innovative response to discrimination of Romani communities by creating non-segregated multigenerational play spaces in six European countries.

These spaces will be located in areas which are reachable for both Roma and non-Roma families, and will be designed and run by local committees composed by representatives of both communities, school and pre-school teachers, and local authorities. Along with activities aimed to help children develop necessary skills and knowledge for formal education, these spaces will organize play-focused intergenerational activities involving older people with and without a Roma background. As mentioned in the previous section, research has demonstrated that intergenerational activities challenge stereotypes and all involved experience the values of solidarity, respect, and acceptance of the "other" (Jourova 2016). It is expected that discrimination against the very young and older adults as well as against Roma children and their families will be challenged, while cultural heritage of Roma communities will be shared, appreciated, and recognized as an important contribution to the present and future of our European societies. TOY for Inclusion is an ongoing project, however, based on the reactions of participants, as well as practitioners and policy makers, this approach could be an effective tool for tackling social exclusion and isolation amongst children and families with a minority background in other contexts.

Conclusion

The aim of this chapter was to examine the contribution that intergenerational learning makes to the transmission and co-construction of cultural heritage, through re-imaging and re-interpreting spaces, experiences, and memories, and the contribution of this process to the well-being and social cohesion of young and old in diverse societies. With the growth of voluntary and involuntary migration comes an increased risk for social isolation, which can be responded to by supporting intercultural dialogue and cross-cultural contact. In this chapter, through a synthesis of previous research, it is argued that intergenerational learning can be a powerful tool to this end. It can also be a tool for responding to the potential loss of the ability to transmit intangible cultural heritage, both within and across communities, including memories, language, and song from one generation to the next.

Although the path to a cohesive and inclusive multicultural society may not be smooth, IGL paradigms provide a platform for the creation of bi-directional learning relationships between young and old, fostering intergenerational solidarity. The process highlights the value of older adults as cultural models, but also the importance of input from very young children, who transmit cultural ideas to older generations and contribute to the joint transformation of cultural landscapes. By bringing young children and older people together to explore memories, experiences, and traditions, cultural heritage lives in the present and is constantly re-imagined and made relevant to diverse and fast-changing societies. Thus, in response to societal concerns for age integration, aging populations, and multicultural communities, intergenerational processes that foster transmission and co-creation of cultural heritage should be embedded into public heritage preservation policies and programs, as well as in social, educational, and urban policies.

Notes

1. For more information on TOY for Inclusion see <http://www.toyproject.net/project/toy-for-inclusion-2/>.
2. <http://www.who.int/ageing/projects/age_friendly_cities_network/en/>.
3. <http://childfriendlycities.org/>.
4. <http://www.coe.int/en/web/interculturalcities>.

References

Acerbi, Alberto, Stefano Ghirlanda, and Magnus Enquist. 2012. "Old and Young Individuals' Role in Cultural Change." *Jasss* 15(4): 1.

Acerbi, Alberto, and Domenico Parisi. 2006. "Cultural Transmission between and within Generations." *Journal of Artificial Societies and Social Simulation* 9(1). <http://jasss.soc.surrey.ac.uk/9/1/9.html>.

Andreoletti, Carrie, and Jessica L. Howard. 2016. "Bridging the Generation Gap: Intergenerational Service-Learning Benefits Young and Old." *Gerontology & Geriatrics Education* 23: 1–15.

Arnett, Jeffrey Jensen. 2000. "Emerging Adulthood: A Theory of Development from the Late Teens through the Twenties." *American Psychologist* 55(5): 469–480.

Bacallao, Martica, and Paul Richard Smokowski. 2017. "Promoting Biculturalism in Order to Prevent Behavioral and Mental Health Problems in Immigrant Families," in *The Oxford Handbook of Acculturation and Health*, ed. Seth J. Schwartz and Jennifer Unger. New York: Oxford University Press, 433–448. DOI: 10.1093/oxfordhb/9780190215217.013.22.

Bandura, Albert. 1977. *Social Learning Theory*. Englewood Cliffs and London: Prentice-Hall.

Biggs, Simon, and Ashley Carr. 2015. "Age- and Child-Friendly Cities and the Promise of Intergenerational Space." *Journal of Social Work Practice* 29(1): 99–112. DOI: 10.1080/02650533.2014.993942.

Bottery, Mike. 2016. "The Future of Intergenerational Learning: Redefining the Focus?" *Studia Paedagogica* 21(2): 9–24.

Castles, Stephen. 2004. "Why Migration Policies Fail." *Ethnic and Racial Studies* 27(2): 205–227.

Cavalli-Sforza, Luigi Luca, and Feldman, Marcus. 1981. *Cultural Transmission and Evolution: A Quantitative Approach*. Princeton: Princeton University Press.

Cortellesi, Giulia, and Margaret Kernan. 2016. "Together Old and Young: How Informal Contact between Young Children and Older People can Lead to Intergenerational Solidarity." *Studia Paedagogica* 21(2): 101–116.

Danely, Jason. 2013. "Aging: Integration." *Cultural Anthropology*, October 28: <http://www.culanth.org/fieldsights/392-aging-integration> [accessed April 28, 2017].

Dumbrajs, Sivbritt. 2012. "Intergenerational Cultural Transmission." *Procedia—Social and Behavioral Sciences* 47: 109–113.

Este, David, and Hieu Van Ngo. 2011. "A Resilience Framework to Examine Immigrant and Refugee Children and Youth in Canada," in *Immigrant Children: Change, Adaptation, and Cultural Transformation*, ed. Susan S. Chuang and Robert P. Moreno. Lanham, MD: Lexington Books.

Fitz, Nicholas. 2015. "Economic Inequality: It's Far Worse Than You Think. The Great Divide between our Beliefs, our Ideals, and Reality." *Scientific American*, March 31: <https://www.scientificamerican.com/article/economic-inequality-it-s-far-worse-than-you-think/> [accessed April 5, 2017].

Franz, Julia, and Annette Scheunpflug. 2016. "A Systematic Perspective on Intergenerational Learning: Theoretical and Empirical Findings 1." *Studia Paedagogica* 21(2): 25–41.

Geertz, Clifford. 1973. *The Interpretation of Cultures: Selected Essays*. New York: Basic.

Han, Sallie, and Antrosio Jason. 2016. "The Editor's Note: Cultural Heritage." *Open Anthropology* 4(1): <http://www.americananthro.org/StayInformed/OAArticleDetail.aspx?ItemNumber=13443> [accessed April 7, 2017].

Hickey, Andrew, and Louise Phillips. 2013. "New Kids on the Block: Young People, the City and Public Pedagogies." *Global Studies of Childhood* 3(2): 115–128.

Hirschfeld, Lawrence A. 2002. "Why Don't Anthropologists Like Children?" *American Anthropologist* 104(2): 611–627. DOI: 10.1525/aa.2002.104.2.611.

Hoff, Andreas. 2007. "Intergenerational Learning as an Adaptation Strategy in Aging Knowledge Societies," in *Education, Employment, Europe*, ed. European Commission. Warsaw: National Contact Point for Research Programmes of the European Union, 126–129.

Jourova, Vera. 2016. "Progress Made by EU Member States in Roma Integration." *European Commission*: <http://ec.europa.eu/justice/discrimination/files/roma-report-2016-factsheet_en.pdf>.

Kaplan, Matthew. 2002. "Intergenerational Programs in Schools: Considerations of Form and Function." *International Review of Education* 48(5): 305–334.

Konsa, Kurmo. 2013. "Heritage as a Socio-Cultural Construct: Problems of Definition." *Baltic Journal of Art History* 6: 123–149. DOI: 10.12697/BJAH.2013.6.05.

Lewis, Jordan. 2013. "Aging: Translation." *Cultural Anthropology*, October 16: <http://www.culanth.org/fieldsights/389-aging-translation> [accessed April 16, 2017].

Lopez, Shane J., and C.R. Snyder, eds. 2011. *The Oxford Handbook of Positive Psychology*. 2nd edn. New York: Oxford University Press. DOI: 10.1093/oxfordhb/9780195187243.001.0001.

Newman, Sally, and Alan Hatton-Yeo. 2008. "Intergenerational Learning and the Contributions of Older People." *Ageing Horizons* 8: 31–39.

Nicholson, Laurie, and Pauline D. Zeece. 2008. "Grandparents in the Lives of Young Children," in *Enduring Bonds*, ed. Mary Renck Jalongo. New York: Springer, 129–144.

Nilsson, Lena A., and Margaretha Herrman. 2016. "Intergenerational Learning—Children Singing Along with Older People: Possibilities and Complications in a Project Context." *Advances In Social Sciences Research* 3(1): 187–200.

Nsamenang, A. Bame. 2012. "The Intergenerational Continuity of Values," in *The Oxford Handbook of Culture and Psychology*, ed. Jaan Valsiner. New York: Oxford University Press, 767–781. DOI: 10.1093/oxfordhb/9780195396430.013.0037.

Pauw, Leo. 2016. "De vreedzame wijk (The peaceful neighborhood). Een praktische gids voor een samenhangend opvoedklimaat in de wijk." *Uitgeverij SWP*, Amsterdam.

Pearson, M. et al. "Growing Unequal? Income Distribution and Poverty in OECD Countries." OECD Publishing, October 2008.

Phillips, Louise G., and Wajuppa Tossa. 2016. "Intergenerational and Intercultural Civic Learning through Storied Child-Led Walks of Chiang Mai." *Geographical Research* 55(1): 18–28.

Pickering, Michael, and Emily Keightley. 2013. "Communities of Memory and the Problem of Transmission." *European Journal of Cultural Studies* 16(1): 115–131.

Redattore Sociale. 2010. "Palermo, i bambini immigrati 'adottano' un nonno." <http://www.redattoresociale.it/Notiziario/Articolo/307402/Palermo-i-bambini-immigrati-adottano-un-nonno>.

Schönpflug, Ute. 2009. "Theory and Research in Cultural Transmission: A Short History," in *Cultural Transmission*, ed. Ute Schönpflug. New York: Cambridge University Press, 9–30.

Skilton-Sylvester, Ellen, and Alejandro Garcia. 1999. "Intergenerational Programs to Address the Challenge of Immigration." *Generations* 22(4): 58–63.

Smith, Kenny, et al. 2008. "Introduction: Cultural Transmission and the Evolution of Human Behaviour." *Philosophical Transactions of the Royal Society of London. Series B, Biological Sciences* 363(1509): 3469–3476.

Strom, Paris, and Robert Strom. 2011. "A Paradigm for Intergenerational Learning," in *The Oxford Handbook of Lifelong Learning*, ed. Manuel London. New York: Oxford University Press, 133–146. DOI: 10.1093/oxfordhb/9780195390483.013.0049.

Tam, Kim-Pong. 2015. "Understanding Intergenerational Cultural Transmission through the Role of Perceived Norms." *Journal of Cross-Cultural Psychology* 46(10): 1260–1266.

TOY Project Consortium. 2013a. *Intergenerational Learning Involving Young Children and Older People*. Leiden: The TOY Project. <http://www.toyproject.net/publication/latest-publications/literature-review/> [accessed March 12, 2017].

TOY Project Consortium. 2013b. *Reweaving the Tapestry of the Generations: An Intergenerational Learning Tour through Europe*. Leiden: The TOY Project. <http://www.toyproject.net/publication/latest-publications/action-research-and-casestudies/> [accessed March 29, 2017].

TOY Project Consortium (2013c). *Case Studies*. <http://www.toyproject.net/wp-content/uploads/2016/01/TOY-casestudies.pdf> [accessed April 10, 2017].

TOY Project Consortium (2014). *TOY in Action*. <http://www.toyproject.net/publication/toy-in-action/> [accessed May 5, 2017].

UNESCO. 2003. *Convention for the Safeguarding of the Intangible Cultural Heritage*. <https://ich.unesco.org/en/convention> [accessed June 30, 2017].

Vanderbeck, Robert M., and Nancy Worth. 2015. *Intergenerational Space*. London: Routledge.

Ward, Christopher R. 2000. "The Intergenerational Field Needs More Ethnographic Research," in *Intergenerational Programs: Understanding What We Have Created*, ed. V. Kuehne. New York: Routledge, 6–23.

Wentzell, Emily A. 2013. "Aging: Provocation" *Cultural Anthropology*. <http://www.culanth.org/fieldsights/386-aging-provocation> [accessed March 12, 2017].

Yoshida, Hitomi, Nancy Henkin, and Patience Lehrman. 2013. *Strengthening Intergenerational Bonds in Immigrant and Refugee Communities*. Philadelphia: The Intergenerational Center, Temple University.

INDEX

....

Note: Page numbers followed by *f* or *t* indicate a figure or table.